A HISTORY OF
THE FAR EAST

BY

G. NYE STEIGER

ASSOCIATE PROFESSOR OF HISTORY

SIMMONS COLLEGE

GINN AND COMPANY

BOSTON · NEW YORK · CHICAGO · LONDON · ATLANTA
DALLAS · COLUMBUS · SAN FRANCISCO

The Athenæum Press

GINN AND COMPANY · PRO-
PRIETORS · BOSTON · U.S.A.

PREFACE

The way that can be trod is not the eternal way;
The name that can be named is not the eternal name.

IN OFFERING this book for publication I wish first of all to acknowledge my obvious debt to the scholars whose patient labors in innumerable special fields have made available the material upon which such a general survey could be based.

My next acknowledgment is to those contemporary workers in the field of Oriental studies who, from time to time, have aided and encouraged me in my undertaking. In two cases their assistance calls for specific recognition. Professor K. S. Latourette of Yale has been kind enough to read the proof as the book was going through the press, and his constructive criticism has enabled me to strengthen the text at many important points. Dr. C. S. Gardner of Harvard has given invaluable advice on difficult points in connection with the bibliography.

These confessions of indebtedness are not intended to diminish my own responsibility for the book as it stands; any errors of fact or of interpretation are mine alone. The opening lines of the *Tao Te King*, quoted at the top of this page, might be freely interpreted "Any human attempt to state a truth is at best but an approximation"; it is my hope that those who read these pages will feel that the approximation has been reasonably accurate.

CAMBRIDGE, MASSACHUSETTS   G. NYE STEIGER

CONTENTS

MAPS

PHYSICAL MAP OF ASIA

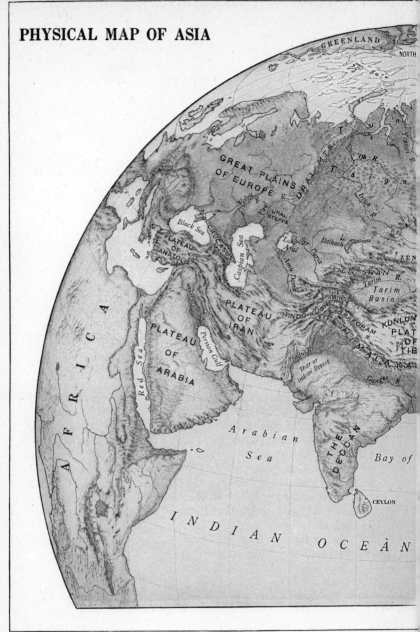

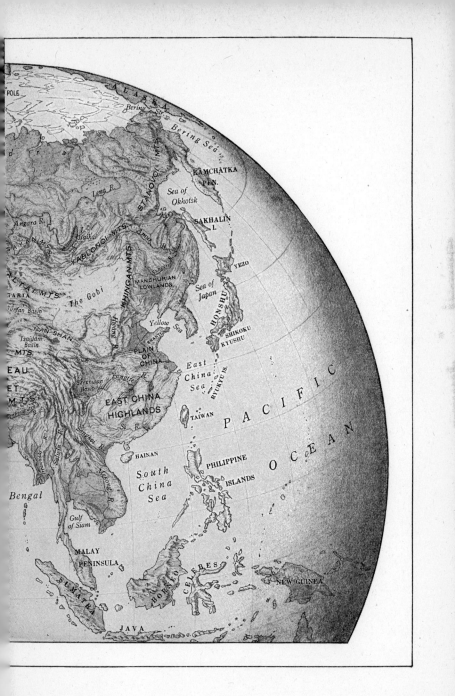

A HISTORY OF THE FAR EAST

I

Introduction

DIAGONALLY across the continent of Asia, from the Iranian plateau of Persia on the southwest to the coast of Kamchatka in the northeast, stretches a mighty system of mountain ranges flanked by broad expanses of sandy desert. This imposing barrier divides southeastern Asia culturally as well as geographically from the lands to the west; it is with the lands and peoples of the Far Eastern world thus separated from the rest of the Eurasian continent that this history deals.

Sometime during the third millennium before the Christian Era there began to develop in the Far Eastern area two of the world's great civilizations, the Chinese and the Indian. Other peoples of the area made at very early dates more or less independent cultural progress, but the less vigorous civilizations were overshadowed and greatly modified by the expanding influence of China and India. During the course of centuries cultural exchange developed between these two civilizations, while central Asia, Indo-China, Korea, and Japan received from them the art, science, philosophy, and religion which became basic elements of their own local cultures.

Of all the influences which tended to create Far Eastern cultural unity the most important was religion. From Ceylon to Japan and from Turkestan to Java all the civilized nations of the Orient, until the coming of Mohammedanism, were profoundly affected by the religious thought of India. Like Europe, the Orient has been a world united, inspired, and enriched by a common religious herit-age. It is this underlying unity of religious thought, more than anything else, that makes it logical to treat the history of the whole area as a single field for study.

"The Occidentals," exclaims a French Orientalist, "have sin-gularly contracted the field of world history, inasmuch as they have grouped around the people of Israel, of Greece, and of Rome the little that they knew of the expansion of the human race. . . . The greatest part of the universe, a civilization different from but certainly as developed as that of the ancient Greeks and Romans, remained totally unknown to those who wrote the history of their little world believing that they were setting forth the history of the world as a whole."

Understandable and excusable though this attitude may have been in the past, it should no longer be possible. In an age which has seen the development of industry and communication to such a point that the peace and prosperity of every part of the world are inevitably affected by the occurrences in every other part we can no longer afford to remain in ignorance of the cultural heritage which vitally influences the actions and the mental attitudes of any important fraction of the human race.

The continental and insular areas included within the scope of this work are at present inhabited by something more than eight hundred and fifty million people, approximately half of the world's total population. The largest two national groups among this teeming multitude of human beings, the Chinese and the Indians, possess civilizations which were already old when Athens and Rome were in their infancy. Despite the recent political weakness of China and India the people of these countries are still factors of incalculable importance in the present development of world affairs. A third national group, the Japanese, has lifted itself during the last three quarters of a century from comparative in-significance to a position among the recognized great powers of the world.

During the last few decades, and especially since the close of the World War, the rising tide of Far Eastern nationalism has awakened in the West a growing appreciation of the fact that the

Orient is an important and not wholly passive part of the world in which we live. Yet even now the treatment of Oriental history in books intended for school and college use is too often limited to the last century or to the last four hundred years. To accept such a treatment as sufficient for the complete understanding of even present-day conditions and tendencies in the Far East is tantamount to assuming that only such events as have been directly connected with the history of Western countries are of vital significance in world history. With such an assumption the author of the present work cannot agree. It is his belief that modern India is conditioned by Gautama, Asoka, and Mohammed Ghori as strongly as by Albuquerque, Clive, and Warren Hastings; that to understand Chinese nationalism it is as important to know something of Confucius and Wang An-shih as it is to have studied about the Opium War and extraterritoriality; that the reforms of the Meiji era in Japanese history will be better understood if the student knows something about the earlier Taikwa reforms and about the origin of the Shogunate.

In Far Eastern countries the events of very ancient history are more intimately connected with the present than is the case in the West. Few of the peoples whose civilization has been derived from Greece and Egypt feel that the history of those countries constitutes part of their own national experience, and a modern Italian would hardly look upon Scipio Africanus or Cato the Censor as having exercised a decisive influence upon the political institutions of the Italian kingdom. In China, in India, and in Japan the people now dwelling in these lands are to a large extent the actual descendants of those who elaborated the civilizations and molded the traditions under which they live. English history hardly begins before the coming of the Angles and Saxons. French history may be started with Clovis and his Frankish followers. But the histories of China, of India, and of Japan stretch back without a break to the earliest records of human existence in those lands, and these records have a real bearing upon the beliefs, the customs, and the institutions of today.

Any attempt to cover within the limits of a single volume the entire history of eastern and southeastern Asia must content itself with giving the barest outline of the story. It is therefore as an introduction and guide to the study of Far Eastern history rather than as an exhaustive treatment of any part of that vast field that this work has been designed. In the selection and arrangement of material there has been a conscientious effort to maintain a proper balance between the various phases of human activity which, taken together, constitute a people's history. Equal care has been exercised to avoid devoting to the history of any single country an undue portion of the total space.

In order to facilitate additional reading and study and in the hope of furnishing helpful guidance in the various fields which may interest the individual student, care has been taken to make the "Suggested References" at the end of each chapter and the general bibliography as useful as possible. With this purpose in mind the "Suggested References" include only such works as are readily obtainable; except for works of outstanding importance books in foreign languages or those long out of print have not been mentioned in these lists. The general bibliography, on the other hand, has been made to include practically every publication which in the author's opinion will be of real use. Because of the policy which has been adopted in compiling the "Suggested References" those for the earlier chapters are quite brief. For the chapters dealing with the more modern periods, in which recent publications in the English language are more abundant, the lists are correspondingly longer and include works containing much important documentary material of an official nature.

The comprehensive nature of the lists of references appended to the chapters dealing with the more modern period is designed to make the book available for courses emphasizing this phase of Far Eastern history. Using the text as an outline, the student will have little difficulty in finding his way to more exhaustive discussions of any important topic.

II

China: from Earliest Times to End of the Ch'in Dynasty

The Geography of China · Sources of Chinese History · Evidences of Stone Age Culture · Origin of the Chinese State · From Legend to History · The Tortoise Shells of Yin · Historical Value of the Tortoise Shells · Expansion during the Yin Period · The Chou Dynasty · The Wei Valley as the Center of China · Organization of the State under the Chou Dynasty · The King: Religious and Political Functions · The Six Boards · Nobles and Peasants · The Ching System · The Ownership of the Land · Transfer of the Capital to Loyang · Decline of the Royal Power · Hegemony of Ch'i and of Chin · The Warring Kingdoms · The Triumph of Ch'in · The Age of Philosophers · Confucius and his Teachings · Lao-tzu and the *Tao Te King* · Mo-tzu · The Legalists · Mencius · Chuang-tzu · The Imperial System of Shih Huang Ti · The Burning of the Books · The Great Wall · The Importance of Shih Huang Ti · The End of the Ancient Period

THE present-day Chinese Republic lays claim[1] to a total area of slightly more than four and a quarter million square miles, almost exactly one fourth of the entire Asiatic continent. Not all this great area is equally "Chinese." Under the nominal sovereignty of the republic as heir and successor of the ancient empire are various regions which, although influenced throughout all ages by Chinese civilization, are usually thought of as outlying possessions rather than as integral parts of "China Proper."

China Proper consists of the eighteen provinces lying south of the Great Wall and comprises a third of the total area now attributed to the republic. On the north the territory of the eighteen provinces is bounded by the Gobi desert of Mongolia, on the west and southwest by the Tibetan highlands and by the southeasterly extensions of this great mountain mass, on the east

---

[1] In various regions China's claims to sovereignty are being disregarded by powerful neighbors, but they are still asserted.

The traces of a paleolithic culture were discovered in the summer of 1923 in the Ordos region, which lies to the north of Shensi Province in the great northern bend of the Yellow River. Here, embedded in the lowest portion of the deep loess deposit[1] or even in the underlying gravel upon which the loess formation rests, were found early paleolithic *artifacts* of roughly shaped quartzite and other kinds of stone. These early works of human hands consisted of points, scrapers, fist hatchets, and so forth, and their great antiquity is further attested by the fact that they were found in company with the remains of long-extinct Pleistocene mammals and birds. Although throwing no light upon the identity of the people by whom they were made and used, these implements clearly prove that northern China was in very early times a place of human habitation.

Almost simultaneously with this discovery of paleolithic evidence came the first extensive discoveries of neolithic culture. In 1921 systematic surveys and excavations at two sites, one in the southwestern part of Fengtien Province in Manchuria and the other in northwestern Honan, brought to light great quantities of neolithic implements and utensils, together with abundant human skeletal remains. During 1923 and 1924 extensive explorations in the river valleys of western Kansu were attended by similar success.

The articles discovered at these various places included stone knives and axes, stone whorls for spinning, bone needles and agricultural implements, and fire-hardened pottery,—painted and unpainted,—some of which had been shaped on the potter's wheel. The Fengtien site was a rather small cave in the side of a cliff, but the Honan and Kansu discoveries came from the sites of ancient villages or—especially in the case of Kansu—from burial grounds, in which were found many of the finest specimens of painted pottery.

As a result of these discoveries and of the geological evidence offered by the discovery sites it seems to be definitely established

---

[1] The loess, a striking characteristic of northern China, is a dustlike loam which has been brought in and deposited, during thousands of years, by the northwest winds. In places this deposit is several hundred feet thick.

that perhaps as early as 3500 B.C. neolithic culture of a high standard existed in southwestern Manchuria, in northern Honan, and in western Kansu. The presence in the first and last of these areas of pottery and other articles closely resembling those found most abundantly at the Honan site also warrants the conclusion that these were not isolated and that the intervening regions were at least partially occupied by peoples of the same stage of development.

At a very early date, probably early in the third millennium B.C., the people dwelling along the lower reaches of the Yellow River —in the modern provinces of Honan, Hopei,[1] and Shantung— began to develop some measure of political organization. Northward, southward, and westward of the area occupied by these people the land was inhabited by "barbarians," inferior in culture but apparently identical in race. Gradually the more civilized valley dwellers extended their influence. They absorbed some of their barbarian cousins, pushed others out of the river valleys draining into the Yellow River, and occupied the great plain lying between the lower reaches of the Yellow River and the sea.

Who these original Chinese were, whence they came, and where they obtained the earliest elements of their civilization are questions upon which there is a wide difference of opinion among the anthropologists and archaeologists who have attempted to answer them. Arguments have been advanced to prove that the first civilized people along the Yellow River were immigrants from southern Asia or from central Asia or even from the distant land of Mesopotamia. Of these various suggestions a central-Asian origin appears the most possible, but the absence of any conclusive evidence in support of this possibility compels us to assume that the basic civilization of the Chinese is indigenous and that they began to receive foreign elements of culture only after this indigenous civilization had reached a high state of development.[2]

---

[1] In 1928, when the Nationalist government of China established the capital at Nanking, the name of the former capital—Peking—was changed to *Peiping* and that of the province of Chihli was changed to *Hopei*.

[2] For a complete discussion of this question from varying points of view see the works of Cordier, Hirth, Maspero, John Ross, Terrien de Lacouperie, and E. T. Williams.

From Legend to History

The myths and legends of the Chinese, as found in the Confucian *Historical Classic* and in other ancient writings, begin the story of their national development more than a thousand years before the dawn of authentic history. Far back in this legendary age stands the "Yellow Emperor" (Huang Ti), whom some Western scholars believe to have been the leader of a band of immigrants from central Asia. Confucius, who makes no mention of the Yellow Emperor, begins his account with the three "Perfect Rulers,"—Yao, Shun, and Yu,—whose combined reigns constituted a Golden Age of peace and virtue.

Yao and Shun, according to the legends, did not hand on the royal power to their descendants; each selected as his chief assistant and ultimate successor the most capable man in the kingdom. With Yu, to whose accession traditional chronology has assigned the date 2205 B.C., the crown became hereditary, and sixteen of his descendants ruled the country as members of China's first dynasty, the Hsia.

Little credit can be given to the list of rulers from Yao to the end of the Hsia dynasty, and no credit at all can be given to the dates traditionally assigned to their reigns. Even the Shang, or Yin, dynasty, which is said to have replaced the Hsia in 1766 B.C., is at best only semihistorical in character. Not until we approach the later reigns of this dynasty do we find contemporary documents supplying actual details concerning the Chinese people and their rulers.

The first reliable historical material relating to the period of the Yin dynasty was made available by an important discovery in 1899. In that year the attention of scholars was drawn to the existence of thousands of inscribed bone and tortoise-shell fragments being offered for sale in certain parts of northern Honan. The characters with which these fragments were inscribed, although archaic in form, were sufficiently like early Chinese to be decipherable, and they were soon identified as the records of divinations which had been performed for a number of the later rulers of the Yin dynasty. Hundreds of the inscriptions have now been deciphered; and, although there remain thousands still to be translated, the light which they throw upon the Yin dynasty already suffices to push back several centuries the dividing line between the legendary and the historical in China's past.

The tortoise-shell inscriptions, which are attributed roughly to the twelfth and eleventh centuries B.C., are the oldest known documents in the Chinese language, and it is difficult to exaggerate the importance of the information to be derived from them. In the first place, they are conclusive evidence that the Chinese had developed by this early date an elaborate system of writing very similar to that which is now in use. In the second place, they mention by name something more than half of the thirty Yin monarchs included in the ancestral lists of their later descendants, the Dukes of Sung[1]; thus the historical validity of the traditional list of the Yin dynasty is greatly strengthened. Finally, the subject matter of these appeals which the Yin rulers made to the oracle reveals a living society, a highly organized agricultural state in which the monarch directed his policy and buttressed his political authority by almost daily recourse to the advice of the spirit world.

China of the Yin period, like China of today, was predominantly agricultural; the crops which were cultivated included millet, wheat, and even rice. The climate of the Yellow River valley, in those days as today, offered little certainty of favorable conditions during the growing season; hence the sovereign, as high priest and father of his people, showed at all times a deep concern over the prospects for an abundant harvest, and a large part of the questions asked of the oracle relate to the agricultural outlook. Other appeals bear evidence to the fact that hunting still constituted an important supplement to agriculture as a means of support. Many questions also relate to the prospects for a satisfactory increase in the flocks and herds, considerable anxiety being displayed concerning the supply of animals suitable for use at the sacrifices, from which it is possible to see how largely the religious function occupied the head of the nation.

[1] With the deciphering of additional inscriptions the number of monarchs mentioned will probably be more complete.

In addition to being the high priest of the nation the king was, in theory at least, an absolute political head; yet the tortoise shells betray the fact that his wishes were often opposed by the council of great and small nobles. Where the oracle's response was favorable, the monarch was able to have his way and to force from the council support for the policy which they disapproved. Even when the "small and great" expressed no opposition to the royal policies, an appeal to the oracle usually preceded any important undertaking of peace or war.

Although the traditional chronology places the accession of the first Yin monarch at 1766 B.C., modern scholarship assigns the establishment of the dynasty to a considerably later period, sometime in the sixteenth or fifteenth century B.C. Except in their partial verification of the traditional dynastic list the tortoise shells do not provide us with any new chronological material, and it is not until the middle of the ninth century B.C. that the dates of Chinese history become thoroughly dependable; but from the days of Yin the Chinese state and its government assume a substantial reality which is lacking for earlier ages.

Under the monarchs of this dynasty the Chinese state entered upon a period of expansion. Bodies of Chinese settlers pushed westward and established detached colonies along the upper Yellow River and in the valleys of the streams which flow into this great river near the point where it ceases its southerly course to turn abruptly toward the east.

Compelled to maintain themselves by force of arms against the barbarians whom they had displaced, these colonies gradually developed into semi-independent states. Their dukes and princes continued to acknowledge the overlordship of the Yin ruler, who alone, as high priest of the nation, was competent to offer sacrifice to the supreme Lord of Heaven; but for self-defense and in the management of local affairs they were thrown almost completely upon their own resources. Thus there slowly developed during this period of expansion the condition of feudal decentralization which was to endure for nearly a thousand years before being destroyed by the reforms of Shih Huang Ti.

THE CHOU DYNASTY

Of these outlying vassal states the duchy of Chou, which occupied the Wei valley in modern Shensi, was in a particularly exposed location and was compelled to struggle for existence. Established early in the twelfth century B.C., Chou, under a succession of energetic dukes, was able not merely to maintain itself against the incessant attacks of its barbarian neighbors but even to extend its frontiers and to incorporate many of the barbarians into its population. As this western vassal became stronger, the power of the royal line declined, and about the middle of the eleventh century B.C.[1] Duke Fa, the ruler of Chou, rose in revolt against his suzerain. Leading his war-hardened forces eastward from the Wei valley, he stormed the capital, put to death the last Yin monarch, seized the royal power, and, as Wu Wang ("Warrior King"), became the founder of a new dynasty known as the *Chou*.

Under the Yin dynasty the political center of the Chinese state had been located in northern Honan, several cities having enjoyed at different times the distinction of being the royal headquarters. Wu Wang, on his seizure of the power, transferred the seat of government westward to his Wei-valley ancestral home, where he built a new capital at Hao, near the modern Sianfu. At the same time he dismembered the royal domain of the Yins. One portion was left to the descendants of the late dynasty, henceforth known as the Dukes of Sung; the greater part of western Shantung, including the state of Lu (the native state of Confucius), was given as a fief to Wu Wang's brother, the Duke of Chou (Chou Kung); a considerable section of northern Honan was retained by the new monarch as a part of his personal domain, while the remainder of the old royal domain was granted out as fiefs to those who had assisted the successful rebellion.

The ambitious ruler of Chou had shown himself to be strong enough to overthrow the Yin dynasty, but he lacked either the power or the political wisdom to destroy the feudal system which

[1] The traditional date for the beginning of the Chou dynasty is 1122 B.C., but modern scholarship is inclined to place this event at a somewhat later date.

had grown up during the period of Yin expansion. The status of the already existing vassal states was unchanged, save for their acceptance of the new ruler as their lawful suzerain, while the infeudation of portions of the Yin domain added to the number of semiautonomous local rulers. This decentralizing political system, which was continued and even extended by the founder of the Chou dynasty, proved fatal to his descendants and during the last five centuries of the Chou regime involved the Chinese people in almost continuous strife.

In addition to a voluminous political history the literature of the Chou dynasty provides for the social life of the period a mass of information which in its scope and its detail is unequaled for any contemporary civilization.

Like their Yin predecessors, the Chou monarchs combined the functions of sovereign and high priest. The priestly function, indeed, has been regarded throughout the entire history of China as an essential attribute of sovereignty. At all times the head of the state has been looked upon as deriving his authority from the "mandate of Heaven"; he alone was competent to appeal to Heaven on behalf of the nation; his "virtue" kept the life of the nation in a state of harmony with the heavenly forces and thereby ensured peace and prosperity to the people under his rule. Thus the proper observance of all the rites and the correct performance of the sacrifices appropriate to the changing seasons were duties which the king could never safely neglect. Since the maintenance of harmony between Earth and Heaven depended upon the regular performance of all the seasonal sacrifices, an accurate calendar was needed to fix the correct dates for the sacrifices. Therefore it was the duty of the monarch or of his board of astronomers to establish and maintain an official calendar.[1]

As the ruler of a feudal state the Chou monarch enjoyed varying degrees of political power, ranging from absolute sovereignty in the royal domain to an extremely tenuous authority over his more distant vassals. In the performance of his political functions he was assisted by a well-organized body of administrative

[1] The acceptance of the Chinese calendar by the rulers of neighboring states was regarded down to modern times as a recognition of China's suzerainty.

officials. This central administrative body was divided into six boards, each presided over by a minister. Above the six boards was placed a Prime Minister, the king's "other self" and often, in the case of feeble monarchs, his real master.

The activities of the six boards, taking them in their established order, dealt with agriculture, war, public works, finance, religious affairs, and punishment. With their aid the king, in theory at least, regulated the more important affairs of the whole country, sending military expeditions against the barbarians, settling disputes between his feudatories, and receiving from these their payments of tribute and their visits of homage. Within the limits of the royal domain practice accorded with theory, and the central administration regulated the most minute details in the life of the people.

The Minister of Agriculture ("Director of the Multitude") regulated the planting, the harvesting, and the rotation of the crops. He also had under his supervision all the details relating to the markets at which the peasants gathered to exchange their surplus produce of field or cottage.

The Minister of War ("Director of the Horses") had in times of peace full charge over the maintenance of the military forces; in time of war he was the commander in chief of the army in the field.

To the *Minister of Public Works* ("Director of the Vast Labors") was confided the oversight of the land. It was his duty to maintain the roads and the dikes, to keep the canals dredged out, and to provide for the digging of new canals as precaution against floods or for the reclamation of swamplands which might be added to the area under cultivation. In addition this officer had under his direct control all the nonagricultural industries of the people.

The Minister of Finance was the "Director of the Royal Household" and in addition to his financial duties had oversight over all the details of the palace economy.

The Minister of Religious Affairs ("Director of Rites") was the chief adviser and expert for all matters relating to the religious functions of the king. He had under his charge the priests, augurers, and interpreters of dreams, he was responsible for the training of the musicians who performed at the sacrifices, and under his control were the astronomers who arranged the calendar.

The Minister of Punishments ("Director of Criminals") had the difficult task of keeping the people in the path of virtue by means of a proper adaptation of punishments to crimes. Thus he and his subordinates administered the law as well as maintaining and, where necessary, revising the already elaborate criminal code.

The population over which the Chou sovereigns thus ruled was divided into two distinct social classes: below were the plebeian artisans and tillers of the soil, above were the patrician nobles. Between these two classes there was an impassable gulf. The nobles had family names and were members of clans each of which traced its descent from some great ancestor to whom ancestral sacrifices were performed. By the virtue which they inherited from their ancestors the noble clansmen were qualified to assist in the affairs of government and to receive fiefs from the king.

Because of the extreme importance of the ancestral cult the marriage of the noble was a religious act, a guaranty that the rites of the clan would be maintained from generation to generation. Authority over the land, which, with the possession of ancestors, was a distinguishing characteristic of the noble, also imposed upon the holder of a fief a variety of religious duties. Although the king alone offered sacrifices to Heaven and Earth, the regular performance of the local rites by his vassals was equally essential to the maintenance of perfect harmony between human affairs and the spirit world. Thus each territorial ruler performed priestly functions for the region over which he had charge and offered sacrifices not only to his ancestors but also to the local god of the soil and to a number of other deities and spirits.

The peasants, on the other hand, had neither family names nor ancestral sacrifices, they were not qualified to hold office or to receive fiefs, and their marriages were without religious significance. Except as beneficiaries of the auspicious conditions which were created by the spiritual observances of their rulers the peasants, as a class, had no part in the religious affairs of the nation. Regulated and directed in all his acts by the officials of the government, the peasant lived out his life in a narrow round of interests and activities. His year was divided into two seasons: winter, which was the time for dwelling in the village; and summer, when he left the village for work and residence in the fields.

The work of the peasant in the fields was organized under the *ching* system. The ching (so called because the interior boundaries resemble the character ching, 井) consisted of a square containing nine hundred *mou*[1] of land divided into nine smaller squares of a hundred mou each. Eight of the nine squares were allotted to as many peasant families, while the central square of each ching was worked in common to provide the government tax or tribute. Different areas were by turn taken under cultivation or allowed to lie fallow, but this was no concern of the peasant; he had only the duty of cultivating each year the particular plot which was assigned to him by his superiors.

The ownership of the land was vested in the monarch as the mandatory of Heaven. By him it could be granted in fief to his vassals, or, as an alternative, the usufruct of a certain region (without any accompanying political authority) might be given to an administrative official as compensation for his services. In neither case did proprietorship in the soil pass to the recipient of the grant. While the grant in usufruct might be hereditary in the family of the official to whom it was made and might be infinitely subdivided in the process of transmission to successive generations, such rights as the grant conferred could not, under the laws of the Chou dynasty, be alienated by sale.

About the middle of the fourth century B.C., when the nominal authority of the Chou monarchs was on the verge of disappearance, the progressive rulers of the vassal state of Ch'in began to permit the free sale and purchase of the right to use the soil, thus legalizing a practice which probably had existed illegally for several centuries. This reform, which during the next cen-

---

[1] A mou is approximately one sixth of an acre.

tury became the law for all China, left the fundamental theory of the sovereign's ownership unchanged; but the right to the *use* of the soil was henceforth regarded as property. With the spread of this reform the peasants as well as the nobles were able to secure permanent rights in the land. A body of small landholders gradually developed, and the old ching system disappeared.

For about a century after the death of Wu Wang the kings of the Chou dynasty are shadowy figures concerning whom we have little information, but toward the end of the tenth century B.C. they are found extending the boundaries of the kingdom and endeavoring to reorganize and to strengthen the royal power.

With Li, the tenth sovereign of the dynasty, we arrive at the first date upon which all Chinese sources are in agreement—the first date therefore which can be accepted as presumably reliable. In the year 842 B.C. Li was driven from his capital by a palace revolution and was compelled to take refuge in a neighboring feudal state, where he remained until his death in 828 B.C. During the fourteen years of Li's exile the throne remained vacant, since the religious aspects of the royal office precluded the possibility of having two kings at the same time.

The long reign of Li's son and successor, Hsüan (827–782 B.C.), was marked by almost incessant military activity. On the north the king's armies were compelled to struggle against the Hsiungnu Tartars who occupied the upper valley of the Yellow River. These ancient ancestors of Attila's Huns were redoubtable foemen; in 822 B.C. they succeeded in capturing and plundering the royal city, but were driven out and decisively defeated later in the same year. To the south Hsüan sent his forces across the mountains into the fertile plain of modern Hupeh, at the junction of the Han and Yangtze rivers. After this expedition, which resulted in the temporary conquest of the invaded region, he turned his attention toward the southeast and extended his dominions to include the valley of the river Hwai.

Although temporarily successful, the wars of Hsüan appear to have exhausted the resources of the royal government. In 771 B.C. a fresh Hsiungnu invasion from the north swept down into the

Wei valley and destroyed the capital. Hsüan's successor upon the throne lost his life in the catastrophe, and two years later the next ruler, abandoning the ruined city of Hao, established a new capital at Loyang in the valley of the Lo River, near the modern city of Honanfu.

If the ambitious military undertakings of Hsüan were disastrous in their effect upon the royal power, the transfer of the capital eastward from Hao to Loyang was fatal. For more than five centuries after the transfer the royal title remained with the descendants of Wu Wang; but with their abandonment of the Wei-valley outpost in favor of the sheltered valley of the Lo the Chou sovereigns lost their pre-eminence as defenders of the realm, and the real power quickly fell into the hands of their nominal vassals.

By the beginning of the seventh century B.C. the central government had so declined in power as to be almost wholly ignored by the more powerful vassals. Three of these vassal states—Ch'i, Chin, Ch'in[1]—were, by reason of strategic position and sound organization, especially important. Ch'i occupied the greater part of modern Shantung and overshadowed its smaller neighbors of the eastern plain. Chin was situated in the valleys of Shansi, whose mountain ramparts afforded valuable protection on the east and south, while the counts of Ch'in held the old Wei-valley home of the early Chou rulers and, like them, were forced to maintain a constant struggle against the barbarians to the north and west.

In addition to these three powerful feudatories of the east, north, and west there was to the south a fourth state, which was to play an equally important part in the wars and intrigues of the next four centuries. This was the independent kingdom of Ch'u, which had come into existence through the spread of Chinese culture among the barbarians of the Yangtze valley and whose development had in the last part of the ninth century received considerable impetus from the invasion of the Yangtze valley by King Hsüan. Occupying the valley from the gorges to the

[1] Ch'i and Ch'in are pronounced as spelled, while Chin is pronounced as if it were spelled *Jin*.

delta, on the west this southern kingdom was separated by the mountains of modern Shensi and Honan from the Wei-valley state of Ch'in; in the east, however, the kings of Ch'u had pushed northward across the fertile coastal plain until their frontier met that of the Chinese in modern Anhui and northern Kiangsu. The independent but semi-Chinese Yangtze power therefore came inevitably into conflict with Ch'i and Chin, each of which held at times a dominating position among the states occupying the eastern lowland district of China.

Ch'i, already an important state during the days of Yin, was the first of the feudatories to seize upon the decline of the Chou power as an opportunity for self-aggrandizement. In 681 B.C. Huan, the prince of Ch'i, compelled the rulers of four neighboring states to conclude a treaty whereby they placed themselves under his protection and leadership. In the course of a few years this confederation had grown to include within its members practically all the states lying southeast of the lower course of the Yellow River. Under the energetic leadership of the prince of Ch'i wars were carried on against the various barbarian tribes occupying the mountainous districts of Shantung and Honan, as well as against the ever threatening kingdom of Ch'u, while any local ruler who wavered in his duty to the federation was promptly and sternly punished. So long as Huan remained at the helm the operations of the federation were crowned with success, but with his death in 643 B.C. the power of the state of Ch'i completely collapsed; the league, torn by dissensions among its secondary members, began to dissolve, and the armies of Ch'u were soon busily reducing to submission the disunited states.

These circumstances prepared the stage for the appearance of a new hegemon. In 634 B.C. the prince of Chin, in response to an appeal for aid against the aggressions of Ch'u, led his armies down from Shansi and put himself at the head of the league forces; Ch'u was repulsed, and the league was reorganized with Chin at its head. Although Chin retained the hegemony for nearly a century, its leadership was much less energetic than had been that of Ch'i. Unable to rely upon the head of the league for effective support, the states along the Hwai River

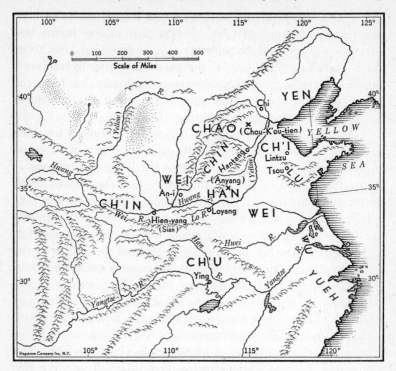

China in the Fourth Century B.C.

therefore began to make terms with Ch'u and to form under its leadership a rival confederacy.

By the middle of the sixth century B.C. the position of the prince of Chin, threatened by Ch'u on the south and by Ch'in on the west, had become almost impossible. To free himself from the danger of a hostile combination between these powerful foes, he therefore sought an alliance with the kingdom of Ch'u. The rapprochement between these two former rivals was facilitated by a proposal put forward by Hsiang Hsü, a minister of the duchy of Sung, who suggested that all the states of the two rival leagues should enter into a solemn treaty for the renunciation of war as an instrument of policy. In 546 B.C. fourteen states, including Chin, Ch'u, and Ch'i,—the last of which had recently regained something of its earlier importance,—signed the treaty and formed themselves into a new league under the joint presidency of Chin and Ch'u. In 541 this solemn league and covenant was renewed for a further term of five years. For about three years after the renewal the pact was faithfully executed, but in 538 the king of Ch'u, observing the steady decline in the power of Chin, decided that the arrangement was no longer advantageous; accordingly he broke the league.

The collapse of this league of nations was followed by three centuries of war and disorder. This period is commonly referred to by Chinese historians as the Age of the Warring Kingdoms.

By the middle of the fourth century B.C. the regions north of the southern boundary of the Yangtze valley had been consolidated into seven states,[1] whose rulers, completely ignoring the feeble descendants of Wu Wang, had assumed royal titles and dignities. During the hundred years from the middle of the fourth century to the unification of the country under the Ch'in dynasty the seven kingdoms were engaged in almost constant war, either against each other or—in the case of Yen, Chao, and Ch'in—against the ever dangerous Hsiungnu Tartars on the north.

By the end of the fourth century B.C. the kingdom of Ch'in was easily the most powerful of the seven kingdoms into which China was divided. Various factors contributed to produce this superiority. For several generations the state had enjoyed a

[1] In the extreme northeast was the kingdom of *Yen*, including the greater part of modern Chihli, with its capital almost on the site of Peiping and extending eastward as far as the Liaotung peninsula. West of Yen was the kingdom of *Chao*, occupying central and northern Shansi together with the western portion of Chihli. The kingdom of *Ch'in*, with its center in the Wei valley, included most of Shensi and a portion of Kansu. In the east the kingdom of *Ch'i*, having recovered from its seventh-century collapse, included the whole province of Shantung. *Ch'u*, in the south, was the largest of the seven, occupying the entire Yangtze valley and extending northward to include the valley of the Han River and the formerly independent states along the Hwai. In the center was the kingdom of *Han*, straddling the Yellow River in southeastern Shansi and northern Honan. The kingdom of *Wei* consisted of two widely separated holdings: a western section in southwestern Shansi and eastern Shensi, and an eastern section in southern Chihli and northeastern Honan.

Three of these kingdoms—Chao, Han, and Wei—had come into existence during the fifth century B.C. through the partition of the old duchy of Chin; the other four—Yen, Ch'in, Ch'i, and Ch'u—had existed since the end of the eleventh or the beginning of the tenth century B.C.

succession of capable rulers and intelligent ministers. In their frequent wars against the Hsiungnu Tartars the military officials of the kingdom had learned to appreciate the advantages possessed by mounted horsemen over the clumsy war chariot and had discarded the chariot to fight on horseback à la Tartar; thus in their subsequent campaigns against the other Chinese states the armies of Ch'in had the advantage of greater mobility. To a certain extent also the strength of Ch'in may be attributed to the reform which, about the middle of the fourth century, had been made in the laws regarding the tenure of land (see page 19). This reform had brought about the gradual disappearance of the old peasant system and the substitution of a system of small landholders, with a consequent improvement in agricultural methods. Finally, Ch'in by reason of its location had been shut out from the intrigues and civil wars which occupied the other states during the greater part of the fifth and fourth centuries B.C.

In the closing years of the fourth century the energetic rulers of Ch'in turned their forces toward the east and began to seize territory on both banks of the Yellow River, thus opening for themselves a path along which they could advance into the eastern plain. The other kingdoms, alarmed by the threatening advance of Ch'in, attempted to save themselves by forming a defensive coalition. Before this new league could come into effective operation the armies of Ch'in had overrun modern Shansi, reducing to a state of vassalage the three kingdoms of Wei, Chao, and Han. Shortly after this the kingdom of Yen, always bitterly hostile to Ch'i, became an ally of the rising western power.

For nearly half a century after this development China was torn by a fresh series of civil wars in which the nominal sovereign of the warring rulers was completely ignored by all. In 256 B.C., however, the Chou monarch rashly determined to assert himself and summoned his loyal vassals to combine their forces against Ch'in. In response to this declaration of war the ruler of Ch'in acted with promptness and decision. He entered Loyang at the head of his army, drove the last king of the Chou dynasty into exile, where he died the following year, and carried away to his capital in the Wei valley the symbols of sovereignty. After eight centuries of rule the "mandate of Heaven" passed from the descendants of Wu Wang into more capable hands; the Chou dynasty gave way to the new dynasty of Ch'in, from whose name, it is generally believed, the present name of China has been derived.

THE AGE OF PHILOSOPHERS

Although the political history of China during the last four centuries of the Chou regime presents a picture of almost uninterrupted turmoil and confusion, it was in this period that China produced the great teachers whose philosophical ideas were destined to have such a permanent influence not only upon their own country but also upon the neighboring lands which borrowed so heavily from Chinese culture. It is reasonable to believe that the political turmoil which afflicted the country during the seventh to third centuries B.C. actually contributed in no small degree to the philosophical and literary achievements of the age. Educated and intelligent men, who in normal times would have found steady employment in honorable government positions, were shaken out of their accustomed grooves by the spectacular rise or calamitous fall of the governments which they served. Political refugees from dozens of petty courts wandered through the land, seeking employment for their talents, and in the course of their wanderings enriched their minds by wider observations or by the exchange of ideas with their fellows in misfortune. The obvious and steadily increasing ills from which the country was suffering aroused a healthy skepticism concerning every detail in the existing social system and inspired thoughtful men to attempt the elaboration of a set of principles upon which society could be more solidly founded.

Priority of place among the philosophers belongs beyond all question to Confucius (Kung-fu-tzu, or "Kung the Teacher"), whose social and ethical teachings have been for more than two thousand years the chief cornerstone of Chinese society. Con-

fucius was born in 551 B.C. in the petty state of Lu, south of T'ai
Shan (Mount T'ai) in Shantung, where his father held a minor
official post and where after the death of his father the widow
and her orphaned son maintained themselves in genteel poverty
upon the land which had been granted to them as a pension.
"When I was young," he is quoted as saying in later years, "I
was in humble circumstances, and for that reason I developed
a variety of abilities in common matters."

Attaining manhood, Confucius entered into official service in
his native state and rose to a post of considerable importance
which, on his mother's death, he resigned. During the three years
of retirement which the rites prescribed for an official mourning
the death of a parent he gave himself over to the study of the
ancient writings, in which even before this time he had developed
an absorbing interest. A visit to Loyang enabled him to witness
the royal sacrifices and still further increased his reverence for
the virtues of antiquity. On returning from the royal city Confucius re-entered official service, first in his native state, later in
Chi (in eastern Shantung) and in Ch'i. About 492 B.C. a change
in the government of Ch'i compelled him to withdraw from the
court. It was not possible for him to retire to Lu, which at this
time was dominated by its powerful neighbor; so Confucius,
accompanied by a small group of intimate friends who formed
the nucleus of his school, set forth upon the wanderings which
lasted until his return, a few months before his death in 479, to
the state where he was born.

At various times in his earlier years when not holding official
position Confucius had occupied himself with giving instruction
in history and the ancient rites. During the thirteen years of his
exile he elaborated his ideas and founded the school by which
these teachings were carried on after his own death. Confucius
had no desire to be looked upon as a philosopher; in his teaching
he repeatedly described himself as a transmitter rather than as
an originator. Regarding himself as primarily a man of action,
he looked forward to the time when some wise ruler would entrust him with the administration of a state and thus give him
an opportunity to put his theories into practice. As a reformer

he was concerned not with morals but with behavior, not with the individual but with society.

The fundamental object of Confucius, as of all the other teachers during the period, was the establishment of good government for the state. The basis of good government he found to lie in the "virtue" of the prince, not merely—or even primarily—as an example to the people but as a positive force which was capable of transforming them by its influence. Also important, although less so than the virtue of the prince, was that of the minister; hence it was the duty of every member of the patrician class to cultivate his virtue in order that, if summoned to high office by his ruler, he should become a force for the transformation of society.

How was this cultivation of virtue to be accomplished? In two ways. First, by the diligent study and the scrupulous observance of the ancient rites and ceremonies. Second, by the cultivation and practice of altruism, which was to show itself in filial and fraternal piety as well as in observing the maxim "Do not do unto others what you would not have others do unto you." Around these two points—the observance of the rites and the practice of altruism—Confucius formulated his rules of behavior which, if put into practice by a prince or a minister, would reform society and bring back the golden days of Yao and Shun.

During Confucius's lifetime his theories of government were little appreciated. "No intelligent monarch arises," said he a few days before his death. "There is not one in the empire that will make me his guide." But, although he died a broken and disappointed man, his labors were not wasted. His work of instruction was carried on and his ideas were kept alive by the band of devoted followers whom he had gathered around him. For a few generations the Confucian school appeared to be lost in the medley of philosophical schools with which the age abounded, but gradually the practical common sense of his teachings began to be recognized in all parts of the country. With the spread of this recognition came a growing reverence for the dead teacher. Temples were erected in his honor; sacrifices were offered to the spirit of the "Perfect Sage"; and Confucianism, the philosophy of Confucius, came to be accepted as the embodiment of all truth and all wisdom.

The substance of the Sage's teachings, as preserved and handed down by his disciples, is incorporated in nine works known as the Confucian Classics, although these nine are usually divided into the Five Classics and the Four Books. The Five Classics include the *Book of Changes*, the *Book of History*, the *Book of Poetry*, the *Book of Rites*, and the *Spring and Autumn Annals*, which is a very brief history of the state of Lu. Only the last of these is supposed to have been written by Confucius,[1] but he is credited with having edited and revised the others. The Four Books are the *Analects*, the sayings of Confucius as recorded by his disciples; the *Great Learning*, written after Confucius's death (and possibly from his notes) by his disciple Tseng-tzu; the *Doctrine of the Mean*, attributed to his great-grandson Tzu-ssu; and the *Book of Mencius*, written in the third century B.C. by the disciples of Mencius, who is regarded as the most brilliant of Confucius's successors.

For more than twenty centuries the Confucian Classics have enjoyed in China an influence even greater than that of the Bible in Christian lands. During the greater part of this time all aspirants to official position have been required to pass rigid examinations upon the content and interpretation of these books. Thus Confucianism, besides furnishing a guide for the daily life of the people, has supplied the Chinese Empire with the code of political ideals by which it has been governed. Nor did the influence of Confucianism stop at the frontiers of China. In Korea, in Japan, and in the states of Indo-China the Great Sage was long held in high esteem. In all these countries scholars devoted themselves to the study of the Classics, and Confucian ideas of ethics and of social morality contributed to the establishment of well-ordered society.

In striking contrast to the founder of Confucianism is the author of the little volume known as the *Tao Te King*. Although

---

[1] Present-day scholars, both Chinese and Western, are inclined to deny the Confucian authorship even of the *Spring and Autumn Annals*.

Lao-tzu (literally, "Old Teacher") is traditionally regarded as having been born in the year 604 B.C., he appears as an extremely shadowy figure about whom nothing definite is known; indeed there is good reason for doubting that anyone bearing that name ever existed. Whether written by its reputed author or compiled by some anonymous writer, however, the *Tao Te King* is known to have been in existence as early as the end of the fifth century B.C., and it is cited by numerous writers during the century which followed.

Unlike the practical rules of conduct taught by Confucius, the ideas set forth in the *Tao Te King* are a combination of mysticism and philosophical anarchism. The author believed that there was a "natural order" of the world, which he called *Tao*, and that man could attain true virtue, *Te*, only to the extent that he succeeded in putting himself in harmony with this natural order. It was his belief that rites and ceremonies were utterly worthless, that humility of spirit was necessary above everything else for the man who wished to make life harmonize with *Tao*. In the opinion of the author government was a snare and delusion; the affairs of mankind could not be improved by legislation. "The more warnings and prohibitions there are in the world," he writes, "the poorer the people become; the more laws and commands there are, the greater the number of thieves and robbers."

In later ages the mysticism of the *Tao Te King* became the foundation of the superstitious cult known as Taoism, which at times has enjoyed great influence in China. The ethical teachings of the book, however, have a simple purity which puzzled the early Christian missionaries. "He who knows men is wise, but he who knows himself is understanding; he who subdues others is strong, but he who can conquer himself is mighty." "To the good I am good, to the bad also I am good, for virtue is goodness." "Repay hatred with kindness." These and similar passages from the *Tao Te King* led many early missionary Sinologues to assume that there must have been a close connection between ancient China and the Old Testament sources of Christianity.

During the century which followed the lifetime of Confucius the most brilliant thinker and writer was Mo-tzu, who lived in the last half of the fifth century B.C. and the first two decades of the fourth. Although Mo-tzu, like Confucius, was a native of the state of Lu, he was not a member of the Confucian school, and his teachings differed in a number of essential points from those of his great fellow countryman. Mo-tzu cared less for the glories of antiquity and denied that rites and ceremonies had any value in themselves; to him religion was a more personal and spiritual matter than it was to Confucius. Especially did he differ in regard to the principle which should control the superior man in his relations with his fellows. Whereas Confucius had advocated *altruism*—a discriminating humanitarianism—as the proper basis for these relations, Mo-tzu insisted that "universal love" was necessary.

In method even more than in the substance of his teachings Mo-tzu was unique. His predecessors and contemporaries poured out their ideas with little attempt at logical arrangement or development; Mo-tzu, in his writings and in his lectures, strove to develop his ideas, defining his terms and supporting his statements by arguments designed to meet the objections which might be raised against them. Thus the school of Mo-tzu, in which the students were trained in the art of discussion, introduced the logical element into Chinese philosophy.

About the middle of the fourth century B.C. there came into prominence a group of political theorists who denied the possibility of discovering from study of the past any fixed principle which could serve as the foundation of the state. This group, the Legalists, insisted that the only basis of government was law and that law could not be fixed once and for all time but must constantly change so as to adjust itself to ever changing conditions. The single criterion by which a law could be judged was its effect: if the result was good, the law was good. Inasmuch as there could be no unanimity with regard to the nature of a result, the application of this criterion implied the dominance of a single will. Law therefore was the expression of the will of the prince, to which he secured obedience by a judicious use of rewards and punishments. The prince, having made the law, should himself respect it so long as it remained in force; but he could not be bound by it, since changing conditions might at any moment render it necessary to proclaim new and contradictory laws. The logic of the Legalists thus led inevitably to the advocacy of an absolute state ruled by an autocratic sovereign.

After the death of Confucius his disciples were chiefly anxious that no part of their master's instruction should be lost or altered. In their writings, therefore, they systematized the Confucian teachings but did little or nothing to develop them, and it was not until the appearance of Mencius (or Meng-tzu) that the school produced a thinker of original genius. Mencius, like Confucius and Mo-tzu, was a native of Lu, and he is said to have studied for a while in the school established by Tzu-ssu, the great-grandson of the Sage. Although he is regarded as the bright and shining light of the Confucian school and although the *Book of Mencius*, written by his disciples, is included in the list of the Confucian Classics, Mencius was not purely Confucian in his thought. He was a Confucianist to the extent that he accepted the Confucian teachings as a reasonable middle ground between two unacceptable extremes: on the one hand, the ideas of the *Tao Te King* and of Mo-tzu; on the other, the belief of the Legalists that society could be reformed by the simple application of law and force. In his development of Confucianism, however, he reflects the influence of the non-Confucian ideas with which his wanderings into the various neighboring states brought him into contact.

In his ideas of government Mencius was revolutionary where Confucius had been conservative; instead of looking back to the glories of the early Chou dynasty and hoping for a restoration of the royal power in the hands of its descendants he looked forward to the establishment of a new and more vigorous line of sovereigns. He was revolutionary also in the importance which he attached to the people. To him the people were not only the most important single element of the state; they were also the true source of all political power: "Heaven sees as the people see, heaven hears as the people hear." According to Mencius the ruler who oppressed his people destroyed thereby his own princely character, and the murderer of such a ruler should not be regarded as guilty of regicide.

While Mencius was elaborating and modifying the teachings of Confucius, his contemporary, Chuang-tzu, a native of the kingdom of Wei, was performing a similar service for the ideas set forth in the *Tao Te King*. Like the author of this work, Chuang-tzu taught that the life of the mystic was the only path to perfection. "Those who wish to attain Tao by study," he writes, "seek that which study will not give; those who wish to obtain it by effort seek that which effort can not bring." Chuang-tzu's attitude toward government was frankly contemptuous. Brilliant in his satire and rich in imagination, Chuang-tzu has been characterized by modern critics as the most versatile writer of ancient China and probably the most profound thinker of his time.

SHIH HUANG TI (246–209 B.C.)

Under the first three sovereigns of the Ch'in dynasty some progress was made toward forcing upon all parts of the country the recognition of the central power; but it remained for the fourth monarch of this line, coming to the throne in 246 B.C., to accomplish the sweeping changes which make the half-century of Ch'in rule a turning point in the history of China. Cheng Wang, as he was called during the first part of his reign, succeeded to the throne at the age of thirteen, and the first ten years of his reign were marked by intrigues and disorders which threatened to bring the dynasty to an early ruin. In 236 B.C., however, a conspiracy which was headed by some of the chief court officials was overthrown, the prominent leaders were put to death or sent into exile, and the young king assumed personal control of the government. After a few years devoted to reorganizing and bringing under control the administration of the state Cheng turned his attention to the task of establishing his absolute authority over all parts of China.

By the year 221 B.C. the work of subjugation had been completed, and the Ch'in monarch wielded a power more absolute than that of any previous Chinese ruler. Hitherto the sovereigns of China had borne the title of Wang ("King"), but Cheng now determined to assume a new and more distinguished title as evidence of the new order which had been established. The title which he created for himself was Huang Ti ("Sovereign Lord" or "Emperor"); he was to be known as Shih Huang Ti, "First Emperor," while his successors upon the throne were to be crowned as "Second Emperor," "Third Emperor," and so on "throughout a thousand generations."

The assumption of this new designation was not a mere indulgence of the monarch's desire for a more imposing title. From the time when Shih Huang Ti seized direct control over the government he had been strongly influenced by the political theories of the Legalists (see page 31), and he was now determined to make those theories the basis of a new political organization. In the empire which he had conquered, law promulgated and enforced by an autocratic sovereign was to replace the traditional principles of social relations which had been handed down from primitive antiquity.

In the place of the old feudal divisions the First Emperor divided his vast domains into thirty-six provinces ruled by salaried military and civil officials answerable to the emperor for every act and liable to be transferred at the emperor's will from one province to another. On the south bank of the Wei River, near the site of the modern Sianfu, he erected a new and splendid capital to which, in order that it might become the real metropolis of his realm, he forcibly transported a hundred and twenty thousand well-to-do families from all parts of the empire.

Among the various other reforms with which he is credited should be mentioned the simplification of the Chinese written character. This reform was facilitated, and perhaps occasioned, by the invention of improved writing materials: the hair brush pen, and an early form of paper made from bamboo pulp.

The drastic reforms whereby Shih Huang Ti centralized and unified the administration of his empire met, very naturally, with widespread opposition. Prominent in this opposition were the scholars, particularly those of the Confucian school, who

bitterly criticized every innovation as an unpardonable violation of sacred tradition. In addition to thus constantly criticizing
the emperor's innovations the Confucian scholars lost no opportunity to compare unfavorably the condition of China under the
new regime with the conditions which had existed during the
great days of Chou or in the Golden Age of Yao and Shun.

To the autocratic war lord this persistent opposition was adequate justification for drastic action; but the emperor may also
have thought that the obliteration of all record of Chinese history prior to the establishment of his new regime would increase
his own glory in the eyes of posterity. Whatever may have been
his dominating motive, he issued in 213 B.C. a decree commanding that all books of history, except the *Annals of the State of
Ch'in*, and all other writings, except those dealing with divination,
medicine, or agriculture, should be destroyed. In the following
year hundreds of books collected from all parts of the empire
were burned, while four hundred and sixty of the scholars, accused
of continuing their criticism of the new regime, were put to death
by imperial command.

The importance of this literary holocaust has often been exaggerated, for in 206 B.C., six years after the event, the second
Ch'in emperor—the successor of the "Book Burner"—was overthrown by a revolution which terminated in the establishment of
the Han dynasty. The rulers of the new dynasty soon repealed
the decree against the ancient writings, and the surviving Confucian scholars were encouraged to reproduce from memory as
much as they could recall of the lost Classics. In 154 B.C. complete copies of a number of the books were discovered hidden
in the wall of a house where Confucius had once lived. Other
fragments were discovered later, and the Classics were gradually
restored almost to the form in which they had existed when
Shih Huang Ti attempted to destroy them forever.

The great Ch'in emperor did not content himself with the
unification of those territories which traditionally belonged to
the Chinese state. Even before his assumption of the new title
he had brought under his control the Yangtze-valley kingdom of
Ch'u, which, although long involved in Chinese affairs, had never

acknowledged the sovereignty of the Chou dynasty. After 221 B.C. he sent expeditions to the south, far beyond the frontiers of this Yangtze kingdom, and extended his authority, nominally at least, over southern China and Annam.

During the reign of Shih Huang Ti the armies of China also carried on frequent campaigns in the north against the Hsiungnu Tartars, whose plundering raids had troubled the Chinese for the preceding thousand years. Although several decisive victories were obtained against the hard-fighting northern barbarians, there was little or no territorial expansion in this direction. Instead of attempting to annex the lands of the Hsiungnu the emperor determined to erect a barrier which would protect his dominions against a continuation of their raiding activities. The idea of such a barrier did not originate with him or his advisers. As early as the beginning of the fourth century B.C. the rulers of Yen and Chao, as well as his own ancestors on the throne of Ch'in, had begun to build walls along portions of their northern frontiers in order to block the passes against the invading horsemen and thus to simplify the problem of the defense. Now, however, the Chinese government undertook the stupendous task of linking together and extending these earlier constructions so as to form an unbroken wall which, beginning at Shanhaikuan on the coast, would reach westward until it lost itself in the sands of the desert.

The work thus undertaken was completed during the reign of the first Han emperor; as it stands today, most of the wall was constructed or reconstructed by later dynasties, but the Great Wall of China always will be associated with the name of Shih Huang Ti. Running over hill and valley, reinforced at the more accessible passes by two or three interior lines of defense and broken only where it crosses the great northern loop of the Yellow River, the Great Wall and its slender garrison may have offered little opposition to the advance of an organized army; against bands of plundering horsemen armed only with bow and spear it provided throughout the ages useful protection for the peaceful Chinese farmers in the valleys and plains to the south.

In 209, after a reign of thirty-seven years, Shih Huang Ti died. Three years later his son and successor was overthrown by a rebellion, and in 202, after four years of civil war, the throne was seized by Liu Pang, the founder of the Han dynasty. In most of the things which he hoped to accomplish Shih Huang Ti failed. His dynasty, which was to endure for "a thousand generations," expired with the three years of mourning for his own death. His effort to give China a government in which the emperor enjoyed absolute power was hardly more successful than his attempt to destroy all memory of past traditions and past glories. In spite of these failures, however, the reign of the great Ch'in emperor had a lasting influence upon his country. While the Great Wall did not end all invasions from the north, it undoubtedly checked many petty plundering expeditions from this quarter, and along its western sections it served for many centuries to mark the northern frontier of the empire. His conquests toward the south set an example for later rulers and thus ensured the permanent establishment of an empire which, although sometimes larger and sometimes smaller, roughly corresponded to the present Chinese state. Finally, China, though frequently broken into fragments during the intervals between strong dynasties, never completely lost the tradition of unity which Shih Huang Ti had endeavored to establish.

END OF THE ANCIENT PERIOD

The half-century of Ch'in rule may conveniently be taken as marking the end of the ancient period in China's history. Throughout the legendary age and a thousand years of authentic history the people of China had slowly evolved the essential features of their distinctive civilization. The climax of this indigenous development came in the reign of Shih Huang Ti, who united the separate political fragments and formed the Chinese Empire. Up to this point in their development the Chinese had received little from outside, yet even during the half-century preceding the Ch'in dynasty there had begun to appear upon the western frontiers the first emissaries from foreign civilizations: India and the Greco-Bactrian world. In the new era which is to follow, the Chinese people, united into an empire, will be found in ever increasing contact with a hitherto unknown world, while the indigenous civilization of China will be compelled to meet and adjust itself to an increasing inflow of ideas from foreign lands.

SUGGESTED REFERENCES

ANDERSSON, J. G. An Early Chinese Culture.

ANDERSSON, J. G. Preliminary Report on Archaeological Research in Kansu.

CARUS, P. The Canon of Reason and Virtue. (A translation of the *Tao Te King*.)

CHARDIN AND LICENT. The Discovery of Palaeolithic Industry in North China.

DUYVENDAK, J. J. L. The Book of Lord Shang.

GILES, H. A. Chuang Tzu: Mystic, Moralist, and Social Reformer.

GRANET, M. Chinese Civilization.

HIRTH, F. The Ancient History of China.

LATOURETTE, K. S. The Chinese: their History and Culture.

LEGGE, J. The Chinese Classics.

LI, C. The Formation of the Chinese People.

MASPERO, H. La Chine antique.

MEI, Y. P. The Ethical and Political Works of Motse.

PELLIOT, P. L'origine du nom de Chine. (T'oung Pao, 1912.)

SOOTHILL, W. E. The Analects of Confucius.

SOOTHILL, W. E. The Three Religions of China.

WILHELM, R. A Short History of Chinese Civilization.

WILLIAMS, E. T. China Yesterday and Today.

WILLIAMS, E. T. A Short History of China.

III

India: from Earliest Times to End of the Maurya Dynasty

Antiquity of Indian Civilization · Geography and Population · Chronological
Difficulties in Indian History · Archaeological Records · The Coming of the
Aryans · The Vedas · Aryan Culture in Vedic Times · Brahmanism · Caste ·
Opposition to Brahman Domination · Gautama Buddha · The "Eightfold
Path" · Divisions in Buddhism · Northern India in the Sixth Century B.C. · The
Persian Conquest of the Punjab · Alexander the Great · Consequences of
Alexander's Invasion · Magadha in the Fourth Century B.C. · The Maurya
Dynasty · Asoka · Asoka and Buddhism · Decline and End of the Maurya
Dynasty · Art and Literature of the Maurya Period · Southern India · Summary
of Early Indian History

INDIA, like China, is the scene of one of the oldest continuous
civilizations in the world's history. Originating at a time
when Egypt and Mesopotamia were transmitting their culture
to uncivilized peoples around the Mediterranean Sea, the civilization of India has been handed down throughout the ages in the
form of institutions and beliefs which still direct the lives of
a large part of the three hundred million people who now inhabit
the land. Although the beginnings of Indian civilization were
contemporary with—or perhaps even antedated—the earliest
known civilization in China, the reliable record of Indian antiquity cannot be traced back nearly so far as that of the Chinese;
the absence of any satisfactory system of chronology presents
well-nigh insuperable difficulties to any authoritative reconstruction of India's ancient record.

The total area of India is almost equal to that of Europe with
Russia excluded. Although not so large as China if all the outlying Chinese dependencies are included, India is considerably
larger than the eighteen provinces of China Proper. Thus in
dealing with India we are dealing with a region which is almost
continental in size. In addition to the great size of the country

there is the further important fact that India is divided into a number of clearly defined geographical units. The lowland region of the north, from the foothills of the Himalayas down to the Vindhya Mountains, is occupied by the Indus and Ganges river basins, which are almost completely separated from each other by the highlands and deserts of Rajputana. To the south of the Vindhyas and reaching southward to the Krishna River is the Deccan plateau, a rough inhospitable region difficult of access and covered in its valley regions with tropical jungle. South of the Deccan lies the even more tropical, but less forbidding, region of Tamil-land, or Dravida. In modern times engineering science has reduced the importance of the mountains and the river gorges by which these areas are marked off from each other; but in earlier ages so formidable were these obstacles to communication that only on a few occasions in India's history did a single ruler extend his dominions to include two of these three great divisions, while never, until the establishment of British rule, were all three brought together under a single crown.

In its population, as in its geographical features, India exhibits a high degree of diversification. The people of the northern lowlands, where the tall, fair-skinned type predominates, belong to two separate groups: one, the Indo-Aryans, who probably absorbed various non-Aryan invaders during early historic times; and the other, the Mohammedans, who after the tenth century poured down into the country from central and western Asia and who, because of religious differences, resisted absorption. In the Deccan the predominantly Dravidian population has adopted much of the Aryan culture, but the people are shorter in stature and darker in skin than those of the north. The population of the extreme south is almost purely Dravidian and, although it has accepted to some extent the religion and the general organization of the Aryans, has retained its own language and culture. Scattered through the Deccan, moreover, there are to be found various aboriginal hill tribes, such as the Gonds; while the states of the extreme north, in the Himalaya region, contain a considerable element of Tibeto-Burman Mongolians. The failure of these various population groups to amalgamate into a single people—a failure which may be attributed partly to geographical conditions and partly to the Hindu system of caste—left India throughout the greater part of its long history divided into a multitude of warring states, each with its separate traditions and with its own local heroes.

A serious obstacle to the satisfactory reconstruction of early Indian history lies in the absence of any dependable chronological skeleton. The extensive literature of the Indian peoples furnishes an abundant supply of facts and traditions for the use of the historian; but even in the case of such limited areas as the Punjab or the kingdom of Magadha the absence of a trustworthy system of dates makes it often impossible to determine with any degree of accuracy the order in which events occurred or the extent of time between any two given events. While Chinese history, chronologically, is on solid ground by the middle of the ninth century B.C. and while a fairly reliable chronology can be constructed for the four or five centuries preceding that point, the earliest precise date in Indian history is fixed by the invasion of Alexander the Great in the spring of 326 B.C.

Upon the cornerstone thus provided by Western chronology modern research has succeeded, by synchronizing the fragmentary historical evidence in Indian literature, in building up for northern India an approximated chronological framework which reaches back to the middle of the seventh century before the Christian Era. Even for northern India, however, the period from the seventh century B.C. to the end of the sixth century A.D. can be dated only tentatively; there are many gaps in this constructed chronology, and the only thoroughly dependable dates are those which have been established by the contacts between India and her neighbors. For southern India there are no reliable historical dates before the last quarter of the sixth century A.D.

The archaeological record of human existence in India goes back to the Paleolithic Age, and the remains of this period seem to indicate that the peninsular south was occupied even earlier than were the lowlands of the north. As elsewhere, so in India, the roughly shaped stone implements of the Paleolithic Age were gradually replaced by the polished stone of the Neolithic. In northern India an Age of Copper intervened between the Neolithic Age and the introduction, probably about 1000 B.C., of the use of iron; but in southern India, where the use of iron probably began several centuries later than in the north, there is no evidence of an intervening use of copper implements. There appears to have been no Bronze Age in India, either northern or southern. The people of neolithic India used the potter's wheel, cultivated the land, had domesticated animals, and appear also to have engaged in mining for gold. They lived in settled communities, had established religious rites, and, unlike their paleolithic predecessors, disposed of their dead by burial.

During the last few years excavations by archaeologists in the Indus valley have brought to light evidence which seems to prove that this section of India was, during the third millennium B.C., connected with or influenced by the Sumerian civilization of Mesopotamia. The intimacy of this connection and the degree to which it may have influenced the subsequent development of Indian culture are points upon which modern scholarship is still at variance. According to an eminent British scholar,[1] this ancient Indus-valley civilization was a highly "individualized" branch of a great culture which covered all western Asia and the eastern Mediterranean. In the Indus valley it was completely obliterated by the subsequent Aryan invasion, but it is altogether possible that elements of this civilization, carried southward by fugitives from the Indus, may have exerted a strong influence upon cultural development in the Deccan.

THE COMING OF THE ARYANS

Even during the early Neolithic period the population of India was composed of diverse elements. The most important group were the Dravidians, who occupied the northern plains as well as the peninsula and who may have extended into modern Baluchistan on the northwest; but there were also, scattered around in different parts of the land, various even more ancient

[1] Sir John Marshall, in the *Times* (London), February 26, 1926, p. 18, and in the Archeological Survey of India Annual Report, 1923-24 (1926), p. 49.

occupants of the country whose descendants still compose a part of the population. About two or three thousand years before the Christian Era there began to arrive in the upper portion of the Indus valley a taller, fair-skinned race: the Aryans. The newcomers, who were related to the Persians, to the Iranians, and, more distantly, to most of the present peoples of Europe, occupied at first only the Punjab: the basin of the upper Indus and its tributaries. To the south and southeast the Punjab is cut off, by a dry sandy waste, from the other parts of India; but after several centuries the invaders worked their way along the foothills lying to the north of this semidesert area and entered the upper part of the Ganges basin, which they eventually occupied to its mouth.

This Aryan occupation and conquest, which thus gradually extended over the two great river basins of the north, did not reach south of the Vindhya Mountains. In later ages a certain amount of commercial intercourse with the south was carried on by way of the coastal lowlands of the eastern coast, and Aryan culture gained a limited influence in the Deccan; but the Deccan and the extreme south both remained Dravidian in population, while even the earliest Aryan traders who entered these regions found there and in the island of Ceylon organized communities with a well-developed and thoroughly independent civilization.

Our knowledge of the history and the institutions of the early Aryans is drawn from a single source: the body of literature known as the Vedic scriptures. The Vedas are four in number,— the Rigveda, the Samaveda, the Yajurveda, and the Atharvaveda,—consisting of collections of hymns, prayers, spells, and incantations. Supplementing these collections, but usually regarded as an integral part of the Vedic scriptures, were prose writings known as Brahmanas and Upanishads. The Brahmanas were theological and ritualistic treatises serving as explanations of the hymns or as manuals to guide the priests in performing the sacrifices, while the Upanishads were still later compositions of a more philosophical nature.

Among the scholars who have devoted themselves to the study of Vedic literature there is a wide difference of opinion with respect to its age. One prominent scholar attributes the oldest hymns of the Rigveda to the period between 6000 B.C. and 4000 B.C., while he believes that a number of the Brahmanas were composed between the years 2500 B.C. and 1400 B.C. In contrast with this view is the opinion of an equally eminent authority who suggests 1500 B.C. as the earliest limit of Vedic literature. A larger number place the date of composition somewhere between 2500 B.C. and 1500 B.C., but admit that this vague dating is mere conjecture.

An effort has been made by some scholars to synchronize the composition of the Vedas with the advance of the Aryan occupation by proving that the Rigveda was composed while the Aryans were still confined to the Punjab, the Samaveda and the Yajurveda when they had occupied the upper portions of the Gangetic plain, and the Atharvaveda after they had completed their conquest of the Ganges valley. Critics of this view, however, point out that all four of the collections remained "open" for a number of centuries and that consequently the mention or the failure to mention certain geographical features does not serve to show where the Aryans were located at the period when the bulk of the hymns in any one collection were being composed.

Although the Vedas deal primarily with matters of religion, incidental allusions in many of the hymns throw valuable light upon the life and culture of the early Aryans. Like the early Greeks who, at about the same time, were pushing down into the Balkan peninsula, the Aryan invaders of India consisted of a number of related tribes. Each tribe was governed by its own chief and tribal council. The Aryans brought with them domesticated animals, including the horse, and they were skilled in the cultivation of the soil. In battle they fought from chariots, chiefly with the bow and arrow, and they wore defensive armor to protect themselves from the weapons of the enemy. They were acquainted with the arts of weaving, tanning, and metalworking; but the use of iron appears to have been unknown to them in the earliest Vedic period. Unlike their descendants of a much later date, the earliest Aryans had no objection to the eating of flesh, but their chief articles of diet were milk, grain, vegetables, and fruit. Where they settled they built fortified villages, but these villages showed little tendency to develop into towns. At times the various Aryan tribes fought against one another, but when occasion arose they were usually ready to put aside their private quarrels and to make common cause against the earlier inhabitants of the country which they were slowly occupying.

The religion of the early Aryans consisted in the worship of the "bright gods" of nature, to whom were addressed the hymns which compose the Vedas. Unlike the contemporary deities of the Dravidians, the Aryan gods were regarded as essentially benevolent in their attitude toward mankind and as making war against the forces of evil. The hymns of the first three Vedas, which appear to be least affected by non-Aryan influence, therefore sound the note of praise and thanksgiving rather than that of propitiation. The Atharvaveda, however, appears to have been more influenced by the religious ideas of the pre-Aryan inhabitants with whom the conquerors were coming into contact, and it contains a large number of spells or propitiatory incantations designed to avert the dangerous activities of malignant spirits.

This difference in tone between the Atharvaveda and its predecessors is significant. Although the Rigveda has been said to contain "the germs of the whole afterdevelopment of Indian religion and polity," it is generally recognized that Brahmanism —the fully developed religion of India—has been immeasurably affected by non-Vedic and non-Aryan religious elements. Except for Indra, the god of thunder, who continued to hold high rank, the Vedic gods found themselves reduced to subordinate positions, and their places were taken by Brahma, Vishnu, and Siva, supported by a multitude of other deities unknown to the Vedas. The doctrine of rebirth, which does not appear in the Vedas, has become since Vedic times a fundamental tenet in the faith of the Indian Aryans. Along with the doctrine of rebirth there was adopted the belief that the nature of the new incarnation depended upon the soul's Karma: the totality of its actions in previous incarnations.

Even the priestly sacrifices, which from Vedic times have formed the essential feature of the Aryan religion, underwent modification. Instead of being regarded as offerings of praise and thanksgiving these sacrifices, performed in accordance with strict Vedic regulations, came to be looked upon as appeasing the gods and inclining them to grant the wishes of their worshipers. Hence the priests, or Brahmans, who alone had power to perform these mysteries, gradually became first the necessary intermediaries between the gods and man, and later, with the growing belief that the response of the gods was automatic, the actual masters of the divine forces. Brahmanism in its final form may therefore be considered as the religion of the Brahmans rather than that of the god Brahma.

Probably the most unique and certainly the most widely known feature of Indian social organization is the caste system with its hundreds or even thousands of closed social groups, each group hedged about with strict rules and regulations pertaining to matters of diet, birth, marriage, physical contacts, and the like. This institution, which was already well established at the time of the Macedonian invasion in the fourth century B.C. and which probably had existed for six or eight centuries before that date, is unknown to Vedic literature.

The origin of the caste system has been frequently attributed to the classification of the population into four orders: (1) the Brahmans, who were the priestly and learned class; (2) the Kshatriyas, who were the rulers and warriors; (3) the Vaisyas, who comprised the merchants and farmers; and (4) the Sudras, the slaves or serfs. Other peoples than the Indo-Aryans, however, have had a similar classification without having evolved anything even remotely resembling the Indian system of caste.

Perhaps the most satisfactory explanation of the development of the institution is that suggested by the late Dr. Vincent A. Smith, who finds its germ even in Vedic times in the great preeminence of the Brahman sacrificers. This learned, priestly, and intellectually superior class, according to Dr. Smith,

gradually framed extremely strict rules to guard their own ceremonial purity against defilement through unholy food or undesirable marriages. The enforcement of such rules on themselves by the most respected members of the Indo-Aryan community naturally attracted the admiration of the more worldly classes of society, who sought to emulate and imitate the virtuous self-restraint of the Brahmans. It being clearly impossible that ordinary soldiers, business men, peasants, and servants could afford to be as scrupulous as the saintly or at least professedly religious Brahmans, a separate standard of *Dharma* (law) for each section of society necessarily grew up by degrees. Kings, for instance, might properly and must do things which subjects could not do without sin, and so on. The long-continued conflict with the aboriginal Indians, who held quite different ideals of conduct, made both the Brahmans and their imitators more and more eager to assert their superiority and exclusiveness by ever-increasing scrupulosity concerning both diet and marriage.[1]

Gautama Buddha, or Sakyamuni (563?–483? b.c.)

The people of India, Aryan and non-Aryan alike, seem to have been throughout all periods of their history peculiarly addicted to religious speculation; but the two most important rivals of Aryan orthodoxy, Buddhism and Jainism, arose almost simultaneously as revolts against the domination of the Brahmans and against the rigid formalism of their ceremonial. Mahavira, the founder or at least the reviver of Jainism, and Gautama Buddha both lived during the sixth century b.c. and were, according to the most commonly accepted dates for their lives, close contemporaries of Confucius, the great Chinese sage. Mahavira and Gautama both belonged to the Kshatriya, or ruling class, and both taught, in opposition to the ritualistic religion of the Brahmans, doctrines in which the existence of the gods was either ignored or expressly denied, while emphasis was placed upon the suppression of desire and upon the cultivation of a compassionate attitude toward all living beings. Jainism appears never to have extended its influence to regions outside India, where it still has, however, a number of adherents; but Buddhism, now almost negligible in the land of its origin, spread to all parts of central and eastern Asia and is today one of the great world religions.

[1] V. A. Smith, *The Oxford History of India*, p. 37.

Because of the influence which his teachings have exerted throughout the Far Eastern world the founder of Buddhism deserves more than a mere passing notice. Gautama, or Siddhartha, was the son and heir of the rajah of Kapilavastu, a little state of northern India situated just inside the borders of modern Nepal. He is often referred to as Sakyamuni ("Sage of Sakya") from the name of the tribe to which his family belonged; usually, however, he is called Gautama Buddha, which means "Gautama the Enlightened." The dates of Gautama's life cannot be definitely stated; the Ceylon chronicles put his birth at 623 B.C. and his death at 543 B.C., while the chronology now most generally accepted substitutes for these dates the years 563 and 483 respectively. According to the traditions handed down in Buddhist literature the young prince was brought up in luxury and was given a good education, but instead of finding satisfaction in the pleasures by which he was surrounded he brooded over the mysteries of human life: the problems of sin, suffering, sickness, and death.

At the age of twenty-nine he decided to abandon the wealth and position to which he had been born and to devote himself to a life of asceticism. Acting upon this decision, he left his home and submitted himself to six years of rigid self-discipline and penance, only to find that mortification of the body brought no peace to his soul. Finally he came, through meditation, to the conclusion that all these formal observances were useless and that the only way to spiritual peace lay in complete forgetfulness of self. From the date of this "enlightenment," which he attained at the age of thirty-five, until his death forty-five years later he spent his time in meditation and in expounding his faith to an increasing body of followers.

In the form originally taught by its founder Buddhism was a purely human religion. While Gautama did not actually deny the existence of the Hindu gods, he completely ignored them and denied the value of the Vedas. He accepted the common Indian theories of rebirth and of Karma, but he was wholly uninterested in the discussion of such matters as the origin of the universe or the nature of the soul. His one concern was with the question of human sorrow. The cause of sorrow he found in human desire; only as self was forgotten and all desire eliminated could mortal man be freed from sorrow. This condition, however, could not be achieved so long as the soul was lodged in a physical body, and the doctrine of rebirth seemed to condemn the soul to an endless treadmill of successive incarnations. From this gloomy prospect Gautama saw a possibility of escape in the acquisition of a Karma which by becoming progressively more pure and perfect would eventually entitle the soul to be set free from the treadmill and to enter Nirvana: a state of absorption into the "All-soul" of the universe.

This goal of ultimate perfection was not to be secured by the performance of ritual ceremonies or by rigorous fasting, since such activities, being selfish in themselves, would serve only to strengthen the ties which bound the soul to its physical prison. Instead, Gautama taught his disciples to strive above all else for purity in thought, in word, and in deed. As a guide to this threefold purity he put before them the "Eightfold Path": "Right Belief," "Right Feelings," "Right Speech," "Right Actions," "Right Means of Livelihood," "Right Endeavor," "Right Remembrance," "Right Meditation." As further guidance he gave them also ten commandments: not to kill, to steal, or to commit adultery; not to lie, to gossip, to indulge in faultfinding, or to use profanity; to abstain from covetousness or hatred; and to avoid ignorance. The founder of Buddhism made no direct attack upon the caste system of the Brahmans; but the ideal of self-forgetfulness which he taught was utterly opposed to the basic principle of caste, and among his disciples all caste distinctions were ignored.

In 483 B.C., the year of Gautama's death, his disciples held a council for the purpose of fixing authoritatively the substance of their master's teachings. This object was accomplished by the composition of the Tripitaka (the "Three Baskets"), of which the first portion contained the discourses of Gautama, the second portion the rules of monastic discipline, and the third portion a systematic outline of the doctrine. As formulated by this first council the doctrines of Buddhism retained the primitive simplicity of its founder, but it was not long before the spirit of innovation began to appear among the members of the faith. Gautama was deified as the savior of mankind, to whom prayer and praise were to be addressed; numerous other gods, borrowed from the Brahman pantheon, were associated with him, and a complicated theology was evolved.

These innovations were resented by a conservative minority and eventually resulted in a definite separation of the two parties. The doctrine of the conservatives was known as the Hinayana, or "Lesser Vehicle," because it rejected all the proposed additions, while the "enriched" Buddhism of the majority group became known as the Mahayana, or "Greater Vehicle."

Both forms of Buddhism were carried from India into other parts of Asia; but the Mahayana form was the more successful in extending its influence and spread into central Asia, Tibet, China, Korea, and Japan, in all of which countries it underwent still further transformation and subdivision. The Hinayana branch, which became the Buddhism of Ceylon, found its most fruitful field for missionary work in Malaysia and in Indo-China, especially Burma. But the division between these two branches of the Buddhist faith was not marked by an impassable gulf. Such is the religious eclecticism of Oriental peoples that Mahayanists and Hinayanists were frequently found in the same religious community, while the Chinese pilgrims of the fifth, sixth, and seventh centuries A.D. were in the habit of visiting both Mahayanist northern India and Hinayanist Ceylon in their search for more perfect knowledge of the law.

Western Invaders in the Punjab

From the religious writings of the Jains, Buddhists, and Brahmans of the sixth and succeeding centuries B.C. it is possible to collect around the chronological framework supplied by the first two of these religions a certain amount of historical material relating to the contemporary political situation in the valley of the Ganges. Of the numerous states which then occupied the Gangetic plain three stand out as especially prominent. The first of these, Avanti, occupied the southwestern portion of the plain, with its capital at the still important city of Ujjain, and was at this time probably the most powerful state in the north. The kingdom of Kosala, which lay to the north of the middle Ganges, had its capital at Sravasti, while Magadha was farther to the east in the modern district of South Bihar, with its capital at Rajagriha. Kosala and Magadha, the latter of which was destined to become the center of the first great Indian empire, were especially prominent in the writings of the Jains and the Buddhists; and it has therefore been possible to reconstruct a list of the sixth-century and fifth-century Magadhan rulers with fairly dependable dates for their reigns.

Although the Punjab (the "Five Rivers") of the Indus basin lay outside the scope of this religious literature, the closing years of the sixth century B.C. saw also the beginning of dated, or datable, history for this section of the north. Sometime between the years 517 and 509 B.C., Darius I of Persia extended his empire eastward into the Indus valley and annexed the western part of the Punjab. In obedience to the orders of Darius his Greek admiral, Skylax, assembled a fleet of boats on the upper Indus and explored the river to its mouth. The conquered portion of the Punjab, which was organized into the twentieth satrapy of the Persian Empire, remained under Persian rule for a century and a half, paying annual tribute and supplying Xerxes with a contingent of troops for the expedition with which that monarch, in 480 B.C., invaded Greece. The Persian conquest of the Indus valley made it possible for a considerable amount of information concerning India to reach the peoples of the Mediterranean world; and the merchants of Arabia and Phoenicia, who probably began to trade even earlier with southern India, now began to develop commercial relations with the Punjab. One of the two early Indian alphabets, the Kharoshthi, is closely related to the Persian; and it appears almost certain that it was introduced at this time into the Punjab, where it continued to be used until the fourth century A.D.

In the year 330 B.C., Alexander the Great, having made himself the master of the Persian Empire, started eastward upon his ambitious campaign of exploration and conquest. After more than three years of marching here and there through the regions lying between the Caspian Sea and the Himalayas, the Macedonian conqueror finally led his army into the plains of the upper Indus. In February, 326, he crossed the Indus and entered the Punjab, which at that time was occupied by a number of independent states. The rivalries of the local rulers facilitated the task of the invader, and the Macedonians in their march southeastward across the Jhelum, Chinab, and Ravi rivers to the banks of the Bias met no united opposition. Arriving at this point, Alexander was informed that a great kingdom, probably Magadha, mightier and more wealthy than any of the Punjab states, lay still farther to the southeast.

Against this new objective the conqueror immediately determined to advance, but at this point his soldiers failed him. Four years had elapsed since he had started eastward from Ecbatana, while it had been eight years since his European contingents had first crossed the Hellespont to battle against the Persians. Flatly refusing to proceed farther to the east, the troops demanded that they be led toward home, and Alexander, after pausing long enough to erect altars to mark the eastern limit of his conquests, yielded to the demand.

Retracing his route as far as the river Jhelum, the conqueror turned southwestward along this river, accompanied by a great flotilla of boats under the command of Nearchos. As he passed down the Jhelum to its junction with the Indus and down the Indus to its delta, Alexander everywhere summoned the local rulers to make their submission; those who obeyed were confirmed in their rights, while such as presumed to ignore his call were conquered. At the head of the delta, while Nearchos made a survey of the main channels leading to the sea, the conquering Macedonian laid the foundations of a garrison city for his newly won provinces; then, in October, 325 B.C., twenty months after his first crossing of the Indus, he led his army out of India upon the long and difficult homeward march.

Prior to his departure from India, Alexander had organized his conquests into provinces and had appointed governors and viceroys supported by garrison forces to govern in his name. Upon his death in 323 B.C., however, his vast empire quickly fell apart, and his recently conquered Indian subjects, rebelling against their foreign rulers, were among the first to regain their independence. Although every vestige of the conquest thus quickly disappeared from the Indus valley, the eastern expedition of Alexander appears to have had important indirect consequences for India. Before entering the Indus valley he had established in Bactria and Parthia a number of Greek colonies. These colonies, more lasting than his Indian garrisons, became permanent centers of Hellenized culture, whose influence, especially in the realm of art, had a decided effect upon India.

Even more important, although quite as indirect, was the effect of the invasion upon the political situation in the country. By crushing a majority of the independent states of the Punjab and by bringing the region momentarily under a single rule the Macedonian conqueror had decidedly modified the existing balance of power in northern India and had made possible the emergence of new combinations. Moreover, the political and military methods by which these conquests had been achieved, although they may have passed unnoticed by most of the Indian rulers and leaders, appear to have made a deep impression upon a young Magadhan prince who lost little time in taking advantage of the new opportunities and in utilizing the new ideas.

During the sixth century B.C. and the greater part of the fifth the kingdom of Magadha had been under the rule of a dynasty known as the Saisunaga. Two of the Saisunaga kings, Bimbisara and his son Ajatasatru, occupied the throne during the lifetime of Gautama Buddha, and their interest in the teachings of Gautama and of his Jain contemporary ensured to these monarchs considerable prominence in the religious literature of the period. Toward the end of the fifth century (the date has been put tentatively at 413 B.C.) the Saisunaga dynasty was overthrown and Magadha came under the rule of a new line of kings known as the Nandas.

At the time of Alexander's campaign in the Punjab, Chandragupta Maurya, a young prince who appears to have been descended from the last ruler of the Saisunaga dynasty and who had been exiled from Magadha, was among the number of Indian nobles who responded to the conqueror's summons by attending his court. When the news of Alexander's death reached the Indus valley, Chandragupta became the leading figure in the uprising against the foreign garrisons. At about the same time, approximately 322 B.C., a revolution in Magadha drove the last of the Nandas from the throne and placed this area also under the rule of Chandragupta, whose power was thus established over an empire stretching across northern India from the Ganges delta to the northwestern limits of the Punjab.

THE MAURYA DYNASTY, 322?–185 B.C.

With the accession of Chandragupta Maurya the history of northern India emerges for a while at least from the shadows of uncertainty. For the hundred and thirty-seven years of the Maurya dynasty the recorded observations of Greek visitors and the numerous inscriptions of the great emperor Asoka provide a wealth of historical material, while the frequent contact during the first three Mauryan reigns between India and the Western world make it possible to establish almost certain dates for the important events of the period. Yet this emergence of Indian history is only partial and temporary. Almost no correlation between the Mauryan dates and events in the extreme south has been possible, while the breakup of the Mauryan empire plunged the whole of India again into a state of historical semidarkness.

As the capital of his extensive empire the first Maurya ruler selected Pataliputra, modern Patna.[1] From this capital, whose palaces are described by the Greek Megasthenes as excelling in splendor those of Susa or of Ecbatana, Chandragupta and his ministers governed the empire by means of a highly organized civil administration supported by a regular army of nearly three

[1] At that time the site of the city was a point of land between the Ganges and Son rivers, the latter being a southern tributary which now joins the Ganges somewhat farther to the west than it did in the fourth century B.C.

quarters of a million. Although the Maurya ruler had risen to power as the champion of Indian liberties against the foreign oppressor, his own rule was marked by great severity; heavy taxes were imposed upon the people, and harsh penalties were meted out to all violators of the law.

In the year 312 B.C., Seleukos Nikator, one of Alexander's generals, succeeded in making himself the master of Babylon and of the greater part of Alexander's Asiatic possessions. Having established his authority over the regions nearer at hand, he determined to reconquer the lost Indian provinces and in 305 invaded the Punjab. Instead of regaining the lost provinces Seleukos was so severely repulsed by the forces of Chandragupta that in the subsequent treaty of peace he ceded to the Indian ruler the region comprising modern Afghanistan and Baluchistan. By this treaty permanent friendly relations were established between the two empires; and a few years later, probably in 302 B.C., Chandragupta received at his court as an ambassador from Seleukos the celebrated Megasthenes, whose observations at Pataliputra have been the source from which the classical writers of Greece and Rome derived most of their information concerning India.

Chandragupta was succeeded on the throne by his son Bindusara, to whom he bequeathed an empire extending from Bengal on the east to the western limits of Afghanistan and including all of India north of the Narbada River. In the Indian records Bindusara stands out less clearly than does his father, but he is known to have carried on friendly correspondence with Antiochos I of Syria and to have received at his court ambassadors both from that monarch and from Ptolemy Philadelphos, the Macedonian ruler of Egypt. Along with the empire the second Mauryan emperor appears to have inherited a considerable amount of his father's energy and ability. He governed successfully for a quarter of a century and at the end of that period bequeathed to his own successor a domain which was not only unimpaired in size but had been expanded by the establishment of a certain degree of control over the Deccan as far south as the Krishna.

While Bindusara stands out less clearly than his father as a historical figure, his son and successor Asoka is better known to the modern reader than is any other Indian ruler before Akbar. Asoka's numerous and lengthy edicts, inscribed sometimes in living rock and sometimes upon stone pillars which he erected for the purpose, furnish a wide variety of information not only with regard to the events of the reign but also concerning the policies, the motives, and the character of the emperor himself. Beginning with the ninth year after his formal coronation, which did not take place until the year 269 B.C., these inscriptions are dated by regnal years, a fact which makes it possible to fix definitely both the sequence and the actual dates of the events which they record.

Although some historians are inclined to attribute to Asoka rather than to his father the conquest and annexation of the Deccan, Asoka himself in his inscriptions lays claim to only one conquest: that of Kalinga, on the east coast between the Mahanadi and Godavari rivers, which occurred in the year 261 B.C. In the field of political history the Kalinga war is the one striking event of Asoka's reign, the single military achievement in the record of a peaceful and benevolent despot.

It was as a professor and patron of the Buddhist faith that the third Mauryan emperor achieved his greatest fame. Prior to his reign the adherents of Gautama's teachings appear to have constituted merely one of the numerous petty religious sects which existed in the northwestern districts of India; Asoka made Buddhism for a while one of the leading Indian religions and gave it, or helped to give it, the impetus which carried it far beyond the boundaries of his own empire into the most distant regions of the Far East.

The emperor's own conversion to Buddhism, according to the account given in one of his most important inscriptions, came as the direct result of his Kalinga campaign:

Directly after the annexation of the Kalinga began His Sacred Majesty's zealous protection of the Law of Piety, his love for that Law, and his inculcation of that Law. Thus arose His Sacred Majesty's remorse for having conquered the Kalingas, because the conquest of a country previously un-

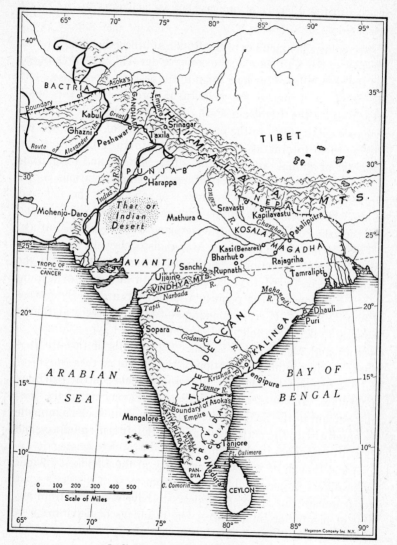

India in the Third Century B.C.

conquered involves the slaughter, death, and carrying away captive of the people. That is a matter of profound sorrow and regret to His Sacred Majesty.

Becoming a lay member of the Buddhist brotherhood in 261 B.C., the year of the Kalinga war, the emperor devoted himself throughout the remainder of his long reign to the task of spreading among his people and among the peoples of foreign lands the noble principles of the Eightfold Path. His numerous edicts contain repeated admonitions to the people and officials of the empire, exhorting them to practice the "law of piety," to refrain from the slaughter of animals and from the eating of flesh, and to be compassionate toward all living creatures. These exhortations Asoka supplemented by his own example: he abolished the imperial sport of hunting, built hospitals and resthouses, and dug wayside wells for the comfort of the travelers and their beasts of burden.

Outside his own dominions Asoka dispatched Buddhist missionaries in all directions: northward into the countries of the Himalayas, eastward to Indo-China, southward to Ceylon and to the kingdoms of the peninsula, and westward to the realms of four "Yavana" (Greek) monarchs—Antiochos, the grandson of Seleukos Nikator; Ptolemy Philadelphos of Egypt; Magas of Cyrene; and Alexander of Epirus. The records of the Mediterranean world contain no mention of the arrival of these missions, and any attempt to establish a connection between the teachings of Gautama and subsequent religious developments in the west must remain in the field of pure conjecture; but Asoka's missionary enterprise to the north, east, and south left lasting impressions upon his neighbors in these directions.

Ardent though he was in his advocacy of the Buddhist "Way," Asoka differs in one notable respect from most of history's royal propagandists: his advocacy appears to have been free from any taint of bigotry or intolerance. The teachings of Gautama were to him not a body of dogma but a way of life; therefore, while urging all men to choose and to follow this way, he was careful to avoid making any attack upon the existing beliefs and religious practices of his subjects.

One possible political motive may have supplemented the genuine religious enthusiasm of the great Buddhist emperor. The caste system of the Brahmans, already well established, was dividing the people of his empire into an ever increasing number of rigidly closed communities, but the Buddhist brotherhood ignored all caste distinctions. It is conceivable that Asoka, regarding himself as the father of his people, hoped that the expanding influence of the Buddhist faith would break down the barriers of caste and make of the Indian people a single undivided family. If this hope existed, it was doomed to disappointment. Brahmanism, although somewhat modified by Buddhist influence, has remained throughout the ages the dominant religion of the Hindu people, while Buddhism after the death of its powerful advocate steadily lost ground in the land of its origin until at present Nepal and Ceylon are the only areas south of the Himalayas which can be called Buddhist.

Following the death of Asoka the Mauryan empire entered upon a rapid decline. Asoka's dominions were inherited and partitioned by two grandsons, and this division of the empire was promptly attended by a decline in the strength of the military forces defending the frontiers. In the year 206 B.C., Antiochos III of Syria invaded and occupied the province of Gandhara in the extreme northwest. Some forty years before this event the Hellenized provinces of Bactria and Parthia, breaking away from Syrian rule, had established themselves as independent kingdoms. Thus when Antiochos proved unable to hold Gandhara permanently the province fell into the hands of the neighboring Hellenic king of Bactria. The possession of Gandhara carried with it control over the mountain passes by which the Indus valley can be invaded from the north, and in 185 B.C. the Bactrian ruler Demetrios led his forces down into the Punjab, annexing the greater portion of this region to his kingdom. The same year that saw this invasion witnessed also the end of the Maurya dynasty; the last Maurya ruler of Magadha was murdered by one of his military officials, and the murderer, Pushyamitra, set up a new dynasty known as the Sunga.

Although Megasthenes, residing at the court of Chandragupta about the year 300 B.C., describes the palaces of the Indian ruler as more splendid than those of Susa or Ecbatana, little remains of Mauryan art to enable the modern critic to judge for himself the excellence of its attainment. With the possible exception of the "stupa" at Sanchi, there is today no example of Indian architecture which dates back to the time of the Mauryan empire. It was not until the last part of the Mauryan period that the builders of north India began to substitute for perishable wood the more enduring materials of stone and brick. The few existing fragments of stone sculpture, however, bear evidence to the fact that the men who produced them possessed a very high degree both of artistic conception and of skill in execution.

In literature, aside from the frequently mentioned edicts of Asoka and the purely religious writings of the Buddhists, Jains, and Brahmans, the most important single work of the Mauryan period is a political treatise known as the *Arthasastra,* which has been attributed to Kautilya, the able and unscrupulous minister of the first Mauryan emperor. Kautilya, a Brahman by birth, had been Chandragupta's fellow conspirator in the revolution which drove the Nandas from the throne of Magadha, and his authorship of the *Arthasastra,* although questioned by some scholars, appears to be not improbable, for this ancient Indian treatise on statecraft might well have come from the pen of Machiavelli himself. With all its cynicism the *Arthasastra* displays a thorough comprehension of the important problems of government and marks its author as a practical man of affairs rather than a mere political theorist; it also reveals the existence under Chandragupta of a thoroughly organized and extremely modern administrative system.

Southern India

From the period of Mauryan rule come the earliest records of contact between northern India and the peoples of the peninsular south. As early as the time of Megasthenes' visit to Pataliputra the kingdom of Andhra, or Vengi, situated between the mouths of the Godavari and Krishna rivers, was known to be a powerful state, while the inscriptions of Asoka seem to indicate that during his reign the Andhras had become vassals of the Mauryan empire. From the same ruler's edict of 257 B.C. comes the earliest mention of the Tamil kingdoms of Chola and Pandya, which were located south of the Krishna, while a later edict mentions the two additional Tamil states of Keralaputra and Satiyaputra. But it was with Ceylon, the most fruitful field of his missionary enterprise, that Asoka came into closest contact. Buddhist missionaries—led, according to tradition, by the emperor's brother Mahendra—reached Ceylon in 251 B.C., while a second mission was under the leadership of Mahendra's sister, Sanghamitra.[1] King Tissa, the newly crowned king of Ceylon, had encouraged the coming of the mission, and his ardent support of the new faith through his long reign of forty years enabled it to secure a permanent foothold in the island. Such accounts as we possess of Ceylon during this period were written almost entirely from a religious point of view, but the friendly intercourse between King Tissa and the emperor Asoka throughout the nineteen years in which they ruled as contemporaries may be taken as evidence not merely of a community in their religious enthusiasm but also of a growth in commercial relations between Ceylon and the northern empire.

SUMMARY OF INDIAN HISTORY

The disappearance of the Mauryan empire in India, like the fall of the Chinese Ch'in dynasty twenty-one years earlier, provides a convenient and satisfactory point at which to close the early history of the country. By the opening of the second century B.C., India, like China, had evolved the ideas and institutions which were to determine the character of a great and lasting civilization. As in China also, this evolution in India, at least since the arrival of the Aryans, had been essentially indigenous. It is true that the art of writing, which was acquired probably during the seventh or sixth century B.C., came to India from the west, that the impact of the Macedonian invasion in the fourth century B.C. probably contributed to the formation of the Mauryan empire and that the art of the Mauryan period shows unmistak-

[1] Buddhist records of Ceylon refer to Mahendra, or Mahindra, and Sanghamitra as the children of Asoka.

able evidence of Persian influence. It is also true that the civilization of the Tamil south, developing independently along different lines from that of the north, was influenced, to an extent which cannot be measured, by foreign maritime contacts, probably with the Arabs and the Phoenicians. Yet the distinctive culture which we know as Indian and which during the succeeding centuries was to impress itself upon successive waves of invaders from the north was the achievement of the people who for two thousand years or more had occupied the regions south of the Himalaya Mountains.

In this cultural development the most striking achievements were in the field of religion. Unlike the Chinese, who by the time of Shih Huang Ti had succeeded in evolving an imperial tradition, the people of India seem never to have developed either in theory or in practice the organization of political unity. At long intervals in their history, as under the Mauryas, the Guptas, or the eighteenth-century Marathas, great portions of the country were united for a brief period under Hindu rule; but only in the *Arthasastra* of Kautilya do we find Indian thought producing in the realm of political theory anything comparable to the work of contemporary Chinese political philosophers. In the field of religious thought, however, India stands alone. Of the two great religious systems developed by the Indians before the second century B.C., Buddhism was destined to become one of the greatest of world religions, while Brahmanism, in addition to remaining the faith of the majority of the country's population, was to spread eastward and exert a powerful influence upon Indo-China and the islands of Malaysia.

It has been customary to attribute the great religious contributions of the Indians almost exclusively to the peculiar genius of the Aryan invaders. This judgment is now being revised. Not only is there reason to believe that the doctrine of rebirth existed in the land before the time of the Aryan invasions, but it also has been pointed out that much of the thought of the later Vedic literature has been derived from non-Aryan sources and that many of the gods of later Hinduism are unknown to the Vedas. Moreover, some students of Indian history and religion contend that both

Gautama and Mahavira, whose teachings in addition to giving rise to new and independent systems of belief produced important modifications in the Brahman religion, were of non-Aryan origin. Whatever may be the true explanation of this peculiar genius of the Indian people, whether it be the happy combination of diverse racial endowments or some occult influence exerted by the soil and climate of the land, early India's greatest contribution to the later civilization of the country and to the history of the entire Far Eastern world was its formulation and elaboration of systematic religious thought.

SUGGESTED REFERENCES

BANERJEA, P. Public Administration in Ancient India.

ELIOT, SIR C. Hinduism and Buddhism.

HAVELL, E. B. A Short History of India.

HOPKINS, E. W. The Great Epic of India.

KETKAR, S. V. The History of Caste in India.

MACPHAIL, J. M. Asoka.

MARSHALL, SIR J. "Exploration and Research at Harappa and Mohenjo Dara," Archæological Survey of India, Annual Report, 1923–1924.

PRATT, J. B. The Pilgrimage of Buddhism and a Buddhist Pilgrimage.

RAPSON, E. J. Ancient India, from the Earliest Times to the First Century A.D.

RAPSON, E. J. (editor). The Cambridge History of India, Vol. I.

SHAMASASTRY, R. (translator). Arthasastra.

SMITH, V. A. Asoka: the Buddhist Emperor of India.

SMITH, V. A. The Oxford History of India.

STEVENSON, MRS. S. The Heart of Jainism.

IV

The Land and Peoples of Central Asia

Mountains, Deserts, and Pasture Lands · Sources of Central-Asian History ·
Changing Names and Shifting Peoples · Indian Influence North of the Hindu
Kush · China's Land Route to the West · The Nan Lu and the Pei Lu

THROUGHOUT all ages of human history the development
of the peoples inhabiting the marginal regions of eastern
and southern Asia has been constantly influenced by the inhabitants of the great central portion of the continent. Although many
anthropologists avoid expressing an opinion in regard to the original home of the human race, a plurality—perhaps even a majority—of those who have risked a conjecture on the question
have favored the plateau region of central Asia to the north of
the Himalayas. Whatever may be the truth of this conjecture,
there have undoubtedly been from the earliest known time outward migrations of central-Asian peoples to the east and south
as well as westward into Europe. Against these periodic out-
pourings of surplus population even the most formidable natural
obstacles have offered little protection. Wave after wave of invasion has poured southward through the Hindu Kush passes into
the Indus valley, has swept across broad stretches of desert to
flood the northern provinces of China, or has flowed westward and
southward into Europe and Asia Minor.

A very large part of this central-Asian region is taken up by
mountains. Immediately to the north of the Indus valley lies a
mass of mountains composed of the Hindu Kush, the Karakoram,
and the Pamir ranges. Here almost innumerable peaks rise far
above the twenty-thousand-foot level, while even the passes by
which the ranges must be crossed rise to fourteen or fifteen thousand feet. On the west this wild mass of mountains slopes off
to the Iranian plateau; on the east it joins the great plateau of

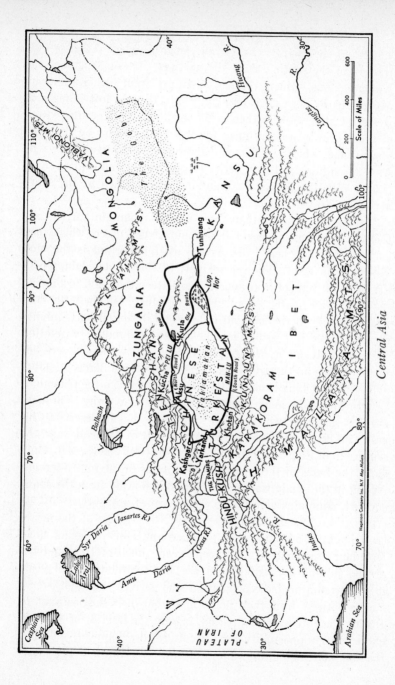

Central Asia

Tibet and the mighty Himalayan range by which Tibet is buttressed on the south. Along the northern side of Tibet lies the Kunlun range, which reaches eastward from the Karakoram Mountains to slope away gradually into the less lofty ranges of western China. Still farther to the north the Pamirs (the "Roof of the World") are continued toward the northeast by the Tien Shan range, which, in turn, is continued northeastward by the Altai Mountains and by a series of gradually diminishing ranges ending with the Stanovoi Mountains, which reach to the shore of Bering Strait.

Hardly less striking than these mighty mountain barriers are the vast expanses of "near" desert and "true" desert which they enclose. Of the "near" deserts the most important is the high tableland of Tibet. The greater part of this broad plain, which lies at an altitude of from fourteen to sixteen thousand feet above sea level, is adequately supplied with moisture; but the bitter cold which prevails at this high altitude except during a short summer season makes it possible for the region to produce vegetation sufficient only for a slender population. The "true" desert lies farther to the north, stretching along the northern border of Tibet and of north China from the Pamirs on the west to the plateau of eastern Mongolia, more than two thousand miles away. Throughout this vast area, which includes the Taklamakan desert of Chinese Turkestan, the Gobi (or Shamo) desert of Mongolia, and the arid basin of Zungaria, rain and snow practically never fall. Only along the bases of the encircling mountains or, at rare intervals, far out in the sandy wastes do the waters flowing from the snow-covered mountains give life to vegetation of any sort.

Northward of this broad desert belt the valleys of the northern mountains and the plains of Siberia have offered at all times abundant grazing land. In recent years much of this land has proved suitable for agricultural use, but for thousands of years it supported a nomadic population who derived their subsistence almost entirely from their flocks and from their skill as hunters. During the entire historic period, indeed, the interior of Asia has offered little opportunity for agricultural development. In Tibet the high plateau and the valleys toward the Chinese frontier have yielded a slender return to the persistent labor of a frugal population, while the narrow strip of irrigated land around the western end of the Taklamakan desert has enabled this portion of Chinese Turkestan to support a permanent agricultural civilization. Still farther to the west, where the Amu Daria (ancient Oxus) and the Syr Daria (ancient Jaxartes) flow through a semidesert region from the Pamirs to the Aral Sea, a plentiful supply of water for irrigation resulted in the development of narrow strips of settled agriculture. Elsewhere the hunter and the wandering herdsman reigned supreme.

For the history of this vast region, the bulk of whose inhabitants remained for many centuries in the most primitive stages of cultural development, we are largely dependent upon the records of their more highly civilized neighbors, especially the Chinese. During the last half-century or so, archaeological research carried on by scholars of different nations has drawn supplementary historical information from the cultural remains that the central-Asians have left behind them; but little has been discovered which can serve to carry our knowledge of this part of Asia to a period antedating the earliest records of the Chinese.

From earliest times the nomadic peoples of central Asia have constantly shifted their locations. Temporary failure of pasturage in a particular region or defeat or victory in their wars with a neighboring people frequently sufficed to dislodge a group of related tribes from their accustomed haunts and to start them off on a long course of wandering. Not only did such wanderings often carry the dislodged peoples far afield before they finally settled upon a new abode; the wanderers, in the course of their travels, often absorbed alien contingents into their loose organization and on a few occasions assumed new names as they occupied their new homes. For example, the Yuehchi, who during the days of the Ch'in dynasty were located on the western frontier of China in what is now a part of Kansu Province, were driven from their homes early in the second century B.C. by the hostility of their Hsiungnu neighbors. Two centuries later the Yuehchi, now calling themselves the Kushans, pushed southward from present-day Afghanistan, where they had been settled for somewhat more than a hundred years, and made themselves for a time the masters of a great part of northwestern India.

This one example, for which a number of parallels can be found in still later periods, sufficiently illustrates what may be termed the fluidity of a great part of this central-Asian population. Only when the development of an agricultural civilization tended to fix them to the soil or when superior grazing lands were occupied by tribal groups strong enough to resist the attacks of their neighbors did these restless people continue to dwell for long centuries in a fixed habitat. Even when there was little actual displacement of the population the emergence of new dominant tribes, establishing their authority over more or less extensive groups of related peoples, brings new names into the record and strengthens the impression of a constant ebb and flow.

The first of the nomadic "barbarians" to find place in the historical records of the Chinese were the Hsiungnu Tartars, the ancestors of Attila's Huns. Twelve centuries before the westward-moving forces of the Huns swept across Europe to the battlefield of Châlons their ancestors, dwelling along the northern border of China, were periodically raiding the territories of the Chinese. Occupying at this time a broad strip of territory in the northern part of modern Hopei, Shansi, and Shensi, as well as the mountain grazing land north of the Gobi desert, the Hsiungnu, early in the eighth century B.C., sacked and destroyed the Wei-valley capital of the Chou monarchs, forcing the later rulers of the dynasty, as we have seen, to seek security by transferring their headquarters to the more sheltered valley of the Lo River. During the course of the half-millennium of Chou rule which followed this transfer the northern states of feudal China gradually pushed their Hsiungnu neighbors out of the arable land south of the desert. In the fourth century B.C. the dukes of Ch'in, Chao, and Yen undertook to minimize the danger of fresh Hsiungnu invasions by erecting barrier walls in all the important passes which opened northward into the Gobi, an undertaking which reached its climax in the great project of Shih Huang Ti for an uninterrupted line of masonry reaching from the Gulf of Pohai to the desert of northern Kansu.

Although these centuries of contact were marked by almost incessant struggle, there was inevitably a certain amount of cultural exchange between the Chinese and their less civilized neighbors. Most of China's borrowing from the Hsiungnu was in the art of war, and reference has been made in a previous chapter to the military advantage obtained by the armies of Ch'in through the adoption of mounted horsemen to replace the earlier war chariot. The Hsiungnu borrowings from the Chinese, on the other hand, were more widely diversified. Although these northern Tartars continued to remain primarily herdsmen and hunters, the numerous Chinese captives whom they brought back from their raids gradually introduced among them hitherto unknown arts of peace.

The most important consequence of this infiltration of Chinese ideas among the Hsiungnu, however, was the development of a political organization in imitation of the Chinese. Even while the great Ch'in monarch Shih Huang Ti was consolidating his Chinese dominions into an empire, Tou-man, a contemporary Hsiungnu chieftain, was gathering under his rule the loosely associated Tartar tribes and was extending his authority over a steadily widening range of territory. Thus unified, the Hsiungnu promptly drove out the Yuehchi, who occupied northwestern Kansu, and re-established themselves on the southern side of the Gobi desert.

While the Chinese during the centuries preceding the unification of the empire under Shih Huang Ti were struggling to secure complete control over the fertile land south of the Gobi desert and were spreading some of their culture among the people against whom they fought, Indian influence, far to the west, was spreading up through the passes of the Hindu Kush to gain a foothold among other groups of central-Asian peoples. The northward extension of Indian influence received a great impetus from the missionary enterprise of the emperor Asoka, who dispatched members of the Buddhist brotherhood up into the mountains to spread among the "outside people" a knowledge of the Eightfold Path. By the end of Asoka's reign the teachings of Gautama had been carried at least as far as the banks of the Oxus, and the peoples of this section of central Asia had some knowledge of the fact that a great and prosperous country lay southward across the mountains.

Even before the middle of the third century B.C. foreign traders from central Asia appear to have reached the banks of the upper Yellow River, bringing with them goods from western lands unknown to the Chinese, and it has even been suggested that certain religious teachers who arrived in China during the reign of Shih Huang Ti were early Buddhist missionaries. Yet it was not until the close of the second century B.C., during the reign of the Han emperor Wu, that a Chinese emissary sent to conclude a treaty of alliance with the wandering Yuehchi brought back to the imperial capital definite information concerning a great country called T'ien Chu (India), far to the southwest of China. Later in the reign of the same Han emperor the Hsiungnu were again forced to retire to the north of the Gobi desert, and there were opened the long, perilous caravan routes along which for many centuries goods flowed back and forth not only between China and India but also between China and the Mediterranean west.

From the oasis town of Tunhuang in northwestern Kansu two ancient caravan routes led westward. The first of these routes—the Nan Lu (or "South Road")—passed to the south of the almost dry salt lake of Lop Nor and followed the line of oases lying at the foot of the Kunlun Mountains, through Khotan to Yarkand. From Yarkand the route led through the difficult passes of the Pamirs and the Hindu Kush to the upper waters of the Oxus, or by even more dangerous passes found its way southward into the Indus valley. The somewhat longer "North Road" (Pei Lu) avoided many of the difficulties which must be faced by those who took the southern route. Starting from Tunhuang, the Pei Lu followed along the northern edge of the Taklamakan desert through Kurla, Kucha, and Aksu to Kashgar. From Kashgar the road led by way of Ferghana to the valley of the Jaxartes and the west.

These two routes, beset with perils, were of tremendous importance in the history of China. Along them went the precious shipments of silk destined for far-western markets. Along them came and went ambassadors and Buddhist pilgrims. By these roads came artistic and scientific additions to Chinese civilization, brought from India, from Persia, or from the distant Mediterranean. Because of their importance the Chinese government in the days of its strength put forth every effort to keep in its hands the control of these routes as far westward as Yarkand and Kashgar, and the history of China's relations with central Asia for a full thousand years after the reign of Han Wu Ti is bound up with China's struggle to hold or to regain the control over these two channels of trade and communication with the west.

SUGGESTED REFERENCES

BUXTON, L. H. D. China, the Land and the People.
HEDIN, S. Central Asia and Tibet.
HEDIN, S. Through Asia.
HEDIN, S. Trans-Himalaya.
HUNTINGTON, E. The Pulse of Asia.
PUMPELLY, R. Explorations in Turkestan.
PUMPELLY, R. Prehistoric Anau.
STEIN, SIR M. A. Innermost Asia.
STEIN, SIR M. A. Serindia.

V

China: from the Han Dynasty to the Southern Sungs

The Middle Period of Chinese History · The Han Dynasty · Expansion of the Empire · China and Central Asia · The Introduction of Buddhism · Wang Mang the Usurper · The Eastern Han · Relations with Central Asia · The Roman World · India · Japan · Internal Developments under the Han · Rehabilitation of Confucianism · Ssu-ma Ch'ien · Invention of Paper · Art of the Han Period · Fall of the Han Dynasty · The "Three Kingdoms" · Barbarian Invasions · The Northern Wei Dynasty · Sculpture of the Northern Wei · The Five Southern Dynasties · The Naturalization of Buddhism · Pilgrimages to India · Fa Hsien and Others · The Sui Dynasty, China Reunited · Foreign Relations under the Sui · Fall of the Sui Dynasty

DURING the fifteen centuries which elapsed between the fall of the Ch'in dynasty in 206 B.C. and the conquest of China by the Mongols in the last half of the thirteenth century A.D. the history of the Chinese Empire is marked by frequent and extreme variations of fortune. At times, united under strong dynasties, the Chinese people enjoyed internal peace and good government while their rulers extended their authority to regions lying far beyond the limits reached by Shih Huang Ti, ambassadors from distant lands came to the Chinese capital to do homage to the emperor, and scholars from equal distances made their way thither to study at this center of civilization the arts and sciences which were the foundation of the country's greatness. At other times incompetent rulers or the outbreak of civil war brought periods of disunion and disorder. Weak at home, the empire was unable to impress with its power the frontier peoples, invading armies replaced tribute-bearing embassies, and barbarian conquerors not infrequently set themselves up as rulers over more or less extensive portions of the country.

Even in these periods of political weakness, however, China continued to be the cultural center of eastern Asia. Art and literature continued to develop, often enriched by the increased inflow of foreign ideas, while foreign scholars continued to visit China as the source and origin of all knowledge. Moreover, because of this recognized superiority of Chinese civilization, the conquering invaders, when they came, were always ready to become Chinese and were quickly absorbed into the population of the country. Each humiliating conquest thus served to add fresh physical vigor to the Chinese nation and contributed something to the subsequent revival of the ancient empire: ever different, yet always the same.

THE HAN DYNASTY, 202 B.C.–221 A.D.

Four years of turmoil followed the overthrow of the last ruler of the Ch'in line, and it was not until 202 B.C. that Liu Pang, who in 206 had assumed the title "King of Han," was able to seize the imperial power and to proclaim himself emperor as the first of the Han dynasty. The new emperor, who is known in the dynastic list of the Hans as Kao Tsu ("High Ancestor"), continued the policy of his Ch'in predecessors in making the Wei valley the center of the empire and erected near the site of Shih Huang Ti's capital the new imperial city of Changan.

Having ascended the throne as a result of a revolution which transformed him from a soldier of fortune into an emperor, the founder of the Han dynasty was compelled to reward his supporters with extensive grants of power. Kao Tsu recognized the importance of the great First Emperor's reforms, and he retained as far as possible the Ch'in system of provincial officials directly responsible to the central government; but this partial restoration of feudalism had serious consequences for himself and for his earlier successors on the throne. Vassal after vassal, inspired by the hope of attaining complete autonomy, rose in revolt against the imperial authority. The suppression of these revolts was usually followed by the destruction of the disloyal vassal, but it was not until about eighty years after the establishment of the dynasty that the Han emperor Wu finally succeeded, in 127 B.C., in bringing all parts of the empire under the absolute control of the central administration.

Wu Ti, the sixth and greatest monarch of the Han line, ascended the imperial throne in the year 140 B.C. In the domestic history of China this reign of fifty-four years was a period of peaceful consolidation and reorganization. The central administrative system, the personnel of which was recruited entirely from the non-feudal classes, was completely reorganized and became an important counterbalance to the particularistic tendencies of the provinces. To improve the economic condition of the country the central government undertook the digging of canals and the construction of harbors in various parts of the empire, while in the year 119 B.C. a uniform system of currency was established.

Externally the reign was marked by the extension of China's boundaries in all directions. On the southwest considerable portions of modern Yunnan and Szechwan were conquered and annexed. In 110 B.C. the Han emperor reconquered Kwangtung and Annam, which after the death of Shih Huang Ti had broken away from the empire. To the northeast his armies advanced far beyond the Great Wall, and by 108 B.C. Manchuria, as far north as the line of the present North Manchuria Railway, together with the northern part of the Korean peninsula, had been brought under Chinese sway. Elsewhere along the northern frontier the reign of Wu Ti saw almost constant warfare against the Hsiungnu Tartars, who continually threatened to pass the Great Wall and to ravage the territories of the Chinese.

Because of this constant Hsiungnu menace Wu Ti in 138 B.C., two years after his accession, determined to seek an alliance with some of the central-Asian tribes which had reasons for hostility toward his northern neighbors. With this end in view he dispatched an officer named Chang Ch'ien, with a retinue of a hundred men, as ambassador to the Yuehchi, who at one time occupied the valley of the Ili but who, unknown to the Chinese court, had been driven from this region to a more distant home toward the southwest. On his way to the Ili, Chang Ch'ien fell into the hands of the Hsiungnu, by whom he was held captive for nearly ten years. Escaping at last from his captors, the ambassador continued his journey westward until he finally reached the Yuehchi in Tokharestan, south of the Amu Daria (Oxus) River.

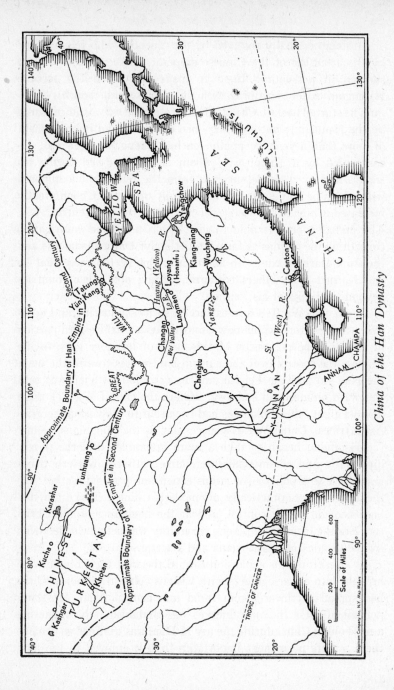

China of the Han Dynasty

Although cordially received by the Yuehchi, who felt honored by the attention of the Chinese emperor, Chang Ch'ien did not succeed in persuading them to make war upon the terrible Hsiungnu. After remaining with them for several months, therefore, he started back to China. On his return he was again captured by the Hsiungnu; but escaping once more after an imprisonment of more than a year, he finally reached Changan in 126 B.C., accompanied by a Tartar wife whom he had married during his travels and by a single survivor from the retinue of a hundred with which he had started. The embassy of Chang Ch'ien greatly increased China's knowledge of the countries of central Asia. The ambassador was able to give much first-hand information concerning the regions as far west as the Syr Daria (Jaxartes) and the Amu Daria (Oxus); in addition to this he reported what he had learned from others concerning India and other countries beyond the limits of his journey.

In 121 B.C. Wu Ti's armies succeeded in conquering and occupying the territory which now comprises the northwestern portion of Kansu. The possession of this strip of territory gave to the Chinese the control over the natural land routes toward the west, the Nan Lu and the Pei Lu, and in 115 Chang Ch'ien was sent westward on a second embassy. Before the end of Wu Ti's reign at least eight other embassies had been sent to the various central-Asian tribes. Under Wu Ti's successors, as the campaigns against the Hsiungnu began to take a more favorable turn, the purely diplomatic and commercial intercourse with the western tribes gave place to a policy of vigorous expansion in this direction. By the year 59 B.C. practically all modern Chinese Turkestan had been brought under control, and at the beginning of the Christian Era the Chinese emperor's suzerainty was acknowledged even by the peoples of Transoxiana and Bactria.

As a result of this expansion toward the west the Chinese were brought into closer contacts with various cultural elements which had spread northward from India into central Asia. Most important of these Indian influences was Buddhism, which, gaining a foothold in China during the age of Han, was destined to achieve there a more permanent importance than it enjoyed in the land of its origin. Chinese Buddhist tradition attributes the introduction of Gautama's teachings to Ming Ti (58–76 A.D.). According to this tradition Ming Ti, in the year 61 A.D., having dreamed of a man sixteen feet tall, clothed in golden vestments, with the light of the sun about his neck, sent to the west messengers who after several years returned bringing with them an image of Buddha and copies of the Buddhist scriptures.

This tradition, which dates only from the closing years of the second century A.D., is unquestionably a pure myth. There is positive evidence[1] that the religion was known to the Chinese as early as 2 B.C., in which year, sixty-three years before the alleged date of Ming Ti's dream, a set of Buddhist scriptures is known to have been presented to the emperor Ai (6 B.C.–1 A.D.).

During the opening quarter of the first century A.D. the regular succession of Han emperors was interrupted by the usurpation of Wang Mang. This ambitious and remarkably capable statesman first rose to prominence in the closing years of the reign of Ch'eng Ti (32–6 B.C.). Relegated to a position of unimportance during the reign of Ai Ti, Wang Mang after the death of this ruler conspired with the empress dowager, widow of Ch'eng Ti, to seize control of the government. For ten years he was content to rule as chief minister for two successive puppet emperors, but in the year 9 A.D. he deposed the second of these, a child of five, and openly assumed the imperial title.

In his efforts to make himself popular and to establish himself firmly as the founder of a new dynasty Wang Mang instituted a series of sweeping reforms. Slavery was abolished, a system of fixed salaries for officials was introduced, and an income tax was imposed to provide the central government with a more adequate revenue. In order to protect the people against wide price fluctuations, especially in foodstuffs, Wang Mang erected government storehouses throughout the empire and established maximum and minimum prices for all important commodities; during periods of low prices goods were bought up and stored in the warehouses, to be sold when prices rose above the established maximum. These and other equally radical innovations had the result of arousing

---

[1] According to Professor Paul Pelliot.

against the new emperor the bitter hostility of the merchants, the property-holders, and the former slaveholders, all of whom made common cause with the loyal adherents of the Hans in stirring up revolt.

In spite of this powerful combination against him Wang Mang's efforts to establish a new dynasty might have been crowned with success if he had not become involved at the same time in a struggle with the Hsiungnu Tartars. For somewhat more than half a century these warlike northerners had remained at peace with the Han empire, their rulers acknowledging the supremacy of the Chinese emperor but being recognized by China as independent sovereigns. Upon his assumption of the imperial title, however, Wang Mang sent to the ruling Hsiungnu chieftain a new official seal so inscribed as to proclaim that the recipient was a *subject* of the Chinese emperor. When the northern ruler promptly protested against this insult, Wang Mang attempted to make him a prisoner, and war resulted. Caught between his domestic enemies and this powerful foreign foe, the usurper's position became steadily more desperate. In the year 23 A.D. a rebel army led by a prince of the Han imperial line captured the capital, Wang Mang was put to death by his own troops, and his short-lived dynasty—the Hsin—came to an inglorious end.

In the struggle which overthrew Wang Mang the capital, Changan, was almost completely destroyed. Two years after his overthrow, therefore, the new emperor of the restored Han dynasty abandoned the Wei valley and, following the example of the Chou rulers eight centuries earlier, transferred the central government to Loyang in the valley of the Lo River. As a result of this move, although Chinese historians refuse to include Wang Mang and his Hsin dynasty in their lists of rulers, the Han emperors after the year 25 A.D. are customarily called the Eastern Hans.

When the ancient Chou rulers in 769 B.C. moved their capital eastward from the Wei valley to the Lo, they quickly lost all pretensions to sovereign power. Such was not the result of the similar move by the Hans. The first two emperors who ruled at the new capital were capable and energetic men; and although all but two of the subsequent rulers ascended the throne as infants, the government at Loyang continued for more than a century and a half to administer the country's affairs with a strong hand. At home and abroad, down to the outbreak of fresh internal troubles in 184 A.D., the regime of the Eastern Han was a period of greatness for the Chinese Empire.

During the usurpation of Wang Mang and as a result of his arousing the antagonism of the Hsiungnu Tartars, China's influence among the peoples on her western frontier underwent a marked decline. From fifty-five, at the beginning of Wang Mang's reign, the number of western rulers acknowledging China's suzerainty had been reduced, at the time of his overthrow, to about twenty. Kuang Wu Ti, the first of the Loyang emperors, was concerned primarily with the establishment of internal peace and made no effort to re-establish Chinese authority over the lost vassal states, with the result that the Hsiungnu had a clear field for the extension of their own imperial control. In the year 58 Kuang Wu Ti was succeeded on the throne by the emperor Ming. Under the new emperor the government displayed fresh interest in the central-Asian peoples and began to respond to their appeals for aid against the Hsiungnu. During Ming Ti's reign, therefore, the Chinese armies reappeared in the region now known as Chinese Turkestan, where they administered several checks to Hsiungnu expansion.

The closing years of Ming Ti's reign saw the appearance of a Chinese commander who during an active career of more than thirty years was destined to extend the influence of the empire westward until it came into contact with its great European contemporary, imperial Rome. Pan Ch'ao was born in the year 32 A.D., and in 69 he served as a minor officer in his first western campaign. Between the years 73 and 83 he was nominally the second in command of the western expeditionary forces; actually he had direct supervision over the operations which in 74 A.D. created the Chinese protectorate-general over the four important oasis states of Khotan, Karashar, Kucha, and Kashgar and a number of smaller tribal organizations. The death of Ming Ti in the year 75 A.D. was followed by an uprising against the Chinese protectorate, but by the year 78 Pan Ch'ao had restored order and had strengthened his Chinese army by the addition of ten thousand soldiers recruited from among the protected peoples.

In the year 83 Pan Ch'ao became in name, as for the last ten years he had been in fact, the commander in chief of the imperial armies in central Asia. Within eleven years after this promotion his military activities had so raised the prestige of China that "more than fifty kingdoms had sent hostages," while countries as far away as Mesene,[1] Parthia, and the shores of the Caspian Sea sent regular tributary missions to Loyang. In 100 A.D. Pan Ch'ao received permission to resign his post as "Protector-General of the Western Countries"; two years later, at the age of seventy-one, he died at Loyang. During his career of thirty-one years this capable soldier and administrator had firmly established the authority of China over the routes leading to the west. After his retirement, however, this authority began to wane, and by the middle of the second century A.D. only a few of the states which Pan Ch'ao had reduced to submission continued to acknowledge Chinese suzerainty.

The Chinese appear to have obtained their first definite knowledge of Rome during the reign of Wu Ti, who is reported to have exchanged embassies with the king of Parthia; from this period until the days of the T'ang dynasty Rome, or that part of western Asia under Roman influence, was known to the Chinese writers by the name *Ta Ch'in*. The first recorded attempt to open direct communication between the two countries, however, was made in 97 A.D. by Pan Ch'ao, who dispatched toward the west one of his officers, named Kan Ying, with instructions to make his way to Ta Ch'in and to bring back firsthand information concerning that country.

Kan Ying traveled through Parthia, at that time the intermediary for all the trade between the Far East and the Mediterranean world, until he reached the head of the Persian Gulf. Here he was informed that it would be necessary to continue his voyage by ship (down the Persian Gulf, along the southeastern coast of Arabia, and up the Red Sea), and the Persian sailors, inspired

---

[1] Mesopotamia (?), Persia (?). See J. P. A. Rémusat, *Nouveaux mélanges asiatiques*, Vol. I, pp. 215–216.

by the hope of keeping control over the trade between East and West, pictured to him so graphically the dangers and discomforts of the sea voyage that he retraced his steps to China.

The next attempt to establish direct relations between the two empires was made by the Romans. In the year 165 the outbreak of war between Rome and the Parthians resulted in the interruption of the customary trade routes, and the following year saw the arrival at Loyang of a commercial embassy which represented itself as having been sent by the emperor Marcus Aurelius. This embassy, which probably had no official status, had traveled by ship from the Red Sea to Burma and thence overland to the Chinese capital. Sixty years later, during the period of the "Three Kingdoms," a merchant from Ta Ch'in is said to have arrived at Nanking, at that time the capital of the kingdom of Wu, where he was received with official honors. Although these attempts to establish diplomatic intercourse were unsuccessful, a considerable volume of trade flowed overland between China and the Mediterranean, while ideas as well as material products were exchanged by the two regions.

China's first definite information about India, like that concerning Rome, appears to date from the reign of Wu Ti. The earliest mention of this country in the Chinese annals is found in connection with the report submitted in 122 B.C. by Chang Ch'ien on his return from his first mission to central Asia. From information which he secured among the Yuehchi in Bactria, Chang Ch'ien reported that India, or Sind (transcribed into Chinese sometimes as *Shen Tu* and sometimes as *T'ien Chu*), lay to the southeast of Bactria at a distance of several thousand *li*. He believed that the country could not be very far from southern Szechwan in a southerly direction, and Wu Ti, acting on this suggestion, made several unsuccessful attempts to open communication with India through Szechwan and the mountains of Tibet. Embassies from India, coming by way of central Asia, reached China during the reign of Ho Ti (89–105 A.D.), the period when Pan Ch'ao was making China feared and respected by her western neighbors, and in 159 an embassy from India arrived at Loyang from the south, having come by way of Burma. About the beginning of the third century A.D., because of the confused conditions accompanying the collapse of the Han dynasty, land communication with India was broken, and it was not resumed until the end of the fourth century.

As in the west and the south, so also in the east the conquests of Wu Ti opened the way for intercourse with peoples dwelling beyond the conquered regions. It seems possible that the Chinese had some faint knowledge of Japan as early as the fourth century B.C., and their legends state that Shih Huang Ti in 219 B.C. dispatched an officer attended by three thousand youths and maidens to visit the "Islands of the Eastern Sea" and bring back the "Elixir of Immortality." Wu Ti's conquest of northern Korea in 108 B.C. enabled the Chinese to replace their earlier fantastic beliefs concerning Japan with more accurate information gained from the Koreans and from the Japanese with whom they came in contact in the peninsula.

For something more than a century and a half Korea served as the intermediary through which Chinese and Japanese received knowledge of each other; but in 57 A.D., the last year of the reign of Kuang Wu Ti, an envoy from the ruler of "Ito" (modern Chikuzen in Kyushu) arrived at Loyang and offered tribute to the emperor. The envoy was presented with an official seal for his master, and a Chinese embassy accompanied him on his return to Japan. Other embassies from Japan were received at long intervals during the next five centuries and a half by the Chinese sovereigns, but it was not until the beginning of the T'ang dynasty that active direct intercourse between the two countries was established.

Spectacular as were the undertakings whereby the Han emperors extended their territories and brought their country into communication with more and more distant parts of the world, the internal developments in the Chinese Empire during the four centuries of Han rule were of equal or even greater importance. Except for the years of Wang Mang's usurpation and the last two or three decades of the dynasty's tenure of power the Han period was one of internal peace and prosperity. Although Kao Tsu, the founder of the dynasty, had been compelled to make extensive grants of feudal power to those who had aided him in his rise, the decentralization of authority was even during his reign only partial; his successors,.as has been pointed out, steadily reduced both the number and the powers of the feudatories until in the reign of Wu Ti all real authority was centralized in the hands of the emperor and his appointed officials.

While the ambitious wars of expansion were at times a heavy strain upon the economic resources of the empire, the people suffered less from these than their ancestors had suffered from the interminable civil wars of the feudal era. Unification under a strong government naturally resulted in a more active exchange of goods and ideas between the different sections of China; with this exchange there developed a healthy and stimulating competition in all fields of activity, while China's steadily increasing intercourse with the outside world brought into the "melting pot" a constant flow of new artistic skill and new knowledge.

No sooner had the first Han emperor seated himself upon the throne than he was besieged by the Confucian literati with requests that he repeal Shih Huang Ti's decree against the possession and the reading of the ancient books. This step Kao Tsu at first refused to take. In vain did the scholars strive to convince him of the unique and inestimable value of the Confucian Classics as handbooks in the science of government. "I have conquered the empire upon my horse," he replied; "I have become your master without your *Shu King* and your *Shi King*; what need have I of your books?" Toward the end of his reign, however, Kao Tsu considered it advisable to conciliate the literary class in order to win their support, and in the year 195 B.C. he paid a visit to the ancient state of Lu, where he offered sacrifice at the tomb of Confucius. Kao Tsu died the following year, and three years later his successor finally repealed the ban upon the Classics.

The task of re-creating the works of the Confucian school from memory and from scattered fragments required much time and labor, and some portions of the original Classics were permanently lost; but from the repeal of the Ch'in emperor's proscription Confucianism quickly gained the position which it was to occupy for the next two thousand years. Although Taoism—

based upon the *Tao Te King* or upon the even older beliefs from which Lao-tzu derived his ideas—and, later, Buddhism are joined with Confucianism as constituting the "three religions of China," the first two of these are supplements rather than rivals of the last. Throughout the ages Confucian scholars have turned for spiritual comfort to Taoism or to Buddhism, yet they have continued to uphold the social philosophy of Confucius as the basis of public morality and good government.

Closely connected with the restoration of the Confucian Classics and with the permanent influence of Confucian philosophy upon the government of the empire is the establishment of the system of literary examinations as prerequisites for official appointment, a system which antedated by many centuries the institution of civil-service examinations in Western lands. Kao Tsu during the greater part of his reign depended entirely upon military men as the officers of his government, but even he, toward the end of his life, made some use of the literati as advisers and recommended a similar policy to his vassals. After the repeal of the book-burning decree an increasing number of the Confucian scholars found employment as officers of the central administration, and in 140 B.C., the first year of Wu Ti's reign, one of these scholars recommended to the new emperor the establishment of a college for instruction in the Confucian Classics, the graduates of the college to be eligible for appointment to posts in the civil offices.

Although Wu Ti was deeply impressed by the argument that such an arrangement would provide the imperial government with a body of trained men who were wholly independent of the landed aristocracy, he was not yet prepared to entrust the affairs of state to the hands of impractical bookmen. In 128 B.C., however, the emperor issued a decree summoning the scholars of the empire to make suggestions for the improvement of the government. In response to this appeal one of the literati enlarged upon the fact —already appreciated by the emperor—that the chief threat to national unity lay in the territorial power of certain great vassals. At a subsequent private interview with the emperor the writer of this memorial pointed out that without any use of force the great feudal estates could be gradually broken up by permitting a vassal to transmit a half of his fief to his eldest son and to divide the other half equally among his younger sons.

The shrewdness and simple practicability of this solution of one of his greatest problems convinced Wu Ti that the trained scholar could be decidedly useful to the government. In 124 B.C. therefore, he issued a decree establishing a great college and providing for a regular system of examinations; those who completed the prescribed courses and passed the appropriate examinations were to be qualified for appointment to the various grades of official service.

The reign of Wu Ti, which thus saw the restoration of scholarship to high honor in the empire, produced its full share of outstanding literary figures: poets, philosophers, and scientific writers. The most justly famous writer of the reign and of the entire Han era was Ssu-ma Ch'ien, who has been accorded by common consent the title "Father of Chinese History." Carrying to completion a work commenced by his father, Ssu-ma T'an, who had spent many years in patient research, Ssu-ma Ch'ien produced a history of China from the days of the Yellow Emperor down to the opening of the first century B.C.

For many centuries prior to the time of Ssu-ma Ch'ien, China had had official historians (annalists) whose duty it was to record in minute detail the words and acts of their sovereigns. Earlier writers, moreover, had attempted to write more or less connected histories of their country. But Ssu-ma Ch'ien compares with these earlier historians very much as Thucydides compares with his famous predecessor Herodotus. Although he began his history, *Shih Chi* ("Historical Records"), at a point many centuries before the opening of what we regard as the historical period and although for this early section of his work he was dependent upon a body of unreliable tradition, Ssu-ma Ch'ien even in his treatment of ancient tradition was critically minded and remarkably free from superstitious bias. In the later portions, for which more and more abundant source material was available, he collected and carefully weighed all the evidence bearing upon any important statement of fact.

It would be difficult, perhaps impossible, to estimate the extent to which Ssu-ma Ch'ien was influenced in his thought by the philosopher Mo-tzu, who lived and wrote some three centuries earlier. He performed for Chinese history, however, a service similar to that which Mo-tzu rendered to Chinese philosophy, introducing the critical, logical, and scientific method which, continued by later historical writers, makes Chinese history a sound basis for the study not only of China but also of the neighboring peoples of the Far East.

The development of scholarship and literature in Han China was aided in no small degree by an invention which constitutes one of China's greatest contributions to world civilization—paper. Before the opening of the Han dynasty the Chinese scribe was compelled to work under difficulties, carving his characters with a sharp-pointed instrument upon smooth slips of wood or bamboo. Under these conditions writing was a slow process and books were both bulky and extremely rare. At some date during the first or second century A.D., however, the art of paper-making was discovered; this discovery and the almost simultaneous invention of ink in conjunction with the writing brush, a much earlier invention, made writing easier and books less cumbersome.

From the land of its origin the art of making paper spread westward, and one step in its transcontinental journey, although properly belonging in the succeeding chapter, may be given here. Among the captives taken by the Arabs in the battle of Athlach (751) were a number of workmen trained in the paper-making craft, who were taken to Bagdad, where they taught their art to their Arab captors.

For the ages preceding the Han dynasty the available specimens of Chinese art are limited. A small quantity of neolithic pottery, a few jade ornaments and a number of bronze utensils attributed to the Yin period, and a larger number of bronze vessels from the ages of Chou and Ch'in are all that have escaped the ravages of time. Even these remains, however, prove that the Chinese of the Yin, Chou, and Ch'in periods had evolved a highly developed art. The earliest bronzes, with their geometrical and highly conventionalized animal designs, display high standards of artistic conception and technical skill in execution.

From the opening of the second century B.C. there is a great increase in both the quantity and the variety of China's artistic remains. Like the artists of the earlier periods the Han artists did much work in bronze and clay; but from this period there also come specimens of stone sculpture, both in bas-relief and in the round. The earliest piece of Chinese stone sculpture to which a date can be assigned is a monument erected in 117 B.C. at the tomb of General Ho Ch'i-ping, in the Wei valley to the west of Sianfu. According to a French authority[1] this group of figures carved in massive granite "appears to represent the adaptation to a new and still rebellious medium—stone—of an art which had been already perfected in bronze, wood, and jade."

Throughout the Han dynasty the growing contact with the peoples of central, southern, and western Asia made China the recipient of artistic influences from India, Bactria, Persia, and the Mediterranean world. To these influences, the most important of which accompanied the introduction of Buddhism, the Chinese readily responded, and the age of Han became in consequence one of the great periods in the history of Chinese art.

FOUR CENTURIES OF CONFUSION

By the closing years of the second century A.D. intrigue and corruption had begun to undermine the power of the imperial government. Under a succession of feeble emperors, all of whom ascended the throne as infants, the control of the administration fell more and more completely into the hands of the palace eunuchs. At Loyang assassination by poison or dagger was the order of the day; in the provinces, neglected by all except the tax-collector, the growing discontent showed itself in sporadic uprisings. In the year 189 the leaders of the army combined to destroy the power of the palace eunuchs. As soon as they had achieved this success, however, the army chiefs began to struggle among themselves for the control over the throne. For a period of thirty years, 190–220 A.D., the power of the central government steadily

[1] Captain Lartigue, quoted by R. Grousset, *Histoire de l'Extrême-Orient*, Vol. I, p. 226.

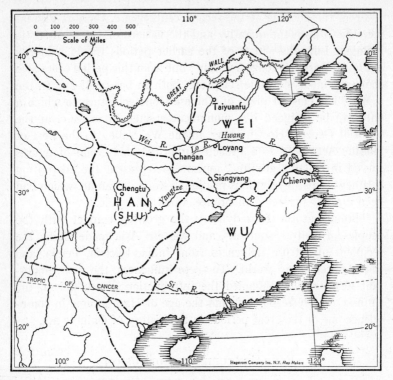

China at the Time of the Three Kingdoms

declined; at the end of this time the last Han emperor was dethroned and the empire fell into a state of disunion which, with a single brief interruption, was to continue for nearly four centuries.

For about fifty years after the collapse of the Han dynasty, China was divided into the three kingdoms of Wei, Wu, and Shu, or Han. The kingdom of Wei, with its capital at Loyang, was ruled by the descendants of General Ts'ao Ts'ao. It consisted of the northern portion of the empire and coincided approximately with the area nominally ruled by the Chinese monarchs prior to the days of Shih Huang Ti. Wu, ruled by the descendants of General Sun Chien, consisted of the Yangtze valley eastward from the gorges, together with the provinces to the south. Its capital was located at first at Wuchang, but in 229 A.D. the monarch of Wu transferred his headquarters eastward to Chienyeh, modern Nanking. Shu, or Han, under a cadet branch of the old imperial family, corresponded roughly with the modern province of Szechwan and had its capital at Chengtu.

Between these rival kingdoms, whose respective monarchs all hoped to reconstitute the empire, there was almost continuous war, and the "Age of the Three Kingdoms," with its profusion of military heroes, has furnished the inspiration for the greater part of China's romantic literature and popular drama.

In the year 264 the western kingdom of Shu was conquered and absorbed by Wei. A year later the ruler of Wei was forced to abdicate in favor of Ssu-ma Yen, who was descended from a collateral branch of the family to which Ssu-ma Ch'ien belonged. The new ruler, who is known as Wu Ti, became the founder of a dynasty to which he gave the name of Chin.[1] In 280, fifteen years after the inauguration of the new dynasty, the kingdom of Wu was conquered and China was once more united into a single state.

Unity under the Chin emperors was destined to be brief. Even while the armies of Chin Wu Ti were conquering the Yangtze valley, barbarian invaders from the north were pushing their way down into the provinces bordering on the Great Wall. During the reign of Wu Ti these intruders—the Hsiungnu, the Sienpi, and the Toba—maintained toward the Chinese government an attitude of respectful obedience; but after his death, in the year 290, the imperial court at Loyang was torn by intrigues and the northern tributaries took advantage of this internal confusion to throw off their allegiance. In 311 Loyang was captured and sacked by a rebel Chinese army; five years later the third successor of Chin Wu Ti was driven from the throne and the dynasty's rule over a united empire came to an end.

For two and three-quarters centuries after the collapse of the Chin dynasty, while southern China was ruled by a succession of Chinese dynasties, the north was under the rule of invaders. Although the eight dynasties which during this period held sway

[1] Not to be confused with the Ch'in dynasty of earlier fame.

over part or all of the north are characterized as "barbarian" by Chinese historians, all these warlike invaders had adopted a considerable amount of Chinese civilization even before their invasion of the empire, while their ruling families could claim relationship, on the maternal side, with former Chinese dynasties.

Five of these eight barbarian dynasties, short-lived and overlapping in their brief careers, dominated north China for a space of seventy years; but in 386 the ruler of the Toba tribe extended his authority over a number of adjoining tribes and established a dynasty known in history as the Northern Wei. From 386 until 535, a period of a hundred and forty-nine years, this dynasty ruled over a united empire containing all of north China between the Great Wall and the Yangtze River.

The monarchs of the Northern Wei were enthusiastic Buddhists and patrons of literature, but it was with the development of Chinese art, especially sculpture, that the period of Northern Wei rule is most closely identified. The sculpture of the Northern Wei artists exists in great abundance at two places: in the grottoes of Yünkang, near Tatung, the earlier dynastic capital in northern Shansi, and at Lungmen, not far from Loyang, which became the capital in 494. At these two centers the artists of the fifth and sixth centuries executed a multitude of carvings—in outline, in bas-relief, and in the round—which have come down to the present day in almost perfect condition. Since the art of Northern Wei was inspired by Buddhism, most of these carvings deal with religious subjects, although some also depict purely historical subjects; religious or historical, all of this sculpture bears evidence to a growing influence from central Asia, Bactria, and the Mediterranean.

The transfer of the Wei capital southward in 494, from Tatung to Loyang, was followed by a decline in the power of the dynasty. In 535 the Wei empire was divided into two parts, eastern and western, which were governed for a few years by rival branches of the family; then these two feeble lines gave place to two new ruling families, between whom the north continued to be divided until the rise of the unifying power of Sui.

During the period covered by the eight barbarian dynasties of the north the south was under the rule of five successive dynasties, each of which had its capital at Nanking and for a longer or shorter period held undisputed sway over all the empire south of the Yangtze. Of these five southern dynasties, Eastern Chin, Sung, Ch'i, Liang, and Ch'en, the first enjoyed the longest term of power. Founded in 317 by a prince of the family which had just been driven from Loyang, the Chins of Nanking ruled in the south until 420. The Sung and Liang dynasties, second and fourth in the order of their appearance, each lasted slightly more than half a century: the Sung from 420 until 479, and the Liang from 502 to 557. The Ch'i sovereigns, seven in number, held the throne for a period of only twenty-three years, between 479 and 502. The five monarchs of the Ch'en line, which seized the power in 557, ruled for thirty-two years, the last Ch'en emperor being overthrown in 589 by Yang Chien, who reunited all China under the Sui dynasty.

The collapse of the Han dynasty during the opening years of the third century had been attended by the almost complete interruption of cultural intercourse between China and India. In the century which followed this interruption, however, the Buddhist faith in China, although cut off from its source, appears to have held its ground. About the beginning of the fourth century the arrival of Arab ships at Canton marked the opening of maritime communication, by which a restoration of direct contact between China and India became possible; and in the year 310 the Indian monk Buddhojanga arrived in China as a Buddhist missionary. In 335 Buddhojanga secured from the reigning monarch of one of the northern dynasties (the Northern Chao) permission for Chinese believers to take the vows of monasticism. Probably many Chinese had previously taken the vows illegally; but this permission, which later was secured also for the other parts of China, enabled the religion to become thoroughly naturalized.

Partly as a result of this improved status and partly because of the turbulent political conditions, which drove many to seek escape from the world in a life of religious meditation, the fourth century witnessed a tremendous expansion of Chinese Buddhism. The rulers of the Northern Wei dynasty, which came to power toward the end of the century, were, as we have noted, ardent Buddhists, and their unification of the region between the Yangtze and the Great Wall enabled them to restore much of China's earlier prestige among the central-Asian peoples. As the land route to India was thus reopened, the growth of Buddhism aroused in many of the Chinese believers a desire to visit the land where their religion had originated. Some of these enthusiasts were actuated merely by the wish to visit the places which had been made sacred by the earthly life of Gautama; but others, realizing that their scriptures had necessarily undergone considerable corruption in the process of translation, desired to secure at the original fountain of the faith more accurate versions of the Buddha's teachings.

Of the many Chinese pilgrims to India, the first whose name and travels are definitely known to us is the monk Fa Hsien. A native of Shansi, in the empire of the Northern Wei, Fa Hsien was distressed at the imperfect state of the scriptures which contained the rules of monastic life. In the year 399 therefore he departed from Changan (modern Sianfu in Shensi), accompanied by a number of fellow pilgrims who were also inspired by a desire to visit India.

From Changan the little band traveled northwestward along the ancient trade route by way of Tunhuang to Karashar; thence they took the road southwestward to Khotan; from Khotan they found their way to Kashgar and turned southward to penetrate the mountain passes of the Hindu Kush, reaching the Indus River at Peshawar. Arriving finally in the valley of the Ganges, Fa Hsien spent several years visiting the sacred places of Buddhism and copying for transmission to China all the religious writings upon which he could lay his hands.

From the mouth of the Ganges the pilgrim proceeded by ship to Ceylon, where he remained for two years and obtained copies of many sacred writings hitherto unknown to the Chinese Buddhists. After this sojourn at Ceylon he returned to China by the sea route, stopping off for five months in Java, "where heresies and Brahmanism were flourishing while the faith of Buddha was in a very unsatisfactory condition." In 414, after an absence of fifteen years, Fa Hsien returned at last to his native land. He had spent six years in journeying by foot across burning deserts and freezing mountain passes to reach India; six years had he spent studying in India, and two years in Ceylon, while the sea voyage homeward had required nearly twelve months.

The example thus set by Fa Hsien, and recorded in the account which he left of his travels, was followed during the next few centuries by many of his fellow nationals. Some of these later pilgrims also have left accounts of their journeys and descriptions of the conditions which they found in the various parts of central Asia or India. Hence the Chinese Buddhist travelers of the fifth, sixth, and seventh centuries are important not only because of their influence upon the religious development of their country but also for the light which they throw upon the condition of Buddhism outside of China and because of the material which they provide for the study of Indian and central-Asian history.

In 518 Sung Yun, a native of Tunhuang, and Hwei Sang, a monk from Loyang, traveled as far as Peshawar, returning to China in 521 with a hundred and seventy volumes of sacred writings.

Hsüan Chuang, who was born near the city of Honanfu, started in 629 on a pilgrimage which kept him abroad for sixteen years. During his sojourn in India he visited all sections of the country, and on his return he wrote an account of his travels which was even more complete than that of Fa Hsien.

Unlike Fa Hsien, Hsüan Chuang used the land route on his return trip as well as on his outward journey; but the latter half of the seventh century saw a large number of religious devotees, including the scholarly monk I Tsing, making the trip to India and back by sea. Still later, with the growth of Buddhist influence in Sumatra and Java, it became customary for Chinese Buddhists to regard these islands as an antechamber to India and either to spend a few years there in preliminary study before proceeding to India or to return to China after studying in this more accessible secondary Buddhist center.

By the beginning of the Christian Era, Chinese ships were carrying on an extensive trade along the coast of Asia from Korea to Indo-China. Beyond the southern point of the Malay peninsula the Chinese navigators of the first Christian centuries appear not to have ventured; but the closing years of the third century A.D. witnessed the arrival of Arab merchant ships at Chinese ports, and about the year 300 A.D. Chinese sources record the existence of a flourishing foreign-merchant community at Canton.

Fa Hsien describes the ships upon which he traveled early in the fifth century A.D., from Ceylon to Java and from Java to China, as each carrying "more than two hundred souls"; among his fellow travelers on the second of these ships he notes a number of merchants and traders who were returning to their homeland. The voyage from Java to Canton was expected to require fifty days, but the ship was driven from its course by storms and sailed for ninety days before finally making land on the coast of Shantung.

In the thirteenth century Marco Polo, although brought up in the great commercial city of Venice, was filled with wonder at the number and the size of the ships which he saw in the ports of China. Marco Polo's account may have been tinted with exaggeration, but it seems probable that to a European of the fifth century the contemporary maritime activity of China and southern Asia would have seemed even more remarkable.

THE SUI DYNASTY, 589–618 A.D.

The last quarter of the sixth century saw the territories of China reunited once more into a single empire. Although the dynasty which accomplished this feat enjoyed but a brief tenure of power, the unification was destined to endure for more than three centuries and marked the beginning of a period more glorious even than the Golden Age of Han.

Yang Chien, by whose energy the disunited fragments were gathered into a single whole, first rose to power as a minister in the court of the Northern Chou, one of the two petty dynasties which ruled the north after the disappearance of the Northern Wei. In 581 this ambitious minister, who had been created Duke of Sui, compelled the abdication of the nine-year-old occupant of the Northern Chou throne and proclaimed himself emperor. Four years before this usurpation Yang Chien, as minister of the Northern Chou, had achieved the consolidation of all north China; in 589 he led his armies down into the Yangtze valley, captured the Ch'en capital at Nanking, and brought the whole of south China under the sway of his newly established Sui dynasty.

In the dynastic list of the Sui dynasty Yang Chien is known as Wen Ti ("Literary Emperor"); yet he had in him little of the scholar, and in the year 601 he suppressed as useless all the public institutions of learning except the small imperial university at Changan. In other respects, however, the founder of the Sui dynasty showed himself to be a ruler of unusual energy, ability, and common sense. As soon as he had united the empire under his rule, he effected a number of important internal reforms, and at Changan, in the Wei valley, he maintained a simple court where he worked steadily at the affairs of state.

During nearly four centuries the northern and northwestern neighbors of the Chinese had repeatedly invaded the frontier provinces of the empire. The successive waves of barbarian invaders were slowly but inevitably absorbed by the earlier population, and probably the most important result of the invasions was the infusion of new vigorous elements into a population whose vitality had been sapped by long centuries of civilization. Yet the constant invasions of the northern provinces had also contributed to the long period of disorder and confusion and had threatened to swamp the Chinese under a barbarian flood too great for assimilation.

Under the Sui dynasty and under its T'ang successors this danger was definitely averted. At this time the Hsiungnu, as the dominant people on China's northwestern frontier, had been replaced by the Turks, or Tou-chüeh. Impressed by the energy of the new imperial government, the Turks ceased their attacks upon the frontier and dispatched embassies to Changan to render homage to the emperor. Wen Ti was naturally pleased at the respectful attitude of his barbarian neighbors; but he was sufficiently shrewd to realize that this attitude was subject to change without notice, and he adopted a policy calculated to weaken the power of the Turkish organization. Taking advantage of the fact that the Turks were divided into "Northern" and "Western" branches, each with its separate line of "Kagans," the Sui emperor began to confer favors—decorations, honorific titles, and occasionally the hand of an imperial princess—with careful discrimination upon the princes of the two lines.

In a short time the Northern and Western Turkish Kagans were jealously competing for the favor of the Chinese court, even to the extent of protecting against their rivals the integrity of the Chinese frontiers. During the brief Sui tenure of power the results of this policy did not reach full fruition, and Turkish attacks upon the frontier played some part in the fall of the dynasty. Under the T'ang emperors, however, the constant application of the principle "divide and rule" broke the power of the Turks and led to the steady expansion of Chinese influence throughout central Asia.

In 604 Wen Ti was succeeded on the throne by his second son, who is known as Yang Ti. The rule of the new emperor differed in many ways from that of his father. Simplicity and economy gave place to extravagant ostentation, and the administrative center of the empire was transferred from Changan to Loyang, where Yang Ti devoted himself to the task of building a capital of surpassing splendor. Although the imperial court was soon moved eastward to the new capital, the former capital at Changan was not wholly abandoned. Great sums were spent on the maintenance of the palaces which had been erected there by Wen Ti, while forty new palaces at convenient stages along the road from Changan to Loyang were erected for the accommodation of the court whenever the emperor might desire to travel between the two cities.

Not all of Yang Ti's expenditures, however, were for luxurious palaces and charming gardens; reversing his father's policy, he patronized education, re-established schools, and patronized the various branches of literature. During his reign, also, there was carried out at great expense one monumental internal improvement, the completion of a system of canals which linked up Loyang with the Yangtze-valley cities and which subsequently became the basis of the larger portion of the famous Grand Canal.

In the field of foreign affairs the transfer of the capital eastward to Loyang was followed, or attended, by a new orientation of imperial interests. As early as the closing years of Wen Ti's reign the Chinese forces had invaded the southern kingdom of Annam, which, although formerly subject to the empire, had enjoyed about sixty years of complete independence. During the first three years of Yang Ti's reign the conquest of Annam was completed and the country was divided into three administrative districts under resident Chinese officials. Champa, the southern neighbor of Annam, was also invaded and plundered; but the unfavorable climate of this region soon forced the Chinese armies to retire, and the fugitive Cham monarch returned to his throne. In 607, ambassadors were also sent to Siam, returning the following year accompanied by an embassy to the imperial court.

Even more important than this renewed interest in the southern lands was the development of intercourse with and interest in the countries which lay toward the east. Relations with Japan, which appear to have been broken off about the beginning of the sixth century, were renewed in 607 by the arrival at Loyang of an embassy from the famous Japanese regent Shotoku Taishi (see page 223). At about the same time, either in 607 or in 610, Yang Ti dispatched an expedition against the island kingdom of Luchu. According to Chinese sources the expedition reached the islands, defeated the Luchuans in battle, and returned to China with much booty and several thousand prisoners; but no permanent conquest of the kingdom was effected.

The country most seriously affected by this new eastward turn of China's interests was Korea. About the time of the expedition against the Luchus, Yang Ti was reminded of the fact that Korea in the days of the Han dynasty had been a tributary of the Chinese emperor and that Wen Ti had intended to re-establish this relationship between the two lands. A demand was therefore sent—apparently to the king of Koguryu, the northernmost of the three Korean kingdoms (see page 202)—for the recognition of Chinese suzerainty. The Korean monarch refused to comply with the demand, and Yang Ti prepared to punish him for his rebellious attitude. Two expeditions were repulsed by the Korean forces; but a third army, led by the emperor in person, invaded the peninsula in 614 and was in a fair way to complete the subjugation of Koguryu when news of a revolutionary outbreak at home compelled Yang Ti to abandon his undertaking and to hasten back to the relief of Loyang, which was besieged by rebel forces.

The extravagant court expenditures, the ambitious internal improvements, and the military undertakings of Yang Ti all combined to burden the Chinese people with constantly increasing taxes and requisitions. At the same time the transfer of the capital to Loyang and the emperor's growing interest in the countries to the east and south led to a comparative neglect of China's dangerous neighbors on the northwestern frontier.

The revolt of 614, which had forced Yang Ti to return from Korea for the defense of his capital, was successfully suppressed; but the fall of the dynasty was not long delayed. In the late summer of the following year, while the emperor was making a tour of inspection in the northern provinces, the Northern Turks poured down across the poorly guarded frontier. Yang Ti escaped capture at the hands of the invaders; but rejecting the advice of his ministers, who urged him to rally his forces at Changan, he fled southward to Yangchow in the Yangtze valley.

This precipitate abandonment of the northern provinces practically marked the end of the dynasty. By the spring of 616, revolts had broken out in all parts of the empire, and at least six of the rebel leaders, reading correctly the fate of Sui, had established themselves as independent rulers or, more ambitious, had proclaimed themselves the founders of new imperial lines. After a brief attempt to cope with these outbreaks Yang Ti, in 617, abdicated in favor of his thirteen-year-old grandson, who was supported by the loyal armies under the command of Li Yüan, the Duke of T'ang. A general amnesty issued in the name of the new emperor had no effect upon the rising tide of revolt, and in June, 618, the brother of the boy emperor was named co-emperor. On the eighteenth of the same month, however, both boys abdicated their imperial authority in favor of the Duke of T'ang, and the Sui dynasty came formally to an end.

SUGGESTED REFERENCES

BUSHELL, S. W. Chinese Art.

CARTER, T. F. The Invention of Printing in China.

GILES, H. A. A History of Chinese Literature.

GILES, H. A. The Travels of Fa-hsien.

GROUSSET, R. Histoire de l'Extrême-Orient.

HIRTH, F. China and the Roman Orient.

LATOURETTE, K. S. The Chinese: their History and Culture.

LAUFER, B. Sino-Iranica, Chinese Contributions to the History of Civilization in Ancient Iran.

PETRUCCI, R. Chinese Painters: a Critical Study.

WALEY, A. Introduction to the Study of Chinese Painting.

WILHELM, R. A Short History of Chinese Civilization.

WILLIAMS, E. T. A Short History of China.

YULE, H. Cathay and the Way Thither.

VI

China: from the Han Dynasty to the Southern Sungs (continued)

THE new dynasty—the T'ang—which rose to power in place of the fallen Sui was to hold the throne until the year 907, and its rule of nearly three centuries was to be one of the most glorious periods in the history of the empire. Before his assumption of the imperial title, Li Yüan (known to history as T'ang Kao Tsu, "Exalted Ancestor of T'ang") was the Duke of T'ang, a portion of Shansi which included the present provincial capital Taiyuanfu. Himself a man of more than average ability both as a soldier and as a statesman, Li Yüan was the father of four unusually able sons, of whom the second, Li Shih-min, must be rated one of the outstanding men in Chinese history. In 615, when the Sui emperor Yang was besieged by the Turks in the northern Shansi city of Soping, it was Li Shih-min, at that time a mere boy of sixteen, who raised the siege and enabled the emperor to escape capture; and the last three years of the Sui regime saw this youth constantly in command of important bodies of imperial troops. Still in his teens when his father ascended the imperial throne, Li Shih-min was the guiding spirit of the new regime during the six-year struggle by which the rule of T'ang was firmly established in the land.

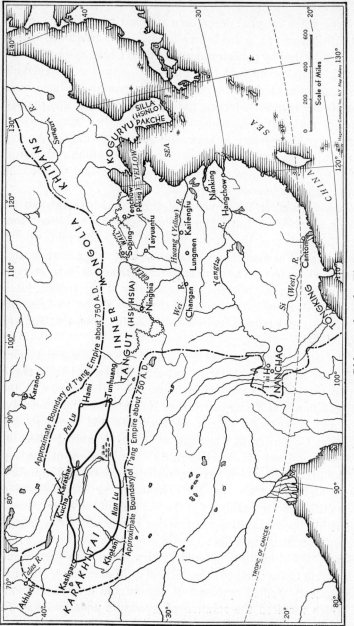

China under the T'ang

Hardly had internal peace been restored when there came, in the autumn of 624, a fresh invasion by the Turks. The elderly Kao Tsu, seized by panic, proposed to burn Changan and to transfer his capital southward to a place of safety, but his energetic son vetoed this timid policy and insisted upon presenting a brave front to the invader. Meeting the Turkish forces outside the very gates of the capital, Li Shih-min convinced their Kagan, Hie-li, partly by his resolute bearing and partly by diplomacy, that peace with the Chinese Empire was more profitable than war. A treaty was concluded between the two rulers, and the invading army withdrew beyond the frontier.

Two years after the removal of this Turkish threat and following a period of fratricidal strife among his ambitious sons, Kao Tsu abdicated the throne in favor of Li Shih-min, who, as the emperor T'ai Tsung, now became the head of the state in name as well as in fact. The new emperor, during his long reign of twenty-three years, restored the prosperity of the empire, established the dynasty in the esteem of the whole nation, and regained for China the dominant position in the affairs of eastern and central Asia.

The second T'ang emperor, besides being a warrior and a statesman, was himself a scholar of no mean ability and fully appreciated the social importance of education. As evidence of this appreciation T'ai Tsung reorganized the national educational system and consistently patronized literature and learning. The Imperial University at Changan, as it was organized under his decrees, consisted of six colleges: (1) the "College of the Sons of the State," to which were admitted the sons and grandsons of the highest officials; (2) the "Great College," for the sons of less exalted official families; (3) the "College of the Four Classes," admitting by competitive examination the sons of petty officials and of nonofficial families; (4) the "School of Laws"; (5) the "School of Calligraphy," a study which has always been highly honored in China; and (6) the "School of Mathematics," in which the students studied problems of algebra and arithmetic "some of which required the solution of quadratic equations and the extraction of square and cube root."

During T'ai Tsung's reign the enrollment of these six schools was fixed at 3260, and the graduates, after a thorough examination, passed into the ranks of the civil service. Supplementing the Imperial University and providing it with a constant stream of competent candidates for admission were the provincial colleges in each province of the empire, which, in turn, drew their students from the great number of prefectural preparatory schools.

The reorganized educational system assured to the empire an adequate supply of educated civil officials. Trained officials had been sadly lacking since the fall of the Han dynasty, and they now gave the government the prestige and the administrative intelligence which were needed for long survival. Hardly less important was the effect of the new institutions upon China's position among her neighbors. The rulers of the three Korean kingdoms, of the Uighurs (see page 171), and of the Tibetans sent their sons to the Imperial University, while numerous Japanese scholars, attracted by the intellectual supremacy of the Chinese capital, flocked thither for study and returned to their native land deeply impressed with respect for China and things Chinese.

The restoration of a body of trained civil officials was followed in due time by a complete revision of the laws, and in 643 the *T'ang Lü* ("T'ang Code of Law") was completed and put into force. By the opening of the seventh century China's foreign trade, the greater part of which was concentrated at Canton, had grown so large that many foreign merchants of various nationalities were residing at the ports. One section of the new code is therefore of particular interest as illustrating the method by which the T'ang legislators dealt with the problem of administering justice to these "outlanders." The *T'ang Lü* provided that civil disputes between foreigners of a single nationality should be settled in accordance with the laws of that nation; but that those between foreigners of different nationalities or between foreigners and Chinese should be settled in accordance with Chinese law, which was also to be applied in all criminal cases.

Each group of foreigners, containing all the merchants of a single nationality, was required to have its chief, or "headman." To this chief the officials gave instructions as to the rules and regulations which must be obeyed, and the headman, in addition to settling the disputes between the members of his group, was held responsible for the proper behavior of all his fellow nationals. This arrangement, by providing for the settlement of most disputes within the group concerned, made it unnecessary for all the foreigners to understand the Chinese language, while it was not necessary for the Chinese officials, in order to avoid making an unjust decision, to become acquainted with all the different customs and laws of the various foreign nations.

The Northern Turks, with whom T'ai Tsung in 624, as his father's adviser and lieutenant, succeeded in negotiating a satisfactory settlement, still constituted a serious threat to the peace of the empire. Hie-li, their Kagan, had granted asylum to the widow and the grandson of the Sui emperor Yang, and it soon became apparent that he was preparing to support their imperial claims by a fresh invasion of Chinese territory. To avert this danger the Chinese government relied upon intrigue rather than upon military force. Imperial emissaries, sowing rivalry and discontent, were sent among the tribes which acknowledged the overlordship of the Turkish Kagan, and in 628 Hie-li found his power undermined by a widespread revolt. Refusing to receive an ambassador from the now penitent Turkish ruler, in 630 T'ai Tsung dispatched an army to co-operate with the most powerful of the rebels, and Hie-li was taken prisoner. The T'ang emperor showed himself to be a generous victor and gave his defeated enemy courteous treatment at Changan, but this triumph of Chinese policy reduced the Northern Turks to impotence. Turkish princes were honored with Chinese titles; Turkish troops were incorporated into the Chinese army; and for the next half-century the expansion of Chinese influence to the north and west was achieved by the utilization of these Turkish auxiliaries.

During his struggle against the Northern Turks, T'ai Tsung had maintained cordial relations with the Western Turkish tribes, who occupied the valley of the Ili River, and had made considerable use of their jealousy toward their northern cousins. After the elimination of all danger from the Northern Turks, however, the Chinese government adopted toward the more western tribes, as the surest way of preventing the rise of any dangerous combination on the frontier, the same policy of fostering internal dissension and winning individual chieftains to the support of the empire.

While the Turks, like their Hsiungnu predecessors, were so placed as to be able to threaten the northern of the two caravan routes along which Chinese goods found their way to the markets of the west, the mountaineers of Tibet, from their almost inaccessible retreat beyond the Kunlun Mountains, were similarly able to threaten the Nan Lu, or South Road, which ran along the southern edge of the Taklamakan desert.

Toward the Tibetans, who at the close of the sixth century had begun to achieve political unity, T'ai Tsung adopted a policy of friendly conciliation. In 634 an embassy from the Tibetan king Srong-tsan Gam-po arrived at Changan to render homage to the Chinese emperor. The embassy was received with marked honor, and four years later T'ai Tsung reciprocated by dispatching a number of distinguished officials on an embassy to the Tibetan king. Srong-tsan Gam-po, perhaps convinced by this courtesy that the Chinese government feared him or had special need of his friendship, now demanded in marriage the hand of an imperial princess, and, when this demand was rejected, invaded the empire at the head of a powerful force. After defeating the Tibetan army and driving it back to its mountains, T'ai Tsung in 641 conciliated his vanquished neighbor by bestowing on him an imperial princess.

The steady expansion of Chinese influence into central Asia secured for the T'ang emperor respectful recognition from his most distant contemporaries. In 641 Harsha Siladitya, the ruler of the Indian kingdom of Kanauj, sent an embassy to the Chinese court. Two years later T'ai Tsung dispatched a return embassy which, after visiting Kanauj, returned to China by way of Nepal, where it was cordially received by the Nepalese king. In 647 Wang Hiuen-ts'e, who had been a member of the first embassy to Kanauj, was sent again at the head of a second embassy. Arriving at the capital of Kanauj, Wang found that Harsha was dead and that his throne had been seized by a usurper. The new ruler seized the gifts destined for his predecessor and attempted to massacre the ambassador with all his escort; but Wang escaped with a single companion and made his way to Nepal, where he recruited an army of seven thousand Nepalese and twelve hundred Tibetans. Re-entering India at the head of this force, the Chinese ambassador besieged and took the capital and captured the usurper, whom he carried back in chains to Changan.

Eminently successful in the policy which he adopted toward his neighbors on the north and west, T'ai Tsung was less fortunate in his effort to carry out in Korea the conquest which had been attempted by Yang Ti of the Sui dynasty. In 643 the Korean kingdom of Silla (see page 203), called Hsinlo by the Chinese, appealed to the Chinese emperor for aid against its two hostile neighbors. Disregarding the cautious advice of the officers who had participated in Yang Ti's ill-fated expedition, T'ai Tsung in 645 invaded the peninsula at the head of a powerful army. Several battles were won, and a number of Korean cities were occupied; but the approach of winter found the Korean forces still unbroken, while the Chinese army was in such an unsatisfactory position that it was compelled to withdraw into its own territory.

For this humiliating failure T'ai Tsung stubbornly refused to forgive the Koreans. A peace embassy from Koguryu in the spring of 646 was unable to secure an audience at the court, and the following spring saw another Chinese expedition launched against Koguryu and its ally Pakche. This expedition, however, was little more than a hurried raid, and T'ai Tsung was compelled to leave to his successor on the throne the actual subjugation of the peninsula.

In the summer of 649 T'ai Tsung, who deserves to be regarded as the real founder of the dynasty, died, leaving a powerful empire and a well-organized government over which a succession of T'ang rulers were to hold the power for an additional two hundred and fifty-eight years. This period of two centuries and a half is regarded by Chinese writers as the Golden Age of their country's history, yet the greatness of the period must be attributed to the sound organization established during the reign of T'ai Tsung and to the inherent genius of the Chinese people rather than to the ability of the later T'ang monarchs. Indeed, of the nineteen rulers who nominally controlled the destinies of the empire between the death of T'ai Tsung and the final collapse of the dynasty in 907, only two stand out as having been endowed with more than average ability.

The first, and probably the greater, of these two rulers was a woman, the empress Wu, the concubine and later the empress of T'ai Tsung's immediate successor, Kao Tsung. After dominating the government during the last twenty-three years (660–683) of Kao Tsung's reign and after experimenting in 684 as regent in the name of two successive puppet emperors, this strong-minded woman boldly ascended the throne and from 684 until her death in 705 exercised all the prerogatives of the imperial office. Energetic, unscrupulous, and resembling Catherine the Great of Russia in private life as in her political ability, the empress Wu succeeded in inspiring the government to a high degree of energy and efficiency.

The second notable ruler was Hsüan Tsung, who came to the throne in 712 for a long reign of forty-four years. The death of the empress Wu had been followed by a period of political intrigue and general disorder, but Hsüan Tsung was able to restore the government to good working order. During his early years upon the throne this prince showed himself to be a stern—even puritanical—ruler, and the empire enjoyed peace at home and prestige abroad. After 735, however, he fell more and more completely under the sway of the famous beauty Yang Kwei Fei. Luxury and extravagance now quickly replaced the simplicity which had characterized his court, while an unfortunate turn of affairs brought disaster upon the imperial forces abroad. The resultant popular discontent showed itself in a widespread revolution which in 756 drove the former puritan from the capital and finally compelled him to abdicate the throne.

The internal troubles which preceded and terminated the reign of Hsüan Tsung were characteristic of the entire period of T'ang rule. Intrigues, conspiracies, and popular uprisings marked almost every reign. Yet the sound legal and administrative systems established during the early years of the dynasty enabled it, until the opening of the tenth century, to weather each successive storm.

Although the foreign policy of the T'ang emperors made abundant use of diplomacy and intrigue, the centuries of T'ang rule were marked by frequent struggles against the turbulent peoples on the frontiers. Nor did the foreign wars of this Golden Age result always in victory for the empire. Disastrous, or at least unsuccessful, foreign campaigns were quite as common throughout the period as were the domestic uprisings.

Between the years 660 and 668 the emperor Kao Tsung reduced to submission the three Korean kingdoms of Koguryu, Pakche, and Silla and established over the peninsula a Chinese hegemony which was recognized until the end of the T'ang regime. On the northern and western frontiers, however, the armies of Kao Tsung were not so fortunate. In 670 the Tibetan forces attacked and captured the four "garrison towns" of Turkestan,—Kucha, Khotan, Kashgar, and Karashar,—which insured to their possessors the domination of the two important trade routes toward the west. In 679 the Western Turks allied themselves with the victorious Tibetans, and China's predominance in Turkestan appeared to be definitely lost. With the assumption of full power five years later by the empress Wu, Chinese affairs in the west took a more favorable turn. By 692 the Tibeto-Turkish alliance had been broken, the four garrison towns regained, and China's control over the northern and southern trade routes re-established.

Almost immediately after this recovery in the west, however, a new threat to China's peace and prestige appeared on the northern frontier, where the Khitan Tartars, allying themselves with the Northern Turks, had established themselves in southern Manchuria and were invading the northeastern districts inside the Great Wall. A number of Chinese armies were defeated by this hostile combination; but here, as in the west, the imperial government resorted successfully to diplomacy where military effort had failed. The Northern Turks were won away from the alliance, and the Khitans were driven off to the north, where, however, they continued to remain a source of danger to the empire.

At the close of the reign of the empress Wu in 704, Chinese influence was strongly established in the neighboring regions to the north and west, while the long reign of Hsüan Tsung (712–756) saw China's prestige in central Asia at its zenith. In 720 Chandrapida, the ruler of distant Kashmir, solicited and received from the Chinese emperor a formal recognition of his royal title. Thirteen years later Chandrapida's son and successor sent an embassy to Changan to render homage and to seek an alliance with the empire against Tibetan aggression. Hsüan Tsung confirmed the new king's accession to his father's throne, but the proposed alliance against Tibet did not meet with his approval.

During the years which followed Hsüan Tsung's rejection of the appeal from Kashmir the Tibetans, allied with the Mohammedan Arabs, rapidly extended their power in central Asia, subjugating a number of China's tributaries and undermining Chinese influence throughout the region. In 747, aroused by the defection of some of his former vassals, the emperor determined to assert his power. General Kao Hsien-chih, with a force of ten thousand infantry and cavalry, was sent from Kucha across the Pamirs and the Hindu Kush as far as Yasin and Gilgit on the upper branches of the Indus. Here the Chinese army inflicted severe punishment upon a former tributary who had renounced his allegiance to the Chinese throne and had attached himself to the Tibetan-Arab cause. This spectacular campaign, which was followed in 748 and 749 by the infliction of similar punishment upon a number of recreant vassals in Western Turkestan, made a great impression upon the rulers of central Asia, many of whom hastened to renew their tributary relationship with the Chinese government.

Impressive though these military activities were at the time, they had only a momentary effect upon the fate of central Asia. The power of the Arabs was steadily expanding, and the crushing defeat of a Chinese army under Kao Hsien-chih in 751, at the battle of Athlach (see Chapter VIII), marked the substitution of an Arab hegemony for that of the Chinese. The Chinese government quickly accepted the loss of its far-western domination and began to cultivate the good will of the Arabs, who, for their part, were quite willing to reach a friendly understanding with their great eastern neighbor. In 756, five years after the battle of Athlach, when the aged Hsüan Tsung had been driven from his capital by revolution, his successor was able to save the tottering dynasty only by calling to his assistance Turkish and Arab troops.

Fresh troubles for the empire soon appeared from another source. Encouraged by the foreign disasters and the internal disorders of China, the Tibetans, between the years 763 and 801, repeatedly invaded the T'ang dominions. On the first of these dates the invaders took and sacked the capital, Changan, while several of the later Tibetan expeditions spread ruin and panic through the western frontier districts of China. In 798 an alliance against the Tibetans was concluded by the T'ang emperor Te Tsung and the famous caliph Haroun al Raschid; the Tibetans were defeated and in 822 were compelled to make a definitive treaty of peace with China.

The eighth-century decline of China's imperial domination was attended by the rise, within the area now included in the Chinese Republic, of a new independent state: the kingdom of Nanchao, which occupied the modern province of Yunnan and the southern part of Szechwan. The peoples of this region belonged to the racial group known as the Shan, or Tai, and from early in the seventh century had acknowledged the supremacy of the T'ang emperors. Between 728 and 738 one of the Shan princes, who had succeeded in gaining authority over his neighbors, assumed the title "King of Nanchao"; he secured the emperor's confirmation of this title and established his capital at T'ai Ho, just south of modern Tali. In 751 the second king of this new state rebelled against Chinese suzerainty and gained his complete independence; but forty years later, when the Chinese were engaged in their desperate struggle against the Tibetans, Nanchao allied itself with China against the Tibetans and contributed in no small degree to the final outcome of the conflict.

After the decline of Tibetan power Nanchao was tempted to assume the role hitherto played by Tibet. In 863 the Shan kingdom broke off relations with China and invaded the province of Tongking, at that time a part of the empire. Driven from Tongking by the forces of the Chinese general Kao P'ien, they next invaded the Chinese portion of Szechwan, only to be defeated once more, in 875, by the same general and compelled to sue for peace. After the conclusion of a new treaty in 877, Nanchao remained independent until 1253, when it was conquered by the Mongols.

For more than a century after the death of T'ai Tsung in 649 T'ang China, in spite of occasional reverses, was the dominant power in central and eastern Asia. Even after the rise of the Arabs, the aggressions of the Tibetans, and the emergence of the Shan kingdom of Nanchao had combined to deprive the Chinese rulers of much of their far-flung power, their armies were sufficiently strong and their diplomacy sufficiently skillful to retain for them until the last quarter of the ninth century an influential position in the affairs of the continent. Yet the lasting glory of T'ang is to be found in the cultural consequences of China's international contacts under the dynasty rather than in the mere fact of her imperial pre-eminence.

Throughout the seventh, eighth, and ninth centuries China was, in a new and more glorious sense, the "Middle Kingdom." From Japan and Korea, from Burma, Cambodia, and the kingdoms of the East Indies, from the camps and cities of central Asia, from the shores of the Caspian and Black seas, from the banks of the Ganges, the Indus, and the Euphrates, there came during these three centuries an endless stream of foreigners of every nationality and of every description. Scholars and religious devotees, artists and poets, merchants, soldiers of fortune, and solemn embassies, all found their way along the converging roads which led to this great central state of the Oriental world.

The influence of this multitude of "strangers coming from afar" was supplemented by that of the many Chinese travelers who during these centuries found their way outward along the same roads to India, central Asia, Indo-China, and other distant regions of the earth. At no time in their history, except in the present century and perhaps under the Mongol regime, have the Chinese received in greater volume and variety the impact of foreign ideas; at no period since the days of Confucius has there existed in China more complete liberty for the individual thinker; and rarely, if ever, in the history of mankind has this combination of new ideas and intellectual freedom produced more brilliant results in the fields of art, literature, religion, and philosophy.

One important feature, already noted, of T'ai Tsung's reign (626–649) was the establishment of a well-organized educational system in which instruction was based primarily upon the Confucian Classics. Later reigns saw modifications and reforms in this system (such as the creation, by the emperor Hsüan Tsung, of the Han-lin Academy, a body of specially selected scholars of highest attainments), and throughout the entire life of the T'ang dynasty the Confucian scholars played an important part in the affairs of the country. During several of the reigns, also, high imperial favor and a considerable amount of popular support were accorded to Taoism, which by this time was so altered by superstitious accretions that it could hardly be recognized as the doctrine taught in the *Tao Te King* and in the writings of Chuang-tzu.

However, in spite of the prominent place held by Confucian scholarship and the occasional popularity of Taoist necromancy the dominating influence in T'ang China was Buddhist, and the three centuries which followed the unification of the empire saw the Indian religion strengthen steadily the position which it had gained during the troublous period of the fifth and sixth centuries. The pious pilgrimage of Fa Hsien, at the beginning of the fifth century, was imitated during the T'ang period by many Chinese Buddhists. Hsüan Chuang, whose pilgrimage extended from 629 to 644, and I Tsing, between 671 and 695, are merely two of the most famous figures in this veritable army of devotees who made their way to the land of Gautama Buddha.

Upon his return from India, Hsüan Chuang received from the emperor T'ai Tsung repeated evidence of imperial favor; dying in 664, the great traveler-scholar was given an official funeral by T'ai Tsung's successor. Both these rulers, moreover, regarded it as a privilege to be permitted to compose prefaces for Hsüan Chuang's translations from Indian Buddhist texts. I Tsing also, after his return from India, was received with highest honors by the empress Wu, who was an ardent supporter of Buddhism.

The steady growth of Buddhist influence was strenuously combated by the Confucian scholars and at times by the Taoists; yet it was not until the last century of the T'ang regime that the opponents of the foreign religion were able to record any noticeable success. In 845 they succeeded in obtaining from the emperor a decree ordering the dissolution of the Buddhist monasteries and the return of their inmates to family life. Even this triumph was of short duration; and fifteen years later the decree was repealed by a new occupant of the throne, who conferred fresh favors upon the Buddhists and their institutions.

Nor was the strength of Buddhism during these centuries shown only by the increasing number of its adherents or by the extent of imperial favor which it received. In their struggle to maintain themselves against the Buddhist advance both Confucianism and Taoism were forced to modify their teachings by borrowing ideas from their rival. In the case of Taoism, which had a fundamental resemblance to Buddhism, this exchange of ideas was reciprocal; and it is difficult to estimate which of the two parties to the exchange was the greater gainer. But even the Confucianists, although resisting the temptation to develop a religious organization, assimilated a certain more spiritual outlook on life, and Confucian philosophy after the middle of the T'ang regime is noticeably different in this respect from the earlier teaching of the school.

The flourishing condition of Buddhism under the T'ang was, as we have seen, a more or less normal development of the importance which the religion had acquired during the immediately preceding period; hence this would not of itself constitute conclusive evidence as to the philosophical and religious tolerance of Chinese thought at this era. Supplementary evidence on this point, however, and on the far-reaching effects of T'ang imperialism is furnished by the appearance in China of four other foreign religions,— Mazdaism, Manichaeism, Nestorian Christianity, and Mohammedanism,—all of which owed their introduction to the contact between the T'ang empire and the peoples of central and southwestern Asia.

Mazdaism, which reached China shortly before 631, and Manichaeism, which was introduced in 694, appear to have had little lasting influence, and they owed their appearance to the desire of the T'ang rulers to conciliate, respectively, the Persians and the Uighurs. But Nestorianism and Mohammedanism, although they both seem to have been professed only by the non-Chinese elements of the population, occupy places of some importance in the history of the country.

The doctrine of Nestorius, which was condemned as heresy by the Council of Ephesus in 431, was brought to China in 635 by a Nestorian monk whose name is recorded by the Chinese as Alopen. Three years after Alopen's arrival the emperor T'ai Tsung issued an edict permitting him to preach his doctrine and to erect a church at Changan. With the exception of the empress Wu, whose support of Buddhism amounted to fanaticism, all the subsequent T'ang rulers continued to protect and to patronize the Nestorians. Hsüan Tsung even permitted the Nestorian clergy to hold their services within the precincts of the imperial palace, while he honored their church building by placing in it portraits of his ancestors.

Most of our information concerning the fortunes of Chinese Nestorianism during the first hundred and fifty years of its domicile, is obtained from the famous Nestorian tablet erected in 781 on the property of the church at Changan. This tablet, which was discovered in 1625 by the Jesuits, contains a statement of the doctrine, a short history of the mission, and eulogies of the T'ang monarchs who had distinguished themselves in showing favor to the religion.

With the collapse of the tolerant T'ang dynasty at the beginning of the tenth century this eastern branch of Christianity underwent a series of persecutions which drove it from the empire. It continued to flourish in central Asia, however, and reappeared in China three and a half centuries later under the protection of the equally tolerant Mongols.

The precise date of the introduction of Mohammedanism into China has not been established. In central Asia, as we have seen, the Chinese came into contact with the expanding power of the Mohammedan Arabs about the end of the seventh century; but the doctrines of Islam may easily have reached China by way of the sea at least half a century earlier, and indeed even before the death of the Prophet. At the beginning of the T'ang regime the greater part of China's sea-borne foreign trade was in the hands of the Arabs, who constituted the most numerous element in the foreign communities at Canton and at the other seaports; and in 651 an embassy from Arabia reached the Chinese capital by way of Canton.

In 758 the Mohammedan population at Canton, probably swelled by a large number of unpaid Arab mercenaries who had assisted in the restoration of the T'ang power and who were now being returned to their own country by way of Canton, precipitated a serious riot with much destruction of property. For more than a century after this outbreak the presence of this alien community with its foreign religion caused no trouble; the Arab merchants were nonaggressive, and they met with complete tolerance on the part of the Chinese. Toward the close of the ninth century, however, the growing maritime activity of the Chinese resulted in the development of hostility toward the foreign traders, and in 879, in the midst of the disorders which attended the decline of the T'ang dynasty, a violent antiforeign outbreak drove the Arabs from Canton.

This anti-Arab development appears, however, to have been produced by economic rather than by religious considerations. In other parts of the empire, where similar economic grounds for hostility did not exist, the followers of Mohammed were not molested; and the gradual infiltration of Mohammedanized central-Asians resulted in the steady growth of the religion in the western provinces, especially in Kansu and Yunnan, where it now numbers some fifteen or twenty million adherents.

Although the doctrines of the Buddhists penetrated and modified the teachings of the Taoists and even of the Confucianists, it is in the field of art, especially sculpture and painting, that the Indian religion has made its most splendid permanent contribution to Chinese culture. At Lungmen in northern Honan, where Buddhist sculpture of the T'ang period is found side by side with the earlier work of the Northern Wei, at Tunhuang in western Kansu, where the explorations of Stein and Pelliot have brought to light a wonderful collection of sculpture and painting dating from the eighth, ninth, and tenth centuries, and at various other points in the empire the artists of T'ang China have left behind them convincing evidence of noble religious inspiration coupled with a high degree of technical proficiency.

In its technique, as in the religious thought which called it forth, T'ang art owed much to foreign influence; Greek and Hindu models can be easily discerned in the features of Buddhas and Bodhisattvas and in the graceful flow of their draperies. Yet, while the art of the period bears additional testimony to the manifold cultural influences which were pouring in upon the empire, the sculpture and painting of Lungmen and Tunhuang are no slavish imitations of foreign compositions; the borrowed elements, like Buddhism itself, underwent a process of naturalization, and out of them the Chinese artist produced art which was wholly Chinese. Not all of T'ang art, however, was religious. The secular art of the period included landscape and portrait painting, and painted terra-cotta statuettes of human beings and of animals. Many of these latter, which were placed in the tombs of the dead, were strikingly modeled figures of horses, concerning which a present-day French author writes: "The spirit, the boldness, and the elegance of these works permit one, without blasphemy, to compare them with the cavalcade of the frieze of the Parthenon."

In poetry, as in sculpture and painting, the age of T'ang produced some of the greatest figures in the history of China. For more than a thousand years the poetry of T'ang has retained its high position among Chinese readers; translated into foreign languages, it has fairly earned the praise of readers to whom the Chinese language is a closed book. Among the many poets the most famous were Li T'ai-po—sometimes known as Li Po—(701?–762), Tu Fu (712–770), the devout Buddhist Po Chü-i (772–846), and two Taoist poets, Ch'ang Chien and T'ao Han, both of whom were contemporaries of Li T'ai-po.

Several of these writers enjoyed the patronage of the T'ang emperors, and much of their verse deals with the brilliant life of the court or with the great achievements of their patrons in peace and war. But princely favor has never sufficed, in China or elsewhere, to produce great poets and great poetry. Moreover, the T'ang poets, far from being subservient eulogists of the existing order, were extremely independent, criticizing as often as they praised, and their caustic satire often brought upon them the disfavor of their imperial patrons. Li T'ai-po, commonly regarded as the greatest poetical genius produced by the Far East, spent the last years of his life in disgrace, as also did Tu Fu, to whom the Chinese have accorded the title "God of Poetry." Other writers, although avoiding the disgrace which fell upon these two men, wearied of their efforts to combine the functions of poet and courtier and became voluntary exiles from the court in order to live their lives in closer communion with nature.

As in the days of Han, so also during the T'ang period, the development of literature owed much to the inventive genius of the Chinese; for this period saw the invention or, more correctly, the evolution of a means whereby many copies of a literary work could be reproduced at little cost. The first step in the evolution of printing appears to have come in the fifth century, when carved seals smeared with ink were used by officials for stamping documents. About the same time, moreover, "rubbings" began to be taken from stone inscriptions by spreading a sheet of paper over the inscribed surface, pounding the paper with a brush so as to force it down into the interstices, and then rubbing with ink so as to blacken the entire surface except where it had sunk into the lines of the carving.

During the eighth century, block prints of page size were produced by the simple expedient of adapting to a larger surface the principle of the inked seal, and the ninth century saw the printing by this method of the first complete book, a Buddhist *sutra*. The completion of the evolutionary process came in the Sung dynasty when, about the middle of the eleventh century, the substitution of movable type for the full-page carved block put an end to the danger that a whole page would be spoiled by a single slip of the engraver's tool.

The last quarter of the ninth century saw the empire torn by a series of internal disorders which finally brought the dynasty to ruin. The first of these outbreaks, which began in 875, swept the entire country and in 881 drove the emperor from his capital. Two years later, with the aid of a Turkish force under a Turkish leader named Li K'o-yung, Changan was retaken, the chief rebel leader put to death, and apparent order restored. But the restoration of the imperial power was only nominal. Although the T'ang emperors retained to the very last the loyal support of their Turkish allies, they now found themselves almost without aid from their

A History of the Far East

own people. The struggle dragged on for two decades, but the end could not be long deferred. In 905 the most powerful of the rebel leaders, Chu Wen, imprisoned the reigning emperor and put him to death after having compelled him to abdicate the throne in favor of an infant son. Two years later this boy meekly surrendered his empty title to his father's murderer, and the T'ang dynasty was at an end.

THE FIVE "LATER" DYNASTIES

The fifty-three years following the abdication of the last T'ang sovereign saw only a continuation of the anarchy which had characterized the closing decades of that once glorious dynasty. Between 907 and 960, when the accession of the first Sung emperor brought some degree of peace to the distracted country, five short-lived dynasties held sway. Since each of these five assumed the name which had been borne by some earlier line of emperors, they are known in Chinese history as the five "Later" dynasties: the Later Liang (907–923), the Later T'ang (923–936), the Later Chin (936–946), the Later Han (946–950), and the Later Chou (950–960). None of these dynasties succeeded in gaining actual control over more than a small fraction of the empire.

The half-century of the five "Later" dynasties, like the period which followed the collapse of the Han regime, witnessed a marked increase of barbarian influence in the northern portions of the empire. The second of the five dynasties, the Later T'ang, was founded by a son of the Turkish general, Li K'o-yung, who had so faithfully supported the last rulers of T'ang, and the Later Chin and the Later Han were also established by leaders of Turkish extraction.

Even more important than the temporary rule of these military chieftains from the western frontier was the growth of a new and formidable state, the empire of the Khitans, on the northeast. In the closing years of the seventh century this branch of the northern Tartars had been sufficiently strong to attack the T'ang empire and had been repulsed only after a bitter struggle. Two centuries later, when the power of T'ang declined, the Khitans again pushed down from the north into southern Manchuria. In 916 the Khitan chief, Ye-lü A-po-ki, assumed the title of Huang Ti ("emperor") and took for his dynasty the name *Liao*, meaning "Iron." By the end of his reign in 926 A-po-ki had extended his dominion north-eastward to include all the territory between Korea and the Amur River. In 936 A-po-ki's son and successor, Te-kwang, assisted the founder of the Later Chin to seize the imperial title, for which assistance he was rewarded with the northern districts of the modern provinces of Chihli and Shansi. Two years later Te-kwang established a southern capital at Peking, then known as Yenchow and now called Peiping, and made himself the master of north-eastern China as far south as the Yellow River.

In 946, when the Later Chin emperor attempted to break away from the control of his recent benefactors, the Khitans invaded the regions south of the Yellow River and pillaged the Chinese capital. This catastrophe brought to an end the rule of the Later Chin. But neither the Later Han (946–950) nor the Later Chou, which seized the power in 950, was able to offer successful resistance to the steadily growing Khitan empire.

THE FOUNDING OF THE SUNG DYNASTY

Out of this desperate struggle against the Khitans arose a leader capable of reuniting and restoring the empire. In 960 the officials of the Later Chou, acting in the name of a nine-year-old puppet emperor, sent against the Khitans an imperial force commanded by General Chao K'uang-yin. Hardly had the army left the capital, at that time located at K'aifengfu, when the subordinate officers united to demand that their commander assume the imperial title. After some hesitation Chao K'uang-yin acceded to the demand, on condition that no harm should be done to the little emperor at K'aifengfu. At the head of his army he returned to the capital and was proclaimed emperor as the first of the Sung dynasty, in whose dynastic list he is known as T'ai Tsu ("Great Ancestor").

The political situation in China at the moment when Chao K'uang-yin ascended the throne was such that few of his contemporaries could have predicted any great success for the dynasty.

From his capital at K'aifengfu the authority of the emperor extended only over the three modern provinces of Shantung, Honan, and Shensi. To the north the Khitans held Chihli and the northern part of Shansi, while southern Shansi, with its capital at Taiyuanfu, was held by the independent prince of Pei Han, who had allied himself with the Khitans. South of the imperial domain the old empire was shared among a half-dozen petty kingdoms and a large number of smaller subdivisions.

Nor were the qualifications of the new emperor, on the surface at least, such as would have warranted the hope that the dynasty which he was founding would prove different from its recent predecessors. A competent but hardly a great general, handsome, personally popular with his subordinates, Chao K'uang-yin was neither a scholar nor an experienced administrator. Yet the passage of time showed that this unlettered soldier and untried statesman was endowed with the patient determination, the activity, the simplicity, and the native good sense needed to overcome the difficulties by which he was confronted; and the first Sung emperor succeeded, by virtue of these qualities, in establishing his dynasty so firmly that it ranks with the Han and the T'ang as one of the three great dynasties of the middle period of China's history.

During the reign of T'ai Tsu (960–976) and during that of his brother T'ai Tsung[1] (976–997) the disunited fragments of the empire were brought once more under the control of the central government. Within less than twenty years after the founding of the dynasty all the territory south of the Great Wall, except that held by the Khitans, had been induced to acknowledge the authority of Sung.

In his labors for the reconsolidation of the empire T'ai Tsu did not depend solely upon force of arms but endeavored in every possible way to improve the administration and to strengthen the bonds which would hold the people together. Uneducated though he was, the founder of the new dynasty patronized education and restored to the civil-service examinations the importance which they had held under the early T'ang emperors. A soldier by train-

---

[1] Not to be confused with T'ang T'ai Tsung, the second emperor of the T'ang dynasty (627–649).

ing, he fully appreciated the evils which China had suffered from military rule, and he strove throughout his reign to place the power once more in the hands of civil officials directly answerable to the throne. In order to lessen the probability of revolt in the reconquered provinces he confirmed the appointments of the local officials and even, where possible, appointed the defeated rulers to act as his representatives; but he strictly limited the powers of all these appointees and introduced into the criminal code the sound principle that all death sentences should be referred to the Imperial Board of Punishments for approval. Since his policies on these points were continued by his successor, the various conquests and annexations were quickly followed by the restoration of internal peace and by a consequent revival of prosperity.

In 979 the emperor T'ai Tsung made a determined effort to bring under his sway those portions of Chihli and Shansi which were held by the Khitans. Repulsed in his first attempt to take Peking, he did not again attack his northern neighbor until seven years later. This time he succeeded in reconquering northern Shansi, together with some districts of southern Chihli, but northern Chihli remained in Khitan possession. Under Chen Tsung, the third emperor of the dynasty (997–1022), the long struggle was terminated in 1004 by a treaty whereby the Khitans evacuated southern Chihli but received in return the northern districts of Shansi and an annual subsidy, or tribute, in the form of a hundred thousand ounces of silver and two hundred thousand pieces of silk.

At the same time that the Sung government was thus definitely checked in its effort to recover the northeastern territory it was suffering a fresh loss on the northwest, where the kingdom of Tangut, or Hsi Hsia, succeeded in establishing its independence. The Tanguts, a people belonging to the Tibeto-Burman linguistic group, had been loyal supporters of the imperial power during the closing decades of the T'ang regime, and their leader had been rewarded for his loyalty by being given the title of Duke of Hsia. Practically independent throughout the half-century which followed the T'ang collapse, the Duke of Hsia submitted unwillingly to the rising power of Sung, and in 990 he took advantage of the

Sung-Khitan struggle to renounce his allegiance. The new kingdom, which was promptly recognized by the Khitan emperor, had its capital at Ninghia and occupied northern Kansu as far west as Karanor, together with a considerable section of Inner Mongolia immediately north of the Great Wall.

Although the Tangut kingdom included a portion of China Proper and controlled the caravan routes leading to the west, the Sung emperors made no move for its reconquest. Indeed, after the treaty with the Khitans in 1004 the Chinese were quite satisfied to remain at peace with their two northern neighbors, and for more than a century after that date the only interruption of peaceful relations came in the form of a Tangut attack, in 1040, upon the Chinese territory on their southern frontier. This attack was repulsed, and the Sung government showed its pacifist tendencies by arranging for an annual "gift" to the Tangut king similar to that which it was already paying to the Khitans.

The territory of the Tangut kingdom contained little fertile land, and the rulers of the country supplemented their scanty income by levying heavy toll upon such trade as passed through their dominions between China and western Asia, a practice which frequently proved irritating to their more civilized neighbors. On the other hand the Tanguts, like the Khitans, rapidly adopted a considerable degree of Chinese civilization. In 1037 they developed a written language of their own, using for this purpose modifications or imitations of the Chinese characters, in which they produced a respectable body of national literature.

At peace on the frontiers and renouncing all idea of foreign conquest either to the north or to the south, Sung China turned its energies to the solution of internal social and political problems. The law code was thoroughly revised; education was fostered by the erection of public schools in every city of the first or second rank; and an unsuccessful effort was made, by the construction of drainage canals, to put an end to the periodic ravages of the Yellow River.

In the third quarter of the eleventh century the movement for social and economic reform through government action reached its climax under the leadership of the radical statesman Wang An-shih.

Born in 1021, Wang An-shih first gained notoriety by his unorthodox interpretations of the Confucian Classics. In 1067 he was recommended to the emperor, and the following year saw him appointed, by the new emperor Shen Tsung, to a post in the central administration. In spite of the opposition of those who distrusted his unconventional views, Wang quickly won the complete confidence of the emperor, and in 1069 he was raised to the rank of chief minister.

Declaring that the general welfare of the nation demanded a return to the patriarchal system of antiquity, he now embarked upon a program of sweeping reform. The land tax was greatly reduced and was made payable in grain or other produce instead of in coin. In the spring of the year the government advanced to the farmers the necessary seed grain, and these advances were repaid at harvest time with interest at the rate of 2½ per cent *per month*. In order to prevent great fluctuations in the price of foodstuffs the government was to buy up grain when prices were low and sell it when the price rose above a fixed maximum. Stability of general prices was to be maintained by the careful regulation of the amount of money in circulation. Government works were no longer to be carried out by forced labor; instead this labor was to be paid, and an income tax was levied to provide the government with the additional funds necessary to meet the expense thus incurred.

These reforms, many of which sound strangely modern, aroused strenuous opposition. The scholars felt that Wang An-shih was departing from the principles of Confucius and that his new laws were therefore fundamentally wrong; the business and financial classes were bitterly antagonistic to changes which would limit their prospective profits, while the people as a whole feared the growth of government interference in their daily affairs. In 1075 Wang resigned his post as minister and was appointed governor of Nanking; dismissed from his office a few years later, he spent the remaining years of his life in retirement, a disgraced and disappointed man. The conservative statesmen who replaced Wang abolished all but one of his many innovations. In order to lessen the power and the expense of the military organization, he had instituted for the maintenance of internal order a system of local militia called the Pao Chia. This militia system continued to exist for more than eight centuries, and, as we shall see later, had an important part in the development of the Boxer movement of 1900.

Among the numerous tribes which during the eleventh century acknowledged the overlordship of the Khitan emperor were the Juchen (or Nuchen) Tartars, who lived in northern Manchuria in the vicinity of the Sungari River. In 1114 the chief of the Juchen broke off relations with his Khitan suzerain and invaded southern Manchuria. The Khitans, whose long contact with Chinese civilization had modified their earlier warlike character, were unable to resist the attack of these former vassals, especially since the Sung government co-operated with the Juchen and attacked the Khitans from the south. The conquest of southern Manchuria was completed in 1116; in 1122 the Juchen forces gained control of northern Shansi, and the following year saw the conquest of the Khitan territory in Chihli. A fragment of the Khitans, under the leadership of one of their princes, fled westward to the valley of the Ili River, where they founded a new state known as the kingdom of Kara Khitai, while the chief of the Juchen, now completely master of the former Khitan dominions, seated himself upon the vacant throne as the first emperor of the Kin ("Golden") dynasty.

THE SOUTHERN SUNGS (1127–1279)

In aiding the Juchen Tartars against the Khitans the Sung statesmen at K'aifengfu had hoped to destroy the empire on their northeastern frontier and to prepare the way for the reannexation of the former Chinese territories held by the Khitans. Too late they were to realize that their assistance had been given to the stronger of the two warring powers and that they had "exchanged King Log for King Stork." The warlike Kins who now occupied the place of the peaceful and extremely civilized Khitans lost little time in attacking their recent ally. In 1125 they raided the Sung territories lying north of the Yellow River. The following year their armies crossed the river and after a brief siege took the

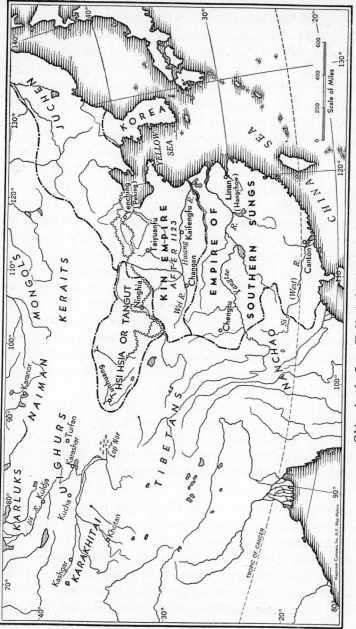

China in the Last Half of the Twelfth Century

capital. The emperor, with most of his family, was taken away into captivity; but one of his sons, escaping from the general disaster, took refuge at Nanking, where later in the same year he was proclaimed emperor.

Even at Nanking the Sung court was not safe from its enemies. In 1129 the Kins crossed the Yangtze and overran the provinces south of the river, capturing both Nanking and Hangchow. For a while it looked as if all China was destined to fall under the rule of the invader. But the Kins, although momentarily successful in their southern expedition, were unable to maintain their gains south of the Yangtze. Between 1130 and 1141 the Sung armies, under the command of the famous hero Yo Fei, drove them steadily northward until a treaty was arranged fixing the boundary between the two empires at the watershed which divides the Yangtze valley from that of the Yellow River.

The treaty of 1141 did not restore to the Sung rulers their former capital, and after a brief sojourn at Nanking the imperial court established itself at Hangchow. From the time of their expulsion from K'aifengfu in 1127 the rulers of the Sung dynasty are known in Chinese history as the Southern Sungs, and Hangchow (the "Kinsay" of Marco Polo) remained the capital of their diminished empire for a century and a half until it was finally conquered by the Mongol armies of Kublai Khan.

The Han dynasty, which rendered itself illustrious by its conquests in central Asia, is the warrior dynasty of Chinese history. The T'ang, which bound these same countries by a vast confederation under its patronage, is its political dynasty. That of the Sungs, which neglected the defense of the frontiers in order to occupy itself almost exclusively with the development of great literature, is the essentially literary dynasty of these annals.[1]

In many respects the China of the Sung period appears as a mere continuation of the T'ang empire. Buddhist pilgrims continued, as late as the middle of the eleventh century, to make their way to the holy places of India. In art—in sculpture as well as in portrait and landscape painting—the artists of the Sung period maintained or even surpassed the high standard set by those of T'ang. From Japan and Korea, from central Asia, and from Indo-

[1] E. Biot, *Essai sur l'histoire de l'instruction publique en Chine*, p. 321.

China foreign scholars still made their way to China as to the great center of culture and knowledge.

Over against these points of resemblance, however, there are other points in which the two periods were strikingly different. During the seventh, eighth, and ninth centuries the culture of China can be most fittingly characterized as international. The far-reaching interests of the T'ang emperors opened the country to the impact of new ideas from every part of Asia. Li T'ai-po, the greatest of the T'ang poets, is said to have been born of Chinese parents residing in the distant valley of the Chu River, in what is now Russian Turkestan; General Kao Hsien-chih, the commander of the remarkable expedition in 747 across the Pamirs and the Hindu Kush, was a Korean by birth; Abe-no Nakamaro, who came to China about 750 as an ambassador from Japan, took service under the T'ang emperor and held office as governor of Annam, while many high imperial officials, especially during the ninth century, were of Turkish or other central-Asian origin.

Although China under the Sung rulers continued to have considerable contact with the outside world, the period was decidedly nationalistic in temper and in culture. It was a time in which the Chinese turned their attention inward and devoted themselves to the task of digesting the new cultural elements introduced during the expansive days of T'ang; Buddhism continued to have great influence, especially in art, but the dominating factor in Chinese thought during the eleventh and twelfth centuries was Confucianism.

The Confucian philosophy of Sung China, however, especially that of the twelfth century, was far from being the simple practical code originally taught by the Great Sage. In the eleventh-century struggle between Wang An-shih and his conservative opponents each party accused the other of taking unjustifiable liberties in interpreting the Confucian Classics, yet both were still using the Classics as the basis of a purely utilitarian social program. The philosophers of the twelfth-century Southern Sungs, although Confucian in name, borrowed heavily from Buddhist and Taoist mysticism to expand the earlier simple code of social relations into a complete and satisfactory explanation of the universe.

The influence of Buddhism is particularly evident in the case of Chu Hsi (1130–1200), who is regarded as the greatest philosopher of the Sung period and whose commentaries on the Classics are still accepted as authoritative. Chu Hsi was brought up under Buddhist influence, but at the age of twenty-five he renounced this religion and applied himself to the study of the Classics. In view of his early training there is little reason for wonder that he read into the Confucian writings, especially into the *Book of Rites* and the *Great Learning*, ideas which were wholly foreign to primitive Confucianism.[1]

SUMMARY

During the long period of nearly fifteen hundred years which elapsed between the fall of the Ch'in dynasty of Shih Huang Ti and the final conquest of Sung China in 1279 by the Mongols, the Chinese Empire was ruled as a united country by three great dynasties—Han, T'ang, and Sung—whose combined tenure of power totaled slightly more than a thousand years. The one serious break in the national unity, the four centuries between the Han and the T'ang, saw China divided first into the "Three Kingdoms" and then, after a brief reunion under the Chin emperors, into a "Barbarian" North and a "Chinese" South, each governed by a succession of comparatively short-lived ruling families. Yet even during this period of disunion and during the turbulent interval between the downfall of the T'ang and the appearance of the Sung, China's institutions and her political ideas were maintained.

Throughout this millennium and a half the Chinese advanced steadily in civilization until by the twelfth century A.D. they were probably the most highly civilized people on earth. In their cultural development they had drawn heavily upon the ideas of the outside world. The armies of Han and the diplomacy of T'ang, the religious devotion awakened by the teachings of Gautama Buddha, the profit-seeking activities of the traveling merchant, and even the hungry aggression of barbarian neighbors all combined to bring into the Chinese "melting pot" the ingredients

[1] For an excellent analysis of the "Neo-Confucianism" of the Sung period see K. S. Latourette, *The Chinese : their History and Culture*, Vol. I, pp. 257–264.

from which Chinese genius evolved its finished product. Nor was China the sole beneficiary of this development. Like ancient Greece and Renaissance Italy, she gave freely to the outside world the fruits of her labor. To Europe and to the Mediterranean world she gave silk, the art of making paper, and possibly the mariner's compass, gunpowder, and some contributions to the painting of the Renaissance. To her Asiatic neighbors her gifts were innumerable; Korea and Japan were perhaps her heaviest debtors, but central Asia, Indo-China, the Malay world, and even India, Persia, and Arabia all profited greatly from their centuries of intercourse with the Chinese Empire. Not only is it possible to say that China in the twelfth century was probably the most highly civilized nation on earth; with even more assurance it may be said that in the twelfth century and for many centuries to come the civilization of the greater part of the Far East was that which had been worked out by the Chinese and by them transmitted to their neighbors.

SUGGESTED REFERENCES

AYSCOUGH, F. Tu Fu, the Autobiography of a Chinese Poet.

BEAL, S. (translator). Si-Yu-Ki: Buddhist Records of the Western World.

BRUCE, J. P. Chu Hsi and his Masters.

BUSHELL, S. W. Chinese Art.

BUSHELL, S. W. "The Hsi Hia Dynasty," *Journal of the Royal Asiatic Society*, 1895–1896.

FERGUSON, J. C. "Wang An-shih," *Journal of the Royal Asiatic Society* (North China Branch), 1903-1904.

HIRTH, F., and ROCKHILL, W. W. The Chu-fan-chi of Chau Ju-kua.

HOWORTH, H. H. "Hia or Tangut," *Journal of the Royal Asiatic Society*, 1883.

LATOURETTE, K. S. The Chinese: their History and Culture.

LATOURETTE, K. S. A History of Christian Missions in China.

LAUFER, B. Chinese Clay Figures.

LEVI, S. "Les Missions de Wang Hsiuan-tse dans l'Inde," *Journal Asiatique*, 1900.

OBATA, S. The Works of Li Po.

PELLIOT, P. Les Grottes de Touen-houang.

PETRUCCI, R. Chinese Painters: a Critical Study.

WALEY, A. Introduction to the Study of Chinese Painting.

WILHELM, R. A Short History of Chinese Civilization.

WILLIAMS, E. T. A Short History of China.

VII

India: from the Second Century B.C. to the Delhi Sultanate

THROUGHOUT the fourteen centuries which follow the disappearance of the Maurya dynasty in 185 B.C. the history
of India has hardly more unity than that imposed by its geographical boundaries and by the possession of a common religious
heritage. Even northern India during this long lapse of time
only twice achieved any considerable degree of political union:
from the early years of the fourth century A.D. to the opening of
the sixth century the Gupta dynasty, founded by a new Chandragupta, reigned over a united empire which included the territory north of the Narbada and east of the Punjab, and a century
after the fall of this dynasty almost the identical districts were
again united for the single reign of the adventurous Harsha
Siladitya. Apart from these two empires, the second of them
exceedingly short-lived, we have only the separate histories of a
large number of independent states. These separate histories,
however, are frequently drawn by the contacts of peace or war
into parallel channels; and from century to century one or an-

other of the independent states, by virtue of its military power, commercial activity, artistic achievement, or religious enthusiasm, stands out prominently among its contemporaries.

The Punjab, the broad basin of the upper Indus and its tributaries, occupies a peculiar position with respect to the rest of India and plays a unique role in Indian history. Open on the northwest to invasion through the passes of the Hindu Kush—almost the only practicable military land route into India—the Punjab, as we have seen, is almost completely cut off from the rest of India by the highlands of Rajputana and the adjoining strip of desert which stretches northward nearly to the foothills of the Himalayas. Successive invaders of India by land have thus found the Punjab a sort of vestibule to the Indian world. Only on rare occasions has a foreign invasion after occupying the Punjab retained sufficient momentum to carry it forward into the more eastern portions of northern India. The earliest Aryans appear to have spent several centuries in the plain of the upper Indus before pushing their way along the slopes of the Himalayas into the upper part of the Gangetic valley, while Alexander the Great, because of the weariness of his soldiers, never advanced farther than this antechamber. The history of the Punjab, therefore, has always been more frequently affected by foreign invaders than has that of India as a whole.

The first of the numerous invasions of the Punjab after the time of Alexander came in 185 B.C., the same year which saw the end of the Maurya dynasty. In that year Demetrios, the Greek (or at least Hellenic) king of Bactria, led his forces southward from his recently acquired province of Gandhara. Some ten years after this invasion, which overran and conquered the whole Punjab, the throne of Bactria was seized by a rebellious lieutenant named Eukratides, who succeeded in extending his authority southward to include the western part of the Punjab, leaving to Demetrios and his descendants only the regions to the east of the Jhelum.

About the year 135 B.C. the kingdom of Bactria, in its turn, was invaded and conquered by the central-Asian Sakas, or Scythians; but the Bactrian possessions in the western Punjab remained under the rule of the descendants of Eukratides until about the middle of the first century B.C., when they were invaded and seized by the Sakas. In the eastern Punjab the descendants of Demetrios, with their capital at Sialkot, continued to reign until about the same date, the conquest of this region by the Sakas being placed at about the year 58 B.C. For the most part the Greek rulers of the eastern Punjab made little effort to extend their power eastward at the expense of their Hindu neighbors, but in the year 155 B.C. Menander, one of the earlier successors of Demetrios, invaded the Ganges valley and advanced as far as the Magadhan capital at Pataliputra before he was finally repulsed by the forces of Magadha.

The conquest of the Greek states of the Punjab by the Sakas terminated, so far as India was concerned, the political consequences of Alexander's eastern expedition. Land communication between India and the west, which had existed since the days of Darius, was practically broken off, and the arrival of the Kushans, about a century after the Saka invasion, substituted for this western contact a new and growing intercourse with the Chinese world.

So complete was the ultimate disappearance of the Indo-Greek kingdoms that only a few ancient coins unearthed by the research of archæologists now bear unimpeachable testimony to the existence of such states and to the rule of their once powerful monarchs. Yet the century or more of Greek rule in the Punjab had a permanent influence upon the art, especially upon the Buddhist art, of India and of the entire Far East. The sculptured representation of Buddha and of Buddhist saints first occurred in the regions under Greek rule and must be regarded as a Buddhist borrowing from Greek religious customs. Along with this practice Buddhism borrowed much of the technique and form of Greek art, with the result that the whole body of Buddhist sculpture, from Gandhara to Kamakura, is permeated with the influence of ancient Greece.

In Bactria and in the Punjab the Indo-Greek rulers, like all the Greek rulers in Asia beginning with Alexander, attempted to establish a cordial relationship between themselves and their Asiatic subjects. The Brahmans, with their rigid barriers of

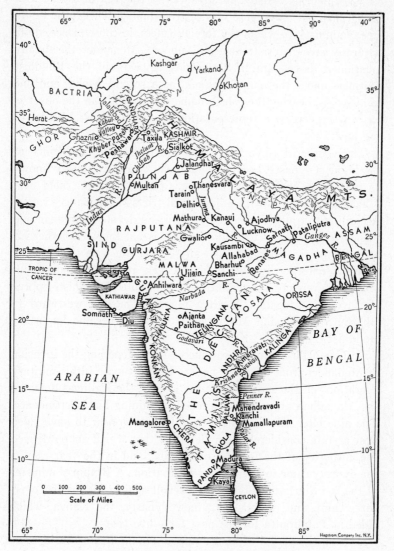

India to the Mohammedan Conquest

caste, stubbornly resisted all advances on the part of the unclean barbarians, but an entente was easily established with the caste-free Buddhists, to whom the foreign rulers, in consequence, quite naturally gave their patronage and support. Menander, the already mentioned descendant of Demetrios, appears in the Buddhist writings, under the name *Melinda*, as a second Asoka, and one of his coins, bearing the ruler's name and portrait on the obverse, has on the reverse a representation of the Buddhist "Wheel of the Law."

The usurper Pushyamitra, who overthrew the last prince of the Maurya dynasty, became the founder of a new dynasty known as the Sunga, which from 185 B.C. to about 73 B.C. ruled over Magadha and some of the adjoining districts of the Ganges valley. According to tradition the new ruler was a devoted Brahman and was bitterly opposed to Buddhism. It is not known whether his attitude toward Buddhism had any connection with the invasion of his territories by the Punjab Greek ruler Menander; but during the reign of Pushyamitra the persecuted Buddhists appear to have left Magadha in great numbers, moving westward to Bharhut, Sanchi, and Mathura, all of which became important Buddhist centers.

Although Pushyamitra was successful in repelling the invasion of Menander from the west, he was less fortunate in his military operations on the south, where the king of the Kalingas defeated the Magadhan army and succeeded in gaining his independence. The nine later rulers of the Sunga dynasty appear to have ruled over a state considerably smaller than that which acknowledged the authority of the founder of the line, and in the year 73 B.C. the dynasty came to an end by a usurpation. A Brahman minister of the last Sunga monarch rose in revolt against his master, overthrew him, and established a new dynasty, the Kanva, which ruled at Pataliputra for the next forty-five years.

During the period of Sunga rule at Pataliputra a considerable number of the states of the Deccan, formerly vassals of the Maurya rulers, were drawn together into a single state under the rule of the kings of Andhra. The kingdom of Andhra, originally a rather small state on the east coast between the lower reaches of the

Godavari and Krishna rivers, had itself been in the days of Asoka a vassal of the Mauryan empire. Shortly after Asoka's death, however, the Andhras, apparently under a new royal line, had renounced their allegiance and had commenced their expansion into the interior of the Deccan. By the beginning of the first century B.C. they had extended their domain westward to the west coast of the peninsula and northward along this coast so as to include the western portion of Malwa.

The acquisition of a frontage on the west coast enabled the Andhras to participate in the flourishing and profitable maritime trade with the Persians and Arabs, while their northward expansion into the district of Malwa brought them into early conflict with the Saka invaders. After the disappearance of the Sunga line at Pataliputra the Andhra kingdom began also to extend its power northward along the east coast, and in 28 B.C. the last prince of the Kanva line was overthrown by the contemporary Andhra monarch. This event put an end to the long pre-eminence of Magadha, which since the sixth century B.C. had been the most important state of the Gangetic plain; three centuries and a half were to elapse before Pataliputra, under the Gupta rulers, was to become again the center of a great north-Indian state.

Whether or not the Andhra rulers after their destruction of the Kanva dynasty exercised political authority over the territory of Magadha is uncertain; but from this date for more than two centuries the Andhra kingdom was the paramount Brahman state of central and northern India. Against the casteless Saka, Pahlava, and Kushan invaders the Andhras stood forth as the champions of Brahman orthodoxy. The assumption of this role by a Deccan state whose people were predominantly Dravidian (or at least non-Aryan) in race strikingly illustrates the extent to which the Aryan religion of the Brahmans had become, by the first century B.C., the "national" religion of the Indian peoples, irrespective of their racial origin.

As we have already seen, the Indo-Greeks of the Punjab, whose Bactrian territories were conquered in 135 B.C. by the Sakas, did not enjoy a long tenure of their Indian possessions. About the year 75 B.C. the Sakas were driven southward into Gandhara by the pressure of the Yuehchi and commenced an invasion of the Punjab which in 58 B.C. resulted in the complete conquest of the two Indo-Greek states. Almost immediately after this new conquest of the Punjab the conquering Sakas, who appear to have been an eastern branch of the Iranian people, were forced to acknowledge the overlordship of the Parthians, or Pahlavas,[1] who were Iranians like themselves. In addition to occupying the entire Indus valley, including Sind, the Saka-Pahlava combination extended its power into the western part of the Gangetic plain as well as to Gujarat and to the Konkan on the western coast of the peninsula, coming into conflict in the last of these regions with the power of the Andhras.

Even as the Sakas, after having taken Bactria from its Greek rulers, followed the Greeks down into the Punjab, so also were they in turn, pursued southward into India by the people who had driven them from Bactria. These people, the Yuehchi, were of central-Asian origin (see above, p. 67). Like most of the nomadic peoples of central Asia, as has been seen in an earlier chapter, the Yuehchi at the time of their conquest of Bactria consisted of a loose confederacy of independent tribes, each under its separate tribal chieftain.

Somewhat more than a century after their occupation of Bactria the tribes of the confederacy were brought together into a strong union under the rulers of the Kushan tribe, and the name of this dominant tribe was extended to the entire Yuehchi people. The first Kushan ruler, Kadphises I, who appears to have reigned between the years 40 A.D. and 78 A.D., found himself at the head of a powerful people whose long-fixed residence in Bactria had enabled them to attain a stage of civilization much higher than that of their nomadic ancestors. About the year 48 A.D. Kadphises I led his forces southward, conquered Gandhara, and occupied the district of Taxila in the northern part of the Punjab.

---

[1] Not to be confused with the Pallavas of southeastern India.

RISE OF THE KUSHAN EMPIRE

After extending his power southward into the northern portion of the Punjab the first Kushan ruler appears to have spent the remaining years of his reign in consolidating his authority; but under his successors the Kushan empire expanded southward to include a large part of northwestern India, while to the north of the Himalayas it reached as far as Kashgar and Khotan. A great part of this expansion occurred during the reign of Kadphises II, who succeeded his father in 78 and ruled until the year 110.[1] This second Kushan ruler conquered the entire Punjab, together with the upper Ganges valley as far eastward as Benares and the districts of western India lying north of the Narbada River. North of the Himalayas, where their empire came into contact with that of Han China, the Kushans were less fortunate. In the year 90 A.D. the armies of Kadphises II were defeated in Chinese Turkestan by the forces under the Chinese general Pan Ch'ao. About the year 125 the Kushans took advantage of a temporary decline in Chinese power and established their suzerainty over Yarkand and Kashgar, but the Chinese almost immediately returned to the attack and compelled the abandonment of these distant possessions.

Kadphises I and his son had retained their Bactrian capital as the headquarters of their government, and this policy was continued by the third Kushan ruler; but Kanishka, who ruled over the Kushan empire from 120 to 162, moved his capital southward to Peshawar, on the Indian side of the Khyber Pass. Partly as a result of this transfer and partly as a result of the repulse at the hands of the Chinese in Turkestan the Kushan empire became under Kanishka and his successors more pronouncedly Indian than it had been during the preceding reigns. The earlier Kushan rulers were foreign invaders; Kanishka made himself an integral part of Indian history.

Like the Indo-Greek Menander, Kanishka is represented by the contemporary Buddhist writers as a new Asoka, devoted to

[1] The chronology of the Kushan period is a debated question; I follow here the dates adopted in his later writings by Dr. Vincent Smith.

the teachings of Gautama and patronizing the Buddhist church. The poet Asvaghosha, a Buddhist monk, is reported to have been one of the Kushan monarch's most influential advisers; and under Kanishka's patronage a council of Buddhist theologians, assembled for the purpose of establishing anew the canon of Buddhist faith, drew up official commentaries upon each division of the Tripitaka.

Although Kanishka's conversion to the faith of Gautama has become the subject of pious legends resembling the story of Asoka's conversion, there is every reason for believing that in his favorable treatment of the Buddhists the Kushan monarch was actuated primarily by the same political motives as had directed the policy of the Indo-Greeks. Uncompromisingly rejected by the caste-bound Brahmans, Kanishka's only hope of creating a bond of sympathy between himself and his Indian subjects lay in winning the support of the Buddhists and in enabling the Buddhists to become the dominant religious group throughout his Indian possessions.

Since the Kushans during their century and a half of residence in Bactria had imbibed freely of the Hellenized Bactrian culture, Kanishka's alliance with the Buddhists of northwestern India contributed to the spread of Greco-Bactrian artistic ideas in India itself. These ideas, being more acceptable to the Mahayanist form of Buddhism than to the simpler Hinayana form, had much to do with the ultimate triumph of the Mahayana as the Buddhism of the north. At the same time the fact that the Kushan empire extended far beyond the Himalayas into central Asia and Chinese Turkestan was an important element in the rapid spread of the Buddhist faith, during the first two centuries of the Christian Era, into these regions and into China.

Although the cordial relations between Buddhism and the foreign invaders of the northwest thus contributed to the rapid spread of the religion outside of India, these same relations appear to have been partly, perhaps largely, responsible for the decay of Buddhist influence in its native land. Throughout four centuries of struggle between the Indian people and the foreign invaders—Greek, Saka, and Kushan—Buddhism consistently allowed itself to be identified with the fortunes of the foreigner, while Brahmanism, stubbornly refusing to regard even the most powerful conqueror as other than an "outcaste," became more and more definitely the religion of Indian nationalism. In this connection it seems highly significant that the two regions in the Indian world where Buddhism still prevails, Nepal and Ceylon, are the regions which were most completely removed from this conflict between the earlier inhabitants of India and the later invaders.

For nearly two centuries, from the middle of the first century A.D. until the first quarter of the third century, the Kushan empire and that of the Andhras shared the power over northern and central India. While the Kushan sovereigns or their Saka vassals controlled northwestern India as far south as the Narbada and as far east as Benares, the Andhra rulers of the Deccan dominated the west coast to the south of the Narbada and appear to have been recognized as suzerains by the petty states of the eastern Ganges valley. During the first quarter of the third century the power of both empires began to decline. Under the successors of Kanishka the Kushans appear to have been driven steadily backward by their Hindu enemies; but the actual breakup of the empire probably resulted from the rise of the Persian Sassanid empire, which was established in 226 A.D. and which was so placed as to be able to attack the Kushans in the rear.

The collapse of the Andhra empire coincided almost exactly with that of its northern rival. This coincidence was not altogether accidental, since the steady decline of the Kushans relaxed the bond of a common fear because of which the Aryan states of the north had been willing to acknowledge the suzerainty of the Dravidian Deccan. Yet the Andhra empire, like the Kushan, had its power definitely broken by an attack from the rear; in the year 225 the Andhras were crushingly defeated by their Pallava neighbors on the south, and the whole Deccan empire fell into fragments.

THE GUPTA EMPIRE (320–535)

The simultaneous collapse of the Kushans and the Andhras left India for almost a century without any state which could pretend to paramountcy. The early years of the fourth century, however, saw the ancient state of Magadha become once more the center of a powerful northern empire. In the year 320 a Magadhan ruler, who, like the founder of the Mauryan empire, was named Chandragupta, succeeded in extending his authority over the entire eastern half of the Ganges valley.

The reign of this new Chandragupta came to an end in 330; but he was succeeded on the throne at Pataliputra by a son, Samudragupta (330–380), under whose administration the Gupta empire steadily increased in size and power. After spending some years consolidating his authority and acquiring fresh territories in the Ganges valley Samudragupta embarked upon a campaign of conquest in the Deccan. In the course of this campaign, the date of which cannot be definitely fixed, Samudragupta subdued momentarily a number of the states of the Deccan and even levied tribute from the kingdom of Pallava; but he seems to have made no permanent annexations to his empire. Returning from the southern expedition, the Gupta monarch turned his attention to the north and succeeded in forcing the kingdom of Nepal to submit to his authority.

The conquests of Samudragupta were still further extended by his son and successor, Chandragupta II (380–415), who conquered the Saka states of Malwa and Gujarat, formerly vassals of the Kushan rulers, and brought under his protection the eastern Punjab as far as the river Chinab. Because of this westward expansion of his empire Chandragupta II abandoned Pataliputra and moved his capital first to Ajodhya and later to Kausambi, on the Jumna River, a point from which he could give adequate attention to the defense of his western frontier.

It was in the reign of Chandragupta II that Fa Hsien, the Chinese Buddhist pilgrim, arrived in India to spend the years from 404 to 410 in visiting the holy places of Buddhism and in collecting copies of all the available Buddhist scriptures. Some five years of Fa Hsien's visit were spent within the frontiers of the Gupta empire, and for three of these years he resided at the ancient capital of Asoka.

During the reigns of Chandragupta II and of his two immediate successors the Gupta empire was at the height of its power; these reigns, with those of the first two rulers of the dynasty, constitute what has been characterized as the most brilliant period of Indian history, one which "is, in the annals of classical India, almost what the Periclean age is in the history of Greece."

In his writings Fa Hsien undoubtedly exaggerated the devotion of the Gupta monarch to the teachings of Buddha; Chandragupta II, like the other rulers of the dynasty, appears to have preferred the worship of Vishnu. Yet the royal preference for Vishnuism and the general revival of Hinduism in the Gupta empire did not interfere with the full religious liberty of either the Buddhists or the Jains; tolerance in matters of religious belief was one of the outstanding characteristics of the period, and perhaps one of the most important factors in its greatness.

Interested primarily in matters of religion, Fa Hsien tells all too little about the prosperity and the artistic achievements of the India which he saw, but this little is more than confirmed by contemporary Indian records and by the still existent specimens of Gupta art. In literature this period produced Kalidasa, who is commonly regarded as the greatest of all Sanskrit poets, and the dramatist Sudraka, the author of *The Little Clay Cart*. Science, philosophy, and, as Fa Hsien has pointed out, music all made considerable progress.

But it is in architecture and in the related arts of sculpture and painting that the students of Indian culture find the greatest glory of the Gupta period. Only a few scattered specimens of Gupta temple architecture escaped destruction, six centuries later, at the hands of the Mohammedan invaders; but these few specimens and the remains of the magnificent stone temples at Sarnath, near Benares, suffice to prove the greatness of Gupta achievement in this field. In the matter of sculpture and painting the modern student of Indian art is even more fortunate. The many pieces of Gupta sculpture which have been recovered at Sarnath,

Mathura, and elsewhere and the noble fresco paintings in the grottoes of Ajanta reveal Indian art at its climax. Unquestionably indebted to Gandhara and Bactria, and through them to the art of Greece, the sculptors and painters of the Gupta period developed a new art, essentially Indian in spirit, which was to influence and inspire the development of all subsequent schools of Indian art.

Skandagupta (455–485), the fifth Gupta ruler, was the last great monarch of the dynasty. When he ascended the throne the empire was still at the height of its power, but before the end of his thirty-year reign a fresh invasion of India had shaken this power and had started the empire definitely upon its decline. The invasion which thus began the downfall of the Gupta empire was that of the Hephthalites, or "White Huns," warlike central-Asian nomads who appear to have come originally from Mongolia and to have been related both to the early Hsiungnu Tartars and to the later Mongols.

About the year 425 the Hephthalites, after sweeping southward through central Asia, made themselves the masters of Bactria and turned their arms against the Persian Sassanid empire, by which in 428 they were repulsed and forced to retreat into Bactria. Defeated on this side, the Hephthalites advanced southward into the Punjab and in 455 made their first attack upon the western frontier of the Gupta domain. The recently crowned Skandagupta succeeded in repelling this attack, and the invaders withdrew into Gandhara and Bactria, where they remained for nearly thirty years in more or less continual conflict with the neighboring Sassanids. In the year 484 the Hephthalites, under the leadership of Toramana, met the Persians in a decisive battle and won a sweeping victory.

Freed for the time being from all embarrassment on his western frontier, Toramana now led the full force of his armies southward in a second invasion of India. The Indus valley was completely conquered, the Gupta armies were defeated, and the invaders established their headquarters at Sialkot, from which advantageous location they carried their ravages into Malwa and into the western districts of the Gangetic plain.

With their defeat at the hands of the Hephthalites the Guptas lost much of the prestige which had enabled them to hold sway over all northern India. The successors of Skandagupta continued, for half a century after his death, to rule a greatly diminished domain; but the Gupta political system was broken up, and a number of new kingdoms arose to share the territories which in the days of its greatness had composed part of the empire.

In 502 Toramana was succeeded as chief of the Hephthalites by his son Mihiragula, who continued for a quarter of a century to spread ruin and desolation through the western provinces. Toward the end of this period, however, a new leader of ability, in the person of the king of Ujjain, arose to champion the cause of India against the invader, and in 528 the forces of Ujjain administered a decisive defeat to the Hephthalites at Multan in the Punjab. Following this battle the invaders withdrew to Kashmir, where Mihiragula and his descendants continued to hold sway until 565 or 566, when their power was finally crushed by the combined forces of the Turks and the Persians.

In their progress across central Asia from Mongolia to the Hindu Kush Mountains the conquering Hephthalites had collected under their banners a motley array of unrelated tribes and peoples. After the Hephthalite defeat in 528 many of these associated peoples were left behind as stragglers from the retreating army. Most important of these stragglers were the Gurjaras, who with various other smaller groups settled permanently in the region lying to the east of the lower Indus valley. Rapidly assimilating Hindu culture and intermarrying with the inhabitants of the region, the Gurjaras became the ancestors of the so-called Rajput clans who gave their name to modern Rajputana. By the middle of the seventh century the Rajputs succeeded in forcing their way into the "closed community" of Indian caste and secured recognition as Kshatriyas. The barren uplands of Rajputana command the narrow passageway from the Punjab eastward into the upper portion of the Gangetic plain, and these warlike recruits to Hinduism were to play an important part in the history of their adopted land for several centuries, serving it well as a wall of defense against fresh invasions from the northwest.

HARSHA SILADITYA (606–647)

Out of the turmoil which followed the breakup of the Gupta empire there rose to prominence toward the end of the sixth century the state of Thanesvara, which, located to the north of Delhi in the upper valley of the Jumna River, held the position of a "county palatine" guarding the Ganges plain against attacks from the Punjab. In 605 the old rajah of Thanesvara died, leaving to his son a small but well-organized kingdom; and in the following year the assassination of the new rajah brought to the throne his seventeen-year-old brother, Harsha Siladitya. Within six years the young prince had brought under his sway almost all the territories which formerly acknowledged the rule of the Guptas. Most of the petty north-Indian states submitted in good grace to the authority of the new hegemon, but several of the stronger kingdoms were subjugated only after hard fighting. Abandoning Thanesvara, Harsha established the capital of his new empire at Kanauj, on the Ganges River to the northwest of the site of modern Lucknow, where a splendid city was erected.

In 620, following the example of the second Gupta sovereign, Harsha attempted to extend his empire southward into the Deccan. He therefore led his forces across the Narbada River and attacked the strong kingdom of the Chalukyas, which after the dissolution of the Andhra empire had grown up in the western part of the peninsula south of the Narbada. This southern expedition was a complete failure; Harsha suffered what appears to have been the only serious defeat of his military career and was forced to content himself henceforth with the Narbada River as his frontier.

Unlike the founders of the Maurya and Gupta dynasties, Harsha did not succeed in uniting his possessions into an empire which would survive his own death. Instead of developing an organized civil administration, such, for example, as was being perfected in China by his great T'ang contemporary T'ai Tsung, Harsha established a purely personal rule and depended upon the services of the formerly independent local princes who had submitted to his power and over whom he maintained constant supervision. Despite the fact that he reigned for forty-one years, Harsha at the time of his death was only fifty-eight years of age; he therefore retained his energy and ability, and the empire was firmly administered practically until the end of his reign. As soon as his strong hand was withdrawn from the helm, however, his empire promptly dissolved into its component parts.

An accomplished scholar himself and accredited with the composition of several dramatic works, Harsha was a generous patron of literature. Among his protégés were the poet Mayura and the Brahman Bana, the latter of whom composed a historical romance, the *Harshacharita*, containing an account of his patron's reign.

In matters of religion Harsha combined devoutness with an exceedingly wide tolerance. Toward the end of his reign he inclined more and more to the Buddhist faith, although his Buddhism is said to have been of a decidedly eclectic type, and he endeavored to follow the example of Asoka in building up the strength of the Buddhist church. Even with this royal patronage, however, Buddhism was now steadly losing ground in northern India; although the Buddhist monasteries at Harsha's capital are said to have numbered more than a hundred, the temples of the Brahmans were even more numerous.

It was during the reign of Harsha, between the years 630 and 643, that the Chinese Buddhist pilgrim Hsüan Chuang made his visit to India. At the very beginning of his visit the Chinese pilgrim was personally entertained by Harsha at a great imperial assembly at Kanauj, which was attended by a number of the ruler's most important vassals, and at a religious gathering at Allahabad, where Harsha distributed alms to a multitude of Buddhist, Brahman, and Jain religious devotees. Some eight years of Hsüan Chuang's visit were spent within the boundaries of Harsha's domains, and his account, more full in such matters than that of the earlier Fa Hsien, contains a wealth of geographical, political, and historical information concerning the country.

In addition to his eight years in the north, Hsüan Chuang spent several years traveling through the Deccan and the extreme south, in the course of which travels he visited almost every province of India. Sections of his account refer to Assam, Orissa, Kalinga, Kosala,[1] Andhra, Chola, the Pallava kingdom of Kanchi, the Maratha kingdom of the Chalukyas, and many others which he visited. Although he states that he did not visit the island of Ceylon, Hsüan Chuang also incorporates in his description of India the information which he received from others concerning that kingdom.

During the last years of his reign Harsha established friendly diplomatic relations with Tibet, where Srong-tsan Gam-po was consolidating the Tibetans into a strong kingdom, as well as with the T'ang empire of China, which, under T'ai Tsung, was extending its sway over the peoples and tribes of central Asia. About 641 Harsha bestowed the hand of his daughter upon the Tibetan monarch, and the influence of this Indian princess is believed to have been an important factor in the establishment of Buddhism in a modified form as the religion of her adopted country. In 641 also, as we have seen in the preceding chapter, Harsha sent an ambassador to the Chinese imperial court, to which T'ai Tsung responded by sending two embassies to Kanauj. It was the chief of this second embassy who, arriving at Kanauj in 648 and meeting rough treatment at the hands of the usurper of Harsha's throne, stormed the city at the head of a hastily recruited Tibeto-Nepalese army and carried the culprit back to Changan in chains.

For more than five centuries after the death of Harsha no state of northern India succeeded in establishing a hegemony over its neighbors. Divided among a large number of independent and warring rulers, it was not until the Mohammedan conquest in the last part of the twelfth century that this region was again brought under a single sovereignty. Although these five centuries saw notable achievement in architecture, sculpture, and literature, the histories of the separate states offer few events of such importance as to deserve special mention in a brief survey.

The capital and center of Harsha's vanished empire, after eighty years of obscurity, regained a certain momentary importance under King Yasovarman, who became famous as a patron of literature

---

[1] In the Deccan and distinct from the early Gangetic kingdom of the same name.

and who also, in the year 731, dispatched an embassy to the T'ang emperor of China. In 740, however, Yasovarman was defeated and slain in a war against the kingdom of Kashmir, and Kanauj again relapsed into unimportance. About the beginning of the ninth century Kanauj was conquered by a branch of the Gurjara Rajputs. Under Bhoja, the most famous ruler of this line, the kingdom was extended by the inclusion of several neighboring states, and this extended power was retained for a brief period by Bhoja's immediate successors on the throne.

About the middle of the eighth century, after a long period of anarchy, the districts of Bengal and Magadha were united under a royal line known as the Pala dynasty, which held the throne until 1060, when it was replaced by a new line of kings known as the Senas. The Pala rulers were ardent patrons of Buddhism,— in the form known as Tantric Buddhism, which was considerably affected by magic rites borrowed from Sivaism,—and in 1038 the tenth Pala monarch sent to Tibet a religious mission which had a permanent influence upon the development of Tibetan Lamaism. The Sena dynasty, which ruled in Bengal from 1060 until the Mohammedan conquest of the lower Ganges in 1202, was Brahman, and their overthrow of the Palas may be regarded as indicative of the declining influence of Buddhism in this region.

In the western portion of Harsha's former dominions and in the present Rajputana the various Rajput states dominated the picture and, especially after the appearance of the Mohammedans in the upper Indus, played an important role. The most powerful of these states appears to have been the kingdom of Gurjara, in southern Rajputana; but Rajput rulers also held sway at Delhi, at Kanauj, and at other places. Ever ready for warlike adventures, the Rajput military aristocracy frequently engaged in struggles among themselves; but their position between the Punjab and the rest of India enabled them, until the early part of the eleventh century, to protect the peoples of the Ganges valley from the Mohammedan attack.

SOUTHERN INDIA

In the earlier pages of this chapter and in the chapter dealing with the ancient period of Indian history occasional references have been made to the Tamil states of the south and of the Deccan. Although little is known of the early history of the southern kingdoms, the statements of Megasthenes and the references in the edicts of Asoka establish the fact of their existence as kingdoms as early as the third or fourth century B.C., while archaeological research has proved that the early culture of the south was in many respects different from that of the Aryan north. At an early date, moreover, it is known that the Tamil states had commercial relations by sea with the Arabs and with Egypt. When this maritime connection commenced is unknown; but Strabo, who died in 21 A.D., describes a flourishing trade between Egypt and India, while an embassy to Augustus Caesar, in 20 B.C., from "King Pandion" is believed to have come from the king of Pandya.

About the beginning of the Christian Era three kingdoms, Pandya, Chola, and Chera, appear to have shared between them the triangular southern point of the peninsula. The first-named occupied the portion of the coast facing the island of Ceylon, while Chola and Chera lay to the north, on the east and west coasts respectively. At an early date Chola and Chera appear to have adopted the cult of the Brahmans; but the kingdom of Pandya was strongly influenced by Jainism, having been, according to tradition, the asylum of a large number of Jain devotees who were driven from Magadha in 360 B.C. During the days of Asoka, Buddhism appears to have found a favorable reception here; and it is recorded that Asoka's younger brother[1] Mahendra, who in 251 B.C. carried the teachings of Gautama to Ceylon, went to the island kingdom from Madura in Pandya, where he had previously established a flourishing monastery.

Toward the end of the second century A.D. a new state began to assume importance in the east-coast region around the mouth of the Penner River. This state, the kingdom of Pallava, first gave evidence of its real power about the year 225, when its

[1] Or son (see footnote on page 61).

armies invaded the territories of the Andhra kingdom and inflicted upon the Andhras a defeat which, coupled with simultaneous developments in the north, caused the downfall of that once powerful empire. After this auspicious beginning the Pallavas steadily expanded their power at the expense of their neighbors on the south, and King Simhavishnu in the closing years of the sixth century claimed to have conquered the rulers of Pandya, Chola, Chera, and Ceylon. In 642 Narasimha-varman (625–645) invaded the Chalukya kingdom, captured the capital, and put an end to the dynasty. This victory, which occurred only five years before the death of Harsha, made the Pallava kingdom, after the disintegration of Harsha's empire, the most powerful state in the Indian world. The original Chalukya kingdom, lying along the west coast south of the Narbada, was not broken up; but all of India to the east of the Chalukyas, between the latitude of the Narbada and that of the southern Penner, acknowledged the suzerainty of the Pallava king.

It was during the reign of Narasimha-varman that the pilgrim Hsüan Chuang visited the Pallava kingdom, which he calls Dravida, and stayed at the capital, Kanchi, the modern Conjeeveram. "The capital of the country," he writes, "is called Kanchipura and is about thirty li [ten miles] around. The soil is fertile and regularly cultivated, and produces abundance of grain. There are also many flowers and fruits. It produces gems and other articles. The climate is hot, the character of the people courageous. They are deeply attached to the principles of honesty and truth, and highly esteem learning; in respect of their language and written characters, they differ but little from those of Mid-India. There are some hundred of sangharamas [many-storied monasteries] and ten thousand priests. They all study the teaching of the Sthavira school belonging to the Greater Vehicle. There are some eighty Deva temples and many heretics called Nirgranthas" [Jains of the nude or Digambara sect].

Hsüan Chuang's account of Kanchi thus records the presence of a flourishing Mahayana Buddhist community, but also mentions "some eighty Deva [that is, Brahman] temples" and a large number of Jains. Here, as in other districts visited by the Chinese pilgrim, the different Indian religions appear to have dwelt side by side in mutual tolerance. Although the earliest datable Pallava king, who ruled during the fifth century, is definitely reported to have been a Buddhist, the later rulers were usually supporters of Brahmanism, favoring either the special cult of Vishnu or that of Siva.

It was during the first half of the seventh century, in the reigns of Mahendra-varman I (600–625) and of his successor, Narasimha-varman, that the Pallavas constructed the splendid stone buildings which stand as a lasting monument to their greatness. To the reign of Mahendra are attributed a number of rock-cut temples and caves as well as a great reservoir near his ruined town of Mahendravadi. Narasimha founded the town of Mamallapuram, on the coast to the southeast of Kanchi, and here were executed under his orders the wonderful "Seven Pagodas," each carved out of a single gigantic boulder. In their relief sculptures upon these and other rock surfaces near Mamallapuram the Pallava artists displayed a high degree of ability. The temples at Kanchi, erected during the reigns of the later Pallava kings, appear to have been the earliest examples of *structural* stonework in southern India. Thus the transition from wood to stone as building material, which began in northern India during the third century before Christ, did not occur in the south until near the end of the seventh century A.D., a difference of nearly a thousand years.

Although defeated by Narasimha-varman in 642, the Chalukya state on the west coast had not been crushed. Within thirty years after their defeat these warlike westerners, whose rulers were Rajputs of the Gurjara stock, recovered their strength and began to attack the far-reaching territories of the Pallavas. The intermittent warfare between the Chalukyas and the Pallavas reached its climax in 740, when the Pallavas suffered a severe and, apparently, decisive defeat. Although Pallava monarchs continued for another century and a half to reign at Kanchi, they ruled over a greatly diminished domain, and their power never rivaled that exercised by their predecessors during the seventh century and the first part of the eighth.

The decline of the Pallavas after their defeat by the Chalukyas soon showed itself in a weakening of their control over the Chola, Pandya, and Chera territories of the extreme south, and it was from this direction that the Pallavas were to receive their final defeat. In the closing years of the ninth century Aditya, the king of the Cholas, made himself the head of a confederacy composed of the three ancient southern kingdoms, and destroyed the remnant of the Pallava state. The date of this victory and the date of Aditya's succession to the Chola throne are both unknown; but from 907, when Aditya was succeeded by his son Parantaka I, the Cholas enjoyed more than three hundred years of supremacy in southern India, and it was not until after the Mohammedan invasion of the south, in 1310, that the dynasty finally disappeared.

At the beginning of the period of Chola supremacy Pandya, although an ally in the struggle against the Pallavas, had been conquered and reduced to the rank of a vassal. Held in subjection during the eleventh and twelfth centuries, this southern kingdom of the mainland took advantage of the thirteenth-century decline of the Chola power to regain its independence. During the last part of the century Pandya was probably the most prosperous of the Tamil kingdoms. Its principal port, Kayal, was visited by every merchant ship trading between Arabia or Persia and the Far East; and Marco Polo, who stopped there in 1293 on his homeward journey from China, described it as a "great and noble city" where much business was done. Seventeen years after this visit, however, came the Mohammedans, and Pandya, like Chola, ceased to exist as an independent state.

THE MOHAMMEDANS

While the Ganges valley, the Deccan, and the south during the centuries which followed the dissolution of Harsha's empire were thus working out their several fates, the clouds of a fresh storm which was to involve the whole land were gathering on India's northwestern frontier. By the year 642, five years before the death of Harsha and only a decade after that of the prophet Mohammed, the followers of the prophet had overthrown the Sassanid empire of Persia and had established the new faith of Islam in the Iranian plateau. In 711, the same date that saw their brothers in religion cross the Strait of Gibraltar to gain a foothold in Spain, Arab Mohammedan forces under the command of Mohammed ben Kasim reached the mouth of the Indus and conquered the region of Sind. At the same time, as we have seen in an earlier chapter, Mohammedan influence was pushing farther and farther into central Asia, and in 751 the Arabs defeated the Chinese in a battle that determined which of the two civilizations was to prevail in this great region. About 865 Yakub ben Layth ben Muaddal, an ambitious and warlike vassal of the Caliphate, extended his authority over both Sind and the Kabul valley and annexed them to his fief of eastern Bactria, or Afghanistan.

Until nearly the end of the tenth century the Indian world was little affected by the growing Moslem power. Although the followers of the prophet had occupied Sind and the valley of Kabul, they were held in check by the Rajput kingdoms which extended from Gurjara northward through the Punjab to include Gandhara and the Khyber Pass. In 977, however, control over the Mohammedan state of Ghazni, in the Kabul valley, passed into the hands of a new and energetic ruler. Sabuktagin was by birth a non-Mohammedan Turk. He had been captured, while still a young man, by the Mohammedans, and had become a convert to the faith of Islam. The zeal and ability of the young Turkish convert soon won the favor of his Arab masters, and his rapid promotion brought him in 977 to Ghazni with the rank of Amir. During the remaining twenty years of his life the Amir played an increasingly important part in the eastern affairs of the Mohammedan world, and before his death in 997 he had made himself, by his skillful manipulations, the complete master of all the Mohammedan provinces south of the Amu Daria. In the winter of 986–987, nine years after his appointment to Ghazni, Sabuktagin led his first raid into the Indus valley; and by 991, in spite of the opposition presented by a Punjab confederacy headed by the rajah of Bathinda, the lord of Ghazni had extended his possessions by the annexation of Jalalabad and Peshawar, an extension which put into his hands the Khyber Pass: the gateway to India.

In 997 the government of Ghazni passed into the hands of

Sabuktagin's son Mahmud. The new Amir soon gained for himself power more extensive even than that exercised by his father, and in 999 he assumed, at least for court purposes, the more imposing title of Sultan, although he was still referred to in ordinary speech as Amir. With the accession of Mahmud the Mohammedan storm broke over northern India in all its fury. Attracted by the opportunities for loot in the rich lands to the southeast and taking as his pretext the duty of extending the faith by holy wars, Mahmud is said to have assumed the obligation of making each year an expedition into India. This program was not carried out to the letter; but, between 999 and his death in 1030, seventeen incursions into India are recorded.

The earlier expeditions of Mahmud, like those of his father, were confined to the Punjab. For a while he met with stubborn resistance, and on one occasion narrowly escaped a crushing defeat at the hands of the confederated Rajputs. When his numerous invasions of the Punjab had resulted in exhausting the possibilities of that region as a field for plunder, he turned his attention to the valley of the Ganges, into which, between the fall of 1018 and the spring of 1022, he led at least three separate expeditions. Kanauj was taken and looted; the splendid city of Mathura, a center of Indian art since the days of the Guptas, was sacked and its beautiful temples burned to the ground; and devastation was spread throughout the entire valley of the Jumna and into the districts to the south of the Ganges.

In December, 1023, Mahmud started from Ghazni upon the greatest of his Indian expeditions. With thirty thousand horsemen he proceeded first to Multan, in the Punjab, from which point he made his way directly southward across the desert to Gujarat. After spending the greater part of a year in this region, looting and destroying to the top of his bent, Mahmud proceeded southwestward to Somnath, a city on the seacoast northwest of modern Diu. Somnath was plundered and destroyed, and the invader, heavily laden with booty, turned homeward by way of Gujarat and Sind, arriving at Ghazni, after more than two years' absence, in the spring of 1026.

By the end of Mahmud's reign, in 1030, all or the greater

part of the Punjab had been annexed to his domain. So far as the rest of the invaded districts are concerned, however, the consequences of his expeditions had been purely destructive. There had been a tremendous loss of human life, an immense amount of wealth had been carried away, and many irreplaceable monuments of ancient Hindu culture had been ruthlessly destroyed; but Mahmud's raids had effected no permanent change in the political organization of the invaded territories. The successors of Mahmud were too deeply involved in political intrigues to attempt a repetition of their ancestor's freebooting expeditions, and the Rajput states and the kingdoms to the south and west resumed their normal course of peace and war; almost a century and a half were to elapse after Mahmud's death before northern India witnessed the advance of a Mohammedan force bent upon permanent conquest.

Among the vassals of the Sultan of Ghazni during the days of Mahmud and of his immediate successors was the petty state of Ghor, which lay to the east and southeast of Herat. Early in the twelfth century the decline in the fortunes of the Ghazni dynasty gave to the rulers of Ghor an opportunity to assume an independent status, and in 1150 a feud between Ghor and the reigning descendant of Mahmud resulted in the sack and almost complete destruction of Ghazni. Twenty-three years after this event the Sultan of Ghor annexed the entire territory of Ghazni and put it, with all its dependencies, under the rule of his younger brother Mohammed, who is best known as Mohammed *Ghori*—"of Ghor."

The new ruler of the Ghazni sultanate lost little time in undertaking his first operations in India. Assuming power in 1173, he descended into the Punjab during the winter months of 1175–1176 and subdued the important city of Multan. Three years later he advanced southward into the rich district of Gujarat, only to be defeated and repulsed with heavy losses by the warlike Rajputs. For thirteen years following this serious check, Mohammed devoted himself to the task of bringing thoroughly under his control the Punjab and Sind. In 1191, having completed the consolidation of his power in the Indus valley, he gathered the full force of his armies and advanced eastward for an invasion of the rich

Ganges valley. Against this invasion, as against the earliest expeditions of Sabuktagin and Mahmud, the Rajput and Hindu rulers of northern India united in self-defense. For once the Hindu confederacy was successful. The two armies met in battle at Tarain, in the upper valley of the Jumna, and the invaders were driven from the field. This defeat, however, served merely as a temporary check to the Afghans. Reorganizing his forces, Mohammed advanced again the following year. Once more the Mohammedan army and the combined forces of the Hindu confederates met upon the same field of battle, but this time it was the defending army which broke and gave way. Defeated, the confederacy fell apart, and the Ganges valley lay open to the victorious invader, to be conquered in detail at his leisure.

Having defeated the Hindu confederacy in the second battle of Tarain, Mohammed Ghori returned to his Afghan capital, leaving to his ablest lieutenant, Kutbu-d din Aibak, the task of completing the conquest. Among the conquering Mohammedans lowly origin counted for little when weighed in the balance against unusual abilities—a fact which may go far toward explaining their success as conquerors. Kutbu-d din Aibak was, like Sabuktagin, a native of Turkestan; captured by the armies of Islam and sold as a slave, he was still, technically at least, a slave of Mohammed Ghori when that ruler entrusted to him the conduct of the Indian campaign. The choice was a wise one. By 1206, the year of Mohammed Ghori's death, the power of the Moslems had been permanently established over the whole Gangetic plain from Delhi and Gwalior in the west to the eastern borders of Bengal. In addition the capital of Gujarat had been temporarily occupied by the invaders in 1197, although the permanent subjugation of this kingdom was not achieved.

Apart from the almost ridiculous ease with which it was carried out, the most notable feature of the conquest was its ruthless destruction of almost every great monument of ancient Hindu culture. The earlier invasions of Mahmud had spread ruin and desolation through a great part of the Jumna valley; the forces under Kutbu-d din, actuated either by avarice or by religious fanaticism, completed what Mahmud had begun and spread the same ruin to regions into which Mahmud had not penetrated. Few indeed were the specimens of Hindu architecture which were left standing. The Mohammedan conquerors of northern India, like the medieval Christians of Rome, regarded the most splendid structures of the "idolators" as useful only in providing building material for the erection of edifices consecrated to the true religion. Brahman temples and Buddhist monasteries throughout the land thus promptly disappeared to rise anew as mosques and minarets.

Down to the Mohammedan conquest north-Indian Buddhism had continued to survive chiefly in Magadha, where it enjoyed the patronage of the Pala rulers; elsewhere in the north Brahmanism had long since regained the supremacy, and the Buddhist faith had comparatively few followers. Although the fury of the invader fell indiscriminately upon the adherents and the property of both religions, one survived while the other perished. Brahmanism was far too deeply rooted in the daily lives of millions of individual Hindus to be displaced by anything short of a general extermination of the population. Buddhism, on the other hand, existed primarily in its organized religious communities, and it was upon these communities that the hand of the invader fell with most deadly force. The buildings and books were burned, thousands of their "shaven-headed" inmates were put to the sword, and the monks who survived the massacre fled northward to Nepal and Tibet or south into the states of the peninsula. After the beginning of the thirteenth century, therefore, Buddhism in northern India was practically dead.

In the year 1203 Mohammed Ghori succeeded his older brother as supreme ruler over all the family dominions. Upon Mohammed's own death in 1206 this power descended to his nephew, who bestowed upon Kutbu-d din Aibak authority over all the conquered Indian territories with the title "Sultan of India."

In order to be located strategically for the oversight of affairs both in the Ganges valley and in the Punjab, Kutbu-d din established his capital at Delhi, now the political center of British India but at that time an unimportant village in the upper valley of the Jumna River. Here the line of Kutbu-d din, called because of the lowly origin of its founder the "Slave Dynasty," ruled for a period of eighty-four years; and here the later Mohammedan dynasties of northern India continued to hold their court until the sixteenth century, when Babur, the descendant of Tamerlane, came down from central Asia to found the empire of the Moguls.

During the rule of Kutbu-d din and his descendants the Mohammedan penetration of the peninsula went steadily forward; but this conquering movement was completed only in 1310, after the establishment of a new ruling line at Delhi. In 1221–1222 India was threatened by the advance of the conquering Mongols. Twenty years later the Mongol hordes again arrived on the northeastern frontier and sent bodies of raiders down into the Indus valley. Under Kutbu-d din and Iltutmish, the ablest sultans of the dynasty, a number of splendid buildings were erected to adorn the capital; aside from these two the dynastic list contains only a series of absolute despots who are distinguished primarily by their fanaticism or their debaucheries—or both.

SUMMARY

Fourteen centuries of troubled history lay between the collapse of the Mauryan empire and the commencement of Moslem rule at Delhi. During the two centuries of the Gupta empire and the forty-one years of Harsha's reign the regions north of the Narbada enjoyed the benefits of political unity, wise administration, and a general prosperity which was reflected in noteworthy cultural development. Before, between, and after these periods of unity the northern plains were divided into a multitude of petty states, while the Punjab was invaded in turn by Greco-Bactrians, Sakas, Kushans, and Hephthalites, each of whom ruled for a time over considerable portions of the Indus valley. In the Deccan and in the far south the kaleidoscopic changes of these fourteen centuries brought into prominence a succession of powers. Andhras, Chalukyas, Pallavas, Cholas, and Pandyas each enjoyed in turn their rise and decline; yet seldom did one of these central or southern kingdoms succeed in dominating for any extensive period the affairs of Dravida or of the Deccan.

By the opening of the Christian Era the coastal regions of India were in maritime commercial contact with the ports of the Red Sea and the Persian Gulf; how much earlier this contact existed cannot be stated. Early in the Christian Era, if not during the first century B.C., similar maritime connection existed between southern India and the Eastern Archipelago, while from the end of the third century A.D. Arab merchantmen, calling at southern Indian ports, were trading as far eastward as the coasts of China and Korea. This maritime intercourse between India and the other countries of Asia was supplemented by equally important land contacts. The Greco-Bactrians, the Sakas, and the Kushans brought with them cultural contributions from Persia and from the Hellenic world, while Fa Hsien, Hsüan Chuang, and Wang Hiuen-ts'e were only the most notable of the many Chinese travelers who, from the beginning of the fifth century A.D., made their way backward and forward along the difficult paths between India and China, knitting together these two great civilizations.

In the theory and practice of government the Indian people appear to have made little if any advance since the days of Chandragupta Maurya, when Kautilya, his unscrupulous Brahman minister, wrote the *Arthasastra*. The armies of the Hindu confederacy, on the battlefield of Tarain, employed against Mohammed Ghori the same tactics that had failed fifteen centuries earlier against Alexander of Macedon. But in the field of religious thought and in the closely related field of religious art the achievements of India were of the first importance. By the end of the period under review Buddhism, indeed, had practically ceased to exist as one of the religions of India; but long before this date the faith of Gautama and the rich art which is so intimately associated with it had become vital parts of the civilizations of Tibet, China, Korea, Burma, and Japan, while Brahmanism—without its caste features—as well as Buddhism had been implanted in Champa, Cambodia, and the islands of Malaysia. Invaded and conquered at last by a people whose own militant faith made them impervious to the influence of Brahmanism or Buddhism, India before suffering this fate had been for a thousand years the religious teacher of the Far Eastern world.

SUGGESTED REFERENCES

AIYANGAR, S. K. South India and her Muhammadan Invaders.

BEAL, S. (translator). Si-Yu-Ki: Buddhist Records of the Western World.

CODRINGTON, H. W. A Short History of Ceylon.

DUTT, R. C. The Civilization of India.

FOUCHER, A. The Beginnings of Buddhist Art.

GILES, H. A. The Travels of Fa-hsien.

GRIFFITHS, J. The Paintings in the Buddhist Cave Temples of Ajanta.

HAVELL, E. B. Indian Architecture.

HAVELL, E. B. A Short History of India.

JOUVEAU-DUBREUIL, G. Pallava Antiquities.

MOOKERJI, R. Harsha.

MOOKERJI, R. A History of Indian Shipping and Maritime Activity from the Earliest Times.

RAPSON, E. J. Ancient India, from the Earliest Times to the First Century A.D.

RHYS-DAVIDS, T. W. Buddhist India.

SMITH, V. A. A History of Fine Art in India and Ceylon.

SMITH, V. A. The Oxford History of India.

WARMINGTON, E. H. The Commerce between the Roman Empire and India.

VIII

Central Asia: the Tartars, Turks, Uighurs, and Tibetans

Eastern Turkestan · Han China and the Trade Routes · Recent Archaeological Discoveries in Eastern Turkestan · The Hsiungnu and the Yuehchi · The Juan-juan and the Hephthalites · The Turks: their Relations with China and with the Byzantine Empire · The Arabs in Central Asia · The Uighurs · The Rise of the Tibetan Kingdom · Relations between China and Tibet

ON THE extreme northwest of China Proper a long penin-sulalike extension of Kansu Province, including the oasis settlements of Kanchow, Suchow, and Tunhuang, thrusts its way up between Tibet and the Gobi desert to the eastern end of the Eastern Turkestan desert. Except during periods of extreme po-litical disintegration the Chinese, since the closing years of the second century B.C., have been able to retain possession of their Kansu "corridor" toward the northwest; but only in 1755, when it was conquered by the armies of the Manchu emperor Ch'ien Lung, did Eastern Turkestan become an integral part of the Chi-nese Empire. Yet this forbidding desert, which stretches west-ward for nearly a thousand miles from the end of the Kansu cor-ridor to the foot of the Pamirs, constituted an all-important link in China's communications with the west. Along the two chains of oases which fringe the barren Taklamakan desert ran the an-cient caravan routes by which China for many centuries exchanged goods and ideas with central Asia, with India, and with Europe.

CHINA AND THE TRADE ROUTES

Although venturesome traders probably found their way east-ward along the edges of the Taklamakan desert many centuries earlier, the history of the Turkestan trade routes begins in the last part of the second century B.C. with the dispatch of Chang

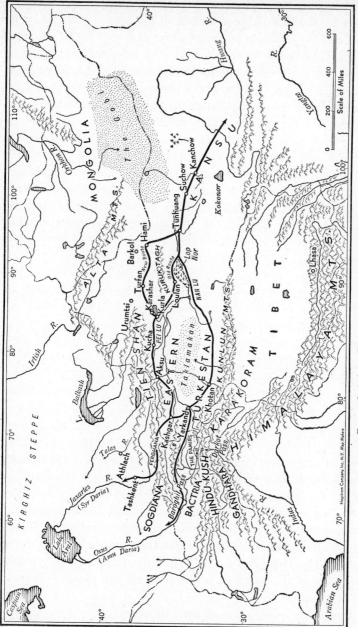

Central Asia: China's Corridor to the West

Ch'ien by the Han emperor Wu Ti, in 138 B.C., as ambassador to the Yuehchi. Upon his return to China twelve years later Chang Ch'ien was able to furnish Wu Ti with information concerning the peoples to the west and southwest, and he also brought back knowledge of the road by which these distant regions could be reached. After unsuccessful attempts to discover a road into India by way of Tibet the great Han emperor turned his attention to the task of driving off the Hsiungnu Tartars, whose occupation of the Kansu corridor effectively barred the Chinese from access to the path along which Chang Ch'ien had found his way homeward. By 115 B.C. the Hsiungnu had been forced to withdraw once more to the grazing lands north of the Gobi desert and the Tien Shan range, and in 108 B.C. an earthen rampart, leading westward from the extremity of the already completed Great Wall, had been carried as far as the present site of Tunhuang.

While thus establishing themselves at the eastern end of the desert routes, the Chinese also endeavored, by means of embassies and by show of force, to overawe the people who occupied the oases through which the trade routes passed. Even before 115 B.C. Chang Ch'ien, as Chinese commander in chief for the "Western Regions," established Chinese garrisons at the four important oasis settlements of Kashgar, Khotan, Kucha, and Karashar. In 104 B.C., in consequence of the mistreatment of Chinese merchants by the people of Ferghana in the upper valley of the Jaxartes, a Chinese army was sent to inflict punishment upon the wrongdoers. This punitive expedition was a total failure, but two years later a second army, after making its way around the desert and through the passes of the western Tien Shan, inflicted upon the offending state of Ferghana such exemplary punishment that all the peoples of the Turkestan basin hastened to recognize the suzerainty of the Han emperor. In spite of this impressive display of Chinese strength the nomadic Hsiungnu, from their grazing grounds to the north of the Tien Shan range, frequently made their way southward through the mountain defiles to attack and plunder the passing caravans.

During the early years of the first century A.D. domestic disorders in China and the usurpation of Wang Mang (see page 77) enabled the Hsiungnu to break the Chinese control of the caravan routes and to levy exactions upon the petty states which had recognized the overlordship of the Han emperors; but with the restoration of order at home the "later" Han monarchs returned to the task of making secure the trade routes toward the west. In 73 A.D. a Chinese army marching directly northward from Tunhuang took from the Hsiungnu the oasis of Hami. Hitherto the Chinese caravans proceeding westward by the northern road (the Pei Lu) had been compelled to follow a route across the eastern end of the dry lake of Lop Nor and along the southern side of the Kuruk Tagh ("Dry Mountain") to Kurla. With the occupation of Hami and Turfan, which were reoccupied in 88 A.D. after temporary reverses, the Chinese gained control over the far more satisfactory route by way of Tunhuang, Hami, Turfan, Karashar, Kurla, Kucha, and Aksu to Kashgar. This new route was henceforth adopted as the "true" north road, while the earlier route from Tunhuang to Kurla became known as the "middle" road and fell into comparative disuse.

The opening decades of the twentieth century have seen the discovery of much material to supplement the already adequate records of Chinese literature on the subject of the western trade routes. Of the numerous archaeological explorations in Eastern Turkestan and northwestern Kansu the most strikingly successful have been those undertaken by Sir Aurel Stein. From the vicinity of Tunhuang, from Loulan on the northern shore of Lop Nor, and from various stations along the north and south caravan routes Stein in the course of three expeditions was able to secure an almost incredible quantity of historical "treasure," some dating from as early as the first century B.C. and much more from the first three centuries of the Christian Era. Copper coins and arrowheads from the time of the early Han dynasty, varnished leather scales from the "scale armor" worn by the soldiers of that period, utensils, pottery, and decorative wood-carving are, perhaps, no more than might reasonably be expected from the sites of ancient military outposts.

In addition to these, however, the British archaeologist brought to light many relics of a more fragile nature: a roll of silk whose written label shows that it was manufactured in the province of Shantung about the end of the first century A.D., a large number of wooden slips bearing written records in Chinese and other languages, and a more limited number of fragmentary documents on paper. The oldest of the wooden records in Chinese go back almost to the beginning of the first century B.C., while the late Professor Chavannes, the eminent French Sinologue who was entrusted with the task of editing and publishing the Chinese documents, assigns a few of the paper fragments to the period of the Eastern Han, the first two centuries A.D.

The fragmentary Chinese documents on wood and paper consist principally of official orders and accounts dealing with the administration of the military forces garrisoning these distant outposts of the Chinese Empire, although a number of personal letters also have been recovered. One of these personal letters, discovered at Loulan and dating from the end of the third or the beginning of the fourth century A.D., is an almost perfectly preserved piece of paper, 8½ inches long and 1¾ inches wide, upon which a woman, probably the wife of an officer of the garrison, wrote to tell her uncle in China of her loneliness and of her longing for news from home.

From the same location and the same general period, but dated definitely as of the year 330 A.D., comes a fragmentary wooden document which bears eloquent testimony to the complete isolation of the Loulan garrison. The last year-period of the Chin dynasty, known as *kien hing*, lasted only four years (313–316 A.D. inclusive), but the date on the document, a record of money paid to a "barbarian" named Lou, reads "eighteenth year of *kien hing*"; for fourteen years the Loulan garrison, cut off from all communication with the home government, had continued to make use of a year-period which no longer existed.

Other documents, some with dates and others undated, make it possible to reconstruct in considerable detail the arduous life in these military outposts. The first duty of the garrisons was to maintain a constant watch against the approach of barbarian forces. On the approach of an enemy the news of the danger was "telegraphed" along the line of stations by means of signal fires, which were of two kinds: those intended for the daytime were constructed to produce great columns of smoke, while those used for night signaling were of dry wood and burned with a bright, clear flame. In addition to maintaining this constant watch the soldiers were employed in a number of less military occupations. To maintain an adequate supply of fuel for the signal fires, parties of soldiers were sent out, often to considerable distances, to gather firewood. They also built or repaired the ramparts, labored to reclaim fresh areas from the desert, and on the land thus brought under cultivation raised the grain necessary for their own food and for supplying the passing caravans.

Perhaps even more important as throwing light upon the history of the region are the documents in Indian Kharoshthi script, in Tibetan, and in unknown scripts of central-Asian origin. The Indian documents, some of which were found in close juxtaposition to the Chinese records of the Han period, consist chiefly of religious writings and indicate the strength of Buddhism, at the very beginning of the era of Chinese political influence, in this region so far removed from the scene of Gautama's life. The Tibetan writings date from the seventh and eighth centuries A.D., a period which saw the temporary domination of the Turkestan basin by the recently consolidated peoples of the neighboring plateau on the south. Finally, the writings in hitherto unknown scripts, upon which a number of Orientalists have been working, prove the existence of an independent central-Asian culture sufficiently advanced to have developed its own system of writing before the arrival of the Indians and the Chinese.

During the first three centuries after the establishment of Chinese control over the desert trade routes the Hsiungnu Tartars on the north were a constant threat to the safe development of trade. Against this danger the Chinese authorities adopted the policy of "using barbarians to attack barbarians." A large portion of the forces by whom the military outposts were garrisoned consisted of barbarian recruits, while every effort was made to secure the loyal allegiance of the powerful western tribes against the northern Tartars. In spite of this policy the Hsiungnu, between 107 A.D. and 131 A.D., succeeded in recapturing Hami; and when the Han dynasty finally collapsed in 220 A.D., these warlike Tartars once more gained supremacy along the entire length of the road to the north of the desert.

Toward the middle of the first century A.D. a new power rose in the far southwest to rival the Hsiungnu as a source of anxiety to the Chinese government. About 125 B.C. the Yuehchi, to whom Chang Ch'ien had been sent for the purpose of securing an alliance against the Hsiungnu, advanced southward from the Oxus valley into Bactria, where, under the name Kushan, they gradually developed into a strongly organized nation. About 48 A.D., as we have seen, the Kushans occupied the northern portion of the Indus valley, and almost simultaneously they began to extend their power northward into central Asia.

By the year 87 the Kushan power had been extended as far to the northeast as Kashgar and Yarkand, and the Kushan monarch Kadphises II demanded that the Chinese emperor bestow upon him a Chinese princess. When this demand was refused, Kadphises dispatched a strong army into Eastern Turkestan; but his army was defeated, and the Kushan monarch, according to Chinese accounts, was forced to acknowledge Chinese suzerainty. About 125 A.D. the Kushans again exercised power for a brief period over the western portion of Eastern Turkestan; after this they became more involved in affairs in India, with the result that their influence north of the Hindu Kush quickly disappeared.

The fifth century A.D. saw the disappearance of the Hsiungnu —at least under their ancient name—as an important factor in central-Asian history. In part this disappearance of the Hsiungnu was the result of the great western migration which brought the "Huns" under Attila to the battlefield of Châlons; for the rest the disappearance was nominal rather than real. By the fifth century many of the Tartars living close to the northeastern frontier of China, in Manchuria and eastern Mongolia, had become semi-Chinese and were losing their old nomadic habits. Farther to the west the still nomadic tribes of Tartars became known by new names, but continued their former depredations.

From the middle of the fifth century until the middle of the sixth the history of central Asia was dominated by two branches of the Mongols, the Juan-juan and the Hephthalites, or "White Huns."[1] In 455, as has been seen in the preceding chapter, the Hephthalites pushed their way down through the passes of the Hindu Kush into northwestern India, where they were repulsed for the time by the armies of the Gupta empire. After this first repulse, however, they gathered fresh strength and until about the end of the fifth century played a conquering role in Persia and in the Punjab. At the same time the Juan-juan, in the east, enjoyed supreme power over the regions north of the deserts from Karashar on the west to the boundary of Korea.

THE TURKS

Among the many non-Tartar peoples upon whom the Juan-juan and the Hephthalites were able to impose their yoke were a number of disunited tribes known to the Chinese historians as the Tou-chüeh (that is, the Turks). In 552 a Turkish chieftain who had succeeded in uniting a number of the related tribes under his leadership destroyed the power of the Juan-juan and made his people the dominant factor in the grazing lands of the northeast. Following this initial success the Turkish confederacy rapidly extended its power toward the southwest, and within fifteen years after the defeat of the Juan-juan the Turks inflicted a crushing defeat upon the Hephthalites in the valley of the Oxus.

The rise of this new power completely changed the situation in central Asia and had a decided influence upon the highly civilized countries of the east, west, and south, between whom this region provided an important line of communication. To India and to Persia the destruction of the Hephthalite power meant instant relief from the ravages of a destructive neighbor; to the Byzantine Empire the substitution of the Turk for the Tartar as master of the regions now known as Eastern Turkestan and Western Turkestan meant the reopening of the caravan routes along which the Mediterranean world had long been accustomed to

---

[1] Some authorities regard these two groups as identical and explain that the first name is the one by which they were known to the Chinese, while the second is the name by which they were known in India and in western Asia.

receive the silks of the East; to China it meant the appearance upon the northwestern frontier of a new and formidable neighbor against whom defenses must be prepared.

In 589, less than a quarter of a century after the Turkish triumph over the Hephthalites, the Chinese Empire, after centuries of disunion, was reunited under the Sui dynasty, which in 618 was superseded by the glorious dynasty of T'ang. During the brief rule of the Sui emperors and during the first two decades of T'ang rule, the Chinese territories were frequently invaded by the new masters of central Asia; and it is highly probable that the Turks, if they had been able to maintain unity among themselves, would have succeeded, as did the Mongols six centuries later, in establishing their power over part or all of the Chinese Empire.

Fortunately for China, however, divisions among the Turks had begun to develop as early as 582, a circumstance of which the Chinese government, under the Sui emperors and their T'ang successors, took every possible advantage. The division among the Turks, which thus provided Chinese diplomacy with an opportunity for "balance of power" politics, split the confederacy into two parts: the Eastern or Northern Turks, occupying a region north of the Gobi desert to the east of the Orkhon, and the more powerful Western Turks, whose power extended westward and southwestward from the headwaters of the Orkhon to the valley of the Oxus.

Inasmuch as the Eastern Turks, because of their location, constituted an immediate threat to the safety of the empire, the Chinese government first curried favor with the Western Turks and encouraged them to make war upon their eastern cousins. By 599, however, Chinese fears were aroused by the growing power of the western branch, whose Kagan, Ta-t'ou, had forced practically all the eastern tribes to recognize his overlordship. Chinese intrigue therefore fomented an outbreak among the western subordinates of Ta-t'ou, who was overthrown.

Freed for the time from the attacks of their western relatives, the Eastern Turks embarked upon a series of attacks upon the Chinese Empire. These invasions from the north led, in 618, to the fall of the Sui dynasty, and in 624, when the Eastern Turks under Hie-li Kagan advanced to the very walls of Changan, only the fortitude of Li Shih-ming, the son and future successor of the first T'ang emperor, saved the T'ang dynasty from destruction. Li Shih-ming, who as the emperor T'ai Tsung succeeded to the imperial throne in 627, promptly turned his energies to the destruction of his dangerous northern neighbor; in 630, largely as the result of revolts incited by Chinese intrigue, Hie-li was overthrown, and the Eastern Turks were brought under Chinese control as vassals of the empire.

Toward the Western Turks the great T'ang emperor assumed at the outset a policy of conciliation, but after his defeat of the Eastern Turks he turned with equal energy to the task of regaining from the western tribes the control over the trade routes as far westward as the Pamirs. This task, in which the Chinese ruler had the assistance of the recently subdued Eastern Turks as well as that of various discontented tribes among the western confederates, was finally carried to completion by Kao Tsung, T'ai Tsung's son and successor, about the year 660. The four "garrison cities" of Kashgar, Karashar, Khotan, and Kucha, as well as the less important oases along the northern and southern roads, were once more brought under Chinese control; the suzerainty of the Chinese emperor was recognized by the tribes occupying the regions far to the north, west, and southwest; and central Asia was brought more completely under Chinese cultural influence than ever before in history.

In the southwest, as in the Far East, the Turks, as masters of central Asia, quickly became involved in the political affairs of powerful and highly civilized neighbors. Although the emperor Justinian, 527–565, had succeeded in introducing into the eastern Mediterranean the art of producing silk, this industry never flourished, and the Byzantine Empire continued to be dependent upon the Far East for its silks and satins. For this reason the rise of the Turkish power was immediately recognized by the Byzantine government, and in 568 Justin II, the successor of Justinian, dispatched an ambassador to the Turkish Kagan Istami,[1]

[1] Known to the Chinese as Che-tie-mi and to the Greek authors as Dizabul.

at that time the ruler of the united Turkish people. A second embassy from Constantinople was sent to the Turkish ruler Tar-dou[1] eight years later, and the Turks reciprocated by sending several embassies to the Byzantine capital.

After the separation of the Turks into eastern and western branches the Western Turks, as a result of their intercourse with Constantinople, became involved in wars in alliance with the Byzantine Empire against the Persians, and later against the combined forces of Persia and Byzantium. An incident which occurred in the second of these wars throws some light upon the eastward expansion of Nestorian Christianity: in one of their battles against the Turks the Persians took a number of prisoners whose foreheads were marked with the sign of the cross.[2] In 626, once more allied with the Byzantine Empire, the Turks engaged in a new war against the Persians. The Persians were defeated, but the net result of the struggle was so to weaken all three of the belligerents as to prepare the way for the rise of a new power, that of the Mohammedan Arabs, in southwestern Asia.

From about the middle of the seventh century both branches of the once formidable Turkish people quickly lost their importance as independent factors in central-Asian history. Chinese intrigue, which had helped to bring about the original schism, had reduced the Eastern Turks to the status of obedient vassals of the Dragon Throne, while the Western Turks, who might have blocked the northeastward advance of Mohammedanism, had so exhausted themselves by their ambitious military undertakings that they offered little effective resistance to the conquering Arabs.

The Arabs in Central Asia

During the second half of the seventh century the Arabs, having conquered the Sassanid empire of Persia, began to push their way northeastward into those portions of central Asia whose rulers

[1] Ta-t'ou in the Chinese records.

[2] These prisoners the Persian ruler handed over to his Christian ally, the emperor Maurice, who, upon inquiring about the Christian symbol, was informed that the mark had been placed on them in childhood upon the advice of certain Christians, as a charm against pestilence.

acknowledged to some degree the suzerainty of the T'ang emperors of China. About the year 670, according to the account of the Buddhist pilgrim I Tsing, the Arabs closed the route from China to India by way of Gandhara; and about 682, after having made earlier plundering raids to the north of the Oxus River, an Arab force for the first time spent the winter in this region.

The advance of the new power during this period was slow, partly because the Arabs were chiefly interested in acquiring plunder and partly because of the difficulty which they found in adapting themselves to conditions of land and climate so different from those to which they were accustomed. In 705, however, an energetic general named Kotaiba (or Qutayba) was sent to the far northeast as the caliph's viceroy. Under Kotaiba the Arab domination was rapidly extended; by the time of his death, in 715, Arab governors appear to have been established over the valley of the Jaxartes, and Kotaiba's armies are said to have advanced eastward of the Pamirs to Kashgar.

The *Hui-ho,* or Uighurs, one of the many tribes which were united in the sixth century to form the Turkish confederacy, had been known to the Chinese historians during the fourth century as the *Kao-che,* "High Carts," because of the high-wheeled vehicles which they used in their wanderings. The writers of the early T'ang period describe these people as being "of a wicked and cruel nature. They excel in riding horses and in archery. They surpass all other people in rapacity, and they live by brigandage." Despite this unfavorable description the Uighurs proved on various occasions during the seventh and eighth centuries to be useful allies of the T'ang emperor, while their history after the dissolution of the Turkish confederacy is evidence of the fact that their rapacity and their tendency toward brigandage were accompanied by a high degree of cultural adaptability.

About the middle of the eighth century the Uighurs became the masters of the grazing lands north of the Altai Mountains and the Gobi desert, with their headquarters in the valley of the Orkhon. In their new home, which they occupied from 744 until 840, the Uighurs, although far enough to the north to be removed from the danger of Mohammedan domination, were so located as to be influenced by Arab culture, while they also retained their earlier contact with the Chinese. Either during this period or at some earlier date the Uighurs had developed an alphabetic form of writing based upon the ancient writing of Sogdiana, which, in turn, was derived from the Aramean;[1] now subjected to the cultural influence of both the Arabs and the Chinese, this Turkish people made remarkable progress in civilization. Some twenty years after they had established themselves as rulers of Mongolia the Uighurs adopted Manichaeism, and this remained for about a century the religion of the nation. After the decline of their political power Manichaeism was abandoned, and the Uighurs divided their favor between Buddhism and Nestorian Christianity.

In 840 the power of the Uighurs was overthrown by the warlike Kirghiz, their neighbors on the west. After this defeat a part of the Uighurs migrated to the west and settled among the Karluks, who dwelt beyond the Altai Mountains near the river Irtish. Others made their way southward and occupied Hami, Barkol, Urumtsi, Turfan, and other scattered localities to the north of Eastern Turkestan. Although they never regained their former power, the Uighurs during the next five centuries played a prominent role in the history of central Asia. Scattered among the other Turkish tribes of the north, they became the transmitters of the culture which they had absorbed from the Arabs and the Chinese; their occupation of Hami, Turfan, and other strategic positions enabled them to control the greater part of the trade between east and west, while the Uighur alphabet, besides being adopted by the other Turks, eventually became the written language of the world-conquering Mongols.

THE RISE OF THE TIBETAN KINGDOM

For many centuries before the consolidation of the Chinese Empire by Shih Huang Ti the mountain valleys of eastern Tibet and the high plateau farther to the west were inhabited by barbarian tribes known to the Chinese writers as the "Ch'iang." One of the early references to these western mountaineers relates that

---

[1] The alphabet used in Persia under the Sassanids.

when Ping Wang of the Chou dynasty transferred his capital eastward from the Wei valley to Loyang the Ch'iang began to harass the western frontier. Nearly seven centuries later the Han emperor Wu Ti issued commands that the Ch'iang dwelling on the frontier should be strictly barred from entering the territories of the empire. During the four centuries which followed the collapse of the Han dynasty (220 A.D.) the people of China appear to have had little contact with their neighbors of the Tibetan highlands.

Early in the seventh century A.D. a certain Lung-tsan, the chieftain of a part of the Ch'iang, subdued some neighboring tribes and established a kingdom which became known to the Chinese as T'u-fan or T'u-bot. Under Lung-tsan and under his successor Srong-tsan Gam-po, T'u-fan (Tibet) rapidly developed in power. In 641, as has been pointed out in an earlier chapter, King Srong-tsan Gam-po received in marriage a Chinese princess and also the daughter of Harsha Siladitya, king of Magadha. As both these royal brides had been brought up in Buddhist surroundings, this double marriage of the Tibetan king led to the establishment of strong Buddhist influence at Lhasa, the capital of the kingdom; and Buddhism, as well as the more material elements of Chinese and Indian civilization, spread among the Tibetan people.

The newly organized kingdom soon began to take an active part in the already complicated affairs of central Asia. The Tibetan rulers were steadily extending their power at the expense of their highland neighbors, and in 663 the conquest of the "Tungusic" (Mongol) Tukuhuns, who occupied the region around Kokonor, brought them to a position from which they were able to threaten the Kansu corridor and the trade routes of Eastern Turkestan. In 670 T'ang Kao Tsung sent an army into Kokonor for the purpose of restoring the independence of the conquered Tukuhuns. Taken in ambush by the Tibetans in a mountain valley to the west of Kokonor, the Chinese army was practically annihilated; and the Tibetans followed up this victory by invading Eastern Turkestan, where they seized the four garrison cities of Kashgar, Karashar, Khotan, and Kucha.

After their seizure of the "Four Garrisons," the Tibetans took advantage of the T'ang empire's difficulties on its northern frontiers and invaded the western provinces of China. In 692 the Chinese succeeded in regaining the lost cities, and two years later they defeated a Western Turk chieftain with whom the Tibetans had formed an alliance. From this time, however, the Tibetans were a constant source of trouble to the Chinese. Safely established behind their mountain bulwarks, which enabled them to repulse the strongest threats of invasion, the Tibetans sallied forth on all auspicious occasions to plunder the western provinces of China or to attack the trade routes on their northern frontier.

During the last years of the seventh century and the first few years of the eighth the Tibetan rulers followed the policy of allying themselves with such of the Western Turkish leaders as were ready to co-operate with them in their sporadic attacks upon the far-flung power of the Chinese. About 715, however, Tibetan policy took a new turn, and the Lhasa government, abandoning its erstwhile Turkish allies, entered into an alliance with the Arab followers of Mohammed, who by this time had pushed their way up into central Asia from the southwest.

When the Tibetans in 715 allied themselves with the conquering Arabs, Chinese influence in central Asia was threatened as never before during the T'ang regime. In 717 the allies sent their combined forces against the "Four Garrisons," and the Chinese protector-general at Kucha reported to the imperial government that the situation was desperate. Against this threat to the prestige of his imperial throne Emperor Hsüan Tsung attempted, for a while successfully, to organize the forces of the various princes and chieftains who acknowledged him as their suzerain. Honors and titles were conferred with a lavish hand upon those who loyally adhered to their allegiance, and a strong Chinese army was sent into eastern Turkestan for the double purpose of rendering support to the loyal and of punishing such as failed to perform their duty.

In spite of these energetic measures, which reached their climax in 747 when Kao Hsien-chih led an army across the Baroghil and Darkot passes for the purpose of punishing a disloyal vassal in the valley of the upper Indus, China's claims to sovereign power in the western regions were doomed to destruction. In 750 the Tibetans succeeded in taking Tunhuang and in making themselves masters of the Kansu corridor at the Chinese end of the caravan routes, which they held until early in the ninth century. The following year saw an even more decisive blow to the imperial power. In 749 the king of Tashkent had repudiated his allegiance to the Chinese emperor, and in the closing months of 750 Kao Hsien-chih advanced upon Tashkent to punish this act of desertion. At the approach of the Chinese force the frightened king hastened to make his submission; in spite of this he was promptly put to death, and his city was given over to plunder by the Chinese troops. The son of the unfortunate monarch appealed to the Arabs for assistance against Chinese tyranny, and in July, 751, Kao Hsien-chih's army of thirty thousand men, caught between the Arabs and the forces of Tashkent, was almost annihilated in a battle fought at Athlach, near the river Talas.

For some forty years after this double disaster, the loss of the Kansu corridor and the battle of Athlach, isolated Chinese officials continued to exercise authority at several places in Eastern Turkestan, but the actual power of the Chinese government in this region was lost beyond restoration. From this time the habitable region in the western part of Eastern Turkestan, as well as the entire region west of the Pamirs, came more and more completely under the influence of Mohammedanism; and not until the thirteenth century, when the Mongols under Genghis Khan swept down from the northeast, was the influence of the Arabs broken.

During the three quarters of a century which followed the seizure of northwestern Kansu by the Tibetans the history of Tibeto-Chinese relations presents a bewildering succession of border raids and of peace negotiations. In contrast with the Arabs, whose victory over the Chinese was soon followed by the establishment of cordial relations with the T'ang empire, the Tibetans appeared quite incapable of settling down to normal peaceful intercourse with their powerful neighbor. During the early years of the ninth century the forces of the Chinese emperor inflicted a series of convincing defeats upon the Tibetans, and in 821 the Tibetan government "sent an envoy to ask for a sworn treaty."

As a result of this request negotiations were begun, and in 822 a solemn treaty was concluded. The terms of this treaty, engraved in Chinese and in the Tibetan script upon a stone which still stands at Lhasa, read in part as follows:

The learned, warlike, filial, and virtuous Emperor of the Great T'ang and the divine and all-wise Tsanpu (King) of the Great Fan (Tibet), two sovereigns allied as father and son-in-law, having consulted to unite the gods of the land and of grain, have concluded a sworn treaty of grand alliance which shall never be lost or changed . . . They have reconnected the bonds of affectionate kinship, strengthened anew the right policy of neighborly friendship, and made this great peace. The two countries, Fan and Han (China), shall keep the lands and boundaries which they now rule: all to the east shall be within the borders of the Great T'ang, all to the west shall be the territory of the Great Fan. Neither the one nor the other shall slaughter or fight, they shall not move weapons or armor, nor shall they plot to encroach on each other's territory. Should any men be liable to suspicion, they shall be taken alive, and their business inquired into, after which they shall be given clothes and food and sent back to their own country . . . Should they not keep these oaths, and either Fan or Han disregard the treaty and break the solemn agreement, may there come to them misfortune and calamity. Provided only that the work of rebels against the state or secret plotters shall not be included as a breach of the sworn ceremony. . . .

Very shortly after the conclusion of this treaty internal dissensions began to develop in Tibet; the royal power rapidly declined, and by the end of the ninth century the Tibetan kingdom had ceased to be an important factor in the affairs of central Asia.

SUGGESTED REFERENCES

BARTHOLD, W. Turkestan down to the Mongol Invasion.

BELL, SIR C. Tibet: Past and Present.

BRETSCHNEIDER, E. Mediaeval Researches from Eastern Asiatic Sources.

BRETSCHNEIDER, E. Notices of Mediaeval Geography and History of Central and Western Asia.

BUSHELL, S. W. "Early History of Tibet," *Journal of the Royal Asiatic Society*, 1880.

CHAVANNES, E. Documents sur les Tou-kiue (Turcs) occidentaux.

CURTIS, W. E. Turkestan, the Heart of Asia.

CZAPLICKA, M. A. The Turks of Central Asia in History and at the Present Day.

Das, S. C. "Early History of Tibet," *Journal of the Bengal Asiatic Society*, 1881.

Francke, A. H. A History of Western Tibet.

Gibb, H. A. R. The Arab Conquests in Central Asia.

Laufer, B. Sino-Iranica.

Rockhill, W. W. "Tibet: a Geographical, Ethnographical and Historical Sketch, derived from Chinese Sources," *Journal of the Royal Asiatic Society*, 1891.

Skrine, F. H., and Ross, E. D. The Heart of Asia.

Stein, Sir M. A. Ancient Khotan.

Stein, Sir M. A. Innermost Asia.

Stein, Sir M. A. Ruins of Desert Cathay.

Stein, Sir M. A. Serindia.

IX

Indo-China and Malaysia: to the Era of Mongol Invasions

The Population · Indian and Chinese Influence · Annam and Champa · Early History of Annam · Independent Annam · Early History of Champa · Champa's Relations with China · Cham Art · The Khmers of Cambodia · United Cambodia · Angkor Thom and Angkor Vat · Cambodia and her Neighbors · Siam before the Siamese · Early History of Burma · Anawrata, the Burmese Asoka · The Greatness and Decline of Pagān · Sumatra and Java · The Empire of Sri-Vishaya · The Javanese and the Sri-Vishayans · The Kingdom of Singosari · Javan Architecture; the Borobudur · Kartanagara and Buddhism · Kawi Language and Literature

FROM the eastern portion of the great Tibetan highland and from the adjoining Chinese province of Yunnan numerous parallel mountain ranges, separated by narrow river valleys, run southward to form the framework of the Indo-Chinese peninsula. Along these valleys there has been from earliest times a constant migration of peoples southward into the region. Occasionally when new bodies of these immigrants pressed down upon earlier arrivals, the two groups amalgamated; sometimes the earlier occupants of the land proved strong enough to repel the intruders, and sometimes the more powerful later arrivals drove their predecessors up into the hill regions or forced them out of the peninsula into the islands of the archipelago.

By the opening of historic times, which in the case of Indo-China means about the beginning of the Christian Era, the bulk of the population of the region was divided into four linguistic groups.

Numerically, and perhaps culturally, the most important of these groups was the Mon-Khmer family, which held the lower part of the Salwin and Irrawaddy valleys in the west as well as the greater part of the Menam valley in the center of the peninsula and the plains of the lower Mekong farther to the east.

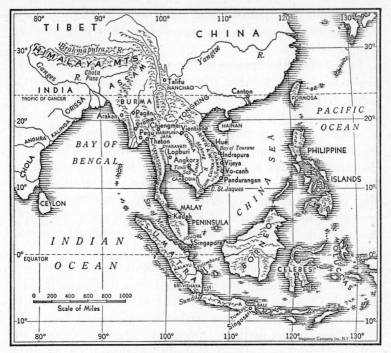

Indo-China and Malaysia in Earliest Times

North of the Mon-Khmers, in the valleys of the Salwin and the Irrawaddy, were the so-called Tibeto-Burmans, a people closely allied to the inhabitants of eastern Tibet.

In the southern part of the Malay peninsula and in the islands of the archipelago the dominant element was that known as Malaysian, a people formed by the amalgamation of the various groups which had found their way into the islands in prehistoric times. On the extreme eastern side of the peninsula the narrow coastal strip between the mountains and the sea was occupied by the Chams, a people who belonged linguistically to the Malaysian group.

North of the Chams, in modern Annam, were the Annamese, who seem to have been closely related to the Shans, or Tais. The principal body of the Shan, or Tai, people, who were later to become the dominant element in the peninsula, were still located in the southern provinces of China, particularly in Yunnan, where they had been pushed by the expansion of their more civilized Chinese relatives.

Even before the opening of the Christian Era contacts had begun to develop between the peoples of Indo-China and the highly civilized nations to the north and west. The mountain barrier between the peninsula and India on the west constitutes a serious obstacle to travel by land in this direction; but the seafaring people of the Indian east coast were able to ignore this difficulty and make their way across the Bay of Bengal to the Indo-Chinese shore. As the Chinese had not yet taken to the sea, their influence at this early date was chiefly in Annam, which was contiguous to the province of Kwangtung and easily reached by land from it. The influence of India was more widely scattered. From Orissa, from Kalinga, from Andhra, and from the Tamil states of the south, Indian merchant adventurers made their way eastward in their ships and established their trading posts along the Indo-Chinese coast from the delta of the Irrawaddy to the Strait of Malacca; others had settled in Sumatra and Java, while still others, sailing northward from these islands or crossing the narrow Malay peninsula, established themselves at the mouth of the Mekong or on the narrow strip of coast occupied by the Chams.

Annam, because of its proximity to China, tended from an early date to become an integral part of the Chinese Empire. The more extensive zone of Indian influence, on the other hand, showed no tendency to become so closely allied with India. The various Indian commercial settlements, having little feeling of political unity with their distant homeland, were at first mere centers of cultural diffusion; later, when their superior culture had taken root, the descendants of the Hindu settlers constituted the governing classes in the various local states which were evolved.

Under the influence of the civilizing Indians Sanskrit became at an early date the official language of the Chams and of the Mon-Khmers, but the most important contribution of India to the civilization of Indo-China was in the field of religion. Brahmanism in its various forms, but with the cult of Siva predominating, appears to have been the first religion introduced into the peninsula. Buddhism followed Brahmanism into the region, in some places to supplant the older cult and in others to combine with it in forming a synthetic religion.

As in other parts of Asia, the spread of Indian religious ideas was accompanied by the introduction of Hindu architecture and art. Great temples and pagodas—many of them now in ruins—and the wonderful carving upon these buildings show the influence of India upon the architects and artists of Indo-China and the Malay Archipelago.

While India was the chief source of religion and art, the Chinese furnished the people of Indo-China with the greater part of their political institutions and their science. Although these Chinese contributions during the earlier centuries of the Christian Era found their way only into the northeastern corner of the peninsula, by the eighth century even the Hinduized peoples of the south and west had begun to be deeply influenced by their powerful northern neighbor. Indo-Chinese embassies to the T'ang court at Changan brought back to their lands both a knowledge of Chinese institutions and Confucian political philosophy and a deep admiration for these. Chinese legal codes were imitated, and Chinese titles were given to the officers of government. The Chinese calendar was adopted as official by most of the Indo-Chinese courts, and the Chinese system of astronomy naturally accompanied the calendar.

ANNAM AND CHAMPA

During the latter part of the fourth century B.C. the kingdom of Yueh, lying to the south of the Yangtze delta, was overthrown by its powerful neighbor, the kingdom of Wu, which at that time occupied practically the entire lower Yangtze valley. As a result of this conquest the people of Yueh, who were of Tai stock, moved toward the south. Some settled in modern Fukien, Kwangtung, and Kwangsi; but others, proceeding still farther to the southeast, entered the region now known as Tongking, where they conquered the earlier inhabitants and laid the foundations of the kingdom of Annam.

When Shih Huang Ti, toward the end of the third century B.C., had succeeded in uniting all the Chinese kingdoms into a single empire, he turned his attention toward the more southern regions occupied by these semi-Chinese Yueh refugees. The Yueh settlements in the present-day Chinese provinces were conquered about the year 221 B.C., and by 214 the Ch'in monarch had established his authority over Annam, which at this time included all of Tongking and extended southward along the coast to a point a little beyond modern Hué.

In 208 B.C., during the disorders which followed the death of Shih Huang Ti, a Chinese general named Chao T'o set himself up as the ruler of an independent southern kingdom including Annam, Kwangtung, and Kwangsi, with its capital at Canton. This kingdom, known as Nan-yueh or Nam-viet ("Southern Yueh") lasted until 110 B.C., when it was conquered and annexed to the Chinese Empire by Wu Ti of the Han dynasty. After this second annexation the region of Kwangsi and Kwangtung rapidly became thoroughly Chinese; but Annam, although divided into districts and administered by Chinese officials, retained its local traditions and customs.

The Annamese remained under Chinese rule until the second quarter of the tenth century. During this period of more than a thousand years Confucianism, Chinese Buddhism, the use of the Chinese written character, and Chinese political institutions were firmly rooted among the ruling class of the Annamese, which class through intermarriage became increasingly Chinese. The bulk of the common people, however, were little affected by a culture designed primarily for scholars.

The fall of the T'ang dynasty in 907, as we have seen in an earlier chapter, was followed by half a century of anarchy in the Chinese Empire, and in 939 the Chinese-Annamese ruling class took advantage of the situation to throw off the Chinese yoke and to establish an independent kingdom of Annam.

From this date until 1400, a period of approximately five centuries, five national dynasties successively ruled the country. Without exception the monarchs of these dynasties adopted the political and religious institutions of the Chinese. An official hierarchy, in which the civil officials took precedence over the military as well as over the Buddhist and Taoist clergy, was established in 971. Thirty-six years later an embassy to China from the reigning sovereign secured from the Sung emperor a set of the Confucian Classics as well as a Chinese version of the Buddhist canon, while later rulers piously built Buddhist and Taoist monasteries and gathered into their libraries the writings of both religions.

Even during the centuries when Annam was still under Chinese rule, its southern districts along the coast were frequently invaded by the forces of Champa, the kingdom of the Chams. Under their national dynasties the Annamese were engaged in an almost constant struggle with the Chams over territorial questions; and these wars came to an end only in 1257, when the Annamese found their dominions invaded from the north by an army of the great Mongol khan Mangu.

When the armies of Han Wu Ti, in 110 B.C., conquered and annexed the country of Annam, they found on the southern frontier of the civilized Annamese a people so savage that "they knew only hunting and fishing and had no knowledge of cultivating the soil." These southern barbarians were the Chams, a Malaysian people who at some unknown early date had settled on the narrow strip of coast land between the Bay of Tourane on the north and Cape Saint Jacques on the south. For about three centuries after the Chinese conquest of Annam the Chams appear to have had only a primitive tribal organization, but they were turbulent neighbors and made frequent inroads into the southern frontier districts of Annam.

In 137 A.D., when the Han emperor Shun Ti called a meeting of his Grand Council to determine what action should be taken with regard to a particularly serious Cham incursion, it was decided that the climate of the country and its great distance from the Chinese capital were insuperable barriers to any effective military operations. "If there are among these insurgents any men capable of exercising authority over the rest," said the Minister Li Ku, "the Emperor should permit them to be appointed feudal princes of the second rank. In this way the country will be brought under the control of the officials in Annam." This advice, which accorded with China's time-honored policy toward troublesome frontier peoples, was accepted by the emperor; but the Chams were not destined to be thus assimilated into the Chinese imperial organization. Sometime during the preceding century Indian merchant adventurers from the Andhra country, the region between the Godavari and Krishna rivers, had begun to arrive at Pandurangan on the Champa coast. By the time the Chinese government had felt the need of adopting a definite policy with respect to the Chams the influence of this Hindu merchant colony was already beginning to spread through the country, and about the year 192 A.D. a Hindu ruler known as Sri Mara appears to have established an organized kingdom of Champa.

Although the local Cham rulers offered at first considerable resistance to the unifying efforts of the Hindus, a rock inscription at Vo-canh, attributed either to the son or to the grandson of Sri Mara, indicates that the royal power was at last solidly established. The Vo-canh inscription is in the Sanskrit language, and the letters used are those which were in use during the second and third centuries in southern India; it has therefore been attributed to an early date in the third century and is believed to be "the most ancient inscribed monument in Champa or even in Indo-China." By the middle of the third century Champa, which now begins to appear in the Chinese records as the "Kingdom of Lin-yi," was completely Hinduized. Indrapura, the first capital, which was located in the extreme north on the Bay of Tourane, was obviously Hindu in name, while the ruins of the many Brahman and Buddhist edifices at that spot are predominantly Indian in architecture. By the end of the fourth century, morever, the Cham monarchs had begun to assume names with the terminations "varman" and "dharma," both of which were typical of southern-Indian royalty.

Under the guidance of their Hindu tutors the Chams gradually turned from their primitive pursuits of hunting and fishing to the more civilized occupations of agriculture and trade. The cultivable area of the country was not extensive, but the numerous bays and estuaries along the coast looked upon a growing commerce between the Chinese on the north and the western merchants—Arab, Indian, and Persian—who came up from the Strait of Malacca. By legitimate commerce or by piracy the Chams drew rich profits from their location and at times were able to control the important spice trade between the Indies and the ports of China. But the sea brought them perils as well as profits; during the last half of the eighth century the prosperity of Champa made her a shining mark for her neighbors, and her coasts were ravaged by buccaneering expeditions from Malaysia, especially from Java.

Partly by reason of their contiguity to Annam and partly as a consequence of their maritime activity the Chams were drawn into frequent contact with China. When the T'ang dynasty assumed the imperial authority in China, Champa, like most of the other Indo-Chinese states, was greatly impressed by the splendor and power of the empire; throughout the seventh century and the first part of the eighth, therefore, tributary missions from Indrapura made regular visits to Changan to lay their gifts at the feet of the Chinese emperor. Toward the end of the eighth century, as the power of T'ang began to wane, these tributary missions were discontinued.

With the accession of the Sung rulers to the imperial throne of China the tributary missions of the Cham monarchs were resumed, and one of these missions furnished Ma Tuan-lin, the thirteenth-century Chinese historian, with the following story:

Jaya Harivarman IV, king of Champa, sent in 1167 a tribute so considerable that the emperor promptly ordered that only one tenth of the presents offered should be accepted. Soon afterwards the Chinese authorities at Fukien transmitted to the imperial court the complaints of a certain Wou-che-tien and a number of other Arab merchants who accused the king of Champa of having forcibly taken from them the precious objects with which he had thus dared to attempt to gain honor for himself. This communication greatly moved the Emperor. He refused to accept any of the present and decided to write to Jaya Harivarman to let him know the reason for this refusal. With regard to the honorific title which the Chinese Emperor was accustomed to confer upon the kings of Champa, it was the opinion of the council of ministers that, before investing Jaya Harivarman, it would be necessary to wait until this affair of the Arabs had been settled and the Cham monarch had sent to the imperial court a fresh tribute such as could properly be accepted.

In addition to their struggle against the Annamese on the north the sovereigns of Champa, from the closing decades of the ninth century, frequently found themselves involved in war with the powerful Khmer empire of Cambodia. This intermittent struggle proceeded with varying fortunes, and in the first part of the thirteenth century Champa was reduced for a brief period to a mere province of the Cambodian empire.

The oldest specimens of Cham sculpture which have been preserved date from about the fifth century, while the most ancient of their existing buildings were erected in the seventh century, at which time brick began to replace wood as building material. Aside from the royal palaces at Indrapura and at Vijaya, the later capital, the most important Cham structures were the Brahman temples and Buddhist monasteries, in the erection of which the various sovereigns displayed great enthusiasm. The existing specimens of sculpture also are chiefly religious,—Buddhas, Bodhisattvas, and statues of the various Brahman deities,—although the bas-reliefs with which the buildings were ornamented present in addition a considerable variety of nonreligious human figures.

While the art of the Chams, both sculpture and architecture, was based upon that of southern India and especially upon that of Pallava, it was not mere servile imitation of the work of Indian artists. The Indian elements were modified both by indigenous ideas and by the infiltration, especially during the seventh and eighth centuries, of Chinese influence, with the result that Champa became in time an "autonomous province" in the world of art.

CAMBODIA

Among the Khmer people occupying the plains at the mouth of the Mekong River the first Hindu settlements were made and the introduction of Hindu civilization commenced perhaps as early as the third century B.C. By the second century A.D. two Hinduized kingdoms, both of which were ruled by monarchs claiming Indian descent, existed in the Mekong valley. In the south, occupying modern Cochin China and the southern part of the present French province of Cambodia, was a kingdom known to the Chinese historians as Funan. North of Funan lay Chenla, which occupied the valley of the Mekong almost to the site of Vientiane.

Although established by Hindus, the southern-Cambodian kingdom had come into contact with China at least as early as the first quarter of the third century A.D. In the year 225 the ruler of Funan dispatched an embassy to Nanking, which during the period of the "Three Kingdoms" was the capital of the kingdom of Wu; and in 245 Sun Ch'üan of Wu sent a return embassy to his southern neighbor.

This return embassy throws an interesting light upon the extent of international intercourse at that time in the Far Eastern world. At the Funan capital the Chinese envoy met the ambassador of an Indian monarch who was bringing to the king a gift of horses from Transoxiana. From this Indian ambassador the Chinese representative was able to secure and to carry back to his own government a considerable amount of new information concerning the affairs of central and western Asia.

From the middle of the sixth century the two kingdoms of the Khmers were united for more than a hundred years, but the country was not permanently unified until the year 802, in the reign of Jayavarman II. This sovereign first applied to his domain the name Kambuja, or Cambodia, and he may be regarded as the real founder of the Cambodian empire. The new ruler was related to the royal family of the Sumatran empire of Sri-Vishaya, which at this time appears to have gained sufficient influence in Indo-China to be able to establish upon the throne of the Khmer state a prince of its own choice. For just three quarters of a century the line of Jayavarman II reigned over Cambodia; then it was replaced by a new royal family, whose first sovereign is known as Indravarman I.

Indravarman I determined to create a new and more splendid capital for his empire. On the shore of Tonlé Sap, therefore, he commenced the erection of the famous city of Angkor, "Angkor Thom." The building of Angkor Thom, which for four centuries was to be the capital of Cambodia and the most magnificent city in all Indo-China, was carried to completion by Indravarman's son and successor. The later rulers of the dynasty, which continued in power for a century and a quarter, upheld the tradition established by these two monarchs and left behind them, in the form of numerous temples, splendid architectural monuments. About 1115 the second monarch of a new ruling family commenced to erect outside the city of Angkor the great temple of Angkor Vat, which has been called the Cambodian Parthenon.

The early architecture of the Khmers, like that of their Cham neighbors, was predominantly Indian in form and was constructed first in wood and later in brick. From the ninth century, however, the Cambodians began to build in stone, while their Indian architectural style was now considerably modified by Chinese influence. In sculpture, particularly in the bas-reliefs with which Angkor Thom and Angkor Vat are so richly decorated, the Indian influence continued to predominate; but Chinese influence is evident in the bronze statues, whose construction the Khmer artists learned from their Chinese neighbors.

The two great periods of building —the one at the close of the ninth century, when the construction of Angkor Thom was commenced, and the other during the first half of the twelfth century, which resulted in the erection of Angkor Vat—were periods of Brahman rather than Buddhist influence. In Cambodia, however, as in other parts of the Indo-Chinese world and in India itself, the relations between the two religions were usually marked by mutual tolerance, and the theology of Buddhism as well as that of Brahmanism can be discovered in the sculpture at Angkor.

Under the various dynasties which held the throne after its permanent unification Cambodia was, until the first half of the thirteenth century, the most powerful state in the Indo-Chinese peninsula. During the greater part of this period the Cambodians were frequently engaged in war against their eastern neighbors, the Chams, whose territory at the beginning of the thirteenth century was temporarily incorporated into the Cambodian empire. With the Annamese Cambodia was usually at peace, while the Cambodian monarchs, after 615, usually dispatched tributary missions to and recognized the suzerainty of the Chinese emperor. With the peoples of the Malay Archipelago Cambodia's relations were chiefly commercial, although Sri-Vishaya was able on at least two occasions to influence and perhaps to control the succession to the Cambodian throne. In the upper valley of the Mekong the territories of Cambodia appear never to have extended much farther north than the limits reached by the old kingdom of Chenla. On this frontier, early in the thirteenth century, the Cambodians began to come into contact with the southward-moving bodies of Tai peoples by whom the empire was destined eventually to be destroyed.

SIAM BEFORE THE SIAMESE

The valley of the Menam River, to the west of Cambodia, was occupied by Khmer peoples who were closely related to the people of Cambodia. During the early centuries of the Christian Era these Khmers of the Menam valley, like all the other peoples in southern and western Indo-China, were subjected to the influence of Hindu civilization which reached them partly from India, partly from Sumatra, and partly from their Mekong-valley relatives on the east. About the sixth century the effect of this higher civilization was seen in the organization of the kingdom of Dvaravati, in the region of Lopburi. This kingdom, unlike Cambodia, was Buddhist rather than Brahman in its religious ideas. During the eighth century a group of Hinduized Khmers from Dvaravati migrated to the upper portions of the Menam valley and established an independent kingdom, also predominantly Buddhist, known as Haripunjaya, with its capital near the present-day Chiengmai. Early in the eleventh century the southern of these two Menam kingdoms was annexed to Cambodia, but the Cambodian monarchs were unsuccessful in their efforts to extend their control over Haripunjaya. Until the middle of the thirteenth century the northern kingdom retained its independence while the southern continued as a province of the Cambodian empire; then came the great southward migration of the Tai people, who were to effect a complete change in the political condition of the peninsula.

BURMA

During the early centuries of the Christian Era the present Burma was inhabited by three groups of people. The plain at the mouths of the rivers and the narrow strip of Tenasserim coast were occupied by Mons. Tibeto-Burman tribes held the Arakan coast and the greater part of the Irrawaddy valley. The Tais, or Shans, occupied the mountainous regions of the north and northeast, and even at this time they had begun to settle in the upper valleys of the Irrawaddy and the Salwin.

As early as the second century B.C. there appear to have been Chinese trade routes through Yunnan to the Irrawaddy and Salwin valleys. The Tibeto-Burmans of the upper Irrawaddy had at an early date some contact with India by way of Tibet and Assam. But the earliest and most continuous civilizing influence came by sea from India. Along the coast of the present Burma there began to arrive, perhaps even before the Christian Era, the merchant adventurers from south India. By the third century A.D. this overseas expansion of Hindu peoples had resulted in the establishment of numerous commercial colonies along the coast of Tenasserim, at the mouths of the principal rivers, and even at points on the coast of Arakan. These newcomers brought with them many elements of Hindu culture. At the various trading centers where they settled, the Indian immigrants and their descendants gradually came to constitute, if not a majority of the inhabitants, at least the ruling classes. The more prosperous trading towns, dominating the neighboring hinterland, developed into commercial kingdoms, such as Prome, Thaton, and Pegu.

The Hindu influence was especially strong in the region occupied by the Mons, as is demonstrated by the fact that in time the people of this territory became known as Talaings. The name appears to have been derived from Telingana on the coast of India, a region from which a great part of the Hindu settlers had come. The Talaings introduced the art of writing into Burma, and the probable date of this introduction is suggested by the fact that the oldest known inscription in Burma is a Talaing inscription in Pallava letters such as were used in southern India during the fifth century A.D.

Among the numerous Tibeto-Burman tribes of the Irrawaddy valley the most important were the Pyu, whose chief town was Prome. As the delta land of the Irrawaddy, twelve or fifteen hundred years ago, was far less extensive than it is today, Prome in the fifth to seventh centuries was practically at the mouth of the river and was quite as accessible to the Indian merchants as were the ports in the Mon territory. During the eighth century Prome appears to have been governed by a dynasty of Indian or semi-Indian origin and to have exercised a sort of hegemony over the Pyu tribes in a rather extensive region.

About the middle of the eighth century the Shan state of Nan-chao, in Yunnan, extended its authority over the tribes in the upper part of the Irrawaddy, and in 802 an embassy from the Pyu —called by the Chinese the P'iao—arrived at Changan accompanying a mission from Nanchao. The visit of this mission, which appears to have been the first case of official intercourse between China and Burma, was recorded by the great Chinese poet Po Chü-i in one of his poems. The Pyu embassy of 802 was not repeated, and the states of Burma had no further direct official contact with the Chinese government until the beginning of the twelfth century.

Shortly after the date of the Pyu embassy to Changan, Prome lost its hegemony over the neighboring Pyu tribes and rapidly disintegrated. With the decline of Prome the people of the city and of the surrounding districts moved northward about two hundred miles to the Tibeto-Burman town of Pagān. Aided by the addition to its population of this new element, whose culture was decidedly superior to that of the up-river tribes, Pagān from about the middle of the ninth century steadily increased in importance until, from the eleventh to the thirteenth century, it became the political center of all Burma.

With the seizure by Anawrata in 1044 of the royal power at Pagān, Burmese history emerges from the confusion of tribal legend and becomes for a while the record of an organized kingdom. The new king was an able administrator, a zealous reformer, and a successful military leader. He established the kingdom of Pagān so firmly that it endured for more than two centuries after his death and did not finally disappear until broken by the armies of the all-conquering Mongols.

The kingdom over which Anawrata found himself supreme in 1044 was limited in area and in natural resources, and the new sovereign's first concern was to strengthen it by improving its organization and by adding to its resources. In the field of national economy his most important achievement was the development of an irrigation system which tremendously increased the production of rice. This addition to the country's resources enabled Anawrata to maintain a military organization much more powerful than that of any former ruler of Pagān.

Even more important was the part which Anawrata played in the introduction of a purer form of Buddhism in place of the extremely corrupt and degraded form which hitherto had been prevalent at Pagān. In the thirteenth year of his reign there arrived at his court a Talaing monk of the Hinayana branch of Buddhism. This monk, Shin Arahan, quickly impressed the king with the purity of his doctrines and the saintliness of his character. Anawrata summoned from the Talaing monasteries a number of other Hinayana teachers, to whom he gave the full support of the royal power, while the ignorant and gross-living Mahayanist parasites were exiled from the country or were forced to work for their living. Like the great Asoka, Anawrata made his court the center of the country's religious life and a place where really devout Buddhist monks from every land could be sure of support and protection.

Anawrata's religious enthusiasm led to—or at least provided a pretext for—his first great undertaking in the field of war. Desiring to secure reliable versions of the Buddhist scriptures, he sent an envoy in 1057 to the king of Thaton to ask for one of the thirty copies of the Tripitaka in that monarch's possession. When the Talaing ruler refused this request, Anawrata marched down at the head of his forces, besieged and captured Thaton, and carried back to Pagān not only the desired books but also the defeated king, a large part of the population of the conquered city, and an immense quantity of loot.

After the overthrow of Thaton the local rulers of southern Burma hastened to make their submission to the conqueror, and Anawrata quickly found himself the supreme ruler of all the region hitherto dominated by the Talaings. Turning now to his northern neighbors, he invaded and conquered the northern districts of

Arakan and is reported to have led his armies westward into the territories of Bengal. On the north and northeast a number of Tai, or Shan, tribes were forced to pay him homage, and his troops even advanced northward into the kingdom of Nanchao as far as its capital, Talifu.

Partly through his victories, partly through the labors of the many skilled artisans brought back as captives to his capital, but most of all through the new contacts which he established with the outside world, Anawrata was enabled to transform Pagān into the cultural as well as the political and religious center of the Burmese world. A library was erected to house the sacred scriptures brought from Thaton, the Talaing alphabet was adopted and adapted for writing the Burmese language, and the Buddhist scriptures were translated for the first time into Burmese. At the same time the cordial relations which developed between Pagān and Ceylon, which was the spiritual capital of Hinayana Buddhism, brought to the Burmese people the architectural and artistic ideas of Ceylon and of southern India.

Anawrata had commenced the work of transforming Pagān into a royal city whose splendor should rival that of Angkor; this work was continued by his successors. The year 1090 saw the dedication of the beautiful Ananda temple, the first and the greatest of a series of splendid buildings which still stand as monuments to Pagān's two centuries of glory. During this period of greatness the court of Pagān entered into formal diplomatic relations with the imperial court of China. In 1106 a Burmese embassy, the first to appear at the Chinese court since the Pyu embassy of 802, reached the capital of the Sung emperors, where, after deliberation by the Board of Rites, it was received as representing a fully sovereign state and was given precedence over missions from the various tributary countries.

Throughout the entire twelfth century Pagān continued to enjoy the power and prosperity inaugurated by Anawrata, but the opening of the thirteenth century saw the beginning of its decline. The three monarchs who reigned at Pagān between 1210 and 1254 delegated the actual political power to others and devoted themselves to works of piety or abandoned themselves to lives of frivolous luxury. In 1254 the last ruler of the kingdom, Narathihapate, ascended the throne. Already the Shans from the north were beginning to push their way southward in order to escape from the pressure of the conquering Mongols, and Narathihapate was to see his kingdom invaded and destroyed by the forces of Kublai Khan.

SUMATRA AND JAVA

From the earliest times the two great islands of Sumatra and Java have been intimately connected with Indo-China and especially with the Malay peninsula. About the beginning of the Christian Era this already intimate connection was strengthened by the arrival of Indian colonists from the west. Of the southern-Indian settlements which are known to have been established between the first century B.C. and the second century A.D., one was in Sumatra on the Palembang River, one in central Java, a third near the southern extremity of the Malay peninsula, and a fourth in the upper part of this peninsula near Kedah.

In the islands, as on the mainland, the Indian commercial settlements eventually became the centers of organized states. According to the Chinese chronicles of the Han dynasty an envoy from the Javan king Devavarman arrived at the Chinese capital in the year 132 A.D., and the name of this king may be regarded as conclusive proof that at least a part of Java was at that date already under Hinduized rule.

In the islands and in the Malay peninsula, as in Indo-China, the early Indian colonists were Brahman rather than Buddhist in religion. In 412–413, when the Chinese pilgrim Fa Hsien visited Java on his return voyage from India, Brahmanism was the prevailing religion of the island. In Sumatra and in the Malay peninsula, which was under Sumatran control, Buddhism began, about the fifth or sixth century, to replace the earlier Brahman cult; and many of the seventh-century Buddhist pilgrims from China and from Korea pursued their religious studies in Sumatra for a time before continuing their pilgrimage to India.

About the first century A.D. there appear to have been two important kingdoms in Sumatra: Sri-Vishaya, which was situated in the eastern portion of the island, and Malayu, which was located slightly to the northwest of its rival. Toward the end of the seventh century Sri-Vishaya, under a dynasty known as the Sailendra, reduced Malayu to vassalage and became the dominant state of Sumatra. During the seventh and eighth centuries the rulers of this growing kingdom extended their authority over the whole of Sumatra and the Malay peninsula as well as over the western and central portions of Java; and in the early part of the ninth century, as we have seen, they were sufficiently powerful to place upon the throne of southern Cambodia the prince by whom that country was permanently united into a single kingdom.

The power and wealth of Sri-Vishaya resulted from the fact that the colonies and settlements of the state were so located as to control the most important trade routes of the Malay world. The first Sri-Vishayan expansion had been along the Sumatran side of the Strait of Malacca, but opposite their ports on this side of the strait the Sri-Vishayan rulers soon acquired corresponding ports on the coast of the peninsula. A settlement on the island of Singapore and another on the site of present-day Johore gave to the Sumatran kingdom control over the much-used intervening strait and enabled it to levy tribute upon all passing ships. A similar pair of tribute-levying ports faced each other across the Sunda Strait, one settle-ment on the Sumatran shore and its mate on the Java side, while the mouth of every river which might serve as a port of refuge was made the site of a Sri-Vishayan colony.

About 1030 Rajendra Choladeva I, one of the great rulers of the southern-Indian kingdom of Chola, dispatched to Sumatra a fleet which conquered the Sri-Vishayans and reduced them tem-porarily to vassalage. Forty years later, however, Sri-Vishaya threw off the Chola yoke and reduced to subjection its late con-querors. By 1180 the empire of Sri-Vishaya appears to have reached the height of its power. In the west, Chola and the island of Ceylon acknowledged the authority of the Sumatran ruler; in the north, his power extended over the entire Malay peninsula, and his au-thority was recognized by commercial settlements as far away as Formosa and the island of Hainan; about half of the neighboring island of Java was under his sway, while Sri-Vishayan colonies in Borneo, Celebes, the Philippines, and the Moluccas gave the Sumatran empire almost complete control over the commerce of the entire East Indian Archipelago.

When the Sailendra rulers of Sri-Vishaya, toward the end of the seventh century, overthrew Malayu and made themselves the masters of Sumatra, they also extended their power eastward, as we have seen, into the island of Java. The petty states into which Java was at that time divided could offer little effective resistance to their powerful neighbor, and Sri-Vishaya, by the middle of the eighth century, was in complete control of the western and central portions of the island. Shortly after the middle of the ninth century the Javanese princes organized and succeeded in pushing the Sumatran conquerors out of the central-Javan plain, but early in the tenth century the Sri-Vishayans were able to reoccupy this lost territory.

The ninth-century league of east-Javan states had been able to gain only temporary success against the Sri-Vishayan masters of the central plain; but early in the tenth century, at the very moment when the Sumatrans were regaining their lost ground, there began in eastern Java a process of consolidation which was to unite the multitude of petty states into more powerful political organizations, and about 1025 the entire eastern third of the island came under the sway of a ruler named Erlangga. Upon the death of Erlangga the kingdom was divided, but the opening years of the thirteenth century saw the beginning of a new and more vigorous movement of consolidation.

About the year 1220 an adventurer named Ken Arok (or Ken Angrok), said to have been the son of a peasant, established himself as the ruler of a petty state known as Tumapel, with his capital in the village of Singosari. By the date of his death, in 1247, he had built up his state, now known as Singosari, into a kingdom more powerful than any that had hitherto existed in eastern Java. Under the third successor of Ken Arok the expansion of Singosari steadily continued, while his capital, although not a seaport, became a great city whose fame spread to all parts of the Far East. The fifth ruler in line after Ken Arok, Kartanagara, who ruled from 1268 to 1292, was the last as well as the greatest ruler of the kingdom.

By the date of Kartanagara's accession the power of Sri-Vishaya had begun to wane, and the twenty-four years of his reign saw steady encroachments by Singosari upon the territories which formerly had acknowledged the sway of the Sumatran commercial empire. The entire island of Java was brought at least nominally under the hegemony of Singosari, Bali and a number of other islands to the east and northeast were conquered, Javan overlordship replaced that of Sumatra in southern Borneo and in parts of the Malay peninsula, and a considerable portion of southern Sumatra was reduced to vassalage. Finally, in 1275, Kartanagara dispatched a great expedition to Sumatra for the invasion and conquest of the very center of the Sri-Vishayan power. This expedition spent eighteen years in Sumatra and did not return to Java until after the death of Kartanagara. While it did not actually succeed in taking the Sri-Vishayan capital, it effectively destroyed the power of that once mighty empire.

While the early east-Javan states were predominantly Brahman in their religious belief, the Sailendra rulers of Sri-Vishaya were ardent disciples of Buddhism. Thus the struggle between the Sri-Vishayans and the eastern Javanese for the control over the central plain of Java was a struggle between Buddhism and Brahmanism. Perhaps it was the religious nature of this struggle that impelled the victorious Sumatrans to commemorate their triumph by erecting in central Java the great Borobudur monument, which has been called the supreme masterpiece of East Indian art. The Borobudur, erected between the middle and the end of the eighth century, is purely Buddhist in the subject matter of its rich bas-relief sculpture; but some fifty miles to the southeast of this great structure, at Prambanan, eighth-century Buddhist edifices are to be found side by side with Brahman temples dating from the tenth and eleventh centuries, while an equal distance to the northwest of the Borobudur there are a number of purely Brahman monuments which were erected between the ninth and thirteenth centuries. The religious edifices of the central-Javan plain thus commemorate the changing domination of the Buddhist Sri-Vishayans and the Brahman princes of eastern Java.

Until the latter part of the thirteenth century the hostility of the eastern Javanese toward the Sri-Vishayans served to keep alive a patriotic opposition to Buddhism as a "foreign" religion. By the date of Kartanagara's accession, however, the power of Sri-Vishaya had declined to such an extent that Java had nothing more to fear from her former conquerors. Kartanagara, who was deeply interested in all branches of literature and philosophy, also threw his influence on the side of greater tolerance in religious matters, inviting Buddhist monks to his court and spending much of his time in listening to their expositions of Gautama's "Eightfold Path."

For a while this tolerant attitude of their king aroused bitter opposition among the people of Singosari, who were still inspired by their ancient religio-patriotic prejudice; but gradually the Buddhist faith began to gain a strong foothold among the people of eastern Java. By the end of Kartanagara's reign Buddhism appears to have become the dominant religion of the kingdom, and the empire of Madjapahit, which rose upon the foundations of Singosari, was from the beginning thoroughly Buddhist.

One small fragment only of Kartanagara's domains resisted this religious transformation. The little island of Bali, which lies off the eastern extremity of Java, stubbornly maintained its Brahman traditions. Here Brahmanical Hinduism, in the form of the special cult of Siva, had acquired in the lives and habits of the people a position as strong as it held in any part of India itself.

Nor did the Hindu cult succeed in maintaining itself only against the encroachments of Buddhism. Two centuries later it opposed with equal success the introduction of Mohammedanism; the fifteenth-century rulers of Bali laid down an absolute prohibition against the admission of any Mohammedans to their domain, and at the present day rites and customs of Sivaite Hinduism are still observed in the island.

Under the Indianized rulers of Sumatra and western Java, as in those parts of Indo-China which looked toward India for their early culture, Sanskrit appears to have been the official written language; the earliest inscriptions in the Malay Archipelago to which dates have been assigned are in this Indian writing. In eastern Java and in the island of Bali, however, there was developed, possibly as early as the time of these oldest Sanskrit inscriptions, a local written language known as Kawi, in which an extensive Javanese literature was produced.

Most of the Kawi literature takes the form of poetry, romance, or religious writing, and even those parts which purport to record historical events are devoted primarily to folklore and to traditional tales of ancient heroes. Although the historian finds the Kawi records of little assistance in the task of reconstructing the formal history of the Malay world, the very existence of these writings is itself a fact of historical importance; and a thorough study of Kawi literature, like the study of the sculpture and the architecture of the ancient temples, should lead to a more perfect appreciation of the culture which flourished between the eighth and fifteenth centuries in Java and in the adjacent islands of Malaysia.

SUGGESTED REFERENCES

AYMONIER, E. Un aperçu de l'histoire du Cambodge.

BOSE, P. The Hindu Colony of Cambodia.

CAMPBELL, D. M. Java: Past and Present.

CANDEE, H. C. Angkor the Magnificent.

COEDÈS, G. "Le royaume de Çrīvijaya," *Bulletin de l'École française d'Extrême-Orient*, 1918.

COLLET, O. J. A. Terres et peuples de Sumatra.

FERRAND, G. "L'Empire sumatranais de Çrīvijaya," *Journal Asiatique*, 1922.

HARVEY, G. E. History of Burma.

HIRTH, F., and ROCKHILL, W. W. The Chu-fan-chi of Chau Ju-kua.

KROM, N. J. Barabudur, Archaeological Description.

LAUNAY, A. Histoire ancienne et moderne de l'Annam.

MAJUMDAR, R. C. Ancient Indian Colonies in the Far East.

MASPERO, G. Le Royaume de Champa.

MOOKERJI, R. A History of Indian Shipping and Maritime Activity from the Earliest Times.

O'CONNOR, V. C. S. Mandalay and Other Cities of the Past in Burma.

PHAYRE, SIR A. History of Burma.

SCHELTEMA, J. F. Monumental Java.

STERN, P. Le Bayon d'Angkor et l'évolution de l'art khmèr.

STUART, J. Burma through the Centuries.

X

Korea: from Earliest Times to the Mongol Conquest

The Peoples of Korea · Dawn of Korean History · Conquest of Korea by Han Wu Ti · The Three Kingdoms: Koguryu, Pakche, and Silla · Early Korea and Japan · Korea's Indebtedness to China · The Rise of Silla · Destruction of Koguryu and Pakche · Greatness and Decline of Silla · Wang Kien · Korea under the Wang Dynasty · The Mongols · Submission to Mongol Domination · Summary

AT THE beginning of its historic period Korea appears to have been inhabited by two quite distinct major population groups. To the north of the Han River there were people who had found their way into the peninsula by the land route from Manchuria and from regions lying still farther to the west. The people who lived to the south of the Han differed from the northern group in language, in customs, and in physical characteristics, in all of which they resembled the people of southern Japan and of the Luchu Islands. In addition to these two major groups there was a smaller but already considerable body of Chinese settlers who had found their way to the peninsula either by way of Manchuria or by crossing the Yellow Sea. During historic times there have been constant additions to the population by further immigration, but all these varied elements have gradually amalgamated into a single people.

After a purely mythical period, during which the country is said to have been governed for twelve centuries by a superhuman being named Tan Gun and his equally superhuman son, the historical legends of Korea record the arrival, in 1122 B.C.,[1] of a Chinese exile named Ki Tse, with a band of five thousand followers, who established a kingdom to which he gave the name "Chosen." The only real basis for the tradition, however, is the existence, about the sixth century B.C., of a Chinese colony in the northern

---

[1] Even if this legend be accepted as fact, the traditional date is obviously too early, probably by a century or more.

Korea in Earliest Times

part of the peninsula governed by a ruling family named Ki, who claimed Ki Tse as their ancestor and as the founder of their state.

This Chinese colony, with its center at Pyongyang on the north bank of the Taitong River, introduced among the less civilized Koreans some knowledge of Chinese arts and industries: house-building, agriculture, the production of silk, and so forth. Under the Ki rulers Chosen included the northern provinces of present-day Korea, together with the Liaotung portion of Manchuria, and appears to have been, from early in the third century B.C., a vassal of the kingdom of Yen in northeastern China.

During the reign of Shih Huang Ti in China the stream of Chinese migration to Korea was swelled by the many malcontents who refused to submit to the domination of the Ch'in sovereign, while still more numerous refugees made their way to the penin-sula during the closing years of the third century B.C., when the founder of the Han dynasty was establishing his authority over the fragments of the short-lived Ch'in empire. Many of these later emigrants settled in the neighborhood of the Yalu River, and in 193 B.C. one of their leaders, marching upon Pyongyang, seized the capital and drove the last ruler of the Ki dynasty to the south-ern part of the peninsula.

For eighty-five years the new rulers of Chosen were able to main-tain themselves at Pyongyang; but in 108 B.C., as we have seen in an earlier chapter, the emperor Wu Ti of the Han dynasty invaded the northern part of the peninsula and annexed it to the Chinese empire. The domination of the Han emperors, which ex-tended only to the western provinces north of the Taitong, lasted only about seventy years. After the disappearance of Chinese au-thority there was a considerable period of anarchy, but by the opening of the Christian Era the greater part of the peninsula had been incorporated into three well-organized independent kingdoms.

The largest and most northern of these three kingdoms was Koguryu,[1] which was established in the year 37 B.C. During most of its history Koguryu was bounded on the south by the Taitong River, although its power was occasionally extended for short periods of time southward into the valley of the Han. On the east

---

[1] Also called by Chinese or Japanese writers Kaoli, Kaokaoli, Korai, or Koma.

its territories extended to the seacoast, while on the west they stretched beyond the Yalu River and included a considerable part of eastern Manchuria. At times the rulers of Koguryu even felt themselves sufficiently powerful to send their armies west of the Liao River and to attack the northern provinces of China Proper.

South of Koguryu, on the western side of the peninsula, was Pakche,[1] which was organized in 16 B.C. The name of this kingdom, which in Chinese means "hundred crossers," indicates its growth from a Chinese colony; and its frontage upon the western coast, with its numerous harbors, insured ready access to Chinese influence.

The more mountainous region to the east of Pakche was occupied by Silla,[2] which was the oldest of the three states, having been founded in 57 B.C. The territory of Silla was less extensive than that of Koguryu, her lands were less fertile than those of either of her two rivals, and she lacked the harbors with which Pakche was so plentifully provided. Less exposed to the cultural influence of China than were the people of Koguryu and Pakche, the Sillans were usually behind their neighbors in the development of their civilization; but in their narrow eastern valleys they developed the useful virtues of frugality, simplicity, and hardihood.

In addition to these three organized kingdoms which occupied the greater part of the Korean peninsula there was, in the extreme south, a region known as Kaya,[3] which formed a sort of wedge between the southern portions of Pakche and Silla. Kaya was occupied by a loose confederacy of tribes which appear to have been closely related to the Japanese people. During the first five centuries of the Christian Era, Japanese influence was dominant in this southern region; Japanese adventurers frequently succeeded in establishing themselves here as local rulers, while the Japanese chronicles habitually referred to Kaya as the Miyake (that is, "State Granary") of Mimana.

During the seven centuries of their existence as separate states the three Korean kingdoms were engaged in frequent and bitter

---

[1] Known as Paichi and Kudara.

[2] Hsinlo, Sinra, or Shiragi.

[3] Also known as Kara or Mimana.

struggles, sometimes among themselves and sometimes against the Japanese, whose dominant position in Kaya led them to attempt to extend their power over the more northern portions of the peninsula. The wars which originated as purely Korean affairs usually ended by assuming an international aspect, since one side or the other generally appealed for aid to the Chinese or to the Japanese. In the long period of their own national disunion which followed the disappearance of the Han dynasty the Chinese had little interest in Korean affairs and took practically no part in the Korean wars. Japan, on the other hand, was usually both interested and active.

Koguryu, the most powerful of the three, was also the most aggressive, and frequently combined with one of her local rivals in an effort to destroy the other; hence it was against Koguryu, either alone or in combination, that foreign assistance was most often invoked. Silla, whose location on the east coast brought her into frequent contact with piratical Japanese freebooters as well as with the Japanese adventurers of Kaya, was usually hostile to the warlike islanders; on one or two occasions, however, the hard-pressed Sillans found themselves forced to appeal to Japan for aid against the forces of Koguryu. In 467 A.D. Silla narrowly escaped conquest at the hands of a formidable Japanese expedition; fighting desperately, the Sillan army held the invaders to a drawn battle, and the Japanese expedition, disrupted by dissension among its leaders, subsequently abandoned the campaign. Pakche, on the west coast, appears to have feared China more than Japan and was consistently pro-Japanese. The government of this kingdom, therefore, usually maintained cordial relations both with the court at Yamato and with the local Japanese rulers in Kaya.

For several centuries prior to the conquest of northern Korea by Han Wu Ti there had been, as we have noted, a faint but continuous flow of Chinese civilization into the peninsula. The Han conquest marked the beginning of closer contact with China and resulted in a considerable increase of Chinese influence. After the formation of the three Korean kingdoms Chinese influence was especially strong in Koguryu, whose land frontiers touched those of China, and in Pakche; yet even the people of mountainous Silla, on the eastern side of the peninsula, were constantly receiving from China important additions to their civilization.

Although it seems almost certain that many of the early Chinese colonists must have had some knowledge of the art of writing, there is no evidence of the general use of this art in Korea until early in the first century A.D., when Chinese characters were used in Koguryu. In Pakche it was not until 375 A.D. that the use of Chinese written characters became general and the events of history began to be recorded in official chronicles. In Silla the art of writing appears to have been introduced during the second quarter of the fifth century.

The first Buddhist missionaries to Korea began to spread their doctrines in Koguryu in the year 372 and in Pakche about twelve years later; in both these states the new religion became almost immediately the official religion of the court. Silla did not receive its first Buddhist missionaries until about the middle of the fifth century, and it was not until some time after this that the Sillan government adopted Buddhism as the state religion.

Along with these two great gifts from China—written language and Buddhism—there came other important contributions to Korea's culture. The introduction of Chinese writing enabled the Koreans to become acquainted with the teachings of the Chinese philosophers and with all that the Chinese had learned in the fields of medicine, geography, and astronomy. Buddhism, on the other hand, brought with it all the beauties of Chinese art and all the artistic influences which China had received from India and central Asia. In science and philosophy the Koreans appear to have made practically no addition to the Chinese originals; but in art they soon displayed decided independent genius, and as early as the sixth century the Korean sculptors were producing original work of great beauty.

Early in the sixth century the kingdom of Silla began to increase in power and to expand its territories at the expense of its neighbors. In 527 the king of Silla was strong enough to annex certain districts which had been included in the southern part of Koguryu, while twenty-five years later the Sillan armies overran and conquered the whole of Kaya. Several Japanese expeditions were sent to Korea for the purpose of re-establishing Japan's supremacy over the lost districts; but these invasions produced no tangible or permanent results, and Kaya remained in the possession of the Sillan conqueror.

Japan's failure to regain her power in Kaya appears to have been due, in part at least, to a decline of the Japanese interest in Korea. By the beginning of the seventh century the Japanese were turning to China as the source of the civilization which hitherto had reached their shores by way of Korea, while the ruined condition of Kaya, in consequence of the almost continuous local wars, made the region of little real value to the Japanese as a source of foodstuffs.

Simultaneously with the decline of Japanese interest in Korean affairs there came a renewed interest and activity on the part of the Chinese, who in 589 were reunited into a single empire under the short-lived Sui dynasty. In 611 Yang Ti, the second Sui emperor, was reminded by his courtiers of the fact that Korea during the days of Han was a province of the empire; accordingly the emperor summoned the monarch of Koguryu to recognize the suzerainty of China. This summons was ignored, and in 613 Yang Ti dispatched a punitive expedition against the recalcitrant ruler. After some partial successes Yang Ti's expedition was forced to retreat, while another invading force, which crossed the Yalu the following summer, was compelled to abandon its operations against Koguryu in order to deal with a rising rebellion at home.

The first emperor of the T'ang dynasty, which replaced the Sui line in 618, was so fully occupied with other matters, domestic and foreign, that he had no time for Korean affairs, and the kingdoms of the peninsula were left to their own resources. With Japan's abandonment of her Korean interests after 622 the power and prestige of Silla were greatly increased, but the Sillans were soon called upon to meet a serious attack from the north. In 637 an ambitious general of Koguryu, Hoh Su-wen, made himself "Mayor of the Palace" at Pyongyang, and six years later he invaded the territories of his southeastern neighbor. Threatened with destruction at the hands of the forces of Koguryu, the Sillan king appealed to Changan, where T'ai Tsung, the second emperor of the T'ang dynasty, now held the scepter. In response to this appeal T'ai Tsung led a powerful expedition into Koguryu. Like the earlier expeditions of the Sui emperor, T'ai Tsung's invasion failed to conquer the warlike northern kingdom, but Silla was relieved from invasion and was saved from possible extermination.

For something more than a decade after the death of T'ai Tsung, Koguryu, although free from fresh Chinese invasion, was so completely exhausted by the recent struggle that its attack upon Silla was not renewed. In the year 660, however, an alliance was concluded between Koguryu and Pakche, and the two kingdoms simultaneously declared war against their rival. Once more the Sillans appealed to Changan for assistance, and once more the Chinese government responded. A powerful army marched through Manchuria to invade Koguryu by land, while a Chinese naval expedition was sent against the coast of Pakche to co-operate with the forces of Silla in attacking this weaker member of the alliance.

Pakche was conquered in 660 in the course of a single campaign, and the somewhat tardy intervention of the Japanese on behalf of their unfortunate friends resulted only in the crushing defeat of a Japanese fleet in 662 by the Chinese naval force. Koguryu offered more stubborn resistance; but in 668 Pyongyang was captured, and the northern kingdom, after seven hundred and five years of national independence, ceased to exist. The Liaotung portion of Koguryu and the Korean districts north of the Taitong were annexed to the Chinese Empire, while all the peninsula south of the Taitong was united to form a new and larger kingdom of Silla.

Up to this point in their career the rulers of Silla had been extremely punctilious in the performance of their duties as vassals of the Chinese emperor. With the increased power which resulted from the annexation of Pakche and southern Koguryu, however, the Sillan monarch believed himself sufficiently strong to terminate his vassalage and to wrest from Chinese control the more northern portions of the peninsula. A severe defeat by the Chinese soon showed him the error in his calculations, and the kings of Silla, until the decline of the T'ang dynasty, continued to send their tributary missions to the Chinese court. For more than two centuries the enlarged kingdom of Silla, like the other vassals of the Chinese Empire, shared in the greatness of the T'ang period, and rapid progress was made in all the arts of civilization. Princes and nobles of the Korean court went to China to be educated in the imperial university at Changan. Korean Buddhist monks spent years of study in the monasteries of China. Commercial relations between the two countries steadily increased. At times, ambitious Koreans of the official class took service under the Chinese government, and at least one of these officials—Kao Hsien-chih, who led the spectacular expedition across the Pamirs in 747—rose to high office under the T'ang sovereigns.

Progress in culture, however, was accompanied by a decline in the virtues which formerly had made Silla strong. The hardy mountaineers lost much of their earlier simplicity and bravery; among the ruling class, loyalty gave way to conspiracy and intrigue, and the later monarchs of the kingdom gave themselves up to lives of luxury and dissipation. By the close of the ninth century corruption and misgovernment had led to the outbreak of revolutionary movements in various parts of the country, and a long period of internal struggles brought the kingdom to the verge of ruin.

While Silla was thus torn by internal strife, the decline of the T'ang dynasty in China enabled the districts of northern Korea to throw off Chinese control, and a number of nationalist uprisings broke out in this part of the peninsula. One of these northern insurrections numbered among its leaders a man named Wang Kien, who claimed descent from the ancient royal family of Koguryu. Although at first only a subordinate officer, Wang Kien eventually became the commander in chief of the revolution with which he was connected, and by 919 he had made himself the actual ruler of northern and central Korea, with his capital at Sunto (modern Kai Seng). Sixteen years later the successful rebel leader forced the abdication of the last king of Silla and united into a single kingdom all the territory south of the Tumen and Yalu rivers. Wang Kien, who was nearly sixty years old when he became the ruler of the united peninsula, lived only a few years after his triumph; but his descendants held the Korean throne until 1392, when the last of the line was overthrown by a new nationalist uprising.

Throughout the four and a half centuries of the Wang dynasty Korea's contacts with Japan, except at the time of the Mongol attempts to invade the island empire, were few and unimportant. With China and her other continental neighbors, on the other hand, Korea's relations during this period were most intimate. Immediately after the abdication of the king of Silla, Wang Kien appealed to the ruling Chinese emperor—Kao Tsu of the Later Chin dynasty—for imperial confirmation of his title to the Korean throne. This formal recognition of Chinese suzerainty was followed by a thorough reorganization of the Korean government and the establishment of an administrative system in which, as in China, the power was exercised by educated civil officials. The successful operation of the Chinese institutions, however, was soon compromised by the growing power and political activity of the Buddhist clergy and by the rapid development of rival parties in the court, with the result that the history of Korea under the descendants of Wang Kien is marked by frequent periods of internal strife.

More serious than these domestic disturbances of the peace were the developments upon Korea's land frontier—developments in which the peninsula kingdom could not avoid being involved. In China, after the Later Chin dynasty had been succeeded by two others equally short-lived, the imperial power fell into the hands of the Sung dynasty, to whom, as to their predecessors, the Korean monarchs pledged their allegiance and paid tribute. But the Sung emperors, although they ruled central and southern China for more than three centuries, never exercised more than nominal control, and even this for less than half a century, over the northeastern provinces.

Before the end of the tenth century the Khitan Tartars had established their supremacy over all southern Manchuria and over the northern portion of the modern Chinese province of Hopei; and in 1011 these powerful neighbors invaded Korea, advancing as far as the capital, which they plundered and burned. For protection against the Khitans the Korean rulers allied themselves with the Kins of northern Manchuria. When the Kins, after having been called in by the Chinese government as allies against the Khitans, made themselves in 1123 the masters of the northern provinces of the empire, the Koreans transferred their allegiance to this new paramount power and rendered to the Kin dynasty the tribute formerly paid to the Sungs. Korea's vassalage to the Kin emperors of northern China lasted for ninety years, at the end of which time the Kins were overthrown by the rising power of the Mongols.

In 1218, three years after his seizure of Peking (see Chapter XII), Genghis Khan sent an expedition eastward into the Korean peninsula. Against the world-conquering Mongol horsemen the Korean army could offer no effective resistance; and as city after city fell before the invaders, the king and his court abandoned the capital. Fleeing southwestward to the coast, they finally took refuge upon the island of Kangwha, which lies at the mouth of the Han River. As the Mongols were wholly unaccustomed to the use of boats, Kangwha was a safe refuge; here, for the next thirty years, the king and his court were virtually prisoners, while the Mongol khans ruled the kingdom through their military officers. In 1259 the old Korean king died; and Kublai, who succeeded in the following year to the Mongol authority as Great Khan, induced the new Korean monarch to acknowledge the overlordship of the Mongols and to take up his residence at the old capital.

From the date of the Korean king's return to Sunto his country became to all intents and purposes an integral part of the Mongol empire. In submitting to the suzerainty of the Sung and Kin emperors and later in acknowledging the overlordship of the Mings and the Manchus the monarchs of Korea willingly assumed a status which most of China's smaller neighbors regarded as both honorable and advantageous—a status, moreover, which involved only nominal submission and carried with it no interference by the suzerain in the country's internal affairs. The submission to the Mongols, on the other hand, brought with it the most degrading servitude; Mongol officials, appointed by the Mongol ruler, filled all the important offices in the kingdom and administered the government in accordance with the khan's instructions, while the Korean kings, forced to accept Mongol princesses as their queens, were nothing more than puppets in the hands of the alien ministers.

In 1274 and again in 1281 Korea was compelled to provide ships and large contingents of fighting men for Kublai Khan's expeditions against Japan. In addition to imposing a heavy tax upon the country's resources Korea's participation in these two disastrous undertakings was productive of later misfortunes, since it aroused the bitter resentment of the Japanese and furnished Hideyoshi, three centuries later, with a colorable pretext for demanding that the Koreans co-operate in his proposed attack upon the Chinese Empire.

As a result of this absolute subservience to the Mongols and the constant infusion of Mongol blood into the royal family the later descendants of Wang Kien soon ceased to be in any real sense national rulers. So long as the Mongols retained their supremacy in China and Manchuria, Mongol support sufficed to maintain these princes upon the Korean throne; but the expulsion of the Mongols from China in 1368 was followed by nationalist uprisings in Korea, and in 1392 the last ruler of the discredited dynasty was overthrown.

During the first six centuries of the Christian Era the Korean peninsula, divided among the three kingdoms of Koguryu, Pakche, and Silla, played a more actively important role in Far Eastern history than in any subsequent period. The disintegration of the Chinese Han empire in the later years of the second century A.D. and the fact that Japan had not yet become a great power made it possible for the three Korean states to pursue their local rivalries, if not without intervention by these neighbors at least without the domination of either. At the same time these local rivalries and the consequent appeals, particularly by Pakche, for the military support of the Japanese quickened the flow of continental civilization through Korea into Japan.

From the opening of the seventh century, changing conditions condemned the Koreans to an increasingly passive role in international affairs. Japan had by this time begun to develop intercourse directly with China, and Korea's importance as a "cultural bridge" permanently declined. Although the peninsula now achieved a greater degree of political unity, first under the kings of Silla and later under the line established by Wang Kien, this fact was more than offset by the development of continental neighbors more formidable than those in previous centuries. The peninsula consequently lost its earlier freedom from political entanglements and was compelled to become a satellite to the successive empires which rose on its western frontier, the extreme depths of national humiliation being reached in the thirteenth century, when Korea was transformed into a mere province of the Mongol empire.

SUGGESTED REFERENCES

BRINKLEY, F., and KIKUCHI, D. A History of the Japanese People.
GRIFFIS, W. E. Corea, the Hermit Nation.
HULBERT, H. B. The History of Korea.
LONGFORD, J. H. The Story of Korea.
MURDOCH, J. A History of Japan, Vol. I.
ROSS, J. History of Corea.

XI

Japan: from Earliest Times to the Kamakura Shogunate

The Beginnings of Japan · The Legendary Character of Early Japanese History · Shinto, the "Way of the Gods" · Yamato in the Third Century · Contacts with Korea and with Chinese Culture · The Coming of Buddhism · The Growth of the Imperial Power · Shotoku Taishi · Direct Intercourse with China · The Taikwa Reforms · Nara and Kyoto · Cultural Development · The Rise of the Fujiwara · Tenth-Century Japan · Luxury and Frivolity of the Court · Condition of the Provinces · The Daimyo · The Monks of Hiyeisan · The Cloistered Emperors · Taira and Minamoto · The Military Domination of Kyoto · The Rule of the Taira · Minamoto Yoritomo · The Establishment of the Kamakura Shogunate · The Bakufu Organization · The Hojo Shikken · New Sects of Buddhism · Japan's Relations with China after the Ninth Century · Summary

THE group of islands which now constitute the Japanese Empire was certainly inhabited by man for many centuries before the dawn of history. Archaeological research has unearthed no certain evidence of paleolithic culture in the islands, but the existence there of a well-developed neolithic culture has been definitely established. It is possible, but not certain, that the authors of this neolithic culture were the ancestors of the modern Ainus, the Yemishi of the early Japanese chronicles, who are found chiefly in the island of Yezo and in the northern part of the main island—Honshu, or Hondo. The neolithic inhabitants and after them the Ainus—if indeed the Ainus are a different people— probably entered the islands from that part of the Asiatic mainland near the mouth of the Amur River, occupying first the island of Yezo and then the main island.

Sometime during the first millennium B.C., probably between the years 1000 and 500, the Ainus, having already occupied Yezo and a large part of Honshu, began to push their way southward in the island of Kyushu. In this southern island the Ainus soon found themselves confronted by a warlike people who seem to

Japan in Early Times

have entered Kyushu from the south not long before this meeting.
The origin of these newcomers, the ancestors of the present Japanese, has not been definitely determined. They certainly entered
Kyushu by sea, and they appear to have been closely related to
people who at about the same time settled in southern Korea. The
most generally accepted theory is that these new arrivals in Japan
and Korea were part of a maritime migration, possibly of Malay
origin, which had come northward along the eastern coast of Asia.

The newcomers gradually drove the Ainus out of Kyushu and followed them northward into Honshu, where, generations and perhaps centuries after their first arrival in the islands, they succeeded in gaining a firm foothold. Before the opening of the Christian Era the conquerors had made themselves the masters of western and central Honshu as far as the Gulf of Owari.

At this early period in their history the ancestors of the Japanese had developed very little political unity, and for a long time the area from which the Ainus had been expelled was occupied by a number of independent clans, each governed by its own chieftain. The most powerful of these clans was one occupying a region known as Yamato,[1] near the eastern end of the Inland Sea. In the course of time the chief of this clan gained more and more authority over the other local rulers, becoming at last the supreme ruler of a united people, but at the beginning of the Christian Era the real authority of the Yamato chief probably did not extend beyond the limits of the present province of that name. In the year 57 A.D., as we have seen in a previous chapter, the ruler of the state of Ito, which was located in the island of Kyushu, dispatched an envoy to the Chinese Han emperor at Loyang. The authority of the Yamato ruler was naturally less regarded in the southern island than in western Honshu, but even in the main island the local chieftains were at this time practically independent. The Chinese ambassador who visited the islands in reply to the Ito embassy records that there were thirty-two provinces in the country and that the rulers of these provinces, although acknowledging some duty to the Yamato overlord, each claimed the title of king.

The officially accepted history of Japan begins in the year 660 B.C., with the accession of the emperor Jimmu (Jimmu Tenno), the first human sovereign of the empire. Jimmu is regarded as the direct descendant of the Sun Goddess, whose divine descendants ruled for many ages before the accession of the first human ruler. Beginning with Jimmu Tenno, the Japanese histories record an unbroken line of monarchs directly descended from him, with

[1] With the unification of Japan the name *Yamato* was applied to the whole country; it is so used in the ancient histories and also in modern poetry.

the exact date of the beginning and the end of each reign. Yet the whole of this history, for more than a thousand years after the date given for Jimmu's accession, is decidedly legendary. The art of writing was not introduced into Japan until the beginning of the fifth century A.D., while the oldest existing historical works, the *Kojiki* ("Record of Ancient Matters") and the *Nihongi* ("Chronicles of Japan"), were not compiled until early in the eighth century. These two earliest historical collections were based partly upon oral tradition and partly upon older writings which have since been destroyed. From the year 405 A.D., which saw the introduction of writing into the country, the dates may be regarded as trustworthy; but exact dates for events which occurred before that time can be satisfactorily fixed only when such events are mentioned in the contemporary records of China or Korea.

It must not be assumed, however, that Japanese history prior to the fifth century is merely a collection of myths. Although rich in legendary and supernatural incidents, the *Kojiki* and the *Nihongi* were the result of painstaking efforts to reduce to writing what the eighth-century Japanese knew of their country's history. Modern historical scholarship, Western and Japanese scholars arriving independently at the same conclusion, has discovered the interesting fact that the chronology of the *Nihongi* for several centuries prior to 405 A.D. shows a consistent error of a hundred and twenty years.[1] With allowance for this error the Japanese and Korean records show a reasonable degree of harmony upon a number of events involving the relations between the two countries. It is therefore possible, while rejecting the obviously supernatural elements, to accept the Japanese chronology, with a discount of a hundred and twenty years, as fairly reliable for the events of internal history since the opening of the Christian Era.[2]

The present state religion of the Japanese, Shinto (the "Way of the Gods"), was already well developed at an early period in

[1] Events were assigned to dates a hundred and twenty years before they actually happened.

[2] But the officially accepted date for the accession of Jimmu Tenno, 660 B.C., is probably five or six centuries too early.

the history of the Yamato people. Essentially a nature worship and originating in sacrifices performed in honor of the *Kami* (the spirits of various natural objects and forces), Shinto at an early date became complicated by the injection of ancestor worship. The Kami of nature were innumerable; not merely sun and moon, thunder and lightning, and similar great natural forces, but also rivers, mountains, lakes, and even unusually large trees or peculiarly shaped rocks all had their separate Kami which must be worshiped with appropriate sacrifices. In addition to this multitude of nature spirits deceased ancestors and ancient heroes also came to be regarded as Kami.

Among these ancestral Kami a regular hierarchy developed. The deceased ancestors of a private family became the especial guardian spirits of the household; those of the clan chieftains became the chief Kami of their respective clans, while those of the Yamato clan—which eventually became the imperial clan—were accepted as the supreme Kami of the entire nation. In time also the two sets of Kami, the nature spirits and the deceased ancestors, tended to amalgamate. This amalgamation was especially notable in the case of the imperial family, whose earliest ancestor, as we have seen, has been identified for many centuries with the Sun Goddess. As a result of this identification the Japanese emperor has enjoyed for some two thousand years—and still enjoys—a "divine right" such as has been unknown to Western history since the days of imperial Rome.

The worship which was accorded to the Kami of Shintoism consisted almost exclusively of propitiatory sacrifices. Although there was some development of the art of divination, the practice of praying to the spirits appears never to have grown up. Unlike Christianity, Mohammedanism, Buddhism, and Brahmanism, the Japanese religion never evolved a body of sacred writings, a peculiarity which may be attributed to the fact that Shinto never became an ethical religion. It was from the beginning, and still is, the religion of a race of warriors by whom loyalty was regarded as the all-important virtue, and its moral teaching may be summed up in the single sentence "Honor the Gods and serve loyally their descendants."

By the opening of the third century A.D. the chieftains of all the clans in western Honshu, from the Gulf of Owari to the Strait of Shimonoseki, had recognized the descendant of the Sun Goddess as their suzerain. From this time, therefore, it is permissible to refer to these suzerains as the "sovereigns" of Yamato, although the Yamato organization was still essentially tribal in character. In the two southern islands of Kyushu and Shikoku the districts along the northern coasts also comprised a part of the Yamato state; but the southern portions of these two islands, although inhabited by related peoples, still remained wholly independent. In the eastern portion of Honshu the district around Tokyo Bay— the region later known as the Kwanto, or Eastern Plain—was also occupied by independent tribes whose rulers and peoples were closely related to those of Yamato. The remaining parts of Honshu and the northern island of Yezo were still held by the Ainus.

Since a large part of the people of southern Korea were related to the invaders who had reached Japan from the south, there had been from very early times considerable intercourse between the two countries. This intercourse was particularly active between Yamato and the loosely organized tribes of Kaya, at the southern extremity of the peninsula, and as late as the fifth century the Yamato government appears to have had more authority in Kaya, called by the Japanese Mimana, than it had over the people in the southern part of the island of Kyushu.

During the opening years of the third century A.D. Japanese history records the invasion of Korea by a great expedition under the empress Jingo. This ruler is said to have conquered the three Korean kingdoms, forcing their monarchs to do homage, to pay tribute, and to promise perpetual allegiance. According to the Korean records, which for this period must be regarded as more reliable than those of the Japanese, there was no great invasion of the peninsula at the date given by the Japanese historians, nor was there either a complete or even a partial subjugation by Japan of the kingdoms north of Kaya. Korean histories, however, do record, in 219, 233, and 249, three Japanese attacks, of increasing severity but all successfully repulsed, upon the eastern kingdom of Silla.

Although the alleged glorious expedition of the empress Jingo must be rejected as unsubstantiated, there is ample evidence that from early in the third century the Yamato state was in close contact with the several Korean kingdoms. With the kingdom of Pakche, on the western side of the peninsula, Yamato was usually on good terms, and in the course of the constant wars among the three Korean kingdoms the Pakche rulers frequently appealed to their Japanese friends for military assistance against their rivals. With Silla, on the other hand, the relations of the Japanese were almost as uniformly bad, and it was the rise of the power of this kingdom during the sixth and seventh centuries which finally destroyed Japanese influence in the peninsula.

Although it is possible that immigrants from China, as from Korea, had reached Japan in small numbers at various times before the opening of the Christian Era, such elements of Chinese civilization as reached the Yamato people before the third century A.D. appear to have come by way of the Korean kingdom of Pakche. After the collapse of the Chinese Han dynasty early in the third century the subsequent disorders impelled a considerable number of Chinese to take refuge in Korea and even in Japan.

During the fourth and fifth centuries the pressure of the Tartar invasions and conquests in northern China increased this flow of exiles into Korea and from there into the Japanese Islands, and a Japanese census taken about the year 450 recorded 18,670 Chinese or persons of Chinese descent among the population of western Honshu. These immigrants brought with them a number of China's industrial arts, some of which—such as the arts of sericulture and silk-weaving—were gradually adopted by the Japanese people.

As the refugees of this period included people of the upper classes as well as skilled artisans, they must have possessed some knowledge of the art of writing and some acquaintance with the socio-political ideas of Confucianism. Neither Confucianism nor the use of the Chinese ideographs, however, appears to have spread from the Chinese immigrants to the people and rulers of Yamato. The introduction of the use of written characters at the Yamato court can be definitely fixed as taking place in 405 A.D. In that year the king of Pakche sent to the Japanese sovereign a present of two fine horses, whose attendant was an accomplished scholar able to read and explain the Confucian Classics. This scholarly keeper of horses was appointed tutor of the heir apparent and instructed him in the mysteries of the Chinese written character as well as in the social maxims of Confucianism.

Like the art of writing, the faith of Gautama Buddha appears to have reached Japan some time before the date given for its formal introduction. In 522 a Chinese monk arriving in Yamato by way of Korea erected a temple containing an enshrined image of Buddha and attempted to spread Buddhist teachings among the people. This first missionary venture appears to have produced no results, and it was not until thirty years later that Buddhism was brought to the attention of the Yamato government.

In the year 552 the king of Pakche, threatened with a combined attack by Koguryu and Silla, appealed to the Yamato ruler for military assistance. Accompanying this appeal, he sent as presents a gold-plated copper image of a Buddha and a number of volumes of Buddhist scriptures. Kimmei Tenno, the Yamato sovereign, was deeply impressed by the statement of the Pakche envoys extolling the virtues of Sakyamuni's teachings, but he cautiously referred to his ministers for discussion the question as to whether the golden image should be worshiped.

The head of the powerful Soga family, the highest civil official of the court, expressed the opinion that Buddhism, having been accepted by the great nations of the west, should be adopted also by Japan. The more conservative military officials, on the other hand, argued that the worship of foreign gods would call down upon the nation the righteous anger of the national deities and would result in national disasters. Unable to decide this difficult question, Kimmei Tenno avoided committing himself; the new religion was neither definitely rejected nor officially adopted, and the image of Buddha was committed for safekeeping to the hands of the Soga chief.

During the century which followed this inconclusive debate the religious question gave rise to constant friction between the Soga family, who had become enthusiastic advocates of the cause of Buddhism, and their more conservative opponents. Throughout this century an increasing number of missionaries, artists, and scholars from Korea swelled the ranks of the Buddhist party, making it the party of art and learning, while in 660, after the conquest of Pakche by the Chinese, several thousand refugees from the defeated kingdom arrived in Japan, where they were cordially welcomed and were given lands upon which to settle. Long before 660, however, Buddhism had gained a definite ascendancy over the Shinto religion in court circles.

The ascendancy of Buddhism at the Yamato court was closely connected with the success of its patrons, the Sogas, in gaining absolute control over the affairs of government. Since the triumph of the Soga family was achieved by tactics which were subsequently imitated by each of the noble families whose dominance in governmental affairs marks the various periods of Japanese history, the story of their rise is of more than passing interest.

Soga Iname, the first champion of Buddhism, had married two of his daughters to the emperor Kimmei. As a result of these marriages his son, Soga Umako, who succeeded him as head of the family and as chief civil official of the Yamato court, was the uncle of three successive emperors, Bidatsu, Yomei, and Sushun, who ruled between 572 and 592, and of the empress Suiko, widow and half-sister of Bidatsu, who occupied the throne from 593 to 628. Soga Umako, moreover, still further strengthened the political position of the family by marrying one of his daughters to the famous Prince Shotoku (Shotoku Taishi), who as regent for his aunt, the empress Suiko, was later to administer the government in her name.

In 587, upon the death of the emperor Yomei, the opponents of the Soga family conspired to secure the accession of an anti-Soga and anti-Buddhist half-brother of the Soga nominee, Sushun. This conspiracy was promptly discovered and defeated; the unlucky rival candidate for the throne was killed, and the extermination of the prominent military officials who had organized the plot left the Sogas absolute masters of the situation.

Although the immediate outcome of the struggle reduced the nominal sovereign to the position of a mere puppet in the hands of the all-powerful Soga chieftain, the Soga triumph was an important step in the consolidation of the Yamato state and in the transformation of its ruler from the suzerain of a feudal aristocracy into an actual emperor. Two generations of further development were required for the completion of this transformation, and the feudal idea was destined to reappear in subsequent periods of Japanese history; but the triumph of the civil official, as represented by the Sogas, was a deathblow to the ancient quasi sovereignty of the military clan chieftain.

To no small extent this centralization of power under the emperor and his civil officials was aided by the rising influence of Buddhism. The military officials and the clan chieftains had long acknowledged the pre-eminence of the Sun Goddess and of her reputed descendants, who alone could pretend to the imperial throne; but from their own divine ancestors—despite the fact that these were less exalted than the Sun Goddess—they claimed independent powers which could not lawfully be infringed upon, even by the emperor himself. The decline of Shinto belief during the century which followed the introduction of Buddhism therefore made possible for the imperial government an assumption of authority which in an earlier period would have been regarded as an impious usurpation.

Prince Shotoku, who administered the government for twenty-eight years as regent for the empress Suiko, was both an imperial prince and, on his maternal side, a Soga; in addition he was a devout Buddhist, an accomplished Confucian scholar, and a man of extraordinary natural abilities. Throughout the entire period of his regency, which ended only with his death in 621, Shotoku labored for the attainment of two ideals. As a moral leader he strove to put the government of the nation upon a moral and religious basis rather than upon a foundation of sheer force. As acting head of the state he endeavored to complete the consolidation of the central power at the expense of the clan chiefs.

In the year 604 Shotoku drew up and issued an edict, known as the Seventeen-Article Constitution, in which he set forth the principles to be followed by all the officers of the state in the performance of their functions, repeatedly emphasizing the duty of ruling justly and benevolently the people under their control. The seventeen articles—really moral maxims—of Shotoku's so-called constitution are remarkable for their radicalism on two points. In the first place, this edict said absolutely nothing about the observance of Shinto rites or the worship of the Kami, while the second of the seventeen articles exhorted officials and people alike to reverence the "Three Treasures" of Buddhism—Buddha, the Law, and the Priesthood—as the only sure guides to a righteous life. The second, and even more revolutionary, feature of the edict is its unequivocal statement of imperial supremacy. The principle that the nobles and the officials of the empire are vassals of the emperor and have no authority except such as the emperor permits them to exercise in his name appears repeatedly throughout the seventeen articles, but it is most clearly asserted in the third and twelfth.

III. When you receive the Imperial Commands, fail not to obey scrupulously. The lord is Heaven; the vassal, Earth. Heaven overspreads; Earth upbears. When this is so, the four seasons follow their due course, and the powers of Nature develop their efficiency. If Earth attempts to overspread, Heaven falls in ruin. Hence when the lord speaks, the vassal hearkens; when the superior acts, the inferior yields compliance. When, therefore, you receive an Imperial Command, fail not to carry it out scrupulously. If there be any want of care in this respect, a catastrophe naturally ensues.

XII. Let not the provincial authorities or the *kuni no miyatsuko* levy exactions on the people. In a country there are not two lords; the people have not two masters. The sovereign is the master of the people of the whole country. The officials to whom he gives charge are all his vassals. How can they, as well as the Government, presume to levy taxes on the people?

Since the political ideals of Shotoku Taishi, as set forth in his edict of 604, were based on the political philosophy of Confucianism, the great regent realized that the ultimate triumph of these ideals demanded the support of a body of officials and scholars as well grounded as himself in the teachings of the Confucian Classics. In 607, therefore, Shotoku determined to open direct relations with the Chinese Empire, which had recently been reunited by the Sui precursors of the T'ang dynasty; and a Japanese embassy was dispatched to the imperial court at Loyang. A year later he sent a group of eight carefully selected scholars to China for the purpose of studying the institutions, laws, and political philosophy of the Chinese. Ten years after the dispatch of this educational mission the accession of the powerful T'ang dynasty to the Chinese imperial throne marked the beginning of the most glorious period in Chinese history, and the T'ang capital at Changan became the cultural center of the Far Eastern world, attracting to its great university an increasing number of scholars from Japan as well as from other countries of eastern and central Asia.

Of the eight scholars originally sent by Shotoku in 608, several remained in China until 632, while two of them—the *literatus* Kuromaro and the Buddhist priest Bin—returned to their native land only in 640, after an absence of thirty-two years, and played important roles in the political reorganization which occurred shortly after their return.

THE TAIKWA REFORMS

The work of Shotoku Taishi was incomplete. Connected through his paternal grandmother, his mother, and his wife with the Soga family and compelled to depend upon the assistance of his powerful uncle and father-in-law, Soga Umako, Shotoku had reduced the political influence of all the rival clans only to leave the Soga clan in the enjoyment of unlimited power. During the twenty-four years which followed his death the evils of the clan system, as exemplified in the growing power and arrogance of the Sogas, became more and more glaring. They jealously excluded from the throne any of the Shotoku family and selected puppet monarchs through whom they ruled the country to their own profit. In 643 Soga Umako's son and grandson, who now dominated the government, exterminated the family of Shotoku and began to plot the actual seizure of the throne. Aroused by this development, Prince Naka-no-Oye organized a counter-conspiracy which overthrew the Sogas and put to death the two leaders.

The overthrow of the Sogas put the control of the imperial government in the hands of two unusually able men: Prince Naka-no-Oye, who was later to become the emperor Tenchi, and Nakatomi-no-Kamatari, one of the shrewdest statesmen in Japanese history and the ancestor of the famous Fujiwara family. Before carrying out their coup these two leaders determined upon a complete reorganization of the government, to be accomplished by abolishing the old administrative system and by establishing new institutions patterned after those of T'ang China. The hereditary officialdom was to be abolished, the whole nation was to be brought directly under the authority of the throne, and the emperor's title to the ownership of all the land in the empire was to be established.

Through the next twenty-five years Kamatari and Prince Naka-no-Oye, aided by a number of the scholars who had spent years in China studying the philosophy and the institutions of that country, worked out the practical details of this reorganization. Because of the fact that the year 645, in imitation of the Chinese system of naming year-periods, was made the first year of the Taikwa period, the sweeping changes which began in that year are known as the Taikwa reforms.

Upon the overthrow of the Soga domination the reigning sovereign, the empress Kogyoku, immediately abdicated the throne. Prince Naka-no-Oye, who was her lawful heir, could have succeeded to the imperial title. Upon the advice of Kamatari, however, he chose to carry out the work of reform in the less exalted position of regent, and he allowed an uncle, brother of the recent empress, to assume the nominal power. Not until 668, twenty-three years after the inauguration of the reform movement, did Naka-no-Oye finally ascend the throne, as Emperor Tenchi, for a brief reign of three years. Throughout the twenty-three years of his regency and the first year of his reign as emperor, Naka-no-Oye had the loyal support of Kamatari, who occupied the important but inconspicuous post of Minister of the Interior. After the death of Kamatari in 669 the emperor conferred upon his descendants the family name of Fujiwara ("Wisteria") in memory, it is said, of the wisteria arbor where, many years before, the two conspirators had met to lay their plans.

In order to avoid arousing the suspicions and the hostility of the conservatively minded officials and of the still influential fragments of the old clans the first steps taken by the reformers were slow and cautious. They began by adopting the Chinese calendar and by creating three high ministers of state, whose titles were new but whose duties seemed to be little different from those of the earlier court officials. At the coronation of the new emperor all the officers were required to take a new oath of allegiance. The next move was the appointment of imperial governors, rather than hereditary territorial lords, for the eight eastern provinces, where the recently displaced Ainus still made it necessary to maintain strong military garrisons. In imitation of the early rulers of China the imperial government instituted a "complaint box," in which any injured subject might deposit petitions for redress or formal complaints against unjust officials.

From these cautious first steps the reformers proceeded with steadily increasing assurance. Each step served to strengthen their position still further, and each increase in strength made it possible for them to take fresh measures for the centralization of political power. The appointment of imperial governors for the eastern provinces was followed by the creation of similar officers for the less troubled areas. Many of the new posts were filled by the appointment of men who formerly had been clan chieftains in the same districts, but the strict regulations and the detailed instructions issued by the throne left these appointees with but a vestige of their earlier power. Finally, as the culminating step, Prince Naka-no-Oye and his associates annulled all existing titles to private ownership of land, declared all the land in the empire to be the property of the crown, and allowed the former owners to occupy and to cultivate the soil on payment of an annual rent or tax.

By the end of the reign of the emperor Tenchi in 671 the reorganization of the central government had been completed. In the general administration of national affairs the emperor was assisted by a Great Council of State consisting of five members: the Chancellor, the Minister of the Left, the Minister of the Right, the Minister of the Interior, and the head of the Ministry of the Imperial Household, who served as Lord of the Privy Seal. Below the Great Council were eight boards, or ministries: the already mentioned Ministry of the Imperial Household, the Ministry of Ceremonies and Civil Offices, the Ministry of Rites, the Ministry of Domestic Affairs, the Ministry of War, the Ministry of Justice, the National Treasury, and the Treasury of the Imperial Household. Subordinate to these eight ministries were various bureaus, about a hundred in number, with oversight over the multitude of administrative details.

Although the machinery of the reorganized government closely imitated the institutions of contemporary China, the Taikwa reformers failed to adopt the most important feature of the Chinese system: the selection of imperial officials by means of competitive examinations open to all men of ability, without family or class distinction. They did establish an imperial university and draw up regulations providing that official appointments and promotions should depend upon knowledge and ability rather than upon rank, but only the sons of noble families could obtain admission to the university and thus meet the educational qualifications for official appointment. As a result of this failure officeholding in Japan remained a caste privilege. The imperial officials were recruited from a small upper-class group of the nation, while capable and ambitious men of other classes, whose lack of family rendered them ineligible for a political career, were attracted into the Buddhist priesthood or into the career of arms, both of which remained open to all classes. Church and army thus became more and more powerful as rivals of the imperial government. On the other hand, the aristocratic official class, unlike the widely recruited civil officials of the Chinese Empire, had little sympathy for the common people or interest in the general welfare, and they constantly strove to utilize their power for the special benefit of the highly privileged social group to which they belonged.

NARA AND KYOTO

Prior to the Taikwa reforms the Japanese sovereigns had felt no need for a permanent capital, and the imperial court had been accustomed to change its location with the accession of each new emperor. After the reorganization of the government, however, it was felt necessary to establish the court permanently at some convenient place where the Great Council, the eight boards, and the hundred or so subordinate bureaus could be provided with suitable offices in which to carry on their work of administration. In

710 Nara was chosen as the site for the capital, and a splendid city was built, resembling as closely as possible the imperial city of the T'angs at Changan.

For seventy-four years Nara continued to be the capital of the empire and the center of its artistic, literary, and religious life. In 784, however, the emperor Kwammu, in order to diminish the political influence of the numerous Buddhist institutions which had grown up around Nara, decided to transfer his government to a new location. For a few years the court resided at Nagaoka, but in 794 this site was abandoned and Kyoto was chosen as the capital. Here the emperor's architects, once more taking the Chinese capital as their model, built the city which was to serve for more than a thousand years as the capital of the Japanese Empire.

Throughout the seventh and eighth centuries the influence of Chinese ideas, supplemented during the seventh century by those of Korea, was apparent in every phase of Japanese development. In the regency of Shotoku and in the period of the Taikwa reforms, as we have seen, Chinese political institutions and Confucian philosophy were the guide and inspiration of the architects of the new social order. In matters of government and law the dominance of Chinese ideas continued until the end of the eighth century, and the two great eighth-century law codes—the Taiho Laws of 700–701 and the Yoro Code of 718—were both based upon the code of the T'ang dynasty.

In nonpolitical matters Japan's debt to her continental neighbors was equally notable. From the days of Shotoku Taishi we find the imperial court patronizing architecture, sculpture, painting, and literature, in all of which continental models were followed. Similar encouragement was given to the development of ceramics, the casting of metals, and the various other arts and crafts which the Chinese and the Koreans had introduced into the land.

Pre-Buddhist architecture in Japan was of a most primitive sort, and the temple buildings at Horyuji, erected in 607 by Shotoku with the assistance of Korean architects and workmen, began the development of the splendid religious architecture of Japanese Buddhism. The Chinese-Korean influence also extended to domestic architecture, and Japanese dwelling houses from this time gradually lost their earlier half-subterranean form. The almost exclusive use of wood as building material during the early periods quickly led to certain modifications in details, but Japanese architecture down to the nineteenth century showed clearly its Korean origin.

Equally permanent was the continental influence upon the related arts of sculpture and painting, which were especially affected by the great artists of T'ang China, while the Kamakura Daibutsu, erected in the thirteenth century, marks the culmination of the art of bronze-casting which was introduced in the seventh century by the Korean artist Tori Busshi.

Until the invention, in the ninth century, of the *Kana* syllabic script the Japanese had no form of writing other than the Chinese ideographic characters. From China, therefore, came also their models of literary excellence. The extent to which the Japanese writers imitated their Chinese models can best be illustrated by a comparison of their two early historical compilations, the *Kojiki* and the *Nihongi*. In the older of these two works, compiled in the year 712, the legends and traditions of ancient times were collected and written down in very simple style. This work, however, failed to measure up to Chinese literary standards; and eight years later the task was performed in more approved style by the authors of the *Nihongi*, who made their chronicle more impressive by the inclusion of events borrowed from Chinese history and by putting into the mouths of their own early rulers long speeches taken from the recorded utterances of Chinese emperors.

From China and Korea came the earliest standardized weights and measures, while the closing years of the seventh century or the opening years of the eighth saw the introduction from China of the use of gold, silver, and copper coins.

Even the name *Dai Nippon*, by which the empire is now known to its own people, and the western derivative *Japan* are of Chinese origin. Early in the Nara period a communication from the Chinese emperor addressed the island ruler as emperor of "Tai-nyih-pung-kok" (literally: "Great-Sun-Origin-Kingdom"). This fine-sounding designation impressed the Japanese scholars and officials as being highly appropriate, and it quickly displaced the earlier indigenous name *Yamato*. Centuries later the Venetian

Marco Polo, while in China, heard the island empire referred to as *Nyih-pung-kok* or *Jih-pung-kok*. When Marco, still later, dictated in a Genoese prison the story of his travels, his fellow prisoner and amanuensis, Rustician, transcribed the name as *Chipango*, from which ultimately came the modern western form, *Japan*.

THE PERIOD OF FUJIWARA DOMINATION

Although the Taikwa reformers had hoped by their thorough reorganization of the imperial government to free the country for all time from the evils of clan domination, less than two centuries were to elapse before a new family succeeded in gathering into its hands powers even more absolute than those wielded by the Sogas. By the irony of fate the family which was thus to frustrate the hopes of the reformers was the Fujiwara, descended from Nakatomi-no-Kamatari and bearing the name given by the emperor Tenchi to this faithful lieutenant in memory of the wisteria arbor under which the reforms had been planned. After the death of Kamatari his son held high office in the imperial government and married his daughters to two successive emperors. For a short period during the first part of the eighth century the Fujiwara family fell into disfavor, but the minister who secured the accession of the emperor Kwammu in 782 and that monarch's most trusted adviser both were Fujiwaras. The real supremacy of the family, however, did not begin until about half a century after Kwammu, acting on the advice of his Fujiwara minister, had transferred his capital to Kyoto.

In 842 Fujiwara Yoshifusa, two of whose sisters were wives of the reigning emperor, succeeded in having the heir apparent sent into exile and his own young nephew designated as heir to the throne. Nine years later this nephew ascended the throne as the emperor Montoku and married one of Yoshifusa's daughters. At the same time Yoshifusa was appointed Minister of the Right, and a few years later he was promoted from this post to that of chancellor. In 858, on the death of Montoku, Yoshifusa's infant grandson became emperor, and the grandfather assumed the office of regent, which hitherto had never been held by anyone except a prince of the imperial family. Father of the empress dowager, grandfather of the emperor, chancellor and regent of the empire, the head of the Fujiwara family was now firmly established in a position of dictatorial power.

For more than two hundred years the supremacy of the Fujiwara family was maintained by tactics similar to those adopted by Yoshi- fusa. Successive emperors were compelled to accept in marriage ladies of the Fujiwara clan, and only the sons of Fujiwara em- presses were permitted to ascend the throne. If the emperor was a child, as was usually the case, his Fujiwara uncle or grandfather assumed the office of regent. During the usually short period between an emperor's attainment of his majority and his forced abdication in favor of an infant son the Fujiwara regent took the title *Kwampaku* ("Mayor of the Palace") and continued to rule with unimpaired powers.

The centralization of the imperial power by the Taikwa reforms had been followed by a steady expansion of the territory over which the emperor's authority was recognized. By the end of the ninth century the whole of the islands of Kyushu and Shikoku acknowl- edged the imperial power; imperial governors ruled over the Kwanto and over the region lying between the Kwanto and Kyoto, while the imperial commanders in the northeast were driving the barbarian Ainus farther and farther toward the northern extremity of the main island. This expansion of the empire involved a con- stant increase in the functions of the central government. The maintenance of internal order, the administration of justice, the collection of taxes, the organization and direction of the military forces operating against the Ainus, all combined to throw an in- creasing burden of responsibility upon the bureaucratic officials at Kyoto.

In the face of these increasing responsibilities the tenth century witnessed a correspondingly steady decline in the efficiency of the central organization. Fujiwara Yoshifusa and his two earliest suc- cessors, Mototsune and Tokihira, had been men of unusual ability; after them the successive heads of the Fujiwara family were con- spicuous chiefly for their extravagance and for the jealousy with which they guarded their traditional privileges. At the capital the

Fujiwara domination of the court remained absolute, but in the provinces the power and prestige of the Kyoto government steadily declined.

During the tenth century the luxury, extravagance, and frivolity of court life at Kyoto were carried to an extreme which has seldom been equaled in the history of Japan. In the mad rivalry of competitive spending which prevailed, there was more than one case of a noble's laying out a whole year's income for a single suit of clothes or for a single banquet. Men as well as women plucked their eyebrows, powdered and rouged their faces, and stained their teeth black. Popular pastimes among the court nobles and ladies took the form of competitions in writing love letters or in recognizing the fragrance of the various kinds of perfumes. When the cherry trees were in bloom or during the season for any of the favorite flowers, the whole court went on picnics to enjoy the beauty of the scene, and prizes were given to the persons who composed the most graceful verses describing the occasion. Music, dancing, the writing of dainty verses, and the display of taste in landscape gardening were the accomplishments best calculated to win favor and promotion at the court.

Chinese was still the language of all serious literature, and scholarship was still held, nominally at least, in high esteem; but few men of ability or ambition were attracted by the empty rewards of scholarship, and the serious writers of the period produced little that was either original or lasting. Alongside this dead or dying scholarly literature in Chinese, however, a new style of literature was developing to reflect the real interests of the age. This new literature, written in Japanese idiom by the use of the syllabic Kana script, flowered first in the graceful verses of the poetry contests. Later the Kana writing came also to be used for prose works, the most important of which in the tenth century were a number of monogatari,[1] or romantic narratives, written chiefly by ladies of the court or by male authors masquerading under feminine noms de plume.

[1] *The Genji Monogatari* ("*The Tale of Genji*"), by Lady Murasaki, is one of the greatest of these narratives and has been made available to Western readers in the translation of Arthur Waley.

Little of the luxury and culture which characterized the court life at Kyoto could be found among the rude rustics and the hard-handed soldiers of the provinces.

Under the emperor Kwammu (782–805) and under his successors down to the middle of the ninth century much had been done to foster agriculture and to encourage the development of trade. In 799 the planting of cotton had been introduced from India, while fifteen years later the tea plant, brought from China, began to be cultivated in some of the central provinces. Nimmyo Tenno (834–850) had encouraged the cultivation of wheat, buckwheat, barley, beans, and sorghum, and had commanded the use of the "paddy loom," upon which the sheaves of rice were dried before being threshed, an innovation which proved to be of considerable value to the rice farmer. For the encouragement of trade Kwammu had constructed roads, had issued coined money, and had ordered the establishment of wayside food shops so that the traveler might be freed from the necessity of carrying with him the food for his journey.

After the rise of the Fujiwaras, however, the central administration ceased to interest itself in these sordid but important matters. The demands of the luxury-loving capital were reflected in a growing burden of taxation upon the farmer and the trader; a constantly increasing supply of forced labor was utilized for beautifying the gardens and palaces of the court, while the roads were neglected and allowed to fall into disrepair. Travel at any distance from the capital became more and more difficult, partly because of the ruined condition of the roads and partly because of the bands of desperate men—brigands on land and pirates on sea—who preyed upon the steadily declining commerce.

With the increasing extravagance and ineptitude of the imperial court and with the development of confusion and disorder in the provinces there came the rise of a new military aristocracy whose power was to rival and eventually to overshadow that of the imperial government.

One of the most important steps taken by the Taikwa reformers had been the abolition of all private ownership of the land, which henceforth was to be exclusively the property of the crown. Hardly more than half a century after the death of the emperor Tenchi, however, the first step was taken in the direction of undoing this all-important reform: in 723 a decree was issued granting absolute title, for three generations, to those who reclaimed and brought under cultivation hitherto unused lands. Twenty years later a fresh decree made the private ownership of such lands perpetual but attempted to restrict the area of a single manor, or *shoen*, to 1250 acres; this limit, however, was not enforced, and the manors became steadily larger. Since the reclaimed lands were not liable to the regular land tax, the peasant holders of "old" lands evaded the tax by settling upon the land of some near-by manor; their former holdings, thus becoming wasteland, would eventually be reclaimed and taken into the expanding manor as tax-free. In addition to these fraudulently reclaimed lands other tracts of land passed from the control of the crown by being granted in perpetuity as rewards for distinguished service or as marks of favor to the nobles of the court.

The tax-free lands, especially those reclaimed from waste, went by the name of the family which held them and came to be known as *myoden*, or "name land"; the holders of great tracts of land were called *daimyo* ("great names"), while those whose manors were less extensive were known as *shomyo* ("small names"). Unable to exercise effective control outside the districts in the immediate vicinity of Kyoto, the tenth-century Fujiwaras made increasing use of the daimyo, who with their armed retainers were more successful than any civil official could hope to be in the suppression of highway robbery or in the collection of taxes.

In the eastern districts of the main island, where the lands conquered from the Ainus were granted in great tracts to the military leaders by whom the wars had been conducted, the daimyo became especially powerful. By the middle of the eleventh century the territorial magnates of the Kwanto were practically independent rulers who regarded with open contempt the civil officials of the imperial government. Many miles of mountainous country, almost without roads, lay between the Kwanto and the capital; and the Kwanto daimyo, when not engaged in campaigns against the Ainus, waged bitter private wars among themselves without fear of inter-

ference from the Kyoto authorities. To the Fujiwara organization
the rise of this military aristocracy was especially dangerous because of the fact that a number of the most powerful daimyo families of the Kwanto were founded by men whom the Fujiwara
dictators had jealously forced into practical exile. So long as the
daimyo were engaged in their private feuds the capital had little
to fear; but if at any time one great family should succeed in crushing its local rivals, the civil government would be helpless to resist
its power.

While by the middle of the eleventh century the rising power
of the daimyo had replaced the authority of the imperial government in the distant provinces, a second decentralizing factor, almost equally serious, was growing up at the very gates of the
capital.

When the emperor Kwammu in 784 moved his court from Nara
and eventually established a new capital at Kyoto, one of his purposes had been the withdrawal of the imperial administration from
the influence of the powerful Buddhist institutions which had
grown up at the old capital. The Nara monastic orders, which
belonged chiefly to the Hosso and Kegon sects, were so firmly
rooted by their extensive buildings that they were unable to transfer themselves to the new metropolis; but the opening years of
the ninth century saw the founding of two new Buddhist sects:
the Tendai, established in 805 by Dengyo Daishi, and the Shingon,
which was founded four years later by Kobo Daishi. Both these
new schools of Buddhism established themselves at the capital:
the Tendai located on Hiyeisan, a hill to the northeast of the
city, while the Shingon had its headquarters in the temple known
as Toji.

Although both the new sects played important roles in the subsequent development of Japanese Buddhist thought, the Tendai
sect, which from the beginning of its career enjoyed imperial
patronage, combined with its spiritual importance a great deal
of political power. On the slopes of Hiyeisan there grew up a
number of great monasteries, such as the Kofukuji, the Onjoji,
and the Enryakuji, endowed with immense wealth and sheltering
thousands of monks. Many of these monks, perhaps a majority,

were worthy followers of the founder of their religion; but the monasteries of Hiyeisan also sheltered many others of less saintly character: able-bodied peasants who chose the tonsure rather than brigandage as an avenue of escape from crushing taxation, and learned scholars whose abilities or ambitions found no opening in the aristocratic monopoly of civil office.

To this dangerous body of none too docile churchmen on the hills above the capital the Fujiwaras unwittingly provided a capable political leadership. In order to retain in their own hands the supreme control of the government the Fujiwara chiefs had adopted the policy of excluding from office all non-Fujiwaras who gave evidence of unusual ability or ambition, and they usually compelled such individuals to disqualify themselves for any further part in public affairs by taking the tonsure. As a result of this policy the Hiyeisan religious communities contained a number of clever politicians who were quite ready to work against the government and who had at hand in the thousands of turbulent monks a group of followers willing to lay aside the weapons of the spirit and to take up the sword.

Shortly after the middle of the eleventh century a shrewd and almost successful attempt was made to restore to the imperial family the power which had been wielded for more than two hundred years by its Fujiwara ministers.

In the year 1072 the emperor Sanjo II ("Go-Sanjo"), the first sovereign in many generations who was not the son of a Fujiwara mother, voluntarily abdicated the throne in favor of his son Shirakawa and retired to a monastery, where he planned to direct from cloistered seclusion the government of his successor. Sanjo II lived only about a year after his abdication, but fourteen years later Shirakawa, following his father's example, also retired to the cloister and ruled as the power behind the throne during the reigns of his son Horikawa and grandson Toba. In 1123 Toba likewise abdicated in favor of his infant son Sutoku and joined his grandfather in retirement. In 1128, after having dominated from the cloister for a period of forty-two years the governments of his son, grandson, and great-grandson, Shirakawa died, and the cloistered dictatorship was assumed by Toba.

For an additional twenty-eight years, until his own death in 1156, Toba continued the system of Sanjo II and Shirakawa. Throughout the seventy years following Shirakawa's abdication the "cloistered court" had left to the Fujiwara officials of the imperial palace only the outward ceremonies of government, all important decisions being made by the ex-emperor and his monastic entourage. In any clash of opinion between palace and cloister the former always had to give way, and Shirakawa, or in later years Toba, arranged the marriages in the imperial family, nominated successors to the throne, and controlled the all-important official appointments and grants of land.

THE TRIUMPH OF THE SOLDIER

From earliest times until the closing years of the eighth century all the sons of an emperor, together with their descendants to the fifth generation, were regarded as princes of the imperial clan. Beginning with the emperor Kwammu, however, a new policy was instituted: the younger sons of each sovereign, usually the sixth and succeeding sons, were reduced from imperial rank to the status of mere nobles and were given family names. As the emperors were usually plentifully supplied with sons, the number of new families thus created was considerable. The most prominent of these noble families of imperial origin were the Taira and the Minamoto. The Taira families were four in number, being descended from the four younger sons of Kwammu Tenno; the more numerous Minamoto families traced their descent from the sons of various later emperors.

The jealous monopoly of all the higher political offices at Kyoto by the Fujiwara family after the middle of the ninth century forced the more ambitious of the Taira and Minamoto nobles into the military profession. In this capacity they were utilized by the Fujiwara civilians as guardians of the peace in the capital and the home provinces or as commanders of expeditions against the Ainus and as military governors of the provinces at a distance. Although the semi-independent daimyo of the eastern provinces belonged to many different families and included even cadet

branches of the Fujiwaras, the most numerous and the most powerful members of this new military aristocracy were those of Taira
and Minamoto descent.

So numerous, indeed, were the various branches of these two
families that they adopted for convenience distinguishing territorial names, and Minamoto or Taira daimyo frequently engaged
in violent intrafamily feuds; but they never lost sight of the fact
that they were Minamoto or Taira, and the daimyo of each family
could usually be depended upon to support their kinsmen against
any outsider. Until early in the eleventh century the power in
the Kwanto was about equally divided between the two families.
In 1028, however, Taira Tadatsune undertook to bring the entire
Kwanto under his control; and the resulting struggle between
Taira and Minamoto ended in 1031 with the destruction of Taira
power in this region, where the Minamoto henceforth ruled supreme. Although thus defeated in the Kwanto, the Taira still possessed great power in the districts between the Kwanto and the
capital, especially in the province of Ise, which during the next
century became the center of the family organization.

Upon the death of the cloistered emperor Toba in 1156 the
political situation at the capital became chaotic. Toba in 1141
had forced his son Sutoku to abdicate and had replaced him by a
second son who ruled until 1155 as the emperor Konoe. Upon the
death of Konoe still a third son of Toba had ascended the throne
as Shirakawa II ("Go-Shirakawa"). Sutoku, already bitterly resentful because of his forced abdication in 1141, had been further
incensed by his failure to secure the accession of his own son as
the successor of Konoe. When Toba's death left Sutoku as the
single cloistered emperor, he therefore planned to set aside his
younger brother and to return to the throne. While this serious
split was developing in the imperial family, a similar division
was taking place in the ranks of the Fujiwaras; the *kwampaku*
Tadamichi supported the cause of the reigning emperor Shirakawa II, and his father and younger brother rallied to the side
of the ex-emperor Sutoku.

Both the party of the palace and that of the cloister now
turned for military assistance to the Taira and Minamoto fam-

ilies, and here also division occurred inside the families; Taira Kiyomori and Minamoto Yoshitomo supported Shirakawa II and the kwampaku, while the uncle of Kiyomori and the father of Yoshitomo took service on the side of the ex-emperor. After a brief but bitter struggle known as the Hogen insurrection Shirakawa and his supporters were victorious; the cloistered emperor was sent into exile, and his Fujiwara, Taira, and Minamoto supporters were put to death. In 1158, after reigning for two years, Shirakawa II abdicated in favor of his son and attempted to continue the policy of ruling from the cloister. But the real power at Kyoto had now definitely passed from the hands of the civilian to those of the soldier, against whom cloister and palace were equally defenseless.

After the defeat of Sutoku's attempt to return to the throne jealousy and friction quickly developed between the Taira and Minamoto leaders to whom Shirakawa had owed his triumph. In January, 1160, this jealousy came to a head in a desperate struggle known as the Heiji Tumult. Taira Kiyomori was victorious, and Minamoto Yoshitomo, with all his kinsmen at the capital except four of his young sons, was put to death. Of the four Minamoto children who escaped the general slaughter one was the fourteen-year-old Yoritomo, who twenty years later was to be the avenger of his family. For the present, however, the Taira was supreme.

For twenty-one years after his triumph over the Minamoto, Taira Kiyomori held dictatorial power at Kyoto and in the provinces. Setting aside the unwritten law which excluded military men from the higher civil offices, Kiyomori had himself appointed councilor of state, while the appointment of his relatives and trusted friends as provincial governors gave him control over the military forces of the empire.

Nor did the Taira chieftain neglect to consolidate his political position by the time-honored methods of the Fujiwaras. In 1160 he gave his sister in marriage to the cloistered emperor Go-Shirakawa, and in 1169 a child of this marriage ascended the imperial throne. Uncle of the reigning emperor, Kiyomori now had himself appointed to the offices of chancellor and regent. Seven years later the imperial nephew received in marriage one of

Kiyomori's daughters, and the prince who was born the following year was immediately recognized as Prince Imperial. Finally, in 1180, Kiyomori forced the abdication of his nephew and placed upon the throne his three-year-old grandson.

The fortunes of the Taira family were now at full flood. Kiyomori ruled the empire in the name of the infant emperor, the majority of the important civil and military posts were occupied by his relatives, and during the last twenty years he had gathered into his hands enormous wealth. But already the ground was beginning to crumble beneath his feet. At the capital the arrogance and avarice of the Taira family had aroused the smoldering hatred of all the non-Taira nobility and had reduced the common people to almost indescribable misery. Already, in 1177 and 1179, Kiyomori had been called upon to crush incipient insurrections, and in 1180 a fresh revolt against his domination narrowly missed success. This insurrection at Kyoto, like the others, was suppressed; but in faraway Kwanto, Minamoto Yoritomo had now raised the standard of a revolt far more formidable than the half-hearted plots of the intriguers at the capital. In March, 1181, Kiyomori died, demanding of his sons and grandsons that no tomb or tablet be erected to his memory until the head of Yoritomo had been placed upon his grave.

For twenty years following the Kyoto disaster of 1160, Yoritomo had resided in the Kwanto, at first in the custody of a Fujiwara daimyo, Ito Sukechika, and later under the oversight of a Taira named Hojo Tokimasa. The Minamoto fighting men matured early, and Yoritomo at the age of fourteen had carried arms against the Taira; but the twenty years of his quasi imprisonment brought to him an intellectual activity and maturity which were less common among the nobles of his day. It was only natural that a Minamoto should brood over the humiliation of his family and plot vengeance against the victorious Taira; in addition to this, however, he appears to have pondered the causes for the disaster and to have reached the conclusion that military men residing in the capital could not hope to hold their own with court intriguers or to escape the corrupting influence of unaccustomed luxury.

In his political education and in establishing valuable contacts with the daimyo of the Kwanto the young Minamoto exile was greatly assisted by the second of his two custodians. Hojo Tokimasa was a real political genius who, although a member of the Taira family, had no love for his powerful relatives at the capital and hoped that a revolt organized in the Kwanto might furnish him with an opportunity to achieve national power and distinction. In time, also, a new bond developed between the prisoner-pupil and his tutor-custodian. Yoritomo won the heart of Tokimasa's young daughter, and the calculating Hojo daimyo, giving his consent to a marriage which might have involved him in ruin, became the father-in-law of Japan's future dictator.

In the late summer of 1180 Yoritomo learned that Taira Kiyomori had issued orders for his execution. Realizing that the time for action had arrived, he raised the white standard of the Minamoto and assumed the aggressive. At first his little handful of retainers barely escaped annihilation at the hands of the local Taira military governor, but soon his forces were swelled by a steady stream of recruits from all parts of the east and north. Not only the Minamoto but all who had suffered from the oppression of Kiyomori hastened to take the field to strike a blow for the destruction of Taira rule.

By the summer of 1182 the Taira forces in the Kwanto had been destroyed, and the Minamoto armies were free to advance upon the capital. In August of the following year the Taira were driven from Kyoto. They still held a great deal of power in the west; but the two years which followed their expulsion from the capital saw the Taira standard steadily pushed back, and the last remnants of their force were finally destroyed in April, 1185, in the naval battle of Dan-no-ura, which was fought at the western end of the Inland Sea near the Strait of Shimonoseki.

The three years following the decisive battle of Dan-no-ura saw the ranks of the Minamoto momentarily broken by a fratricidal struggle in which Yoritomo was arrayed against his young half-brother Yoshitsune, the most brilliant military leader of the period. Yoshitsune's failure to return promptly to the Minamoto headquarters and his continued sojourn at Kyoto after the defeat of the Taira had aroused in his merciless superior the suspicion that he had fallen under the influence of the court, which would forthwith adopt its old policy of playing off two military leaders against each other. Nothing that the younger brother could say or do served to dissipate this suspicion, and Yoritomo did not rest content until Yoshitsune had been hounded to death and his descendants exterminated.

By the summer of 1189 Yoritomo had gained military control over the entire empire and had established at Kamakura, near the modern city of Yokohama, a "camp capital" from which his military administration was to be directed. Not until the winter of 1190–1191, however, did the Minamoto chief visit Kyoto, for the first time since he had left it as an exile after the Heiji tumult of 1160, to pay his respects to the emperor. During the course of this visit, which lasted only a few months, he received appointment as lord constable of the empire, and in 1192 a commission was issued appointing him to the post of *Sei-i-tai-Shogun* ("Barbarian-Subduing Great General").

The office of Sei-i-tai-Shogun (briefly, Shogun), which conferred upon its holder absolute authority over all the military forces of the empire, had been created about the beginning of the ninth century. Hitherto appointments to this post had been made only at times of great national emergency, and the Shogun, like the dictator of ancient Rome, had always resigned his office at the end of the crisis for which he had been vested with supreme command. Yoritomo's appointment, however, was not limited in time; he was to be Shogun for life, and on his death the title was to pass to the person whom he should designate as his successor.

With the creation of the Shogunate as a hereditary office the administrative control of the empire passed definitely from Kyoto to the military capital which Yoritomo had established at Kamakura. At Kyoto the emperor still sat upon his throne, and the courtiers still plotted and intrigued; but the actual government of the country was centered at Kamakura, where it was administered by the Shogun and his advisers. The Kamakura Shogunate, established by Yoritomo in 1192, held the supreme power until it was overthrown a hundred and forty-one years later by Emperor

Daigo II ("Go-Daigo") ; but the Shogunal system, whereby the supreme authority lay in the hands of a military vice-regent, continued for more than five centuries longer and was finally abolished only in 1867 at the beginning of the Meiji era.

For the systematic administration of the affairs under his control Yoritomo created at Kamakura an organization known as the *Bakufu*, or "camp office." The name, however, belies the character of this administrative machine. Because of the military basis of the Shogun's authority emphasis was naturally placed upon the ordering of military affairs. Yet the problems of taxation, of the administration of justice, and the like required for their solution qualities of mind which are not always found in the warrior, and this fact was recognized by Yoritomo. The highest posts in the Bakufu were entrusted to daimyo of proved loyalty and ability, but the Shogun strengthened his organization by attracting to Kamakura a large number of trained scholars to serve as members of his various boards. Indeed, the long period of supremacy enjoyed by the Kamakura Shogunate is only partly attributable to the military power of the Minamotos; to an equal, perhaps to a greater, extent it may be attributed to the fact that, while in Kyoto the holding of office was still a matter of birth and favoritism, at Kamakura appointment and promotion were, for the greater part of the hundred and forty-one years, determined by ability and character.

Even as the Japanese emperors had long been figureheads in whose name the government was directed by the Fujiwaras, by the "cloistered emperors," by the Taira, and finally by the Shoguns, so also the successors of Yoritomo, after his death in 1199, became mere puppet rulers, and the actual power of the Shogunate was exercised by ministers who managed affairs in the Shogun's name. By far the most important of the ministers at Kamakura, and the one who quickly became the real power behind the puppet Shoguns, was the *shikken*, or regent.

During the lifetime of Yoritomo this office was held by his astute father-in-law and early preceptor, Hojo Tokimasa. The career of Tokimasa ended in 1205, when he was exiled in consequence of his participation in an unsuccessful intrigue. Although the direct line of Yoritomo became extinct in 1219, the office of Shogun after this date being held by collateral members of the Minamoto family or by imperial princes, the office of shikken remained in the Hojo family throughout the entirer period of the Kamakura Shogunate. In 1221 the cloistered emperor made an attempt to destroy the power of the Shogunate; but on this occasion the prompt action of the Hojo shikken resulted in a decisive victory for Kamakura, and two officials of the Shogunate, usually members of the Hojo family, henceforth resided at Kyoto to maintain a careful watch over the political situation at the capital.

Probably no family in the history of Japan has produced an unbroken succession of public officials who surpass or even equal in ability the nine Hojo who held the office of shikken in the Kamakura Shogunate; and it is also probable that during the thirteenth and early fourteenth centuries no country in the world enjoyed a more efficient government, more complete internal peace, and greater prosperity than Japan.

As we have already seen, there were by the beginning of the ninth century four leading sects, or denominations, among the Japanese Buddhists: the earlier Hosso and Kegon sects, whose principal establishments were at Nara, and the newly formed Tendai and Shingon sects at Kyoto. For nearly four centuries no important addition was made to this list, and such new groups as arose deviated only slightly from the teachings of the older body from which they were offshoots.

After the establishment of the Shogunate the intellectual freedom which prevailed at Kamakura and the especially favorable attitude of the Minamoto toward religion were reflected in a remarkable revival of religious speculation. In little more than half a century, between 1192 and 1252, four important new Buddhist sects arose: the Jodo, the Shin, the Zen, and the sect of Nichiren, which takes its name from the puritanical preacher by whom it was founded. The teachings of these four sects were characterized by an extreme simplicity of doctrine and indicated a growing desire to get away from the metaphysical subleties of the earlier theology. The sect of Nichiren, after a period of considerable activity, gradually declined in influence; but the other three now share with the ninth-century Shingon sect of Kobo Daishi the greatest numerical strength of modern Japanese Buddhism.

The decline of the Chinese T'ang dynasty during the latter part of the ninth century coincided with the decay, under the Fujiwaras, of Japan's central administration, and both developments affected disastrously the relations between the two empires. The waning prestige of the Chinese court led to an almost complete discontinuance of official embassies from Japan, while the prevalence of banditry and piracy in Japan spelled ruin for Japanese commerce, foreign as well as domestic. Even during the periods of greatest disorder, however, some intercourse was maintained between the two countries: Chinese merchant ships arrived from time to time at Japanese ports, especially at those of Kyushu, Chinese goods being eagerly sought by Japanese consumers, and Japanese religious devotees continued to seek instruction at the great Buddhist monasteries in China.

With the overthrow of the Fujiwaras and the establishment of military rule in Japan, relations with China again became more intimate, and in 1173 the Taira regent Kiyomori dispatched an official embassy to the Southern Sung capital at Hangchow, where it was cordially received. The intercourse thus reopened by the Taira dictator was continued under the Minamotos, and the kindly treatment accorded by the Chinese government to the passengers and crews of shipwrecked Japanese vessels indicates both the extent of the growing commerce and the keenness of the Chinese desire to see it continue.

The results of this revived intercourse, which continued for nearly a century after Kiyomori's embassy, were of considerable importance to Japan. In 1191, the year preceding Yoritomo's appointment to the office of Shogun, the Buddhist monk Eisai returned from a long sojourn in China, bringing with him not only the doctrines of Zen Buddhism but also some seeds of the tea plant. On the occasion of its earlier introduction, in 814, tea had failed to achieve any popularity in Japan, and its cultivation had soon been discontinued; but this time the Chinese beverage struck the popular fancy, and the Japanese people quickly came to regard it as a highly prized luxury.

In 1215 Sanetomo, Yoritomo's son and second successor as Shogun, employed a Chinese shipbuilder to oversee the construction at Kamakura of a ship built along Chinese lines. This ship, in which Sanetomo is said to have planned a visit to China, was a failure; but the introduction of "bills of exchange," which made their first appearance about that date in the trade of Kamakura, has been attributed to the young Shogun's Chinese shipbuilder.

In ceramics, as in shipbuilding, the thirteenth-century Japanese were still decidedly behind their continental neighbors. The growing popularity of tea as a beverage, however, soon created a demand for fine pottery to be used in connection with the "tea ceremonial," and in 1223 a Japanese potter visited China to study the methods of the Chinese porcelain-makers, returning in 1230 to become the first producer of glazed porcelain in Japanese history.

After about a hundred years of peaceful intercourse relations between China and Japan were again interrupted, in the second half of the thirteenth century, by the Mongol conquest of China and by Kublai Khan's subsequent attempt to extend his power over the island empire. The Mongol attack was repulsed, and Japan, for another century or more, again reverted to a state of insular isolation.

The establishment of the Kamakura Shogunate in 1192 marks the end of eighteen and a half centuries since the accession of the legendary first emperor, Jimmu Tenno; but only the last eight centuries of this period can be regarded as thoroughly historical. From the last years of the fourth century A.D., when the available material provides us with firm historical footing, until the close of the twelfth century three important stages appear in the political development of the nation.

Between 593 and 671 Shotoku Taishi and the Taikwa reformers transformed Japan from a loosely integrated group of clan states into an empire which was frankly modeled after the Chinese.

The middle of the ninth century saw the control of the imperial government fall into the hands of the Fujiwara family, who monopolized the administrative posts at the capital but who, being civilians, were unable to maintain any semblance of authority over the rising military element in the provinces. The effort of the "cloistered emperors" to regain the lost power of the imperial family may be regarded as the last phase of this civilian rule.

The third and final development was the domination of the soldier, which was established temporarily during the twenty years from 1160 to 1180, when the Taira family ruled at Kyoto, and permanently in 1192, when Minamoto Yoritomo created the Kamakura Shogunate.

Although the attempt in the sixth and seventh centuries to transplant the Chinese political system into Japan was not wholly successful, the influence of Chinese culture in other fields was permanent. After the ninth century the Japanese developed independent literary forms and produced an independent literature in the syllabic Kana script; but Chinese remained the language of scholarship, and Chinese philosophy continued to dominate Japanese thought. In architecture, in painting, in sculpture, in trade, industry, and agriculture, and even in the art of war China was throughout this period a never-failing source of inspiration to the developing civilization of Japan.

Perhaps the most remarkable feature of these eight centuries of Japanese history was the almost complete submergence of the indigenous Shinto cult. For some two centuries after the introduction of Buddhism and for more than a century after the death of Shotoku Taishi, Shinto continued to hold a strong position in the land. About the beginning of the ninth century the Tendai system of Buddhism, established by Dengyo Daishi, put forth the doctrine that the Shinto Kami were incarnations of Buddhist Bodhisattvas. This doctrine, which was also taught by Kobo Daishi, the founder of the Shingon sect, was meekly accepted by the Shintoists; and for nearly a thousand years the Shinto religion ceased to play any important part in the life of the nation.

Yet Japan's borrowings from her continental neighbor should not blind us to the fact that Japanese civilization, as it developed in the course of this long period, was distinctly national. As in the case of her political institutions, so also in other fields, the borrowed elements were steadily modified to fit a Japanese background. The teachings of Sakyamuni, the philosophy of Confucius, the sculpture, painting, and industrial arts of Han, T'ang, and Sung China, all underwent a process of naturalization at the hands of the Japanese; and the resultant civilization at the close of the twelfth century was neither Chinese nor Indian nor Korean nor even an amalgam of these three but unmistakably Japanese.

SUGGESTED REFERENCES

ANESAKI, M. History of Japanese Religion.

ASAKAWA, K. The Early Institutional Life of Japan.

ASTON, W. G. A History of Japanese Literature.

ASTON, W. G. (translator). Nihongi.

BRINKLEY, F., and KIKUCHI, D. A History of the Japanese People.

BRINKLEY, F. Japan: its History, Arts, and Literature.

CHAMBERLAIN, B. H. (translator). The Kojiki.

CRAM, R. A. Impressions of Japanese Architecture and the Allied Arts.

FENOLLOSA, E. F. Epochs of Chinese and Japanese Art.

HALL, J. C. (translator). "Joei Shikimoku (Law Code of the Kamakura Shogunate)," Transactions of the Asiatic Society of Japan, Vol. XXXIV, Part I.

HARA, K. An Introduction to the History of Japan.

LATOURETTE, K. S. The Development of Japan.

MUNRO, N. G. Prehistoric Japan.

MURDOCH, J. A History of Japan, Vol. I.

REISCHAUER, A. K. Studies in Japanese Buddhism.

SANSOM, G. B. Japan: a Short Cultural History.

WALEY, A. (translator). The Tale of Genji.

XII

The Mongols

DURING the last part of the eleventh century and the first part of the twelfth the detached and almost leaderless tribes of certain hitherto ignored peoples dwelling far to the north of the Great Wall of China began to unite. This loose union of the northern barbarian tribes on the Onon, Orkhon, and Selenga rivers was the first step in the creation of the Mongol empire which under Genghis Khan and his successors eventually reduced to temporary submission much of Europe and practically all of continental Asia.

As in the case of other central-Asian tribes and peoples who at various periods have emerged from obscure insignificance to play important roles in history, so also in the case of the Mongols we have little definite knowledge concerning their origin and their early history. During the thirteenth and fourteenth centuries, when the Mongols had established themselves as the rulers of a world empire, official writers and historians endeavored to strengthen the new political edifice by elaborating stately pedigrees for the Mongol people and for their ruling family; but the results of this labor have little historical value.

Amid the kaleidoscopic groupings which constantly occurred among the nomadic peoples of central and northern Asia, language is almost the only reliable test of relationship. By this test the Mongols are now adjudged to have been related more or less closely to the Turks, the Uighurs, and the Khitans, and supporting evidence for this judgment is to be found in the ease with which the peoples named were assimilated into the Mongol empire. In the Chinese records the earliest references to the Mongols, as such, are found in the official history of the T'angs, which was completed shortly after the fall of that dynasty in 907. In these references, as well as in a later work written toward the end of the tenth century, the name given is *Mengku*, and the people thus named are classified under *Shi wei*, a term by which Chinese writers of the period designated detached bodies or tribes belonging to or subject to the Turks.

Until the opening decades of the twelfth century this conglomerate of petty independent tribes, "the world unknowing and to the world unknown," find only occasional place in the contemporary records. Poor and disunited, they were surrounded on all sides, save the frozen north, by powerful and wealthy neighbors. To the east, in the plains of modern Manchuria, were the Juchen Tartars, the founders of the Kin empire; south of the Mongols, in the northern provinces of China, their wealthy Khitan cousins held sway; to the southwest, in central Asia, lay the small oasis states of the settled and civilized Uighurs.

The first quarter of the twelfth century saw important developments to the east and south of the region occupied by the Mongol tribes. Between 1114 and 1123 the Juchen Tartars of Manchuria, henceforth to be known as the Kins, destroyed the Khitan empire of northern China, extending their domain southward to the edge of the Yangtze valley and westward until it reached the kingdom of Hsi Hsia, or Tangut, in northwestern China. Expelled from their Chinese possessions, a remnant of the Khitans fled westward and settled in the valley of the Ili River, where they founded a new state known as the empire of the Kara Khitai.

While these important developments were upsetting the old status quo in the circle of states by which the Mongols were sur-

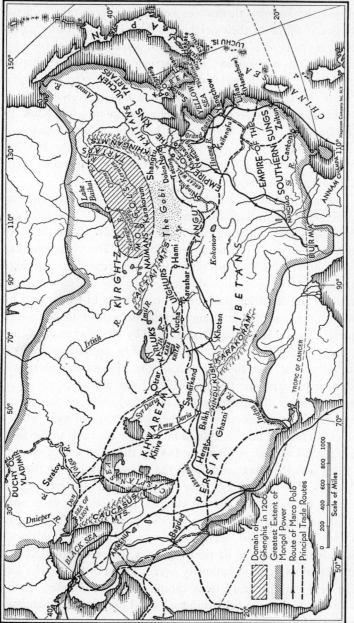

The Expansion of the Mongol Empire

rounded, the Mongols themselves were beginning to take an active part in the affairs of their neighbors. About 1120 a leader named Kabul, at the head of a force of Mongol horsemen, began to accept employment as a mercenary in the struggle between the Kins and the Khitans. When Kabul first involved himself in the Kin-Khitan struggle, he ignored the ties of relationship between his people and the Khitans and served as a hireling of the invading Kins. By 1135, however, he and his warriors had become unacceptable as allies to the rulers of north China. From this date the Mongols, apparently with the aid of subsidies from the Sung rulers of the south, engaged in frequent attacks upon the Kins.

Although Kabul's wars against the Kins, which were continued by his son Bardam Baghatur and by his grandson Yessugei, were little more than plundering expeditions, their effect upon the northern tribesmen must not be underestimated. The booty and captives brought back by these raids introduced new elements of culture among the nomadic Mongols, each successful expedition increased the ambition and the self-confidence of leader and followers alike, and the military reputation gained through these undertakings by Kabul, by Bardam, and by Yessugei enabled them to unite under their leadership a steadily expanding group of Mongol tribes. But the strength of the Mongol confederacy in these early years was not imposing. Even at the height of his power Yessugei, the grandson of Kabul, had under his rule a total population of not more than two hundred thousand men, women, and children, and he was able to muster for his raids to the south an army not exceeding fifteen or twenty thousand horsemen.

Such was the situation among the Mongols when, in the year 1155, the wife of Yessugei gave birth to a son who received the name of Temudjin and who, as Genghis Khan, was to unite under his conquering banners all the warlike nomads of northern Asia. In 1167 Yessugei died, leaving five sons, of whom Temudjin was the oldest. At the age of twelve even a future Genghis Khan is little fitted to exercise authority over a group of tribes who have been held together only by a common love of plunder. Drawn away by ambitious subchieftains who had been held in submission by the mature ability of Yessugei, the tribes composing the Mongol confederacy repudiated the young ruler and separated into a number of rival groups. Only the energy of Temudjin's widowed mother preserved for him some portion of his inheritance. For five years this remarkable woman, as regent for her son, held together in the valley of the Onon River such of the tribes as remained loyal to her husband's heir.

In 1172 Temudjin, at that time seventeen years of age, came into his inheritance and gave first evidence of his political and military ability. At the breakup of the confederacy five years earlier the most important defection had been that of the Taidshuts, who occupied the region to the west as far as the Selenga River and whose chieftain had hoped to secure for himself the undisputed leadership of the associated tribes. Against the Taidshuts, Temudjin now led a successful expedition which added considerably to his power and prestige. Some of the tribes confederated with the Taidshuts rallied to his banner, and he further strengthened his position by an alliance with the Kurulats, who occupied the valley of the Argun on the east. In 1194, when trouble arose between the Taidshuts and the Kin empire, Temudjin took service under the Kins and still further increased his power at the expense of his Taidshut rivals. Two years later the politic Mongol leader allied himself with his neighbor on the southwest, the Keraït[1] chieftain Wang Khan, who had been an ally and a "blood brother" of Yessugei. Between 1196 and 1203 Temudjin and Wang Khan co-operated in several campaigns against their common enemies; but in 1203, apparently as a result of the inveterate hostility of Wang Khan's son toward Temudjin, a break occurred between the Mongol leader and the aged chief of the Keraïts. Wang Khan was defeated and slain in battle, his son fled into exile to the southwest, and the Keraït tribes were incorporated into the Mongol confederacy.

[1] The Keraïts were Nestorian Christians, and Wang Khan is identified by Colonel Yule as the historical person at the foundation of the legend of "Prester John."

Genghis Khan and his Empire

The conquest and absorption of the Keraïts mark an important stage in the history of the Mongols and of their leader. Temudjin was now forty-eight years of age, and in the course of thirty-one years of war and diplomacy he had succeeded in uniting under his rule a much larger aggregation of people than had acknowledged the leadership of any of his ancestors. In appreciation of this fact, therefore, he summoned in the same year (1203) a great *Kuriltai* ("assembly," or "diet") of tribal and clan chieftains, at which he was acclaimed as *khan*, or *khagan* ("supreme ruler"). Three years later, at another great Kuriltai, he prefixed to this title the distinguishing epithet of *Genghis*,[1] meaning "Illustrious," "Resplendent," or "Inflexible," and it was as Genghis Khan that the conqueror was to become world-famous.

The years from 1203 to 1208 witnessed a notable extension of the Mongol power. Immediately after his first great Kuriltai the newly proclaimed khan led his forces westward to attack his most powerful neighbors, the Naimans, who occupied the region of the upper Orkhon and who, after the defeat of the Keraïts, had begun to organize a confederacy against the growing Mongol power. The Naimans were decisively defeated, and a number of their confederated tribes submitted to the Mongol khan. The leading spirit of the Naiman confederacy, however, Guchluk (or Kushluk), the son of the Naiman king, escaped from the field of battle and continued his struggle against the Mongols. In 1206, the year of the second great Kuriltai, Genghis embarked upon a new campaign against Guchluk and his confederates. Guchluk, again defeated, fled southwestward to take refuge in the realm of the Kara Khitai, while Genghis, receiving the submission of the remaining scattered tribes, found himself the undisputed master over a region stretching from the Great Khingan Mountains on the east to the Altai Mountains on the west.

This territorial expansion was accompanied by important political changes. Genghis began to transform himself from the leader of a warlike aggregation of plundering horsemen, held together

[1] Alternative spellings are *Jenghiz, Jingis, Tchingiz, Zingis,* and *Cinggis.*

only by the prospect of rich booty, into the monarch of a compact and organized state. At the defeat of the Naimans in 1203 one of the captives taken by the Mongols was a Uighur who had served as chancelor of the Naiman king. This man now took service under Genghis and instructed him as to the utility of a royal seal. He taught the Mongols the Uighur language and Uighur writing, and he gave them, as the basis of their future legal system, the laws and customs of the Uighurs.

In 1206, the year which saw his assumption of his new title and his final victory over the Naimans, Genghis transferred his head-quarters from the valley of the Onon to the site of Karakorum, on the banks of the more centrally located Orkhon. Although the town or city of Karakorum appears to date only from the reign of Genghis Khan's son and successor, Ogatai, this point now be-came the site of a fairly permanent camp from which written orders and instructions bearing the impress of the imperial seal were issued to the officers in the khan's service.

Although the defeat of the Naiman confederacy had left Genghis the supreme master of the vast region north of the Gobi desert, he looked southward upon a series of powerful states stretching from the shores of the Yellow Sea to those of the Caspian. In the ex-treme east was the empire of the Kins, occupying Manchuria and the northeastern provinces of modern China; west of the Kins lay the kingdom of Hsi Hsia, or Tangut, which held Shensi and Kansu as well as a strip of land along the southern edge of the desert outside the Great Wall; still farther to the west, in Zungaria and in the western part of present-day Chinese Turkestan, was the empire of the Kara Khitai, where Guchluk, the former leader of the Naiman confederacy, had found refuge and was gaining influ-ence in the councils of the Kara Khitan monarch; beyond the Kara Khitans, with its center at modern Khiva, lay the powerful Mohammedan Turkish empire of Khwarezm.

The last named of these four states was at this time probably outside the range of the khan's vision, while to turn either south-eastward against the Kins or southwestward against the Kara Khitans would have involved attacking a state more powerful than his own and leaving his flank exposed to the attacks of a second equally powerful neighbor. Only in one direction could Genghis without too great risk undertake a further extension of his territories. The kingdom of Tangut, directly to the south, was the most easily accessible, and an attack could be made here without any danger of becoming involved in hostilities with any of his other neighbors. The Kins, the Kara Khitans, and the Sung emperors of southern China all agreed in regarding the Tangut state as a brigand organization whose destruction would be a public benefaction. A war against Tangut, therefore, could be carried on with the approval of, and even as an ally of, the Kin emperor; it would be possible for Genghis, throughout the entire undertaking, to keep a close watch upon the activities of the Kara Khitans and also of the wild Kirghiz tribes to the northwest; moreover, if successful, this war would extend his domains southward to the frontiers of the Sung empire and would facilitate a future alliance with the Sungs against the power of the Kins.

Between 1205 and 1209, therefore, Genghis launched a series of attacks upon the Tanguts. Partially successful in his earlier campaigns, he decisively defeated the southern forces in 1209 and compelled the Tangut monarch to sue for peace and to acknowledge Mongol supremacy.

During the course of the second Mongol expedition against Tangut the inveterately hostile Guchluk attempted an invasion of the Mongol homeland from the west. The outcome of this attempt proved the strategic soundness of Genghis's arrangements. Without relaxing his efforts in the south he was able to hurl back the invasion from the west, to reduce to submission the Kirghiz tribes on the northern slopes of the Altai Mountains, and to extend his authority over the oases of Zungaria and Eastern Turkestan. This last achievement was especially important since it gave him control over the great northern caravan route to the west and brought under his sway a large number of the highly cultured Uighurs.

With the great increase of power which resulted from his conquest of Tangut and with his position in the west strengthened by the defeat which he had inflicted upon his enemies in that direction, Genghis now felt himself sufficiently strong to embark upon a more ambitious undertaking, an attack upon the Kin empire on his southeastern frontier. The moment seemed to be propitious. The provinces of north China were seething with discontent against their foreign rulers, and in 1209 a new emperor had ascended the throne at Yenching (modern Peiping). In 1210, therefore, when ambassadors from the Kin court appeared before Genghis to announce the accession of their new sovereign and to receive the respectful submission of the Mongol chieftain, Genghis contemptuously refused to do homage, declaring that such an incompetent prince was unworthy to be the suzerain and ought rather to acknowledge himself the vassal of the Mongols.

This deliberate repudiation of his vassalage was followed in the next year by the outbreak of hostilities. In the spring of 1211 the Mongol army crossed the Gobi desert to invade Shansi from the north, while the forces of Tangut crossed the Yellow River and attacked the western districts of the same province. A simultaneous attack by the armies of the Sung empire from the south and the outbreak of local rebellions in all parts of their domain added to the difficulties of the Kin government and lessened their ability to offer effective resistance to the forces of Genghis. The Mongols found it difficult to make any impression upon the walled cities, but in the open field they were irresistible. In August, 1212, Genghis was wounded in an unsuccessful assault upon the city of Tatungfu in northern Shansi, and his forces, heavily loaded with loot from Shansi and Hopei, withdrew across the Gobi desert. A year later the Mongol horsemen reappeared upon the scene and spread devastation through the provinces of Shansi, Shantung, and Hopei. In 1214 Genghis laid siege to Yenching and compelled the imperial government to make peace upon terms which involved the payment of a heavy indemnity in money, silk, horses, and slaves. Following this humiliating treaty the Kin ruler abandoned the city and moved his capital southward to the city of K'aifengfu in the province of Honan.

The treaty of 1214, humiliating though it was for the Kin emperor, secured for him only a brief respite from the attacks of the Mongols. In the following year they once more attacked Yenching, this time successfully, and the forces of Genghis, after taking and looting this important city, proceeded to force the submission of the province of Hopei and of southern Manchuria. Twenty years of stubborn fighting intervened between 1214 and the final disappearance of Kin rule from Chinese soil, as it was not until 1234 that the last fragments of the once powerful Juchen Tartars withdrew northward into northern Manchuria; but the treaty of 1214 and the destruction of Yenching in 1215 marked, if not the completion, at least the successful development of the greatest undertaking which Genghis had thus far attempted.

Quite apart from the immediate increase in territory and power which resulted from the successful attack upon the Kin empire, the consequences of the war were of far-reaching importance. The Mongol ruler at once assumed a new and more dignified status in the eyes of all the peoples and governments of eastern and central Asia. For more than a thousand years the Chinese Empire, despite its occasional periods of internal weakness, had enjoyed tremendous prestige among its neighbors. The victory of the Mongols in north China therefore affected international opinion in much the same way as, seven centuries later, Japan's military successes against the forces of Russia modified world estimates regarding the importance of the Island Empire. After 1215 the Mongols were a "world power," and the policies, the plans, and the movements of Genghis Khan were matters of importance not merely to his semicivilized immediate neighbors but also to the powerful kingdoms and empires of all Asia and, eventually, of Europe.

Equally as important as this increase in world prestige were the effects of the war upon the culture of the Mongols. Although some measure of Chinese civilization had filtered northward across the Gobi desert and had influenced to a slight degree the manners and customs of the northern "barbarians," the chief outside cultural influence at work among the Mongols, prior to their attack upon the Kins, had been that of the Uighurs, from whom, as recently as 1203, they had received their first instruction in the art of writing and their earliest code of laws. During the campaigns in northern China and after the successful termination of this war the flow of Chinese influence was greatly increased. From this point in Mongol history the social, legal, and political systems of the Chinese were in competition with those of the Uighurs, while Chinese officials found employment in the council of Genghis and his successors alongside the earlier Uighur advisers.

Outstanding among the officials through whose influence the Chinese administrative and legal institutions became firmly established was Ye-lü Ch'u-ts'ai, who, under both Genghis and his first successor, held the post of grand chancellor. Although he was a direct descendant of the Ye-lü A-po-ki who had founded the Khitan dynasty, Ye-lü Ch'u-ts'ai at the outbreak of the Kin-Mongol war was a high official in the service of the Kin emperor. When the Mongol forces took Yenching, he was made prisoner and entered the service of the conqueror. A trained Confucian scholar thoroughly imbued with the political theories of the Classics, Ye-lü Ch'u-ts'ai endeavored to impress upon Genghis the fact that, "although an empire could be conquered on horseback, it could not be governed so." Constantly he labored to substitute a regular system of administration for the arbitrary rule of the Mongol khan and his subordinates, to impose regular methods of taxation in place of indiscriminate and arbitrary levies, to put an end to the destructive policy of pillaging conquered cities, and to establish in the Mongol court some rules of etiquette and a regular order of precedence.

Returning from China in 1216 to his headquarters on the banks of the Orkhon, Genghis soon found opportunity for further indulging his growing appetite for conquest. In the west his old enemy Guchluk, the former Naiman prince, had once more opened hostilities. Five years before this, Guchluk, who had found refuge among the Kara Khitans and had received in marriage a daughter of the Gur Khan of Kara Khitai, had risen in rebellion against his father-in-law and had succeeded, with the assistance of the shah of Khwarezm, in placing himself upon the Kara Khitan throne. Following this usurpation Guchluk brought under his rule a number of his weaker neighbors, and in 1216 his armies were invading the regions which had submitted to the authority of Genghis Khan. In 1217, therefore, Genghis led his forces against this inveterate western enemy. In a single decisive battle the army of Guchluk was utterly routed, and Guchluk himself was slain while attempting to escape from the field. Early in the next year the Kara Khitans submitted to the authority of the Mongol khan.

While the major portion of the Mongol forces had been engaged in the war against Kara Khitai, another army had invaded the Korean peninsula and had forced the descendant of Wang Kien to acknowledge the sovereignty of the Mongol khan. With the successful termination of these two undertakings Genghis showed signs of a willingness to rest on his laurels. He now ruled over an empire which, save where the fragments of the Kin state maintained their losing struggle, extended without a break from the coast of Korea to the boundaries of the great Khwarezmian empire of central Asia. The war with the Kins furnished sufficient occupation for his armies, while the organization of his vast domain would need all the abilities of the khan and of his councilors.

In spite of the fact that the shah of Khwarezm had aided and supported the ever hostile Guchluk, Genghis opened friendly negotiations with Khwarezm, with a view to concluding a treaty of commerce and friendship. Muhammed Shah, the Khwarezmian ruler, apparently reciprocated Genghis's desire for friendly relations, and a commercial treaty was concluded. All hope for peace between the two empires, however, was destroyed by the rash barbarity of one of Muhammed's subordinates, Inal Khan, the governor of Otrar, who arrested and executed as spies a number of Chinese and Mongol merchants. When Genghis sent envoys to Khwarezm to demand reparation for this violation of the treaty, Inal Khan added insult to injury by seizing and executing the envoys.

The empire of Khwarezm was at this time one of the most important states of central and western Asia, reaching from the Syr Daria (ancient Jaxartes) River to the Persian Gulf and from the upper reaches of the Indus to the Caspian Sea. Originally a small province occupying the fertile valley of the Amu Daria (ancient Oxus), and a dependency of the empire of the Seljuk Turks, Khwarezm had become independent about the middle of the twelfth century during the reign of Muhammed Shah's grandfather; and Muhammed himself, who succeeded to the throne in 1200, had extended his territories in all directions. Balkh, Herat,

Western Turkestan, and Ghazni were brought under his sway, and his court was transferred from the early capital on the site of modern Khiva to the wealthier and more centrally located Samarkand.

Undaunted by the apparent greatness of the Khwarezmian empire, Genghis and his followers, at a great Kuriltai which was held in the fall of 1218, decided to avenge by war the insult that had been received. During the spring of 1219, leaving in China an army sufficiently strong to carry on the war against the Kins, Genghis moved the rest of his forces westward from Karakorum to the valley of the Irtish, and in the autumn of that year the invasion of Khwarezm was begun.

In the earlier years of his reign Muhammed Shah had gained wide success as a conqueror, but he offered only a feeble resistance to the Mongol armies which poured down across the Syr Daria into his dominions. Operating in four well-organized armies and combining two or more of their columns whenever circumstances demanded, the generals of Genghis Khan besieged and captured city after city. Here and there an especially strong fortress or a particularly devoted garrison stubbornly resisted their victorious progress; but by the beginning of April, 1220, Samarkand itself had fallen, and Muhammed Shah, accompanied by a few retainers, was fleeing westward in search of a safe refuge from his irresistible enemy. Driven by the pursuing Mongols from one hiding place after another, he finally reached the shores of the Caspian and sought safety on an island. Here the unhappy monarch died, leaving to his eldest son Jelaluddin (or Jelal-ad-Din) the task of regaining the lost empire.

Jelaluddin succeeded in organizing some effective resistance to the conquerors. Hampered though he was by the jealousy and treachery of his brothers, he gathered an army, gained a few victories over detached bodies of Mongol troops, and encouraged some of the conquered cities to throw off the Mongol yoke. These minor successes, however, had little bearing upon the ultimate outcome of the war, and in the fall of 1221 Jelaluddin and his army were brought to bay on the banks of the upper Indus River. Here, in a battle fought on the twenty-fourth of November, the Khwarezmian army was utterly defeated. Jelaluddin, with four thousand of his soldiers, escaped across the river and took refuge with the Sultan of Delhi, pursued by a Mongol force which withdrew after ravaging the upper provinces of the Punjab; the cities which had rallied to the support of the young shah were reconquered and utterly destroyed by the Mongols.

After the fall of Samarkand, Genghis had dispatched a force of twenty-five thousand horsemen under two of his most capable generals to follow and capture the fugitive Muhammed Shah. When Muhammed escaped his pursuers by taking refuge on an island in the Caspian, the Mongol "flying squadron" swept on through northern Persia, turned northward along the western shore of the Caspian, and crossed the Caucasus Mountains into southeastern Russia. Having attacked certain tribes of Kipchak Tartars, whom they drove westward toward the Don River, the Mongol commanders sent envoys to the local Russian princes. The envoys assured the Russians that their master desired only to chastise the Kipchaks, who, being Turks by race, were regarded as deserters and traitors; with Russia he wished peace and friendship. These peaceful assurances were unheeded, the envoys were massacred, and the Russian forces advanced to do battle with the invading Mongols. On May 31, 1223, the two armies met in a battle which ended in an overwhelming defeat for the Russians. After this victory the Mongol column ravaged the districts along the Don and Dnieper rivers down to the Sea of Azov and then withdrew to the banks of the Volga.

During the three years which followed the defeat of Jelaluddin, Genghis remained in central Asia, consolidating his conquests, punishing revolts, and gathering booty and captives to be carried back to Mongolia. In the autumn of 1224 he turned toward home, and in February, 1225, he reached his camp capital on the Orkhon River. The expedition had lasted nearly six years and had extended his power southward and westward until all Asia and eastern Europe trembled with fear at the approach of Mongol horsemen.

While Genghis and his expeditionary forces were carrying fire and sword into central and western Asia and into European Russia as far as the Dnieper River, the armies which had been left in the east were prosecuting successfully their campaigns in northern China. The Kin government, by involving itself in a simultaneous war with the Southern Sungs, diverted from its northern frontier the forces which were needed to repel the Mongol invaders, while intrigues among the Kin generals drove a number of the more capable leaders to take service under the Mongol banner. Under these conditions the Mongol forces were able to invade year after year the steadily diminishing area which remained under Kin rule. The country districts were systematically ravaged, while each year saw the surrender of a number of cities and walled towns.

In the autumn of 1220 the Kin monarch attempted to make peace with his adversary and offered to recognize Genghis as his "elder brother." This offer, however, came too late. By this time the Mongols had gained a sweeping victory over Khwarezm and were able to detach additional troops, if necessary, for the war in the east. A second and even more abject bid for peace two years later was equally unsuccessful. Completely victorious in the west, Genghis was determined upon nothing short of the absolute destruction of his southern neighbor.

After his return in February, 1225, to his headquarters at Karakorum, Genghis soon decided upon a more vigorous prosecution of his operations to the south of the Gobi desert. The new king of Tangut had refused to send his son to Karakorum as a hostage for his loyalty and had still further displayed his hostility by taking into his service an open enemy of the Mongols. Toward the end of 1225, therefore, Genghis led his armies southward for a fresh invasion of the Tangut kingdom. The forces of Tangut were defeated, the country was pillaged, and the adventurous king, dying at the moment of his defeat, was replaced on the throne by a brother, under whom the armies of Tangut once more co-operated with the Mongols in their war against the Kins.

The reign of the new Tangut monarch was short. In the spring of 1227 he also made an attempt to throw off the Mongol yoke, and in July of that year, eleven months after his succession to the throne, he was captured and put to death. From this date the kingdom of Tangut, after a checkered career of nearly three centuries and a half, ceased to exist.

The destruction of Tangut was the final achievement of Genghis Khan. During the summer of 1227, while undertaking a tour of inspection, the great conqueror became seriously ill, and in August[1] of the same year he died.

It is not easy to estimate correctly the characters of the conquerors in world history, among whom Genghis Khan must be ranked as one of the greatest. Considerable space has been given in the preceding pages to the successive steps by which Genghis achieved authority over his vast empire, an empire which under his successors was destined to attain even wider limits before it began to fall apart. But what can be said of the character of the leader under whom this world conquest began?

Genghis was essentially a destructive genius; war and conquest were the dominant purposes of his life, cruelty and treachery were the constantly employed weapons of his policy. In addition to these characteristics, however, which may be attributed equally to the numerous rivals whom he defeated and conquered, Genghis possessed certain qualities of leadership which raised him above the crowd. To his fondness for war were added a genius for military organization and an ability to select capable generals for the command of his armies. His cruelty and his treachery were accompanied by a foresighted shrewdness which enabled him to succeed in his alliances and intrigues, while his strong will and his dominating personality made it possible for him to enforce strict discipline upon his soldiers and also to impose upon the nomadic tribes which came under his sway a greater degree of unity than had hitherto existed.

The essentially warlike nature of Genghis's genius, moreover, should not blind us to other aspects of his character. Despite the fact that he was educated in the rough school of the nomad tribesman and despite the cultural poverty of the Mongol people, Genghis showed himself capable of appreciating the richer civilization of the regions which he brought under his rule. Himself unlettered (apparently ignorant, until past the age of forty, even of the use of writing), he found employment at his court for educated men from all the nations which he conquered.

[1] The exact date is given by some sources as August 18, by others as August 24.

This appreciation and utilization of the achievements of more civilized peoples were naturally most thorough in the field of military science, and in all their later campaigns the Mongols made abundant use of the war machinery with which they first became acquainted during their early invasions of China. But in other fields, also, Genghis displayed a constant readiness to employ foreign advisers and to utilize foreign methods. Mention already has been made of the Uighur from whom the Mongols first learned the art of writing, and of the former Kin official Ye-lü Ch'u-ts'ai; but the biographical section of the *Yuan Shih* ("History of the Yuan Dynasty") is filled with the names and the achievements of Chinese, Uighurs, Arabs, Persians, Armenians, and other non-Mongols whom Genghis and his successors employed in the central government or in the administration of local affairs.

Thousands of less conspicuous individuals, moreover, also benefited by the Mongol khan's growing appreciation of a higher civilization. The wholesale slaughter which so frequently accompanied the capture of a hostile city and so fully justifies the charge that cruelty or at least a ruthless disregard for human life was an outstanding characteristic of Genghis's policy was seldom wholly indiscriminate. Usually, if not in every case, such massacres were preceded by a careful segregation of all the skilled workers whose training and ability could be turned to advantage by the conqueror. Thus the far-reaching conquests of Genghis, although accompanied by an incalculable destruction of human life, did not result in the eradication of the cultures developed in the regions through which his victorious armies passed. Indeed, barbarian though he was, the effect of his conquests was rather to stimulate the further development of culture by bringing into fruitful contact civilizations hitherto separate in their growth.

In his treatment of the diverse forms of religious belief which existed among the peoples of his mighty empire the record of Genghis, like those of his successors, is extremely creditable. All religions—Buddhism, Taoism, Nestorian Christianity, Judaism, Mohammedanism, and Confucianism—were tolerated; their places of worship were protected, and exempted from taxation; their teachers were respected, and on occasion were treated with distinguished honors.

One instance of his conferring honor upon an outstanding figure in the religious world, occurring during his campaign in central Asia, has provided modern historians with a valuable contemporary source for the history of the period.[1] Having heard of the venerable Taoist monk Ch'ang Ch'un, who was famed throughout China for his wisdom and piety, Genghis in the midst of his campaign invited this saintly man to come and explain his philosophy of life. Ch'ang Ch'un, who was living in the province of Shantung, was seventy-two years of age when he received the imperial invitation from central Asia. Undeterred by the gloomy forebodings of his disciples, who had little expectation that their master would ever return to them, the aged monk set forth, in company with the honorable escort placed at his disposal by Genghis, upon a journey which after more than two years of hard traveling brought him to the Mongol camp in the Hindu Kush Mountains on the frontier of India. After several interviews, at which some effort was made to explain to him the Taoist philosophy, Genghis allowed his guest to depart; and Ch'ang Ch'un, again accompanied by an escort, set out on his return trip to his home in Shantung, where he finally arrived in 1224 after a four years' absence.

There is no evidence that the khan in his interviews with Ch'ang Ch'un showed more than a perfunctory interest in the religious and philosophical teachings of Taoism or that he subsequently modified his own way of life. Yet this imperious summoning of the aged monk from easternmost China to the border of India throws light upon the character of the Great Khan. The patronage which he extended to Ch'ang Ch'un and to other religious teachers, his protection of the places of worship consecrated to diverse religious beliefs, and his preservation of artistic and literary treasures did not reflect any real personal interest on the part of Genghis as an individual. It was the ruler, not the man, who was interested in these matters, shrewdly calculating their value in enhancing the prestige of his imperial throne and in reconciling to his rule the recently conquered peoples for whom religion and art and literature had real significance.

[1] The diary of Ch'ang Ch'un's journey is found in Bretschneider, *Mediaeval Researches from Eastern Asiatic Sources.*

THE SUCCESSORS OF GENGHIS

By his first wife, to whom he had given the title of empress, Genghis had four sons: Juji, Jagatai, Ogatai, and Tului. Juji, the eldest, had been one of the leaders of the expedition which invaded southeastern Russia; and after ravaging that country as far west as the Dnieper he had retired to the valley of the Volga, where he died in the spring of 1227. On the death of Genghis the empire was divided into four parts: one for each of the three surviving sons, and the fourth for Batu, the eldest son of Juji. Batu received the conquered regions of western Asia north of the Syr Daria and of the Aral and Caspian seas, together with the Volga and Don valleys in Russia. To Jagatai were given the conquered territories of the west lying south of the Syr Daria. Ogatai, the third son, received Zungaria, the conquered provinces of northern China, and the western portion of present-day Mongolia, while to Tului, the youngest son, or "hearth child," was given the original Mongolian homeland together with the conquered territory in Manchuria and Korea.

For his successor as head of the entire empire Genghis during the last years of his life had fixed his choice upon Ogatai, in whose ability to win and hold the friendship of all associates seemed to lie the best assurance for continued unity. For nearly two years no step was taken to fill the vacant post, but in the spring of 1229 all the Mongol chiefs and their followers assembled in a great Kuriltai on the banks of the Kerulen. Here, largely through the efforts of Tului, supported by the influential Ye-Lü Ch'u-ts'ai, the choice of Genghis was ratified and Ogatai was elected. For forty days Ogatai coyly resisted the honor, at the end of which period he finally accepted on condition that the post should remain in his line so long as he had descendants.

The twelve years of Ogatai's khanship (1229–1241) have been described as a compromise between the Chinese party, which did not wish the empire to be governed "on horseback" but dreamed of restoring under a sufficiently civilized Mongol dynasty the ancient glory of Han and T'ang, and the Mongol party, which desired only a continuation of the "empire on horseback," with its policy of conquest to the limit. In the organization and administration of the Mongol government the influence of the Chinese party was supreme. Under the new khan, Ye-lü Ch'u-ts'ai enjoyed even more power than had been conferred upon him by Genghis. The system of taxation was made to approximate more nearly that of China; customhouses and public granaries were established; and a regular courier service was inaugurated, enabling the imperial commands to be transmitted promptly to all parts of the empire. With this growing complexity of the administration Ye-lü succeeded in convincing Ogatai of the necessity of having only literate officials in charge of the governmental machinery, and educated Chinese came to fill an increasing proportion of the official posts. In 1236, also apparently at Ye-lü's suggestion, Ogatai created two great colleges, one at Yenching and the other at Pingyang in Shansi, for the education of sons of officials and nobles.

The increasing complexity of the administration and the development of a regular bureaucracy made it necessary for the Mongol khan to give his government permanent quarters. Since 1206, when Genghis had moved his headquarters westward from the Onon valley, Karakorum, on the banks of the Orkhon, had served as the political center of the growing empire. Here had been located the "home camp" of the Great Khan, and here great assemblies of Mongol leaders had been held from time to time to decide momentous questions of peace and war. Yet Karakorum, for nearly thirty years after Genghis made it his headquarters, remained merely a centrally located camping place. In the spring of 1235, after his return from the final campaign against the Kins, Ogatai ordered the construction of a walled enclosure some two miles in circuit, within which his Chinese architects and workmen erected buildings for the residence of a mighty ruler. The camp was changed into a city; the Mongol khan dismounted from horseback and took up his residence in a palace.

Nine years after the erection of these first buildings William of Rubruck visited Karakorum as the ambassador of Louis IX to the successor of Ogatai, and William's report to the French king contains the following interesting description of the Mongol capital:

Of the city of Caracarum you must know that, exclusive of the palace of the Chan, it is not as big as the Village of Saint Denis, and the monastery of Saint Denis is ten times larger than the palace. There are two quarters in it; one of the Saracens in which are the markets, and where a great many Tartars gather on account of the court, which is always near this city, and on account of the great number of ambassadors; the other is the quarter of the Cathayans, all of whom are artisans. Besides these quarters there are great palaces, which are for the secretaries of the court. There are there twelve idol temples of different nations, two mahummeries [that is, mosques] in which is cried the law of Machomet, and one church of Christians in the extreme end of the city. The city is surrounded by a mud wall and has four gates. At the eastern is sold millet and other kinds of grain, which, however, is rarely brought there; at the western one, sheep and goats are sold; at the southern, oxen and carts are sold; at the northern, horses are sold.

While the Chinese party was thus successful in its efforts to create an imperial government modeled along Chinese lines, the Mongol party had its way in matters of foreign policy. Throughout the entire reign of Ogatai his military forces were occupied in wars of conquest on the east, south, and west.

In China, where the influence of the Chinese administrative officials led the Mongol government to abandon the earlier policy of giving over captured cities to pillage and destruction, the Kin empire was completely conquered; and a beginning was made in the conquest of the Sung empire.

Korea, which had suffered its first Mongol invasion in 1218, was again invaded in 1231 as punishment for an attempt to throw off the Mongol yoke. Unable either to resist the Mongol forces or to make peace, the Korean king transferred his court to the island of Kangwha, in the estuary of the river Han, and abandoned the remainder of his kingdom to the mercies of the invader.

In the regions of western Asia south of the Syr Daria the withdrawal of Genghis Khan in 1224 had been followed by the return of Jelaluddin from his Indian refuge. Within two years after his return the young Khwarezmian ruler had gathered an army, and upon the death of Genghis all of west-central Asia rose in revolt against the Mongols. The forces of Jagatai, aided by Batu and by troops sent from the east, reconquered the insurgent regions and finally, after four years of fighting, destroyed the army of Jelaluddin, who fled westward and lost his life at the hands of the Kurds.

The most important of all the military enterprises during the reign of Ogatai was the great expedition into Europe. After the final defeat of Jelaluddin in 1231 and after the termination of the struggle against the Kins in 1234 the Mongol military leaders were left without any satisfactory employment for themselves and their troops. At a Kuriltai held in the summer of 1235 at Karakorum it was therefore decided to undertake a great campaign beyond the Volga River. As the field of the undertaking lay within the region which had been assigned to Batu, this prince was made the nominal commander in chief of the entire force. The actual direction of the military operations, however, was given to Subutai, the most able of the generals trained in the school of Genghis Khan; and the expedition, which included the elite of the Mongol troops, numbered among its subordinate leaders descendants of all four of the sons of Genghis.

In the spring of 1236 the expedition arrived in the valley of the Volga. The first eighteen months were devoted to the systematic subjugation of the southeastern portions of Russia, the region which had been hastily ravaged by the earlier invasion, and it was not until December, 1237, that the Mongol forces appeared on the frontier of the grand duchy of Vladimir. The somewhat leisurely beginning of the campaign appears to have been utterly ignored by the governments of the West, but the Mongol storm now broke upon Europe with a fury which astonished and dismayed the entire Christian world.

Between February, 1238, when the city of Vladimir was taken by storm, and March, 1242, when the news of Ogatai's death was received at the Mongol headquarters in Hungary, the invading forces swept over central and southern Russia, Poland, Silesia, Moravia, Hungary, and eastern Austria. City after city was taken by storm, army after army was defeated and annihilated, and then, just when it appeared that nothing could prevent the conquest of all Europe, the arrival of the news that Ogatai had died put an end to the advance. The sons and nephews of the late khan, together with many of the prominent officers, left the army and hastened back to Karakorum to play their part in the election of a new ruler.

For more than a year the bulk of the Mongol army remained in Hungary and carried on a few minor operations; then, loaded with plunder, it withdrew slowly into southern and eastern Russia. The Mongol withdrawal, however, brought no peace of mind to the terrified peoples and rulers of Europe. Ignorant of the cause for the unexpected relief, Christendom tremblingly awaited a fresh attack and made frantic efforts to organize a defense against the irresistible forces of Asia. Innocent IV, who was elected to the papal throne in 1243, proclaimed a crusade and promised to those who took the cross against the Mongol the same spiritual blessings as for a crusade to the Holy Land. In 1245 a general church council at Lyons, presided over by the Pope, decided to dispatch envoys to the Mongol rulers in an effort to dissuade them from making a fresh attack. In accordance with this decision two missions were sent: one to the Mongol leaders in Armenia, and the other to the leaders of the forces in Russia.

The first of these missions, which was confided to the Franciscan friar Lawrence of Portugal, is of little interest to the student of Far Eastern history. The second was entrusted to Friar John of Plano Carpini (or Pian di Carpini), who was some fifty years of age and the provincial of the Franciscan order at Cologne. Friar John left Lyons in April, 1245, and so well performed his mission that he delivered the Pope's message not only to the Mongol commander in Russia but also to Ogatai's son and successor, Kuyuk. To accomplish this feat he and his companion, Benedict of Poland, had traversed Russia and the greater part of Asia to a point not far from Karakorum, where they found the Mongol princes and leaders assembled at a Kuriltai for the election of their new khan. The two Franciscans remained at the Mongol camp long enough to witness the election and coronation of Kuyuk; then, with the new khan's reply[1] to the Pope's letter, they returned to Europe, reaching Lyons in the autumn of 1247 after an absence of more than two years.

[1] Kuyuk's letter to the Pope, written in the Persian language, was discovered a few years ago in the archives of the Vatican; for a translation and full discussion see Paul Pelliot, "Les Mongols et la papauté," in *Revue de l'Orient chrétien*, 1922–1923, pp. 3–30.

Although Kuyuk's reply to the Pope's letter contained no assurance that the Mongols would not again invade Europe, the mission of John of Plano Carpini had far-reaching consequences, since it brought to the rulers of Europe their first accurate information concerning the Mongols and opened the way for further diplomatic intercourse. Other missions were sent by the Pope to the Mongol princes in Asia Minor and in western Asia.

In the year 1248 Louis IX of France, who was at that time engaged in a crusade against Egypt and the Holy Land, conceived the idea of securing Mongol co-operation against the Mohammedans. With this object in view St. Louis dispatched to the Mongols several embassies, the most important of which was that committed to William of Rubruck, who, like John of Plano Carpini, was a Franciscan friar. Leaving Constantinople in the spring of 1253, Friar William reached the camp of Mangu, who had succeeded Kuyuk, on December 27 of the same year. He remained at the camp until nearly the end of March, when he proceeded to Karakorum, where he stayed for nearly five months. About the middle of August, 1254, William set forth on his return journey; and on August 15, 1255, he finally arrived at Tripoli, where he wrote his report for the French king.

Friar William found the Mongol ruler thoroughly tolerant on questions of religion but without any inclination either toward the acceptance of the Christian doctrine or toward a war of extermination against the adherents of Islam. At the camp of Mangu and in the city of Karakorum, however, he found a great number of Europeans who had been captured during the Mongol invasion of Europe and who were now pursuing their European arts and crafts in distant Mongolia. During his stay of nearly eight months at the camp and the capital William, who appears to have been an unusually competent observer, was able to gather a great quantity of valuable information concerning the Mongols and their Asiatic neighbors; and his report to Louis IX, although disappointing the pious hopes of this monarch, is an important historical source for the study of the Mongols.

The death of Ogatai, which checked the Mongol invasion of the west, occurred in December, 1241; but his successor, as we have seen, was not elected until the summer of 1246, after the arrival of John of Plano Carpini at the Mongol camp. During this interregnum of four and a half years Tourakina, the widow of Ogatai, acted as regent, and she used her power to bring about the election of her son Kuyuk instead of an elder son whom Ogatai had designated as his successor. Kuyuk, who died in the spring of 1248 after a reign of less than two years, was a member of the "war party" and recommenced the wars of conquest to the south and southwest, against Sung China and Persia.

The election of Kuyuk had constituted a triumph for the families of Ogatai and Jagatai over the Chinese party and the descendants of Juji and Tului. The election of his successor Mangu, who was proclaimed khan in July, 1251, was a victory for those who had been defeated five years earlier. In violation of the pledge which had been given to Ogatai in 1229 the princes of the houses of Juji and Tului rejected the claims of Ogatai's surviving descendants and chose the oldest son of Tului as head of the empire. The outcome of this family quarrel was a triumph for the Chinese party, the party of the administrative officials whose power had developed under the leadership of Ye-lü Ch'u-ts'ai. Under Mangu, and more rapidly under his famous brother Kublai, the Great Khan of the Mongols was steadily transformed into a Chinese emperor. But the election of Mangu also meant the beginning of disruption for the vast empire which had been built up by the conquests of Genghis and Ogatai, and from this time there was almost constant strife between the supporters of the Great Khan and the irreconcilable princes of the houses of Ogatai and Jagatai.

Although a triumph for the Chinese party, the election of Mangu did not mean an abandonment of the policy of conquest, and the new khan carried out in the south and southwest the military projects which had been commenced by his predecessor.

Kublai, the next younger brother of Mangu, was appointed lieutenant general for the conquered regions south of the Gobi desert, where he busied himself in repairing, with the aid of his Chinese advisers and officials, the damages caused by the long period of warfare. In addition to carrying on this work of peaceful reconstruction, however, Kublai embarked energetically upon the task of extending still further the Mongol domination. In 1252 he led his armies southward through the present province of Szechwan against the kingdom of Nanchao. The forces of Nanchao were defeated, the capital was taken, and the conquered country was organized into districts under Mongol and Chinese officials. Following the subjugation of Nanchao a Mongol army was sent in 1257 into the kingdom of Annam. Here the conquerors from the north were not so completely successful as they had been in Nanchao, but in 1258 an Annamese embassy appeared at the court of Mangu to recognize the suzerainty of the Great Khan.

By these extensions of their power the Mongols succeeded in establishing themselves upon the western and southwestern frontiers of the Sung empire, and even before the submission of Annam they had embarked upon the task of conquering this great neighbor. This undertaking, commenced in the fall of 1257, was destined to be completed in the reign of Mangu's successor, Kublai.

The reign of Mangu also saw the continuation and completion of the conquest of Korea. So long as the Korean monarch remained in his island refuge of Kangwha, beyond the reach of the Mongol armies, the Mongol forces in the peninsula were in constant danger of popular uprisings inspired by royal agents. In 1253, therefore, the armies of Mangu undertook the thorough subjugation of the kingdom. This task was carried out with great energy, and by the end of 1255 the Korean people were completely cowed. The old king steadfastly refused to abandon his safe retreat; but in 1259 this monarch died, and his son, submitting to the invaders, took up his residence at Sunto as the vassal of the Mongol khan.

While these conquests were being carried on in the east, the Mongol armies were busy also in southwestern Asia. In January, 1253, only a few months before William of Rubruck set forth on his embassy to secure Mongol co-operation against the Mohammedans, a great Kuriltai decided upon the invasion of Persia; but this was to be a war for conquest and not for religion. Under the command of Hulagu, the younger brother of Mangu and Kublai, the Mongol forces crossed the Amu Daria in January, 1256, and by the following January they had destroyed the kingdom of the Assassins, which occupied the mountain region to the south of the Caspian Sea.

After this conquest Hulagu turned southwestward through Persia and pushed on toward Bagdad, conquering as he went. In September, 1257, he summoned the Abbassid caliph to dismantle the fortifications of Bagdad and to acknowledge himself the vassal of the Great Khan. This summons having been ignored, Hulagu advanced to the attack. Bagdad was besieged on January 18, 1258; on the tenth of February the caliph surrendered, and ten days later the last of the Abbassids was put to death by the Mongol conqueror.

Kublai Khan Becomes a Chinese Emperor

In the autumn of 1259 Mangu died from wounds received in an unsuccessful assault upon a Chinese city. The military operations against the Sung empire were immediately suspended, and in the spring of 1260 a partial assembly of the Mongol leaders, meeting at Yenching, chose Kublai as successor to his brother. The election, since it had been accomplished by an irregular assembly, was repudiated by many of the Mongol princes; but Kublai was supported by a majority of the most powerful leaders, and after some fighting his claim to the succession was finally recognized.

The accession of Kublai practically completed the disruption which had commenced with the election of Mangu. Mongol Persia under Hulagu, and the Mongols in Russia (the "Golden Horde") under the successors of Batu, still supported loyally the authority of the Great Khan; but, situated as they were on the western edge of the Mongol world, these were allies rather than vassals of Kublai. Between the actual domains of Kublai and these loyal but distant supporters lay the great central regions of Asia, ruled by the Ogatai and Jagatai princes, who had grudgingly acquiesced in Kublai's seizure of power in the east, but who were always ready to rebel or to aid rebellion against him.

Nor was the disruption of the empire which had been founded by Genghis the result merely of rivalry among his descendants; to an even greater degree it was caused by the cultural development of the Mongols. In the various regions over which they had established their sway the garrisons and the local rulers gradually assumed the culture of the particular people among whom they were domiciled. In southeastern Russia, Batu and his Golden Horde became tinged with Russian and European civilization. Hulagu's descendants and the descendants of his conquering armies became Persians. In central Asia the Jagatai and Ogatai princes became Khwarezmians and Uighurs. In China, Kublai and his supporters became Chinese. Only in Mongolia did the Mongol leaders and people remain wholly Mongol.

This disruptive process, therefore, had been in operation throughout a long period prior to the election of Kublai, but the year 1260 may be taken as the date on which the history of the Mongols as a united people comes to an end. From this date also the separate histories of the far-western Mongol khanates cease to be an integral part of the history of the Far East. Although the eastern empire of Kublai and his descendants continued for more than a century to have economic and diplomatic intercourse with the other parts of the Mongol world, this intercourse was little, if at all, more intimate than its relations with Europe. On the other hand, the descendants of Hulagu, of Batu, and of the Jagatai and Ogatai families were drawn into ever closer contact with Europe, Africa, Asia Minor, and India.

Long before he became khan, Kublai had given abundant evidence of his preference for Chinese culture and Chinese administrative methods, and his partiality for the Chinese party was one of the grounds upon which the "old Mongol" party combined to oppose his election. After his accession to supreme power he lost little time in transforming himself into a Chinese emperor. In 1263 he erected at the former Kin capital Yenching an ancestral hall similar to those of the other imperial families of China. In this hall he placed the tablets of the Mongol rulers beginning with Yessugei, bestowing upon them the customary Chinese posthumous titles and proclaiming this line of rulers as the *Yuan* ("Original") dynasty.

As early as 1255 Mangu had recognized the inappropriateness of the old Mongol capital at Karakorum as the center of a great empire and had begun the construction of a new capital on the Chinese side of the Gobi desert, in the region of Dolon Nor. To this new city, in 1264, Kublai gave the name *Shangtu* (the Xanadu of Coleridge), and here, according to Marco Polo, he built a grand palace of marble and stone. Even Shangtu, however, was located too far to the north to be a satisfactory administrative center for an empire in which China was bound to be the most important part; and Kublai soon fixed upon Yenching, where he had already established his ancestral hall, as a more suitable location. In 1267, therefore, on the present site of Peiping, to the northeast of the old Kin city, he commenced the erection of Khanbalik (Cambalech, Cambalu, or Cambaluc), the "City of the Khan."

The death of Mangu had brought a halt in the Mongol campaign against southern China, and Kublai during the first few years of his reign was too fully occupied with his domestic struggle to be able to resume the enterprise. But in 1267, the year in which the construction of Khanbalik was begun, the Mongol armies once more took the field against the Sung empire. In 1276 the Sung capital Linan (modern Hangchow) surrendered to Bayan, the commander in chief of Kublai's army. Three years later the last of the Sung fighting forces were destroyed, and the last Sung emperor, a child of nine, was drowned in the destruction of the fleet. By the Chinese historians the year 1279 is regarded as the last year of the Sung era; from that date the Yuan emperor is acknowledged as the ruler of all China.

To the administration of the now united Chinese Empire, Kublai brought much of the boundless energy which had characterized his less civilized grandfather. Coupled with this energy were a hearty appreciation of Chinese culture and a readiness to depend upon Chinese intelligence for the working out of details. As a result of this combination his reign was marked by a number of noteworthy innovations.

One of Kublai's enterprises, commenced in 1289 on the suggestion of the local authorities in Shantung, proved to be of great value to the empire. In that year he authorized the construction of a canal to connect the Yellow River, which at that time flowed into the sea to the south of the Shantung promontory, with one of the rivers flowing northward to Tientsin. This canal, about eighty miles in length, linked the northern rivers to the ancient system of artificial waterways completed by Sui Yang Ti[1] and established

[1] Cf. ante, p. 96.

an unbroken line of internal water communication between Khanbalik and Hangchow. The Chinese engineers who executed this project approached but did not actually attain a modern "lock" system for their canal: in the stretch of eighty miles they introduced thirty-one dams or sluices and thus created a canal of varying levels, separated by short rapids up which the boats were drawn by means of windlasses. For six centuries this great internal waterway, the Grand Canal, was an important artery in the trade of the Chinese Empire.

As a patron of education Kublai Khan lived up to the traditions established by the great earlier dynasties of China. The two colleges established at Yenching and Pingyang by Ogatai had suffered from neglect during the reigns of Kuyuk and Mangu; they were now restored and considerably expanded by the new monarch. Kublai also built in 1279 an astronomical observatory on the southeast corner of the city wall at Khanbalik; and the original bronze instruments, which were constructed at his command by the Chinese astronomer Ko Chu-king, are still in existence.

Prior to the reign of Kublai the Mongols, having no written symbols of their own, had made use of either the Uighur or the Chinese form of writing. In response to Kublai's orders a scholarly Tibetan lama named Mati Dhwadsha undertook to produce a distinctive system of writing for the Mongol language and elaborated forty-one phonetic symbols by means of which the Mongol speech could be accurately transcribed. Although Kublai, like his predecessors, was consistently tolerant of all varieties of religious belief, he entertained a marked partiality for the Tibetan (Lamaist) (see page 503) form of Buddhism, and Mati Dhwadsha, as a reward for having developed a Mongol script, enjoyed until his death the highest favor of the emperor. The death of this lama favorite did not lessen Kublai's interest in the Tibetan religion, and it is from this period that Lamaism became the dominant religion of the Mongols.

The use of paper currency, whereby Kublai (to the surprise and delight of Marco Polo) was able to keep himself in funds, was neither an innovation nor a blessing for the Chinese. According to the Chinese historian Ma Tuan-lin, squares of white deerskin were used for money as early as the reign of Han Wu Ti (140–86 B.C.). Paper money was used during the ninth century A.D. by the monarchs of the T'ang dynasty, while the Southern Sungs and the Kin rulers of northern China both issued large quantities of paper currency during the twelfth century. Although the Mongols began to issue paper money in 1236, the issues before the accession of Kublai were quite small. Kublai's first issue of paper was in 1260. In 1277 a new issue was put out, and in 1288 he issued a complete new currency which was to exchange at half its nominal value in silver. As the new notes were to exchange for five times their face value in the older issues, it is easy to see how badly the older issues had depreciated. Under Kublai's successors more and more paper was issued, and the value of the currency steadily declined.

Ma Tuan-lin, who wrote during the Mongol regime, makes the following remarks on the subject of paper money:

Paper should never be *money*; it should only be employed as a representative sign of value existing in metals or in produce, which can thus be readily exchanged for paper and the cost of its transport avoided. At first this was the mode in which paper currency was actually used among merchants. The government, borrowing the invention from private individuals, wished to make a real *money* of paper, and thus the original contrivance was perverted.

The constant increase in the amount of paper currency under the Yuan emperors and its steady depreciation in value caused much distress and discontent among the people of the country and helped to bring about the fall of the dynasty.

If Kublai was thoroughly Chinese in his administrative methods, he was quite as thoroughly a Mongol in his unquenchable thirst for world conquest and domination. Even before his armies in southern China had completed their task of crushing the forces of the Sungs, the Great Khan embarked upon a series of aggressive foreign wars which continued to the end of his reign. These wars of conquest fall naturally into two classes: the campaigns for the subjugation of the several states of the Indo-Chinese peninsula, and the overseas expeditions against Japan, the Luchus, and Java.

In his wars against China's continental neighbors to the south
—Burma, Annam, and Champa—Kublai and his generals achieved
a certain measure of apparent success. Yet even here the victories
gained by the Mongol invaders added little to the authority of
their ambitious ruler. Burma, Champa, and Annam all dispatched
tributary missions to Khanbalik, and all were enrolled among the
states recognizing the overlordship of the Yuan emperor. But in
Burma, after winning a victory over the Burmese armies in 1287,
the Mongols were forced to withdraw from the country; the king
of Champa, driven from his capital by the Mongols in 1283, found
a safe refuge in the mountain districts of his little kingdom and
returned to his capital upon the retirement of the enemy; and
the conquest of Annam, which was undertaken in 1282, occupied
the Mongol armies until the end of Kublai's reign, costing him the
life of his eldest son and accomplishing nothing save the ravaging
of some invaded territory.

Two of the overseas expeditions were equally unimportant in
their results. The fleet which was sent in 1291 to conquer the
Luchu Islands lost its commander and returned to the coast of
China without having even sighted the islands for whose conquest
it had been fitted out. The expedition against Java, which was dispatched to punish an insult inflicted upon one of Kublai's ambassadors, reached its objective and carried out in appearance its
punitive task, although the actual punishment fell upon an innocent person. Arriving in Java in the autumn of 1293, Kublai's commanders discovered that the guilty monarch against whom they
had been sent—Kartanagara, the king of Singosari—had been overthrown and put to death by a rebellious vassal, the king of Kediri.
This new potentate offered resistance to the Mongol forces, who
with the assistance of Kartanagara's son-in-law defeated him and
took his capital. After this success their Javanese ally turned against
them, and the Mongol commanders had considerable difficulty in
extricating themselves from the interior of the island. When they
finally succeeded in reaching the coast, Kublai's generals decided
to abandon the campaign; and the expedition returned to China
with a number of prisoners and much booty, having spent four
months in the island and having lost some three thousand men.

The greatest and the most disastrous of Kublai's foreign enterprises, however, was his attempt to conquer the Island Empire, Japan. His attention appears first to have been turned toward Japan by the piratical activities of the Japanese along the coast of Korea, and in 1265 a Korean official is said to have suggested that he call upon the Japanese government to acknowledge his suzerainty. Kublai was incited to action by exaggerated reports[1] concerning the wealth of Japan, and in 1268 he sent his first envoy to Japan with a demand for "the establishment of friendly relations" and with the warning that a rejection of this demand would lead to war. Three years later a second envoy was sent in the person of Chao Liang-pi, former governor of Shensi Province. The Japanese received the new envoy with suspicion and hostility; but Chao, while neglecting no opportunity to spy out the land and to gather such information as might be useful in case of war, succeeded in clearing away the prejudice against him and established himself firmly in the good graces of the Japanese officials. On his return to Khanbalik in 1273, after having spent a year and a half in Japan, Chao Liang-pi advised his emperor against attempting the invasion and conquest of the country. In addition to setting forth the dangers and uncertainties involved in an expedition by sea he pointed out that the Japanese were a brave people, soldiers from birth, and well trained in the arts of war. Moreover, even if the invasion should prove successful, he argued that Japan was really a poor country and that the conquest would benefit neither Kublai nor the Chinese.

In spite of the wise advice of his envoy the emperor decided upon war. In the autumn of 1274 an armada of nine hundred Korean ships, manned by Korean sailors and carrying twenty-five thousand Mongol soldiers, put forth from Korean ports against Japan. The weakly garrisoned islands of Tsushima and Iki were easily captured, and on November 18 the expedition arrived at the port of Hakata, in northern Kyushu. Landing in force on the following morning, the invaders were immediately engaged in battle by the Japanese troops. In the fighting, which lasted throughout the day, the Mongols appear to have enjoyed a slight

[1] These reports are reflected in the tales of Marco Polo.

advantage; their troops were better disciplined and better organized, while their bows and arrows proved more deadly than the long swords of the Japanese. That night, however, the western coast of Kyushu was swept by a typhoon. The Korean navigators did not dare to face the storm in the poorly sheltered harbor of Hakata; hence the entire expedition hastily re-embarked and put to sea. A few of the ships were lost in the storm, and the remainder were driven back to the ports of Korea.

Although the first expedition had failed with a cost of some thirteen thousand men, Kublai was not ready to abandon his ambitious project. In 1275 and again in 1279 he dispatched to Japan envoys who demanded the submission of the empire under threat of invasion; on each occasion the Japanese authorities executed the envoys and defied the Mongols.

In the summer of 1280, having completed the subjugation of the Sung empire, Kublai set to work definitely upon the organization of a second and greater expedition against the Japanese. A hundred thousand picked Mongol troops, twenty thousand Korean soldiers, and fifty thousand Chinese constituted the fighting strength of the expedition. Half the Mongols were sent by land to the Korean port of Fusan, where they embarked with their Korean auxiliaries upon a thousand ships, while the Chinese and the remainder of the Mongols sailed from Zaitun and effected a union with the Korean fleet off the coast of Japan. On June 23, 1281, the combined fleets landed their forces in the province of Hizen, flanking the Japanese, who had assembled a great army of defense at Hakata. For nearly eight weeks the invaders fought desperately to dislodge the Japanese and to establish a firm foothold on Japanese soil. Then, on August 14, the typhoon came once more to the aid of the defenders. More than half the ships of the Mongol armada were destroyed by the storm, and only a fragment of the great expedition succeeded in making good its retreat.

Furious at the failure of his undertaking, Kublai determined upon a third expedition and gave orders for the organization of a fresh armada. The heavy taxes, the commandeering of property, and the requisitioning of labor for carrying out these preparations, however, soon aroused serious discontent, especially in the coast provinces; the civil and military officials all opposed the venture, and Kublai was eventually persuaded to postpone his new attack until the passage of time should have lulled the Japanese into a relaxation of their vigilant defense. The project was therefore allowed to lapse, and the khan soon found sufficient occupation in the prosecution of his other foreign conquests, with the result that the third expedition never materialized. After the death of Kublai his grandson and successor, Timur, countermanded all warlike preparations and even attempted to revive friendly relations with the Japanese. Timur's friendly advances, however, were in vain, and peaceful relations between China and Japan were restored only after the last Mongol ruler had been expelled and the Chinese Empire had been reorganized under the founder of the Ming dynasty.

If to the Western reader Kublai Khan stands out among the rulers of China as an actual person rather than as a mere name, this fact must be attributed in no small measure to the famous Venetian Marco Polo. In 1263 or 1264 Nicolo and Maffeo Polo, two Venetian merchants who had made their way eastward from a Venetian trading post in Crimea, reached the court of Kublai and remained there long enough to gain his favor. In 1269 the Polo brothers returned to Europe, charged with a mission to the Pope: the Great Khan requested that a large body of well-educated missionaries be sent to spread among his people the doctrines of Christianity and the scientific knowledge of the West. Upon their arrival in Europe, Nicolo and Maffeo found some difficulty in discharging the mission with which they had been entrusted; Clement IV was dead, and more than two years elapsed before the election of his successor to the papal throne. In 1271 they decided to return to the East and explain to Kublai the reason for the failure of their mission, and they had actually started back, accompanied by Nicolo's seventeen-year-old son, Marco, when the election of a new Pope finally made it possible for them to deliver the khan's letters into the hands for which they were intended. The new pontiff, however, could send with them only two friars instead of the hundred for whom Kublai had asked, and even these two quickly lost heart and turned back, leaving the three Polos to go alone.

Marco Polo was about twenty-one years of age when he arrived with his father and uncle, in the spring of 1275, at Kublai Khan's headquarters north of the Great Wall; he was thirty-eight when, in 1292, the three Venetians finally departed from China on the return voyage which brought them three years later to their native city. During the seventeen years of their residence in China the Polos, especially young Marco, rose high in the favor of the Mongol emperor. The annals of the Yuan dynasty show that in the year 1277 a man named Polo was appointed an agent of the privy council; between the years 1282 and 1287 Marco, according to his own account, served for three years as chief magistrate of the important city of Yangchow; on several occasions the young Venetian was sent by Kublai on tours of inspection or on missions to the courts of vassal kings; and the last use which Kublai made of the Polos was to appoint them as an escort of honor to accompany a Mongol princess on her voyage to Persia as the chosen bride of Arghun, the grandson of Hulagu.

In the account which as a prisoner of war in a Genoese prison he dictated to his fellow prisoner, Rustician of Pisa, Marco Polo was therefore able to draw upon a wealth of firsthand information concerning the personal characteristics of Kublai as well as the manners, customs, industries, and institutions of the Chinese. Like Herodotus of old, Marco also frequently reported matters of which he had only secondhand information, and such information was not always accurate; but his record of his own experiences and observations has proved to be unusually reliable. His descriptions are substantiated by those given by contemporaneous and later Western travelers, while his accounts of political events at the capital of the khan are verified by Chinese historical records.

Although Marco Polo is by far the best known, he was but one of many Europeans who found their way to the Far East during the period of Mongol domination. Before his time we have John of Plano Carpini and William of Rubruck; after him came John of Monte Corvino, Friar Odoric, John of Marignolli, and others. All these visitors left accounts of their journeys, and in their accounts we find frequent references to hundreds of other Europeans whom the writers had found residing in central or eastern Asia. The authors of most of these records were missionaries, and many of the European residents whom they mention were either fellow missionaries or prisoners of war whom the Mongols had brought back from their western expeditions. But there is ample evidence also of flourishing commercial intercourse between the eastern and western extremities of the Eurasian continent. About 1340 Francesco Balducci Pegolotti, an agent in the employ of the great Florentine commercial house of Baldi, compiled a handbook of information for those who wished to engage in overland trade with "Cathay." Pegolotti had never been to China; apparently he had never been farther east than the island of Cyprus, but the fact that he could and did write such a book bears evidence to the existence both of a considerable body of attainable information concerning the Far East and of an equally considerable interest in Far Eastern trade.

Even more numerous, perhaps, than the European travelers of this period were the non-Europeans who made their way westward across the wide expanses of Asia, and the diary of one such eastern traveler, an Oriental counterpart of the *Book of Marco Polo*, is particularly interesting as furnishing us with a picture of thirteenth-century Europe seen through Far Eastern eyes. At almost the very moment when Marco Polo was starting eastward with his father and his uncle two Nestorian Christians—one of whom, by a curious coincidence, also was named Marco—set forth from Khanbalik on a pilgrimage to the Holy Land. As these two pilgrims, Marco and Sauma,[1] followed in a reverse direction almost the same route as that over which the Polos were traveling, it is possible that the two parties actually met each other on the road. Arriving at Bagdad, the two Nestorians discovered that political conditions made it impracticable for them to continue their pilgrimage to Jerusalem; so they attached themselves to the Christian community at Bagdad, in which both achieved high reputations for piety and learning. In 1281 the Nestorian patriarch died, and Marco was elected to fill this supreme post in the Nestorian church, taking Yaballaha as his patriarchal name.

Six years after the accession of Yaballaha to the patriarchal chair Arghun, the Mongol ruler of Persia, determined to send a

[1] Sauma was the author of the diary.

letter to the Pope, and appointed Yaballaha's fellow pilgrim as his envoy. The embassy went by way of Constantinople to Rome, where Honorius IV died just before its arrival and where Sauma spent some time discussing doctrinal questions with the members of the college of cardinals. From Rome he proceeded to Paris, where he visited Philip IV of France, and to Bordeaux, where he met the English king, Edward I. After these visits Sauma returned to Rome, where he was received by the newly elected Pope Nicholas IV, before whom on at least one occasion he celebrated the Holy Communion according to the Nestorian ritual. He delivered to Nicholas the letter of Arghun and another from Yaballaha; answers to these communications were put into his hands by the Pope, and the envoy finally made his way safely home to Bagdad.

After the death of Kublai Khan, in 1294, the power of his Mongol-Chinese empire rapidly declined. During the space of seventy-four years nine Yuan emperors succeeded to his imperial throne at Khanbalik; then, in 1368, the last of these successors was expelled from the capital and driven northward beyond the Gobi desert. Even during the reign of Kublai, in spite of his efforts to transform himself into a Chinese monarch and to administer his empire in accordance with Chinese traditions, the people of China never lost sight of nor ceased to resent the fact that he was a foreigner; under his less capable and less politic successors this antiforeign opposition to the dynasty steadily increased. But the nationalist uprisings which swept the Mongols from the country and put in their place the founder of the great Ming dynasty were not inspired solely by antiforeign sentiment. The vast military and naval expeditions undertaken by Kublai had thrown a tremendous burden upon the resources of the country and had gained little prestige for him in the eyes of the Chinese people; under his successors the imperial government was unable even to defend the coasts of the empire against the piratical raids of the Japanese. In addition there was widespread economic distress resulting from the mass of steadily depreciating paper currency, while the powers and favors enjoyed by the Tibetan lamas cost the Mongol government the support of the influential Confucian scholars.

THE LATER MONGOLS

In eastern Asia the expulsion of the Mongols from China and the simultaneous disappearance of their influence in Korea marked the end of their career as a dominant people. Driven back into the mountainous region north of the Gobi desert, the Mongols quickly broke up into tribal divisions such as had existed before their unification at the hands of the great Genghis. In one important respect, however, these later Mongols of Mongolia differed from the ancestors who had inhabited the same region. During their domination of China they had come into contact with the doctrines of Tibetan Lamaism and had been deeply influenced by these. This close religious connection between the Mongols and the Tibetans has persisted to the present day. During the fifteenth and sixteenth centuries it gave to certain Mongol chieftains considerable influence in Tibetan affairs, political as well as religious. Many writers, however, regard the establishment of Lamaism among the Mongols as the principal factor in their transformation from the turbulent, warlike tribesmen of earlier times into the peaceful and spiritless herdsmen which they are today.

In central, western, and southern Asia the Mongols were destined still to play an important role. At the very moment when the founder of the Ming dynasty was expelling the descendants of Kublai from China the Mohammedanized Mongol conqueror Tamerlane was making himself the lord of Samarkand. Having established himself as the ruler of central Asia, Tamerlane turned to the northwest and subdued the Golden Horde in southeastern Russia. In 1398 he led his armies southward into India, where he spread ruin and desolation as far as Delhi. Returning from India with his plunder, Tamerlane marched westward into Asia Minor, where in 1402 he inflicted upon the forces of the Seljuk Turks a crushing defeat at Angora. Unable to lead his central-Asian horsemen across the Bosphorus into Europe, he reluctantly returned to Samarkand and was planning a great expedition for the reconquest of China when, in 1405, death overtook him.

Upon the death of Tamerlane his empire fell apart even more quickly than it had been conquered. In Russia the power of the

Golden Horde, who immediately regained their independence, persisted until the middle of the sixteenth century, while the central-Asian domains were divided among a number of petty rulers. A hundred and twenty years after Tamerlane's death one of his descendants, Babur, succeeded in re-establishing a portion of his ancestor's empire; then, marching down into India, he conquered the northern districts of that great country and laid the foundations of the Mogul empire.

Summary

From the assumption of the title of khan by Genghis in 1203 until the expulsion of the last Yuan emperor from China in 1368 the Mongols were the dominating factor in the history of eastern Asia, while their power extended over almost the entire continent of Asia, together with a large portion of Europe. From Genghis to Kublai a line of extremely energetic rulers, aided by military subordinates who displayed real genius in the art of war, advanced by an almost unbroken series of victories to world domination, Kublai's two ill-fated expeditions against Japan being the only important setback suffered during this period by the Mongol arms. Even before this wide-flung empire had reached its zenith, however, disintegration began to set in. At the very moment that Kublai was extending his authority over the last fragments of the Sung empire, central Asia was breaking up into independent Mongol states; after his death all vestiges of Mongol unity rapidly disappeared.

The disintegration of the Mongol power was quickened, if not caused, by the readiness with which they adopted the culture of the more civilized peoples whom they had conquered. Endowed with a real genius for war, the Mongols as administrators appear never to have risen above mediocrity,[1] and their often superficial adoption of superior alien culture resulted in the decay of their military virtues without any compensating development of the qualities needed for the establishment of a permanent well-ordered society.

---

[1] Genghis and Kublai, perhaps, should be regarded as exceptions.

In spite of their failure to establish a permanent empire and in spite of their feeble contributions to civilization the Mongols should not be dismissed as a merely destructive influence in the development of Far Eastern history. Destructive they unquestionably were, and certain portions of central Asia never recovered, probably never will recover, from the devastation which they inflicted; but they were also a powerful integrating force, and the result of the Mongol conquests was to establish throughout Asia, and between Asia and Europe, a degree of cultural intercourse hitherto unknown. After the dissolution of the Mongol power this exchange of ideas gradually died out, and the two worlds—European and Far Eastern—once more became absorbed in their own domestic affairs.

Even in Europe, however, the effects of this century or more of intercourse never wholly disappeared. In Russia the domination of the Golden Horde continued down to the moment when the Muscovite rulers were strong enough to commence their eastward expansion through Siberia to the shores of the Pacific Ocean. Farther west, although the writings of John of Plano Carpini, William of Rubruck, John of Monte Corvino, and others gathered the dust of ages in royal or papal archives, the tales told by Marco Polo remained in circulation and kept alive some measure of interest in the wonderful lands of Cathay and Chipango.

Of all the regions over which the Mongols extended their sway China was the country which, despite the incapacity and misgovernment of the later Yuan emperors, derived the most permanent benefits from the period. As an offset to this misgovernment and to the destructiveness of the Mongol invasions China saw herself, for the first time since the decline of the T'ang dynasty, reunited into a single state which henceforth included the ancient independent kingdom of Nanchao, the modern province of Yunnan. This political unity, which coincided closely with a unity in general culture, has been maintained down to the present. In addition China benefited, probably more than did any of her Asiatic neighbors, from the cultural exchange which went on during the high tide of Mongol power. Like the great age of T'ang, the Mongol age was for China a period in which the nation's horizon was broadened by new contacts, and much of the artistic, literary, and economic activity which characterizes the days of the Ming dynasty must be attributed to the new and enriching elements that found their way into the country during the reigns of Kublai and his successors.

SUGGESTED REFERENCES

BARTHOLD, W. Turkestan down to the Mongol Invasion.

BRETSCHNEIDER, E. Mediaeval Researches from Eastern Asiatic Sources.

CAHUN, L. Introduction à l'histoire de l'Asie.

CURTIN, J. The Mongols: a History.

CZAPLICKA, M. A. The Turks of Central Asia.

D'OHSSON, C. Histoire des Mongols.

HOWORTH, SIR H. H. The History of the Mongols.

KOMROFF, M. Travels of Marco Polo, the Venetian.

LAMB, H. Genghis Khan.

LAMB, H. Tamerlane.

LATOURETTE, K. S. The Chinese: their History and Culture.

LATOURETTE, K. S. A History of Christian Missions in China.

MONTGOMERY, J. A. The History of Yaballaha III.

PELLIOT, P. "Les Mongols et la papauté," *Revue de l'Orient chrétien*, 1922–1923, pp. 3–30.

ROCKHILL, W. W. (translator and editor). The Journey of William of Rubruck.

WILLIAMS, E. T. A Short History of China.

YULE, SIR H. The Book of Ser Marco Polo.

YULE, SIR H. Cathay and the Way Thither.

XIII

China and Korea: from the Expulsion of the Mongols to the End of the Fifteenth Century

The Rise of Chu Yüan-chang · Expulsion of the Mongols · The Ming Dynasty · Hung Wu and the Empress Ma · The Usurpation of the Prince of Yen · Yung Lo · Ming China and its Neighbors · Relations with Japan, Nepal, Burma, Korea, and the Luchus · The Voyages of Cheng Ho · Consequences of Cheng Ho's Missions · Closure of the Western Trade Routes · The Disappearance of Christianity · Prosperity and Culture of Fifteenth-Century China · Korea's New Dynasty · The Reforms of Yi Tai-jo · Yi Tai-jo's Successors · Relations with China and Japan · The Yalu River Frontier · Fifteenth-Century Korea

THE half-century which followed the death of Kublai Khan saw the outbreak of anti-Mongol rebellions in all parts of China, and by the middle of the fourteenth century there had appeared among the various rebel leaders one who was able eventually not only to drive the foreign rulers from the country but also to subdue his many rivals and to reunite the Chinese Empire under a lasting dynasty. Chu Yüan-chang, the future founder of the Ming dynasty, was born in 1327 of peasant parents. At the age of seventeen, having been left an orphan without means of support, Chu entered a Buddhist monastery and became a monk. After some seven years, however, he wearied of monastic life and took service as a soldier in the forces of Kuo Tzu-hsing, an anti-Mongol leader in the modern province of Anhui. The abilities of the ex-monk soon attracted the attention of his leader and brought him rapid promotion. In 1356 the young adventurer, who by this time had risen to the command of a separate rebel army, crossed to the south bank of the Yangtze, where he besieged and captured the important city of Nanking.

Upon his capture of Nanking, Chu proclaimed the re-establishment of the ancient lower-Yangtze state of Wu; he assumed the title Duke, and the death of his former leader, Kuo Tzu-hsing, soon left him without a serious rival in the lower Yangtze valley.

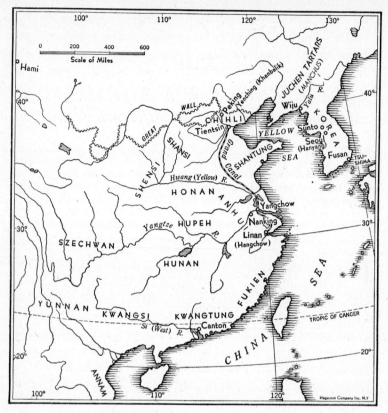

Fifteenth Century China and Korea

While many—perhaps most—of the other rebel leaders were little more than bandits, plundering the defenseless people and fighting among themselves for the richest booty, Chu Yüan-chang distinguished himself both by the strictness with which he repressed the pillaging of his troops and by his constant efforts to secure the co-operation of all Chinese patriots in one great undertaking, the expulsion of the Mongols. As a result of these statesmanlike policies Chu became more and more widely recognized as the outstanding leader of Chinese nationalism, and an ever increasing stream of recruits from all parts of the country took service under his banner. By the summer of 1366, ten years after his assumption of the title Duke of Wu, his authority was firmly established over the entire Yangtze valley east of the gorges, and he had abandoned to his generals the purely military aspects of the struggle in order to devote his energies to the task of organizing for his growing domain an efficient administrative system based upon the soundest of Chinese traditions.

During 1367 and the first half of 1368 the power of the Duke of Wu was extended southward, with little actual fighting, over the provinces of Fukien, Kwangtung, and Kwangsi, while the spring of 1368 also witnessed a steady northward advance of the Chinese armies into Honan and Shantung. By midsummer of 1368 only two—Hopei and Shansi—of the eighteen provinces south of the Great Wall remained in Mongol hands, and at the beginning of the "seventh moon" Chu moved northward at the head of a mighty army to complete the liberation of the country. This northern campaign proved to be a triumphal parade; city after city opened its gates with hardly a show of resistance, and on the twenty-first day of the "eighth moon" (about mid-September) the southern forces entered Khanbalik, from which the Mongol court had fled to seek safety beyond the frontier.

During the twelve years following his assumption of the title Duke of Wu, Chu had repeatedly refused to adopt the more pretentious title Emperor. After the unification of the empire under his rule every reason favored his taking this long-delayed step, and he proclaimed himself emperor, giving to his dynasty the name *Ta Ming* ("Great Brilliance") and dating the commencement of his reign from the first day of the first moon of the year 1368. In the dynastic tables the first Ming emperor, like the founders of a number of other Chinese dynasties, is listed as *T'ai Tsu* ("Great Ancestor"). From the beginning of the Ming regime down to the end of the empire, however, the emperors of China are known not by their "temple names" but by the *nien hao* ("auspicious designation") of their reigns.

Since the days of Han, in the second century B.C., *nien hao* had been employed to designate special periods,[1] of varying length,

---

[1] The reign of Han Wu Ti, for instance, was divided into eleven *nien hao* periods, some of four years and some of six.

within a single reign, and this system had been introduced about the beginning of the seventh century into Japan; henceforth, however, each reign in China was to have but a single *nien hao*. Such designations, selected by each new sovereign at the time of his accession, were intended to foreshadow the policy and the nature of the ensuing reign. In view of the warlike exploits which had paved the way for the foundation of his dynasty Chu Yüan-chang adopted for his reign the *nien hao* "Hung Wu" ("Vastly Martial"); he is consequently referred to as the Hung Wu emperor or, less accurately but more frequently, as Emperor Hung Wu.

During the first few years after his assumption of the imperial title the new emperor, who had retained Nanking as his capital, was busily engaged in pursuing and crushing the fugitive princes of the Mongol royal family and in forcing the submission of local rulers in the more distant parts of his empire. By the year 1372 these military undertakings necessary for the consolidation of the Ming power had been completed. In 1374 there was a brief revival of hostilities by the Mongols on the northern frontier, and in 1381 the southwestern province of Yunnan, whose leaders had submitted nine years earlier to the new regime, was the scene of a revolt which was not finally suppressed until the end of 1383. With these exceptions, however, the last twenty-six years of the reign were characterized by an almost complete absence of the martial activity foreshadowed by its *nien hao*.

Once firmly established on the throne, indeed, the founder of the Ming dynasty appears to have turned definitely from his earlier warlike interests to the more prosaic task of giving to his people the best possible government. Fully appreciating the fact that the success of a government depends upon the character and ability of its subordinate officers quite as much as upon the good intentions of the monarch, he made every effort to build up and to maintain throughout the empire a body of well-qualified civil officials. To ensure the training and appointment of men who, being thoroughly imbued with the social philosophy of Confucius, would be guided in their public acts by the principles of justice and propriety, the ancient system of literary examinations was reorganized. In order to preclude as far as possible favoritism in local administration (perhaps, also, in order to draw the different sections of the empire more closely together) he inaugurated the policy of appointing all officials to posts outside the provinces in which they were born. Knowing that the officials, especially those of the more distant provinces, were prone to conceal unpleasant truths from the eyes of the emperor, he issued a decree providing severe penalties for any officer who should fail to report promptly the occurrence of a drought, flood, or other disaster within his jurisdiction. The ancient laws of the T'ang dynasty were revived, and in 1373 a new code, based upon that of the T'ang, was issued. Abolishing the four ministries of the Mongol regime,—finances, justice, rites, and war,—the Ming ruler reorganized the central administration by creating six "boards": Civil Appointments, Finances, Rites, War, Justice, and Public Works.

The greatness of the emperor Hung Wu as a ruler lay primarily in the fact that he never lost his contact with and his understanding of the common people from whom he had risen. Throughout his long reign he appears to have retained his simple peasant tastes, and his ideal continued to be a government under which the poorest subject would be protected in his rights. But he realized that the people, on their side, ought to be properly educated as to their part in the maintenance of peace and good order. With this end in view he drew up and issued in the form of an imperial decree six moral exhortations to the people: "Practice filial piety toward your father and your mother." "Respect your elders and your superiors." "Live in harmony with the people of your district and your village." "Instruct your children in good manners." "Occupy yourself peacefully with your trade." "Do no evil." Trite as they may seem, these pious maxims served to strengthen the position of the Ming dynasty among the Chinese people; and three centuries later the great Manchu emperor K'ang Hsi elaborated them into his famous "Sacred Edict" which he issued for the same general purpose.

During the first fourteen years of his reign Hung Wu appears to have been greatly influenced in his policy and his important decisions by the advice of the empress Ma. This capable and level-headed woman was the daughter of Kuo Tzu-hsing and had married the future founder of the Ming dynasty about the time of his assumption of the title Duke of Wu. Until her death in 1382 she was a constant influence on the side of mildness and peace. After this date the rule of Hung Wu was noticeably more harsh than it had been in earlier years. This change may have been due in part to the growing irritability of advancing age, but there is reason to believe that it was partly attributable to the removal of the steadying influence of the empress.

The death of Hung Wu, in the summer of 1398, opened the way to four years of domestic turmoil in the recently united empire. The first Ming ruler was survived by six of his sixteen sons, each of whom had been entrusted with the administration of a division of the empire. The most capable and energetic of these six surviving sons was Chu Ti, who, having been created prince of Yen, had authority over the northeastern provinces, with his capital at Yenching (Peking, or modern Peiping). In spite of the outstanding ability of Chu Ti, Hung Wu had designated as heir to the throne his oldest son, Chu Piao; and in 1392, on the death of Chu Piao, Chu Ti was again passed over in favor of a ten-year-old son of the deceased heir apparent. In the spring of 1398, apparently realizing that his end was near, the aged emperor had ordered his six sons to leave the imperial court at Nanking and to take up residence in their respective appanages; as a result of this step the officials at Nanking were able to proclaim the accession of the sixteen-year-old Chu Yun-wen before his uncles had learned of their father's death.

The young emperor, who is usually known by his *nien hao* "Chien Wen," had no sooner seated himself upon the throne than he began to take energetic steps against his powerful uncles, all of whom were suspected of entertaining dangerous ambitions. Within a year after his accession five of the six had been satisfactorily dealt with: one had been sent into exile in Yunnan, one had committed suicide, three had been stripped of their powers and reduced to the status of private subjects. The prince of Yen, however, was too capable, too powerful, and too far removed from Nanking to be caught off his guard, and the harsh treatment which had been inflicted upon his brothers transformed him from a possible supporter to an irreconcilable enemy of the Nanking government.

In the spring of 1400 Chu Ti issued at Yenching a manifesto denouncing the ministers on whose advice the young emperor had laid impious hands upon the sons of Hung Wu, and he declared his intention of proceeding to Nanking at the head of an army for the purpose of redressing the wrong which had been committed. The role of redressor of wrongs served but to cloak the ambitions of a usurper. By the end of 1402 Chu Ti was completely master of the northern provinces, and the following spring saw him advancing southward upon the capital. Against this advance the disorganized forces of Nanking were able to offer little resistance. The capital surrendered without a struggle; the unfortunate young emperor, abandoning his throne, took the tonsure as a Buddhist monk, and the prince of Yen, in the sixth moon of 1403, assumed the imperial power.

For his *nien hao* the new emperor chose "Yung Lo" ("Eternal Happiness"), a designation which seems hardly more appropriate than that chosen by his father. Founded upon usurpation and consolidated by the ruthless slaughter of all who had supported the cause of his nephew, the rule of the third Ming emperor was characterized by harshness and severity rather than by happiness. Yet the emperor Yung Lo, usurper though he was, must be counted among the great emperors of China. His reign of twenty-one years served to complete the task begun by Hung Wu and to consolidate the power of the Ming dynasty so thoroughly that his successors were able to hold the imperial throne for more than two centuries after his death.

Yung Lo had no love for the city of Nanking, and in 1409 he transferred the offices of the imperial administration northward to his own city of Yenching, whose name was now changed to Peking. Twelve years later Peking was formally proclaimed the capital of the empire, a dignity which it was to enjoy for slightly more than five hundred years. Although the emperor's personal preference for the northern city unquestionably had much to do with this transfer, there were other good reasons why the capital of China should at this time be located in the north rather than in the Yangtze valley. The recently expelled Mongols were still far from being a negligible factor in China's foreign relations, and Yung Lo was compelled to maintain a close watch upon the northern frontier in order to protect his country against fresh invasions. Even after the close of his reign these warlike northern neighbors continued to threaten the peace of the empire, and Yung Lo's successors at Peking were in constant need of keeping them under close observation.

In addition to carrying on these wars on the northern frontiers the warlike Yung Lo, in 1406, sent an army into the neighboring kingdom of Annam, where continued internal disorders appeared to provide a suitable pretext for intervention. In 1407 Annam was reannexed to the empire, of which it remained a part until 1428, four years after Yung Lo's death, when it once more regained its independence.

At the same time that his forces were subduing the Annamese, Yung Lo also re-established Chinese authority at Hami, in Chinese Turkestan, partly in order to possess an outpost from which to keep watch over the Mongols and partly for the purpose of regaining control over the western caravan routes. This western extension of the imperial authority was accomplished by peaceful means; but half a century after the death of Yung Lo the local Turfan chieftain revolted against his Chinese overlord, and the resultant struggle between the Turfans and the Chinese lasted intermittently for about forty years before the local rulers finally submitted to Chinese rule.

Except for these two enterprises of Yung Lo, only the first of which may be regarded as aggressive, the Ming period in Chinese history appears to have been entirely free from attempts at territorial expansion. Even Yung Lo was usually content to live at peace with his neighbors and to devote his energies to the internal problems of government. Yet the period of Ming rule, at least during the first century and a half, was not marked by the same neglect of foreign relations as had characterized the Sung regime. Both Hung Wu and Yung Lo realized the importance of commercial and diplomatic intercourse with the outside world. Less warlike than the emperors of the Han dynasty and less ambitious in their diplomatic undertakings than the great rulers of the T'ang, the early monarchs of the Ming dynasty exerted themselves to secure the respect as well as the good will of the other Far Eastern nations, and the capital of their empire became once more the goal of diplomatic missions from the greater part of the Orient.

As a result of Kublai Khan's two disastrous attempts, in 1274 and 1281, to bring Japan under his imperial sway the remaining period of Mongol rule in China saw the interruption of all official intercourse and of practically all commercial contact between the Chinese and their island neighbors. During this period of eighty-odd years a considerable number of Chinese Buddhists made their way to Japan as missionaries, while in 1342 the first Ashikaga Shogun, Takauji, opened a limited trade with the southern ports of China for the purpose of obtaining articles necessary for the equipment of the Tenryu-ji temple; otherwise the contact between the two empires was limited to the piratical expeditions of Japanese freebooters, who avenged the Mongol attacks by ravaging the coasts of China as well as those of the Korean peninsula.

These depredations were at their height when the Ming dynasty came into power, and Hung Wu lost no time in protesting to the Japanese government against the lawless actions of its unruly subjects. Satisfactory negotiations between the Chinese and Japanese courts were impeded by the fact that Japan at this time was engaged in the bitter civil war known as the War of Succession.[1] In 1380 a Buddhist monk sent by Hung Wu as ambassador to the so-called Southern Court was thrown into prison by the Japanese authorities; and the next Chinese ambassador, who was sent to the same court a year later, was able to obtain no satisfaction on the subject of piracy, although his threatening language induced the southern authorities to release the imprisoned envoy. Learning now, apparently for the first time, of the existence of a rival government, the Chinese emperor subsequently directed his attention to the Northern Court at Kyoto, where Yoshimitsu, the third Shogun of the Ashikaga line, held the power.

Ashikaga Yoshimitsu, like the other Shoguns of his line, was a patron of Zen Buddhism; and his Zen councilors were anxious to see the restoration of friendly intercourse with China, from whose monasteries of the Zen cult they derived their spiritual inspiration.

[1] See Chapter XVII, p. 390.

The Shogun therefore met the Chinese complaints by handing over for punishment a number of notorious pirates. In 1392 the termination of the dynastic conflict left the Shogun at the head of a re-united—and comparatively peaceful—state. He now entered upon a course of negotiations which resulted, about the year 1401, in the conclusion of a formal treaty of friendship and commerce between the two countries. The Japanese government pledged itself to put an end to the piratical expeditions, while the treaty further provided for an exchange of embassies at ten-year intervals.

Yoshimitsu, whose subservience to the Chinese emperor was carried to such a point that it has brought upon him the bitter reproaches of Japanese historians, made earnest and decidedly effective efforts to put an end to the activities of the Japanese pirates and to promote legitimate commerce with China. His immediate successors in the Shogunal office also attempted to keep on cordial terms with China, and the trade between the two countries continued to flourish until practically the end of the fifteenth century. After this date, however, the decline of the Ashikaga power in Japan removed all domestic checks upon Japanese piracy.

In the years 1384 and 1385 formal diplomatic relations were established between the Ming emperor and the rulers of Nepal and Burma respectively. Intercourse with the first of these countries was opened by Hung Wu, who in 1384 sent a Buddhist monk as his ambassador to the Nepalese king. Three years later a return embassy arrived at Nanking, and tributary missions from Nepal continued to arrive at the Ming court at regular intervals until 1427.

Between China and Burma official intercourse was opened on the initiative of the ruler of the recently established kingdom of Ava in the upper Irrawaddy. In 1383, being seriously troubled by attacks on his northern frontiers by the Shans, this monarch sent an embassy to the Chinese court, by way of Yunnan, to lodge a complaint against his troublesome neighbors. The Burmese embassy, which arrived at Nanking in 1385, secured for its sender imperial recognition as lord of Ava and brought to his Shan neighbors a pious exhortation to keep the peace. The Chinese government, fully appreciating the value of the trade routes through Burma to the ports on the Bay of Bengal, consistently endeavored to maintain peace among the warring tribes of this region, and about the middle of the fifteenth century the official records list at least three Burmese states—Ava, Pegu, and Hsenwi—among the countries whose rulers were regarded as vassals of the Chinese imperial throne.

In 1392 the Korean people, as will be seen later, took advantage of the Mongol collapse to overthrow their old, discredited dynasty and to establish a new line of rulers upon the throne. The new dynasty promptly restored Korea to its ancient position as vassal of the Chinese Empire. The Chinese calendar was adopted, and tributary missions were dispatched at regular intervals to the imperial court. In the same year, also, the king of the Luchu Islands acknowledged himself a vassal of the Ming emperor and dispatched his sons and his younger brothers to Nanking to be educated in the imperial college.

The emperor Yung Lo, whose armed intervention in and subsequent annexation of Annam have already been mentioned, sent embassies in the first year of his reign to Java, Sumatra, Siam, and Bengal. Two years later he dispatched the eunuch Cheng Ho upon the first of a series of remarkable expeditions to the maritime countries of the south and west.

Sailing in the summer of 1405 from the mouth of the Yangtze River with a fleet of sixty-two ships manned by an impressive force of sailors and soldiers, Cheng Ho in the course of slightly more than two years visited the Philippine Islands, Sulu, Borneo, Cochin China, Cambodia, Siam, the Malay peninsula, Sumatra, and Java. The fleet under Cheng Ho's command was well loaded with gold, silks, and other valuables intended for use as presents to the rulers of the various states at whose ports it touched, and the commander of the expedition appears to have made more use of the presents than of the fighting force at his disposal. On his return to China in the fall of 1407 he was accompanied by envoys from the various states which had willingly acknowledged the suzerainty of the Ming emperor and by the ruler of Palembang, in Sumatra, who had been made prisoner for having plotted an attack upon the Chinese.

After a year spent in repairing and reorganizing his fleet Cheng Ho sailed again in the fall of 1408, with forty-eight ships, upon a fresh expedition. Many of the places at which he had touched on his first voyage were again visited, but this time the Chinese fleet passed also through the Strait of Malacca and proceeded westward as far as Ceylon and the coast of India. During the visit at Ceylon the ruler of the island attempted to surprise and capture the Chinese envoy. The plot was discovered, and Cheng Ho brought the indiscreet monarch back to China as a prisoner, together with his family and his principal officials. Upon the return of the expedition in 1411 Yung Lo liberated the captives; but the guilty king was deposed, and the Chinese emperor appointed a successor who appears to have occupied the throne of Ceylon until 1462 and to have paid regular tribute to China as late as the year 1459.

Cheng Ho's third expedition, which lasted from November, 1412, until late in the summer of 1415, was chiefly occupied with the one serious military undertaking which arose out of this extended effort to spread China's prestige: the conquest of Acheh, or Achin, in northern Sumatra. According to the account written by Ma Huan, who accompanied the expedition as an interpreter, this campaign in Sumatra was directed against a usurper and resulted in restoring to the throne the son of the monarch whom the usurper had murdered. During the last twenty years of his life Cheng Ho made four other voyages, the last of which—between the years 1430 and 1435—took him as far to the west as Ormuz, on the Persian Gulf.

Partly by their imposing military strength but even more by their dazzling opulence the expeditions under Cheng Ho succeeded in raising China's prestige among the Indo-Chinese and Malay states to a height which probably never had been attained at any earlier period in the history of the Far East. In Ceylon and in northern Sumatra force had been employed to overcome the opposition of hostile rulers, but in the other countries visited by Cheng Ho the mere show of power and wealth had sufficed to convince the local monarchs of the greatness of their northern neighbor and to persuade them to dispatch tributary missions to the Ming court. In 1405 and in 1407 envoys came to Nanking from the king of Malacca; 1406 saw the arrival of envoys from the petty rulers of Borneo, Luzon, and Bruni, while in 1408 the rulers of the two latter came in person to pay their respects to the Chinese emperor. In 1411 the king of Malacca also visited the Chinese court in person, and three rulers of Sulu are said to have come with their families and their retinues in the year 1417. From a number of the Malaysian states the envoys to China appear to have continued only throughout the reign of Yung Lo, or at most until Cheng Ho ceased his periodic visits to the archipelago; but the rulers of Malacca, from 1411 until the arrival of the Portuguese just a century later, maintained their tributary relationship with the Chinese court.

Behind this diplomatic intercourse, with its stately trappings of official embassies and tributary missions, was the even more important growing commercial contact between China and the Malay world. Except with Malacca, which was the focal point for the trade of the archipelago, China's diplomatic intercourse with the region south of Cambodia and Siam quickly lapsed; but throughout the entire fifteenth century Chinese merchants, especially those from the provinces of Fukien and Kwangtung, carried on a flourishing commerce with all the principal islands of the East Indies. Silk and cotton cloth, iron implements and porcelain, gold, silver, and copper were exported from China and were exchanged for the various products, particularly the spices and fine woods, of the Malay Islands. Even after the arrival of the Europeans in the sixteenth century this commercial activity of the Chinese persisted, and the Chinese colonies established in the regions under Portuguese, Spanish, and Dutch control were merely a continuation of the colonizing tendency which had been displayed when these same islands were under non-European rule.

Even the official tribute missions to the Chinese court seem, indeed, to have constituted so many thinly veiled commercial transactions, and this aspect of China's relations with her vassals persisted at least to a late date in the nineteenth century. In 1889 W. W. Rockhill, who was traveling westward from Peking to the Tibetan frontier, fell in with a Nepalese mission on its homeward journey, of which he writes:

The mission was in no hurry to get home, as the chiefs and even the servants were in receipt of a daily allowance from the Chinese government as long as they were in the empire, and were transported, fed, and lodged free of all expense, nor did they have to pay any duties or octroi dues on their goods, either when going to Peking or when returning home. There were about forty persons in the mission, a number of them Chinese from the Tibetan border-land or from Lhasa, these latter acting as interpreters for the Goorkhas, with whom they conversed in Tibetan. All tribute missions to the Court of Peking are treated with the same liberality as was this one, and as the members of such missions can bring to Peking a very large amount of goods to sell free of all charges, and carry back to the frontier of their own country an equally large quantity under the same favorable conditions, it is no wonder that the right to present tribute to the emperor is considered a valuable privilege, and is eagerly sought after by tribes and peoples living near the Chinese border.

The diplomatic and commercial activity of Ming China in the regions to the south appears to have been caused, in part at least, by the closure of the ancient land routes to the west, along which, for a millennium and a half, trade had been carried on between China and the Mediterranean world. In the first year of his reign the emperor Yung Lo had taken steps to cultivate friendly relations with the Tibetans, summoning to his court the lama Ha-li-ma, upon whom he conferred the titles "Sovereign of the Great and Precious Law" and "Grand Excellent Buddha of the Western Paradise." Three years later, as we have seen, the same emperor established a Chinese government at Hami, on the old trade route through Eastern Turkestan.

Beyond Tibet and the more eastern portions of Turkestan, however, all Asia was in chaos. The western portion of Eastern Turkestan and a considerable portion of Western Turkestan were under the rule of the various descendants of Jagatai, the second son of Genghis Khan, while to the southwest of the territories ruled by the Jagatai princes lay the empire of the conquering Tamerlane, which, after Tamerlane's death in 1405, quickly broke up into its component parts. Yung Lo and his successors were able to maintain China's prestige among such of the western tribes as were situated on the frontier of the empire; but the constant strife among the warlike peoples of central and western Asia made travel through these regions extremely hazardous, and the Ming period saw the prompt disappearance of the voluminous trade which had traversed Asia during the days when the authority of the Great

Khan was acknowledged from the Sea of Japan to the banks of the Danube.

Partly by reason of this interruption of land communication across Asia the fall of the Mongols in China was quickly followed by the collapse of the Franciscan mission which had been built up by John of Monte Corvino and his successors. This mission appears never to have admitted any of its local converts to holy orders, but to have depended entirely upon European reinforcements to recruit the ranks of its clergy. Even before the actual expulsion of the Mongols from Peking the chaotic conditions in the west had interrupted these reinforcements; and although appointments to the see of Cambaluc continued to be made as late as 1475, there is no evidence of the arrival of new missionaries in China after the middle of the fourteenth century.

Another cause for the disappearance of Christianity from China after the establishment of the Ming dynasty may be found in the patronage which the Franciscan mission had enjoyed under the Mongol emperors. In the eyes of the Chinese people Christianity was not merely a foreign religion with a purely foreign body of clergy; it was also a religion closely identified with the foreign conquerors who held the empire in bondage. Like Nestorian Christianity, which also received the patronage of the Mongol khans, the Roman form of Christianity appears to have made few, if any, converts among the purely Chinese elements of the population and therefore to have failed to secure any real foothold on Chinese soil.

It is even possible that the active interest of Kublai Khan and his successors in Europeans, merchants as well as missionaries, served to involve the latter in the patriotic hostility which the Chinese displayed toward their alien rulers and that the prompt disappearance of Christianity came, in part, as a result of a positive anti-Christian trend in Chinese patriotism. Yet the following passage from the *Ming Shih* ("History of the Ming Dynasty") seems to indicate that the first Ming emperor, at least, was quite anxious to remain on cordial terms with the European countries:

At the close of the Yuan Dynasty a native of this country [*Fulin*, the Chinese name for the Roman Empire], named *Nieh-ku-lun* [possibly a Chinese transcription of Nicholas], came to China for trading purposes.

When after the fall of the Yuan, he was not able to return, the Emperor T'ai Tsu, who had heard of this, commanded him to his presence in the eighth month of the fourth year of Hung Wu [September, 1371] and gave orders that an official letter be placed in his hands for transmission to his king, which read as follows : "Since the Sung Dynasty had lost the throne and Heaven had cut off their sacrifice, the Yuan Dynasty had risen from the desert to enter and rule over China for more than a hundred years, when Heaven, wearied of their misgovernment and debauchery, thought also fit to turn their fate to ruin, and the affairs of China were in a state of disorder for eighteen years. But when the nation began to arouse itself, We, as a simple peasant of Huai-yu, conceived the patriotic idea to save the people. . . . We have established peace in the Empire and restored the old boundaries of Our Middle Land. We were selected by Our people to occupy the Imperial throne of China under the dynastic title of 'the Great Ming,' commencing with Our reign styled Hung Wu, of which We now are in the fourth year. We have sent officers with this Manifesto except to you Fulin, who, being separated from Us by the western sea, have not yet received the announcement. We now send a native of your own country, Nieh-ku-lun, to hand you this Manifesto. Although We are not equal in wisdom to our ancient rulers whose virtue was recognized all over the universe, We cannot but let the world know Our intention to maintain peace within the four seas. It is on this ground alone that We have issued this Manifesto."

At peace with their neighbors except for occasional disturbances created by the border tribes on the north and northwest, and content to follow a purely defensive policy on the frontiers, the emperors of the Ming dynasty were able to devote their energies to the internal affairs of the empire, and in this field much was done to foster the welfare of the Chinese people. Imperial commissions were appointed to inspect and to improve the waterways throughout the country ; reservoirs and irrigation canals were maintained to provide adequate supplies of water for agriculture in times of drought ; river channels were dredged and dikes were constructed to guard against the danger of floods. Public granaries were established in all parts of the country in order to ensure a food reserve in case of poor crops. Taxes were revised downward, and the actual burden of taxation was further reduced by employing the army to transport the "tribute rice" from the provinces to the capital instead of making this transportation, as in earlier days, an additional charge upon the provincial treasuries. The dredging of the river channels, undertaken primarily as a measure for the prevention of floods, greatly improved the internal transportation facilities of the empire. Especially in the coastal provinces, domestic trade rapidly increased, and this growth of domestic trade reacted favorably upon the foreign commerce which had been so energetically fostered by the expeditions of Cheng Ho.

For nearly a century after the reign of Yung Lo the political history of Ming China is characterized by a dull monotony in which few events or rulers stand out as especially worthy of mention. Yet the drabness of this political record, punctuated only by border troubles or by the follies of mediocre occupants of the throne, covers an era of prosperity and general well-being such as probably has never been surpassed in Chinese history. During this period art and architecture flourished as in the great days of Han, T'ang, and Sung; lacking, perhaps, the originality which had characterized the work of the earlier periods, the painters of the Ming Age nevertheless produced pictures rivaling those of contemporary Italy, while splendid buildings were erected at Peking, at Nanking, and at other important cities throughout the land.

Even more notable was the development of the industrial arts, in which beauty of design and skill of execution were carried to new heights. The bronzes and porcelains of the Ming dynasty are especially famous for their graceful shapes and beautiful workmanship; the making of cloisonné and damascene ware—introduced into China from the West during the Mongol period—was firmly established among the country's industries, while the weaving of plain and brocaded silks was carried on with increasing skill. In spite of the fact that by the year 1500 the Italian Renaissance had been in progress for more than a century, China at that date was far ahead of any European country in wealth, industry, and general culture.

KOREA'S NEW DYNASTY

The expulsion of the Mongols from China by the forces of the first Ming emperor had been followed almost immediately by the utter collapse of their authority in the neighboring kingdom of Korea. For almost a quarter of a century the descendants of Wang

Kien, freed from the domination of their Mongol masters, continued to occupy the throne at Sunto; but their long subservience to the Mongols had destroyed their claim to be regarded as a national dynasty, and their wild misgovernment soon aroused against them the hatred of the heavily burdened Korean people. The last monarch of the Wang dynasty came to the throne in 1389, and the popular discontent with his rule found a leader in the person of one of his ablest advisers, General Yi Syeng-kyei,[1] who was the commander in chief of the Korean army as well as the father-in-law of the king.

Yi appears to have enjoyed the respect and confidence both of his colleagues in official life and of the people at large. For three years he attempted with little success to curb the excesses of his royal son-in-law, but in 1392, recognizing the hopelessness of this task, he deposed the king and with the general approval of the nation seated himself upon the throne as the founder of a new dynasty. In the annals of his country the new monarch is known as Yi Tai-jo[2] ("Great Ancestor of the Yi"), and the royal line which he established was destined to occupy the Korean throne for five hundred and eighteen years, surrendering the royal power only in 1910, when the peninsula was annexed to the Japanese Empire.

As king in his own right, Yi Tai-jo devoted himself to the task of reforming the manifold abuses which had developed during the later reigns of the Wang dynasty. To facilitate this reform program he transferred the capital from Sunto, where it had been located under the previous royal line, to a newly built city on the banks of the river Han. To this new city he gave the name *Hanyang* ("Fortress of Han"), but popular usage, ignoring the official name, fixed upon the designation *Seoul* ("capital"), by which it has been known down to the present day. At the same time the new monarch discarded the name *Korai,* by which the kingdom had been known during the four and a half centuries of the Wang regime, in favor of the more ancient name *Chosen.*

The change of name and the transfer of the capital, mere symbols of Yi Tai-jo's determination to break with the traditions of the Wang dynasty, were followed by a complete reorganization

---

[1] Called, by the Chinese historians, Li Tan.   [2] Chinese: Li T'ai Tsu.

of the government. The Buddhist monastic institutions, whose wealth and political influence under the Wangs had led to constant intrigue and disorder, were deprived of their vested privileges, and Buddhism ceased to be the "official" religion of the kingdom. In place of Buddhism the cult of Confucius was made the recognized religion, and the study of the Confucian Classics was fostered by the re-establishment of official literary examinations, based upon the Classics, as a prerequisite for civil appointment. The feudal powers of the great landholders were much reduced, and the kingdom was divided for administrative purposes into eight districts, each under a royal governor; at the same time the inefficient and often unruly feudal levies were replaced by an organized royal army.

For about a century after the accession of Yi Tai-jo the sovereigns of the new royal line appear to have been men of character and ability, and fifteenth-century Korea, like contemporary China under its Ming emperors, enjoyed prosperity and internal peace. The taxes of the heavily burdened people were lightened, and Yi Tai-jong,[1] the younger son and second successor of Tai-jo, had recourse to the ancient Chinese device of the "complaint box," into which the humblest subject was privileged to drop petitions addressed to the king.

Under these early monarchs of the Yi dynasty, moreover, the Koreans made at least two important steps in cultural progress. In 1403 Yi Tai-jong gave orders that types should be molded of copper for the purpose of printing fresh editions of all the ancient Classics. For a good many centuries the Koreans as well as the Chinese had been using the printing press, and the Chinese, at least, had developed the use of separate type as more convenient than a single page-sized block which might be marred by an error in carving a single character. There is evidence also that the Chinese had already experimented in the use of metal type, but the use of metal type in Korea, if not the earliest, may at least be regarded as an independent invention.[2] The second important

---

[1] Chinese: T'ai Tsung.

[2] See E. Satow, "Notes on Movable Types in Korea," in the *Transactions of the Asiatic Society of Japan*, Vol. X.

innovation, which appears to have been adopted in the reign of Tai-jong's son and successor, was the invention of the *on-mun* alphabet. Hitherto the Koreans had been dependent upon the Chinese ideographs, supplemented by a syllabic phonetic script somewhat resembling the Japanese Kana; but the *on-mun* script was a true alphabet, admirably adapted to the reproduction of the spoken language. After the invention of this new form of writing, Chinese characters continued to be the medium of scholarly authors, but the *on-mun* alphabet came to be extensively used for correspondence and for the production of nonscholarly literature.

The last rulers of the Wang dynasty, influenced perhaps by sympathy for their Mongol relatives, had adopted a hostile attitude toward the Ming government at Nanking, but the accession of Yi Tai-jo saw the prompt restoration of the ancient friendly relationship between Korea and the Chinese Empire. The new king dispatched a mission to inform the emperor of his assumption of the royal power, and Hung Wu replied to this notification by sending a formal letter of investiture and by bestowing upon the Korean monarch an official seal. In further recognition of its vassalage the Korean court again adopted the Chinese calendar, and Korean princes were sent to Nanking to study at the imperial university.

From 1392 the official relation of vassal and suzerain was maintained, with the single break accompanying the overthrow of the Ming dynasty by the Manchus, for almost exactly five hundred years, that is, until the defeat of China by Japan in 1894–1895. At regular intervals tributary missions from Seoul made their way to the Chinese capital. On the accession of a new king in Korea or of a new emperor in China these ordinary missions were supplemented by the dispatch of a special embassy with a renewed declaration of loyalty, to which the Chinese emperor responded by sending an imperial envoy to confer upon his loyal vassal a fresh patent of investiture.

As during the centuries which preceded the subjugation of Korea by the Mongols, Korea's formal acknowledgment of Chinese suzerainty involved no Chinese interference in the domestic affairs of the weaker nation, and the connection with China appears to have been regarded by the Korean rulers as an honorable privilege rather than as a humiliating limitation upon their sovereignty. The frequent embassies, like those which came to the Chinese court from the other tributary states, were a medium for carrying on a considerable volume of profitable commerce, which supplemented the more spontaneous and less dignified trade relations across the land frontier and between the seaports on the two shores of the Yellow Sea.

For several decades preceding the accession of Yi Tai-jo to the Korean throne the Japanese Empire, as we have already noted, had been torn by a desperate civil war. During this long-continued state of anarchy in Japan, Korea, like China, had suffered greatly from the depredations of Japanese pirates, who were often organized and led by powerful daimyo of the outlying Japanese provinces. As soon as he ascended the throne, therefore, the new Korean king dispatched an official embassy to Kyoto for the purpose of announcing his accession and also to lodge a formal protest against the Japanese depredations on the coasts of his kingdom. The Korean envoys reached Japan just after the Japanese civil war had been brought to a close, and the Ashikaga Shogun Yoshimitsu, who was extremely anxious to promote legitimate commerce between Japan and her continental neighbors, did what he could to remove the just cause of the Korean complaints. A number of Korean captives, victims of the pirates, were liberated and returned to their native land, while the Korean government was notified that the Shogun intended to repress the lawless activities of his fellow nationals. As a result of this conciliatory attitude on the part of Yoshimitsu the Korean government entered into the negotiation of a commercial treaty and concluded an arrangement whereby Fusan and two other Korean ports were opened to Japanese merchants for residence and trade.

In spite of their good intentions, however, Yoshimitsu and his successors were unable to put a complete stop to piracy, and the Koreans, like the Chinese, continued to suffer from Japanese incursions. In 1420, as reprisal for these attacks, a Korean fleet was sent to attack the Japanese island of Tsushima, which at that time appears to have been the headquarters both of the piracy and of the legitimate trade with Korea. Korean and Japanese accounts differ exceedingly as to the success of this expedition; but peace between the two countries was soon restored, and Japanese trade at the three Korean ports continued without further interruption until after the close of the fifteenth century.

In one direction, on the northwest, where the Yalu River separates Korea from the plains of Manchuria, the peace of the peninsula was threatened even more seriously than by the depredations of the Japanese sea-rovers. The armies of the first two Ming emperors had established Chinese authority over the southwestern portion of Manchuria, but the northern and northeastern districts of this great region were occupied by a number of warlike Tartar tribes wholly independent of Chinese authority although influenced to some extent by the culture of their southern neighbors. Among these northern tribes the most powerful were the Manchus, who appear to have been descended from the remnants of the earlier Kin Tartars and who in the seventeenth century were to become the new conquerors of eastern Asia. Even in the fifteenth century these active tribesmen were a constant source of trouble both to the Chinese and to the Koreans, and the successors of Yi Tai-jo, after the middle of the century, maintained to the northwest of their Yalu River frontier a "no man's land" whose western boundary was marked by a palisade of wooden stakes. Between the river and the palisade no one was allowed to settle, and this uninhabited strip of territory, crossed only by the main road from Wiju to Peking, served for a century or more to defend the Korean frontier from the ravages of the semibarbarian northerners.

For Korea, as for the Chinese Empire, the fifteenth century was a period of general peace, prosperity, and cultural development. Although the second half of the century saw the appearance of rival court parties whose later intrigues were to become a source of weakness to the kingdom, the monarchs of the Yi dynasty continued to be men of more than average ability, while the reforms of Yi Tai-jo and his immediate successors had established sound governmental institutions manned by a body of capable and well-trained officials. Despite the continued activity of the irrepressible Japanese pirates the official relations between Korea and Japan were usually cordial, and the legitimate trade at the three Korean open ports attained a respectable volume, much to the benefit of both countries. With China the political and commercial contacts of the Koreans were supplemented by an intimate cultural relationship. The re-establishment of Confucianism as the official cult, the revival of the system of official literary examinations, and the constant stream of Korean students to the Chinese institutions of learning all served to foster among the Koreans a deep respect for the Ming empire and a ready acquiescence in the existing status of vassal and suzerain. Only on the northwest frontier, between the wasteland and the palisade on the far side of the Yalu River, did real danger exist, and here the somewhat primitive frontier defense served its purpose so long as the turbulent Manchus remained disunited and disorganized.

SUGGESTED REFERENCES

HENKE, F. G. The Philosophy of Wang Yang-ming.

HOBSON, R. L. The Wares of the Ming Dynasty.

HULBERT, H. B. The History of Korea.

LATOURETTE, K. S. The Chinese: their History and Culture.

LONGFORD, J. H. The Story of Korea.

ROCKHILL, W. W. Notes on the Relations and Trade of China with the Eastern Archipelago.

ROCKHILL, W. W. China's Intercourse with Korea from the XVth Century to 1895.

SATOW, SIR E. M. "Notes on Movable Types in Korea," Transactions of the Asiatic Society of Japan, Vol. X.

TSCHEPE, A. Japans Beziehungen zu China.

WILLIAMS, E. T. A Short History of China.

YULE, SIR H. Cathay and the Way Thither.

XIV

Indo-China and Malaysia: from the Thirteenth Century to the Arrival of the Europeans

General Effects of the Mongol Era · Annam and Champa · Annam Reannexed to China · The Le Dynasty in Annam · Expansion of the Annamese Kingdom · Annam at the End of the Fifteenth Century · Siam; the Coming of the Tai · Tai Culture · The Decline of Cambodia · Siam and the Malays · Siam's Other Neighbors · Burma: the Fall of Pagán · Ava, Pegu, and Toungoo · Early European Visitors · The Rise of Toungoo · Unification of Burma · Fourteenth-Century and Fifteenth-Century Malaysia · The Rise and Decline of the Madjapahit Empire · The End of Indian Domination in Malaysia · The Mohammedan States · Malaysia at the Beginning of the Sixteenth Century

WE HAVE seen in our survey of the Mongol conquest that the Mongol armies, during the reigns of Mangu and Kublai, pushed their way southward beyond the frontiers of China into Annam, Burma, and Champa, while one of Kublai's overseas expeditions was dispatched against the Javanese state of Singosari. The direct consequences of these southern enterprises were insignificant. While all the invaded countries were plundered by the armies of the khans, no territory was annexed, and the Mongol rulers were forced to content themselves with the same formal tributary missions as previously had been dispatched without compulsion to the Sung emperor at Hangchow.

Indirectly, however, the rise of the Mongol power on the continent of Asia had a far-reaching influence upon the subsequent history of Indo-China. Prior to the thirteenth century the Tai, or Shan, peoples were located in Yunnan and in the upper valleys of the Mekong, the Salwin, and the Irrawaddy. The Mongol conquest of the Tai kingdom of Nanchao, shortly after the middle of the thirteenth century, dislodged these people from their ancient Yunnanese habitat and started them on a series of invasions to the south. During the course of the next hundred years they overcame the Mon-Khmer states and established new political organizations.

ANNAM AND CHAMPA

Between 1257 and 1286 the Mongol khans sent three expeditions into Annam and one into Champa. The Annamese and their Cham neighbors, although they had acknowledged the suzerainty of the new masters of China, stubbornly resisted every attempt to incorporate them, as Korea had been incorporated, into the Mongol empire. There are indications that Kublai contemplated a new expedition against Annam. With his death in 1294, however, the government of the Mongol empire passed into less vigorous hands, and the Annamese were freed from the danger of a fresh invasion.

During their struggle against the Mongols, Annam and Champa had been drawn into more friendly relations with each other, and this improved relationship continued even after the removal of the Mongol danger. In 1307 the two royal families were united by a matrimonial alliance; but the new family tie was soon utilized by the Annamese monarch as a pretext for reducing his weaker neighbor to vassalage, and the greater part of the fourteenth century was filled with attempted conquests on the one hand and retaliatory border raids on the other.

In the year 1400 a capable Annamese general, having repulsed a Cham attack upon the southern frontier, overthrew his lawful sovereign and usurped the throne of Annam. Although the new king, in the hope of gaining popular support for his dynasty, threw himself energetically into a fresh war of conquest against Champa, his reign was brief. The adherents of the deposed royal family appealed to the emperor Yung Lo against the usurper, while the ruler of Champa simultaneously begged the Chinese emperor to intervene for his protection. In 1406, as we have seen, Yung Lo sent an army into Annam. The usurper was taken prisoner and exiled, and the emperor, instead of restoring to the throne the old royal family, formally incorporated the territory of Annam into his empire. A Chinese governor-general was installed, and a corps of Chinese officials undertook a thorough reorganization of the administrative system.

If the work of reform had been carried on less energetically, the reannexation of Annam to the Chinese Empire might have be-

The Malay World after the Mongol Period

come permanent. In culture the Annamese were sufficiently close
to their northern neighbors to make political union a possibility.
Nearly five centuries of independence, however, had imbued the
people of the kingdom with a spirit of national patriotism. For
the first decade after the imposition of Chinese rule the growing
popular discontent was sternly repressed, but in 1418 the anti-
Chinese elements found a capable leader in the person of Le Loi.
From this date the imperial officials in Annam had to maintain
themselves against an ever spreading guerrilla warfare. After the
death of the emperor Yung Lo in 1424 the strength of Chinese
control declined; by 1427 the Chinese held only the city of Hanoi;
in 1428 Le Loi captured this last Chinese stronghold and freed
his country from foreign rule.

By 1431 the Ming emperor had abandoned all hope of reconquering the Annamese; Le Loi's tributary mission was received at Peking, and his assumption of the royal power was confirmed by the grant of an official seal and a patent of investiture. Under Le Loi and his successors, from 1428 until 1527, Annam enjoyed ninety-nine years of good government and prosperity. Bitterly though the Annamese had resented the reforms introduced by the Ming officials, the rulers of the Le dynasty were quick to appreciate the real value of these innovations and to adopt them in their own administration. The old code of laws was revised, and the law courts were reorganized, both along Chinese lines. From China also came the new systems of weights, measures, and coinage. The revival of industry and prosperity was quickened by an unprecedented development of foreign commerce. Annam, like all the other states of Malaysia and Indo-China, had been aroused to new commercial activity by the voyages of Cheng Ho, which coincided with the brief period of Chinese rule. Under the Le regime this activity continued, and the Annamese ports were visited by increasing numbers of ships and merchants not only from China but also from Siam and from the Malay Islands.

The political and economic progress of the kingdom was attended by an advance in national culture. During the last decades of the fourteenth century the Annamese, hitherto dependent upon the Chinese ideographs, evolved a modified and less difficult form of character writing. They began to develop a "vulgar" literature written in these simplified characters. Even the scholarly literature, still written in the Chinese characters, began to display a more nationalistic spirit. The reign of the third Le monarch saw the compilation of a national history covering the preceding two centuries; in the following reign this history was revised and extended to include the glorious first half-century of Le rule. In art, as in literature, the Annamese continued to be strongly influenced by the Chinese, but here also the fifteenth century was marked by a newly aroused spirit of nationalism. A number of recently discovered specimens of sculpture in stone, attributed to this period, are dedicated to the memory of Le Loi, the liberator of his people from foreign domination.

Prosperous, well governed, and strongly nationalistic, fifteenth-century Annam soon began to expand to the west and south at the expense of its less powerful neighbors. The reigns of the first two Le monarchs saw the establishment of Annamese authority over a number of semibarbarous tribes occupying the hilly districts along the western frontier, and henceforth any turbulent activity on the part of these aborigines was promptly suppressed. The reign of Le Thanh-tong (1460–1497) was the most glorious in the entire history of the Le dynasty and saw the final victory of the Annamese in their ancient struggle with the people of Champa. In 1471 Vijaya, the Cham capital, was destroyed; the last king of the Cham royal line was taken prisoner, and two of the five provinces of Champa were promptly annexed to Annam. Before the end of Thanh-tong's reign two of the remaining three provinces suffered the same fate, leaving only the southernmost province of Binhthuan to be ruled by a vassal Cham prince until its annexation by Annam in the seventeenth century.

In 1498, when Le Thanh-tong was succeeded on the throne by a capable and energetic son, the Annamese ship of state was sailing upon an untroubled sea with no apparent sign of either storm or mutiny. The Le monarchs regularly dispatched tributary missions to Peking in recognition of their allegiance to the great Ming emperor and regularly petitioned their Chinese suzerain for the official confirmation of their accession to the throne, but the Chinese government did not presume to interfere with them in their domestic affairs or to dictate in regard to their relations with the neighboring people of the peninsula. In Indo-China, indeed, the Annamese rulers were emperors in their own right, and from the accession of Le Loi they had assumed, except for their communications with the Chinese court, the imperial title. The conquests of the fifteenth century had given to the Annamese the entire stretch of Champa coast as far as Cape Padaran. The mountains marking the western frontier of the Cham provinces guarded this portion of the Annamese empire from attack save in the extreme south, while the territorial expansion in the north had extended the power of the Le sovereigns inland to an equally defensible mountain frontier on the northwest.

SIAM

Nowhere in the Indo-Chinese peninsula did the southward migrations of the peoples set in motion by the Mongol conquests produce more far-reaching changes than in the region now occupied by the Siamese kingdom. Here the invading Tai tribes—the same people as the Shans of Burma—replaced the Khmers in the broad central valley of the Menam, destroyed the ancient empire of Cambodia, and laid the foundations of the one Indo-Chinese state which has succeeded in maintaining down to the present day, in the face of European expansion, an independent sovereign status.

The Menam valley at the close of the twelfth century was occupied by two Khmer kingdoms. In the south was the kingdom of Dvaravati, with its capital at Lopburi, which had become a vassal of the Cambodian rulers; in the north, with its capital near the modern city of Chiengmai, was the kingdom of Haripunjaya, over which the twelfth-century Cambodians had not succeeded in extending their authority. Even before the opening of the thirteenth century, Haripunjaya appears to have been the recipient of a certain amount of Tai immigration from the north.

With the conquest of Nanchao by the Mongols in 1253 the Tai movement toward the south was greatly accelerated. Apparently as early as 1256 some of these immigrants had succeeded in setting up a mixed Tai-Khmer state, Sukotai, in the southern part of Haripunjaya. Six years later a purely Tai state, Chiengrai, was established in the northern part of Haripunjaya. By 1292 Haripunjaya had ceased to exist. Its northern districts were conquered and annexed by the ruler of Chiengrai, who now proceeded to set up the Tai state of Chiengmai with the conquered capital as the seat of his government. The southern districts of Haripunjaya at the same time were absorbed by the rapidly growing kingdom of Sukotai.

By the end of the thirteenth century the suzerainty of Sukotai was recognized by most of its neighbors from Luan Praban in the north to Ligor on the Malay peninsula, and from Vientiane on the east to the frontiers of Pegu on the west. The Khmer kingdom of Dvaravati in the lower Menam, supported by its Cambodian overlords, held out for a time against the domination of the new-comers, but it too was destined to give way to the invaders.

As a result of these various invasions petty states of Tai origin were springing up rapidly in the regions formerly held by the Khmers. Until the middle of the fourteenth century Sukotai remained the dominant state of the Menam valley; then in 1350 the ruler of Utong, or Supan, a Tai state which had appeared about half a century earlier in the territory of Dvaravati, conquered Lopburi, the Dvaravati capital. This conquest marked the end of the southern Khmer kingdom. The year following the capture of Lopburi the ruler of Utong, who assumed the title *King* and took the name *Rama Tiboti*, built the city of Ayuthia, which almost immediately became the capital of a unified and rapidly expanding Tai state. The hegemony over the various states, formerly exercised by Sukotai, now passed to this new power. To the warlike Tai invaders the Cambodians had applied the name *Syam*, and about this time the name *Siam* was adopted by the Tais themselves as the official designation of their growing state of Ayuthia.

The Tais of Siam appear to have brought with them into the Menam valley a civilization considerably higher than that of their Shan cousins who at the same period were invading the valleys of Burma. From their earliest arrival in their new habitat the Tais were zealous adherents of Hinayana Buddhism, which apparently had made its way northward into Nanchao from Pagān in the days of Anawrata. About the year 1283 Rama Kamheng, the second king of Sukotai, invented (or had his scholars invent) a form of writing for the Siamese language. The same monarch, who has left stone inscriptions recording the important events of his reign, made two visits to the Mongol court at Khanbalik and brought back with him on his return Chinese artisans who introduced into Siam their highly developed industrial arts. Equally strong was the Chinese influence upon the political institutions and laws of Siam. A passage from the laws of Rama Tiboti of Ayuthia, promulgated between 1350 and 1360, may be cited to show their unmistakable Chinese origin: "If any worthless and unfilial man attempts to bring a case against his parents or grandparents, let him be soundly flogged as an example to others; and his claim shall not be admitted."

The steady growth of Tai power in the valley of the Menam and in the upper reaches of the Mekong spelled ruin for the ancient Khmer empire of Cambodia and for the glorious city of Angkor. As early as 1296 the Chinese ambassador of the Mongols, Chou Ta-kuan, who has left us the most adequate contemporary description of the Cambodian capital,[1] wrote that the country of Cambodia had been completely devastated by the recent war with the Siamese. With the establishment of Ayuthia and the consolidation of the Siamese state the Tai attacks upon the Khmer empire became increasingly serious. During the hundred and ten years between 1350 and 1460 the Siamese armies invaded Cambodia on four or five separate occasions. Partly as a result of these repeated attacks, partly because of a disastrous flood which inundated the extensive cultivated area around Angkor, the Cambodians about the middle of the fifteenth century definitely abandoned "Angkor the Magnificent." Deserted by its inhabitants, the great city and the once fertile fields by which it was surrounded quickly became the prey of the rapidly growing jungle.

After the abandonment of their ancient capital the collapse of the Cambodian power was complete. For the next four centuries they constituted a petty state at the mouth of the Mekong River, sometimes paying homage to the Siamese and sometimes to their Annamese neighbors on the east, finally becoming in the last half of the nineteenth century a part of the French possessions of Indo-China. During these four centuries, indeed, all memory of the once mighty Khmer empire was completely lost; and when, in the closing decades of the nineteenth century, French archaeologists stumbled upon the wonderful ruins of Angkor, the tribesmen of the jungle region in which the ruins were located knew only that the buildings had been erected by a "race of giants" who had once dwelt in the land.

Even before the founding of Ayuthia the power of the Tai peoples, as we have seen, reached southward along the Malay peninsula as far as Ligor. These southern Tai settlements, like those in the Menam valley, were quickly brought to acknowledge the

---

[1] Chou Ta-kuan's description of Angkor has been translated by Professor Pelliot in *Bulletin de l'École française d'Extrême-Orient* for 1902, pp. 123 ff.

sovereignty of the kings of Ayuthia, and Rama Tiboti, the founder of Ayuthia, extended his conquests southward as far as Malacca at the extremity of the peninsula.

About 1380 a large number of refugees from Sumatra, fleeing from the tyranny of the Javanese Madjapahit empire (see page 334), settled at Malacca, and by the year 1400 this port had become the greatest commercial center of the Malay world, practically monopolizing the spice trade of the archipelago. The cosmopolitan population of this important commercial city, in addition to the Sumatran refugees, soon included many Mohammedan Indian and Arab merchants, and shortly after 1400 the political power of the city fell into the hands of the Mohammedan element.

Although a flourishing city, Malacca could hardly be called a powerful state, and its commercial importance made it a very desirable possession to the Siamese as well as to the Javanese empire of Madjapahit. Threatened by conquest from these two directions, the Mohammedan rulers of Malacca turned for protection to the recently established Ming dynasty in China. Malacca was duly enrolled in the list of states paying tribute to the Chinese Empire, and the voyages of Cheng Ho between 1405 and 1435 appear to have been intended, in part at least, as notice to the two most aggressive powers in the Indo-Chinese-Malaysian world that the political independence of Malacca was to be respected. The Siamese were able to establish their authority over the more northern portions of the Malay peninsula; but Malacca, until the arrival of Albuquerque in 1511, remained an independent state, protected by its Ming suzerains.

Although the Siamese aspirations for Malacca were blocked by Chinese intervention, the relations between the Tai kingdom and its great northern neighbor were uniformly cordial. Seventeen years after the founding of Ayuthia, Chu Yüan-chang completed the expulsion of the Mongols from China and assumed imperial power. Three years later, in 1371, a Siamese embassy appeared at Nanking to announce the accession of a new king to the throne of Siam, and other Siamese embassies were sent in 1373 (this mission included Prince Nakon In, who later was to occupy the throne) and in 1384. In 1408 Nakon In became king of Siam; and during his reign, which coincided with that of the emperor Yung Lo, there were regular tribute-bearing embassies from Ayuthia to Peking, while the Siamese capital was visited on several occasions by envoys from China.

So long as the Tai peoples of the Menam and upper Mekong valleys were struggling to supplant the earlier Khmer domination, they usually maintained a united front against the common enemy. After the completion of their victory, however, and after the rise of Ayuthia the spirit of co-operation was replaced by bitter jealousy between the southern Tai, now united into the kingdom of Siam, and their northern cousins of the kingdom of Chiengmai. Between 1376, when an army from Chiengmai marched down into the Menam valley to aid a revolt against the power of Ayuthia, until 1557, when Chiengmai was destroyed by the Burmese, the pages of Siamese history are filled with the accounts of invasion and counterinvasion. The southern kingdom was the larger and the more powerful, and the armies of Chiengmai usually retreated northward as soon as they had acquired any considerable plunder from their operations. In spite of their superiority in numbers and resources, however, the Siamese were unable to gain a decisive victory.

Over the disunited states of Burma, on their western frontier, the fourteenth-century and fifteenth-century Siamese enjoyed a decided superiority, and Siam was able during much of this period not merely to hold the Tenasserim coast on the western side of the peninsula but also to interfere in the domestic affairs of the Burmese, especially in those of Pegu. The first ruler of Pegu after the disintegration of the old Pagān empire was Wareru (1287–1296), a Tai adventurer from Sukotai who strengthened his position by becoming the vassal of the Siamese king. In 1317 Wareru's successor renounced his vassalage and seized the two cities of Tavoy and Tenasserim, together with the intervening coastland. The coast provinces were reconquered for Siam by Rama Tiboti, the founder of Ayuthia, and were held until early in the fifteenth century, when they appear to have become for a time an independent principality; they were again brought under Siamese rule in 1488.

In 1511, when the Portuguese envoys dispatched from Malacca by Albuquerque arrived at Ayuthia, Siam was a powerful and well-organized kingdom. For a hundred and sixty years the power of the royal line at Ayuthia had been recognized by the people of the Menam valley and by the greater part of the Malay peninsula. Cambodia, the ancient rival on the eastern frontier, had fallen into insignificance, while the troublesome northern-Tai kingdom of Chiengmai was able to do little more than launch occasional raids into the northernmost districts of the Siamese domain. On the western frontier the Burmese were still divided, and there was as yet no indication of the rise of the unifying conqueror who, in little more than half a century, was to reduce Siam to temporary vassalage.

As in Annam, the administrative system of Siam was modeled after that of China, and the introduction of Chinese industrial methods had contributed greatly to the wealth of the country. The prevailing religion was Hinayana Buddhism, and many of the monarchs who held power at Ayuthia distinguished themselves by their zealous patronage of Buddhist institutions. But the Siamese, although zealous Buddhists, were usually tolerant in matters of religious faith. The Christian Portuguese, when they began to arrive in the land, were accorded the same freedom of worship as formerly had been extended to the Brahman Hindu and to the Mohammedan Arab.

BURMA

The Burmese kingdom of Pagān, for a century and a half after the death of Anawrata, was ruled by a succession of capable kings; then the royal line began to deteriorate, and in 1254 Narathihapate ascended the Pagān throne. The new king probably was no more incapable than his recent predecessors, but in 1253, the year before his accession, the conquering Mongols had established their authority over the kingdom of Nanchao; the Burmese kingdom could not long continue undisturbed by this change on its northern frontier.

In 1271, the seventeenth year of Narathihapate's reign, a Mongol envoy appeared at Pagān to demand from the Burmese sovereign the tribute which his predecessors had been accustomed to render to the emperors of China. The demand was ignored; and two years later ambassadors again arrived bearing a letter from Kublai, in which the khan, under threat of war, summoned the Burmese monarch to fulfill his duties as a loyal vassal. Irritated, according to Burmese accounts, by the failure of the ambassadors to observe the customs of his court, Narathihapate had them and their entire retinue put to death.

Kublai at this time was too busy with his other projects to punish the unpardonable crime of the Burmese monarch; the first clash of arms between Burma and the Mongols came in 1277, when a Burmese army raiding the territory of Yunnan was defeated and driven southward across the frontier. In 1283 fresh Burmese raids into Yunnan were punished by the invasion and conquest of the northern districts of Narathihapate's domain. Although the Mongol forces made no attempt to advance upon the capital, the king fled southward in panic and in 1287 was murdered by one of his numerous sons. Seizing the throne of the now chaotic country, the parricide emulated his father by massacring the members of a Chinese embassy. Once more the Mongol forces swept down into the country; the Burmese army was crushed, Pagān was taken and looted, and the invaders laid the country waste as far south as the ancient city of Prome.

With the capture of Pagān in 1287 the kingdom went to pieces. Twelve years later the once glorious capital of Anawrata was practically destroyed by the wild Shan tribesmen who poured down the Irrawaddy valley, pressed southward by the spread of the Mongol power. The Shans made themselves masters of a large part of the country and established their rule over the more cultured inhabitants of the land.

After the collapse of Pagān and the Shan invasions Burma was divided into a number of petty states, frequently warring with each other and almost constantly torn by internal intrigues. Of these various petty states three were important. The first of these was the Burmese-Shan state occupying the middle and lower Irrawaddy valley. For a while the capital of the Irrawaddy state was migratory, but in 1365 it was permanently established in the new city of Ava. The second important state, Pegu, occupied a broad belt at the mouths of the Irrawaddy, Sittang, and Salwin rivers and a strip of land stretching southward along the Tenasserim coast. Here, with Martaban and later with Pegu as their capital, a line of Shan rulers held sway over a mixed population of Mons and Shans. The third, smaller than its two rivals and populated almost entirely by Burmans, was the Sittang-valley state of Toungoo, which had been established in 1280, seven years before the fall of Pagān, and which eventually was to provide a new line of conquerors for the reunification of Burma.

To the north and east of these three states—in the upper Irrawaddy and along the entire course of the Salwin—the land was occupied by the Shans, for the most part wild tribesmen with little or no political organization, whose constant immigration steadily increased the Shan element in the population of Ava and Pegu. To the west, beyond the mountains which bound the Irrawaddy valley, the Arakanese, who had been partially subject to Pagān, regained their independence and except for occasional raids from Ava and Pegu remained wholly apart from the turmoil on their east.

Throughout the fourteenth and fifteenth centuries the history of Burma is principally a record of the struggles between Ava and Pegu. They waged war almost constantly, but neither was able to gain a decisive triumph over the other. In their foreign relations both states had frequent contacts with the Shans on the east. In the case of Ava there was some intercourse with China. The Ming emperors, as we have seen, constantly exhorted their southern neighbors to keep the peace, and tributary missions were dispatched by the sovereigns of the Burmese kingdom, at long intervals, to the Ming court.

By the middle of the fifteenth century Ava had fallen into a condition of almost utter chaos. In Pegu, on the other hand, the last half of the fifteenth century and the opening decades of the sixteenth were marked by peace and prosperity. This period of approximately three quarters of a century, however, prefaced the extinction of Pegu as an independent kingdom; in 1539 the country was conquered by the forces of Toungoo.

The fifteenth century saw the arrival in Burma of a few hardy European travelers. The exact number of these early European visitors to Burma is not known, but there were at least three during the course of the fifteenth century whose recorded descriptions of the land have been preserved. Nicolo di Conti, the first of these visitors, was a Venetian merchant who arrived on the Tenasserim coast, apparently by way of India, about the year 1435. After wandering along the coastal plains as far northward as Arakan, Di Conti found his way across the mountains from Arakan to the Irrawaddy, which he describes as "larger than the Ganges," and sailed up this river for a month, arriving at "a city more noble than the rest, called Ava." After his stay at Ava, where he heard of a land to the north named Cathay, "superior to all others in the world," Di Conti journeyed southward to the sea and proceeded to the "very populous city" of Pegu. About thirty-five years after Di Conti's visit a Russian merchant named Nikitin visited Pegu in the course of his travels, and in 1496 an Italian merchant, Hieronimo de Santo Stephano, arrived at Pegu but was unable, because of the troubled conditions in the interior, to go to Ava.

With the opening of the sixteenth century the European visitors became more numerous. When Albuquerque in 1511 established the Portuguese flag over Malacca (see page 362), he dispatched an envoy to Tenasserim, Martaban, and Pegu. Eight years later a second Portuguese envoy concluded a treaty whereby the merchants of that country secured trading privileges at the port of Martaban. The Burmese themselves appear never to have taken an active part in the overseas trade proceeding from their ports; prior to the arrival of the Europeans it had been carried on by foreign merchants of Indian or Malay origin. After 1519 a steadily increasing portion of the trade fell into European hands, and the Europeans became a steadily increasing factor in the affairs of the country.

Throughout the fourteenth century and the greater part of the fifteenth the little Burman state of Toungoo had played but an insignificant role in the affairs of the Burmese world. This kingdom was a haven for the Burmans who fled from the Shan domination in Ava and Pegu, and its population rapidly increased during the especially turbulent fifteenth century. Until nearly the end of this century, however, the state in the Sittang valley had rather more than its share of dynastic troubles; assassinations and usurpations were of common occurrence, and only the bitter struggle being waged between its more powerful neighbors saved Toungoo from destruction at the hands of one or the other. In the last quarter of the fifteenth century there came to the throne of Toungoo a powerful monarch, Minkyinyo (1486–1531), under whose guidance the kingdom began to expand its territory and to increase in military power. By the date of Minkyinyo's death, at the age of seventy-two, Toungoo was the most powerful state in Burma.

Tabin Shwehti, the son of Minkyinyo, was only fifteen years old when he ascended the throne of Toungoo in 1531. During the first seventeen years of his nineteen-year reign the young prince showed that he had inherited the energy and abilities of an empire-builder. In 1535 he began his conquests by leading an army into the delta of the Irrawaddy; by 1539 he had overrun the delta region and had made himself master of the city of Pegu. In 1541 he advanced against the wealthy city of Martaban. After a siege which lasted more than six months Martaban was taken and sacked, and the fall of the city was followed by the recognition of the young prince's authority over the coast as far south as Tavoy. The following year saw the capture of Prome, and Tabin Shwehti, returning to Pegu, was crowned king of all Lower Burma. Within four years after his coronation the conqueror had extended his sway northward as far as Pagān and had assumed the title *King of all Burma*.

In 1546 Tabin Shwehti led an expedition westward in an attack upon Arakan. For this undertaking he had strengthened his army by employing a body of well-armed Portuguese mercenaries; but the Arakanese sovereign, also assisted by Portuguese adventurers, offered stubborn resistance, and the ruler of Burma was compelled to abandon the attack in order to defend his own territories against an invasion by the Siamese. In reply to this Siamese raid Tabin Shwehti, in the winter of 1547–1548, led an expedition against

Ayuthia. Here again, however, he found the fighting ability of his Portuguese mercenaries offset by the presence of foreign fighting men among the defenders, and he was compelled, after much hard fighting, to retire to his own domain.

In 1550 Tabin Shwehti was assassinated by a group of palace officials who attempted to place one of their number upon the throne. Bayin Naung, the foster brother of the murdered king and the actual ruler of the country during the closing years of his reign, promptly summoned to his assistance the Portuguese leader De Mello, who had served with him in the campaigns of Tabin Shwehti. By 1551 Pegu had fallen and Bayin Naung had established his authority over all the region which formerly submitted to the rule of his predecessor. Having thus gained control over central and southern Burma, the new ruler embarked upon a career of conquest far more ambitious than that of Tabin Shwehti. In 1555 he took Ava and subdued the adjoining districts of the upper Irrawaddy. The following year saw the commencement of a series of campaigns against the Shan states to the east, and in 1557 he marched southward from the upper Salwin valley to attack and destroy the northern Tai kingdom of Chiengmai.

With all Burma and a great part of the Shan states under his sway, Bayin Naung in 1563 led his assembled armies into Siam and besieged Ayuthia. The Siamese monarch capitulated after a short siege; but in less than four years the defeated people rose against their conqueror, and a fresh invasion became necessary. This time the siege of Ayuthia lasted ten months. Once more the city was garrisoned by a Burmese force, but the army of Bayin Naung was hardly across the frontier when the conquered country was again in revolt. The exhaustion of his military resources and the outbreak of petty revolts in various parts of his domains made it impossible for the Burmese ruler to renew his attack, and under the new king, Phra Naret, Siam resumed its position as an independent nation. After the death of Bayin Naung, in 1581, Burma remained united; but his constant foreign wars had left the country exhausted, and his successors ruled over an impoverished land.

Fourteenth-Century and Fifteenth-Century Malaysia

The history of the Malay Archipelago between the disappearance of the kingdom of Singosari at the end of the thirteenth century and the arrival of the Europeans early in the sixteenth falls into two fairly well-marked periods. The first of these, almost exactly covering the fourteenth century, saw the rise and fall of the Javanese empire of Madjapahit, while the second, from the opening of the fifteenth century until the arrival of the Portuguese, was marked by the steady spread of Mohammedanism throughout the archipelago and the establishment of a number of petty Mohammedan states.

The Javanese kingdom of Madjapahit, which during the last two thirds of the fourteenth century was to hold imperial sway throughout the Malay world, came into existence at the end of the thirteenth century. In 1292 Kartanagara, the last king of Singosari (see page 196), replied in unmistakable fashion to the Mongol emperor's summons to pay tribute and render homage, tattooing his refusal upon the face of Kublai's envoy. Shortly after he had committed this rash act he was overthrown and put to death by a rebellious vassal who promptly established himself as king of Kediri. Immediately after the overthrow of Kartanagara his son-in-law began the erection of a new city, Madjapahit, some thirty miles to the northwest of Singosari.

In the autumn of 1293 Kublai's expedition arrived at the coast of Java for the purpose of avenging the unpardonable insult committed by the recently overthrown Singosari ruler. Upon the arrival of the Mongol forces the founder of Madjapahit hastened to make his submission to the Mongol commanders and offered to assist in the punishment of the guilty ruler, who, he alleged, was his neighbor, the king of Kediri. Upon the destruction of Kediri the ruler of Madjapahit promptly turned against his recent allies; and the Mongols, who had divided their forces for the advance upon Kediri, had much difficulty in withdrawing from the tropical jungle to their ships on the coast. Discouraged by the difficulties involved in a campaign against Madjapahit and having to their credit the destruction of Kediri, the Mongol commanders returned to China to report their success and left Madjapahit to enjoy the fruits of victory.

For some forty years after the destruction of Kediri the power of Madjapahit was confined to the island of Java. About 1331, however, the Javanese kingdom began to extend its authority over other parts of the Malay world. By 1364 Madjapahit had subjugated its neighbors on the east as far as the western portion of New Guinea, was in control of Borneo and the greater part of the Philippines on the northeast, and ruled over all Sumatra except the ancient capital of Sri-Vishaya. In 1377 the city of Sri-Vishaya was finally conquered, and about the same time Madjapahit succeeded in establishing its power over the southern part of the Malay peninsula.

Like the Sri-Vishayans of an earlier age and like the Portuguese who came later, the Javanese rulers of Madjapahit were primarily interested in the commercial exploitation of the regions which they brought under their rule. Imperial governors, adequately supported by armed forces, kept the subjugated peoples under strict control and forced them to pay heavy tribute in such local produce as the Javanese government considered most desirable. This tribute provided Madjapahit with commodities for an extensive trade with China, Indo-China, and India; the rich profits from this trade were supplemented by the not inconsiderable profits derived from commerce between the conquerors and their subject peoples. Wealth poured into the royal treasury; and the capital city, which had risen but a few decades earlier from the jungle, became the metropolis of Malaysia, a veritable beehive of bureaucratic activity. There were broad streets, imposing royal palaces, temples, monasteries, and public buildings in the city, all surrounded and protected by a great city wall. The prosperity of the capital was shared by several other inland cities, especially by the older city of Singosari; but the greatest material advance outside the royal city was in the flourishing coast towns, such as Tuban, Grisseh, and Surabaya, whose ports handled the growing trade with the colonies and the vassal states on the one hand and with the outside world on the other.

In matters of religion the rulers of Madjapahit were thoroughly tolerant. Buddhism and Sivaite Brahmanism both flourished; their institutions enjoyed exemption from the payment of taxes, and their clergy were subject to the jurisdiction of their own ecclesiastical courts rather than to that of the king's court. In the home island, indeed, the ecclesiastical organizations became practically a part of the government machinery, the Buddhist or Brahman religious communities, under the supervision of the king's ministers, exercising political jurisdiction over the rural or semirural districts outside the great cities. But the dominant factor in government and in society was the merchant; the privileges granted to the monks and priests served only to make organized religion the obedient servant of the commercial class, which, throughout the brief period of Madjapahit domination, ruled the Malay world.

The expansion of the Javanese empire reached its climax under Hayam Wuruk; after the death of this monarch in 1389 the process of disintegration began. By 1410 the power of Madjapahit had been reduced to the island of Java and the petty islands immediately to the east. After 1428 the authority of the Madjapahit kings was recognized only by the central and eastern districts of Java, and in 1478, after half a century of comparative insignificance, the last remnant of the once mighty empire was subjugated by the Mohammedans.

Three factors appear to have combined to bring about the speedy decline of Madjapahit power between 1389 and 1410. The first of these was the age-old element of dynastic dissension. Upon the death of Hayam Wuruk a dispute arose with respect to the succession to the throne, and in the year 1400 this dispute developed into a civil war involving the entire island of Java.

The second disruptive factor was the seething discontent among the conquered peoples in all parts of the archipelago. The Javanese were hard taskmasters; and even when the power of the empire was at its height, they were called upon to suppress frequent revolts against their exacting rule. With the outbreak of civil war in Java discontent flared forth in every conquered island; the Javanese garrisons and viceroys were driven out, and a galaxy of petty states replaced the unified imperial system of Madjapahit.

The third factor contributing to the decline of Madjapahit was the appearance in Malaysian waters of the Chinese expeditions commanded by Cheng Ho (see page 301). It is difficult to say whether the naval demonstrations organized by the Ming emperor of China helped to cause the widespread revolts among the peoples under Javanese rule or whether Cheng Ho's first expedition came as a result of appeals made to the Chinese throne by the peoples already in revolt. Whatever may have been the connection between the revolts and the Chinese intervention, Cheng Ho's first expedition, as we have seen, resulted in the establishment of vassal relationships between many of the petty Malay states and the Ming empire, while the subsequent periodic visits of the Chinese admiral effectively precluded any attempt on the part of Madjapahit to restore its lost supremacy.

The fall of the Madjapahit empire marked the end of the Hindu power which for nearly a thousand years had dominated the Malay Archipelago. Under the leadership of Sri-Vishaya, Singosari, and Madjapahit the Hinduized merchants of Sumatra and Java had succeeded in exploiting their less powerful and less civilized island neighbors, while Hindu culture, considerably modified by its passage through the two larger islands, was carried throughout the archipelago, eastward as far as New Guinea and northward as far as the shores of Luzon. It is impossible to determine which elements of this Hinduized culture were scattered abroad by the Sumatrans and which by the Javanese, but the fact remains that the culture was widely diffused and that many traces have survived to the present day. Although more than five centuries have elapsed since the fall of the Madjapahit empire and although the Malay world for the last four hundred years has been increasingly subject to the impact of European civilization, there are still to be found, in the island of Celebes and in the Sulu Archipelago and among peoples of Borneo and the Philippines, commonly used words of Sanskrit origin and forms of writing adapted from the ancient Indian scripts.[1]

---

[1] For a more detailed discussion of these survivals the reader is referred to Chapter XIV, by Professor H. Otley Beyer, in Steiger, Beyer, and Benitez, *A History of the Orient*.

The Chinese maritime expeditions under Cheng Ho, which appear to have contributed so decisively to the collapse of the Madjapahit empire, did not result in the substitution of Chinese imperialism for that of Java. The Ming government was less interested in the extension of political domination than in the maintenance of what we should call a commercial "open door" throughout the archipelago. Having broken the power of the monopolistic Javanese, the Chinese felt perfectly competent to look out for themselves in this part of the world so long as free competition continued to be the rule, and the Ming statesmen viewed with complacency the rise of local independent states sufficiently strong to block the development of any new empire bent upon the establishment of commercial monopoly.

The heirs of Madjapahit and the chief beneficiaries of the Chinese intervention were the Mohammedan Arabs. Since early in the Christian Era the Arabs had played a prominent part in the trade of the East Indian Archipelago. For some centuries after their acceptance of Mohammedanism, however, the Arabs who found their way to the Far East had made little effort to spread their religious beliefs or to achieve political power. Marco Polo, who visited Sumatra in 1292–1293, found two small Mohammedan states, Perlak and Passey, in the extreme northern part of the island; but these appear to have been the only predominantly Mohammedan states in the East Indies until nearly a century later, when the Moslems of northern Sumatra joined with others seeking refuge from Madjapahit domination and flocked across the straits to Malacca. By the year 1400, as we have seen, the Arab merchants had secured political control of this important commercial center; and a decade later, after the decline of Madjapahit had commenced, the Mohammedans began to establish their political power and their faith in all parts of the archipelago.

The rapid expansion of Mohammedan influence in the East Indies during the fifteenth century was the work not of the long established merchants but of a new element, the Sayyids of southern Arabia, who claimed descent from Mohammed's daughter Fatima and who were the most active missionaries of the Moslem world. During the fourteenth century many of these Sayyid missionaries had been actively engaged in spreading the doctrines of Islam among the peoples of India, and there is reason to believe that the invasion of India by Tamerlane in 1398 was an important factor in causing them to transfer their activities eastward to Malaysia. Arriving at Malacca about the beginning of the century and making this commercial metropolis the base of their operations, the Sayyids appear to have turned their attention first to the local colony of merchants from various parts of the archipelago; and their success in winning converts among the traders from the islands made it possible for them to secure a favorable reception in the states from which the new converts had come.[1] So successful, indeed, was this line of attack that by the end of the fifteenth century some twenty states in Java, Sumatra, the Malay peninsula, Borneo, the Philippines, Celebes, and the Moluccas had adopted Islam as their state religion.

Down until its capture by Albuquerque in 1511 Malacca continued to be the leading Moslem state of the East Indies, while its advantageous location made it the commercial capital of Malaysia; through its port passed all the trade between the archipelago and the West. The political self-sufficiency of the petty Mohammedan states and perhaps Malacca's need for Chinese good will as protection against Siamese aggression served to prevent the establishment of a Malaccan empire with a resulting monopoly over the insular trade. But even the Chinese found it more convenient in many cases to make their voyages to Malacca than to trade directly with the islands, while the merchants from Indian ports, from the Red Sea, and from the Persian Gulf made their way to the flourishing city on the strait as the one available source for spices of the East. Throughout the fifteenth century, therefore, the harbor of Malacca was thronged with shipping from every maritime country of Asia, while Chinese, Annamese, Siamese, and Malay rubbed shoulders in the streets with strangers from India, from Persia, and from ports of Arabia.

[1] In this connection it is interesting to note that the first known Japanese convert to Christianity, in whose company St. Francis Xavier made his visit to Japan, was converted at Malacca; and also that several of the early Protestant missionary societies prefaced their entry into China by work among the Chinese merchant communities at Malacca, Singapore, and Batavia.

In addition to Malacca the Mohammedans dominated all the commercially important seaports and interior cities of the archipelago; and, in the cities at least, the doctrines of Islam were zealously propagated. In some parts of Malaysia the labors of Mohammedan missionaries succeeded in establishing their religion in its orthodox form, but outside the more important cities the masses of the people continued to hold their old beliefs and to practice their ancient religious rites in combination with the new cult.

The cultural consequences—other than religious—of the Moslem domination are difficult to assess. The Arabic language, both spoken and written, was introduced as the language of the new religion, and secured a permanent foothold in some parts of the archipelago. More democratic than Brahmanism, or even than Buddhism in the form which had spread through the East Indies, Mohammedanism modified local governmental institutions in the direction of liberalism, and the Malay people, in spite of an occasional tyrannical ruler, were less oppressively ruled during the fifteenth century than during the periods which preceded and followed the Mohammedan supremacy.

SUGGESTED REFERENCES

AYMONIER, E. Histoire de l'ancien Cambodge.

GRAHAM, W. A. Siam.

HARVEY, G. E. History of Burma.

KROEBER, A. L. The History of Philippine Civilization.

LAUFER, B. The Relations of the Chinese to the Philippine Islands.

LAUNAY, A. Histoire ancienne et moderne de l'Annam.

MASPERO, G. Le Royaume de Champa.

PHAYRE, SIR A. History of Burma.

RAFFLES, SIR T. S. The History of Java.

ROCKHILL, W. W. Notes on the Relations and Trade of China with the Eastern Archipelago.

SALMONY, A. La Sculpture siamoise.

STUART, J. Burma through the Centuries.

TCHEOU TA KOUAN. "Mémoires sur les coutumes du Cambodge" (translated by P. Pelliot), *Bulletin de l'École française d'Extrême-Orient*, 1902, pp. 123 ff.

WOOD, W. A. R. A History of Siam.

YULE, SIR H. (translator and editor). The Book of Ser Marco Polo.

YULE, SIR H. Cathay and the Way Thither.

XV

India and the Early Portuguese

THE establishment of the Delhi sultanate in 1206 was followed
by the gradual extension of the Mohammedan power over all
India. By 1310 the Moslem conquerors had pushed their way
southward to the extremity of the peninsula, and even before that
date the last Hindu strongholds in the Himalaya foothills had
been forced to acknowledge the rule of the foreign invader. In the
greater part of the region lying north of the Vindhya Mountains
the results of the conquests were permanent. Constantly recruited
by the stream of warlike and fanatical adherents which poured
down through the northwestern passes, the forces of Islam resisted
Hindu absorption and established themselves as a ruling aristocracy whose ruthless slaughter of idolatrous infidels, coupled with
the tempting economic privileges accorded to converts, steadily
increased the numbers of those who turned in prayer toward the
holy city of Mecca.

Even in northern India, where the conquerors were most successful in establishing their power, the Moslem empire was able to
maintain a semblance of political unity for less than two centuries.
In the hundred and eighty-two years which followed the creation
of the Delhi sultanate three successive lines of sultans held sway
at this new capital of the north. The Slave dynasty founded by
Kutbu-d din Aibak, which held the throne between 1206 and 1290,
was succeeded by the short-lived Khilji dynasty, whose three

sultans reigned for a total of thirty years, and this in turn by the Tughlak dynasty, which lasted from 1321 until 1388. Upon the death of Firoz Shah Tughlak, in 1388, the sultanate collapsed and northern India entered upon a ten-year period of civil strife. At the end of this period the Mongol Tamerlane, fresh from his central-Asian and Russian triumphs, entered the Indus valley at the head of his conquering horsemen and pushed across the Punjab to the gates of Delhi. The city was taken and plundered; and although Tamerlane was himself a Moslem, thousands of his coreligionists were ruthlessly slaughtered in the general massacre which accompanied the sack.

The retirement of the Mongol conqueror to central Asia at the end of 1398 left northern India in a state of complete anarchy; and the sultanate at Delhi was not re-established until 1450, when the Afghan Bahlol Khan seized the power and became the founder of the Lodi dynasty (1450–1526). The Afghan sultans, however, never succeeded in extending their authority over more than a fragment of the territory ruled by the earlier sultans; and four considerable sections of northern India—Bengal, Malwa, Gujarat, and Kashmir—maintained their political independence from the opening of the fifteenth century until the last half of the sixteenth, when they were absorbed into the Mogul empire under Akbar the Great.

Throughout the two centuries (1206–1388) which saw northern India ruled as a unit by its Mohammedan conquerors the Delhi sultans, with one or two exceptions, appear to have been utterly lacking in constructive political ability. At best they were religious bigots, delighting in the slaughter of the infidel and in destroying all vestiges of idolatry; in general they combined with their intolerance insatiable avarice, lustful debauchery, and a positive genius for intrigue and murder. One at least of the list was a parricide; one ascended the throne by murdering a predecessor who was both uncle and father-in-law, while the precautionary elimination of brothers, cousins, and other potentially dangerous relatives was of frequent occurrence. The wealth which they accumulated by their wars of conquest or by the oppressive taxes levied upon their Hindu subjects was poured out in maintaining an

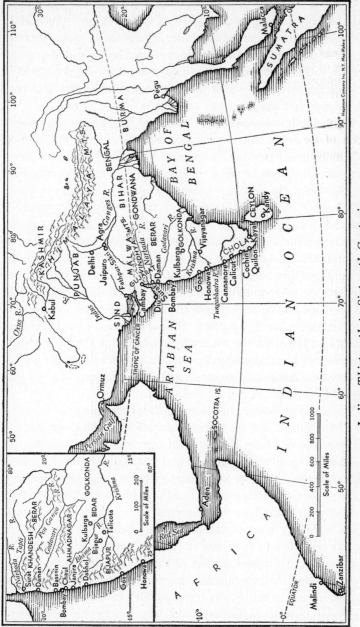

India: Thirteenth to Sixteenth Centuries

elaborate court or in erecting palaces, mosques, and other public buildings to adorn the capital; but little interest was displayed by any of the sultans in the buildings erected by their predecessors, and the splendor of Delhi was always marred by the multitude of dilapidated structures which through neglect had fallen into partial or complete ruin.

In the administration of provincial and local affairs the government of the Delhi sultans appeared at its worst, an undisguised and unmitigated rule by the sword. A crushing burden of taxation—amounting under some rulers to 50 per cent of his total production—kept the unhappy peasant in a state of semistarvation, and in the districts thus deprived of their reserve food supply a poor crop inevitably resulted in the death of thousands by famine. Even under the most enlightened of the sultans thousands of the peasants were enslaved each year by officers authorized to provide the court with an adequate supply of labor; and this policy, while relieving the overpopulation of the agricultural districts, left only the less able-bodied to maintain the unequal struggle against taxgatherer and natural calamities. The not infrequent local uprisings which resulted from the miserable condition of the people were repressed with ruthless severity; but nothing was done for the removal of the causes of discontent, and the restoration of order was followed only by renewed oppression.

Moslem and infidel alike suffered from the misgovernment of the Delhi rulers, and the religious fanaticism of the sultans was sometimes loosed upon the heretical sects among the followers of the Prophet; both misgovernment and intolerance fell with greatest force, however, upon the unfortunate Hindus. The Mohammedan rulers of the thirteenth and fourteenth centuries were still inspired by the belief that those who rejected Islam forfeited all human rights and fully merited extermination. Death was the penalty for any who dared to practice in public the rites of Brahmanism or to replace the ruined temples of their faith. It was the Hindu peasant rather than the Moslem warrior who carried the crushing load of taxation; and it was the same element of the population that saw thousands of its able-bodied members herded into slavery at Delhi, where the acceptance of Islam was the single alternative to death. Fortunately for the conquered people of India, however, the religious zeal of their conquerors did not long remain free from avarice. A living infidel might be an abomination in the sight of Allah, but a dead infidel paid no taxes; and the sultans, appreciating this important fact, gradually adopted the policy of ignoring the religious nonconformity of all save those who publicly paraded their adherence to Hindu beliefs.

During the sultanate of Firoz Shah Tughlak (1351–1388) a new and more insidious campaign was undertaken against the native religion. Firoz Shah, who appears to have been a more enlightened ruler than most of his predecessors, combined a real enthusiasm for Islam with an equally real spirit of humanity; and he issued a decree proclaiming that any infidel who accepted the Mohammedan faith would be exempted from paying the *jizya*, or poll tax. The new arrangement offered a powerful inducement to conversion, and many of Firoz Shah's infidel subjects hastened to embrace the faith of their sultan. If the Delhi sultanate had continued in power and if it had adhered to Firoz Shah's policy of subsidizing conversions, it is possible that Hinduism would have disappeared from northern India as completely as had the doctrines of Gautama Buddha. With the death of Firoz Shah, however, the political unity of northern India came to an end, and the Moslem rulers of the separate northern states which arose from the ruins left by Tamerlane displayed little or no proselytizing zeal. Hinduism, having survived the ordeal of the first two centuries under Mohammedan rule, was not again subjected to serious attack until late in the seventeenth century.

Between the caste-proud Brahmans and the orthodox adherents of Islam there could be no meeting of the minds, and the two religions have remained to the present day bitterly hostile to each other. The Indian people, however, have never lost their ancient genius for creative religious thought, and the fifteenth century saw the rise of a number of eclectic teachers who attempted to blend into a single creed the best elements of Mohammedanism and of Hinduism. The most notable of these teachers was Kabir, a mystic who lived between 1440 and 1518.[1] Originally a Mohammedan, he

[1] Many of Kabir's poems have been translated into English by Tagore.

taught the existence of a Supreme Being who was to be found neither in temple nor mosque and who had no pleasure either in the laws of caste or in those set forth by the Koran, but who could be found by every true seeker. Although these teachings made little impression upon the great mass of Mohammedans or Hindus, Kabir foreshadows both Akbar and the Sikh cult of the sixteenth century and also, perhaps, "Mahatma" Gandhi of the twentieth.

South of the Vindhya Mountains the overlordship of the Delhi sultanate was overthrown almost as soon as it was established. It was not until 1327 that the forces of Mohammedanism completed their conquest of the southern peninsula. Nine years later southern India threw off the foreign yoke and established the Hindu empire of Vijayanagar south of the Krishna River, while in 1347 the tyranny of the Tughlak sultan resulted in the revolt of Zafar Khan, who established in the Deccan the independent (Mohammedan) Bahmani sultanate.

For about a century and a half after this successful revolt the Bahmani sultans, with their capital at Bidar, ruled over the greater part of the Deccan. From Zafar Khan, the founder of the dynasty, to Mahmud Shah, the last of the line, the fourteen Bahmani sultans were, with a single exception, bloodthirsty fanatics who slaughtered countless thousands of their Hindu subjects and waged relentless warfare against the neighboring Hindu empire of Vijayanagar. Like the sultans of Delhi, the Bahmani sultans maintained a sumptuous court upon the taxes wrung from a starving people. Athanasius Nikitin of Russia, who visited Bidar in 1472 or 1473, wrote: "The land is overstocked with people; but those in the country are very miserable, whilst the nobles are extremely opulent and delight in luxury."

Some nine or ten years after Nikitin's visit to Bidar, Mahmud Shah Bahmani (1482–1518) ascended the throne at the age of twelve. This last prince of the Bahmani dynasty reigned but never ruled, and long before his death his title of Sultan had become an empty boast. In 1484 the governor of Berar—the northernmost portion of the Bahmani domain—renounced his allegiance to his nominal lord and established the Imad Shahi sultanate of Berar, which retained its independent power for about ninety years. In

1489, five years after this first successful repudiation of the authority of Mahmud, Yusuf Adil Khan, the governor of the southwestern province of Bijapur, followed suit and established the independent Adil Shahi sultanate of Bijapur. In the following year Ahmad Nizam Shah, governor of the northwestern province of Ahmadnagar, likewise declared independence and established himself as the first of the Nizam Shahi sultans. By 1492 the power at Bidar, the capital of the Bahmani sultanate, had fallen completely into the hands of Kasim Barid, the prime minister of Mahmud. After Mahmud's death Amir Barid, the son of Kasim, set up the Barid Shahi sultanate of Bidar, while a fifth independent Moslem state, the Kutb Shahi sultanate of Golkonda, was established simultaneously in the ancient Andhra territories of the east coast between the Krishna and the Godavari rivers.

Of the five petty sultanates which thus arose in the Deccan after the collapse of the Bahmani power three were, by reason of size and location, of outstanding importance. Bijapur and Ahmadnagar, on the western side of the peninsula, shared between them the ports of the west coast from Honowa to Bassein. The eastern state of Golkonda held the fertile and well-watered plain between the lower courses of the Krishna and the Godavari, as well as the strip of coast including the deltas of these two rivers. Of the two western sultanates Bijapur was the more extensive and held the larger portion of the coast, with the ports of Honowa, Dabhol, and—most important of all—Goa; but the shorter coast line of Ahmadnagar, including, as it did, the ports of Janjira and Bassein and the only partially developed harbor of Bombay, enabled the Nizam Shahi sultans to share in the profitable commerce between the Indian coast and the ports of the Red Sea and the Persian Gulf.

Like the petty states which rose out of the ruins of the Delhi sultanate in northern India, the independent sultanates of the Deccan quickly adopted toward their Hindu subjects a more tolerant attitude than that of their Bahmani predecessors. This growing tolerance in matters of religion was, probably on account of their commercial interests, most noticeable in the three coastal states, and especially in Bijapur, whose first sultan, Yusuf Adil Khan, married a Maratha (Hindu) princess, and whose later rulers commonly employed Hindu officials in the administration of their government. To a certain extent, however, this adoption of a more tolerant policy toward their non-Moslem subjects was forced upon the sultans of the disintegrated Deccan by the bitter hostility of their Mohammedan neighbors; and Bijapur, being the object of frequent concerted attacks by Ahmadnagar, Bidar, and Golkonda, was occasionally driven to ally itself with Hindu Vijayanagar in self-defense. Still another cause for the toleration of Hindu infidelism was the development of heresy inside the Moslem faith; many of the Mohammedan rulers appear to have ignored or even to have condoned the practice of "idolatrous" cults in order to devote their energies the more freely to the extirpation of those who differed with them in interpreting the faith of Islam.

In 1310 the forces of Islam had reached the southern tip of the peninsula, destroying the ancient kingdom of Chola and sacking the busy commercial city of Kayal. During the quarter of a century which followed, successful attacks were made upon various other Hindu states of the Dravidian south. For the districts of India lying south of the Krishna River, however, the Mohammedan invasion at the beginning of the fourteenth century was little more than a raiding expedition, such as Mahmud of Ghazni had led three centuries earlier into the Punjab and the upper Ganges valley. In 1336 a body of Telinga refugees from the northern Deccan under capable leadership commenced the erection of the city of Vijayanagar on the southern bank of the Tungabhadra River. For more than two hundred years Vijayanagar was the capital of an extensive Hindu empire and the bulwark of Hinduism against the Mohammedan conqueror. At the height of its power, from the end of the fourteenth century until the middle of the sixteenth, this empire included all of southern India except one or two commercial cities on the west coast; and its successive rulers waged frequent wars against their Moslem neighbors on the north, first the Bahmani sultans and later the independent sultans by whom the Bahmani territories had been partitioned. Even after the destruction of their capital in 1565 by the allied Deccan sultanates the Hindu rulers of this important empire continued for eighty years to rule over the greater part of southern India.

In 1443 Vijayanagar was visited by Abdu-r Razzak, the ambassador of Shah Rukh, the son and successor of Tamerlane. This learned Persian has left an extremely interesting description of the Hindu capital. He writes:

The capital of Bidjanagar is such that the pupil of the eye has never seen a place like it, and the ear of intelligence has never been informed that there existed anything to equal it in the world. It is built in such a manner that seven citadels and the same number of walls enclose each other. . . . The seventh fortress, which is placed in the center of the others, occupies an area ten times larger than the market-place of the city of Herat. It is the palace which is used as the residence of the king. . . . At the gate of the king's palace are four bazaars placed opposite to each other. On the north is the portico of the palace of the king. Above each bazaar is a lofty arcade with a magnificent gallery, but the audience hall of the king's palace is elevated above all the rest. The bazaars are extremely long and broad. . . .

Each class of men belonging to each profession has shops contiguous the one to the other; the jewelers sell publicly in the bazaar pearls, rubies, emeralds, and diamonds. In this agreeable locality, as well as in the king's palace, one sees numerous running streams and canals formed of chiselled stone, polished and smooth.

As a result of the political disintegration which set in during the last part of the fourteenth century the brief unity imposed by the Moslem conquerors disappeared. Fifteenth-century India was for the moment free from any outside threat; but the situation was obviously such as to facilitate the imperialistic activities of the Europeans who arrived at the end of the century, and of the Moguls who came down from the north a quarter of a century later.

This sketch of fifteenth-century India would be misleading, however, if it presented only a picture of political chaos. In spite of misgovernment, religious differences, burdensome taxation, and constantly recurring wars the people of the country continued to engage in their ancient industries and to produce a variety of commodities for which there existed in other parts of the world a keen demand. Along the west and east coasts of the country, from Cambay to the Ganges, there lay a series of flourishing commercial centers. At these ports Indian, Persian, and Arab merchants were engaged in carrying on trade with Malaysia and Indo-China to the east and with the Persian Gulf and the Red Sea to the west.

In general the more northern of the Indian ports on either coast traded only in one direction, exporting local products in exchange for goods from the east or from the west, as the case might be. But at the more southern commercial cities, such as Calicut, Cochin, and Quilon, local exports to the west were supplemented by goods brought from Indo-China and the East Indies. Chief among the products from the East Indies were the spices which were in such demand in Europe. Here at the southern-Indian ports these goods were transshipped to the Persian Gulf and to the Red Sea; thence they found their way to the Mediterranean. From the eastern Mediterranean the Venetians and, to a lesser extent, the Genoese carried the products of the Orient to the markets of western Europe; for four centuries this trade, which had become increasingly necessary to the peoples of Europe, poured tremendous profits into the coffers of Venice and Genoa.[1] But the European merchant did not always content himself with purchasing his Oriental commodities at the marts of the eastern Mediterranean. During the course of the fifteenth century at least four Western merchants, each of whom has left an account of his travels, went to India on trading expeditions.

The earliest of these visitors was the Venetian Nicolo di Conti,[2] who returned to his native city in 1444 after some twenty-five years of wandering through the East. This wanderer's travels took him as far eastward as Malaysia and Indo-China. He appears to have visited Calicut on his return from these more eastern regions, probably at some date between 1435 and 1440, and he described this port as "a maritime city, eight miles in circumference, a noble emporium for all India."

[1] Professor A. H. Lybyer, in "The Ottoman Turks and the Routes of Oriental Trade," *English Historical Review*, Vol. XXX, pp. 577–588, has pointed out that the rise of the Ottoman power and the capture of Constantinople had no apparent effect upon this trade.

[2] In the course of his travels Nicolo, who was accompanied by his wife and children, had been compelled to renounce his religion, "not so much from the fear of death to himself as from the danger which threatened his wife and children who accompanied him." On his return to Italy, therefore, he petitioned Pope Eugenius IV to grant him absolution for his apostasy. The petition was granted, and Nicolo was required, as penance for his sin, to recount to the Pope's secretary the story of his adventures.

Not long after the visit of Nicolo di Conti came that of the enthusiastic Abdu-r Razzak, who reached Calicut from Ormuz in 1442. He writes:

Finally, after a voyage of eighteen days and as many nights, by the aid of the Supreme King and Ruler, we cast anchor in the port of Calicut. . . .

Calicut is a perfectly secure harbor, which, like that of Ormuz, brings together merchants from every city and from every country; in it are to be found abundance of precious articles brought thither from maritime countries, and especially from Abyssinia, Zirbad, and Zanguebar [Zanzibar]; from time to time ships arrive there from the shores of the House of God [Mecca] and other parts of the Hedjaz, and abide at will, for a greater or longer space, in this harbor; the town is inhabited by Infidels [Abdu-r Razzak was a follower of the Prophet] and situated on a hostile [that is, non-Moslem] shore. It contains a considerable number of Mussulmans, who are constant residents and have built two mosques, in which they meet every Friday to offer up prayer. . . . Security and justice are so firmly established in this city that the most wealthy merchants bring thither from maritime countries considerable cargoes, which they unload and unhesitatingly send into the markets and the bazaars, without thinking in the meantime of any necessity of checking the account or of keeping watch over the goods. The officers of the custom-house take upon themselves the charge of looking after the merchandise, over which they keep watch day and night. When a sale is effected, they levy a duty on the goods of one-fortieth part; if they are not sold they make no charge on them whatever.

In other ports a strange practice is adopted. When a vessel sets sail for a certain point and suddenly is driven by a decree of Divine Providence into another roadstead, the inhabitants, under pretext that the wind has driven it there, plunder the ship. But at Calicut every ship, whatever place it may come from or wherever it may be bound, when it puts into this port is treated like other vessels, and has no trouble of any kind to put up with. . . .

The third Western visitor to Calicut was the Russian merchant Athanasius Nikitin, who arrived in 1472. After commenting briefly on the various ports at which he visited en route he writes: "Calicot [Calicut] is a port for the whole Indian sea, which God forbid any crafts to cross, and whoever saw it will not go over it healthy." Thus writes the Russian landsman; but the Indian and Arab ships, as we have seen, were making regular voyages from Calicut directly across the Indian Ocean to the Persian Gulf and the Red Sea.

The last of the four visitors was Hieronimo de Santo Stefano, a Genoese merchant who embarked upon a commercial voyage to the Far East during the last decade of the century. The Genoese merchant and his partner traveled first to Cairo, where they purchased a stock of merchandise; from Cairo they proceeded overland to a port on the Red Sea, and, after sailing twenty-five days, arrived at Aden. After a stay of four months they embarked for India in another ship and finally arrived at a "great city called Calicut." Santo Stefano reports:

> The lord of this city is an idolator, and so likewise are all the people. They worship an ox, or the sun, and also various idols, which they themselves make. When the people die they are burnt; their customs and usages are various; inasmuch as some kill all kinds of animals excepting oxen and cows; if any one were to kill or wound these, he would be himself immediately slain, because, as I have said before, they are objects of worship. Others, again, never eat flesh or fish, or anything that has had life. . . . In this city there are as many as a thousand houses inhabited by Christians, and the district is called Upper India.

From Calicut, Santo Stefano and his fellow merchant proceeded by ship to Ceylon. From Ceylon they voyaged along the Indian east coast, touching at several ports, and then sailed eastward to Pegu, Malacca, and Sumatra. But what appeared at its outset to be a prosperous undertaking ended in total disaster. In Burma chaotic conditions in the interior interfered with the expected trade; in Sumatra the death of Santo Stefano's partner was followed by the confiscation of the deceased merchant's goods along with much actually belonging to the surviving partner; and on the return trip from the East Indies a shipwreck left the Genoese adventurer penniless. Thanks to the kindly assistance which he received from Mohammedan merchants at Cambay and at Ormuz, the unfortunate Genoese finally succeeded in making his way to Tripoli in Syria, where, on September 1, 1499, he wrote to a Genoese friend the account of the misfortunes "which in my disastrous journey befell me for my sins."

The Coming of the Portuguese

Even at the moment when Santo Stefano was describing to his friend in Genoa the many misfortunes which had overtaken him, there was impending, for his home city as well as for its great rival Venice, an even greater disaster. In September, 1499, less than a month after the date of Santo Stefano's letter, Vasco da Gama entered the port of Lisbon with three Portuguese ships laden with spices, having successfully made his way around Africa to the coast of India and back. The accomplishment of this epoch-making voyage, which shifted the commercial center of Europe from the Mediterranean ports to those of the Atlantic and brought western Europe into direct maritime communication with India and with the entire Far East, marked the culmination of nearly eight decades of patient toil and daring exploration on the part of the Portuguese.

In July, 1497, Vasco da Gama with three small ships had sailed from Lisbon for the purpose of following to its ultimate goal the path explored by his predecessors. Rounding the Cape of Good Hope, Da Gama proceeded up the African east coast, landing at frequent intervals to secure information. At Malindi, a short distance south of the equator, he was able to secure the services of an Arab pilot, and on May 20, 1498, the little squadron entered the harbor of Calicut. At Calicut the Portuguese had little difficulty in exchanging their European goods for a cargo of spices, and in September, 1499, after an absence of twenty-six months, Da Gama returned in safety to the port of Lisbon. Only one third of his men survived the trip, but the cargo which he brought home is said to have been valued at sixty times the entire cost of the voyage.

Six months after Da Gama's return from this first voyage thirteen well-laden ships under the command of Pedro Alvares Cabral set forth to repeat his exploit on a larger scale. Cabral, making a more rapid voyage, returned to his home port in July, 1501, and in February of the following year Da Gama was sent out again in command of a fleet of twenty ships. Spices and other Oriental products were now pouring into Europe in greater quantities and at cheaper prices than ever before, and Lisbon, as the distributing center for this flood of Eastern commodities, quickly became one of the most important commercial cities of Europe.

To the Arab merchants, who had hitherto controlled the eastern end of the route by which Oriental goods found their way to Europe, the opening of Portugal's all-water route was almost as severe a blow as it was to the Venetians and the Genoese. Instinctively recognizing the seriousness of the Portuguese intrusion, the Arabs at Calicut, even in 1498, attempted to obstruct Da Gama's trading operations. In this attempt they were unsuccessful; but two years later the rough-handed tactics of the Europeans made it possible for the Arabs to stir up the people of Calicut to attack the merchants who accompanied Cabral, and the Portuguese were forced to complete their cargo at Quilon and Cochin.

On the Portuguese side the quickly aroused hostility of the Arab traders was met by bitter religious intolerance. The age-old struggle of their homeland against the Moorish invaders who ravaged its coasts had bred in the Portuguese a deep-rooted hatred for all who professed the faith of Islam, and they welcomed an excuse for attacking here in Eastern waters the followers of the Prophet. When Da Gama arrived at Calicut on his second voyage, he inflicted prompt punishment upon the people for their anti-Portuguese riot; on his departure for Portugal he left several of his ships in the East with orders to make war upon the Arabs and especially to attack their ships trading between India and the Egyptian ports on the Red Sea.

By 1505 the Far Eastern interests of the Portuguese king (who with the Pope's consent had assumed the ambitious title of "Lord of Navigation, Conquest, and Commerce of Ethiopia, Arabia, Persia, and India") had become so important that Francisco de Almeida was sent out, with the title of Viceroy, to assume command of the Portuguese forces and to exercise jurisdiction over all Portuguese subjects in the Orient. Under Almeida's energetic leadership the Arab merchants were driven from the seas; in 1509 a combined Egyptian and Arabian fleet was destroyed in a naval battle fought off the port of Diu, and the Portuguese secured complete mastery of the Indian Ocean. In the fall of 1509 Almeida was succeeded by Alfonso de Albuquerque, who as governor directed Portuguese affairs for nearly six years and definitely established the future policy of Portugal in the Far East.

Almeida, believing that preponderance of naval power was sufficient to ensure Portuguese monopoly of the trade, had opposed any suggestion that Portugal should attempt to secure territorial possessions in India or elsewhere in the Orient. The garrisons required to hold such possessions, he argued, would constitute an unwarranted drain upon his country's man power, with the result of weakening the forces available for the all-important naval supremacy.

Albuquerque agreed with his predecessor in regarding command of the sea as essential, but he differed diametrically on the question of territorial acquisitions. He believed, perhaps rightly, that a fleet operating at such a great distance from its home ports must have a certain number of fortified bases for refitting and supply. Between 1510 and 1515, therefore, he seized and fortified four widely separated and strategically important points: Goa, on the coast of Bijapur; Malacca, at the southern extremity of the Malay peninsula; Ormuz, near the mouth of the Persian Gulf; and the island of Socotra, off the entrance to the Red Sea. At these four points Albuquerque established Portuguese administrations and Portuguese garrisons, supplemented by Hindu troops armed and organized in accordance with European methods, and he appears to have hoped that these and subsequent acquisitions would develop into colonial centers from which the political influence of Portugal would gradually spread into the surrounding territories.

After the retirement of Albuquerque, in 1515, his policy was continued under the men who succeeded him. Taking advantage of the political weakness of northern India and the Deccan, the Portuguese seized and garrisoned Chaul, Bombay, and Bassein, on the coast of Ahmadnagar; Daman, on the coast of Khandesh; and Diu, on the south coast of Gujarat. At the same time additional bases of operations were secured in the East Indies, attempts were made to establish footholds on the coast of China, and a number of harbors on the east coast of Africa were occupied as ports of call for ships voyaging to and from the Orient. As a result of this development the Portuguese found themselves in possession of a chain of fortified trading posts extending from Zanzibar on the west to the Moluccas in the east. As Almeida had foreseen, the maintenance of these posts made constantly increasing demands upon the available man power of the homeland, the more so as they had to be defended not merely against Portugal's commercial rivals but also against the growing hostility of the local rulers from whose territories they had been torn.

Although from their first arrival on the coast of India the Portuguese had displayed bitter hostility toward the Mohammedans, it was not until after the accession of John III, in 1521, that they embarked upon a systematic campaign for extending the Christian religion to the peoples of India and of the Far Eastern world. Hitherto each expedition and each commercial post had been provided with its spiritual adviser, but the priests appointed to such posts had been charged merely with the duty of caring for the souls of Portuguese subjects. The new monarch was a religious enthusiast and believed that Portugal's unique position in the Orient imposed upon him the obligation of spreading the Gospel of Christ to the uttermost parts of the world. Missionaries, therefore, were sent in steadily increasing numbers to India, to Malacca, to the islands of the East Indies, and even to regions lying outside the field of Portuguese control. So rapid was the growth of the missionary undertaking that in 1538 a bishopric was established at Goa. Nineteen years later the bishopric was raised to an archbishopric, and the occupants of this office, rivaling the viceroys in dignity and power, exercised jurisdiction over the missionary work throughout the entire Far East.

There is no evidence that this religious enthusiasm of John III modified in any way the energy with which the Portuguese strove to extend their commercial monopoly, but the new activities did complicate and interfere with the attainment of this earlier objective. Hitherto the factor of religious hostility had entered only into the relations between Portuguese and Mohammedan; henceforth the zeal of the missionary was to antagonize the adherents of other non-Christian faiths in India. In 1546 the Portuguese monarch instructed his viceroy "to discover all the idols by means of diligent officers, to reduce them to fragments and utterly consume them, in whatsoever place they may be found, proclaiming rigorous penalties against such persons as shall dare to engrave, cast, sculpture, limn, or bring to light any figure in metal, bronze, wood, clay, or shall introduce them from foreign parts; and against those who shall celebrate in public or in private any festivities which have any Gentile taint, or shall abet them, or shall conceal the Brahmins, the pestilential enemies of the name of Christ." In 1560 the Inquisition was established at Goa, and long before the end of the sixteenth century the attempts of the Portuguese to impose Christianity upon the Indians under their sway had aroused widespread hostility and opposition.

THE MOGUL EMPIRE

For something more than half a century after Vasco da Gama's arrival at Calicut the political situation in India was such as to facilitate the ambitious projects of the Portuguese. At least five independent and mutually hostile Mohammedan states divided the power of northern India. In the Deccan bitter rivalry existed among the five petty sultanates and the kingdom of Khandesh, which, once a part of the Malwa kingdom, now maintained an independent existence between the Narbada and the northern frontier of Ahmadnagar. South of the lower Ganges and northeast of Golkonda the extensive region known as Gondwana was ruled by a number of petty chiefs and rajas. South of the Deccan sultanates lay the Hindu empire of Vijayanagar, almost constantly at war with its Mohammedan neighbors. Under these conditions concerted action against the foreign intruder was out of the question, and even the separate states whose harbors the Portuguese seized were prevented by the attacks of their neighbors from putting forth their full power against the European.

The second quarter of the sixteenth century, however, saw the first steps toward the establishment of the great Mogul empire which, during the second half of the century, was to unite all of northern India and a considerable part of the Deccan under a line of rulers strong enough to administer at least a temporary check to the advance of European domination.

In the year 1504 a central-Asian prince named Babur, a descendant in the fifth generation of the Mongol conqueror Tamerlane, made himself master of Kabul, just beyond the northwest passes through which India, in its long history, has been so frequently invaded. In 1525 the Lord of Kabul, attracted by the wealth and by the political weakness of India, advanced southward into the Punjab. Babur's army consisted of not more than twelve thousand men; but in April, 1526, he defeated the last Afghan Sultan of Delhi and established his power over the upper Ganges valley. During the four and a half years which followed this initial triumph Babur, by a judicious combination of war and diplomacy, steadily extended his dominions. At his death in December, 1530, he was able to leave to his son and successor, Humayun, a realm stretching from the banks of the Oxus River to the frontier of Bengal and from the Himalayas on the north to the highlands of Malwa on the south.

Humayun was less capable or less fortunate than his conquering father. For about ten years he succeeded in maintaining himself against his hostile neighbors, but in the early summer of 1540 he was driven out of India by the Afghan ruler of Bihar. For fifteen years Humayun was a homeless wanderer, but in 1555 he succeeded in regaining Delhi and Agra, together with a portion of the territory over which his father had ruled. In January, 1556, however, less than a year after this favorable turn in his fortunes, Humayun died, leaving to his fourteen-year-old son Akbar the task of establishing the Mogul power.

During the first four years after the death of Humayun the affairs of the Mogul state were directed by Bairam Khan, the loyal and capable minister of the late ruler. Early in 1560 Bairam Khan was driven from office by a court intrigue; and for two years the power was exercised by the successful intriguers, while the young prince gave himself up to a life of frivolity. In 1562 Akbar took the reins of government into his own hands. Although still a mere youth, the new monarch quickly gave evidence of extraordinary ability. His long reign coincided roughly with the reigns of Philip II of Spain and Elizabeth of England, both of whom ascended their thrones at more mature age and both of whom hold prominent places in the history of the sixteenth century. In comparison with these two contemporaries Akbar does not suffer, and it would be quite possible to maintain that, both in vision and achievement, he was the greatest of the three.

The first and most obvious of Akbar's achievements was the establishment of his authority over a territory greater than that ruled by any previous Indian monarch. No sooner had he taken the affairs of government into his own hands than he began a series of conquests which extended in all directions the frontiers of the Mogul empire. In the east he invaded and conquered Bengal. In the north he reconquered Kabul and annexed Kashmir. On the west and southwest he conquered Rajputana, Malwa, Gujarat, and Sind. South of the Vindhya Mountains he established his authority over Khandesh, on the west coast, while many of the independent rajas of Gondwana were forced to acknowledge the suzerainty of the Mogul ruler. The conquest of the state of Gujarat, in 1573, was particularly important. Akbar thereby secured control of Cambay and Surat and profited by the rich commerce of these two ports. At the same time he became the master of that part of the coast upon which the Portuguese footholds of Diu and Daman were located and thus came into direct contact with the Europeans.

Unlike his famous ancestor Tamerlane, Akbar was not merely a conqueror; his accomplishments in political administration and organization rivaled those in the field of war. The extension of his empire was attended by the introduction of reforms intended to centralize the power and to reduce the arbitrary exactions of the local officials. Under the earlier Mohammedan rulers of northern India the administration of local affairs had developed along feudal lines; instead of receiving salaries the local officers were paid by grants of territory or by the privilege of collecting for themselves certain taxes normally payable to the crown. Akbar, abolishing this practice, established a salaried officialdom and a graded civil service. Taxes were regularized, a uniform system of weights and measures was established for the entire empire, and an imperial mint, organized about twenty years after his accession, provided the realm with an adequate supply of reliable currency.

From the very beginning of his personal reign Akbar appears to have realized that the Mohammedans constituted only a small minority of the population under his rule, and that his government, if it was to be anything more than a government by the sword, must win the loyal support of the non-Moslem majority. Throughout the entire course of his long reign, therefore, and often in the face of bitter opposition on the part of the Mohammedans, he adhered to a policy of absolute toleration for all varieties of religious belief. His first wife, the mother of the emperor Jahangir, was the daughter of the Hindu raja of Jaipur, and his subsequent marriage of other Hindu princesses gave unmistakable evidence of his intention to extend imperial favor to the Hindu rulers whom he had brought under his sway. The poll tax formerly levied upon non-Mohammedans was abolished, as was also the tax which his predecessors had imposed upon Hindu pilgrims. The condition of the Hindu was especially benefited by prohibiting the slave raids which during the preceding two centuries had carried millions of their number into servitude. Hindu and Parsee (Zoroastrian) officials occupied high positions in his court, and ordinances were issued forbidding the eating of beef and other kinds of food the consumption of which offended the prejudices of Hindus or Jains.

During the first twenty years of his reign Akbar's tolerance in matters of religion was dictated almost entirely by political considerations. Born and brought up in the Mohammedan faith, the great Mogul emperor appears during this period of his life to have been, with all his tolerance, a sincere follower of Islam. Such tolerance, however, could not fail to react upon his personal religious belief. Constant contact with the adherents of diverse creeds, whom he encouraged to expound their religious views and speculations, steadily undermined his faith in the teachings of the Prophet. At the age of thirty-five Akbar was an agnostic, skeptical with regard to the claims of the Koran but imbued with a strong tendency toward mysticism which compelled him to seek for a more satisfactory explanation of life. At forty he had openly renounced Islam and had formally promulgated a new synthetic religion, monotheistic in form but including elements derived from the Hindu, Jain, Parsee, Mohammedan, and even Christian faiths.

Akbar's venture into the field of religion-building was not a success. A number of his courtiers and officials did lip service during its creator's lifetime, but with his death his new religion disappeared from the memory of all save the historian. In contrast with this failure, however, his policy of toleration was a decided success. Continued by his son and grandson, Akbar's efforts to secure Hindu support placed the Mogul dynasty upon a strong foundation. Not until Aurangzeb, his third successor, abandoned this policy and reverted to the earlier Mohammedan policy of religious persecution did the power of the empire which Akbar had built up by his wise statesmanship begin to decline.

During the last thirty-two years of his reign—that is, after his conquest of Gujarat in 1573—the great Mogul emperor was inevitably drawn into close contact with the energetic Portuguese, who for the preceding three quarters of a century had been steadily extending their monopoly of India's maritime trade. Upon his acquisition of the Gujarat coast Akbar arranged with the Portuguese viceroy terms upon which the Portuguese were to continue in possession of Diu and Daman and were allowed to carry on trade at Surat and Cambay. The consolidation of northern India into a single powerful empire checked the extension of Portuguese power in this part of the Far East; but Akbar was not able to wrest from their hands the ports which they had already gained, and his conquest of Khandesh during the later years of his reign was seriously impeded by Portuguese assistance to the invaded country.

In spite of his dissatisfaction at the existence of these foreign strongholds within the frontiers of his empire, Akbar's relations with the Portuguese were usually of a friendly nature. The rapidly fading Mohammedanism of the Mogul emperor hardly inspired him to make common cause with the Egyptians and Arabs against their victorious rivals, the flourishing trade carried on by the Portuguese at the northern ports contributed in no small degree to the prosperity of the adjoining regions of the empire, and the Portuguese merchants were able to provide Akbar with cannon and other implements of warfare superior to those produced by his own arsenals.

Akbar showed keen interest, moreover, in the doctrines of Christianity, which first came to his attention about 1572 or 1573; and on several occasions he invited to his court learned Jesuit theologians capable of instructing him in these doctrines. The first of these invitations, which reached the authorities at Goa in September, 1579, aroused high hopes in the hearts of the missionaries; and two of their best-qualified members were promptly dispatched to Fathpur-Sikri, near Agra, where Akbar had established his capital. The optimism of the Jesuits was unwarranted. Their two learned representatives remained at the Mogul capital until 1583 and undoubtedly furnished the emperor with many ideas for his new religion, but they made no progress toward the hoped-for conversion. Subsequent missions were sent at Akbar's request in 1590, in 1595, and in 1601; but long before this last date the missionaries had come to realize that the emperor's interest in their teachings was purely intellectual and that his conversion to the Christian faith was not within the realm of probability.

In October, 1605, after a reign of forty-nine years, Akbar died and was succeeded on the Mogul throne by his one surviving son, the emperor Jahangir. Greatest of the Mogul emperors and one of the outstanding rulers in world history, Akbar accomplished much in his long reign. As conqueror and administrator he so extended and consolidated his empire that more than a century elapsed after his death before it began to show evidence of declining power. His broad tolerance in matters of religion served to diminish the long-standing bitterness between the various religious elements in the population of northern India; and if he did not actually succeed in establishing religious unity, he at least gave India a nearer approach to religious peace than she had experienced since the arrival of Mohammedanism. His strong rule made possible the development of commerce, and the general welfare of the empire attested the benefits of his reforms in economic affairs. Like all the Mogul rulers, he was an enthusiastic patron of art, architecture, and literature, and he gathered around him as advisers many of the outstanding scholars and thinkers of northern India.

With the end of Akbar's reign the power of the Portuguese in India, to which the rise of the Mogul empire had been the first serious check, began to wane. Already the ships of Holland and England, following the path opened by Vasco da Gama, were beginning to arrive in Far Eastern waters, and in the last year of Akbar's life an Englishman named Mildenhall, bearing a letter from the late English queen, arrived at the Mogul court to secure for Englishmen a share in Indian trade. During the course of the seventeenth century the Dutch, the English, and later the French were to deprive the Portuguese of the last vestiges of their one-time monopoly of Far Eastern trade. These newcomers, however, made little effort at first to imitate, in India at least, the Portuguese policy of territorial acquisition. For about a century India enjoyed comparative freedom from European aggression; and it was not until the early years of the eighteenth century, when the power of the Mogul rulers had begun to decline, that the European merchants embarked upon the policy of empire-building.

SUGGESTED REFERENCES

DANVERS, F. C. The Portuguese in India.

FOSTER, W. Early Travels in India.

HAVELL, E. B. A Short History of India.

KING, J. S. The History of the Bahmani Dynasty.

LANE-POOLE, S. Bábar.

LYBYER, A. H. "The Ottoman Turks and the Routes of Oriental Trade," *English Historical Review*, Vol. XXX, pp. 577–588.

MAJOR, R. H. (editor). India in the Fifteenth Century. (Contains the accounts of Di Conti, Abdu-r Razzak, Nikitin, and Santo Stefano.)

MALLESON, G. B. Akbar.

MORELAND, W. H. India at the Death of Akbar.

SEWELL, R. A Forgotten Empire.

SMITH, V. A. Akbar, the Great Mogul.

SMITH, V. A. The Oxford History of India.

STEPHENS, H. M. Albuquerque.

TAGORE, R. (translator). One Hundred Poems of Kabir.

WHITEWAY, R. S. The Rise of the Portuguese Power in India.

XVI

Portuguese and Spanish in Malaysia and Indo-China

AT THE moment when the voyage of Vasco da Gama made possible direct maritime intercourse between western Europe and the Far Eastern world the Malay Archipelago was, of all the Far East, the region most perfectly suited to exploitation by the new-comers. Here, even more than in India, were to be found the all-important spices which constituted the bulk of Portugal's rapidly developing trade; and here, more than anywhere else in the Orient, the absence of any powerful political organization facilitated the Portuguese policy, inaugurated by Albuquerque, of basing trade monopoly upon a far-flung line of strategically located fortified posts.

Since the collapse of the Madjapahit empire, more than a century earlier, no paramount power had arisen to exercise imperial dominion over the islands of Malaysia. From 1405 until 1435 the Chinese fleets under Cheng Ho had made periodic voyages through the archipelago and had raised high in the eyes of the local rulers the prestige of the great Ming empire. But the Ming emperors, while welcoming to their court the occasional Malay tributary missions, had displayed no desire to assume direct authority over these distant islands; so long as trade was open for the Chinese merchant

The Malay World in the Sixteenth and Seventeenth Centuries

on terms of equality with the rest of the world, China was willing that the peoples of Malaysia should govern themselves.

Nor did the spread of Mohammedanism and the establishment of Mohammedanized ruling families under Arab influence result in giving to the Arabs at Malacca anything resembling a political hegemony over the scattered island states in which their prose-lytizing methods had achieved success. Possibly from the fear of drawing upon them the wrath of the Chinese emperor, to whom they acknowledged themselves tributaries and whose protection they invoked against the Siamese, the Malaccan Arabs made no attempt at empire-building. Without venturing upon this tempting but dangerous policy, however, they had gathered into their busy port the great bulk of the trade between the Malay Islands and the rest of the world: China, Annam, and Siam on the north, as well as India and all the region which lay to the west.

Shortly after their arrival in India the Portuguese discovered that only a part of the spices came from India itself and that many of the most highly prized varieties were brought there from the east. In 1509, therefore, Diego Lopes de Sequeira was sent eastward with a number of ships to seek out the real source of these much esteemed commodities. Sequeira visited several ports at the western end of Sumatra and, in September, 1509, found his way to Malacca. Here the Portuguese were favorably received, but it was not long before their arrogance and the easily awakened hostility of the Arabs led to trouble. A sudden attack was made upon the Portuguese, and twenty of their number, who were on shore, were seized and thrown into prison. Sequeira's fleet was not strong enough to rescue the captives, so a call for aid was sent to Albuquerque.

Responding to this call with all the forces at his disposal, Albuquerque arrived at Malacca in the summer of 1511. Inasmuch as the government guilty of this act of hostility against his fellow countrymen was Mohammedan, the Portuguese commander had no difficulty in deciding upon a proper course of action. The city was attacked and quickly taken. The power of the hated "infidels" was completely destroyed, and Malacca was transformed into a Portuguese stronghold.

For a hundred and thirty years after its capture by Albuquerque, Malacca remained in Portuguese hands, the cornerstone of their commercial power in the regions to the east of India. Under the Portuguese, as under their Arab predecessors, Malacca continued to be the great central market for the spice trade of the Far East, and efforts were made to attract here the merchants from other Oriental countries. But the Portuguese, unlike the Arabs, were determined to buttress their commercial position by securing positive control over the sources of the spices.

As soon as the city had been taken, Albuquerque dispatched envoys to Pegu, Siam, Annam, and the local rulers of Java and Sumatra; with all these countries he endeavored to develop cordial relations. At the same time a small squadron was sent eastward to explore the archipelago and to discover the more important sources of trade. In the course of an extended cruise this squadron explored the coasts of Java, Sumatra, Borneo, and Celebes, discovered the Moluccas (the "Spice Islands"), and visited a number of other islands, greatly increasing the amount of Portuguese information concerning the East Indies.

Adopting in the archipelago the policy which had already been decided upon for India, and following the earlier examples of Sri-Vishaya and of Madjapahit, the Portuguese now established fortified bases of operations throughout the islands from Malacca to Amboyna. With their headquarters at Malacca this chain of posts enabled the Portuguese ships to maintain an efficient patrol of the archipelago. The merchant ships of other countries were excluded from access to the spice-producing areas and were compelled, rather than invited, to seek their spices at Malacca.

The embassies sent by Albuquerque in 1511 to the states of Indo-China succeeded, especially in Siam and Burma, in opening diplomatic intercourse and in gaining commercial privileges for the new masters of Malacca. In Annam the sixteenth-century Portuguese made little headway. In Siam they established a number of trading stations but appear to have confined their activities to legitimate commerce. Burma, like Annam, lay off the main line of Portuguese trade; few spices were produced here, and Burmese manufactures were inferior in workmanship to those of India, Siam, China, and Japan. For purposes of trade only two ports on the Burmese coast, Martaban and Tenasserim, were important, and the importance of these lay principally in the fact that they provided access to Siamese trade by overland routes more convenient than the difficult sea route around the Malay peninsula.

Although Burmese trade never attained much importance during the century of Portugal's Far Eastern monopoly, Burma provided for many Portuguese adventurers an attractive field for gainful activity. During the constant internal warfare which marked the first half of the sixteenth century, Portuguese soldiers of fortune, deserters from the ships and garrisons of their king, took service under the various warring princes of Burma. Tabin Shwehti (1531–1550), who commenced the unification of Burma, and Bayin

Naung (1551–1581), by whom the unification of the country was completed, both made extensive use of Portuguese mercenaries in attaining their success. Indeed, the attractive possibilities of this service in the Burmese wars must be counted among the factors which undermined and eventually destroyed Portugal's position in the Far East, since the constant loss by desertion of those who responded to its call deprived the Portuguese authorities of hundreds of their best fighting men and rendered all the more difficult the task of maintaining their far-flung line of trading posts.

Among the various Portuguese adventurers of the sixteenth and seventeenth centuries none had a more spectacular career than Philip de Brito, who, starting life as a cabin boy, ruled for a while over a portion of lower Burma. De Brito first achieved prominence, between 1580 and 1590, as a leader of Portuguese mercenaries in the service of the king of Arakan. In 1600 the Arakanese monarch, attracted by the weakness of southern Burma after the death of the conquering Bayin Naung, sent an expedition against the cities of the delta region, and De Brito took advantage of this expedition to establish himself as ruler of Syriam, a seaport on the easternmost mouth of the Irrawaddy. Having decided to set himself up as an independent potentate, De Brito repudiated his allegiance to the king of Arakan and destroyed a force which that monarch sent against him. Realizing the danger of his situation, however, he proceeded to Goa and sought recognition from the Portuguese viceroy, who was so favorably impressed that he bestowed upon the adventurer the hand of his niece.

For about a dozen years De Brito dominated the Burmese delta region. His warships, manned by Portuguese, Eurasians, and Indians, cut off all trade from the rival ports, and Syriam became the single port through which foreign goods could find their way into the interior. In 1612, however, he attacked Toungoo and brought upon himself the full power of the ruler of all Burma. Syriam was besieged by a combined land and sea force which vastly outnumbered the garrisons under De Brito's command. An appeal for aid was dispatched to Goa; but long before Portuguese aid could arrive the city had fallen, and the adventurous De Brito had been tortured to death by his victorious enemy.

By the end of the sixteenth century Portugal's power in the East Indies had begun to decline. For this decline there were many causes. The maintenance of the ambitious empire made constantly increasing demands upon the none too plentiful man power of the home state, demands which were made even heavier by the steady desertion of those who became mercenaries and pirates in the Orient. While the policies adopted in the Far East aroused ever increasing hostility among the peoples over whom Albuquerque and his successors had extended their authority, the great wealth which Portugal derived from her monopoly steadily undermined the hardihood of her people and made them less fit—or less willing —to match the exertions of those by whom the empire had been founded. In the effort to find adequate crews for the ships engaged in the Far Eastern trade, jails were emptied of their prisoners, and eventually foreign sailors were taken into the Portuguese service, thus making it possible for European rivals to learn all the mysteries of the eastern trade route.

Although this employment of foreigners made possible the intrusion of European rivals, the actual cause of this intrusion may be found in the acquisition of the Portuguese crown in 1580 by Philip II of Spain. By this union Portugal became involved in Spain's wars with the Dutch and the English; Lisbon was closed to the ships of these two enemy countries; and the ships of both countries, piloted by men who had visited the Spice Islands under the Portuguese flag, soon appeared in eastern seas bent on destroying the hundred-year monopoly.

In 1602 the Dutch allied themselves with the king of Kandy to drive the Portuguese from the island of Ceylon. Three years later the entire island of Amboyna was seized by the Hollanders, and in 1619 these same energetic rivals established themselves at Batavia near the western end of the island of Java. At the same time the English had shown equal energy in attacking the more western section of Portugal's extremely vulnerable line of trading posts. In 1611 and 1615, Portuguese fleets suffered crushing defeats at the hands of the English in battles fought off Cambay and Surat, while in 1622 the English joined with the Persians to capture the port of Ormuz at the entrance of the Persian Gulf. Against these constant attacks the Portuguese were almost helpless, and in 1641 their power in the East Indies was completely destroyed by the Dutch capture of Malacca. For a hundred and thirty years the possession of Malacca had given them control of the Indies; now their commercial empire in the archipelago had passed into the hands of other and more vigorous European peoples.

While the Portuguese explorers were still seeking to reach India by making their way around Africa, Christopher Columbus, sailing under the Spanish flag, had struck boldly out toward the west and in October, 1492, had reached land on the far side of the Atlantic. In 1493 Pope Alexander VI, in order to prevent conflicts between the Spanish and the Portuguese, issued the famous Bull of Demarcation. An imaginary line was drawn from north to south a hundred leagues west of the Azores;[1] Portugal was to have exclusive rights of exploration and trade in all non-Christian lands lying east of this line, while Spain was to have similar rights west of the line.

For the moment Spain appeared to have received much the better of this bargain. The Portuguese had not yet succeeded in finding their way to India, while Columbus, to the day of his death, believed that the islands which he had discovered were part of the East Indies; and his subsequent voyages were for the purpose of finding his way to the rich empires which must be somewhere in the near vicinity.[2] Six years after the bull was issued, however, Vasco da Gama returned from Calicut with his rich cargo of spices, while the Spanish explorations had led only to the discovery of fresh lands inhabited by savages. For twenty years after Da Gama's voyage, while the Portuguese were deriving fabulous profits from their new discoveries, the Spanish sought in vain for a route which would enable them to share in the rich trade of the Orient; and the discovery of a westward route to the Indies was finally accomplished under the leadership of a Portuguese serving the Spanish crown.

[1] In 1494 Spain and Portugal agreed to move the line two hundred and seventy leagues farther west.

[2] As a matter of fact, Columbus on his last voyage succeeded in reaching a point almost exactly halfway around the world from Malacca.

Ferdinand Magellan (Fernão de Magalhães) had served as an officer under Albuquerque when that great governor was laying the foundations of Portugal's commercial empire in the East. He participated in the taking of Malacca, and he may have accompanied the squadron which Albuquerque sent out, after the capture of Malacca, to explore the Malay Archipelago. After the death of Albuquerque, in 1515, Magellan returned to Lisbon, where he fell into disfavor at the Portuguese court. Believing himself unjustly treated, he renounced his allegiance to the Portuguese crown and became a Spanish subject. From the information which he had acquired in the Orient, either by visiting the Spice Islands or by conversing with fellow officers who had accompanied the exploration, Magellan was convinced that these islands lay so far to the east that they were in the Spanish half of the world.[1] Because of the fact that he had actually been in the Indies, Magellan was able to convince the Spanish government that he could find the long-sought westward route, and in September, 1519, he sailed from San Lucar with five Spanish ships, to discover a way past America.

Steering southwestward until he reached South America, Magellan sailed down the coast, looking for a westward passage. Late in October, 1520, after one of his five ships had been lost by shipwreck, he arrived at the entrance to the passage which, in memory of its discoverer, is now called the Strait of Magellan. A second ship was lost—by desertion—while he was finding his way through the difficult strait; but on November 28, 1520, he led his three remaining vessels out into the open sea, and to this body of water he gave the name *Pacific*.

After sailing northward almost to the equator Magellan turned his ships toward the northwest, expecting to reach the Moluccas at the end of a short voyage. But the distance across the Pacific was much greater than he expected, and his course carried him so far to the north that he finally reached the East Indies a considerable distance to the north of the Moluccas. On March 16, 1521, nearly four months after it had entered the Pacific, the little

---

[1] That is, on the eastern side of a line drawn from north to south halfway around the world from the Demarcation Line.

squadron sighted the first of a group of islands upon which Magellan bestowed, in honor of the date, the name *Archipelago of Saint Lazarus*: the present Philippines.

At the small island of Homonhon, where he first landed, Magellan found little food available. At Limasawa, south of the island of Leyte, he was more fortunate. Here the Spaniards found a prosperous village from which they were able to secure rice as well as coconuts, oranges, bananas, and other fruits. The inhabitants of the village were friendly, and their chiefs exchanged gifts with Magellan. Before leaving the island Magellan solemnly proclaimed the sovereignty of the Spanish king over the entire archipelago; then, having learned of the large town of Cebu, about eighty miles away, he proceeded there with his ships. The people of Cebu, who had long been accustomed to trading with Arab, Siamese, and Chinese merchants, welcomed these new foreigners and showed themselves quite willing to provide them with food in exchange for European goods.

Shortly after his arrival at Cebu, Magellan, anxious to secure acknowledgment of Spanish suzerainty, allied himself with one of the local rulers who was at war with a neighbor. In the ensuing battle the Spanish commander was killed. It was not long, moreover, before the arrogance of the Spanish transformed the earlier friendly attitude of the Cebuans into one of bitter hostility, with the result that the people rose against the strangers and killed some twenty-five of their number.

The survivors now determined to resume their search for the Spice Islands. Destroying one of their ships which was no longer seaworthy, they sailed southward with the two that remained, touching at Borneo and a number of other islands and finally reaching the Moluccas. After exchanging their European goods for spices they decided that one of the ships should return to Spain by the way they had come, while the other should try to get home by the way of the Cape of Good Hope. The first ship fell into the hands of the Portuguese; but the *Victoria*, under the command of Sebastian del Cano, safely found its way around Africa and on September 6, 1522, entered the harbor of Seville. One ship and eighteen men were all that remained of the expedition which had set out nearly three years before, but this ship and its handful of survivors had circumnavigated the earth.

In the same year that saw the start of Magellan's voyage the Spanish, under Hernando Cortez, began their conquest of Mexico, and in 1532 Francisco Pizarro, invading Peru, made this great Inca empire a province of the Spanish crown.

The Far East was affected in two ways by these Spanish conquests on the far side of the Pacific. In the first place, the enormous quantities of gold and silver which flowed into Spain from Mexico and Peru furnished Europe with exportable wealth that could be exchanged for the products of the Orient. In the second place, the occupation of Mexico established the Spaniards permanently on the American shore of the Pacific Ocean and made it certain that they would follow up the claims which resulted from Magellan's voyage.

Magellan had proved that the Moluccas could be reached by sailing westward from the Demarcation Line, while the Portuguese, ten years earlier, had reached the same islands by sailing eastward. Whether the islands lay on the Spanish or the Portuguese side of the Pacific continuation of this line no one knew. A map published in 1523 from data supplied by the survivors of the Magellan expedition represented the extension of the line as passing through the Indo-Chinese peninsula, and the Spanish government was fully prepared to accept this map as authoritative.[1] The Portuguese, on the other hand, denied the correctness of this map and insisted that the line would pass well to the east of the Moluccas. In addition to being more accurate in their geography the Portuguese were first in the field, they held a chain of fortified posts from which their warships steadily patrolled the seas of the archipelago, and they were prepared to resist by force any encroachment by their Spanish neighbors.

In 1525, 1526, and 1527 the Spanish king Charles I[2] fitted out expeditions to the East Indies, the first two sailing from Spain and the third from the coast of Mexico. Only the first and last of these expeditions succeeded in reaching the Orient, and in each case the

[1] See W. C. Abbott, *Expansion of Europe*, p. 222.
[2] Emperor Charles V of the Holy Roman Empire.

few ships which got as far as that were promptly captured by the watchful Portuguese cruisers. Discouraged by the total failure of these undertakings, the Spanish sovereign agreed to negotiate with the Portuguese, and in 1529 the question was settled, for a time, by the Treaty of Saragossa. Spain, in return for the payment of three hundred and fifty thousand gold ducats, agreed that the Demarcation Line in the Pacific should be drawn two hundred ninety-seven and a half leagues east of the Moluccas.

In spite of his treaty with Portugal, Charles made one more effort to secure a foothold in the East Indies. In 1542 an expedition was dispatched from Mexico, under the command of Ruy López de Villalobos, with instructions to avoid the Moluccas and to establish permanent settlements in the Western Islands—a name which was then generally used for the Philippines. Villalobos touched at Mindanao, Sarangani, and Leyte, and named this last island *Felipina* in honor of the Spanish crown prince, who was later to become Philip II. At all these places the people were so hostile that the Spaniards had difficulty in securing food and found it impossible to establish a settlement. Finally Villalobos turned southward to the Moluccas, where, like his predecessors, he was compelled to surrender to the Portuguese.

SPAIN IN THE PHILIPPINES

In 1556 Charles abdicated the Spanish throne in favor of his son Philip, and eight years later the new king determined upon a fresh colonizing effort across the Pacific. By this time the name *Felipina*, given by Villalobos to the island of Leyte, had been extended by the Spanish to the entire archipelago, and Philip II appears to have made up his mind that *Las Felipinas*, since they bore his name, should also recognize his sovereignty.

The new expedition, which started from Mexico in November, 1564, consisted of four ships and three hundred and eighty men under the command of Miguel López de Legaspi. Associated with Legaspi as chief adviser and navigating officer was Andrés de Urdaneta, a soldier-priest-scientist of high character and ability who had participated in the unsuccessful expedition of 1525, nearly forty years earlier. Urdaneta had spent ten years in the Indies after the failure of this earlier expedition and was thoroughly familiar with the geography of the region. Because of the fact that the Philippines and the Moluccas both lay on the Portuguese side of the Demarcation Line he believed that an attempt should be made to colonize the island of New Guinea, a part of which lay on the Spanish side; but the sealed instructions of the Mexican government ordered the colonization of the Philippines, and Legaspi felt bound to obey these orders.

On his arrival in the islands Legaspi, like Villalobos, found most of the people hostile and had great difficulty in securing a fresh supply of food for his fleet. At Bohol, where the more friendly attitude of the people made it possible to secure food, a council of Spanish officers decided that Cebu, where Magellan had met his death, would be the most satisfactory location for the colony; and on April 27, 1565, this town was attacked and captured. After the construction of a fort for the defense of the town Legaspi felt that he could send back to Mexico one of his ships with a report of his success, and reinforcements were soon on their way to assist in the task of conquest and colonization. At last, forty-four years after Magellan's arrival in the Philippines, the Spanish had succeeded in gaining a permanent position in the Far East.

Unlike their cousins in Java and Sumatra, where a far greater population density made possible the rise of strong kingdoms and extensive empires, the Malays of the Philippines dwelt in scattered and isolated villages along the coasts or in the interior valleys of the larger islands. The village (or *barangay*), consisting of fifty or a hundred families, was the political unit. A number of neighboring villages might be grouped together in a loose confederation; and along the coast, where communication was comparatively easy, such a confederation might include a total population of several thousand families. In general, however, the Filipino regarded as a stranger and an enemy everyone from outside his own village. This extreme particularism led naturally to the rise of a great variety of dialects in what was essentially a single linguistic family; and the diversification of language, in turn, constituted an added barrier to the development of a closer unity.

In spite of their failure to evolve a highly integrated political system the sixteenth-century Filipinos were well advanced in civilization. The earliest Spanish arrivals found them living in houses of bamboo and nipa, wearing garments of cotton and linen cloth woven in the islands, mining gold and other metals, and using firearms. Although the firearms were obviously a very recent innovation introduced into the islands by the Mohammedan Arabs, the other features of their material culture were ancient acquisitions.

Perhaps the most striking evidence of the high state of civilization attained by the Filipinos is furnished by their agricultural development. In the valleys of northern Luzon the Spanish conquerors found the slopes of the hills covered by terraced farms similar to those which in China and Japan and the entire Malay Archipelago still arouse the admiration of the Western world. Supported by stone retaining walls, the terraces rose from the edges of the rivers almost to the tops of the valley slopes, while supplies of water, brought long distances by means of ditches or wooden flumes, provided adequate artificial irrigation for the garden patches thus made available. The building and the maintenance of these terraces required foresight as well as much patient labor, while the construction of the irrigation systems proved that the Filipinos possessed, in addition to the capacity for long-time cooperative labor, no small degree of engineering skill.

In an account of the Philippine Islands written about the beginning of the thirteenth century the Chinese writer Chau Ju-kua states that there were numerous copper images of Buddha to be found in various parts of the islands, but he adds that no one could explain how these images got there. These Buddhist images, as well as the Buddhist figures which appear on Philippine bolo handles, and certain Sivaite figures which have been discovered in ancient burial mounds of Cebu and Mindanao, appear to indicate that both Buddhism and Hinduism had found their way into the islands from Sumatra and Java as a result of the commercial activity of Sri-Vishaya and Madjapahit.[1] Chau Ju-kua's observation, however, suggests that all real knowledge of Buddhism had

[1] See Chapter XIV, by Dr. H. Otley Beyer, in Steiger, Beyer, and Benitez, *A History of the Orient.*

disappeared long before the arrival of the first Europeans; and when the Spaniards reached the Philippines, the great majority of the Filipinos held religious beliefs somewhat resembling those of the American Indians. They believed in a Great Spirit, who was the creator of the world; but in addition they worshiped fetishes, ancestral spirits, and certain birds and animals.

In Mindanao and the Sulu chain, Mohammedanism, introduced by the Sayyid Arabs during their fifteenth-century expansion, had become firmly established; and when the Spaniards arrived, the influence of Islam had begun to spread even into some of the more northern islands. The extremely primitive religious beliefs of the non-Moslem Filipinos offered little resistance to the spread of Christianity during the Spanish rule, while the Spaniards quickly destroyed the Mohammedan settlements in Luzon and the other northern islands. In the south, however, the religion of the Prophet successfully resisted all the efforts of Spanish missionaries to spread Christianity; and the Sulu Islands, together with south-western Mindanao, have remained predominantly Moslem to the present day.

If we are to credit the statements of the earliest Spanish observers, the Filipinos must have been the equals or even the superiors of any contemporary European people in the matter of literacy. "So given are these islanders to reading and writing," wrote Father Pedro Chirino in 1604, "that there is hardly a man, and much less a woman, that does not read and write in letters peculiar to the island of Manila." Five years later Antonio de Morga, who served in the Philippines from 1595 until 1603 as chief justice and lieutenant governor, corroborated this statement:

They write very well in all the islands, with some characters something like Greek or Arabic, which are in all fifteen; three are vowels, which serve for our five; the consonants are twelve . . . The way of writing was on canes, and now on paper, beginning the lines from the right hand to the left, in the Arabic fashion; almost all the inhabitants, both men and women, write in this language, and there are few of them who do not write it very well and with correctness.

Most important of the written languages used by the non-Mohammedan Filipinos was the Tagalog; but other groups also had alphabets of their own closely resembling the Tagalog, while the Mohammedans in the southern islands made use of Arabic. Among the Mohammedans, whom the Spaniards called Moros, Arabic has continued in use down to the present day. The other pre-Spanish forms of writing, however, gradually died out. The missionaries zealously destroyed such of the literature as came into their hands, and by the middle of the eighteenth century few of the Filipinos retained any knowledge of the once widely used indigenous scripts.

When the Legaspi expedition reached the Philippines, the Spaniards had knowledge only of the southern islands of this group; and it was for this reason that Cebu was selected as the place for their first settlement. This location, however, soon proved to be unsatisfactory. The continued hostility of the Cebuans made it very difficult for the little colony to secure food, while the Portuguese, suspicious of a Spanish settlement so near the Moluccas, sent an expedition to destroy it. The Portuguese attack was beaten off, but the fact that it had been made convinced Legaspi of the necessity of seeking a more northern location for his colony. The first move was to Capiz, on the northern coast of the island of Panay, but expeditions were sent to explore the regions still farther north, for the purpose of discovering a more suitable location.

In 1570 the Spanish explorers found their way into Manila Bay to the flourishing commercial town of Manila, which was ruled by a Mohammedan prince. This port, situated in the southern part of the island of Luzon, was immediately recognized as an admirable place for the Spanish headquarters. In 1571, therefore, the Spaniards attacked and captured the town, transforming it into the capital of their island empire.

Strong expeditionary forces were now sent to all parts of the islands for exploration and conquest. So energetically was the work carried out that by 1576, eleven years after Legaspi's arrival, the Spanish had established their authority over almost as much of the Philippines as they ever really succeeded in ruling. The mountainous interior districts of the larger islands, together with the islands occupied by the warlike Moros, retained their independence, but elsewhere the power of the European conqueror was supreme.

The compact island empire of the Spanish differed greatly from the far-flung eastern dominion of Portugal. While the fortified posts held by the Portuguese served as centers of trade and as bases of operations for their naval patrol, their effective authority seldom extended inland more than a cannon-shot beyond the lines of their fortifications. In the Philippines, on the other hand, the Spaniards established themselves as territorial rulers over a conquered area and a subject people.

Throughout the regions brought under their control the Spanish rulers exacted from the inhabitants heavy tribute at regular intervals. To this general form of taxation was added the burden of forced labor, and thousands were drafted for road-building or other undertakings of a military nature. Still others, even more unfortunate, were condemned to long years of servitude as galley slaves in the warships of their European masters. To his credit it should be said that Philip II made an honest effort to ensure a decent government in the regions brought under his sway. But in the Philippines, as in Mexico and Peru, the humane "Laws of the Indies," which were intended to check the rapacity and cruelty of the local authorities, did little to alleviate the lot of the unhappy conquered peoples. Many of the Spaniards in the Philippines, caring little for the welfare of the people under their rule, were interested only in wringing from them an ever increasing amount of tribute.

As soon as Legaspi had established Spanish rule in the islands, missionaries were sent in large numbers to Christianize the Filipinos. Philip II, a devoted supporter of the Catholic Church, was extremely anxious to see the Gospel spread to all parts of his domains, and he appears to have hoped that the Philippines, converted to Christianity, might become an outpost of Christendom from which the work of Christianizing the entire Oriental world could be carried on.

In 1581 a bishop was appointed for Manila, and ten years later there were a hundred and forty priests at work in the diocese. By the year 1600 the bishop of Manila had been raised to the rank of archbishop, the number of priests under him had increased to more than four hundred, and Christianity had become firmly established wherever the authority of the Spanish rulers was recognized.

By the date of Philip's death, 1598, the Church authorities had become dominant in the government of the islands, and their influence continued to prevail throughout the remaining three centuries of Spanish rule.

Such benefits as the Filipinos derived from the Spanish rule they owed to the labors of the missionaries. The priests and friars opened schools in various parts of the islands, laying the foundation of a Church educational system which culminated in 1601 with the establishment of a university at Manila. The purpose of this system was, of course, purely religious, and little was taught except those subjects which would serve to prepare Filipinos to assist in the work of spreading the Gospel; yet even such a limited education enabled the recipients to gain some knowledge of the outside world and of European ideas unconnected with religious subjects. Some of the missionaries also attempted to improve the economic conditions of the people by teaching them improved methods of agriculture and by instructing them in other industries; but the effects of this practical education appear to have been very limited, and it is questionable whether the entire three and a third centuries of Spanish rule saw any appreciable advance in the material culture of the Philippine people.

Although the Philippine Islands are admirably located for commerce with the neighboring countries, the Spanish government discouraged all attempts to make the new colony a center of Far Eastern trade. For the adoption of a policy so totally different from that of the Portuguese there were a number of reasons. In the first place, direct trade between the Philippines and the ports of Spain was practically out of the question; the route by the Cape of Good Hope was controlled by the Portuguese, while the voyage by way of the Strait of Magellan was so long and dangerous as to be commercially impracticable. It was quite possible to develop a flourishing trade between the islands and the Spanish possessions in America, but influential and interested groups in Spain succeeded in convincing the king that the growth of such a trade would injure Spain by diverting to the Far East a great part of the gold and silver of Mexico and Peru. The adoption of an active commercial policy was opposed from the outset, moreover, by the representatives of the Church, who had seen their labors in Spanish America frustrated by the rapacity of the *conquistadores* and who hoped to retain the Philippines as a special field for their spiritual labor. In addition to these considerations there was the fact that Philip II, when he secured the Portuguese crown in 1580, pledged himself not to allow his Spanish subjects to trespass upon the commercial monopoly of his Portuguese subjects. Not until the second quarter of the nineteenth century did the Spanish government, having lost by this time nearly all its American possessions, make any real attempt to develop the commercial potentialities of the Philippines.

Despite the unfriendly attitude of royal and ecclesiastical authorities the growth of the Spanish colony was attended by the development of considerable trade between the Philippine Islands and the busy commercial ports of the Orient, especially those of China. For several centuries prior to the arrival of the Spaniards, Chinese merchants had traded with the peoples of the islands, and the appearance of the European conqueror greatly enhanced in Chinese eyes the attractiveness of the Philippine market; the newcomers had luxurious tastes, and their exploitation of the conquered peoples provided them with many commodities for which the Chinese were glad to exchange their own products. From the account of Antonio de Morga we have the following details in regard to this flourishing commerce:

Usually there come from great China to Manila a large number of somas and junks, which are large ships, laden with merchandise; and each year thirty usually come, and sometimes forty ships, and although they do not come in together in the form of a fleet or convoy, they come in squadrons, with the monsoon and settled weather, which most generally is in the new moon of March. They are from the provinces of Canton, Chincheo, and Ucheo, whence they sail; they perform their voyage to Manila in fifteen or twenty days, and sell their merchandise, and return in time before the southwesterly gales set in, which is at the end of May and in the first days of June, so as not to be exposed to danger in their voyage.

De Morga lists at considerable length the various goods brought to Manila by the Chinese: raw and untwisted silk; velvets—smooth, embroidered, and brocaded; damasks, satins, taffetas, and gorvarans; glossy silks, linen, and cotton stuffs; hangings, coverlets, curtains, carpets, and caparisons for horses; musk, benzoin, ivory, pearls, rubies, sapphires, and stones of crystal; vases of copper and cast iron; sheet iron, tin, lead, saltpeter, powder; and wheat, flour, fresh and preserved fruits, live fowls, and salt meat; beds, tables, chairs, and all sorts of furniture; fine crockery of all sorts; and a multitude of other things "to recount all which would be never to come to an end, nor would much paper be sufficient for it."

The extent of the trade thus energetically pushed by the Chinese merchants was limited only by the potential purchasing power of the Philippines, but this purchasing power was restricted by the policy of the Spanish government. The Spanish inhabitants of Mexico and Peru were forbidden to trade with the Philippines, and Chinese goods could be carried from the islands to America only by such residents of the Philippines as received a royal license to engage in trade. The individuals who were thus licensed must either accompany their goods in person or send with them, as their agents, residents of the Philippines; and from the proceeds of the sale of these goods not more than five hundred thousand pesos in any one year could be remitted to the Philippines in bullion or coin.

From 1571, when Manila became the metropolis of the colony, until 1811 the bulk of this permitted trade was by annual ship from Manila to Acapulco, the "Manila galleon." In some years the cargo was divided among two or more ships, but usually a single vessel made the trip, carrying with it the hopes of the entire Spanish community or of such of its members as had been able to secure a trading license for that year.

Sailing from Manila in the last part of June or the first part of July, in order to take advantage of the southwest winds, the great ship passed around the northern end of Luzon and shaped its course to the northeast, past Japan, until it reached about the forty-second degree north latitude, and then eastward to the coast of California, along which it sailed southward to its Mexican destination. With favorable weather the trip could be made in five months, but it frequently required six months or more. The return voyage to Manila usually started between the end of February and the spring equinox and was accomplished in about three months.

On the westward journey the galleon held its course between the tenth and fifteenth parallels north latitude, passing the Ladrone Islands and Guam on the way.

In addition to the perils of storm and of uncharted sea this veritable treasure ship, whose cargo was often valued at half a million pesos, had also to face the dangers of piracy. Thomas Cavendish, the Englishman, fell in with the 1587 galleon off the coast of Lower California, "which ship," he writes, "came from the Philippines, being one of the richest of merchandize that ever passed those seas, as the king's register and merchants' accounts did shew." After Cavendish other buccaneers, Dutch as well as English, frequently made their way to the west coast of America, where they lay in wait for the great galleon. In spite of all these dangers, however, the profits of the trade, usually 100 per cent when the voyage was successful, more than compensated for the risks, and each year the authorities at Manila were flooded with requests for space in the annual ship.

With the spontaneous development of commerce between the Spanish possession and its Oriental neighbors, there began to flow toward Manila a steady stream of Chinese and Japanese settlers. Of these the Chinese were by far the more numerous. In 1590 only a few Japanese had arrived, but there were already about seven thousand Chinese residing at Manila. In 1619, when the number of Japanese reached its highest point, there were three thousand reported to be living in the city, while the Chinese, despite the slaughter of more than twenty-three thousand of their number in the massacre, or revolt, of 1603, were more than twice as numerous; and in 1639 the islands contained more than thirty thousand Chinese residents.

Unlike the Japanese, who never became a serious problem, the Chinese were a constant cause for embarrassment to the Philippine authorities. Capable and industrious workers, the Chinese made themselves practically indispensable to the Spanish community, but they were always both feared and disliked. The missionaries were determined that Christianity should prevail throughout the islands, but most of the Chinese refused to accept the Christian religion. The diligence, shrewdness, and frugality which enabled the Chinese here, as in all parts of the Malay world, to become more prosperous than their neighbors drew upon them the jealousy of the Spaniard and the Filipino alike. Moreover, the constantly growing number of the Chinese community, taken in conjunction with the dangerous nearness of the powerful Chinese Empire, aroused fears of a Chinese attempt to expel the Spanish conquerors from the islands.

To keep the Chinese poor, heavy taxes were laid upon them; to hold them in submission, oppressive restrictions and regulations were imposed upon their activities. In spite of these precautions, however, the spirit of panic periodically seized the Spanish, when the Chinese, having been goaded into revolt, would be massacred by the thousand. The outbreak of 1603, alluded to above, is said to have resulted in the slaughter of twenty-three thousand; in 1639 a second outbreak led to the killing of about twenty thousand, while other thousands were put to death in similar disturbances which occurred in 1662 and 1686.

Although the Spanish fears, so far as they related to the Chinese settlers, appear to have had little justification, the dangers of foreign attack during nearly a century after the arrival of Legaspi's expedition were very real. In its infancy the little colony was threatened by the Portuguese, while in 1574 the Chinese adventurer Limahong almost succeeded in making himself master of Manila. After the union of the Portuguese and Spanish crowns in 1580 the danger from Portugal was removed, while no new threat from the direction of China appeared until 1662, when Koxinga, the piratical supporter of the Ming cause against the conquering Manchus, appears to have contemplated the extension of his power southward from Formosa to the Philippines.

Other dangers arose, however, to take the place of those which disappeared. In 1590 Hideyoshi, who had just succeeded in bringing all Japan under his sway (see page 401), summoned the Spanish governor Dasmarinas to submit to the authority of Japan, and it seemed probable that the Philippines would be called upon to repel an invasion from this direction; but the Japanese conqueror chose as an alternative to turn his hitherto successful armies toward Korea and China.

With the close of the sixteenth century came new European enemies, first the Dutch and later the English. In October, 1600, Oliver van Noort, a Dutch buccaneer, arrived with two ships and remained for two months in Philippine waters, capturing a number of Spanish and Chinese vessels bound to or from the port of Manila. Van Noort was eventually driven away with the loss of one of his ships, but in 1605 the Dutch, after seizing the island of Amboyna from the Portuguese, established a base of operations in the Moluccas. Between 1605 and 1646 the Spanish authorities made several attempts to dislodge their Dutch neighbors, while the Netherlanders, on their side, dispatched several expeditions against the Philippines. The last of these expeditions, in 1646, succeeded in gaining a foothold at Bataan, across the bay from Manila, but the invaders finally withdrew and did not again return.

For about a century after this last Dutch attack the Philippines had little to fear from abroad, although Dutch and English ships frequently appeared among the islands and engaged in smuggling operations. During the Seven Years' War in Europe (1756–1763) Spain became an ally of France against Great Britain, with the result that a British expedition was sent against the Philippines. On October 5, 1762, the British captured Manila; but they were unable to compel the surrender of the Spanish forces in other parts of the islands, and the treaty of peace, concluded the following March, provided for the return of Manila to Spanish rule. This restoration was accomplished in June, 1764. For a long time, in violation of the treaty, the British continued to occupy some of the Sulu Islands. Eventually these also were evacuated. After the re-establishment of Spain's authority at Manila the islands remained for the next hundred and thirty-four years undisturbed by further outside attacks.

Even more serious than these outside attacks were the internal struggles which frequently threatened to destroy the Spanish authority. Some of these disturbances took the form of religious outbreaks and were caused by the zealous efforts of the missionaries to force upon the Filipinos the acceptance of Christianity. More often, however, the discontent arose from economic causes. The Spanish rule was oppressive, and the heavy burden of taxation imposed upon the people frequently passed the limits of endurance. In dealing with these periodic outbreaks, whether religious or economic in origin, the Spanish rulers were greatly aided by the fact that the Filipinos under their rule, although essentially a single people, were divided into a multitude of petty groups. As a result of this division the outbreaks were usually local and seldom spread beyond the particular district in which they originated, while the Spanish were often able to use Filipino fighting men of one district to suppress outbreaks which occurred among the people of a neighboring district.

Whenever the Spaniards had no revolt among the conquered Filipinos to occupy their attention, there were always the unconquered Moros of Mindanao and the Sulu Islands against whom they could direct their military operations. These Philippine adherents to Mohammedanism were the most warlike, the best organized, and the most strongly united people of the islands, and they were able to maintain a fairly equal struggle against the conquering Europeans. At times the Spanish succeeded in inflicting severe defeats upon the Moro forces; but they were never able to break the power of the Moro kingdom, which often retaliated by destructive raids upon the regions under Spanish rule. Not until the middle of the nineteenth century, when the addition of several steam warships to their fleet gave them a definite naval superiority, were the Spanish authorities able to arrange a permanent peace with the Moro Sultan of Sulu, and even then it was a peace by negotiation and not a conquest.

Because of the nature of the empire which they were building for themselves in their part of the East Indies the Spaniards played a less prominent part than did the Portuguese in the affairs of the neighboring Oriental countries. Maintaining their authority over the subjugated peoples, repelling foreign attacks, and waging intermittent war against the Moros furnished adequate occupation for the small group of European conquerors. At the same time the fact that the growing trade between the Philippines and the other countries of the Far East was carried on by Asiatic merchants and in Asiatic ships, rather than by the Spanish themselves, also tended to limit the activities of the Spanish.

In spite of these circumstances, however, Spanish influence was not wholly confined to the islands. From the Philippines the Spanish missionaries hoped and endeavored to extend their labors into all parts of the Orient. In 1575, missionaries from the Philippines made their first attempt to establish their work in the Chinese Empire; eighteen years later the first Spanish missionaries reached Japan, hitherto occupied exclusively by the Portuguese Jesuits.

At the close of the sixteenth century and the opening of the seventeenth, however, the most important field of Spanish activity outside the Philippines was the eastern part of Indo-China—Annam, Cambodia, and Siam. In these countries the Franciscan and Dominican friars from the Philippines soon obtained a foothold, while a few Spanish adventurers engaged in free-lance activities in Cambodia and in Siam. For a while these soldiers of fortune were supported in their operations by the royal officials, who hoped that their success might lead to the extension of Spanish authority over a part of the Asiatic mainland. Later, however, the religious workers discovered that their effort to extend Christianity was seriously compromised by the behavior of their countrymen; the authorities at Manila therefore ceased to approve of the adventurous undertakings, and the Spanish free lances gradually ceased to play an important part in Indo-Chinese affairs.

When Magellan, sailing under the Spanish flag, arrived in the Philippines, Portugal had been engaged for more than two decades in the task of establishing her commercial control throughout the Far East. By 1565, when Legaspi and his men established their little colony on the island of Cebu, the Portuguese trading posts in the Orient extended from Ormuz to Hirado, while Lisbon, as the western center of their Oriental trade, had become one of the most important commercial cities of Europe. Of the two enterprises, however, the Spanish was destined to be the more permanent. Seventy-six years after Legaspi's arrival in the Philippines Portugal's Oriental commercial empire was in ruins, while Spain, now firmly established in her East Indian possessions, could look forward to a further tenure of more than two centuries and a half.

SUGGESTED REFERENCES

BARROWS, D. P. A History of the Philippines.

BLAIR, E. H., and ROBERTSON, J. A. The Philippine Islands, 1493–1898.

BUTTERWORTH, H. The Story of Magellan.

CHAPMAN, C. E. A History of California—the Spanish Period.

CRAWFURD, J. History of the Indian Archipelago.

DE MORGA, A. (translated by H. F. J. Stanley). The Philippine Islands . . . at the close of the Sixteenth Century.

HARVEY, G. E. History of Burma.

JONES, J. W., and BADGER, G. P. The Travels of Ludovico di Varthema.

KROEBER, A. L. The History of Philippine Civilization.

SALEEBY, N. M. Studies in Moro History, Law, and Religion.

STEPHENS, H. M. Albuquerque.

WHITEWAY, R. S. The Rise of the Portuguese Power in India.

WOOD, W. A. R. A History of Siam.

XVII

Japan: from the Fourteenth Century to the Exclusion of Foreigners

FOR more than a century after its establishment by Minamoto Yoritomo the military administration located at Kamakura functioned smoothly and efficiently. After the death of Yoritomo his successors to the office of Shogun quickly became mere puppets in whose name affairs were administered by the *shikken*, or regent. The descendants of Yoritomo's father-in-law, Hojo Tokimasa, were men of unusual ability and as shikken of the Kamakura Shogunate served their country well. By locating the headquarters of the Shogunate in the Kwanto, Yoritomo had hoped to preserve the military organization from the corrupting luxuries which pervaded the court life at Kyoto; and the Hojo shikken, until late in the thirteenth century, maintained to the best of their ability the standards of loyalty, frugality, and even-handed justice which had been established by the first Shogun. Nor were the beneficial services of the Kamakura government during the thirteenth century restricted to the maintenance of internal peace and prosperity. In

1274 and again in 1281 the strict military discipline of the Shogunate and the prompt action of Hojo Tokimune, the sixth shikken,
had enabled the Japanese to hurl back the invading expeditions of
Kublai Khan.

The half-century which followed the repulse of the Mongols saw
a gradual decline in the strength of the Kamakura organization.
The simple military life of the earlier period had given way to
more luxurious standards of living. The vassals of the Shogun, at
Kamakura and elsewhere, were becoming more and more involved
in debt by their increasing extravagance and were beginning to long
for a fresh civil war which, by enabling them to acquire new possessions, might free them from the control of their hungry creditors.
At the same time corruption and favoritism were developing in
the innermost councils of the Bakufu; and by the year 1316, when
the thirteen-year-old Takatoki became the last Hojo shikken, the
Bakufu was hopelessly split by jealousy and intrigue.

The gradual decay of the Kamakura administration was keenly
watched by the imperial party at Kyoto, which had never lost hope
of freeing itself from the domination of the military class; and in
1319 there ascended the throne, in the person of Daigo II ("Go-
Daigo"), an emperor whose character and ability fitted him to be
the leader in a successful revolt against the Bakufu. In 1325
Go-Daigo instigated a thorough canvass of the provincial daimyo
and learned that a large proportion of the military class, including
even a considerable number of the Minamotos, were bitterly resentful of the continued Hojo supremacy. The activities of the court
party were discovered by the agents of Kamakura, and the chief
adherents of the emperor were promptly executed; but the emperor's share in the conspiracy escaped detection.

Six years later, in 1331, the Bakufu finally discovered that Go-
Daigo was actively conspiring for its destruction. Unable to offer
successful resistance to the forces of the Shogunate, the emperor
in 1332 was taken prisoner, deposed, and exiled to the island of Oki.
The exile was not of long duration. In April of the next year Go-
Daigo escaped from his island prison and raised the imperial standard. Loyal daimyo from all parts of the empire flocked to his support; on the Kamakura side defections occurred among some of

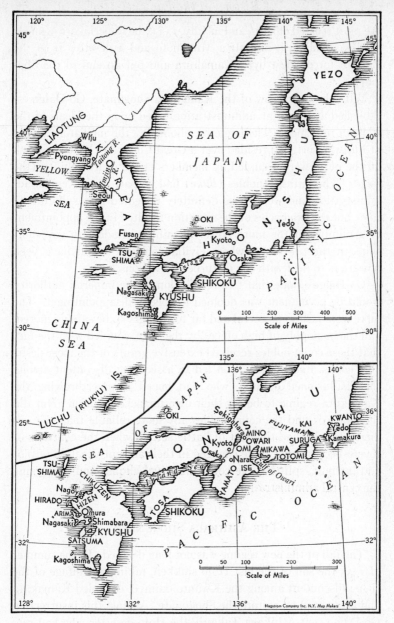

Sixteenth Century Japan

the most trusted officers, and in July, 1333, the imperial army under Ashikaga Takauji, himself a Minamoto and a deserter from the Bakufu forces, destroyed Kamakura and put an end to the Shogunate.

With the overthrow of the Kamakura Shogunate, Go-Daigo established at Kyoto an administration based upon the ideals of the Taikwa reformers. The emperor, abolishing the mediatory offices of Fujiwara origin, presided over a Great Council of State in which all the posts were occupied by members of the court nobility (the *kuge*). The military nobles (*buke*) had no part in the central administration and were to be definitely relegated to a subordinate role ; but the exigencies of the situation resulted in the appointment of a number of the more powerful military leaders to governorships in the provinces, where civilian officials would have been powerless to deal with the disturbed conditions.

Go-Daigo's hope that this restoration of the imperial authority would be permanent was doomed to speedy disappointment. The buke were far too powerful and far too hungry to be safely ignored, and the monopoly of high offices by the kuge, coupled with the fact that these court nobles received extensive grants of the most desirable confiscated estates, soon led to a seething discontent among the disillusioned daimyo, who had hoped by overthrowing the Kamakura regime to better their own financial position. Nor did the emperor find the court nobles any more reliable than the soldiers. Hardly had the dust of battle settled when the courtiers of Kyoto became once more engaged in their ancient vocation of plot and intrigue, splitting the court into rival cliques and paralyzing the central administration.

THE ASHIKAGA SHOGUNATE

The fall of the new regime was not long delayed. In the summer of 1335 the son of the last Hojo shikken, taking advantage of the rising discontent among the Kwanto daimyo, occupied Kamakura and attempted to restore the Shogunate. Against this insurrection Go-Daigo sent Ashikaga Takauji, the Hojo deserter who had rendered such valuable assistance two years earlier. Takauji easily crushed the new Kamakura organization, but instead of suppressing the turbulent daimyo of the Kwanto he secretly fanned their discontent and ultimately put himself at the head of the movement. Defeating the imperial forces which were sent against him, Takauji now moved westward and in February, 1336, entered Kyoto at the head of his conquering army.

After a long struggle in which the emperor received considerable assistance from the warlike monks of Hiyeisan, Takauji became master of the capital and imprisoned the emperor. In January, 1337, however, Go-Daigo escaped and took refuge in the mountainous districts of Yamato. At Kyoto a new emperor was placed upon the throne, and in 1338 Takauji received from this puppet ruler appointment to the office of Shogun; thus was established the Ashikaga Shogunate, which was to continue in power for two hundred and forty-five years.

The period of the Ashikaga Shogunate, 1338–1583, closely resembles the two centuries or more of Fujiwara domination and differs markedly from the Kamakura period as well as from the later Shogunate of the Tokugawas. Like the Fujiwara period, the rule of the Ashikagas was marked by extreme luxury at the capital and by almost unbroken civil disorder in the provinces. In both these respects the Shogunate established by Takauji differed from those founded by Yoritomo and by Tokugawa Iyeyasu. An even more fundamental difference, however, lay in the fact that, whereas the founders of the other two Shogunates established their capitals in the Kwanto, Takauji and his descendants maintained their headquarters at the imperial capital. Domiciled at Kyoto, the Ashikaga Shoguns were inevitably involved in court intrigues which distracted their attention from the more purely military affairs of the provinces, while their efforts to maintain in themselves and their military subordinates the soldierly virtues of simplicity and frugality were of little avail.

When Go-Daigo was made a prisoner by Takauji in the fall of 1336, he was required to surrender the sacred sword and seal—the emblems of imperial power—to the Ashikaga chieftain, who forthwith raised a new emperor to the throne. On his escape from Kyoto the following January, however, Go-Daigo declared that the surrendered insignia were only counterfeits and that the originals were still in his own hands. In possession of the sacred emblems, Go-Daigo denounced the new emperor and the Shogun as rebels and set up at Yoshino, in the mountains of Yamato, a rival court.

For fifty-five years the so-called War of Succession between the Northern Court at Kyoto and the Southern Court at Yoshino involved the entire empire in sporadic fighting. In all parts of the country the daimyo rallied to one or the other of the two rival courts and proceeded to invade and conquer the lands of neighbors upholding the rival cause. In order to avoid attack by stronger neighbors or to have an excuse for attacking those who were weaker than themselves many of the local magnates who had no real interest in the original question at issue changed sides with such bewildering rapidity that the period has been called the Age of Turncoats.

In 1392 peace was made between the two courts; Go-Kameyama, the fourth ruler of the southern line, abdicated in favor of his northern rival and surrendered the authentic sword and seal, receiving in return an adequate pension and official recognition as an ex-emperor. In spite of the agreement reached by the two courts peace was not established in the provinces, where the many private feuds which had arisen during the war were continued for more than a generation longer.

The regime of the third Ashikaga Shogun, Yoshimitsu (1367–1395), saw the restoration of friendly relations between Japan and her two continental neighbors. So long as the conquering Mongols were in control of China and Korea, friendship between Japan and either of these countries was out of the question. In 1368, as we have seen, Chu Yüan-chang, the Chinese nationalist leader, drove the Mongols beyond the Great Wall and as the first emperor of the Ming dynasty became the ruler of all China. Twenty-four years later a new national dynasty was also established in Korea, when Yi Tai-jo overthrew the ruling descendants of Wang Kien and put himself upon the throne.

During the period in which the Chinese were busy expelling the Mongols their coast districts suffered heavily from the depredations of Japanese pirates, chiefly from the ports of Kyushu. In 1390, therefore, the Ming emperor dispatched a formal embassy to the Shogun's court to protest against the depredations and to demand that the Japanese government hand over a number of the principal offenders to the Chinese for punishment.

Yoshimitsu had weighty reasons for desiring to cultivate the good will of China. In the first place, a flourishing commerce between the two empires might reasonably be expected to provide a valuable addition to the Shogun's revenues; in the second place, the Zen Buddhists, of whom the Shogun was a patron and from whose ranks his chief counselors were drawn, were strongly in favor of maintaining close cultural contacts with the great Zen monasteries of China, whence they derived their inspiration and scholarship. For these reasons Yoshimitsu not only complied with the Chinese demands by arresting and handing over for punishment a number of the marauders, but also acknowledged himself to be the Ming emperor's vassal, adopting the Chinese calendar and accepting formal investiture as "King of Japan." Patriotic Japanese writers have bitterly denounced Yoshimitsu for his subservience to the Chinese emperor, but the cordial relations which he reestablished with China contributed in no small degree to Japan's cultural progress during the Ashikaga period.

In 1392 the new Korean monarch, Yi Tai-jo, signalized his accession to the throne by sending a similar embassy to Japan to protest against the piratical activities of the Japanese. Here also Yoshimitsu's desire for commercial intercourse led him to adopt a conciliatory attitude. He released a number of Koreans who had been captured by Japanese raiders, promised effective measures for the prevention of further depredations, and expressed his desire for the establishment of friendly relations between the two countries. As a result of this move the Japanese after some negotiation secured the privilege of residing, for purposes of trade, at Fusan and at two other Korean ports.

Despite the promises and good intentions of the Shogun the piratical raids upon the coasts of China and Korea were not stopped. Even during the administration of Yoshimitsu piracy continued to flourish, while the decline of the Ashikaga power under his successors was attended by a corresponding increase in the profession of freebooting. In 1420 and again during the early part of the sixteenth century, conditions became so bad that the Koreans were aroused to take retaliatory measures against the Japanese island of Tsushima. Because of its greater wealth, however, China furnished an even more attractive field for the armed adventurers of Japan, and the Chinese coasts suffered from almost continuous raids during the entire course of the Ashikaga regime.

From this period, also, commenced the somewhat intricate relations of Japan and China with the Luchu (or Ryukyu) Islands. The inhabitants of these islands are undoubtedly related to the Japanese, and Japanese tradition asserts that the royal family of the Luchus was descended from Minamoto Tametomo, the uncle of Yoritomo. In 1373 the ruler of the islands voluntarily became a tributary of the Chinese emperor, but forty-three years later a Luchu embassy also appeared at Kyoto. In 1441 the Shogun Yoshinori conferred the sovereignty of the Luchus upon the daimyo of Satsuma, and his son Yoshimasa thirty years later forbade any ship to trade with the islands without a Satsuma license. Completely disregarding the Japanese claim to suzerainty,—a claim which appears to have been unattended by any attempt at conquest,—the Luchu monarchs continued until late in the nineteenth century to look upon themselves as vassals of the Chinese emperor, to whom they sent periodic tribute-bearing embassies.

Partly as a result of renewed intercourse with China and Korea, partly as a result of having become once more the sole capital of the empire, Kyoto under the rule of Yoshimitsu and his immediate successors attained to standards of luxury, culture, and extravagance which rivaled or even surpassed those of the Fujiwara period. Chinese architecture, painting, and philosophy—Confucian and Buddhist—were studied and imitated as perhaps never before. In architecture especially the Ashikaga artists followed their Chinese models with far less modification than had appeared in the work of the earlier builders at Kyoto and at Nara; the Kinkakuji ("Golden Pavilion") of Yoshimitsu and the Ginkakuji ("Silver Pavilion") erected by his grandson Yoshimasa display striking resemblance to contemporary Ming architecture.

Like their predecessors of the Fujiwara period, the fifteenth-century courtiers at Kyoto patronized music and dancing, and engaged in poetry-writing and incense-judging contests. Landscape gardening and the artistic arrangement of cut flowers were highly esteemed arts. The Ashikaga period saw also the development of a new feature of Japanese etiquette: the *cha-no-yu*, or tea ceremonial. This elaborate social ritual, in which the actual drinking of the tea plays an insignificant part, was introduced and fostered by the Zen Buddhists as a means of promoting the urbanity, courtesy, and spiritual serenity which would conduce to the acceptance of Zen doctrines.

As in the days of the Fujiwaras, the luxury of the Ashikaga period was largely confined to the capital. Through the medium of the monasteries maintained by the various Buddhist sects some culture and learning penetrated into even the most distant provinces, while communications were facilitated by the roads which the monks constructed; but these attractive features of the situation constitute only a part of the picture. The lower classes were in the depths of ignorance and poverty. The peasants were crushed under a burden of taxation which in one form or another often took from them the equivalent of 70 per cent of their crops. About the middle of the fifteenth century a series of natural calamities spread famine and pestilence over the land; thousands died from disease or starvation, while other thousands abandoned their lands and flocked to the capital in search of food. Worst of all the evils from which the country suffered, however, were the endless feuds and civil wars between the powerful daimyo families. Although the close of the War of Succession saw the Ashikaga Shoguns apparently in absolute control of the situation in all parts of the empire, less than a decade passed before the military power in the more distant provinces began to fall into the hands of the local rulers.

By 1467 the authority of the central administration had almost ceased to exist outside the five provinces—Go-Kinai, or "Five Home Provinces"—in the immediate neighborhood of the capital. That year saw the outbreak of a general struggle known as the Onin War, which lasted for eleven years and which involved more than a score of powerful families, each fighting for an increase in its own landed possessions. Early in 1478 the Onin War, so far as the capital was concerned, came to an end; but a full century was still to elapse before the dawn of any permanent peace for the provinces. Recognizing the fact that none of the provincial daimyo paid the slightest attention to decrees or instructions, the Shoguns even ceased to issue commands to their nominal vassals.

Japan now entered upon the period known in her history as the "Epoch of the Warring Country." Instead of lasting for a brief thirty years, like the contemporary Wars of the Roses in England, this struggle stretched over a full century. Throughout the empire the warrior was supreme. Although the great mass of the peasants continued patiently to till the soil, thousands of their number abandoned the land and sought an easier livelihood in the military service of some powerful daimyo. In the prevailing anarchy sons made war against their fathers, brother turned against brother, and vassals betrayed their lords.

To the general turmoil of the time the warlike members of the rival Buddhist sects added their bitter struggles for lands and influence. The Ashikaga Shoguns, almost without exception, were warm supporters of the Zen sect, and Takauji in 1345 had successfully adopted strong measures against the turbulent inmates of the Tendai monasteries on Hiyeisan. With the subsequent decline of the central administration, however, the Shoguns were as unable to control the monastic orders as they were to impose their will upon the daimyo. At the capital itself, about 1470, the monks of Hiyeisan marched into the city and destroyed by fire the great Hongwanji temple which was the headquarters of the Shin sect. In the provinces the struggles between the different sects were complicated by the feuds, often resulting in bloodshed and destruction, between rival groups inside a single sect or even within a single monastery.

Anarchy in the Japanese Empire had reached its height when in 1542 or 1543 the first Portuguese arrived at the port of Kagoshima, at the southern extremity of Kyushu. These first Europeans, three in number, had been traveling in a Chinese junk from Malacca to Ningpo, and their accidental arrival at the Japanese port had been due to adverse winds; but their return to the Portuguese trading center at Malacca was followed by the fitting out of regular merchant ventures to trade with the newly discovered land.

In addition to Chinese silks and spices from the Indies, which hitherto had reached Japan in Oriental ships, the newcomers brought with them a number of European products. All these articles found a ready market at Kagoshima, but the daimyo of Satsuma, within whose domain the port was located, was particularly pleased and impressed with the weapons of the foreign visitors. Although there is a bare possibility that the Mongol invaders of the thirteenth century had made some use of firearms on Japanese soil, such weapons were absolutely unknown to the sixteenth-century Japanese. The lord of Satsuma was quick to appreciate their superiority over the bow and arrow and to realize the great military advantage which he would have over his neighbors if his troops alone were armed with these superior weapons. He therefore encouraged the Portuguese to continue their trade at Kagoshima and endeavored to discourage their visiting the ports of his rivals.

But Satsuma offered few export commodities to tempt the Portuguese merchants, while the more northern provinces of Kyushu were rich in the attractions which Kagoshima lacked. As the other local rulers, with equally keen appreciation of the benefits to be derived from the trade, were equally cordial in their reception of the foreigners, the Portuguese were soon carrying their silks, their spices, and their highly desirable instruments of warfare to the more northern ports of the island; and the Satsuma daimyo's earlier friendship for the Europeans gave way to a growing antiforeignism as he saw his neighbors reaping all the benefits of the trade.

For just fifty years after their arrival the Portuguese enjoyed complete freedom from European competition in Japanese markets. It was not until 1592 that Spaniards from Manila made their first effort to develop commercial relations with Japan, while the Dutch and English did not arrive until eight years after that date. Although a few of the Portuguese merchants found their way at an early date to the imperial capital, the western ports of Kyushu, especially those of Hizen and Chikuzen provinces, were those to which the ships, almost without exception, directed their course. Indeed, throughout the ninety-eight or ninety-nine years (1542 or 1543 to 1641) during which Japan was open to unrestricted European trade the ports of Kyushu, in spite of the efforts made by eastern daimyo to alter the situation, enjoyed an almost complete monopoly of foreign commerce.

One reason for this monopoly lay in the fact that the ports of Kyushu, having been for centuries the centers of commercial intercourse with China and Korea, had developed a commercial machinery capable of handling satisfactorily this additional foreign commerce. Moreover, since the Portuguese and most of the other European ships approached Japan by way of the Chinese ports, the harbors of Kyushu could be reached with less difficulty and danger than those farther to the east. Only for the Manila galleon, on its annual voyage from the Philippines to Mexico, did the eastern harbors of Japan constitute attractive ports of call, and the commercial policy of the Spanish government prevented any great development of Spanish trade with the Japanese empire. Not until the nineteenth century, when the development of the United States as a Pacific power was one of the factors in the reopening of Japan to Western trade, did the eastern ports of the island empire achieve commercial importance.

THE DAWN OF A NEW ERA

The first Portuguese reached Japan at a time when the country was in the worst stage of anarchy and confusion; but the date of their arrival, if we accept the year 1542 as correct, saw the birth of the youngest of the three great leaders whose united labors were destined to end the disorder and to reunite the empire under a strong government.

Oda Nobunaga, the oldest of the three, was born in 1533. The Oda family was descended from the Taira clan and about the middle of the fifteenth century had acquired an estate in the province of Owari. By the first part of the sixteenth century the original petty holding of the family had so increased that Nobunaga's father exerted considerable influence in the affairs of the adjoining province of Mikawa. In 1549 Nobunaga succeeded to his father's fief. Surrounded by powerful neighbors, all of whom were covetous of his strategically important possessions at the head of the Gulf of Owari, it seemed highly probable that the sixteen-year-old daimyo would soon be deprived of his inheritance. But Nobunaga showed by his choice of capable and trustworthy advisers that he had a wise head on his young shoulders and that he was well able to hold what his father had left to him.

Toyotomi Hideyoshi, to give him the name which he assumed after he had achieved greatness, was three years younger than Nobunaga and was the son of a peasant who lived on the Oda domain. Scarcely five feet tall and with "a face like an ape," Hideyoshi was endowed with an intelligence which made him one of the most able statesmen in Japanese history. Like many other peasants during the "Epoch of the Warring Country," Hideyoshi's father had abandoned the hoe and had taken service as a soldier in the Oda forces.

The life of a farmer, which Hideyoshi's father had found so dull, had equally little attraction for the son; and in 1558 Hideyoshi, at that time twenty-two years of age, was admitted to a humble position in the household of Nobunaga. Tradition says that the shrewd little peasant, after having carefully weighed the merits of various daimyo in that section of the empire, selected Nobunaga as the one most likely to succeed and therefore most worthy of his services. Whatever may be the truth of this story, the rapid rise of Nobunaga's fortunes began in the same year that saw Hideyoshi added to his personal retinue, while the little peasant rose to importance in his lord's council even more rapidly than Nobunaga increased his power in the empire.

Tokugawa Iyeyasu, the youngest of this notable trio, was born in 1542. His original family name was Matsudaira; but in 1562 he adopted the surname Tokugawa, by which he is generally known. Since the Matsudaira family was of Minamoto descent, Iyeyasu alone of the three contemporaries was eligible to the office of Shogun, which could lawfully be held only by imperial princes or by Minamoto daimyo. Less brilliant perhaps than Hideyoshi,

Iyeyasu possessed a high degree of political astuteness, while he was quite the equal of either Nobunaga or Hideyoshi in military leadership. In 1560, however, he was merely a petty daimyo of Mikawa, a vassal of the powerful Imagawa family which controlled the two provinces of Suruga and Totomi and which disputed with Nobunaga the domination of Mikawa Province.

In the summer of 1560 the head of the Imagawa family, having decided to destroy his troublesome Oda neighbor, assembled his forces and invaded Owari. From this struggle Nobunaga emerged victorious. The Imagawa chief was slain, and his forces were driven out of Owari. The outcome of the struggle immediately raised the young lord of Owari to a position of importance in national affairs and awakened in him the ambition to make himself the real master of the Kyoto administration. In order to guard against the invasion of his own domains if he should move westward, Nobunaga strengthened his position by two alliances: one with Takeda Shingen, the lord of Kai, who was one of the most powerful daimyo of the Kwanto; and a second with Tokugawa Iyeyasu, who had been offended by the new head of the Imagawa family and whose position in Mikawa made him a valuable ally for Nobunaga.

Two years after his defeat of the Imagawa daimyo, Nobunaga received from the imperial court a message approving his military operations and inviting him to Kyoto. A visit to Kyoto was, for the present, out of the question; but the message of approval assured Nobunaga that further extensions of his power would find favor in the eyes of the central government, and he proceeded to expand into the neighboring province of Mino, which in the course of the next two years he completely conquered. Turning southward from Mino into Ise, Nobunaga in 1565 attempted to subjugate the daimyo of this province. The campaign in Ise was unsuccessful, but during the course of the next three years most of the Ise daimyo were induced by the persuasiveness of Hideyoshi to place themselves under the banner of Nobunaga.

In November, 1567, Nobunaga received once more an imperial invitation to come to the capital. Two years earlier the Shogun had been assassinated by two disloyal ministers who had subsequently put a three-year-old child in office as their puppet. Nobunaga, after further strengthening his position by new alliances, accepted the imperial invitation and advanced on Kyoto, proclaiming his intention of putting in office the younger brother of the late Shogun. By the end of 1568 he had succeeded in restoring order at the capital; Ashikaga Yoshiaki—the last of his family to occupy the post—had been installed as Shogun, while Nobunaga, as Vice-Shogun, was commissioned to restore order in the empire.

Although nominally a mere subordinate of the Shogun, Nobunaga was now actually the head of the central government, which under his direction assumed renewed vigor in its dealings with the provincial daimyo.

The immediate result of Nobunaga's Vice-Shogunal appointment was to arouse against him the jealousy and fear of every local ruler whose own ambition was thereby frustrated or who saw in the rise of a strong man at Kyoto a threat to the local autonomy hitherto enjoyed by the daimyo. Nobunaga's two principal allies turned against him; only Tokugawa Iyeyasu, whose limited military resources still forced him to be rated as a petty daimyo, and the minor lords of Ise remained loyal to the Vice-Shogun. Between 1570 and 1573 the crucial struggle was fought out, ending with the overthrow of Nobunaga's most formidable opponents. After this important success the fortunes of Nobunaga and his Tokugawa ally steadily improved; by the summer of 1577 the leading Kwanto daimyo had been overthrown and their lands portioned out among the trusted retainers of the victorious allies.

Within less than ten years after his arrival at Kyoto, Nobunaga as champion of the central government had thus established his power not only over the five home provinces but also over the Kwanto and the region between these two important areas. The extreme northern provinces of Honshu, however, together with the western provinces and the two islands of Shikoku and Kyushu, still maintained their independence. Even before the completion of the Kwanto campaign Nobunaga, ignoring the distant and sparsely settled provinces of the north, dispatched Hideyoshi toward the west to begin the subjugation of the districts lying along the coast of the Inland Sea, a task which was not completed until after Nobunaga's own death.

Like the independent military chieftains, the powerful Buddhist monasteries had regarded Nobunaga with jealousy and suspicion from the moment of his first arrival at Kyoto. In 1570–1571, when the Vice-Shogun was engaged in his first desperate struggle against the confederated daimyo, the monks in several provinces as well as those of Hiyeisan had openly sided with his enemies; and the Hiyeisan monasteries permitted these enemies to establish themselves in the strongly fortified monastic buildings, from which commanding position they threatened the safety of the capital.

For the moment Nobunaga's position was too precarious to permit his taking any steps against the Hiyeisan institutions. Such action would arouse the other religious organizations to even more active hostility and might almost alienate the sympathy of some of his supporters. In the summer of 1574, however, he felt strong enough to take his revenge. A powerful army was led against Hiyeisan, and the monasteries were completely surrounded. In spite of the frenzied efforts of the monks to buy peace and in spite of the reluctance of some of his generals Nobunaga now proceeded methodically and ruthlessly to the destruction of the entire monastic settlement. The splendid buildings were burned to the ground, and such of the several thousand inmates as escaped the flames were put to the sword.

Having wiped out this hotbed of intrigue at the gates of the capital, Nobunaga proceeded with equal thoroughness but with modified severity to destroy, throughout the provinces under his control, the political power of the other monastic institutions. One by one these aggregations of soldier-priests were forced to submit, and at the time of his death only the strongly fortified Osaka monastery of the Shin sect remained unsubdued.

In the summer of 1582 Hideyoshi, who was conducting a campaign in the island of Shikoku, appealed to his chief for reinforcements to complete the conquest. In response to this appeal Nobunaga dispatched a fresh body of thirty thousand troops and prepared to go himself to join his lieutenant. While stopping at Kyoto he was suddenly attacked by one of his vassals, Akechi Mitsuhide, to whom he had previously given offense and who, being of Minamoto descent, hoped to establish himself as Shogun. Caught by surprise with only a small bodyguard around him, Nobunaga was overpowered and slain, and his assailant, making himself master of the capital, promptly assumed the title of Shogun.

When the news of Nobunaga's death reached Hideyoshi, the latter acted with his usual promptness. Concluding an advantageous truce with his Shikoku opponent, from whom the calamitous news was successfully withheld, he returned to Kyoto attended by a small bodyguard. Intercepting the thirty thousand reinforcements who were on their way to his assistance, he entered the capital at their head and destroyed the murderers.

Nobunaga's death left as claimants of his estates and titles a grandson, the child of his eldest son, and two of his younger sons. In the council which was held to decide the question Hideyoshi upheld the claim of the infant grandson, and as guardian of the young heir he was soon in absolute control of the imperial court. In 1583 the last of the Ashikaga Shoguns took the tonsure, and two years later Hideyoshi was promoted to the office of *kwampaku*, regent of the empire. The decision of the inheritance question and Hideyoshi's assumption of supreme power at the capital, both of which were bitterly resented by Nobunaga's other prominent retainers as well as by his two younger sons, split the Oda organization into two bitterly hostile factions. Out of the war between the two groups the peasant-statesman finally emerged as victor in December, 1584, having defeated or won over by peaceful means his various opponents.

The last step in this restoration of peace within the districts which had acknowledged Nobunaga's authority was a treaty between Hideyoshi and Iyeyasu; from this point until his death Hideyoshi was able to rely upon the Tokugawa lord for support as loyal as had previously been given to Nobunaga. Within six years after the conclusion of this treaty the unification of the empire was accomplished; by 1590 the entire country, from the northern island of Yezo to the southern extremity of Kyushu, acknowledged the rule of Hideyoshi as regent for the emperor.

Great as had been the work of Nobunaga, the rapid completion of the task of unification must be attributed to the unusual genius of the man who followed him. Nobunaga was a soldier, not a statesman; he won his battles by sound generalship and hard fighting, and he endeavored to consolidate his conquests by the simple expedient of executing every defeated enemy who fell into his hands; but because of the very simplicity of Nobunaga's policy the daimyo who took the field against him, knowing that defeat and death were synonymous, usually fought with a desperate courage. As a soldier Hideyoshi was fully the equal of his former chief, but in addition he was one of the cleverest diplomats and politicians of the sixteenth century in Japan or in any other country. When fighting was necessary, Hideyoshi fought, usually with brilliant success; but he seldom resorted to war if diplomacy could be used to obtain the end in view. Unlike Nobunaga, Hideyoshi understood the art of utilizing his defeated enemies; he almost always spared their lives and either restored them to their former possessions or transferred them to new fiefs in which they would have less opportunity to make trouble. On a few occasions this policy of conciliation proved unsuccessful; but the reverse was more often true, and many of Hideyoshi's earlier foes were thus transformed into loyal supporters.

With the empire united and pacified, Hideyoshi in 1590 faced the difficult problem of finding employment for his soldiers and fresh lands with which to reward his loyal vassals. Although more subtle and politic than Nobunaga, Hideyoshi lacked the statesmanlike qualities which later enabled Iyeyasu to divert the Japanese fighting men from the fields of war to the paths of peace. His only alternative to civil war was a war of conquest on foreign soil, and he undertook to solve his domestic problem by launching his war-hardened veterans against the continent of Asia. This decision was not made on the spur of the moment. As early as 1578, foreseeing the ultimate unification of the country, he had suggested to Nobunaga, as a possible sequel to this achievement, the invasion of Korea in order to make the peninsula kingdom the base of operations for the conquest of China. All this, he believed, he could accomplish "as easily as a man rolls up a piece of matting and carries it under his arm." Again in 1586, just before starting on his successful campaign in Kyushu, he referred to this plan and made use of the same figure of speech.

Although the Japanese merchants still enjoyed the privilege of residing at Fusan for purposes of trade, official communications between the two governments had long since been discontinued, while the piratical activities of the Japanese on the Korean coast had led to the enactment of strict laws against a Japanese landing anywhere in Korea except at Fusan. In 1590 Hideyoshi reopened formal relations with the Korean court by informing the king of his intention to conquer the Ming empire and demanding that Korea offer no resistance to his passage through her territory. The Korean answer was unequivocal in its refusal of this demand:

What is this talk of our joining you against China? From the earliest times we have followed law and right. From within and from without all lands are subject to China. If you have desired to send your envoys to China, how much more should we! When we have been unfortunate she has helped us. The relations which subsist between us are those of parent and child. This you know well. Can we desert both emperor and parent to join with you?

Even before his receipt of the Korean answer Hideyoshi had begun his preparations, and on May 25, 1592, the first Japanese forces landed at Fusan. For a while the invasion of Korea seemed destined to result in one more brilliant success for Hideyoshi. The Korean forces made almost no effort to defend the numerous strategic positions which their mountainous country afforded, and on June 12, eighteen days after the first landing at Fusan, the Japanese advance guard entered Seoul. Abandoning the capital at the approach of the invading armies, the Korean court fled northward to Pyongyang, on the right bank of the Taitong.

Beyond Seoul the Japanese met more determined resistance, especially at the crossing of the river Imjin, where they were delayed for more than a week; but the opening days of July saw the court once more in flight, this time to Wiju, from which point despairing appeals for aid were dispatched to the Chinese emperor. In the brief space of six weeks the Korean government had utterly collapsed. Nearly two hundred thousand of Japan's finest soldiers had been landed in the peninsula, while Hideyoshi had in readiness at Nagoya, in Hizen, an additional force of more than a hundred thousand which could be sent in as reinforcements.

The weak point in Hideyoshi's plan of campaign was the strip of open sea, a hundred and twenty miles in width, which lay between his base of operations at Nagoya and the Korean coast. The sixteenth-century Japanese, although unsurpassed in military prowess and abundantly provided with European firearms, were markedly inferior to the Koreans in naval architecture and in seamanship. Almost at the moment when the Japanese advance guard was entering Seoul the Korean admiral, Yih Sun-sin, inflicted upon the Japanese naval forces the first of a series of crushing defeats by virtue of which Korea secured control of the sea and cut off Hideyoshi's expeditionary forces from their homeland.

The Korean naval supremacy was attributable in considerable measure to a remarkable invention known as the tortoise boat. This strange type of warship, absolutely different from anything that the Japanese had ever seen, derived its name from a strong roof, like the shell of a tortoise, which completely covered it and protected its crew from the missiles of the enemy. The roof, studded with spikes to keep the enemy from boarding the ship and capturing it by hand-to-hand fighting, is said also to have been covered with iron plates as protection against fire darts. The tortoise boats were constructed on long narrow lines which gave them great (comparative) speed, and were heavily timbered so as to enable them to withstand the shock of collision. For purpose of attack they were provided with powerful beaks, or rams, at each end, while their oars were so arranged that the ships could be rowed either end first with equal speed.

Against these true warships, instruments built and maneuvered with the idea of destroying the vessels of the enemy, the Japanese were helpless. Their own ships were, practically speaking, nothing more than transports, and their idea of naval warfare was simply to use these transports as floating platforms from which to discharge their missiles against the enemy or, if opportunity afforded, to board the enemy ship and fight with sword and spear. Against the Japanese, Admiral Yih employed simple and effective tactics. Approaching the enemy fleet, the Korean ships at the first discharge of Japanese missiles would turn and flee as if seized by panic. When the Japanese scattered in pursuit, the tortoise boat would reverse its rowers and dart at the nearest enemy. The Japanese weapons would rattle harmlessly upon the strong shell, while the Japanese ship would be rammed and sent to the bottom.

The Korean superiority on the sea was in itself sufficient to ruin the Japanese expedition. In addition to this, however, Hideyoshi's forces were meeting steadily increasing opposition in their land campaign. Although the organized military forces of the Korean government had collapsed before the first rush of the invading armies, bands of guerrillas quickly formed in all parts of the kingdom, attacking every small detached body of Japanese troops and making it impossible for the invaders to send out foraging parties. At the same time the Chinese emperor, responding to the appeals of his vassal, dispatched troops to his assistance. The first Chinese army, consisting of some five thousand soldiers recruited in Liaotung, arrived in Korea in October, 1592, and was speedily defeated by the Japanese. The following January, however, saw the arrival of a strong Chinese expedition consisting of about fifty thousand men. In February the Japanese were driven from Pyongyang, and on May 9, not quite a year after the arrival of the first Japanese troops at Fusan, a preliminary truce was concluded, providing for the Japanese withdrawal to the southern coast.

In spite of the fact that his troops had been forced to evacuate northern and central Korea, Hideyoshi appears to have believed that the Chinese government was prepared to recognize him as the suzerain both of Korea and of the Chinese Empire. When after more than three years of negotiation the treaty between China and Japan was finally concluded and Hideyoshi received a Chinese embassy at Osaka, he was furiously disappointed to find that the letter from the Ming emperor merely conferred upon him the title "King of Japan" and instructed him to comport himself as a loyal vassal of China. He immediately ordered the resumption of hostilities in the peninsula and in the spring of 1597 sent over a considerable body of reinforcements. Although nothing of importance was achieved, there was much hard fighting, and the war was not finally brought to a close until after the death of Hideyoshi.

On September 16, 1598, Hideyoshi died, leaving a five-year-old son, Hideyori, as heir to his offices and his vast possessions. Shortly before his death Hideyoshi attempted, by creating a board of regents, to safeguard the future of his son and heir. As members of the board he appointed Tokugawa Iyeyasu and four other powerful daimyo. But the restoration of order in Japan had not gone so far that political power could be handed down, like property, from a father to his infant son. Sixteen years earlier Hideyoshi had set aside the political claims of Nobunaga's descendants; now the claims of his own son were to be set aside by Tokugawa Iyeyasu.

The Tokugawa Shogunate

Since his alliance with Nobunaga, thirty-eight years earlier, Tokugawa Iyeyasu had seen his possessions steadily increase until at the death of Hideyoshi he was in direct control of almost one seventh of the empire. These possessions were located entirely in the Kwanto and the immediately adjoining provinces, and in the center of his domain Iyeyasu had constructed the powerful fortified city of Yedo—modern Tokyo. In comparison with the martial Nobunaga or with the brilliant and resourceful Hideyoshi, Iyeyasu appears at first glance slow, methodical, and uninspired; but his statesmanship, although less spectacular than that of Hideyoshi, was perhaps even more subtle and was characterized by inexhaustible patience.

In spite of the precautions which had been taken by Hideyoshi a feud quickly developed between two rival groups of his former generals and advisers. For a short time Iyeyasu was able to maintain an attitude of apparent aloofness; but his immense territorial possessions, together with his position at the head of the board of regents, made him the obvious object for the hostility of his less powerful colleagues, and his apparent inaction masked his careful preparations for the inevitable appeal to arms.

The open break came in the spring of 1600; the outcome of the struggle was determined on October 21 of the same year at Sekigahara, where the Tokugawa forces won a decisive victory over the combined forces of the opposing daimyo. Although the young Hideyori was left in possession of all his father's estates, Iyeyasu now assumed complete control over the government.

Since 1583, when Ashikaga Yoshiaki had resigned his office and "entered religion," the post of Shogun had been vacant. Hideyoshi, as kwampaku, had exercised all the powers of a Shogun, but his non-Minamoto descent had rendered him ineligible to the Shogunal title. Iyeyasu, however, was a Minamoto, and in 1603 he received from the emperor the commission as Shogun which made him legally, as he already was in fact, the supreme military commander of all the forces of the empire.

Like Yoritomo, the founder of the Kamakura Shogunate, Iyeyasu feared the corrupting influence which the imperial court would exercise over any administrative system domiciled at the capital. Although he usually spent several months of each year at Kyoto, the oversight of the court was confided to a trusted deputy residing in the "Nijo" castle; the capital of the Shogunate was established at Iyeyasu's own city of Yedo in the far-off Kwanto, where in imitation of the Kamakura Shogun he organized a Bakufu, or camp court.

After his victory over the opposing daimyo at the battle of Sekigahara, Iyeyasu had embarked upon a redistribution of territorial power in such fashion as to ensure the permanence of Tokugawa supremacy. Of the daimyo who had fought against him many lost their lives, and all their estates were confiscated by the victor. Others were compelled to surrender a large portion of their domains or in some instances to exchange their former holdings for others in a different part of the empire.

The lands which thus came into his possession were allotted by the Tokugawa dictator to two groups of feudatories: the *fudai* daimyo, or "hereditary" vassals, and the *tozama* daimyo, or "outside" nobles. The former group, which included the members of the Tokugawa family and those who, before Sekigahara, had been reckoned among its loyal supporters, received as fiefs lands located in the Kwanto, in the home provinces, and in the region lying between these two important areas. The tozama daimyo, being those who accepted Tokugawa overlordship after Sekigahara, received fiefs in Kyushu, Shikoku, the western and extreme northern provinces of Honshu, and the island of Yezo. By this arrangement the less dependable "outside" nobles were relegated to the outlying portions of the empire, while the central provinces constituted a solid block held by the Tokugawas and their most trusted supporters.

In 1605 Iyeyasu resigned the office of Shogun in favor of his eldest son, Hidetada, a rather dull but conscientious and hardworking man. The remaining eleven years of Iyeyasu's life were spent in training Hidetada in the science of statesmanship and in organizing the Yedo administration. His own outstanding ability and success in the field of politics did not blind him to the fact that many of his descendants would probably be very ordinary men, so he endeavored to create an organization which would function efficiently even under the leadership of a Shogun of average ability. Iyeyasu judged correctly as to the probable character of his successors. Most of them were decidedly mediocre; some were well below the average, and only one or two even approached him in their abilities. But the care with which he built up the Yedo Bakufu enabled the Tokugawa Shogunate to continue as the real government of the Japanese Empire for two and a half centuries after the death of its founder.

In general the Yedo Bakufu was modeled upon the earlier administrative machine of the Kamakura Shogunate. To ensure the smooth running of this mechanism, however, Iyeyasu laid down the rule that members of the fudai families only should be permitted to hold offices in the Bakufu. Thus the fudai daimyo, already established territorially as a compact body, were still further consolidated by being exclusively privileged to hold office at Yedo. The tozama daimyo, although excluded from administrative posts, were not left to while away their time in dangerous idleness. Iyeyasu inaugurated the policy of keeping these "outside" nobles in a state of financial embarrassment by requiring them to undertake the construction of roads, the rebuilding of temples, or other expensive public works. No marriage between daimyo families could take place without the express consent of the Shogun, while Iyeyasu's second successor, Iyemitsu, made it a law that every daimyo should spend alternate periods in residence at Yedo and on returning to his fief should leave behind him at the Shogun's capital his wife and family as hostages.

CHRISTIAN MISSIONS IN JAPAN

Up to this point little has been said of Japan's intercourse with the Europeans; to that phase of the country's history we must now turn our attention. In August, 1549, seven years after the arrival of the first Portuguese traders, the famous Jesuit missionary Francis Xavier landed at Kagoshima, accompanied by two other priests of the order and by a Japanese Christian named Anjiro, whom Xavier had met and converted at Malacca. At Kagoshima, Xavier and his companions were cordially welcomed by the daimyo of Satsuma, who hoped their arrival foreshadowed the return of foreign trade to his port. From Satsuma the Jesuits proceeded to Hirado, which had become the most important center of Portuguese trade. The respectful consideration shown to these missionaries by the Portuguese merchants at Hirado made a deep impression upon the local authorities, who were keenly interested in fostering trade relations. Because of this desire to cultivate the good will of the Portuguese merchants the daimyo of Hirado gave orders that the foreign teaching should be given earnest attention.

After spending several months in Kyushu, Xavier proceeded northward to Honshu and eventually reached Kyoto, where he was received with complete indifference. Returning to Kyushu, where all the daimyo were striving to win favor with the Portuguese merchants, Xavier and his companions, in spite of linguistic difficulties, succeeded in making several hundred converts; but he now determined to transfer his missionary activities to China, since the predominance of Chinese influence, especially in Japanese literature and philosophy, convinced him that the educated Japanese would give consideration only to ideas which reached them by way of China. In the fall of 1551, therefore, he sailed for India, leaving his companions in Japan to carry on the work of the Kyushu mission. The following year Xavier arrived at the island of Shangch'uan, off the coast of China, where he died without being able to reach the mainland.

During the thirty years following the departure of Xavier, Jesuit missionaries came to Japan in increasing numbers, and Christianity made steady progress in some parts of the island of

Kyushu. In the rest of the empire, however, it was not so successful. Not until 1568 did the missionaries secure permission to reside in Kyoto and erect a church there; even then they found the people of the capital little interested in listening to the new doctrine. In 1581 there were reported to be one hundred and fifty thousand Christians throughout the empire. More than 80 per cent of these were in the island of Kyushu, while nearly 70 per cent of them were concentrated in the two small states of Arima and Omura, where trade with the Portuguese was most active. In states where the local authorities, anxious to attract foreign traders to their ports, showed favor to foreign teachers and sided with them against the Buddhists, Christianity had succeeded in gaining a strong foothold; elsewhere it made little or no progress.

When, in 1568, the Jesuits received permission to preach openly at Kyoto, they owed this privilege to the advocacy of their cause by Nobunaga, who was then assuming control over the government. Although the Vice-Shogun never showed any personal interest in the doctrines of Christianity, he favored the missionaries, and his powerful protection enabled them through the fourteen years of his domination to carry on their work at the capital without fear of persecution. Several of his influential vassals became converts to Christianity, and Nobunaga offered no objection when these Christian daimyo compelled their peasants to accept baptism. In 1580 he even gave the missionaries permission to erect a chapel within the walls of his new castle on the shores of Lake Biwa.

Nobunaga's first friendship for the missionaries may have resulted from a favorable personal impression made upon him by the cultured and scholarly Jesuit leader, Froez, but his continued favor appears to have been due primarily to the fact that he and the Christians had, in the Buddhist monasteries, a common enemy. The difficulties created for him by the intriguing monks of Hiyeisan have already been noted, and even after the annihilation of the Hiyeisan establishments the other strong Buddhist communities continued until the end of his career to be a source of trouble. Since there also was bitter enmity between the Buddhists and the Christians, Nobunaga was more than willing to support the latter.

During the first years of Hideyoshi's rule, while he was consolidating his power, the missionaries continued to enjoy government favor and protection. In the spring of 1586, when he was preparing for the conquest of Kyushu, the peasant-statesman treated the Jesuits with especial courtesy, explaining to their leader, Coelho, that it was his intention to divide the island among the prominent Christian daimyo and to hand over the port of Nagasaki to the Jesuits. As convincing evidence of his good will he drew up at Coelho's request a document granting to the missionaries three important privileges: permission to preach their doctrines in all parts of the empire, immunity from the inconvenience of having soldiers billeted in their houses, and exemption from all local taxation. As a result of Hideyoshi's statement of his intentions in Kyushu, a statement apparently confirmed by his generous concessions, the missionaries had high hopes for the future and felt justified in believing that under Japan's new ruler they were to enjoy favors even greater than those which had been conferred upon them by Nobunaga.

The high hopes of the missionaries were doomed to sudden and bitter disappointment. So long as he was engaged in subduing the rebellious daimyo of Kyushu, Hideyoshi heaped favors upon the missionaries and their Japanese adherents; but as soon as this struggle had been brought to a successful conclusion, his attitude abruptly changed. At midnight on July 23, 1587, Coelho was awakened by a messenger from Hideyoshi demanding an immediate answer to the following questions: By what authority did the Jesuits and their converts use force to compel Japanese to become Christians? Why did they encourage their followers to destroy temples? Why did they persecute the Buddhists? Why did they and the other Portuguese eat the flesh of useful animals such as oxen and cows? Why did Coelho permit the Portuguese merchants to make Japanese slaves and carry these slaves to India for sale?

Without waiting for Coelho's answer the Japanese dictator drew up a decree, which was published on July 25, ordering all missionaries to leave the empire within twenty days; any of their number who dared to remain after the expiration of that period would be punished by death. The Portuguese merchants, so long as they obeyed the laws of Japan, might continue to trade at Japanese ports; but if any merchant dared to bring missionaries to the country, his ship and all its cargo would be confiscated.

Like his earlier professions of friendly interest, Hideyoshi's decree of July 25 was simply a move in the political game which he was playing. So long as his enemies in Kyushu were undefeated, his favorable treatment of the missionaries served to keep the Christian daimyo from joining the forces opposed to him. Even before 1586, however, Hideyoshi had begun to take notice of the political activities of the Christians; and his sojourn in Kyushu, where the missionaries had their most numerous following, led him to realize that the adherents of the new religion might easily become a serious danger to the centralized government.

Although convinced that something should be done to check the growing political power of the missionaries, Hideyoshi apparently had no intention of enforcing, at least for the present, his drastic command. At first the twenty-day period of grace was extended to six months; but even when the six months elapsed, no move was made toward expelling or punishing the many missionaries who still remained in the empire. To the end of Hideyoshi's life the Jesuits were allowed to carry on their work, but under conditions which greatly diminished their earlier freedom of action. Wherever they went they were kept under constant surveillance by government officials, and they were fully conscious of the fact that any attempt on their part to interfere in political affairs would bring upon them the punishment threatened in the decree.

Until just half a century after the arrival of the first Portuguese the Jesuit missionaries and the Portuguese merchants had the Japanese field to themselves. By 1590, however, Japanese merchants had found their way to the Philippine Islands, and in 1592 the Spanish governor of the Philippines, Dasmarinas, sent an envoy to Japan to attempt to open relations with the Japanese. This first Spanish embassy was followed a year later by a second, which included among its members four Franciscan friars. Hideyoshi, who was quite as anxious as the Spanish governor to develop trade between Japan and the Spanish possessions, granted the Franciscans permission to remain at Kyoto on condition that they refrain from preaching their religion.

At this time the Portuguese Jesuits, in order to give Hideyoshi no cause for enforcing his decree of 1587, were behaving with the utmost circumspection, but the Spanish newcomers had not yet learned that Hideyoshi was a man whose orders were to be taken seriously. In utter disregard of the conditions upon which they were allowed to remain in the country they were no sooner settled in Kyoto than they began to erect a church and to make converts. In the following year, three additional friars having arrived from Manila, the Franciscans proceeded to establish a branch mission at Osaka and another at Nagasaki.

For the moment Hideyoshi was too busy with his Korean war and other serious matters to pay attention to the Franciscans, but in 1596 an incident occurred which brought the full weight of his wrath upon the men who had dared openly to defy his orders. The Manila galleon of that year, the *San Felipe*, had been caught in a typhoon which carried it off its course and left it, badly battered, near the southern coast of Shikoku. As the *San Felipe* was attempting to make her way into a harbor in Tosa Province, the Japanese who were assisting her deliberately towed her onto a sand-bar. Under the "Strand Law" of Japan the daimyo of Tosa thereupon claimed both ship and cargo, refusing to listen to any protest from the Spanish commander. The Spaniards now attempted to frighten the Japanese into releasing their ship. They produced a map of the world and pointed out the vast possessions of the Spanish monarch, whose hostility would be aroused by this act of injustice. When the Japanese inquired how it had been possible for the Spanish king to bring under his control so many far-distant lands, the Spaniards replied that it was quite simple. First of all, missionaries were sent to these countries; then, when a sufficient number of the people had adopted the Christian religion, soldiers were sent to combine with the converts and overthrow the former government.

This conversation was promptly reported to Hideyoshi, who at the same time was informed of the fact that the Spanish friars, in violation of his orders, had been actively engaged in preaching their doctrines at Kyoto and elsewhere. The commander and crew of the shipwrecked galleon were allowed to return to Manila, but swift and terrible punishment fell upon the Spanish missionaries. The six Franciscans, together with seventeen of their Japanese converts, were seized and taken to Nagasaki, where, early in 1597, they were publicly executed. No harm was done to the Portuguese, but a fresh decree was now issued ordering the immediate departure of all missionaries from Japan; at the same time Hideyoshi took steps to prevent any further spread of Christianity among the daimyo and the upper classes of society. Although the Jesuits ostentatiously prepared to obey the new decrees, only eleven out of more than a hundred who were then in Japan actually left the country. The others were carefully concealed by their Japanese friends until the death of Hideyoshi, in the autumn of the following year, made it safe for them to resume their work in public.

When Iyeyasu began to lay the foundations of the Tokugawa Shogunate, he showed a keen interest in the development of Japan's intercourse with the outside world. Hideyoshi's decrees against the missionaries were therefore not enforced, and every possible encouragement was given the Portuguese traders to continue their visits to Japan. But the existing trade, confined as it was almost exclusively to the Kyushu ports, did not satisfy Iyeyasu, who was especially anxious to see the development of commerce at his city of Yedo, to which the Portuguese seemed unwilling to come. Even before he became Shogun, Iyeyasu began to take steps for the development of Yedo as a commercial center. In December, 1598, he dispatched an ambassador to the governor of the Philippines with a suggestion that the Spaniards make Yedo a port of call for their Manila galleon on its annual voyage to Mexico. The Spaniards, possibly because of the *San Felipe* incident, were slow to take advantage of this friendly suggestion; even when some of them did begin to come to Japan, Iyeyasu discovered that they were less interested in commerce than in religious propaganda. Moreover, the behavior of the Spaniards soon reawakened the old suspicion that their missionary enterprise was intended to pave the way for conquest. Although this renewed suspicion did not lead to any immediate persecution, Iyeyasu henceforth kept the missionaries under careful observation.

Having been disappointed in his efforts to develop any considerable amount of trade with the Spaniards, the Shogun turned his attentions to the Dutch, who were now finding their way to the Far East and whose interest in trade was not complicated by any missionary program. The first Dutch ship to reach Japan, the *Liefde*, arrived in the spring of 1600, and by 1609 the vessels of the Dutch East India Company were making regular voyages to Japan from the Dutch trading posts in the East Indies. Like the Portuguese, however, the Netherlanders preferred to trade at the well-established trading centers in Kyushu rather than to bring their goods to the Shogun's new port at Yedo.

Among the officers of the Dutch ship which reached Japan in 1600 was an Englishman named Will Adams, who because of his knowledge of shipbuilding and navigation soon became quite a favorite with Iyeyasu. Adams built several ships for his powerful patron, taught him some smatterings of geometry and navigation, and gave him a good deal of information, not of a wholly unbiased nature, concerning the Portuguese and the Spanish. At Iyeyasu's request Adams wrote letters to the officials of the English East India Company, urging them to open trade with Japan and advising them to make Yedo their trading port in the country. In 1613 an English ship finally arrived, but instead of taking Adams's advice as to the location of its "factory" the English company joined the Dutch and Portuguese in trading at the ports of Kyushu. After ten years of unprofitable trade at Hirado the English withdrew from Japan, thoroughly disgusted with their venture.

Iyeyasu's efforts to develop foreign trade were not limited to inviting and encouraging foreign merchants to visit his ports. He also encouraged his daimyo to build ships and thus to give Japan an active role in international commerce. During his lifetime and for several years after his death Japanese ships were frequent visitors to the ports of Siam and the Indies, while several vessels made voyages as far afield as the coast of Mexico. So active did the Japanese become that the agents of the English company mentioned the keen competition of the Japanese merchants as one of the chief reasons for the English failure to develop a profitable trade. Even here, however, Iyeyasu's hope that Yedo would become a flourishing seaport was disappointed. The only daimyo who showed any real interest in building ships and in developing trade were the tozama lords in Kyushu; the fudai daimyo of the Kwanto did little or nothing toward assisting in carrying out the Shogun's commercial policy.

In 1613 the suspicions of the Tokugawa government in regard to the missionaries were aroused, and in January, 1614, a decree was issued ordering that all the foreign priests be assembled at Nagasaki and deported from the empire. This edict resulted in the expulsion of more than a hundred missionaries, but about fifty avoided deportation or returned immediately from abroad. In the winter of 1614 and in the following summer Iyeyasu, who retained —even after his abdication as Shogun—the management of Tokugawa affairs, was engaged in overthrowing and destroying Hideyori, the son of Hideyoshi, whose Osaka stronghold had become the headquarters of the anti-Tokugawa faction. In this struggle Hideyori was supported by a large number of Japanese Christians, while at least five foreign missionaries were in Osaka when it was captured in June, 1615.

Although these facts still further convinced Iyeyasu of the dangerous and subversive character of the foreign religion, his actions against the missionaries went no farther than an effort to enforce effectively the decree of expulsion; but the death of Iyeyasu, on June 1, 1616, was followed almost immediately by a stiffening of the policy of the Yedo government toward Christianity and its foreign teachers. On October 1 an edict appeared reaffirming Hideyoshi's two decrees as well as that of Iyeyasu, and the following May saw the execution at Nagasaki of two foreign priests, the first foreigners to be executed in Japan since the six Franciscans whom Hideyoshi had put to death twenty years earlier.

During the next year and a half three other missionaries were put to death, but it was not until 1622 that the Tokugawa authorities deliberately set out to extirpate the foreign religion. In that year began what is known as the "great persecution." On August 19 two priests and the captain of the Japanese ship by which they had reached Japan were burned at the stake; later in the year nine foreign missionaries and nineteen of their converts suffered the same penalty. From this moment the foreign *bateran* ("padres") were ruthlessly hunted down and exterminated, while every possible punishment and torture was employed to force the apostasy of the Japanese converts.

Yet the anti-Christian policy of the Japanese government did not result from its disapproval of the doctrines of Christianity. The authorities determined to destroy Christianity simply because they feared the ambitious designs of the countries from which the missionaries had come and because they felt that in case of an attempted Spanish invasion the Japanese Christians might prove disloyal to their native land.

The campaign against Christian missions was accompanied by a gradual abandonment of Iyeyasu's liberal commercial policy. In 1623, as has been previously noted, the English discontinued their voyages to Japan, leaving the foreign commerce of the country in the hands of the Spanish, the Portuguese, the Dutch, and the Japanese themselves. In 1624 a decree was issued ordering the deportation of all Spaniards and declaring that henceforth only non-Christian Japanese were to go abroad for purposes of trade; even these were strictly forbidden to visit the Philippines or any other place under Spanish control. In 1636 all Japanese, Christian or non-Christian, were forbidden to go abroad for any reason whatsoever; Japanese were forbidden to construct ocean-going ships, and it was declared that any Japanese residing abroad who should attempt to return to Japan would be put to death.

The fall of 1637 saw the outbreak of a rebellion in Kyushu known as the "Shimabara Revolt." Some thirty thousand Christians, including women and children, rose up against the authorities and established themselves on the rocky promontory of Shimabara, near Nagasaki, where they maintained themselves until reduced by starvation. Although there was no proof of Portuguese complicity in the outbreak, a fresh decree now ordered the expulsion of all Portuguese from the empire; and in 1639 the entire Portuguese commercial community sailed away to Macao.

The Portuguese authorities at Macao, regarding the loss of the Japanese trade as a major calamity, made a desperate attempt to regain the favor of the Japanese. In 1640 a Portuguese ship arrived at Nagasaki bearing an embassy which had been sent to negotiate for the reopening of commercial relations. The Japanese, however, had made their decision; the four envoys, together with fifty-seven members of the crew, were put to death, the remaining thirteen of the crew being left alive only that they might report to Macao the Shogun's determination to exclude forever all Portuguese from his domains.

Only the Dutch remained to carry on trade between Japan and the Western world, and even the Dutch were now kept under the closest supervision. As early as 1637, in order to make it impossible for missionaries to move about under false passports, the government had forbidden foreigners of any nationality to travel in the interior of the empire. In 1641, the year following the unsuccessful Portuguese attempt to reopen trade, the Netherlanders were compelled to move their headquarters from Hirado to the little island of Deshima at the mouth of Nagasaki harbor. Here, for more than two hundred years, the Dutch merchants were to carry on their trade under conditions which made them practically prisoners. After ninety-nine years of intercourse with the Europeans Japan closed her once open door and left only a narrow loophole through which her government and people could watch events in the outside world.

The decision of the Tokugawa Shogunate to close the doors of Japan to all save a slender stream of foreign commerce was based primarily upon domestic considerations. The labors of Nobunaga, Hideyoshi, and Iyeyasu had put an end to the long civil war and had established the supremacy of a centralized administration; it was the purpose of Iyeyasu's successors to make this centralization permanent and to eliminate any element which might threaten to disturb its somewhat precarious equilibrium. The power of the Yedo administration lay in the fudai daimyo, who, as we have seen, were concentrated in the central and eastern provinces of Honshu; and the permanence of Tokugawa control depended upon their keeping the "outside" (tozama) daimyo from becoming prosperous and powerful.

If Iyeyasu had succeeded in his attempt to transfer the center of foreign trade from Kyushu to the Kwanto, the policy of the closed door probably would not have been adopted, since the profits of the trade would in this case have enriched the Tokugawas and their fudai vassals, who also would have been the first to receive and to take advantage of any new idea or useful device imported from abroad. But Iyeyasu's efforts to this end had not been successful; and Japan's foreign commerce was still entering the empire almost exclusively through the ports of Kyushu, which were located in the domains of the tozama feudatories. Under these circumstances the continuance of unrestricted foreign trade would have meant the enrichment and strengthening of the dangerous "outside" nobles and a corresponding decrease in the authority of the Yedo administration. After 1641, therefore, all foreign trade —even with the Chinese, whose ships and merchants were submitted to restrictions similar to those enforced upon the Dutch— was confined to the single port of Nagasaki, where the Bakufu maintained a Shogunal governor to control the trade and to collect for the Yedo treasury the heavy taxes levied upon it.

SUGGESTED REFERENCES

ANESAKI, M. Buddhist Art in its Relation to Buddhist Ideals.

ANESAKI, M. History of Japanese Religion.

ASTON, W. G. "Hideyoshi's Invasion of Korea," *Transactions of the Asiatic Society of Japan*, Vol. VI.

ASTON, W. G. A History of Japanese Literature.

BOXER, C. R. A Portuguese Embassy to Japan, 1644–1647.

BRINKLEY, F. Japan: its History, Arts, and Literature.

BRINKLEY, F., and KIKUCHI, D. A History of the Japanese People.

CARY, O. A History of Christianity in Japan.

CRAM, R. A. Impressions of Japanese Architecture and the Allied Arts.

DENING, W. Life of Toyotomi Hideyoshi.

FENOLLOSA, E. F. Epochs of Chinese and Japanese Art.

HARA, K. An Introduction to the History of Japan.

LATOURETTE, K. S. The Development of Japan.

MURDOCH, J. A History of Japan, Vol. II.

NUKARIYA, K. The Religion of the Samurai, a Study of Zen Philosophy.

SANSOM, G. B. Japan: a Short Cultural History.

XVIII

Ming China, the Europeans, and the Manchu Conquest

The Europeans and the Confucian State · Arrival of the Portuguese · Establishment and Destruction of the First Trading Posts · The Nature of the Confucian State · Taxation and Legislation · Provincial and Local Officials · The Examination System · A Commonwealth of Self-governing Communities · Responsibility and Autonomy · Strength and Weakness of the Confucian State · The Portuguese at Macao · The Chinese and the Spanish · Early Dutch and English Attempts to Trade · The Reintroduction of Christianity · Ricci and his Successors at Peking · Spanish Missionaries in China · Chinese Intervention in the Korean War · The Manchu Conquest of China · The Rise of the Manchus · The Manchu Declaration of War · Rebellions in China · The Fall of the Ming Dynasty · Wu San-kuei and the Manchus · Manchu Retention of Ming Institutions · The Emperor K'ang Hsi · Koxinga, the Pirate-Patriot · The Revolt of Wu San-kuei · K'ang Hsi and the Europeans · The Rites Controversy · The Decree of 1717 · China and the Europeans in 1717

WHEN the forces under Albuquerque in 1511 attacked and captured the city of Malacca, the Portuguese commander displayed great courtesy and consideration in his treatment of the Chinese merchants whom he found trading at the Arab spice center. As a result of this treatment the Chinese on their return to China carried a favorable report concerning the Western newcomers, and the Arab appeals to the Chinese court for assistance against their conquerors fell upon deaf ears. Five years after the taking of Malacca a Portuguese squadron under the command of Rafael Perestrello reached the coast of China, and in 1517 a squadron of eight ships under Fernão Perez de Andrade, bringing Thomé Pires as envoy from the Portuguese viceroy at Goa, also reached the China coast. Andrade, with two of his ships, was permitted to proceed to Canton, while the rest of the fleet remained at the island of Shangch'uan, off the coast of Kwangtung.

In spite of the representations of the Arab merchants at Canton, who described the Westerners as piratical barbarians, the Portu-

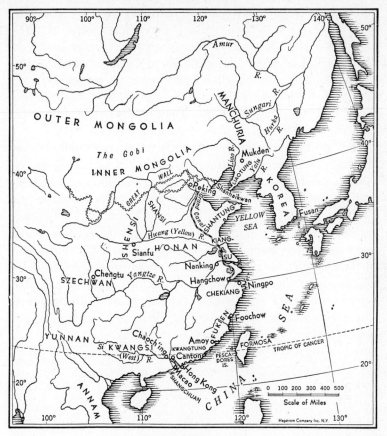

Ming China

guese were hospitably received by the Cantonese officials; and Pires, after some delay, received permission in 1520 to proceed on his embassy to Peking. Shortly after the departure of Pires from Canton on his northward journey, however, the favorable impression which had been created by Albuquerque and by the first Portuguese at Canton was destroyed, and the Chinese were given reason for believing that the Arab characterization of their rivals contained elements of truth. For at this point Simon de Andrade, a brother of Fernão, arrived at Shangch'uan with a fleet of four ships and began to act in a high-handed manner, landing forces on the island, erecting a fort, and assuming jurisdiction over the people. When the news of these proceedings reached Canton, the viceroy fitted out an expedition against the invader and forced him to withdraw. Andrade's violation of China's sovereign rights proved disastrous for his fellow countryman, the ambassador from Goa. When Pires, in January, 1521, arrived at Peking, he was seized and imprisoned as a spy. The following year he was sent back in chains to Canton, where he died in prison in 1523.

For just a quarter of a century after Simon de Andrade's unsuccessful venture the Portuguese attempted to pursue on the Chinese coast the policy which had proved so successful in India and in Malaysia. Fortified posts were established as bases for Portuguese trade at Amoy, Ningpo, and Foochow. These places became important centers of commerce, and the resident Portuguese authorities assumed jurisdiction over the Chinese residents of these districts as if they were conquered people. As usual the Chinese government was slow in taking action against the troublesome outsiders. In 1545, however, an expedition against the three settlements was finally organized by the imperial authorities, and the Portuguese were driven from all three places.

When the first Portuguese ships arrived on the coast of China, the Ming dynasty, established in 1368 by Chu Yüan-chang, had occupied the Dragon Throne for almost exactly a century and a half. Although less powerful than it had been under the emperor Hung Wu and his fifteenth-century successors, the Ming empire was prosperous, well governed, and respected by all its neighbors. Externally the sixteenth-century rulers of China made no effort to attain for their country the greatness which it had enjoyed in the days of Han and of T'ang; even the attempts of Yung Lo to establish control over Annam, Eastern Turkestan, and Malaysia had been abandoned, and the empire was limited practically to the present-day "eighteen provinces" lying south of the Great Wall, while once more, as in the last years of the Mongol rule, Japanese pirates raided and plundered the more exposed districts of the coast provinces of Chekiang, Kiangsu, and Shantung. In spite of the weakness of their foreign policy, however, the Ming emperors still received periodic tributary missions from the rulers of Korea,

Annam, Siam, Malacca, Nepal, and the Luchu Islands, as well as from various chieftains in Manchuria, Mongolia, and Turkestan. In domestic well-being, on the other hand, this period of Ming rule may be regarded as a golden age in China's history. General peace and prosperity prevailed, and the ancient social system which had been organized upon the basis of Confucian philosophy functioned to the satisfaction of rulers and people.

The peculiar organization of the Ming empire, an organization which continued to exist with few modifications until the final overthrow of the Manchu dynasty in 1912, was far from being the "typical Oriental despotism" so often described by Western writers. Equally inaccurate is the characterization "paternalistic," if by *paternalism* we mean a system of government in which the rulers guard, guide, and direct the people in every action of their workaday lives. Three thousand years ago, before the time of Confucius, the government of China was paternalistic, while the government of Kublai Khan and his Mongol successors might properly be described as a despotism; but the rule of the Ming emperors and their Manchu successors was remarkable for its noninterference in the normal economic life of the nation.

Strictly limited in his functions by a tradition more difficult to change than written constitutions, the Chinese emperor reigned rather than ruled. As the holder of the "mandate of Heaven" he offered the various seasonal sacrifices in the name of his nation, rendering thanks for prosperity and doing penance in case of natural calamities, which were regarded as attributable to his lack of princely virtue. Aside from this priestly function the most important duties of the emperor were three in number. First, he was supposed to maintain, chiefly by example and precept, peace and order throughout the empire; only as a last resort and against men utterly lacking in a sense of propriety should force be used. Secondly, he must ensure to the empire, through the selective operation of the examination system, the administrative services of a body of officials who in character, ability, and training stood out as "superior men." In the third place, he must protect the empire against outside attacks from the barbarian peoples upon its frontiers. Only in one respect did the imperial authorities at Peking participate directly in the administration of local affairs: all criminal cases involving the death penalty must be reported to the capital for revision by the Board of Punishments and for the final approval of the emperor before the sentence was actually carried out.

Two functions, commonly regarded as indispensable to the well-being of a modern Western state, were conspicuous by their absence. The imperial government had neither the power of levying new or increased taxes nor the power to make new law. The land tax—the most important source of imperial revenue—was fixed by tradition; other taxes, local in nature, were assessed by the provincial or prefectural officials, with the consent of the communities, or by the communities themselves. Like taxation, law was essentially traditional. From the days of the Chou dynasty or even earlier the Chinese had had written codes of law. Each new dynasty, as it came into power, had issued its own code, modifying on various points the code of its predecessors. Like the edicts of the Roman praetors, these successive dynastic codes had resulted in the gradual evolution of a body of written law which by the time of the Ming dynasty had become very full and complete, at least in criminal law. Once the code of the dynasty had been drawn up and published, however, it was commonly regarded as an unalterable instrument of government, and the legislative power of subsequent emperors of the dynasty was practically limited to amendment by interpretation, not unlike the interpretative power exercised by the United States Supreme Court.

Like the emperor at Peking, the viceroys and governors in the provinces and the prefectural officials, all of whom held office by imperial appointment, exercised traditional and limited powers. Within his particular jurisdiction each was expected to collect for transmission to his superior the customary local taxes, to administer and enforce the established law, and to maintain the peace.

Early European writers saw in these provincial and local officials a feudal aristocracy similar to that of medieval Europe. This parallel, however, has little validity. The fundamental feudal relationship between the official and the soil was wholly absent. From the reign of the first Ming emperor provincial officials were never posted to the provinces of their birth, while both provincial and prefectural officials were forbidden to marry or to acquire real estate within the limits of their jurisdiction. The Chinese local official resembled the feudal lord in the fact that he derived his income from local sources rather than from the imperial treasury; but his tenure of office was subject to the control of the imperial master by whom he was appointed, and this tenure was usually limited, at least in the case of the higher functionaries, to not more than three years at any one post.

A fundamental feature of the Chinese governmental organization was the highly competitive system of literary examinations for admission to civil office. This method of selecting officials, as we have already seen, first made its appearance in the age of Han and was thoroughly systematized by the rulers of the T'ang dynasty. Falling into disuse during the Mongol regime, it had been revived by the first Ming emperor; and under his successors it assumed the form which it was to maintain down to the end of the empire.

The process of selection began in the districts and prefectures, where annual examinations in penmanship, history, and the Confucian Classics eliminated those who were not yet qualified for the higher tests. The successful candidates at the prefectural examinations received the degree of *Hsiu Ts'ai* and became eligible to appear at the provincial examinations, held every third year at the capital of their province. Success at the provincial examinations, which were conducted by special examiners sent from Peking, secured for the candidate the degree of *Chü Jen* and qualified him for the imperial examinations at Peking, which also were held triennially. At the imperial examinations those who passed received the degree of *Chin Shih*. All who attained the Chin Shih became "expectant" officials, eligible for imperial appointment; but about one third of these, by a subsequent palace examination in the presence of the emperor himself, were admitted to membership in the most exalted fraternity of Chinese scholarship, the *Hanlin* ("Forest of Pens"), from which were selected the historiographers and other high literary officers.

The severity of these tests can best be indicated by statistics. It has been estimated that the number of recipients of the Hsiu

Ts'ai degree during each three years amounted in modern times to something more than half a million. Of this number about six thousand Chü Jen, survivors from the provincial examinations, presented themselves each third year as candidates for the Chin Shih degree, and of these six thousand not more than three hundred became eligible to appear before the emperor as candidates for Hanlin honors.

To the modern Western mind this selective process, although admirable in principle, might appear to have been vitiated in practice by the nature of the tests. From the district examinations to the great triennial examination for the Chin Shih degree, success depended entirely upon the candidate's ability to quote accurately from the Classics, to compose poems and formal essays upon assigned topics, to incorporate in his compositions apt allusions to ancient history, and to display in the formation of his written characters a high degree of calligraphic skill. Only in the palace examinations for membership in the Hanlin Academy, where each aspirant was required to write upon some current political problem, did the test become "practical"; and even here success came to the candidate whose solution of the given problem most thoroughly accorded with the examples and precepts of antiquity.

Despite this apparent weakness the Chinese method of recruiting a body of educated officials can claim pragmatic justification. It put control of the government in the hands of a body of men who through long years of study were thoroughly imbued with the social philosophy and ethical ideas of Confucianism; and these men, because of their survival in the rigorous selective process, were looked up to and respected by the whole nation as "superior men." Not all of China's officials followed unswervingly in their public and private lives the principles of Confucian philosophy; but throughout the Ming and Manchu periods, until late in the nineteenth century, a vast majority of the men thus trained and selected conscientiously applied these principles in the administration of the affairs committed to their charge.[1]

[1] The decay of China's administrative system came when corruption and favoritism destroyed the nation's confidence in the true "superiority" of the men whom the later Manchu rulers appointed to office.

Below the network of imperial appointees, few in number and almost unsupported by military force, the Chinese people formed what may best be described as a commonwealth of self-governing communities. In the rural districts the unit was the family village, presided over by a council of elders and the village headman. In the cities the family group was still the social unit, and its elders exercised unquestioned authority in all matters of intrafamily importance; here, however, the importance of the family as an agent of self-government was overshadowed by that of the guild. Each industry and trade had its guild which made rules and regulations governing its own affairs. Although purely family affairs were still settled by the family council, in other matters the individual was bound by the decisions of the commercial or industrial corporation to which he belonged.

Although possessing a highly developed body of criminal law, the Chinese Empire had failed to evolve more than the bare rudiments of civil law. Certain elementary clauses relative to inheritance, mortgages, and the transfer of real estate were embodied in the criminal code, but most of the subjects customarily dealt with in civil-law codes were ignored by the imperial legal system and were placed under the jurisdiction of the various guild organizations. Whenever a civil question involved the members of different guilds, the matter was usually settled by a board of arbitration set up by the guilds whose members were involved. Only when the contending parties, refusing to abide by the decisions rendered by these extralegal bodies, created a disturbance of the peace, did the matter normally come before the political authorities; and then it came as a criminal case. In the urban community, therefore, as in the village, the direction and control of the economic life of the people were vested in the people themselves, while the appointees of the emperor were concerned primarily with the maintenance of peace and the administration of criminal law.

The "Confucian state" was held together by the principle of *responsibility*. Every member of a community—family, village, or guild—was jointly responsible for the debts and for the criminal acts of his fellow members. The local official was responsible to the provincial official, and he, in turn, was responsible to the emperor for the maintenance of peace and order in the region committed to his charge. The circle of responsibility was made complete by the emperor's responsibility to Heaven, which actually meant responsibility to public opinion, for the prosperity and well-being of the empire. Mencius had set forth in no uncertain terms the doctrine that the voice of the people was the voice of Heaven, and this doctrine was no mere philosophical abstraction. The pages of Chinese history bear eloquent testimony to the fact that the loss of popular favor has been tantamount to the loss of the "mandate of Heaven."

As a necessary corollary to the principle of responsibility stood the practice of local autonomy. Full responsibility could exist only if accompanied by an equally full reliance upon the individual initiative of the person who was to be held responsible. Hence the decrees and edicts of the emperor, as well as the proclamations of the viceroys and the governors, dwelt on glittering generalities and expounded the fundamental virtues of justice and propriety; the local official, being the man immediately responsible, must find for any given emergency a solution which, harmonizing with justice and propriety, did not offend the prejudices of the people and thus create fresh difficulties. Failure on the part of an official in dealing with the problems of the area committed to his supervision was punished by demotion, dismissal, exile, or death; conspicuous success was attended by promotion to a higher sphere of activity, but the precise means by which any particular problem should be solved was seldom, if ever, dictated to an inferior officer by those above him.

Based upon the social philosophy of the Confucian school and evolved through two thousand years of practical experience, the Chinese state served the needs of an intelligent and energetic population, predominantly agricultural in occupation and having comparatively little outside contact save with less civilized or less powerful peoples on the frontiers. The upkeep of the government weighed lightly upon the taxpayers; and if it rendered correspondingly limited services to the nation, its traditional noninterference in purely economic affairs contributed in no small degree to develop the initiative and self-reliance of the Chinese people. So long as the literary examinations were honestly conducted and advancement in the government service continued on the merit basis, the empire was assured of the services of a capable and devoted officialdom, while the public confidence in and respect for the official body thus recruited and promoted provided a strong moral foundation for the government and reduced to a minimum its reliance upon armed force. Even in their relations with the neighboring countries of eastern Asia the absence of a powerful executive capable of uniting the empire in an ambitious foreign policy appears to have been beneficial to the Chinese people. Because of her ancient and superior civilization China enjoyed tremendous prestige among her neighbors, and the fact that the empire was not armed for aggressive war made these neighbors the more willing to recognize the imperial claims to a world supremacy which never threatened to become more than cultural.

Like all systems of social or political organization, however, the loosely integrated and almost ungoverned Confucian state contained elements of weakness. Largely self-governing and held together mainly by a sense of cultural unity, the different provinces and local subdivisions developed a high degree of particularism. Provincial restrictions upon the exportation of foodstuffs, combined with difficulties of transportation, impeded the flow of surplus grain from region to region, with the result that the people in one province might be dying of famine while those of another had more than they needed. The defense of the frontiers usually devolved upon the local authorities. In the case of piratical inroads upon the coastal regions this task overburdened the resources of the threatened districts, and imperial aid, called in as a last resort, seldom arrived in time to prevent or even to punish the depredations. With the arrival of the Europeans, whose independently evolved culture precluded the possibility that they would join the Eastern peoples in recognizing the supremacy of China, the inability of the central government to administer directly the affairs in the maritime provinces became a more serious weakness; but it was not until the nineteenth century that the ancient Chinese political system finally gave evidence of being unable to adjust itself to a new and changing world environment.

For twelve years after the destruction of their settlements at Amoy, Foochow, and Ningpo the Portuguese had no port of call on the Chinese coast for their ships trading between Malacca and Japan. A few survivors from the disaster had found refuge on the small island of Lampacao, near the mouth of the West River; others appear to have settled on the island of Shangch'uan. At neither of these places, however, did the foreigners attempt to establish their authority or to engage in activities which might reawaken the jealous suspicions of the Chinese authorities. Having learned to their sorrow that the methods so successful in India could not be employed with equal success in the territories of the Ming empire, the Portuguese altered their policy and set out to win the favor of the Chinese. In 1557 the new policy was crowned with a measure of success, and as a reward for having assisted the imperial authorities in the suppression of piracy the Portuguese secured permission to erect a few buildings at Macao.

In spite of this mark of favor the Chinese authorities showed that they had not forgotten the earlier behavior of their European guests. The little settlement at Macao was kept under careful supervision. Trade with the neighboring city of Canton was strictly regulated; the Portuguese were forbidden to erect new buildings, or even to make repairs on those already erected, until they had obtained official permission to do so; and every precaution was taken to prevent the usurpation of any rights which might be derogatory to Chinese sovereignty. Following the principles which the T'ang dynasty had adopted during the seventh century for the regulation of foreign merchants residing at Chinese ports, the government allowed the Portuguese to settle their private disputes according to their own laws; but all criminal cases and all cases involving the interests of Chinese subjects, if they could not be adjusted by arbitration, were brought before Chinese judges and settled in accordance with Chinese law.

As the first permanent foothold of European trade upon Chinese soil Macao gradually developed into a commercial center of outstanding importance. Until the expulsion of the Portuguese from Japan in 1639 the Japanese trade of the port was even more important than its trade with China, and the action of the Tokugawa government was looked upon at the time as spelling ruin for the community. But the Chinese trade slowly expanded, and Macao, one of the few posts retained by the Portuguese after the middle of the seventeenth century, steadily increased in prosperity for the next two hundred years. Not until the British, as a result of their first war with China, obtained the island of Hongkong and created there a rival distributing point for trade with the Chinese coast did the importance of Macao begin to wane.

Eight years after the establishment of the Portuguese settlement at Macao the Spanish expedition under Legaspi arrived in the Philippines and made the islands a part of Spain's great colonial empire. For centuries the merchants from the seaports along the southeast coast of China had carried on a profitable trade with the people of the Philippines; and with the arrival of the Europeans, whose subjugation of the Filipinos concentrated the wealth of the islands in the hands of the ruling aristocracy, the possibilities of trade greatly increased. The Spanish, as we have already seen, made little effort to develop trade with China, and such efforts as they did make were blocked by the jealousy of the Portuguese at Macao; but the Chinese merchants of Canton, Amoy, and neighboring ports found the Manila market a veritable gold mine and showed great energy in exploiting its possibilities. A large part of the gold and silver which reached Manila from Spain's American possessions eventually found its way to Chinese ports in exchange for Chinese products, while Chinese silks, satins, tea, preserved ginger, and other highly valued commodities furnished the bulk of the cargoes which crossed the Pacific to Mexico in the Manila galleon. In spite of the frequently recurring fears of the Spanish the Chinese government appears never to have contemplated seriously the possibility of extending its rule to the Philippine Islands. Even the massacres of Chinese subjects in 1603, 1639, and 1662 brought only mild protests from the authorities of the provinces along the coast.

During the period of Ming rule the Dutch and the English both attempted, with little success, to open trade with the Chinese Empire. The first Dutch attempt came in 1604, when three ships arrived at Macao and requested permission to engage in trade. By this time the Chinese officials at Macao and at Canton had come to regard all new arrivals with suspicion; and when the Portuguese informed them that the Dutch were a nation of ferocious pirates, the permission to trade was not granted. The second Dutch attempt, in 1622, convinced the Chinese that the Portuguese had correctly characterized their European rivals. In June of that year a Dutch squadron of three ships under the command of Cornelis Reyerszoon arrived at Macao with instructions to take Macao and make it a base for Dutch trade. Completely disregarding the rights of China as territorial sovereign, Reyerszoon attacked Macao with all the forces at his disposal. The attack was a disastrous failure, and the Portuguese, aided by Chinese troops, drove the Dutch back to their ships with heavy losses. Repulsed from Macao, the Dutch squadron proceeded northward to the Pescadores Islands, where they seized a port; and in 1630 they transferred their base of operations to the island of Formosa, where they maintained themselves until 1662, developing a profitable trade with the ports of Fukien Province. Not until 1762, however, did the Dutch succeed in securing permission to engage in trade at Canton.

The first English attempt to open trade with China came in 1637, when Captain John Weddell arrived at Macao with a squadron consisting of four ships and two pinnaces. Although Weddell had stopped en route at Goa and had received from the Portuguese viceroy formal permission to trade at Macao, the local Portuguese merchants did everything in their power to cause trouble between the local officials and the English. Irritated at the long delay in obtaining from the Chinese authorities the necessary permit to proceed to Canton, the English captain forced his way up the river and arrived off Canton with smoking cannon. Here the local authorities, intimidated by a display of force which they were unprepared to resist, allowed the English to exchange their goods for cargoes of sugar, ginger, and other Chinese commodities. Following this stormy episode the English made one or two halfhearted attempts to open trade, but it was not until 1699, fifty-five years after the downfall of the Ming dynasty, that they actually secured a share in the commerce of China.

Two centuries before the arrival of the Portuguese the Franciscan mission established by John of Monte Corvino had introduced Christianity in its Catholic form into China, but with the fall of the Mongol dynasty all traces of this once flourishing work gradually disappeared. In 1552 the Jesuit missionary St. Francis Xavier, who already had spent about two years in Japan, arrived at the island of Shangch'uan with the intention of reintroducing Christianity into China. Xavier's undertaking was unfortunately timed. Only seven years had elapsed since the Chinese emperor had been compelled to send his armed forces against the Portuguese settlements at Amoy, Foochow, and Ningpo, and the officials of the coastal provinces were under strict orders to prevent any Portuguese from entering the country. Xavier tried in vain to find some means of making his way from the island to the mainland. Shortly after his arrival he fell ill, and early in December, 1552, the celebrated "Apostle to the Indies" died without having been permitted to set foot upon the mainland.

When the Portuguese received permission to establish their little settlement at Macao, the door to China became at least partly open for the missionaries. In 1583 two Jesuits from Macao, Michael Ruggerius and the more famous Matteo Ricci, succeeded in making their way to the city of Chaoch'ing, near Canton, where they resided quietly, making no secret of their religion but devoting themselves to the study of the language rather than to the propagation of the Gospel. Both men were well grounded in European science, and Ricci's education had included a thorough training in mathematics, geography, and astronomy. These scholarly attainments enabled the two Jesuits to win both the respect and the friendship of a number of the local officials and scholars. During the next decade the two pioneers were joined by other members of the order, but in 1589 local hostility drove the little mission from Chaoch'ing to seek refuge in a neighboring city. Until 1594 Ricci and his companions, in order to be recognized as teachers of religion, wore the garb of Buddhist priests. After that date, realizing that scholarship rather than religion was the best path to the respect of the educated classes, they threw off their Buddhist garb and assumed the costume customarily worn by the Confucian scholars.

Shortly after this change of costume Ricci decided to make his way, if possible, northward to Peking. As China at that time was engaged in war against the Japanese in Korea (see page 405), the imperial capital was an extremely dangerous place for any foreigner in disguise; and Ricci's first advance toward the north carried him only as far as the Yangtze valley. By 1601, however, he had reached Peking, where he was accorded an audience by the emperor Wan Li and was given permission to remain at the capital. At Peking, as at Canton, Ricci was soon able to win the respect and esteem of the scholars and officials with whom he came in contact, and this success brought with it toleration for his organization. As the result of his favorable impression upon the authorities at the capital his fellow missionaries were able to carry on their work openly in the provinces, and by 1610, the date of Ricci's death, Christianity had obtained in the empire a position even stronger, perhaps, than that which it had held during the Mongol regime.

The Jesuit influence at Peking, thus established by Ricci, was maintained by other able members of the order. About twenty years after Ricci's death Adam Schall, who had arrived in China in 1619, was called to Peking as head of the mission there. Schall rose to a position even more influential than that attained by Ricci. Appointed by the Ming emperor to a post in the Bureau of Astronomy, he served with such distinction that after the fall of the Ming dynasty he was continued in the office by the Manchu conquerors. The new rulers of China also extended their favor to the religious work of the order; and the Jesuits, who hitherto had possessed only a small private chapel for their services in Peking, received from the first Manchu emperor a gift of land and money for the erection of a church.

Hardly had the Spanish established themselves firmly in the Philippines when their missionaries began to press across the China Sea to gain a foothold in the great empire on the mainland. As early as 1575 an Augustinian friar from the Philippines found his way to the coast of Fukien, but he was quickly sent back to Manila by the local officials. During the next half-century unsuccessful attempts to open religious work in China were made by the Franciscans, the Augustinians, and the Dominicans of the Philippines.

In addition to the difficulties presented by the Chinese officials, who were constantly on the alert to arrest and deport the uninvited emissaries of the Gospel, the Spanish missionaries had to face the jealous opposition of their Jesuit predecessors in the field. The Jesuits, who had begun their work in China under the auspices of the Portuguese crown, claimed that Alexander VI's Bull of Demarcation held for spiritual affairs as well as for commerce and that the Christianization of heathen lands lying in Portugal's half of the world was the exclusive privilege of the order expressly authorized by the Portuguese king to undertake this task. On an appeal to the papal curia this claim was upheld, and it was not until 1633 that a modification of the papal decision made it lawful for the Franciscans and Dominicans to enter China from Spain by way of Mexico and the Philippines.

Despite this twofold opposition the Spanish missionaries eventually established themselves on Chinese soil. In 1630 two Dominicans, expelled from Formosa by the Dutch, made their way to the neighboring mainland province of Fukien, where they later were joined by Dominican and Franciscan recruits from the Philippines and from Spain. By the end of the Ming regime the Dominicans and the Franciscans were firmly established in Fukien, and soon after the Manchu conquest the Fukien mission was strong enough to found prosperous branches in the province of Shantung.

The last decade of the sixteenth century saw the Ming empire engaged in repelling the Japanese invasion of Korea, its first serious military undertaking since the days of the warlike Yung Lo. Although the failure of Hideyoshi's disastrous undertaking was attributable in part to the naval superiority of the Korean fleet under Admiral Yih Sun-sin, it was also due in part to the intervention of China. The Chinese government responded with unusual promptitude to its vassal's appeal for aid against the invaders. The Japanese forces landed at Fusan on May 25, 1592, and by the beginning of October a hastily gathered Chinese army of five thousand men crossed the Yalu. This weak detachment was ambushed and cut to pieces by the Japanese, but in less than a year a well-organized Chinese army of fifty thousand soldiers had forced the Japanese to withdraw southward to their base of operations at Fusan. In May, 1593, just a year after their first landing, the Japanese commanders agreed to a truce, and during the three-year negotiation which ensued their forces were concentrated around Fusan. In 1596 Hideyoshi broke off negotiations and recommenced the war, which dragged on until after his death in September, 1598. In their campaigns against the Japanese the Chinese soldiers showed themselves little, if at all, inferior to the war-hardened veterans of Hideyoshi's armies, while the Chinese commanders appear to have displayed military ability quite equal to that of the picked Japanese leaders.

The Manchu Conquest of China

Even before the outbreak of the war with Japan threatening developments were beginning in the far north. Throughout the entire period of Ming rule the Tartar peoples beyond the Great Wall had been a source of danger for the Chinese Empire. The early Ming rulers had established their authority over the southern portions of the great region now known as Manchuria, but in the northern portions, between the Amur River and the present line of the North Manchuria Railway, no attempt had been made to establish Chinese control. During the last quarter of the sixteenth century a Tartar tribe, the Manchus, whose early home appears to have been in the valley of the Hurka River (a branch of the Sungari), began to extend its authority over the neighboring peoples of northern Manchuria. Descendants of the Kin Tartars, who had ruled northeastern China for a century before their overthrow by Genghis Khan, the Manchus were far from being barbarians; their ancestors had been deeply influenced by Chinese civilization, and they themselves during the intervening centuries had been in close contact with peoples living nearer the frontiers of the empire.

Under capable leaders the Manchus steadily extended their power. After uniting under their rule the hitherto disunited tribes of northern Manchuria they pushed southward and occupied all the Liaotung region, the area lying east of the Liao River. In 1606 their ruler, Nurhachu, assumed the imperial title. Although this assumption of a title identical with that of the Chinese ruler might indicate that a conflict between the two powers was inevitable, there existed at this date no grounds for war between the Chinese and the rising power in the north. Such grounds, however, were not slow in appearing. China's south-Manchurian vassals to the west of the Liao River, having been attacked by the Manchus, appealed to their suzerain for protection. In response to this appeal the Chinese sent to their assistance an armed force which, though insufficient to check the advance of the Manchu power, served to arouse in the Manchu leader bitter hostility toward the rulers of China.

In 1618 Nurhachu issued a formal declaration of war against the Ming dynasty, accompanying this declaration by a list of grievances, seven in number, which he and his people had suffered at the hands of the Chinese. Within a short time the Manchu forces had succeeded in conquering all the Ming vassals in Manchuria and in overrunning all Chinese territory north of the Great Wall. From time to time a few of Nurhachu's raiding bodies succeeded in making their way through poorly guarded passages in the ancient barrier, and these spread devastation in portions of the northern provinces; but the triumphal progress of his main army was definitely checked at this point.

Dying in 1626, Nurhachu was succeeded by his son,—commonly known by his *nien hao* "T'ai Tsung,"—who established his capital at Mukden and bestowed upon the Manchu dynasty the official designation of "Ta Ch'ing" ("Great Pure"). Throughout the reign of Nurhachu the Koreans, loyal to their Ming suzerain, had been able to give valuable aid to the Chinese; but in 1627 Korea was invaded by the Manchu armies, and the Korean king was forced to transfer his allegiance to the new dynasty at Mukden. The second Manchu emperor also extended his power toward the northwest, bringing under his rule the hitherto unconquered tribes of western Manchuria and even some parts of eastern Mongolia. Despite these successes outside the Great Wall and despite the obvious military weakness of the Ming organization the Manchus were still unable to gain a firm foothold inside the territories of the empire. Even though China was now torn by internal revolts and Peking had become a hotbed of political intrigue, a strong Chinese army at Shanhaikuan ("Mountain-Sea Gate"), where the mountains reinforced by the Wall come down to the edge of the sea, effectively held the Manchu conquerors at bay until 1644.

As early as 1621 the occurrence of popular outbreaks in various parts of the empire gave evidence that the Ming government was beginning to lose the respect and support of the nation and that the "mandate of Heaven" was about to be withdrawn from the descendants of Hung Wu. The unusual burden of taxation caused by the long military operations, first against the Japanese and then against the Manchus, the widespread destruction of property by Manchu raids in the northern provinces, and the unfortunate coincidence of severe droughts in a number of regions, all combined to cause widespread suffering and discontent. Riots and local uprisings, first appearing in the districts at a distance from Peking, gradually increased in intensity and spread toward the capital. Brigand leaders, recruiting their forces from the thousands of desperate and homeless men of the famine-affected regions, were able to become the actual rulers over large areas, while the authorities at Peking, occupied with the war against the Manchus, dared not withdraw troops from the northern frontier to deal with these marauders.

The most powerful of the robber chieftains produced by this state of turmoil was Li Tzu-ch'eng, who in 1637 was strong enough or bold enough to attempt the capture of the capital of Szechwan. Repulsed from the walls of Chengtu, Li retreated into Hukuang (the vice-royalty comprising Hupeh and Hunan); later he made his way through Szechwan into Shensi, and in 1640 he entered Honan at the head of a powerful army. By the beginning of 1642 Li had established his authority over all of Honan Province south of the Yellow River and had invaded the neighboring province of Shansi. In 1643, at Sianfu, the ancient capital of the T'ang dynasty, he boldly assumed the imperial title; proclaiming that the Ming dynasty had lost the "mandate of Haven," he now decided to lead his forces against Peking.

While the rebel "emperor" was advancing upon the capital at the head of an army three hundred thousand strong, the council of the unfortunate Ming sovereign was torn by intrigue and conflicting opinions. In the capital were a hundred and fifty thousand soldiers, easily capable of defending the massive walls against attack, while at Shanhaikuan lay a well-organized army under Wu San-kuei, the ablest general in the imperial service. Two safe courses of action were open. The army at Shanhaikuan could be recalled and combined with the forces at Peking to meet the rebel in the open field, or the capital could be defended against attack until Wu San-kuei moved down from his post to take the besiegers in the rear. But Wu San-kuei had bitter enemies in the capital, who were jealous of his achievements and were determined that no opportunity should be afforded him to gain fresh distinction; so it was decided to meet the enemy in the field with the forces then at Peking. Other court jealousies caused the division of the Peking troops into two armies under rival commanders. The two forces naturally failed to co-operate. One was decisively beaten, while a large portion of the other force ignominiously laid down its arms; and on the "18th day of the 3rd moon," 1644, Li Tzu-ch'eng, arriving at the gates of Peking, summoned the emperor to abdicate the throne. Deserted by the officials whose jealous intrigues had caused his ruin, the emperor Ch'ung Cheng died by his own hand, and Li Tzu-ch'eng entered the capital to establish himself for a brief period upon the imperial throne.

While the fate of Peking and of the Ming dynasty was trembling in the balance, Wu San-kuei, in obedience to his orders, remained at Shanhaikuan. After the fall of Peking he summoned the Manchus to his assistance and marched upon the capital to avenge his sovereign and to drive the usurper from the throne. With the support of the Manchus, only too willingly given, the rebel army was defeated; and Li Tzu-ch'eng with a fragment of his forces retreated into the western provinces, where he was finally captured and put to death. Wu San-kuei now naïvely suggested to his northern allies that they withdraw to their own territories, but the Manchus had no intention of restoring the Mings to their lost throne. They had been welcomed at Peking as saviors of the country, and their armies were in possession of the city. They now transferred their capital from Mukden to Peking and, placing their own prince upon the Dragon Throne, proclaimed him emperor of China as well as Manchuria.

Up to this point the actions of Wu San-kuei had been such as to command approval. Now, however, he took a step which earned for him the condemnation of Chinese historians as one of the great traitors in the history of his country. Convinced of the hopelessness of the Ming cause, Wu definitely allied himself with the Manchus, whom he regarded as the one faction capable of setting up an orderly government, and rendered them valuable service by bringing about the peaceful submission of the western and southwestern provinces. In recognition of this service the Manchu government rewarded their useful ally by appointing him to rule as viceroy over the provinces which he pacified.

When the Ming capital fell into the hands of the rebel Li Tzuch'eng, several princes of the imperial family succeeded in making their escape to the south, where for almost six years they kept up a losing struggle against the southward advance of the Manchu invaders. First at Nanking, then at Hangchow, and finally at Canton, six Ming emperors followed each other in rapid succession. But province after province submitted to the Manchu sway, and in 1647 the city of Canton was taken by the northern conquerors. After the fall of Canton a Ming prince gathered adherents in Kwangsi and Yunnan, and in the following year several other provinces rallied to his cause. By the end of 1650, however, the conquest of China may be regarded as completed. A few loyal supporters of the old dynasty still continued the struggle on sea, but on land practically all resistance to the Manchu rule had been overcome.

In addition to Wu San-kuei many other Chinese officials had attached themselves at an early date to the Manchu cause, and the support of these Chinese officials was largely responsible for the rapidity with which the conquerors were able to extend their control over the whole empire. Partly because of this prompt adherence of a large part of Chinese officialdom and partly because of their own appreciation of the political institutions which had grown up in China, the Manchus retained practically unchanged the old traditional methods of government. No changes were made in the fundamental laws, the Manchu code—the "Ta Ch'ing Lü Li"—being practically a reissue of the earlier Ming code. No increase was made in the extremely light burden of taxation imposed upon the people. The old system of official examinations was maintained; and a majority of even the highest provincial offices continued to be held by Chinese officers, while in the great administrative boards at Peking an even balance between Manchu and Chinese officials was carefully maintained. As far as the people were concerned, two facts alone gave evidence that there had been a change of dynasties: the wearing of the queue, the Manchu style of headdress, was imposed as a symbol of loyalty, and bodies of Manchu troops were stationed permanently at a number of strategically located cities as a precaution against any attempted rebellion.

While the new rulers of the empire maintained the old institutions of government and endeavored to secure for their rule the moral sanction without which no Chinese dynasty has ever enjoyed a long tenure of the throne, they also brought to the administration of affairs an energy which had been lacking during the last century, and the imperial capital was purged of many of the corruptions which had grown up under the later Ming rulers. In comparison with the pomp and luxury of their predecessors the early Manchu rulers maintained a court of almost Spartan simplicity, and the saving effected by this economy in court expenditure sufficed for the support of the resident garrison forces. The banditry which had grown up during the period of disorder was promptly suppressed, respect for the new government was imposed upon the peoples on the frontiers, and China for the greater part of a century and a half enjoyed an administration which was both efficient and in accordance with ancient traditions.

Shun Chih, the first Manchu emperor of China, held the imperial power for seventeen years. The greater part of this reign was occupied in extending the power of the Manchus over the empire and in adjusting satisfactorily the relations between victors and vanquished. Aside from these tasks of internal organization the most important event of the reign was the arrival at Peking in March, 1656, of the first embassy from Russia. Although the Russian envoys were given an honorable reception, the Manchu emperor's insistence upon the recognition of his universal sovereignty prevented the conclusion of any agreement between the two empires.

In 1661 Shun Chih was succeeded upon the throne by his eight-year-old son, who assumed the *nien hao* "K'ang Hsi." Because of the extreme youth of his heir the dying emperor had created a board of regents composed of four high Manchu officials; this board carried on the government during the first six years of the new reign; but in 1667, although he was only fourteen years of age, the boy emperor took the power into his own hands.

Reigning for sixty-one years over the largest and most populous empire in the world, K'ang Hsi must be regarded as one of the great rulers in world history. Even as a young boy this second Manchu occupant of the Dragon Throne gave ample evidence of his unusual character and applied himself with equal diligence to the military exercises of the Manchus and to the literary studies of the Chinese. Throughout his long reign this twofold activity of body and mind was continued. As a warrior he measured up to the standards which had been set by his warlike ancestors; as a scholar he could meet on a footing of equality the most learned among his Chinese subjects. With his scholarship, moreover, the emperor combined a remarkably open mind on all intellectual topics. Although he regarded the philosophy of Confucius as the best rule of life, he respected the different religious beliefs of the people under his sway; and for many years the Christian missionaries at Peking enjoyed repeated evidences of his favor. K'ang Hsi's toleration of Christianity during the greater part of his reign was merely a phase of his general religious policy, but his extensions of imperial favor to the individual missionaries arose out of a scholar's appreciation of scholarship in others. The aged Adam Schall, who died five years after K'ang Hsi's accession to the throne; Verbiest, whom he appointed in 1669 to the Bureau of Astronomy; Gerbillon and Bouvet, with whom he discussed arithmetic and geometry,—all these and many others of the scholarly Jesuits stationed at Peking were men after the emperor's own heart, men whose talents he was always ready to use and to honor.

After the capture of Canton and the overthrow of the Ming cause in the western provinces, the authority of the Manchu emperor was recognized throughout the entire continental area of the empire. Upon the sea, however, where the Manchus were less powerful than on land, the adherents of the old dynasty continued their armed opposition to the new occupants of the throne. By the time of K'ang Hsi's accession the maritime opposition to the Manchu government had become organized under the leadership of the famous pirate-patriot Cheng Ch'eng-kung, better known as Koxinga (1623–1662). This remarkable man, the son of a Japanese mother and of a Fukienese naval freebooter who had lived at both Macao and Manila, took up arms against the Manchus in 1646.

For fifteen years Koxinga was able to maintain along the island-studded coast of Fukien Province a number of bases of operations, from which he carried on depredations along the entire coast between Macao and the mouth of the Yangtze. In order to deprive the pirate of his means of subsistence the Manchu government finally decreed the removal of all the coast population from a strip of land ten miles wide, while the imperial forces, aided by the Dutch, succeeded in destroying several of his Fukienese strongholds. In 1661, therefore, Koxinga led his forces against the island of Formosa, which since 1630 had been under Dutch rule. After a siege of about nine months the Dutch garrisons capitulated, and Koxinga found himself master of the island. This success against the Europeans immediately inspired him with an ambition to extend his dominion southward over the Spanish-ruled Philippines, and in May, 1662, he dispatched to Manila the Dominican missionary Victor Ricci as his ambassador to demand the submission of the Philippines. Koxinga's demand drew a defiant answer from the Spanish governor at Manila, and frenzied efforts were made to put Manila in a state of defense against the expected invasion. The dreaded attack never came. Before the return of his ambassador Koxinga had died, and the sole result of his ambitious project was the slaughter of thousands of innocent Chinese residents of the Philippines, massacred for fear that they might join hands with the invader and aid him in the attempt to conquer the islands.

For nineteen years after Koxinga's death his son ruled Formosa and defeated every attempt by the Dutch and the Manchus to reconquer it. In 1681 this son died; two years later Koxinga's grandson finally submitted to the emperor and received as reward the title of Duke.

Even more serious than this long struggle against Koxinga and his descendants was the series of outbreaks against Manchu rule in the second decade of K'ang Hsi's reign, precipitated by the revolt of the aged Wu San-kuei. As a reward for valuable services in bringing about the submission of the southwestern provinces to Manchu authority Shun Chih had bestowed upon Wu the title "Prince Pacifier of the West" and had placed under his rule the two provinces of Szechwan and Yunnan. Although the eldest son of Wu had taken up his residence at Peking as a hostage for his father's loyalty, the Manchu government came to entertain suspicions on this point; and in 1672 K'ang Hsi ordered his powerful vassal to proceed in person to the capital and do homage. Warned by his son of the hostility of the Manchu authorities, Wu San-kuei excused himself on the ground of age and requested that his son be permitted to do homage in his stead. When in the following year the demand for his personal appearance at Peking was repeated, Wu decided that the emperor was determined to destroy him. He therefore renounced his allegiance, resumed the Chinese costume, forbade the use of the imperial calendar in his provinces, and took the field in open revolt. The revolt of the powerful "Prince of the West" was the signal for a similar revolt by the Chinese governors of Kwangtung and Fukien, while almost simultaneously the recently subjugated Mongols on the northern frontier rose against their Manchu rulers.

In the face of these widespread outbreaks the young emperor acted with promptness and energy. All the available troops in northern China were led against the Mongol rebels, who were quickly reduced to submission. With the danger in the north removed, K'ang Hsi now sent his forces into the southern provinces, where the rebellious rulers, divided by internal jealousies, were conquered in detail. Only after the suppression of these minor disturbances were the imperial armies turned against the aged precipitator of all this trouble. Wu San-kuei was able to avoid a decisive defeat, but his forces were driven back into the provinces originally under his rule. With his death, in the fall of 1678, the revolt collapsed, and by 1685 peace had been restored throughout the empire.

During the last century of the Ming regime the Chinese government had adopted a policy of strict supervision over Europeans and had permitted them to carry on trade only at the port of Canton. For forty-one years after their seizure of the imperial power the Manchus continued this policy of restriction; but the liberal-minded K'ang Hsi had no fear of the Europeans, and he was firmly convinced that China would be greatly benefited by the increase of commercial intercourse with the outside world. With the restoration of peace in 1685 he repealed the old Ming restrictions and threw open to foreign trade all the ports of China.

K'ang Hsi's liberal attitude toward the Westerners was undoubtedly influenced by the contacts which he had had with many of the missionaries at Peking and by the valuable services which these men had rendered to his government. These services had been particularly valuable during his desperate struggle against the recent revolts, when Verbiest, in response to the emperor's commands, turned his scientific abilities to military account and provided the imperial armies with much-needed weapons.

During the years immediately following the adoption of a liberal commercial policy the missionaries continued to render useful service to the imperial government, and in March, 1692, these services were frankly recognized in the following imperial decree:

The members of the Ministry of Rites, after deliberation, have previously proposed to Us to maintain the ancient churches of the Catholic religion and to permit the men of the west [the missionaries] the exercise of their religion; We have already agreed to this proposal. At present these men, after having corrected the calculation of the calendar and having, at the moment of the war [against Wu San-kuei], repaired the old cannon and manufactured new ones, employing their energies for the Empire and giving themselves much trouble, have recently accompanied the military expedition against the Russians, and in the final arrangement of this affair [the negotiation of the Treaty of Nerchinsk (see page 492)] they deserve well of the Empire. Moreover there is in the conduct of the missionaries nothing bad or improper. If, therefore, their religion is treated as a perverse sect and its practice prohibited, this will be the infliction of punishment upon the innocent. Do you members of the Privy Council therefore meet with those of the Ministry of Rites, deliberate upon this matter, and present Us with a report.

The ultimate loss by the missionaries of the high imperial favor expressed in the above decree may be attributed in large measure to disputes between the Jesuits and the later missionary arrivals on several points, two of which were particularly important: the question of the proper term in the Chinese language for *God*, and the question whether Chinese Christians should be permitted to observe their ancestral rites and the rites in honor of Confucius. On both these points Matteo Ricci had taken a position which he believed would facilitate the spread of the Christian faith among the scholarly and official element in the empire. For *God* he used the terms *T'ien* ("Heaven") and *Shang Ti* ("Supreme Being"), expressions frequently used in the Chinese Classics, and he took the stand that the ancestral and Confucian sacrifices, having no religious connotation, might properly be performed by Christians. The non-Jesuit missionaries, who had begun to arrive in the empire before the fall of the Ming dynasty, took immediate exception to the Jesuit stand on these questions; and the controversy raged with increasing intensity throughout the second half of the seventeenth century.

As a Confucian scholar and as a friend of the Jesuits, K'ang Hsi naturally took the side of the Jesuits in the dispute; but the authorities at Rome, after first approving the policy of Ricci and his successors, finally decided in favor of their opponents and forbade the continuance of the Jesuit policy in regard both to nomenclature and to rites. Angered at the decision and determined to curb the spread within his domains of a religion whose teachers accepted the dictation of a foreign potentate, K'ang Hsi, in December, 1706, decreed that all missionaries who wished to remain in the empire must secure an imperial permit and that such permits should be granted only to those missionaries who adhered to the practices of Matteo Ricci.

The imperial disfavor which resulted from the stand taken by the papal authorities in the rites controversy was soon intensified by the activities of European merchants along the Chinese coast. Many of those who came to the ports of China for the purposes of trade were men who thought little of violating the laws of their own land, and such visitors could hardly be expected to show much regard for the sovereign rights of a foreign country. The continued activity of the missionaries in defiance of the decree of 1706, the steady increase in the number of foreign ships arriving at Chinese ports, and the unruly character of the foreigners all combined to awaken the fears and suspicions of the government officials.

In 1717 these suspicions were clearly and energetically expressed in a report submitted to the throne by a military officer stationed at Canton. This officer emphasized the close connection which had existed in the Philippines and in Japan between the European governments and their merchants and missionaries. Therefore, in order to safeguard the empire against the danger of invasion, he urged the emperor to issue a decree against the further spread of Christianity and to revive the regulations for the restriction of foreign trade.

The Grand Council of State, to which this report was submitted for consideration, approved the recommendations, and the emperor took action as suggested. Trade was again restricted to Canton and Macao, where it was to be carried on under new and more rigid restrictions. At the same time a fresh decree was issued against further teaching of the Christian religion; all missionaries except those who had received special permission to remain in the country were to be arrested and sent to Macao for deportation.

Although the new regulations with regard to trade were promptly enforced, K'ang Hsi's anti-Christian decree of 1717, like the anti-Christian decree issued a hundred and thirty years earlier by the Japanese Hideyoshi, was intended primarily as a warning to the missionaries. So long as they and their converts refrained from political activity, they were allowed to dwell in peace; but any Christians who created disturbances in the country and thus brought themselves to the attention of the authorities were liable henceforth to be treated as outlaws and punished with extreme severity.

K'ang Hsi's decree of 1717, re-establishing trade restrictions and forbidding the free propagation of Christianity, marked the close of almost exactly two centuries of contact between China and the maritime countries of western Europe. During a century and a quarter of Ming rule and during three quarters of a century of

Manchu rule the merchants from the West had frequented the coast of China, while the Christian missionaries, arriving later, had gradually pushed their way into all parts of the empire. At the first arrival of the Europeans the authorities of the Ming empire extended to them a friendly welcome, while K'ang Hsi, a century and a half later, adopted the policy of fostering and encouraging trade with the West. The emissaries of Christianity, although less favorably received at first, also succeeded in winning the favor and respect of the Ming emperors and of their Manchu successors. By the end of the two centuries, however, the great Manchu ruler, like his Ming predecessors, had adopted the policy of restricting European commerce to the port of Canton and had withdrawn from the Christian missionaries much of his earlier favor.

Between these two centuries of Chinese experience with the Europeans and the shorter period of Japan's open-door policy there are certain interesting resemblances. In each country the newcomers met at first a favorable reception; in each the development of commerce was for a while encouraged and fostered by the government; in each the eventual decision to impose drastic restrictions upon the foreigner was the result of political rather than religious considerations.

Equally interesting, however, are the points of dissimilarity. Whereas Japan during her century of experience with European intercourse was transformed from almost complete anarchy into a strong state under a military dictatorship, China at the beginning, as at the end, of the two centuries under consideration was held together and governed by an essentially civil administration. In Japan the spread of Christianity appears to have been closely connected with the desire of the local rulers to cultivate foreign trade; in China, on the other hand, such success as the missionaries attained was attributable in large measure to the scholarship of their earlier representatives, and the development of commerce was detrimental rather than beneficial to their religious propaganda. Finally, the Chinese welcomed the European merchant and missionary with less enthusiasm than did the Japanese—and reacted against them with less violence. After 1640 the Japanese systematically exterminated Christianity and barred their gates for more than two centuries against all foreign contacts save the little Dutch factory on the island of Deshima. In China also, after 1717, maritime trade was restricted to a single port; but here the merchants of every Western country were allowed to carry on commerce, while the Russians in Siberia had a flourishing caravan trade overland to Peking. At the same time, in spite of the formal outlawry of Christianity, mission work was carried on with little hindrance in every province of the empire, while individual missionaries continued throughout the eighteenth century to be employed by the imperial government.

SUGGESTED REFERENCES

BADDELY, J. F. Russia, Mongolia, China . . . 1602–1676.

CAHEN, G. Histoire des relations de la Russie avec la Chine sous Pierre le Grand (1689–1730).

HSIEH, P. C. The Government of China (1644–1911).

LATOURETTE, K. S. The Chinese: their History and Culture.

LATOURETTE, K. S. A History of Christian Missions in China.

MAYERS, W. F. The Chinese Government.

MORSE, H. B. The Gilds of China.

STAUNTON, SIR G. T. (translator). Tu-li-shin's Narrative of the Chinese Embassy to the Khan of the Tourgouth Tartars.

WILLIAMS, E. T. A Short History of China.

XIX

The Dutch, English, and French in the Far East

The Rise of Dutch and English Sea Power · Dutch Voyages to the East · The
Dutch East India Company · The London East India Company · Early Voyages
of the English Company · Nature of the Dutch and English Trade · From Trade
to Empire-building · Anglo-Dutch Co-operation and Rivalry · The Dutch and
the English in Indo-China · Dutch Control of the East Indies · The Dutch-
Portuguese Struggle · Rule of the Dutch East India Company · Oppression and
Misgovernment · Decline and End of the Company · The Dutch East Indies
under the Rule of the Crown · The Growth of British India · The First English
Factories in India · Bombay · The Arrival of the French in the Far East · Decline
of the Mogul Empire · Aurangzeb · Sivaji and the Rise of the Marathas · The
English Company and the Moguls · The Anglo-French Duel for the Control of
India · Clive and Dupleix · The East India Company as a Territorial Sovereign ·
Parliamentary Regulations (1773–1853) · Wars of the East India Company · Na-
ture of the Company's Rule · End of the East India Company · European Rivalries
in Indo-China · Siamese-Dutch Treaty of 1664 · Constantine Faulkon and the
French in Siam · Siam in the Nineteenth Century · Seventeenth-Century Burma ·
Reunification of Burma · British Expansion into Burma · Singapore and the
Malay States · Annam in the Seventeenth and Eighteenth Centuries · Gia Long
and the Unification of Annam · The Beginnings of French Indo-China

FOR just a century after the voyage of Vasco da Gama the
Portuguese and the Spanish shared a practical monopoly of sea
trade with and in the Far East. In the newly discovered continents
across the Atlantic the effective enforcement of exclusive rights
was a physical impossibility; in the Pacific and Indian Ocean
area, however, the exclusion of European rivals was less difficult.
Along the coast of Africa, from Cape Verde to Mombasa, the Portuguese held a chain of naval bases from which their cruisers were
able to protect against trespass by non-Portuguese merchants the
route discovered by Vasco da Gama. The westward route to the
Far East, thrown open by the voyage of Magellan, was less carefully policed than was that around Africa, but the difficulties of this
route were so great as to render it commercially impracticable to
any ships except those of the Spanish.

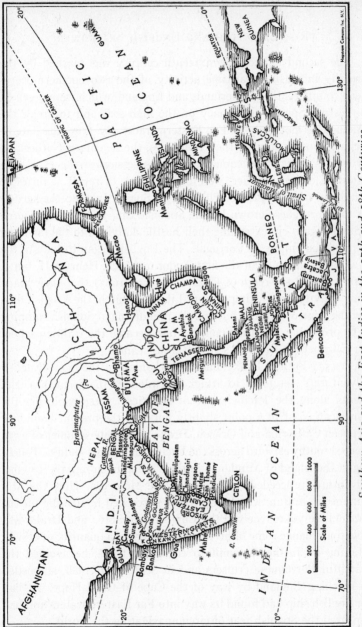

Southern Asia and the East Indies in the 17th and 18th Centuries

Rise of Dutch and English Sea Power

The second half of the sixteenth century was marked by the steadily increasing maritime activity of the two northern European countries, the Netherlands and England, which were destined to destroy Spain's supremacy on the high seas and to break the Portuguese monopoly of Far Eastern trade. By 1565, the date of Legaspi's occupation of the Philippines, the seventeen Netherland provinces, which had come into the possession of the Hapsburg family a century earlier, were on the verge of revolt against the authority of their prince, Philip II of Spain. In 1580 the seizure of the Portuguese crown by the Spanish king justified the Dutch "Sea Beggars" in extending their hostile activities to the far-flung commercial empire of Portugal. The English began to take to the sea during the reign of the first Tudor monarch, Henry VII, but it was not until the reign of Elizabeth (1558–1603) that their maritime activity became important. Like the Dutch, the English during the reign of Elizabeth found the plundering of Spanish shipping very profitable, and the Spanish Main became the training school for Elizabethan England's adventurous seamen.

In 1577 Francis Drake, one of the boldest of the many English adventurers, set forth to attack and plunder the Spanish settlements along the Pacific coast of America. After exploring the American coast to a point slightly north of the present boundary between California and Oregon, Drake in the late summer of 1579 steered southwestward across the Pacific to the East Indies. Touching at the island of Mindanao in the Philippine group, the English adventurer proceeded to Ternate in the Moluccas. Here the Mohammedan Sultan, who had recently succeeded in shaking off the Portuguese yoke, received the English favorably; and Drake was able to exchange some of his Spanish silver for a quantity of cloves. Making no further attempt to engage in trade, he avoided the watchful Portuguese cruisers and in September, 1580, succeeded in reaching England by way of the Cape of Good Hope. At last an English ship had found its way into Far Eastern waters and had repeated the Spanish feat of circumnavigating the world.

Slightly less than six years after Drake's return to England,

Thomas Cavendish, in June, 1586, sailed from London on a similar voyage. Off the west coast of Mexico he fell in with and captured the great Manila galleon *Santa Anna*. Leaving the coast of Mexico in November, 1587, Cavendish crossed the Pacific. On January third he sighted the island of Guam, and twelve days later he reached the Philippines. From here he sailed southward through the Strait of Macassar and the Strait of Lombok; then, after cruising along the southern coast of Java, he crossed the Indian Ocean and rounded the Cape of Good Hope, arriving finally at Plymouth on September 10, 1588.

Seven weeks before Cavendish dropped anchor at Plymouth the Invincible Armada of Philip II had entered the English Channel bent on the conquest of the troublesome island kingdom. The brilliant victory of the English against this mighty armament did more than merely save their country from foreign invasion: it destroyed for all time the vaunted supremacy of Spain upon the high seas and inspired the English henceforth to take to the sea in ever increasing numbers.

Although a squadron of three English ships visited the East Indies in 1591–1594, England's maritime adventurers after 1588 continued for more than a decade to seek their fortunes by preying upon Spanish shipping; and it was left to their Dutch neighbors to make the first serious inroads upon Portugal's spice-trade monopoly. In April, 1595, four Dutch ships under the command of Cornelis van Houtman, who had secured at Lisbon valuable information concerning the Indian trade, sailed from Amsterdam for the Indies. This squadron returned to Holland in August, 1597, and the following spring saw the dispatch of eight fresh ships from Amsterdam and five from the ports of Zeeland. At the same time the merchants of Rotterdam fitted out five ships[1] and dispatched them to the Moluccas by way of the Strait of Magellan. A second Rotterdam squadron, consisting of four ships under Oliver van Noort, sailed in July of the same year, also by the westward route. The two Rotterdam enterprises were not successful as commercial ventures; but one ship out of each squadron

[1] It was on one of these Rotterdam ships, the *Liefde*, that the Englishman Will Adams in the spring of 1600 reached Japan.

succeeded in accomplishing the circumnavigation of the world, and each of these brought back to the Netherlands valuable information concerning the geography of the Far East.

In 1599 the original Amsterdam company of merchants dispatched eleven ships to the Indies, three before the return of their 1598 squadron and eight later, while a new group of merchants of the same city entered the trade by fitting out a venture of four ships. The three ships sent out in the spring of 1599 returned to Amsterdam in the summer of 1601. Besides making a prosperous voyage this squadron had erected and garrisoned a trading-post on the island of Amboyna, which thus became the first Dutch stronghold in the East Indies.

Within seven years after the dispatch of the first four ships under Van Houtman so many rival companies had been formed and so many ships were being sent out for trade with the Indies that there was danger of ruinous competition among the Dutch themselves. In order to guard against this danger the Estates-General of the Netherlands, on March 20, 1602, granted a charter and a twenty-one-year monopoly of Far Eastern trade to a single company. The company was empowered to enter into treaties and agreements with the rulers and peoples of the Indies, to build forts, to establish governors, and to maintain troops and law courts for the preservation of peace and order.

By the terms of the charter every citizen of the United Provinces was entitled to take stock in the company, and the enthusiasm for the Eastern trade was so great that before the end of the year the total amount of capital invested had reached the sum of 6,459,840 florins. Nor was the enthusiasm of the Dutch investors misplaced. In 1605 the company paid a dividend of 15 per cent, and this modest beginning was followed by dividends of 75 per cent in 1606, 40 per cent in 1607, 20 per cent in 1608, 25 per cent in 1609, and 50 per cent in 1610—a total of 225 per cent in six years, or an average of $37\frac{1}{2}$ per cent per annum. The original twenty-one years of the company's charter were extended by appropriate action of the Estates-General at the necessary intervals of time, and the prosperity of the company continued down to the third quarter of the eighteenth century. In 1723 the company's shares, representing an actual investment of 840 florins, were valued at 22,000 florins each; and even in 1774, when mismanagement and corruption had greatly reduced the company's prosperity, its shares sold for more than 13,000 florins each.

After the unpropitious voyage of 1591–1594 the English merchants did not again appear in Far Eastern waters until 1601, when five ships were sent out by the "Governor and Company of Merchants of London Trading into the East Indies." This organization, more commonly known as the London East India Company, had been formed for the purpose of rendering England independent of the Dutch for their spices, and on December 31, 1600, it had received from the queen a charter granting it for a period of fifteen years exclusive rights to trade in the regions of the Far East. The company thus created continued for a hundred and eight years, under charters granted by Elizabeth's successors, to dominate English trade with the Far East. Toward the end of this period the company was forced to struggle against a rival body of English merchants known as "The English Company Trading to the East Indies," but in 1708, by a charter issued by Queen Anne, the two rivals were amalgamated to form "The United Company of Merchants of England Trading to the East Indies." Under the first and last of these companies English chartered trade in the Far East had a continuous history for two hundred and fifty-eight years, and it is convenient—if not wholly accurate—to refer indiscriminately to both, during this long period of activity, as the English East India Company.

Unlike their Dutch rivals, who from the organization of their company carried on their operations on a "joint-stock" basis according to which every shareholder had a proportionate interest in the outcome of every venture, the merchants of the English company at first carried on their trade by "separate voyages"; each voyage was a separate venture in which each member of the company invested as much or as little as he wished, and on the return of each voyage the proceeds were divided among the participants in proportion to their respective investments. Not until 1613, after twelve separate voyages had been undertaken, did the English company become, like the Dutch, a joint-stock organization.

These first twelve years of the company's operations, which may be compared with the Dutch activities from 1595 to 1602, were years of exploration and of prospecting. Most of the voyages, like those of the Dutch company, had as their objective the islands of the East Indies, and the profitable nature of the trade is illustrated by the fact that the third voyage, undertaken in 1606–1609 by three ships, paid the subscribing merchants a profit of 234 per cent. In addition to trading in the East Indies, however, the English during this experimental stage of their Eastern commerce investigated the possibilities of the Red Sea and the Persian Gulf, and the tenth voyage, undertaken in 1612, led to the establishment of permanent "factories" (trading posts) on the coast of India.

It was the establishment of permanent factories, quite as much as the growing confidence in the profitable nature of the trade, that led to the change from separate voyages to joint-stock operation. As early as 1607 a factory had been established at Bantam, in Java, and ten Englishmen were left there to accumulate by trading operations a supply of goods for shipment to England. With the establishment of trading posts it became more and more difficult to keep separate the affairs of the different voyages, and joint-stock management of the company's business became necessary.

Seventeenth-century Europe, with the Industrial Revolution nearly two centuries away in the future, produced very little exportable surplus; and the Dutch and the English, when they began their trade in the Indies, could bring from their home countries comparatively few commodities to exchange for the products of the East. To a certain extent this scarcity of European exports was made good by the existence in Europe of an unusual quantity of gold and silver, then pouring in from Spanish America; but the two East India companies, even so, were compelled to find other means of maintaining the balance of trade between East and West. In the absence of adequate material exports the commodities of the Orient were paid for by "invisible" exports.

The most legitimate of these invisible exports took the form of a carrying trade between the several Oriental countries. Plying between the islands of the archipelago and the ports of India, Indo-China, Japan, and China, the European merchants accumulated profits sufficient to load their homeward-bound ships with cargoes from whose sale in European markets the shareholders would receive their dividends. This legitimate enterprise was profitably supplemented by "exporting" to the Orient the international rivalries and jealousies of European origin. Taking advantage of the fact that Portugal was under the rule of the Spanish king, whom the Dutch and the English still regarded as their bitter enemy, the two companies treated Portuguese ships, wherever found, as enemy property, capturing and condemning them as prizes of war. To these acts of war or piracy the Portuguese, when in a position to do so, replied in kind, and the governments of both Japan and China were compelled to employ force to prevent the use of their territories or territorial waters as stages upon which the Europeans might carry on their private quarrels.

Nor was it only against their European rivals that the Dutch and English traders made use of armed force to guarantee to themselves satisfactory profits from their carrying trade. Like the Portuguese whom they were now displacing, the new Europeans found that the peoples of the Orient—the Hindus, the Malays, the Siamese, the Annamese, the Chinese, and the Japanese—were efficient merchants and capable seamen, quite competent to carry on among themselves the trading activities which for a thousand years before the arrival of Vasco da Gama had flourished along the southern and eastern coasts of Asia. Against this indigenous competition in the carrying trade the Dutch and English employed every available weapon in the attempt either to drive it from the high seas or to force it to become a mere supplement to their own operations.

Faced by the persistent competition of an established trade whose efficiency rendered their own contribution practically superfluous, the Dutch and the English, again following the example of their Portuguese predecessors, had recourse to the policy of securing exclusive control over the sources of various essential commodities. Political domination thus became the most important and most profitable export from Europe to the Orient. Fortunately for the success of this policy, the East Indies offered a field in which the establishment of foreign political domination was comparatively easy. Absolutely lacking in political unity, the multitude of petty states throughout the archipelago—except in the western portion of Sumatra—offered little resistance to the imposition of foreign rule. Often, however, a practical overlordship was established less by actual conquest than by aiding one local ruler against an enemy and securing in return valuable commercial and political rights. By whatever method the control was gained, however, it proved to be a twofold source of profit to those who obtained it, enabling them to sell at their own price in the markets of the East and providing in the form of taxes or tribute a plentiful supply of commodities for export to Europe.

During the early years of the seventeenth century the merchants of the Dutch and English companies, confronted by a common enemy in the person of the Portuguese, frequently co-operated both for defense and for aggression. About 1605 the Dutch representatives at Amboyna, which was then the base of operations for the company's trade, permitted the English merchants to establish a trading post alongside the Dutch factory, and here the two companies carried on their rival trade until 1623. At Jacatra, a port in western Java, both companies also maintained for several years their separate factories.

As the Portuguese were gradually ousted from their entrenched monopoly, however, the relations between the Dutch and the English became steadily worse. In 1618 the English combined with the ruler of Bantam in an unsuccessful attempt to destroy the Dutch factory at Jacatra and to drive them from Java. In the following year the Dutch retaliated by attacking a fleet of four English ships, sinking one and capturing the other three. At the same time, convinced of the need for a strong military base, the Dutch assumed territorial sovereignty over Jacatra, changing its name to Batavia. Here they fortified themselves and established what eventually became the capital of their East Indian empire.

Alarmed at the repeated clashes between their merchants in the Orient, the governments of England and the Netherlands in 1619 concluded a treaty providing for co-operation in defense of their common interests. The trade of the Indies was to be shared equitably by the two companies, and the treaty provided for a combined Anglo-Dutch "defense fleet" operating in Far Eastern waters. One avowed function of this fleet was the prevention of direct trade between China and the Indies, in order that the Chinese should be compelled to obtain their East Indian commodities from the allies.

The effort made by the home governments to establish friendly co-operation between the two East Indian companies was, however, a complete failure. A joint Anglo-Dutch expedition against Manila in 1621 broke up in a dispute between the allied commanders; in 1622 the Dutch governor-general at Batavia wrote that friendship with the English could be maintained only by giving them the whole earth; and in 1623 the Dutch governor at Amboyna, on the ground that they were conspiring against his rule, arrested and executed the entire staff of the English company's factory on that island. This event, commonly referred to by English writers as the Massacre of Amboyna, put an end to all pretense at co-operation between the two companies; and shortly thereafter the English practically abandoned the archipelago to their Dutch rivals, retaining only a foothold in Bantam, where they were allowed to remain until 1682, and the trading post of Bencoolen, on the southwest coast of Sumatra.

Both East India companies, shortly after their arrival in the Orient, opened commercial relations with the states of the Indo-Chinese peninsula. Dutch merchants arrived in 1602 at the Siamese port of Patani, where they secured permission to establish a trading post. Three years after its establishment this factory was attacked and destroyed by Japanese rivals; but the post was promptly rebuilt, and the Dutch continued for many years to carry on trade here. At the same time they extended their operations to Ayuthia and to other Siamese ports. Ten years after the arrival of the Dutch an English ship reached Patani and secured from the Siamese authorities permission to establish a factory. As in Japan (see page 415), the English were less successful here than were the Dutch. In 1623, the same year which saw the Amboyna Massacre and the abandonment of the factory in Japan, the English factory at Patani was closed; for nearly forty years after this withdrawal the English company made no attempt to reopen trade in Siam.

In Burma the English and the Dutch arrived simultaneously, both companies receiving permission in 1619 to establish factories at a number of Burmese ports: the English at Syriam, Ava, and Bhamo; the Dutch at Syriam, Ava, and Pegu. This trade with Burma produced little profit. Neither company succeeded in getting along with the Burmese government; disturbed political conditions in the country obstructed the development of commerce, and both companies frequently closed their factories for more or less extensive periods. Finally, in 1677, the two companies abandoned the attempt and withdrew from Burma. For the Dutch this withdrawal was permanent, but the last part of the seventeenth century saw the English company again participating in Burmese trade.

DUTCH CONTROL OF THE EAST INDIES

The simultaneous abandonment by the English company, in 1623, of its trading operations in Siam, Japan, and the East Indies left the Dutch and the Portuguese to struggle for commercial supremacy over the region lying eastward of India. The outcome of this struggle was not to remain long in doubt. The Portuguese, with their man power exhausted by the efforts of the last century and a quarter, had already lost the greater part of their naval strength, while the Dutch, after a twelve years' truce from 1609 until 1621, were making Batavia a base for unrelenting attacks upon Portuguese shipping wherever it could be found. In 1622 the Portuguese, with Chinese assistance, succeeded in repelling the Dutch attempt to seize Macao; but the Dutch squadron, foiled in this attempt, established a commercial and naval base first in the Pescadores and later at Formosa. This strategically located base of operations, which enabled the Netherlanders to carry on a profitable indirect trade with the Chinese mainland, also made it possible for them to prey upon the Portuguese trade between Macao and Japan.

The expulsion of the Portuguese from Japan in 1639 and the positive refusal of the Japanese to permit their return were serious blows to the declining cause of Portugal, and in 1641 came the crowning disaster. In that year the Dutch, after a short siege, took from their rivals the city of Malacca. For nearly two centuries and a half Malacca had been the great emporium of the spice trade;

for a hundred and thirty years it had been the Eastern stronghold of Portugal's commercial system, second in importance only to Goa. Although the Dutch after this date continued to make Batavia the Eastern administrative center of their commercial empire, the acquisition of Malacca was an event of first-rate importance. It assured to them an almost complete monopoly of the spice trade with the southern coast of Asia; and at the same time it strengthened their position for trade with Siam, Annam, and China, whose merchants had long been accustomed to seek here their cargoes of East Indian products. Although the loss of Formosa, twenty-one years later, deprived the Dutch of a valuable point of contact with the Chinese, their almost complete domination of the East Indies made it possible for them still to secure from China such goods as could be profitably sold in the markets of Europe.

For slightly more than a century and a half after the capture of Malacca the Dutch East India Company dominated the East Indies; from Ceylon to the Moluccas its commercial supremacy was challenged only by occasional smugglers and "free traders," while its political authority was more and more firmly established over the peoples of the archipelago. Over much of this area the company maintained its influence by means of alliances with local rulers, to whom it gave military assistance in return for special trading privileges. In some of the islands, however, and particularly in Java, the company acquired a more direct overlordship. Here the local chieftains became its vassals and were required to pay fixed annual tribute in the products of their particular localities. All other European merchants being jealously excluded from any trade with the islands, the company was able to fix the prices of East Indian spices in the European market, and the commodities received in the form of tribute produced a profit far exceeding the costs of administration.

Although situated within eight degrees of the equator, Java is suited for European settlement, and the company's representatives in the East, almost from the beginning of territorial rule, advocated the policy of encouraging colonization here and in some of the other islands. To this suggestion, and to the related suggestion that the colonists be given complete freedom of carrying on trade within the islands, the directors in the Netherlands turned a deaf ear. So long as the company continued to pay dividends—and its dividends during nearly two centuries of existence averaged slightly more than 18 per cent per annum—the "Committee of Seventeen" steadily opposed any step which might endanger its profits.

In the face of this fear of any important change in the established system the period of company rule witnessed only two innovations: the introduction of coffee plantations and the development of the sugar industry. Coffee was introduced from Arabia in the last part of the seventeenth century or the first part of the eighteenth and soon rose to a position of first importance among the products of the company's possessions. In 1739 the total value of the cargo of a fleet arriving in the Netherlands from the Indies was estimated at 2,316,000 florins. Of the various commodities coffee stood second in value (304,000 florins), being surpassed only by tea (460,000 florins), which came from China, while pepper (212,000 florins) stood third on the list. Sugar, which with a value of 67,000 florins stood fourth among the commodities in this cargo, was produced by employing the skilled labor of the Chinese; for here, as in the Philippines, the establishment of European authority was promptly followed by a stream of immigration from China, and the Dutch, like their Spanish neighbors, found the energy and ability of the Chinese extremely valuable in developing the wealth of their islands.

The purely mercantilist policy of the Dutch company, which led the directors to oppose any attempt at developing colonization, led also to the establishment of a system under which the people of the islands were oppressively misgoverned. From a desire to economize on the costs of administration the direct rule over the people was entrusted to local or tribal chieftains, who, so long as they produced the amount of tribute demanded by the company's officers, were allowed to misgovern the people at will.

The situation was aggravated by the arbitrary fluctuations in the amount of various staple commodities which the company demanded either as tribute or as "forced deliveries" at a fixed price. When certain commodities were selling at high prices in Europe, the company would suddenly demand from its vassals 50 or even 100 per cent additional tribute. At other times, when there was no market for goods over and above the amount of tribute, the coffee and spices which had been produced to fill the anticipated forced delivery were destroyed by order of the company so as to prevent their being sold to the foreign smugglers who were constantly endeavoring to trade with the islands. It may be argued that the local rulers, in the absence of their foreign masters, would have oppressed the people with equal severity; but the fact remains that the tribute demanded by the company was an extra burden added to the rapacity of the indigenous officials, while the wanton destruction of surplus products would never have occurred except under European control.

In spite of the efforts made by the Dutch authorities to suppress smuggling, the people of the islands from the last part of the seventeenth century onward bought in steadily increasing quantities from the English, French, Danish, and unlicensed Dutch traders. By the opening of the eighteenth century the purely commercial activities of the company had ceased to produce a profit, and the bulk of the goods brought out from Europe in its ships were left to rot in the warehouses at Batavia. Long after the decline of its trading operations, however, the company continued to realize splendid profits by selling in Europe the commodities which came to it as tribute from its subject peoples.

During the course of the eighteenth century even these profits began to disappear, wiped out by mismanagement and graft. Money was wasted in futile efforts to carry on a losing trade and in costly wars for the extension of territorial power. The directors in Holland, in order to maintain the company's credit, issued to the stockholders dividends much larger than were justified by the actual profits. Large sums were lost annually through the inefficiency and dishonesty of the company's representatives in the East or through shipwrecks attributable to mistaken economy on the part of its directors in the matter of outfitting and repairs. By 1793 the directors were compelled to admit that the company was hopelessly in debt. Five years later its assets and liabilities were taken over by the government of the Netherlands, and the

Dutch East India Company, after a hundred and ninety-six years of existence, came to an inglorious end.

In 1795, three years before the final dissolution of the company, the armies of revolutionary France had invaded the Netherlands and had set up the Batavian Republic as a vassal of the newly established French Republic; with the rise of Napoleon the Netherlands became first a vassal kingdom and later an integral part of Napoleon's empire. Since Great Britain was, except for a brief period, constantly at war against republican and imperial France, the Dutch possessions throughout the Far East thus became enemy territory which the British might lawfully attempt to conquer. Most of the islands of the East Indies, together with the Dutch bases at Cape Town and Ceylon, were quickly seized, and in 1811 the British captured Batavia and established their authority over the entire Dutch portion of the archipelago. In 1816, in accordance with the decision of the Congress of Vienna, the Dutch possessions, with the exception of Cape Town and Ceylon, which were retained by Great Britain, were handed back to the Netherlands; but from 1811 until 1816 the East Indies were ruled as a province of British India, and the Dutch flag flew at one spot in the world—Deshima.

During the five years of British rule the administration of the islands was in the hands of Sir Thomas Stamford Raffles, who later laid the foundations of British power at Singapore and in the Malay peninsula. Raffles attempted to introduce sweeping reforms in the government of the islands, especially by abolishing the feudal system of administration in local affairs. These changes, which involved a radical readjustment of the social organization, might have proved beneficial if worked out over an extended period. Five years, however, was far too short a period, and the restoration of the territory to Dutch rule put an end to Raffles's experiments.

For thirty-two years after their restoration to the Dutch the East Indies were governed as absolutely and as harshly as during the days of the company's rule. The king of the Netherlands and his ministers held the powers which formerly had been exercised by the directors of the company; the income derived from the islands merely went into the royal treasury instead of going into that of the company. Not until 1848 was the constitution of the

Netherlands so amended as to give to the Dutch Estates-General the power of controlling the management of the country's colonial possessions; before that date the king's authority over these territories was unlimited.

Although the general condition of the East Indians was not improved by their transfer to royal authority, there were changes in the methods by which they were compelled to produce a profit for their rulers. Formerly they had been required to provide annual tribute in the form of fixed quantities of export goods; now the people were compelled to devote a certain portion of their time to the cultivation of such commodities as the government demanded, the crop being bought by the government at an arbitrarily fixed price. This culture system, as it was called, was applied especially to the production of coffee, indigo, and sugar, for all of which there was a good market in Europe.

In theory the culture system demanded only one fourth or one third of a laborer's time, while the land employed for the production of designated crops was to be free from the payment of land tax; in actual practice the land tax was still collected from the culture land, and the farmers of some districts were compelled to spend almost all their working time in the production of the crops demanded by the government. With the consequent forced neglect of the necessary food crops the people in the districts most suitable for the production of export crops were reduced to a stage of semi-starvation, since the prices paid by the government seldom sufficed for the purchase of food from the less heavily burdened areas.

By the second quarter of the nineteenth century public opinion in the Netherlands began to condemn the oppression of the East Indian population, and efforts were made to bring about some reform of conditions in the islands. The revolutionary year of 1848 marked the beginning of a new era for the Dutch East Indies. Since the new constitution of that year gave the Estates-General a voice in the control of the colonies, the influence of public opinion upon the administration of the overseas possessions became much stronger than it formerly had been. The first changes came slowly; but from that time reforms have been made, and the condition of the peoples under Dutch rule has steadily improved.

THE BEGINNINGS OF BRITISH INDIA

While the Dutch merchants were bringing under their control the eastern portions of what had once been the Portuguese commercial empire, the energies of the English East India Company were devoted chiefly to the development of trade with India. The year 1623 had witnessed the abandonment of the English factories in Japan and in Siam and the expulsion of the English from Amboyna by their Dutch rivals. For five years after this date the English were allowed to maintain their factory at the Dutch headquarters, Batavia, and until 1682 the English company maintained a foothold in Bantam at the western end of the island of Java; but not until the beginning of the nineteenth century did the British again assume in the Malay world a position which made them serious rivals of the Dutch.

In India the English faced a situation very different from that which confronted the Dutch in Malaysia. Whereas the Dutch were finding it comparatively easy to extend their territorial authority and to secure exclusive commercial privileges by aiding one local ruler against another, their English contemporaries were confronted by the powerful Mogul empire whose seventeenth-century rulers were striving to complete the unification begun by Akbar. Under Jahangir (1605–1627) and Shah Jahan (1628–1658), the son and the grandson of Akbar, the power of the Mogul empire steadily increased, while Aurangzeb (1658–1707), in spite of the internal weakness which developed during the course of his reign, was able to extend his dominions by the annexation of the Deccan sultanates of Bijapur and Golkonda.

The English company gained its first Indian foothold in 1612, when in the face of Portuguese opposition it secured permission from the Mogul governor of Gujarat to establish a factory at Surat. Between 1612 and 1622, when an English naval force co-operated with a Persian army to drive the Portuguese from Ormuz, the power of Portugal was effectively broken, and the English factories were established at various points along the west coast of India between Cambay and Cape Comorin. About 1622 the English, extending their operations to the eastern coast, founded a factory at Masulipatam, between the Krishna and Godavari rivers, and in 1625 they established another at Armagaon, near the mouth of the Penner. In spite of the fact that the power of the Portuguese was now almost completely destroyed, the local managers of the English company felt a need for fortified ports similar to those possessed by the Portuguese in India and by the Dutch in the East Indies. About three years after the acquisition of trading privileges at Armagaon, therefore, fortifications were erected to protect the factory at that port. In 1639, dissatisfied with the conditions under which trade was carried on at its two east-coast ports, the company secured from the raja of Chandragiri a grant of land adjoining the Portuguese settlement of San Thomé. Here the town of Madras was established, a fort was built, and the company, now in possession of its first piece of Indian soil, began the exercise of territorial sovereign rights.

For about two decades after the founding of Madras, England was torn by civil war, and the activities of the English company in India showed a marked decline. With the Stuart restoration in 1660, however, came the grant of a new charter, and the company began to display fresh energy in the development of trade. In 1661, when the new Stuart monarch married Catharine of Braganza, the Portuguese ceded to the English king as part of Catharine's dowry the island of Bombay. Charles II in 1668 leased Bombay in perpetuity to the East India Company for a merely nominal rent of ten pounds per year. Admirably situated and provided with a good harbor, this port was promptly converted into a commercial and naval base for the Indian west coast.

The Arrival of the French in the Far East

Shortly after the Dutch and the English had opened direct trade with the Far East, efforts were made by the French in the same direction, but it was not until the advent of Colbert, the capable finance minister of Louis XIV, that the French began to become a factor in Far Eastern affairs. Undismayed by the long list of previous failures, Colbert in 1664 drew up articles for a new *Compagnie des Indes Orientales*, and Louis XIV, approving the project, granted the company exclusive right to navigate and trade in the regions of the Far East from the Cape of Good Hope as far as the Strait of Magellan. The new company quickly gave evidence of its determination to secure a share in the Indian trade. In 1668 a French factory was established at Surat, and additional trading posts were soon established at other points along the coast. For a few years the French company confined its activities to the west coast of India; but in 1674 it succeeded in purchasing the town of Pondicherry, about seventy miles south of Madras, and this acquisition rapidly developed into the most important commercial center on the east coast.

DECLINE OF THE MOGUL EMPIRE

When Aurangzeb, in 1658, ascended the Mogul throne, the empire was at the height of its power; when he died, forty-nine years later, he left to his successor a country wasted by war and torn by internal dissension. Aurangzeb's reign had been inaugurated by a successful rebellion against his father, whom he deposed and imprisoned, and by the murder of his brothers, rivals for the throne. Rebellion and fratricide, however, were no novelties in the history of the Mogul dynasty, and the abilities of the new prince seemed to assure him a prosperous reign. Unfortunately, from the beginning of his rule he adopted a policy which destroyed all hope for the preservation of unity in the empire. Abandoning the wise religious toleration of Akbar and Jahangir, Aurangzeb showed himself to be a thoroughgoing religious fanatic. The ancient poll tax was imposed upon all Hindus; Hindu temples in all parts of the empire were ruthlessly destroyed; and various Hindu elements of the population, hitherto loyal supporters of the throne, were driven into open rebellion.

The most serious consequence of this intolerant policy was the alienation of the warlike Rajput clans, who had been the chief dependence of Akbar, Jahangir, and Shah Jahan, and whose location in the northwest made them a valuable defense against any threatened invasion from Afghanistan. Henceforth the support of the Rajputs was lost to the Moguls, and this loss was poorly compensated by Aurangzeb's long and wasteful campaigns in the Deccan which finally resulted in the annexation of Bijapur and Golkonda.

Even before the accession of Aurangzeb to the Mogul throne there had arisen among the Maratha hillmen of the western Deccan a movement which, although insignificant at first, eventually led to the establishment of a new dominant power in India. Sivaji, who as leader of this movement became the founder of the Maratha confederacy, was the son of a Hindu chieftain who had served as a local official under the Mohammedan rulers of Ahmadnagar and Bijapur. Inspired by his mother with a deep devotion to the cause of the ancient religion of the country, Sivaji in 1647, when only about nineteen years of age, took up arms against the Moslems. His first operations were confined to the rugged hill region of the Western Ghats in the vicinity of Poona, near the boundary between Bijapur and Ahmadnagar. By 1655 he had extended his power westward to a part of the Konkan, the coast land south of Bombay, and in 1659 he was strong enough to inflict a crushing defeat upon the forces of the Sultan of Bijapur.

Up to this point in his career Sivaji was little more than a successful brigand inspired with a devotion to Hinduism and a hatred for Mohammedanism. The Marathas, merely a language group in India's population, were Hindus of low caste and had no traditions of existence as a nation. After 1660, however, the Maratha movement assumed new importance. Aurangzeb, now securely seated on the Mogul throne, dispatched an army into the Deccan in an unsuccessful attempt to destroy the troublesome bandit organization. This move created undying hatred between the Marathas and the Moguls; its failure greatly increased Sivaji's prestige and importance in the eyes of his fellow Hindus, while Aurangzeb's fanatical attacks upon the Hindu religion soon created a quasi alliance between the Marathas and the northern Rajputs and made Sivaji the accepted champion of southern Hinduism. In 1667 Aurangzeb attempted to conciliate the Maratha leader by bestowing upon him the title of raja; but by this time conciliation was impossible, and in 1674 Sivaji assumed the royal dignity as an independent sovereign.

At the time of Sivaji's death, in 1680, the Maratha kingdom consisted of a long strip of territory in the Western Ghats and the adjoining Konkan coast, between Bombay and Goa. This territory under Sivaji's direct rule had been united with various other petty states, lying south of the Krishna River, into an extensive but loosely knit Maratha confederacy which acknowledged his leadership. Following a period of reverses after its founder's death the power of the confederacy gradually increased. By the date of Aurangzeb's death (1707) it was the dominating influence of the Deccan, and from 1714 until its defeat by the British in the Third Maratha War (1817–1819) the Maratha confederacy was the strongest organization in all India.

The increasing disorders in Aurangzeb's empire inspired the directors of the English East India Company with the hope of establishing "a large, well-grounded, sure English dominion in India for all time to come." In 1685 the chairman of the directors persuaded James II to dispatch an expedition to Chittagong, on the Bay of Bengal to the east of the Ganges delta, for the purpose of seizing and fortifying that port as a permanent English base. The outcome of this enterprise proved that the decline of the Mogul power had been overestimated. The expedition against Chittagong was a complete failure, the English were compelled to abandon their existing factories in Bengal, and Aurangzeb turned against the English posts in other parts of his domains. Eventually the representatives of the company succeeded in making peace with the enraged Mogul ruler; and in 1690 they again received permission to open trade in Bengal, where they established a modest settlement at Calcutta.

For about half a century after its return to Bengal the company carefully refrained from interference in Indian politics. At Bombay, at Madras, and at Calcutta, the three chief centers of its commercial activities, the management of local affairs of the company was delegated to "select committees," or councils, of the merchants under appointed "presidents," or governors; but all matters of general importance in the "presidencies" were strictly supervised by the directors at London, who now opposed any rash adventures.

During the opening decades of the eighteenth century the French continued to show great activity in the development of their Indian trade. About thirty years after the death of Aurangzeb the brilliant Dupleix, who had been entrusted with the direction of French interests in India, began to intervene with great success in the disputes between rival Indian rulers; as a result of this intervention the French secured valuable commercial privileges in a number of the Indian states. The steady expansion of French political influence was a serious matter for the English company, which found itself in danger of being forced out of the country.

The War of the Austrian Succession (1740–1748) gave the English an opportunity to attack French colonies and French trade in all parts of the world. In India the duel between the two rivals, which commenced in 1745 and continued after the restoration of peace in Europe, involved little actual fighting between opposing European forces. French and English agents intrigued to secure disputed thrones for princes friendly to their respective interests, while Indian rulers, allied with or subsidized by the foreign groups, fought the battles which determined whether the control of India should fall to the French or to their island rivals.

The outstanding figures on the two sides of the duel were Dupleix, who came out to govern Pondicherry for France in 1742, and Robert Clive, a young clerk in the employ of the English East India Company, who arrived at Madras about a year later. To Dupleix may be given the credit for having invented, or for having introduced into India, the technique whereby European domination was ultimately achieved, but it was his young English rival who eventually proved to be the consummate master of this technique. Only eighteen years of age when he reached India, Clive soon found unbearable the monotonous life of a clerk and secured his transfer to the armed forces which the company had organized for the defense of the port. In the field of war and intrigue he found his real calling, and he now entered upon the career which was to make him an empire-builder and the hero of every British schoolboy.

During the early years of the struggle the French appeared to have the upper hand, but France was too deeply involved in European affairs to be able to support her Indian allies. The battle of

Plassey, in 1757, practically settled the outcome of the struggle, and in 1761 the capture of Pondicherry put an end to French aspirations of controlling India. By the peace settlement of 1763 France regained, and she still retains, her ports of Pondicherry, Mahe, and Chandernagore; but after 1761 she ceased to have any real influence in Indian political affairs.

The East India Company as a Territorial Sovereign

At the beginning of the Anglo-French duel for supremacy in India the East India Company exercised territorial jurisdiction over two fragments of Indian soil: Bombay and Madras. With the conclusion of this struggle the company found itself definitely committed to a situation which, despite the occasional misgivings of the London directors, led to the steady development of a territorial empire.

In 1755 the company's forces at Bombay, co-operating with the Marathas against the French, gained possession of Bankot on the adjoining mainland, which became the first British possession on the mainland of western India. Twenty years later the president and council of Bombay, acting upon their own initiative, took advantage of discord among the Marathas as an opportunity for gaining additional territory on the neighboring coast. This venture, which precipitated a war with the Marathas, nearly resulted in the destruction of the English position on the west coast, but the treaty of 1782, at the conclusion of the struggle, gave the company additional territory in this region.

In 1757, immediately after the battle of Plassey, the nawab of Bengal, who owed his position to English support, conferred upon the company the sovereignty over about nine hundred square miles of territory south of Calcutta; two years later the Mogul emperor confirmed this grant by a decree which gave the company perpetual jurisdiction over the land. Almost at the same time an arrangement was made between the government of the Madras presidency and the nawab of the Carnatic whereby the company and the nawab exercised joint rule over the territories of the southeast coast.

These important extensions of the company's power were completely overshadowed by the so-called grant of the diwani in

1765, by which the Mogul emperor conferred upon the company the right of appointing the diwan, or controller of revenue, for the provinces of Bengal, Bihar, and Orissa.[1] For seven years after the grant of the diwani the company exercised its newly acquired power by appointing officers who posed as deputies of the nawab of Bengal, but in 1771 the directors at London decided that henceforth the company itself would "stand forth as Diwan." As a result of this decision the control of the revenue of the three provinces was transferred in 1772 to a Board of Revenue at Calcutta. The new board consisted of the governor and council, and its direct control over the revenue made the company, for all practical purposes, the actual sovereign over the three provinces of the lower Ganges. Simultaneously with this change the company's directors appointed to the governorship of Calcutta, now the most important of its Indian posts, the energetic Warren Hastings.

The company's assumption of virtual sovereignty over millions of Indian people presented a new problem to the British government, and in 1773 Parliament dealt with the situation by passing a Regulating Act which created a new machinery for the administration of the company's Indian affairs and definitely subjected the company to the control of the crown. The new act provided that the presidency of Fort William (Calcutta) in Bengal should be governed by a governor-general and four counselors, in whom should be vested the whole civil and military government of the presidency and all the company's territorial acquisitions "in the Kingdoms of Bengal, Behar, and Orissa." The act declared the supremacy of the Bengal presidency over the other presidencies and empowered the governor-general and council to suspend the governor and council of a minor presidency in case of disobedience of orders. Warren Hastings, the recently appointed governor, was named as the first governor-general, and the act also appointed the four men who were to constitute the new council.

The Regulating Act of 1773 laid the foundation of a constitutional system to which the British Parliament during the subsequent eighty-five years made frequent additions. Most of these

[1] The present district of Midnapur, not to be confused with modern Orissa, acquired in 1803.

additions or changes were made in connection with the periodic renewal, at twenty-year intervals after 1773, of the company's charter; but in 1784, as a result of growing dissatisfaction with the company's administration of its territorial affairs, Parliament passed a measure intended to place the company in direct and permanent subordination to the British government. This was achieved by creating a board of six commissioners, officially known as the Commissioners for Affairs of India but usually referred to as the Board of Control. The Board of Control was to have access to all papers and instruments of the company; it had the power to modify or to veto instructions which the directors sent to the company's officers in India, and it had authority to send direct instructions, without the concurrence of the directors, to the officers in India.

Subsequent to the act of 1784, the most important modifications of the company's position were made in the renewals of its charter in 1813, 1833, and 1853. The first of these acts granted to the company, "without prejudice to the undoubted sovereignty of the Crown of the United Kingdom of Great Britain and Ireland in and over the same," control over its Indian possessions and revenues, together with a monopoly of the China trade for a further term of twenty years; but it provided that the general Indian trade, under certain necessary restrictions, should be thrown open to all British subjects. By the Charter Act of 1833 the company's monopoly of the China trade was abolished, and the directors were required to terminate as soon as possible the commercial affairs of the company. Deprived of its commercial functions, the company was allowed to retain for another term of twenty years administrative and political control over its territorial acquisitions in India, but this power was to be held "in trust for His Majesty, his heirs, and successors." The act of 1853, instead of extending the charter for a further term of twenty years, provided only that the Indian territories should remain under the direction of the company's officials, in trust for the crown, until Parliament should otherwise direct.

The gradual transformation of the East India Company, during the century which followed the battle of Plassey, from a chartered trading organization into a territorial sovereign was accompanied by a long series of wars. In addition to the already mentioned war, between 1775 and 1782, against the Marathas, two other wars with this powerful confederacy occurred before 1819. Two wars were undertaken against the powerful state of Mysore in the Deccan, two against the Afghans, two against the Sikhs, one against Nepal, and two against Burma, while there were numerous minor campaigns against less important enemies. Some of these struggles were undoubtedly defensive; but although the London Board of Directors repeatedly expressed their disapproval of further adventures in imperialistic expansion, the long line of energetic governors-general, beginning with Warren Hastings, seldom had difficulty in finding an excuse for intervening in the affairs of the neighboring Indian states. Such interventions usually brought on war and almost invariably resulted in the annexation of new territory or in the establishment of the company's paramountcy over hitherto independent states. In the first case the company did away with the local rulers and brought extensive areas under its direct rule. In the second case the policy of ruling indirectly through the medium of tributary princes was adopted, these princes becoming by treaty the vassals of the company.

To carry on these wars and to retain its authority over the subjugated peoples the company was obliged to maintain a large fighting force. Only about one fifth of its army, however, was composed of European troops; the other four fifths were sepoys, Indian soldiers armed and drilled after the European manner. Since the expenses of the wars were met by taxes collected in India and since the greater part of the company's army was composed of Indian troops, the extension of British rule in India was accomplished with little or no cost to the English people.

NATURE OF THE COMPANY'S RULE

The people of India reaped little, if any, benefit from the steady extension of the company's power. The wars and diplomacy of its representatives had as their objects only the commercial and financial advantage of the exploiting foreigner. The tribute paid by the vassal princes and the enormous "presents" which these rulers distributed among the company's officials came obviously from the taxes imposed upon the people, and the necessity of making these payments often led to an increase in the already crushing burden of taxation. Nor were the inhabitants of the regions under the company's direct rule appreciably better off than those subject to the rule of its vassals. In these areas taxation was equally oppressive and the administration of affairs equally unaffected by any consideration for the people's welfare. In spite of Parliament's assertion of royal authority the people of India remained subject to a company of merchants primarily interested in commercial and financial profit.

On several occasions during the century following the battle of Plassey the continuance of British control in India was threatened by disaffection among the sepoys who constituted such an important part of the armed force by which this control was maintained. Earlier outbreaks had been suppressed with little difficulty, but in 1857 the great Sepoy Mutiny brought British power to the verge of ruin. Although the mutiny was confined to the sepoys stationed in the northern provinces and was held in check by the aid of other Indian troops which remained loyal, the British government was compelled to send to India a large force of British troops for the complete suppression of the rebellion and the restoration of order.

With the outbreak of the Sepoy Mutiny the British government decided that the management of an Indian empire was a task which no longer could be safely entrusted to "an unprogressive, selfish, and commercial system of administration." An Act for the Better Government of India was therefore passed by Parliament, and on November 1, 1858, a royal proclamation to the princes and people of India announced the transfer of the sovereign authority from the East India Company to the British crown.

EUROPEAN RIVALRIES IN INDO-CHINA

In the sixteenth century, when European influence began to make itself felt in the Far East, Indo-China was divided into the three kingdoms of Burma, Siam, and Annam, while the lower portion of the Malay peninsula, south of Siam, was held by a number of petty Malay states. During the sixteenth century, as we have seen, both the Portuguese and the Spanish developed contact with the countries of Indo-China, the Spanish chiefly with Annam, the Portuguese with all three of the larger kingdoms as well as with the Malay states of the south. Spanish and Portuguese adventurers sought fortune and risked their lives in various questionable enterprises, and Portuguese mercenaries were employed on both sides in the sixteenth-century wars between Burma and Siam; but save for the seizure of Malacca by the Portuguese the century witnessed no serious attempt by either European power to establish its authority on this part of the Asiatic mainland.

The seventeenth-century Dutch and English, like their Spanish and Portuguese forerunners, made little attempt to establish political control over the Indo-Chinese states; and although the French engaged in imperialistic ventures during the seventeenth and eighteenth centuries, it was not until after the commencement of the nineteenth that the first steps were taken toward the establishment of British sovereignty in Burma, and French sovereignty over the territories now included in French Indo-China.

When the English East India Company in 1623 abandoned its factory at the Siamese port of Patani, the Dutch company remained in the field and continued to expand its trade here and at the other ports of the kingdom. After the capture of Malacca in 1641 the Dutch influence in Siam rapidly increased, and in 1664 the company secured from the Siamese government, by a commercial treaty, a complete monopoly in the country's foreign trade. In view of the fact that the Japanese government, twenty-eight years earlier, had strictly forbidden its subjects to leave Japan, it is interesting to note that the Siamese-Dutch treaty of 1664 specifically mentions the Japanese among the merchants who are to be excluded from Siamese trade; the explanation of this anomaly seems to be that the excluded Japanese traders were "men without a country," expatriates who were abroad when the Shogun issued his decree and who were by its terms forbidden to return to their native land.

In spite of their extremely favorable treaty of 1664 the Dutch were not destined to dominate Siam's foreign trade. The management of their insular possessions left them little energy for the extension of their control on the mainland. Even before the date of the treaty, moreover, there had arrived in Siam an adventurer whose growing influence destroyed the Dutch hope of a permanent monopoly of Siamese trade.

Constantine Faulkon, a French protégé and the son of a Levantine innkeeper, arrived at Ayuthia in 1659. Taking service under the Siamese government, he quickly gained favor and from about 1670 became the chief minister of the king, Phra Narai. Faulkon was not actually hostile to the Dutch; indeed, he encouraged them to extend their trading activities at Siamese ports, but he opposed the continuance of their monopoly and induced Phra Narai to adopt a liberal policy toward the English and French merchants for the purpose of bringing them also to the ports of the kingdom. The adoption of this policy resulted in a development of trade which appears to have been decidedly beneficial to Siam; but it also involved the country in the rivalries of the aggressive European nations, and in 1687 James II of England made an unsuccessful attempt to seize the port of Mergui on the Tenasserim coast.

The most serious complications, however, were caused by an ambitious French project to convert Siam into a Far Eastern outpost of "His Most Christian Majesty" Louis XIV. The project originated with Faulkon and three French missionaries, who succeeded in inducing Phra Narai to dispatch an embassy to the French king. Louis sent a return embassy, which was received with great respect, and dispatched to Siam a force consisting of six warships and fourteen hundred soldiers. At the same time the missionaries made vigorous efforts to convert the Siamese monarch to Christianity. In spite of an auspicious beginning, this project resulted only in disaster for those who conceived it. The arrival of the formidable French force and the activities of the missionaries aroused the fears of the people as well as the opposition of a powerful court faction. In 1688 a popular revolt, organized by the dissatisfied court party, drove Phra Narai from the throne; Faulkon was killed, the French force was expelled from the country, and the flourishing missionary enterprise was practically destroyed.

Fortunately for Siam, Louis XIV was too fully occupied during the remainder of his reign to give further serious attention to affairs in the Far East. The outbreak which overthrew Faulkon and saved Siam from French domination was followed by a period of extreme disorder and weakness. A long civil war arising out of a disputed succession to the throne was hardly ended when the armies of Burma, recently united into a strong kingdom by Alaungpaya (see page 480), invaded Siam. In 1767, after eight years of fighting, the Burmese destroyed Ayuthia and compelled the Siamese to submit to the rule of a Burmese viceroy.

As had been the case two centuries earlier after the successful invasion by Bayin Naung, the Siamese quickly threw off the Burmese yoke; and in 1782 the first king of a new dynasty ascended the throne. The new monarch, Rama I, founded a dynasty which has ruled the country to the present day. Siam now entered upon a period of good government in which her internal condition and her foreign relations greatly improved. The capital of the kingdom was established at its present site, Bangkok; capable local officials were appointed to manage affairs in the provinces, and improvements were made in the administration of justice.

In 1826 Siam entered into a treaty of commerce with Great Britain, and seven years later a similar treaty was concluded with the United States. In 1844 there was a brief dispute between Siam and Annam with regard to Cambodia; this dispute ended by Annam's agreeing to recognize Siam as the protector of Cambodia. The steady improvement along all lines during the first three reigns of the new dynasty was continued with conspicuous success by Rama IV. In the seventeen years of his reign, 1851–1868, new commercial treaties were concluded with a number of European powers, modern educational institutions were developed, legal and commercial methods were borrowed from the West, and every effort was made to adopt a policy that would make it impossible for any foreign power to find a pretext for aggressive action.

Exhausted by the sixteenth-century wars of Bayin Naung, the kingdom of Burma rapidly declined in power after his death. In 1600, nineteen years after the conqueror's death, Pegu was sacked and destroyed, and Burma broke up once more into a number of petty states. The very completeness of the anarchy which characterized the history of the next century and a half, instead of marking Burma as a field for conquest, appears to have had a deterrent effect upon European expansion. The factories opened by the Dutch and English East India companies in 1619 accomplished little in the way of trade during the fifty-eight years of their existence, while the meteoric career of Philip de Brito, between 1600 and 1613, fell too far short of ultimate success to arouse emulation among those who superseded the Portuguese in the East.

About the middle of the eighteenth century a new conqueror, Alaungpaya, arose in northern Burma, and in 1753 the petty states of north and south had been reunited into a single kingdom. In his struggle for empire Alaungpaya received assistance, in the form of weapons and munitions, from the English East India Company, while the French, who had a factory at Syriam, gave aid to his enemies. Alaungpaya's triumph therefore enabled the British to conclude an advantageous treaty of commerce. Having reunited Burma, the new ruler in 1759 attempted the conquest of Siam. His death in the following year prevented his achievement of this further triumph, but in 1767 his second successor on the throne destroyed Ayuthia and brought Siam for a brief period under Burmese rule. Although the Siamese quickly regained their independence, the Tenasserim coast remained in the possession of Burma.

Alaungpaya's success in reuniting Burma closely coincided with the triumph of the English East India Company over its French rivals in India, and the later monarchs of the Alaungpaya dynasty found it increasingly difficult to keep on good terms with the new rulers of India. Trouble at first arose between the Burmese officials and the British merchants over questions of taxation, but it was not long before a territorial question was added to the causes for disagreement. The province of Bengal, in which the company had established its direct rule, was separated from Burma by the little state of Assam, lying to the east of the Brahmaputra River. At various times in the past Assam had been subject to the Burmese crown, and King Bagyidaw (1819–1837) was determined that it should again become so, while the East India Company was equally determined that it should remain independent to serve as a buffer state. In 1821–1822, despite the company's proclamation that Assam was under British protection, the Burmese army entered the disputed territory and overthrew its government. In January, 1824, Burmese troops crossed the frontier of Bengal, and later in the same year the company declared war.

The First Burmese War (1824–1826) ended with the defeat of Burma, who abandoned her claims to Assam and also surrendered the Tenasserim coast to the company. Twenty-six years after the termination of this first war Lord Dalhousie, the company's governor-general, found cause for a second war with Burma, and the Burmese king was forced to surrender all his seacoast territories. The transfer of India from the rule of the company to that of the British crown brought no relief to the Burmese. In 1885 the viceroy of British India decided that the rule of King Thibaw was prejudicial to British commercial interests. Burma, therefore, was invaded once more, this time with the result that the remainder of the kingdom was annexed to the British Empire.[1]

Five years before the outbreak of the first war with Burma the British secured a valuable permanent foothold at the southern extremity of the Malay peninsula. Sir Stamford Raffles, the governor of the Dutch East Indies during the five years (1811–1816) which saw this important area under British rule, had protested in vain against the restoration of the islands to the Dutch; and in 1819, with the approval of the company's governor-general, Raffles purchased from the Sultan of Johore the island and port of Singapore. Since the harbor of Singapore is deep enough to accommodate ships much larger than those which can safely enter the shallow water of Malacca harbor, the new British port soon outstripped its neighbor as a commercial center. Within a short time the trade of Malacca had so greatly declined that the Dutch willingly exchanged this once important possession for the British trading post of Bencoolen on the southwestern coast of Sumatra.

---

[1] At the moment of this annexation the British government was anxious to avoid antagonizing the Chinese Empire, whose vassal Burma had been. In order to secure Chinese acquiescence in the extinction of the Burmese state the British representative at Peking therefore concluded in July, 1886, a special convention with China. Article I of this convention provided that "Inasmuch as it has been the practice of Burmah to send decennial Missions to present articles of local produce, England agrees that the highest authority in Burmah shall send the customary decennial Missions, the members of the Missions to be of Burmese race."

Singapore and Malacca became a starting point from which British authority has extended gradually northward until it now dominates the southern portion of the Malay peninsula as far north as the sixth degree north latitude. Along the Strait of Malacca lie the Straits Settlements: the three ports of Singapore, Malacca, and Penang. Until 1867 these three ports were governed from Calcutta as a part of Bengal; since that date they have constituted a separate crown colony. To the northeast of the Straits Settlements and comprising the greater part of the British sphere of control in the peninsula lies an area known as the Federated Malay States. Between 1874 and 1888 the petty Malay sultanates of Perak, Selangor, Negri Sembilan, and Pahang were taken under British protection and agreed to the appointment of British "residents" with supervisory power. In 1896 the four states were federated and placed under the general oversight of a British resident-general, but each retained its local resident. Nominally the states are still ruled by their respective sultans; but the resident-general controls their foreign affairs, while in matters of internal administration all real authority is wielded by the local resident, who is the "power behind the throne."

At the end of the fifteenth century Annam was a strong kingdom, prosperous and well governed. During the course of the sixteenth century Spanish and Portuguese adventurers made several attempts to set themselves up as rulers over parts of the kingdom. At the same time the occupants of the Annamese throne gradually became puppet kings, and all real power fell into the hands of two ambitious court families. In 1600 the rivalry between these two powerful families led to the outbreak of civil war and to the division of Annam into two hostile states. The northern state, with its capital at Hanoi, coincided roughly with the ancient kingdom before its absorption of Champa; the southern state, of which Hué became the capital, included Cochin China and the Cham provinces. Throughout the seventeenth and eighteenth centuries the history of these two states is a record of almost constant turmoil and war. At times they fought against each other, but usually both sections were torn by internal struggles.

About 1785 a defeated claimant to the southern throne was

forced to take refuge in Siam. At Bangkok the fugitive prince, known to history as Gia Long, begged assistance from the missionary bishop of Adran, Pigneau de Béhaine. Bishop De Béhaine believed that Annam offered France a field in which to compensate herself for the recent loss of her power in India. Accordingly he departed for France, accompanied by Gia Long's infant son, and persuaded the government of Louis XVI to conclude a treaty pledging assistance to the Annamese prince. The outbreak of the French Revolution put an end to the hope of securing any real aid directly from France, but the energetic bishop succeeded in recruiting a strong body of volunteers from among the French residents of India. Re-entering Annam in 1792 at the head of this force, Gia Long first established his power in Cochin China and then extended his conquests steadily to the north. By 1801 he had made himself master of Hué; the following year saw the defeat of the northern kingdom and the reunification of Annam under a single crown.

Contrary to the expectations of Bishop De Béhaine, the assistance given to Gia Long did not result in any permanent advantage to French interests in the Far East. Until his death, in 1820, Gia Long showed his gratitude by employing many French officers and advisers. Toward the end of his reign, however, a strong antiforeign party developed in Annam, and his successors on the throne adopted a decidedly anti-French policy. In spite of this hostility the French missionaries were able to continue their religious work in the country, and it was the presence of the missionaries which eventually made it possible for the French to gain their permanent foothold in Indo-China. In 1857, the year of the Sepoy Mutiny in India, Napoleon III took advantage of the execution of a missionary in Annam and sent an expedition against Hué to secure reparation. A year later the French forces seized Saigon, the chief seaport of Cochin China. Unable to drive the French from Saigon, the Annamese government in 1862 finally signed a treaty surrendering Cochin China to France.

In 1863 a French embassy visited Cambodia and concluded a treaty of friendship with the ruler of that once powerful state. The Cambodian king, at that time an unwilling vassal of Siam, welcomed the opportunity to put himself under French protection and promptly repudiated the authority of his former suzerain. For a while there was grave danger of war between France and Siam; but Rama IV, realizing that Siam could have little hope of success in a struggle with a first-class European power, signed in 1867 a treaty by which Cambodia was recognized as a French protectorate. After more than two centuries of fruitless activity in the Far East the French had at last succeeded in laying the foundation of a Far Eastern empire.

SUGGESTED REFERENCES

ANDERSON, J. English Intercourse with Siam in the Seventeenth Century.

CABATON, A. Java, Sumatra, and the Dutch East Indies (translated by B. Miall).

CORDIER, H. La France et la Cochinchine, 1852–1858.

DAY, C. The Dutch in Java.

HARVEY, G. E. History of Burma.

HAVELL, E. B. A Short History of India.

HUNTER, W. W. A History of British India.

ILBERT, SIR C. P. The Government of India.

KAEMPFER, E. The History of Japan, together with a Description of the Kingdom of Siam, 1690–1692.

LANE-POOLE, S. Aurangzib.

LANIER, L. Étude historique sur les relations de la France et du royaume de Siam, de 1662 à 1703.

LYALL, A. Rise and Expansion of British Dominion in India.

MALLESON, G. B. History of the French in India.

MILLS, L. A. British Malaya, 1824–1867.

RAFFLES, SIR T. S. The History of Java.

SMITH, V. A. The Oxford History of India.

SYMES, M. An Account of an Embassy to the Kingdom of Ava.

WOOD, W. A. R. A History of Siam.

XX

The Russian Advance in Northern Asia

Russia's Early Relations with the East · The Rise of Moscow · The Cossacks · The
Stroganovs and Yermak Timofeyevitch · The Russian Arrival on the Pacific ·
Russian Contact with China · Khabarov · Diplomacy and War · Nerchinsk and
Albazin · The Treaty of Nerchinsk, 1689 · Russian Embassies to Peking · A Chinese
Embassy to the Tartars of South Russia · The Kiakhta Caravan Trade · Russians
at Peking · Russian Explorations on the Pacific: Sakhalin, the Kurils, and Alaska ·
Russian Efforts to Establish Relations with Japan · Colonization of Siberia:
Criminals and Political Offenders

FOR more than a hundred years after the thirteenth-century
Mongol invasion of Europe the various states of Russia were
in close contact with their Far Eastern conquerors. Both John of
Plano Carpini and William of Rubruck found tributary Russian
princes at the Mongol camp-capital, Kublai Khan's seventh successor at Peking maintained a regiment of Russian soldiers as part
of the imperial guard, and the lower-Volga city of Sarai continued
until the disintegration of the Mongol power to be the European
terminus of a great trans-Asian caravan trade. After the break-up
of the Mongol empire in the second half of the fourteenth century,
communication with the Far East rapidly declined, but the greater
part of Russia continued for an additional century and a half to
pay tribute and to give allegiance to the powerful khans of the
western Mongols.

In the northern and central portions of Russia the power of the
Mongols had never been so firmly established as in the south and
east. During the fifteenth century, moreover, their authority became steadily weaker, while the centrally located principality of
Moscow in the upper part of the Volga basin gradually became
during the same period the most powerful state in Russia. In the
reign of Ivan III ("the Great"), 1462–1505, Moscow's increase
in power became more rapid, and in 1480 the Muscovite prince
was able to throw off the Mongol yoke and to assume independent

sovereignty. Under this ruler the territory of Moscow was extended northward to the shores of the Arctic, northeastward beyond the Urals, and westward to the frontiers of Poland, Lithuania, and the Swedish possessions on the east side of the Baltic. In 1546 Ivan IV ("the Terrible"), 1533-1584, signalized the growing power of his state by assuming the title of Czar ("Emperor") in place of the earlier title, Grand Prince, by which his predecessors had been designated.

Like his grandfather, Ivan IV was an expansionist, and his adoption of a new title was followed by a steady southward extension of Moscow's domain along the Volga and Don rivers. In 1552 he conquered Kazan, at the junction of the Volga and the Kama, and in 1566 the annexation of Astrakhan at the mouth of the Volga made him the master of the whole of this great river basin. Expansion down the valley of the Don was more difficult, since it was obstructed by the powerful khanate of Crimea; but Ivan pushed the Russian frontier as far as Rostov, beyond which it was not advanced until the reign of Catherine the Great two centuries later.

From an early date the southern and southeastern frontier of the Muscovite state had required the maintenance of a strong military force as a defense against sudden attack by the Crimean and Kipchak Tartars. The burden of guarding against invasion of the border, however, was lightened by the presence of the Russian frontiersmen. Especially attractive was the frontier to the downtrodden peasants, thousands of whom deserted their village communities and their forced labor on the fields of the great landowners to earn here a livelihood as pieceworkers, or—in Russian— *cossacks*. Inside the line of the military frontier these pieceworkers were mere hired laborers, engaging in a variety of gainful occupations. But many of the more adventurous among them did not stop within this line, and the name *Cossack* came to be applied more and more exclusively to this more adventurous element. Employed by the frontier officers as scouts to patrol the country far beyond the line of military posts, the Cossacks gradually developed into a hardy, seminomadic type of frontiersman.

To these turbulent adventurers even the restraints imposed by life in a frontier military post proved irksome; forming into groups

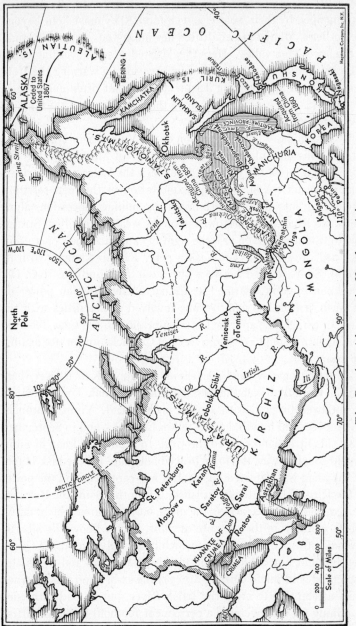

The Russian Advance in Northern Asia

accompanied by their women and children, they moved out beyond the borders. Many of them drifted down into the "debatable land" of the lower Don valley. Here they existed as self-governing clans, still performing valuable service on occasion by warning the frontier officers of approaching Tartar attacks, but often engaging in acts of brigandage which drew upon them the wrath of the Russian government.

By his conquest and annexation of the Volga basin Ivan IV had extended his dominions eastward to the Ural Mountains, the low ridge which forms the watershed between the Volga and the rivers of northwestern Asia. For the exploitation of this new territory extensive grants of land, with important mining concessions along the Kama River, were bestowed upon the wealthy family of Stroganov, to whom was given also the right of extending their operations eastward. Beyond the Urals lay a petty Kirghiz khanate with its capital, Sibir, located between the mountains and the river Ob. The khan of Sibir, alarmed at the advancing Russian power on his western frontier, soon became involved in hostilities with the house of Stroganov, and the latter, appealing to the Czar, received in 1579 permission to recruit a force of Cossacks for service against the khan.

To the Stroganov headquarters on the upper Kama River there came in the fall of 1580 the Cossack leader Yermak Timofeyevitch, an outlawed brigand with a price on his head. Yermak brought with him several hundred of his fellow Cossacks, and in September, 1581, this little band crossed the Urals to attack the khan of Sibir. Small though it was, the force proved adequate for the task before it; the khan was defeated, his capital was captured, and the power of the Kirghiz khanate was crushed. From this point the Russians started their advance across the great northern area which, deriving its name from the khanate of Sibir, is now known as Siberia. Yermak's trans-Ural conquest, which he humbly laid at the Czar's feet, brought him a full pardon for his past crimes and the gift of a splendid gold-inlaid cuirass. In 1584 the ex-brigand was drowned while attempting to cross the Irtish River, but he had succeeded in gaining for his sovereign a permanent foothold in the Ob-Irtish basin.

After the death of Ivan IV, which also occurred in 1584, the Moscow government passed through a period of disorder and turmoil known as the Time of Troubles. Disastrous though this period was in its internal effects, it appears actually to have quickened the progress of Russia's eastward expansion. Civil war and disorder drove additional thousands of peasants toward the frontiers, and the newly opened territory on the east drew its share of these recruits.

Peasants led by Cossacks pushed their way steadily eastward farther into Siberia, meeting little opposition on the way. The year 1587 saw the establishment of Tobolsk on the right bank of the Irtish. In 1604 the town of Tomsk was founded in the upper part of the valley of the Ob. By 1615, the year in which Michael Romanov ascended the throne as the first Czar of that line, the Russian advance had reached the Yenisei, and six years later the town of Yeniseisk was founded. By 1632 the Russians, crossing from the upper waters of the Yenisei to those of the Lena, had pushed northeastward along this river to establish a new outpost at Yakutsk, and in 1638, fifty-seven years after Yermak led his Cossack band across the Urals, another party of Cossacks pushed eastward from Yakutsk and reached the shore of the Pacific at Okhotsk.

For a thousand miles eastward of the Ural Mountains the Russian advance had led through country closely resembling that on the western side of the mountains: extensive plains watered by great rivers, which, however, flowed northward to the Arctic instead of toward the south. About one third of the way across Asia the nature of the land began to change. The great mountain barrier which runs diagonally across the continent turned the Cossack pioneers more and more to the northeast toward the upland region of eastern Siberia. Even after the crossing of the Stanovoi range in 1638 Russian exploration continued to hold a northward trend, and in 1690 it had penetrated as far as Kamchatka, where permanent settlements were established.

In the broad plains just to the east of the Urals, especially in the fertile southern portion, Russian peasants promptly settled down as agricultural colonists. Beyond the limit of these plains the eastward expansion, like the later westward occupation of America, was the work of the hunter, the trapper, and the fur-trader. The cold, rugged country of northeastern Asia, sparsely inhabited by primitive hunting tribes, was rich in fur-bearing animals, for whose pelts Russia furnished a ready market; and the demand for more and more furs was the economic motive which drove the Russians, a half-century after they had reached Kamchatka, still farther eastward to the Aleutian Islands and to Alaska.

In 1638 the Cossacks who reached the coast at Okhotsk heard apparently for the first time of a great river—the Amur—which flowed into the ocean five hundred miles to the south. In the same year a second exploring party, sent out from the settlement at Yeniseisk, pushed southward along the upper branches of the Lena River until it came into contact with some bands of Tungusic Tartars. These Tartars told of other tribes, dwelling still farther southward, who had commercial relations with the Chinese. Upon the receipt of this information the local commander at Yakutsk dispatched an expedition to establish contact with the tribes south of the watershed, but it was not until 1643 that Russian explorers finally succeeded in reaching the Amur River near the present site of Blagoveschensk. In 1648 still another party found its way across the Yablonoi Mountains to the Shilka, which flows eastward into the upper Amur.

These first two expeditions into the Amur region spread terror and destruction among the primitive hunting peoples who inhabited the country. The Cossack explorers looted and destroyed the villages, slaughtered the men, and carried away the women and children into captivity. Thus far, however, the Russians had not come into conflict with the Chinese, nor had they made any attempt to establish permanent posts on the Amur.

In the spring of 1649 Khabarov, having recruited a company of a hundred and fifty men, entered the Amur valley by way of the Olekma and Shilka rivers. In the summer of 1650 Khabarov came unexpectedly upon a village of Dauri Tartars at Albazin on the Amur. The Dauri were defeated with great slaughter, and the Cossack leader found himself in possession of a site suitable for fortification. Pursuing the defeated hunters, he forced them to pay tribute, after which he returned to Albazin for the winter. During the summer of 1651 he continued his advance down the Amur, conquering and plundering as he went. Passing the mouth of the Sungari River, Khabarov about the end of September made his winter camp on the site of the city which now bears his name, Khabarovsk, at the confluence of the Ussuri and the Amur.

At Khabarovsk, in the early spring of 1652, came the first actual conflict between the Russians and the Chinese Empire. Appealed to by their tributary Dauri tribes, the Peking government dispatched a force of about a thousand men with instructions to capture the foreign invaders and bring them alive to the capital. Unhampered by these instructions, the Chinese troops might have succeeded in destroying the little force; but two hundred well-armed adventurers are not easily taken with bare hands, and the Cossacks, when they discovered that the Chinese were endeavoring to capture them without shedding blood, opened a deadly fire which soon drove their opponents from the field. This was the last important achievement of Khabarov as a leader in the Amur region. Later in the spring his little army was reinforced by fresh recruits from Yakutsk; but almost immediately a part of his force mutinied and began independent operations under a rival leader, and in the summer of 1653 Khabarov, surrendering his command to a lieutenant, left the Amur.

In February, 1654, Alexis, the second Czar of the Romanov line, in spite of this border conflict dispatched an embassy to Peking for the purpose of establishing relations between the two empires. This embassy, which arrived at Peking in March, 1656, remained for six months at the Chinese capital but failed to transact any important diplomatic business. In part this failure may be attributed to the ambassador's refusal to perform the *kowtow* (the prostrations required by the ceremonial of the Chinese court) or to deliver the Czar's letter into the hands of anyone other than the emperor himself; but it must also be attributed in part to the continual depredations of the Cossacks in the Amur valley.

In May, 1654, Khabarov's successor, Stepanov, advanced up the Sungari River and came into conflict with a Chinese army which drove him back to the banks of the Amur. Reinforced by a fresh detachment of Cossacks, he fortified a camp at Khamarsk on the Amur, and here in March, 1655, he successfully resisted a siege by the Chinese. For three years longer Stepanov continued his depredations in the lower Amur valley, while other bands of Cossacks were engaging in similar activities along the upper reaches of the river; but in the summer of 1658 his force of nearly five hundred men was defeated and almost exterminated by the Chinese. The commander and two hundred and seventy of his men were killed, while a hundred and eighty of the survivors took to the mountains, only to be wiped out later by a Chinese frontier force.

The destruction of Stepanov's forces practically cleared the lower Amur of the Russians, but the upper part of the valley was still occupied by several bodies of Cossacks, some of them led by government officers and others by uncontrolled outlaws. As bases for their operations, moreover, the Russians held the fortified posts of Albazin, which had been established by Khabarov in the fall of 1650, and Nerchinsk, on the Shilka, which was founded in the early summer of 1658. Nerchinsk, being located well up the Shilka from its junction with the Amur, attracted comparatively little attention from the Chinese; but Albazin was a constant challenge to their territorial claims, and in 1685 a Chinese army was finally sent against this center of disturbance. After a short siege the place was taken. Some of the defenders were carried off to Peking as prisoners of war, while the rest were allowed to join their fellow countrymen at Nerchinsk; the fortifications were destroyed, and the Chinese army withdrew from the scene of its triumph. As soon as the victors had withdrawn, the Russians returned and rebuilt their post. In 1686 Albazin was again besieged. This time the siege was less energetically prosecuted, and in the following year the arrival of a Russian envoy with proposals for a diplomatic settlement of the frontier troubles led the Chinese to transform their operations into a merely defensive blockade.

In August, 1689, the representatives of K'ang Hsi and of the young Czar, Peter the Great, concluded at Nerchinsk the first treaty ever negotiated by China with a European power. The Treaty of Nerchinsk was destined to be one of the longest-lived treaties in diplomatic history. Slight modifications were made in

1727 and again in 1768, but with these amendments it continued to regulate the relations between the two empires until 1858, a hundred and sixty-nine years after its negotiation.

Most pressing of the points to be settled at Nerchinsk was the establishment of a definite boundary between Chinese and Russian territories. On this question the views of the two governments were widely divergent. The Russians, anxious to use the Amur for trading purposes, hoped to make the river the boundary line; while the Chinese, claiming sovereignty over the entire Amur valley, insisted that the boundary should be drawn along the crest of the watershed separating the Amur and its tributaries from the northward-flowing tributaries of the Lena. As finally determined the boundary followed the Shilka River to a point to the east of Nerchinsk and then turned north to follow the watershed, as demanded by the Chinese. This compromise enabled the Russians to retain possession of Nerchinsk; but China retained the entire Amur valley, and the Albazin post was promptly destroyed.

For the preservation of peace and order along the frontier the treaty provided that Chinese or Russians who crossed the frontier illegally or who committed offenses beyond the territorial limits of their respective countries should be apprehended by the authorities of the territory where the crimes were committed and handed over for punishment by their own national officials. Between this agreement and the system of extraterritoriality established by China's nineteenth-century treaties with the Western powers there are obvious fundamental differences. In the first place, the arrangement in the Treaty of Nerchinsk was fully reciprocal, and, in the second place, the sovereign of the state to which the offender belonged, although punishing for crimes committed outside the limits of his territorial jurisdiction, did not maintain officers for this purpose on foreign soil but imposed punishment only when the offender had been returned to his own country.

In addition to delimiting the boundary and providing for the punishment of transfrontier offenses the Nerchinsk Treaty legalized trade between the two empires and thus laid the foundation for lasting and important commercial relations. "All persons, of what condition soever they may be, may come and go reciprocally, with full liberty, from the territories subject to either empire, into those of the other, provided they have passports by which it appears that they come with permission; and they shall be suffered to buy and sell whatever they think fit, and carry on a mutual trade." Under this arrangement Nerchinsk developed a profitable exchange of goods with the inhabitants of the Amur region, while Kiakhta, southeast of Irkutsk, eventually became the point of departure for a voluminous trade across Mongolia to Peking.

Fully appreciating the advantages which might be derived from the commercial clauses of the Nerchinsk Treaty, Peter the Great in 1692 dispatched to Peking a fresh embassy headed by Isbrandt Ides, who was able to secure from the Chinese government a liberal interpretation of these clauses. In 1719 the Czar sent Captain Ismailov to the Peking court for the purpose of adjusting disputes which had arisen out of Cossack activities along the frontier.

Like the Russian ambassador who had arrived at Peking in 1656, Ismailov regarded the performance of the kowtow as humiliating both to himself and to the sovereign whom he represented; at first, therefore, he refused to conform to the Chinese ceremonial. K'ang Hsi was able to convince the ambassador that the performance of the kowtow involved no acknowledgment of Russian inferiority. "Let him be informed," said the emperor, "of my intention to have rendered to the letter which he brings me from his master the same honors which our customs provide for my person. Therefore I desire that he place this letter on a table, and then a high official of the court will go, in my name, and bow his head to the ground before the letter." His objections having been removed by this reciprocal arrangement, Ismailov performed the kowtow and succeeded in bringing to a successful conclusion the negotiations for which he had been sent.

The existing friendly relations between China and Russia were improved during this period by an embassy from the Chinese emperor to the khan of the Turgut Tartars, who occupied a position in southern Russia between the Don and Volga rivers. The Turguts formerly had dwelt in northern Mongolia; and in 1703 the nephew of their chief had traveled to Lhasa to pay his respects to the Dalai Lama, after which he visited the Chinese emperor at

Peking. In 1712, when this prince planned to return to his own country, K'ang Hsi decided to send with him an embassy accredited to the Turgut khan; and he designated for this diplomatic undertaking the vice-president of the Board of War, Tu-li-shin. The Chinese ambassador left Peking in June, 1712, and traveled by way of Irkutsk, Tobolsk, Kazan, and Saratov, at all of which places he was cordially entertained by the Russian authorities; in June, 1715, after an absence of just three years, he returned to Peking. Although Tu-li-shin had no direct diplomatic dealings with the government of Peter, the treatment which he received at the hands of the Russian officials made a favorable impression upon the ambassador and upon the members of his suite. The official report of the mission[1] is interesting both as an account of an unusual diplomatic undertaking and as a record of Chinese impressions of eighteenth-century Russia.[2]

The establishment of Kiakhta as a frontier trading post was an important step in the development of commercial relations between the two empires. From Kiakhta to Peking is a distance of nearly a thousand miles, by air line, and the greater part of this distance is across the barren expanse of Mongolia. In spite of these difficulties Kiakhta quickly assumed prominence in the trade between Russia and China. Across the border from the Russian town there grew up the Chinese town of Maimatchin, populated by Chinese merchants and by the frontier officials appointed for the regulation of trade. From Kiakhta-Maimatchin, caravans crossing the desert to Peking by way of Urga and Kalgan carried chiefly the furs of Siberia, for which China offered an almost insatiable market.

In addition to furs, however, the Chinese received from the Russian traders a variety of European commodities: Russian, French, German, and English textiles, leather, tanned hides, glassware, and hardware. Cattle, horses, camels, and hunting dogs also

[1] It has been translated into English by Sir George T. Staunton as *Tu-li-shin's Narrative of the Chinese Embassy to the Khan of the Tourgouth Tartars.*

[2] The courtesy and consideration of the Manchu court made a lasting impression upon the Turgut khan and his successors, and in 1771, despite the strenuous opposition of the government of Catherine the Great, the Turguts migrated eastward from their south-Russian home to settle in the Ili valley under the sovereignty of Ch'ien Lung, the grandson of K'ang Hsi.

played a part in the trade. In return for all these the Chinese exported all kinds of manufactured silk, cotton cloth, tea, porcelain, sugar, preserved ginger, rhubarb, and lacquered work—both Chinese and Japanese. By 1777 the trade across the frontier at Kiakhta, according to the figures of the Russian customs officials, amounted to 2,868,333 rubles, upon which the Russian government levied duties amounting to nearly half a million rubles. With the inclusion of the inevitable contraband trade, for which no figures are available, it is reasonable to estimate the total trade at about four million rubles.

After the first siege of Albazin, in 1685, some thirty Russian prisoners of war were taken to Peking, where they were held in mild captivity and later were joined by a number of Russian deserters who voluntarily gave themselves up to the Chinese authorities. With the permission of the authorities these Russians settled down in the northeast corner of the capital, where they erected a church. The able-bodied men were taken into the Chinese military service as members of one of the eight "Banner Corps," and they were so well contented with their lot that when the Czar demanded their release they refused repatriation.

In 1715 K'ang Hsi permitted an archdeacon, a priest, a deacon, and seven clerks to come to Peking for the purpose of ministering to the spiritual needs of the little community. Twelve years later, when the Treaty of Nerchinsk was revised, a clause was incorporated providing for the establishment of an ecclesiastical mission at Peking. This mission consisted of four priests and six students of the Chinese language, the students being recalled and replaced as soon as they had become proficient in their Chinese studies. From early in the eighteenth century, therefore, the Russians had assured themselves a regular supply of adequately trained interpreters for their commercial and diplomatic intercourse with China. In addition to the little Russian community permanently residing at the Chinese capital a number of Russians were permitted to visit Peking for commerce. The 1727 revision of the Nerchinsk Treaty permitted a caravan of not more than two hundred persons to come every third year from Kiakhta and to remain temporarily for the purpose of exchanging their goods.

The development of diplomatic and commercial contact with China, important though it was, claimed only a small part of the energy and attention of the Russians. In response to the ever increasing demand for furs the trappers and fur-traders pushed their way into the most remote northeastern regions of the continent, explored the islands along the Pacific and Arctic coasts, and eventually crossed the northern Pacific to the American mainland, which they explored southward until their outposts met those of the British and of the northward-advancing Spanish. Like the advance across the continent, this work of exploration was undertaken at first by private initiative, but in the later stages it was supported and encouraged by the government. From the reign of Peter the Great capable navigators were dispatched to the Pacific to carry out voyages of exploration, while cartographers and other scientists were delegated to accompany these voyages for the purpose of gathering accurate information concerning the new lands which might be discovered.

The island of Sakhalin, which lies along the Siberian coast southward from the mouth of the Amur, was first discovered by the Cossacks, who in 1643–1646 explored the Amur from the site of Blagoveschensk to the sea. As a result of their reports the island appears on the maps of European cartographers after about 1666; but the Treaty of Nerchinsk excluded the Russians from the Amur valley, and their only explorations of this part of the coast after 1689 were those starting from Okhotsk or from Kamchatka.

From the ports of Kamchatka the Russians also gained their earliest knowledge of the Kuril Islands and made their first attempts to establish contact with Japan. By 1698 or 1699 they had completed the exploration of the Kamchatka peninsula, the southern part of which was inhabited by tribesmen known as Kurils. The Kurils were decidedly warlike, and it was not until 1705 that the Russians succeeded in conquering them and making themselves the masters of this part of Kamchatka. From the southern coast of the peninsula the northernmost islands of the Kuril chain were visible; but the Cossacks, who had made their way into Kamchatka by the land route, had no boats at their disposal, and for several years no attempt was made to occupy or even to explore the islands. In the meantime a number of Japanese junks, probably fishing vessels driven north by storms, were wrecked on the Kamchatka coast, and the Russians secured from the survivors information concerning the entire chain of islands as far as the main island of Japan.

In the early summer of 1713 an expedition consisting of sixty-two men, including a shipwrecked Japanese who acted as pilot and interpreter, embarked on several small boats for the exploration and conquest of the Kuril Islands. Although landings were made on only three of the islands, the expedition reported and charted fifteen islands in the chain. To quote: "On the fifteenth, Matsmai, there is a Japanese city. Next to this island is the main island of Japan. In addition to these enumerated islands there are other small islands in different quarters." In 1720 a second expedition to the south, dispatched by Peter the Great, went only as far as the fifth of these islands.

In the summer of 1728 Captain Vitus Bering, sailing under orders which had been drawn up three and a half years earlier by Peter the Great, made a voyage northward from Kamchatka to explore the northeastern coast of Asia and to discover whether—and, if so, where—a connection between Asia and America existed. Bering proceeded as far north as the arctic circle without discovering any connection between the two continents and then turned back to Kamchatka. He had not carried out his instructions to the letter, nor had he proved the existence or nonexistence of an isthmus connecting northeastern Asia with Alaska; but he had sailed through the strait which now bears his name, and his observations made possible a more accurate delineation of the coast along which he had sailed.

In 1732, while Bering was in St. Petersburg, Michael Gwosdef sailed northward along the coast of Kamchatka and then, turning eastward, appears to have reached—without knowing it—a point on the Alaskan coast. Nine years after the voyage of Gwosdef, Bering sailed again from Kamchatka. Passing to the south of the Aleutian Islands, he reached the coast of Alaska on July 20 at a point somewhere to the north of Kodiak Island. In spite of the protests of Steller, the scientist who had been attached to the expedition, Bering remained here only one day—long enough to replenish his supply of drinking water but not long enough to permit any satisfactory scientific study of the land which he had discovered. The commander's fears that the advancing season would render difficult his return to Kamchatka proved only too well grounded. For three months and a half his ship struggled against head winds, storms, and fogs, and on November 6 it was wrecked on Bering Island, some two hundred and fifty miles from the Kamchatka coast. During the voyage and the long winter spent on the island thirty members of the expedition, including Bering, died. In the spring the forty-six survivors constructed a small vessel from the timbers of their wrecked ship, and in August, 1742, they finally succeeded in making their way back to the port of Petropavlovsk in Kamchatka.

In 1738, 1739, and 1742 Captain Spanberg, one of Bering's lieutenants, made three voyages of exploration toward the south. On the second of these he sighted the Japanese coast at thirty-nine degrees north latitude and sailed along it to the latitude of thirty-seven degrees thirty minutes.

From 1739 until the reopening of Japan, more than a century later, to intercourse with the Western world the Russians made repeated attempts to establish commercial relations with the Island Empire. In these attempts to establish friendly relations Japanese sailors who from time to time were shipwrecked on the Kamchatka coast played an important part. Some of these survivors became instructors in the Japanese language at Russian institutions of learning, while one of them, in 1702, was personally interviewed by Peter the Great, who displayed a keen interest in Japan. Besides instructing the Russians in the Japanese language the castaways furnished the Russians with a plausible excuse for approaching the Japanese coast. Captain Spanberg on his voyage of 1739 carried with him a number of shipwrecked Japanese whom he was to restore to their native land. On this voyage the ships of Spanberg's main squadron, as well as the one which became separated from him, stopped at several places along the Japanese coast, where goods were exchanged with the inhabitants and visits were received from the local officials. As an attempt to open diplomatic relations with the Japanese government, however, this voyage was a complete failure.

Subsequent efforts of a similar nature produced equally unsatisfactory results. In 1792, during the reign of Catherine the Great, a Russian ship bringing shipwrecked Japanese arrived at Hakodate. The Japanese officials were polite, but they refused to receive their fellow countrymen and informed the Russians that foreigners were permitted to visit only the port of Nagasaki. Twelve years later the government of Alexander I dispatched an ambassador to Nagasaki to attempt to negotiate a treaty, but the Japanese government rejected his overtures and notified him that Russian ships henceforth should not enter Japanese waters.

Although the Tokugawa government thus refused to enter into any direct communication with the Russian Empire, the steady advance of the Russians in Sakhalin and southward along the Kurils became increasingly a matter of concern for the Japanese authorities. In 1811 the Russian captain Golownin landed on the island of Iterup, the largest of the Kurils and the nearest but one to Yezo. This island having recently been occupied by the Japanese, Golownin and five of his men were captured and were held as prisoners for several years. When the Russians were finally allowed to return to their own country, their only complaint was that the Japanese had used them as "schoolteachers," compelling them to instruct their captors in the Russian language. Determined to keep the Russians at arm's length as long as that was possible, the Japanese took full advantage of this opportunity to learn the language of their neighbors, in order to be able to deal with them when they could no longer be kept at a distance.

Russian emigration into the plains of western Siberia needed little official encouragement, but the more eastern regions long remained the land of hunter and trapper. In 1681 an attempt was made to establish an agricultural colony in the Shilka valley by sending to Nerchinsk a number of families of convicts. This policy might have been successful in the valley of the Amur; but eight years later the Amur was abandoned to China, and the land around Nerchinsk was poorly suited to agriculture. So long as Russia's Far Eastern domain was bounded by the line fixed in the Nerchinsk

Treaty, therefore, its Russian population consisted almost entirely of turbulent Cossacks, outlaws, deported criminals, and exiled political offenders. From the reign of Catherine the Great the mines at Nerchinsk and elsewhere in eastern Siberia were increasingly utilized as places to which criminal as well as political offenders were sent under sentence of penal servitude, and this use continued practically to the end of the czarist regime.

Only with the acquisition of the Amur and Maritime provinces, after the middle of the nineteenth century, did Russian colonization in the extreme eastern part of Asia begin to develop along other and more healthy lines. Up to that point Russia, in the Far East, "showed that she could conquer but she gave little evidence that she could civilize; she subdued the natives but did not enlighten them." Prior to 1850 the Russians appear to have done no more than to explore, occupy, and partially exploit the great open spaces of northern Asia.

SUGGESTED REFERENCES

BADDELY, J. F. Russia, Mongolia, China . . . 1602–1676.

CAHEN, G. Histoire des relations de la Russie avec la Chine sous Pierre le Grand (1689–1730).

GOLDER, F. A. Russian Expansion on the Pacific, 1641–1850.

KRAUSSE, A. Russia in Asia.

MORSE, H. B. The International Relations of the Chinese Empire, Vol. I.

MORSE, H. B. and MACNAIR, H. F. Far Eastern International Relations.

PASVOLSKY, L. Russia in the Far East.

SKRINE, F. H. The Expansion of Russia.

XXI

Central Asia: Lamaism in Tibet and Mongolia

The Origin of Lamaism · Monasticism and the Monarchy in Tibet · Reforms in
Tibetan Buddhism; Tsongkapa and the Yellow Bonnet Sect of Lamas · Lamaism
and the Mongols · The Chinese Government and Lamaism

PRIOR to the second quarter of the seventh century the people of Tibet were followers of the Bon religion, a shamanis-
tic cult which still exists in some parts of the country. About 632,
however, under the royal patronage of Srong-tsan Gam-po, Buddhism was introduced into the kingdom. With the introduction of
Buddhism there were brought into Tibet, also from India, two
systems of writing based upon the Brahmi script, which at first
were used by the Tibetan Buddhists almost exclusively for the
preservation of their sacred writings. The marriage of Srong-tsan
Gam-po several years later to a princess of China and to an Indian
princess, both of whom were Buddhists, contributed in no small
degree to the spread of the new religion.

During the century which followed its introduction the adherents
of Buddhism steadily increased in number. Monasteries were established, and the monks, or lamas, became especially influential
at Lhasa, the capital. About the middle of the eighth century,
Tibetan Buddhism, which was still struggling against the old Bon
cult for popular acceptance, was strengthened by the arrival of the
Indian missionary Padmasambhava. As in Japan, where Buddhism
strengthened its position by adopting ancient Shinto deities as
bodhisattvas, so in Tibet the new faith overcame the ancient Bon
religion by assuming a form in harmony with popular religious
ideas. Padmasambhava was from Nalanda in the Ganges valley,
the stronghold of Tantric Buddhism, and he brought to Tibetan
Buddhism a wealth of mystic beliefs and magic rites which enabled
it to meet the Bon sorcerers on their own ground. The lamas of the

monastic order founded by Padmasambhava, which still exists as the "Red Bonnet" sect, rejected the traditional monastic rules of celibacy and abstinence. Their chief claim to spiritual eminence and to popular respect was based upon the miraculous power of their incantations and upon their ability to invoke the aid of supernatural beings; but these claims sufficed to gain for the Red Bonnet lamas wide popularity at the expense both of the Bon priests and of the more conservative lamas of the older monasteries.

For two centuries after its introduction Lamaism (the Tibetan form of Buddhism) continued to enjoy royal favor, and the successors of Srong-tsan Gam-po bestowed lavish gifts upon the increasingly numerous monasteries, whose lamas, often numbering thousands, exercised a growing influence in the country. About 840, however, the monarchy, instigated by the adherents of the old Bon religion, turned against the lamas and tried to destroy their power. The result of this reversal in religious policy was to plunge the kingdom into civil war. The monasteries were too strongly established to be overthrown, and the outcome of the struggle was the complete disintegration of the once powerful Tibetan kingdom. With the dissolution of the monarchy the monks became all-powerful, and Tibet, divided into a multitude of practically independent districts, passed under the theocratic rule of the monastic clergy.

During the eleventh century the steady development of degrading practices among the lamas aroused some of the Tibetan Buddhists to institute reforms whereby the teachings and practices of Lamaism would be brought into closer harmony with those of the Mahayanist church in other countries. Under the leadership of a Tibetan lama and of an Indian monk who had spent some years in Sumatra a general council was held about 1050 at Lhasa. This council condemned many of the practices of Tantric Buddhism and re-established the monastic rules of celibacy and abstinence. Some thirty years after the date of this council the Tibetan monk Mar-pa, who had studied in India, attempted further reforms and established a new school of contemplative Buddhism. In spite of the partial success of these movements the Red Bonnet lamas continued to be the most numerous and most powerful branch of Tibetan

Buddhism, and their abbots, rejecting the rule of celibacy, became hereditary religious rulers, exercising absolute authority over the great monasteries.

Three centuries after this earlier attempt at religious reform there appeared in Tibet the famous Tsongkapa, the founder of the Gelugpa, or "Virtuous," sect—commonly known as the "Yellow Bonnets." Born in 1357 in the Amdo district of eastern Tibet, Tsongkapa entered a monastery at an early age and soon devoted himself to a life of asceticism and study. The saintly character of this religious enthusiast gradually won recognition, and he gathered around him a body of "reformed" lamas who took the old monastic vows and assumed a yellow garb as a means of distinguishing themselves from the members of the Red Bonnet sect. In 1409 Tsongkapa founded at Lhasa the Galdan monastery, which has since been the headquarters of his order; and before his death, which occurred in 1419, he established two other Yellow Bonnet monasteries.

The distinguishing feature of the Gelugpa sect, as well as the chief source of the great influence which it eventually attained, was its emphasis upon the ancient Hindu doctrine of transmigration, to which Tsongkapa gave a new and "practical" turn. According to the Gelugpa theology each nation, each district, and each chief monastery of the reformed order had as its patron saint a bodhisattva or an arhat of whom the presiding member of the Gelugpa clergy in that territorial division or monastery was believed to be the incarnation. Tsongkapa himself, as head of the entire order, was believed to be the incarnation of Amitabha, or Amida, who, worshiped as the "Buddha of Infinite Light," was a manifestation of Buddha himself. Upon the death of an "incarnation" the patron saint immediately became reincarnate in the person of a newborn infant who, when his identity had been established, was recognized as the divinely constituted spiritual head of the community or area involved. The identification of a new incarnation often became the subject of no little controversy, and the fact that each new incarnation necessitated a period of regency might be regarded as a further inherent weakness in the system; but the claim that the rulers of the church were actual incarnations of the local patron saints, coupled as it was with the esteem in which the Yellow Bonnets were held by reason of their learning and spirituality, enabled the reformed body gradually to gain throughout Tibet the preponderant power which it has held to the present day.

When Kublai Khan in the last half of the thirteenth century became the head of the Mongol empire, he became interested in Tibetan Lamaism partly as an instrument through which he could establish his political control over the Tibetan people and partly as a religion which might have a civilizing effect upon his own warlike Mongol subjects. For both reasons the great Mongol ruler lavished favors upon the members of the Tibetan hierarchy, and Lamaism, with the aid of this imperial patronage, rapidly became the religion of the Mongols in China as well as in the homeland north of the Gobi desert. After the overthrow of the Mongol dynasty in China the religious connection between the Mongols and Tibet continued.

Although these new adherents to the Tibetan form of Buddhism had made their acquaintance with the religion at a time when the Red Bonnet sect was dominant, the Gelugpa sect of Tsongkapa gradually supplanted the older organization in Mongolia as in the greater part of Tibet. In 1577 Altan Khan, ruler of the Tumed Mongols, proclaimed the Gelugpa teaching to be the official religion of his people, and conferred upon the Grand Lama of Lhasa, head of the Gelugpa hierarchy, the title of Dalai ("Universal") Lama, the title by which his successors have since been designated. The prominence of the Mongols in the Gelugpa sect is illustrated by the fact that when the Dalai Lama died, in 1588, his successor was found among the descendants of Altan Khan. The Mongols, in accordance with the system of Tsongkapa, were organized into new religious provinces, each with its own local patron saint whose incarnation, known by the Mongol term *hutukhtu*, exercised powers similar to those of his Tibetan prototype.

The Tibetan form of Buddhism appears never to have made a strong appeal to the Chinese people, and Kublai Khan's partiality for the lamas was severely criticized by his Chinese subjects. In spite of these facts the monarchs of the two dynasties which ruled the Chinese Empire after the fall of the Mongols showed much interest in Lamaism and endeavored in all possible ways to strengthen the power of the hierarchy in the regions where it had become established. In the case of the Ming dynasty this policy related almost entirely to Tibet and was dictated by a realization of the fact that a continuation of the Lamaist regime constituted the best insurance against the rise of a troublesome military power on the western frontier of the empire. During the period of Ming rule in China, Tibetan history is a record of an almost constant struggle between the lama hierarchy, supported by China, and the secular princes, who were allied with the "unconverted" Mongols of the far-western regions. As the power of the Ming dynasty declined, their ecclesiastical protégés in Tibet lost their dominant position, only to recover it when the Manchu rulers of China revived the policy of their Ming predecessors.

For the Manchu emperors the cultivation of friendly relations with the lama hierarchy was a matter of even greater concern than it was to the Ming government. Simultaneously with their conquest of China the Manchus had extended their sway over the eastern—"lamaized"—Mongol tribes, and the task of ruling these subject peoples was greatly facilitated by the establishment of a cordial understanding with Tibetan Lamaism. In 1717 Tsewang Rabdan, ruler of the western-Mongol tribe of Eleuths, sent an army to Lhasa and installed as head of the hierarchy a Dalai Lama favorable to the Eleuths. Three years later, however, the emperor K'ang Hsi dispatched a Chinese expedition to the Tibetan capital; the Eleuth party was driven from power, a Chinese protectorate was established over the country, and a new Dalai Lama was installed with two resident Chinese officials to assist him in the direction of political affairs.

Manchu control over the Tibetan church and state was more definitely established in 1751 by the emperor Ch'ien Lung. An imperial decree of that year placed both spiritual and temporal authority in the hands of the Dalai Lama as supreme pontiff, but it also provided that the two resident Chinese advisers—*ambans*—should exercise control over all his political acts. Ch'ien Lung decreed, moreover, that the two ambans should have a controlling influence in the important question of establishing the identity of the successor to the post of Dalai Lama when that office became vacant; and the imperial government, while officially recognizing the primacy of the Lhasa potentate, took the precaution of strengthening the position of the Panchen Lama of Tashilunpo, in order that this high dignitary, second only to the Dalai Lama in the esteem of the Tibetans, might serve as a check upon the authority of the supreme pontiff.

During the last half of the eighteenth century the Chinese Empire was able once more, as in the glorious days of T'ang, to extend its power far to the west and to bring under its control not only the peoples of Zungaria and Eastern Turkestan but also the tribes dwelling on the western slopes of the Altai and in the valley of the Ili River. This new westward expansion was attributable in no small part to the position which the Manchu rulers had assumed as patrons and protectors of Lamaism. For centuries the warlike Mongols of the north and the turbulent mountaineers of Tibet had been serious obstacles to the establishment of Chinese outposts to the west of Kansu. After the middle of the eighteenth century, as a result of the close entente between the Chinese emperor and the lama hierarchy, it was possible for the imperial patron of the Dalai Lama not only to establish his control in these regions but also to send his armies into the west without fear that they would be cut off by hostile forces from Mongolia or from Tibet.

SUGGESTED REFERENCES

BELL, SIR C. Tibet: Past and Present.

COURANT, M. L'Asie centrale aux XVIIe et XVIIIe siècles.

DAS, S. C. (translator). History of Buddhism in India and Tibet.

DAS, S. C. "Life of Tsongkhapa," *Journal of the Bengal Asiatic Society*, 1882.

FRANCKE, A. H. A History of Western Tibet.

HOWORTH, SIR H. H. History of the Mongols.

ROCKHILL, W. W. The Dalai Lamas of Lhasa, and their Relations with the Manchu Emperors. *T'oung Pao*, 1910.

ROCKHILL, W. W. The Land of the Lamas.

ROERICH, G. Tibetan Paintings.

WADDELL, L. A. The Buddhism of Tibet, or Lamaism.

WESSELS, C. Early Jesuit Travellers in Central Asia.

XXII

Manchu China and the West: 1722–1844

China in 1722 · The Emperor Yung Cheng · The Persecution of Christians · The
Sino-Russian Treaty of Kiakhta · A Chinese Embassy to Russia · The Reign of
Ch'ien Lung · Foreign Trade at Canton · English, French, Dutch, Danes, Swedes,
and Americans · Imperial Regulation of Trade: the Hoppo and the Co-hong ·
Conditions of Residence and Trade · Exports and Imports · Opium · The Macart-
ney Embassy · The Amherst Embassy · Abolition of the East India Company's
Monopoly of English Trade at Canton · His Majesty's Superintendents of Trade ·
Lord Napier at Canton · The Impending Conflict · National Equality and the
Right to Trade · Western Objections to Chinese Law · The Opium Traffic · Com-
missioner Lin Acts · War with Great Britain · The Treaty of Nanking · Additional
Treaties · Most-Favored-Nation Clauses · Extraterritoriality · Modification of the
Edicts against Christianity · Conclusion

WHEN the emperor K'ang Hsi, after a sixty-one-year reign,
died and left the throne to his son Yung Cheng, the Manchu
dynasty was at the height of its power. The empire, consolidated
and pacified by K'ang Hsi's capable administration, enjoyed internal peace and external prestige comparable to that of the "golden
days of T'ang." The uprisings which marked the first twenty years
of the great emperor's reign had been suppressed, but without unnecessary harshness, and K'ang Hsi's just rule had reconciled practically all elements of the Chinese nation to the presence of a
"foreign" dynasty upon the Dragon Throne. The scholar-official
administrators, among whom the emperor himself justly takes high
rank, devoted themselves to the welfare of the people under their
jurisdiction. Six times during his reign K'ang Hsi had made tours
of inspection as far as the Yangtze provinces, and these tours had
done much to create a feeling that the local officials throughout
the empire were being held strictly responsible for the proper
administration of affairs. In imitation of the six moral maxims
promulgated by the founder of the Ming dynasty, K'ang Hsi in
1671 had published a series of sixteen brief commands for the

guidance of the people, thus associating anew the nation as a whole with the imperial government in the task of maintaining peace and prosperity.

From the peoples and states located on its frontiers the Chinese Empire at the close of this long reign commanded general respect and admiration. Nor was this prestige a consequence of an aggressive policy. Unlike his successors on the throne, K'ang Hsi found little pleasure in wars of foreign conquest. After his suppression of the Mongol revolt, which coincided with the outbreak of Wu San-kuei's rebellion, the second emperor of the Manchu dynasty strove only to maintain peace upon his frontiers. Even the depredations of the Russian Cossacks in the Amur valley had been met by essentially defensive operations, and no attempt had been made to exterminate these troublesome neighbors or to drive them northward beyond the mountain barrier.

In his attitude toward the Europeans, those who came by sea as well as those upon his northern frontier, K'ang Hsi combined broad religious tolerance with a statesman's appreciation of the benefits which were to be derived from a flourishing trade. For thirty-two years, from 1685 until 1717, he had permitted the foreign merchants to bring their ships to any port of his empire, reverting to the restrictive policy of his Ming predecessors only upon convincing evidence as to the necessity of such a move. The decrees against Christian missions resulted from no objections to the foreign religious doctrines as such, but from distrust of the powerful institution whose commands the missionaries so implicitly obeyed. Even after the issuance of these decrees the emperor continued to show favor to the Jesuits and to employ them in the service of the government, while the Chinese Christians throughout the empire enjoyed almost complete freedom from persecution.

Succeeding to the throne on the last day of the year 1722, Yung Cheng reigned until October 7, 1735. In his devotion to the tasks of government the new emperor was a worthy successor of his father. His reign was marked by certain useful reforms in internal administration and by a continuance of diplomatic relations with the Russians on the northern frontier. But Yung Cheng lacked the broad tolerance which had characterized K'ang Hsi, while the existence of court cliques which had favored the accession of one or another of his numerous brothers involved him in intrigues and family dissensions.

Partly because of Yung Cheng's suspicions that the Christians were secretly supporting the imperial claims of one of his brothers, the first year of his reign saw the commencement of serious persecution for the foreign religion. In July, 1723, instigated by a group of local scholars, the viceroy of Fukien Province seized the buildings of the Dominican mission at Fuan. In December of the same year this official memorialized the emperor, asking him to exterminate Christianity in all parts of the empire; and in January, 1724, Yung Cheng commanded that all foreign missionaries, save those who were skilled in astronomy and were therefore permitted to remain at Peking, should be deported to Macao and that church property everywhere should be confiscated. There appears to have been no loss of life, either among the foreign missionaries or among their Christian adherents, but Yung Cheng's decree—in contrast with the similarly worded decrees of his father—was vigorously executed. The missionaries were driven from their work in the provinces, and the confiscated mission buildings were converted into schools, public granaries, ancestral halls, and meeting places for the scholars of the districts in which they were located. At Peking the missionaries were allowed to remain and to continue their work, and in 1730 the emperor even contributed to the rebuilding of mission buildings destroyed by earthquake. In the same year, however, the persecution in the provinces broke out afresh, to continue throughout Yung Cheng's reign into that of his successor.

Upon the death of Peter the Great, in January, 1725, the Russian government dispatched an embassy to Peking for the purpose of congratulating the new emperor of China and informing him of the accession of Catherine I to the Russian throne. Russia also wished to negotiate certain desired modifications in the Nerchinsk Treaty of 1689. Count Sava, the Russian ambassador, arrived at the Chinese capital in October, 1726, and remained there until the following April. During his preliminary negotiations at Peking he received valuable assistance from the Jesuit missionaries, to whom he was able to offer the use of the trans-Siberian route for their communications with Europe. In June, 1727, the scene of negotiations was transferred to Kiakhta, on the frontier, and here, on October 21, 1727, the new treaty was signed.

In addition to delimiting the Russo-Chinese frontier in the region west of Manchuria the new treaty gave the Russians the right to send to Peking, once every three years, a caravan comprising not more than two hundred persons. It also gave them, as we have seen in an earlier chapter, the right to maintain at Peking a permanent mission, whose members devoted themselves to the study of the Chinese and Manchu languages.

Having negotiated a new treaty with his great neighbor on the north, Yung Cheng soon gave additional evidence of his desire to cultivate cordial relations with the Russians. In 1730, being informed by the Russians that Peter II had been succeeded on the throne by the empress Anna Ivanovna, he dispatched an embassy to Russia, partly for the purpose of felicitating the new monarch and partly for the purpose of securing co-operation against the troublesome Kalmuk Tartars. The Chinese embassy arrived at Moscow in January, 1731, and exchanged complimentary presents with the Russian sovereign, but no agreement concerning the Kalmuks was reached; in March it set out on its return journey. At the same time Yung Cheng sent a second embassy, also for the purpose of arranging a combination against the Kalmuks, to the Turgut Tartars in the lower Volga; but this embassy, like the one to the Russian court, failed to accomplish any definite result.

Ch'ien Lung, the son and successor of Yung Cheng, actually came to the throne in the autumn of 1735, but according to the reckoning of Chinese historians the dating of the new reign commenced with the beginning of the new year. For a full sixty years he ruled the empire; then, his reign having equaled in length that of his grandfather, he abdicated the throne and spent the remaining three years of his life in peaceful retirement.

Ch'ien Lung takes rank as the great conqueror of the Manchu dynasty and as one of the greatest in the entire history of China. In the north the Mongol tribes were kept under firm control. By 1760 Eastern Turkestan, a part of the empire in the great days of

T'ang, had been reconquered, and China had regained control over the ancient caravan routes to the west. Tibet was brought under Manchu rule, and two imperial residents at Lhasa, leaving spiritual control in the hands of the Dalai Lama, exercised strict supervision over the country's political affairs. In 1792, in reprisal for the invasion of Tibet by the Gurkhas of Nepal, the warlike Ch'ien Lung dispatched into Tibet an army of seventy thousand which drove the invaders back into their own land and, following them into Nepal, forced them to acknowledge the sovereignty of the Chinese Empire. Only in one direction were the armies of the emperor unsuccessful; between 1765 and 1769 four disastrous expeditions were dispatched southward from Yunnan against the kingdom of Burma, at that time ruled by a son of the conquering Alaungpaya. Aided by a tropical climate which took heavy toll of the Chinese armies, the Burmese succeeded in beating off the attacks, but even the Burmese court subsequently acknowledged Chinese suzerainty and dispatched tributary missions at ten-year intervals to Peking.

In spite of his aggressive and successful foreign policy, which made a tremendous impression upon all foreign observers, it is probable that the reign of Ch'ien Lung served to weaken, rather than to strengthen, the position of the Manchu dynasty in China. The Chinese people have never been greatly impressed by the glories of foreign conquest, while they have always resented bitterly any attempt to meet the expenses of war by the imposition of fresh taxes. Thus the victories of Ch'ien Lung's armies were gained at the cost of widespread discontent within his own realms. In every part of the country there began to appear the revolutionary and antidynastic secret societies which, to the end of the Manchu regime, were to be a constant source of trouble. To make matters more serious, this growing weakness at home coincided with growing friction between China and the Europeans.

Even during the period from 1685 to 1717, when all the ports of China were open to foreign trade, most of the European merchants trading with China found it more convenient to trade at Canton than at other points along the coast; after 1717 Canton and Macao were the only ports to which they could legally come. The restrictions imposed by K'ang Hsi were continued by his successors; but the eighteenth century saw a steady growth in China's commercial relations with the maritime countries of the West, and an ever increasing number of ships from all the commercial countries of Europe made their way to Canton for the purpose of securing a share in the rich profits of the "China trade."

For sixty years after Captain Weddell's stormy visit to Canton in 1637 the English made only occasional efforts to trade with China. In 1689, taking advantage of K'ang Hsi's proclamation of free trade at all the ports of his empire, the English East India Company sent a ship to Canton; but it was not until the arrival at Canton of the *Macclesfield*, in August, 1699, that English trade at that port was definitely established. From 1699 until 1715 the English company's trade at Canton was carried on by supercargoes of the various English ships, but the latter date saw the establishment of an English factory with a permanent representative of the company in charge of the trade. By the middle of the eighteenth century the English company held the lion's share of the trade at Canton. Inasmuch as its charter protected it from the competition of other English merchants, the company's ships and the so-called "country ships"—ships built in India and trading at Canton under licenses issued by the company—completely monopolized the importation of Chinese commodities into Great Britain and the British possessions.

French trade at Canton commenced in 1699, but from this date until 1720 the French ventures in this field were not successful. In 1720 the *Compagnie des Indes Orientales*, reorganized under a new charter, entered the China trade; during the fifty years of its existence the French company reaped splendid profits and paid annual dividends ranging from 67 per cent to 141 per cent. In 1770 the company was dissolved, and trade with China under the French flag was thrown open to all French subjects. Almost simultaneously with this change of policy French trade began to decline; in 1786 only one of the forty-eight European ships arriving at Canton was French, and the outbreak of the French Revolution was followed by the closing of the French factory.

For nearly a century after their expulsion from Formosa by the forces of Koxinga the Dutch practically abandoned their efforts to trade at the ports of China, devoting their energies to building up their insular empire and securing from the Chinese merchants who visited their Malaysian ports the Chinese goods desired for export to Holland. Toward the middle of the eighteenth century, however, interest in direct trade with China revived, and in 1762 the Dutch company established a factory at Canton.

A Danish East India Company, founded in 1728, carried on trade with India and at Canton, to which port it usually dispatched one or two ships each year. During the seventeenth century many Swedish ships, sailing under foreign flags, made trips to the Far East, but it was not until 1731 that a Swedish East India Company was chartered. The Swedish company sent a few ships to India; but its principal trade was at Canton, where it maintained a factory until 1814.

After the conclusion of their war for independence the Americans were prompt in making their appearance in the Far East. On February 22, 1784, the first American ship destined for Canton, the *Empress of China*, sailed from New York. She arrived at Canton in August of the same year and returned to her home port in May, 1785. This first venture into the China trade netted a profit of about 25 per cent. In 1786 Major Samuel Shaw, who sailed as supercargo on the *Empress of China*, was elected by Congress to the post of consul at Canton; and in 1790 he was continued in this post by Presidential appointment. By this latter year American trade at Canton was firmly established, and the Americans had become the chief rivals of the British in the maritime trade with China.

For the regulation of the foreign trade at Canton the imperial government after 1702 appointed an official known as the *hoppo*, the name being derived from the *Hu Pu* ("Board of Revenue"), to which he was directly responsible. The hoppo, at least during the first years after the creation of the post, was not a member of the regular official class but a merchant who was exclusively privileged to carry on trade with the foreigner and who, in return for this monopoly, made large annual contributions to the imperial treasury.

By 1720 the inability of a single merchant to handle the trade had become evident, while the exclusion of the other Chinese merchants from any participation in this profitable commerce had aroused a great deal of dissatisfaction among the Cantonese. From this date, therefore, the hoppo ceased to be an active participant in commerce and merely levied certain taxes upon each merchant ship arriving at Canton, while the monopoly of trade on the Chinese side was placed in the hands of a merchant guild known as the *Co-hong*. The number of merchants in the Co-hong varied, tending to increase with the increase in the volume of trade. In 1765 there were ten; in 1807, eleven; and in 1829 the number had risen to thirteen, at which it remained until the system was abolished.

The establishment of the Co-hong made it possible for the officials at Canton to control the trade while avoiding any direct contact with the foreign merchants. As individuals the guild merchants—known as the *hong* merchants or the "security" merchants—assumed full responsibility for the particular foreigner or foreigners with whom they did business, while the guild as a whole was similarly responsible for the behavior of the entire foreign community and for the transactions of the individual guild members.

Each foreign trading house permanently established in the Canton trade or each independent ship arriving at the port transacted all its business through the medium of a single Co-hong member. The hong merchant took charge of the payment of all port dues and taxes, arranged for the accommodation of his client during his stay at port, hired the necessary clerks, interpreters, and household servants, provided lighters and coolies for unloading the cargo, and disposed of the imported goods. With his cargo sold the foreigner arranged with his Chinese guarantor for the purchase of such goods as he wished to load for the return voyage, and the provisioning of the ship, as well as all details connected with securing official clearance papers, was taken care of by the same agency.

In its corporate character the Co-hong had the duty of notifying and explaining to the foreigners the regulations set forth by the civil officials, and the further duty of enforcing these regulations when necessary by putting a stop to the trade of an offending group or of the entire foreign community. In addition the Co-hong, as a whole, guaranteed the solvency of each individual member and maintained a reserve fund to meet the debts of any member who might become bankrupt. Through the Co-hong the foreigners might on occasion petition for redress of grievances or for improvement of trading conditions; directly, however, they had no contact with the officials or right of approach to them.

The trading season at Canton began in the late summer with the arrival of the ships from Europe and from the Indies. The foreign commercial community then left Macao, where it had spent the summer months, and took up its residence in the factories at Canton. The Canton factories occupied a narrow strip of ground, some three hundred yards in length, between the suburbs of the city and the bank of the Pearl River on the south. In the early years of the nineteenth century the factories were thirteen in number; each consisted of a series of buildings, one behind the other, in which the foreign merchants resided and transacted their business as tenants of the hong merchants. Between the factories and the river bank, a distance of about a hundred yards, was an open space—the "square"—which was reserved as a recreation ground. On three days each month the foreigners, if properly attended by Chinese interpreters, were permitted to visit the flower gardens a short distance up the river, but with this exception their only exercise was obtained by walking in the square.

Equally rigid restrictions controlled every detail of residence in the factories. No one was permitted to come up from Macao or depart thither without an official transit pass. Boats coming up from Macao were searched for firearms and other contraband goods. No foreign women were permitted in the factories; they were required remain at Macao when their husbands came upriver. At the end of each trading season, usually about the middle of April, the foreign staffs withdrew to Macao for the summer; they were not allowed to "loiter" at Canton after the ships had departed.

Chief of all the exports from Canton was tea. First introduced into England about 1666, the "Chinese herb" had gradually acquired such popularity that the amount of tea exported from Canton in British ships bound for England averaged during the fifteen years from 1814 to 1828 about 14,225 tons per year, slightly more than half the total cargo capacity of all the ships involved. During the period between 1804 and 1833, with the exception of the years of the embargo and of the war with Great Britain, the American ships seldom carried less than 6000 tons of tea per year; the average amount was about 8000 tons, and in the last year of this period the exportation of tea in American vessels amounted to 13,000 tons. In the less flourishing trade of the Dutch, the French, the Danes, and the Swedes the situation was the same: tea was king. Silk, chinaware, nankeen cloth, sugar, ginger, and rhubarb constituted supplementary exports of varying significance, but for all the countries of the West tea was the outstanding reason for the very existence of the China trade.

In return for this great staple export the maritime traders at Canton brought from their own countries little for which a market existed in China. Like the Russians at Kiakhta, the Americans at Canton found a ready sale for the furs gathered in by their trappers and fur-traders, while their ships also brought ginseng root, quicksilver, lead, iron, copper, and cotton. The total annual value of American commodities imported into China, however, seldom reached two million dollars (Mexican), and the trade was balanced by importing silver to the average annual amount (1804-1833) of some four million dollars. In the trade of the European countries, including Great Britain, the imports into China were even more insignificant. The East India Company's imports from England during the last six years of the company's monopoly at Canton averaged only slightly more than 10 per cent of the value of the tea and other commodities exported to England; the balance was made up by importations from the company's Indian possessions or by goods picked up through trade in other parts of the Far East. The Dutch, likewise, paid for their tea and silks largely by spices from the Indies, while the import trade of the other European merchants consisted chiefly of goods secured from the Dutch possessions, supplemented by large annual importations of silver.

Out of the constant efforts of the foreign merchants to discover some import commodity which would find a ready market in China and would thus obviate the necessity for the constantly increasing importation of silver came the development of the opium trade. Opium, the dried juice from the capsule of the poppy flower, had been known to the Chinese since the days of the T'ang dynasty, but until about the middle of the seventeenth century it had been used only as medicine. About 1620 the use of tobacco reached China from the Philippines, and shortly after that date the Dutch in Formosa appear to have discovered that a combination of tobacco and opium, used in smoking, was valuable for the prevention of malaria. From Formosa this practice spread to Fukien on the neighboring mainland, and by the end of the seventeenth century opium was being smoked by itself, not for medicinal reasons but for its soporific effects.

By 1729 the evils of opium-smoking, which had spread gradually from Fukien to the adjoining provinces, had been brought to the attention of the emperor Yung Cheng, who issued an edict against the opening of opium-smoking dens and against the sale of opium for smoking purposes. This prohibition was repeated, without noticeable effect, in the reign of Ch'ien Lung, and in 1800 the emperor Chia Ch'ing, Ch'ien Lung's successor on the throne, issued a decree strictly prohibiting the cultivation of the opium poppy in China as well as the importation of opium from abroad.

In 1729, when Yung Cheng's first decree appeared, the importation of foreign opium, which was chiefly in the hands of the Portuguese, amounted to approximately two hundred chests per year, each chest containing $133\frac{1}{3}$ pounds. After this date the quantity gradually increased, and in 1773 the English East India Company created an opium monopoly in its Indian possessions for the production of the drug. By 1790 the annual amount of foreign opium imported at Canton had risen to about five thousand chests, with an estimated value of from three million to four million dollars.

The greater part of the imported opium came from India and was imported by the East India Company, either in its own ships or in the ships trading under the company's licenses; but additional quantities of opium came from Turkey and from Persia, and merchants of all nationalities, including the Americans, participated in the trade. Prior to 1800 opium was brought to Canton and sold through the security merchants as any other commodity; after that date the drug was discharged at the mouth of the river into the so-called opium hulks anchored in sheltered havens, from which it was delivered, upon orders from the owners, to the Chinese buyers. At the same time the East India Company formally withdrew from the prohibited trade, at least to the extent of ceasing to bring the drug from India in its own ships. But the company, with its Indian monopoly, continued to produce by far the largest part of the opium brought to China; the opium was transported in ships operating under the company's license, and down until the dissolution of its Canton establishment, in 1834, the proceeds from the sale of the opium thus imported were carried in the company's annual balance sheets.

By the last quarter of the eighteenth century the East India Company, dissatisfied with the restrictions upon residence and trade at Canton, was urging the British government to attempt to secure through diplomatic activity some modification of the Chinese regulations. An embassy dispatched in 1788 was lost by shipwreck, but in 1792 the British sent a second embassy headed by Lord Macartney, viscount of Dervock. Arriving in August, 1793, at the mouth of the Pai Ho, Macartney and his suite were transported up the river from Taku to Tungchow in a flotilla of Chinese boats, upon which the Chinese authorities placed banners with the inscription "Tribute Bearers from the Country of England." At Peking the embassy learned that the aged Ch'ien Lung, now in his eighty-second year, was at Jehol, to the north of the Great Wall. After a brief stay at Peking, during which there was much debate concerning the performance of the kowtow, Macartney proceeded to Jehol.

Whether or not the British ambassador performed the kowtow cannot be definitely asserted. The official report of the embassy states that Macartney proposed two alternatives: first, that he would conform to the Chinese custom if a Chinese official, equal to himself in rank, performed the same prostration before the portrait of the English king; second, that he would kneel on one knee according to the custom of the English court. It is asserted that the Chinese finally decided upon the second of these alternatives; but only a few members of Macartney's suite attended the audience, and one of those who was not present claims that the actual form of the ceremony was never divulged. Whether or not the kowtow was performed, the Macartney mission accomplished nothing. The ambassador and his suite were sumptuously entertained, the elaborate gifts were accepted, and equally costly presents were made in return; but the emperor's reply to the requests put forward by the envoy consisted in a definite refusal to open fresh ports for trade or to change any existing regulations.

For two decades after the fruitless Macartney embassy no further diplomatic steps were taken by the British in connection with the trade at Canton. During the Napoleonic wars and the Anglo-American War of 1812 the British aroused the indignation of the Chinese authorities by landing forces at Macao for the purpose of defending that place against possible French attack and by capturing American ships within the territorial waters of China; both actions resulted in the suspension of trade until the offending forces had withdrawn. Except for these brief interruptions, however, the trade at Canton continued in its accustomed grooves. After the close of the Napoleonic struggle the East India Company again urged diplomatic action at Peking, and in 1816 the British government dispatched a fresh embassy, headed by Lord Amherst, to the Chinese capital.

The failure of this mission was more complete than that of the Macartney embassy. Although the British government had instructed the envoy to perform the kowtow if necessary, the younger Sir George Staunton, who was attached to the mission as junior envoy and who as a boy had accompanied the Macartney embassy, argued vehemently and successfully against conforming to the rules of the Chinese court. Arriving at Peking late at night on August 29, Amherst was hurried to the *Yüan Ming Yüan*, the so-called Summer Palace, where he arrived about five o'clock in the morning and where he was informed that his audience would take place at once. Amherst pleaded his inability to appear before the emperor at such short notice. He was travel-worn, dusty, and exhausted; his court costume and credentials were not at hand; therefore he begged to have his audience postponed. In response to his plea that he was ill the emperor's own physician was sent to examine him; and when the Chinese doctor reported that Lord Amherst was merely shamming illness, the rage of Chia Ch'ing flared forth. Orders were issued that the unmannerly envoy should be at once expelled from the palace and escorted to Canton, where he was to embark without delay for his own country.

The history of these two embassies dispatched by the government whose nationals dominated the trade at Canton throws important light upon the attitude of the Chinese government and of the Western governments, respectively, on the subject of commerce. Both embassies, although dispatched in the name of the British monarch, were undertaken not in the interest of the British people as a whole but in the interest of the East India Company. The company paid the expenses, and its representatives, the elder Sir George Staunton in the first mission and his son in the second mission, held the position of junior envoy. In both cases the company had drawn up the list of requests which were presented to the Chinese government; and, in the case of the Amherst embassy at least, the influence of its representative was so great as to outweigh the government's instructions on the question of conforming to the usages of the Chinese court. Both embassies, in fact, represented the East India Company rather than "the majesty of the British crown," and the Chinese were not far wrong in labeling them "Tribute Bearers."

It is very improbable, however, that the most exact compliance with the demands of the Chinese court ceremonial would have induced the imperial government to look more favorably upon the British requests. Even though the Chinese have been from time immemorial a commercial people, there were, in 1793 and in 1816, weighty reasons for imposing additional restrictions upon the existing trade at Canton rather than granting the foreign traders the privilege of trading at new ports. At the earlier date the foreign ships arriving at the port of Canton brought few commodities needed by the Chinese, and practically none which the Chinese could not procure by means of their own "junk trade" with the East Indies. By 1816 there was even less reason to hope for fresh concessions; the growing dimensions of the opium trade had already become a matter for alarm to the imperial government, and the authorities had begun to question whether foreign trade should not be wholly discontinued.

While the East India Company had hoped that the appeal to diplomacy might result in some extensions of its opportunities for trade, it had been even more anxious to preserve unimpaired its already existing privileges. However humiliating and irksome the conditions of residence and trade at Canton, this trade produced splendid profits and enabled the company to pay handsome dividends to its shareholders. Already, however, these privileges had become the object of increasingly bitter attacks in England itself. By 1830 it became obvious that the renewal of the company's charter in 1833 would be attended by the repeal of the clauses granting it a monopoly of the China trade, and in the winter of 1833–1834 the company was required to terminate its commercial activities. Henceforth all British merchants were entitled to engage in the hitherto monopolized commerce.

Toward the end of 1830 the East India Company's Select Committee at Canton, which hitherto had exercised complete control over all British subjects visiting that port, notified the Chinese authorities, through the medium of the Co-hong, of the impending change and informed them that the committee, after the modification of the company's charter, no longer would be able to exercise jurisdiction over all its fellow nationals. In response to this communication the Co-hong, in January, 1831, informed the committee that in the event of such change it would be necessary for the British government to appoint a "headman" who, as authoritative chief of the British "merchant guild," would act as its representative in all necessary dealings with the Co-hong and would be responsible for the behavior of the British at Canton. In making this demand the Co-hong and the officials for whom they spoke had in mind no essential change from the existing system under which the foreigners at Canton were controlled; least of all had they any intention of opening a way for direct relations between the local authorities and an official representative of the British crown.

To the British government, however, there was but one possible response to the Chinese request, and an act of Parliament authorized the creation of a commission to act as His Majesty's superintendent of trade in China. In accordance with this act of Parliament the British government, on December 10, 1833, appointed three superintendents: Lord Napier, Mr. W. H. C. Plowden,[1] and Mr. J. F. Davis. The second and third superintendents had both resided at Canton as members of the East India Company's staff, and two thirds of the commission could thus be regarded by the Chinese as nothing more than a continuation of the old Select Committee. But Lord Napier was a nobleman of high rank and distinguished career, who regarded himself as a diplomatic representative of the British government. Nor were His Majesty's superintendents to limit their activities to the narrow range of duties imposed upon them by the existing Chinese regulations. An order in council, dated December 9, 1833, authorized the superintendents to constitute a court of justice with "criminal and admiralty jurisdiction, for the trial of offenses committed by His Majesty's subjects within the dominions of the Emperor of China, and the ports and havens thereof, and on the high seas, within an hundred miles of the coast of China."

Lord Napier's natural predisposition to regard himself as the diplomatic representative of his government was strengthened by the instructions which he received from the Foreign Secretary, Lord Palmerston. "Your lordship will announce your arrival at Canton," ran the Foreign Secretary's orders, "by letter to the Viceroy." Other passages in his instructions emphasized the importance of maintaining a conciliatory attitude and of avoiding any steps which might offend against the prejudices of the Chinese, but this one sentence imposed upon him the *duty* of violating, on two points, the established Chinese laws. He was to proceed to Canton without applying for and receiving the permission of the local authorities, and he was to assume the right of communicating directly with the viceroy instead of forwarding his communication, as required by Chinese regulations, through the medium of the Co-hong.

Reaching Macao on July 15, 1834, Lord Napier promptly, and without securing an official permit, proceeded to Canton. As soon as the hong merchants learned that the new British headman had come, two members of the Co-hong, ignoring the irregularity of

---

[1] Mr. Plowden left Canton shortly after his appointment, and the commission as actually established included Sir George Robinson as its third member.

his arrival, visited the British factory for the purpose of transmitting the viceroy's instructions. Napier refused to receive any official communication through this channel, and the two merchants departed without having delivered their message. But when the superintendent of trade attempted to announce his arrival "by letter to the viceroy," he met an equally obstinate refusal on the Chinese side.

The *impasse* thus created was not solved during the two months of Lord Napier's stay at Canton; the viceroy persisted in his refusal to communicate with the British headman except through the hong merchants, while Lord Napier refused to communicate with his Chinese compeer except directly and by letter. On September 4 the viceroy ordered the cessation of trade with the British, surrounded the factories with troops, and ordered all the Chinese in British employ to withdraw from the British factory. Lord Napier attempted to counter this move by summoning British warships from the mouth of the river, but on September 20 he abandoned the struggle and withdrew to Macao. When he left Canton, he was an ill man; three weeks later he died at Macao.

CONFLICT AND READJUSTMENT

For five years after Lord Napier's fruitless controversy with the Liang-Kwang[1] viceroy his successors in the post of chief superintendent carefully avoided taking any step which might reopen the dispute; but the issues raised by Lord Napier's instructions, and by his attempts to carry out these instructions, were such as to make inevitable, sooner or later, an armed conflict between China and Great Britain.

Nor was the impending conflict merely a clash between British and Chinese interests and ideas. Although the British government, when war finally broke out, was bitterly criticized by liberal opinion both in England and in other Western countries, the little international community at Canton and Macao was with few exceptions in sympathy with the British, whom it regarded as the champions

[1] The Liang-Kwang viceroyalty included the provinces of Kwangtung and Kwangsi.

of foreign rights against Chinese arrogance and intolerance. From the British—and Western—point of view three great questions were involved: first, the question of diplomatic intercourse on a basis of equality between the representatives of foreign nations and the officials of the Chinese Empire; second, the question whether China could rightfully refuse to grant the merchants of the outside world free access to her markets; and third, the question of submitting to Chinese jurisdiction over the persons and property of foreigners on Chinese soil or in China's territorial waters.

The Napier controversy, as a matter of fact, did not definitely involve the first of these questions. In spite of his instructions and in spite of the conclusions which he drew from those instructions Lord Napier was not an ambassador; he had no diplomatic credentials, the Chinese government had not been requested to receive him as a diplomat, and therefore he was absolutely without basis for his claim to communicate directly with one of the highest officers of the empire. The fact remains, however, that the Chinese government had persisted in regarding as tributary vassals the nations whose people traded at Canton. The two British missions to Peking, like earlier Portuguese and Dutch missions, had been officially designated as tribute-bearers, while official proclamations with their constant reiteration of the term *barbarian* had aroused bitter resentment among the ranks of those to whom the term was applied. To the rank and file of the foreign community, possessing but a rudimentary knowledge of the rules of international intercourse, the Napier episode appeared as the final and insufferable manifestation of China's refusal to recognize the independent and equal sovereignty of any Western state.

An even more definite grievance was found in the Chinese insistence upon restricting foreign trade to the single port of Canton. The growing industrialization of the West had already led to the development of a theory that the right to trade is a "perfect" right, existing independently of any treaty stipulations, and that a refusal of this right is a just and reasonable cause for resort to arms. Conveniently forgotten was the British Navigation Act, and the American tariff policy was still in its formative stage; public opinion at Canton was convinced that China, willfully and wrongfully refusing to participate freely in the reciprocally beneficial transactions of world commerce, must be "opened"—if necessary, by armed force.

Down until the last quarter of the eighteenth century the various foreign nationalities at Canton admitted without question the jurisdiction of the Chinese courts over crimes committed on Chinese soil. The closing years of the century, however, saw an increasing opposition among the Europeans to the surrender of persons for trial on homicide charges, which, although comparatively infrequent, were practically the only cases in which the Chinese courts insisted upon the assertion of their jurisdiction. As late as 1821 the Americans surrendered for trial and execution a sailor (Francis Terranova) who had caused the death of a Chinese boat-woman; but the last rendition by the English had been in 1784, after which date the East India Company's Select Committee persistently refused to surrender accused persons.

Western objections to Chinese jurisdiction were attributable in part to the wide differences between European and Chinese court procedure. In Chinese courts the accused was not represented by a lawyer and had no right to interrogate witnesses, while the principle that no one could be convicted without an actual confession made the use of torture a recognized feature of Chinese trials. Equally weighty were the objections called forth by the content of Chinese law relating to homicide. Though it was not true, as was frequently alleged, that Chinese law made no distinction between accidental and willful homicide and unfailingly demanded "a life for a life," the Chinese code prescribed the death penalty for many cases where foreign law would have found no guilty intent and therefore no crime. The verdict of "accidental killing" was permissible only where death had resulted from an act which in itself involved no predictable danger to others; when such danger existed in an intentional act, Chinese law proceeded on the assumption that the individual "knows and intends the consequences of his acts." In actual practice, however, the penalties prescribed by the code were customarily abated by one degree: willful and premeditated homicide, for which the code penalty was death by decapitation, was usually punished by the less degrading penalty of strangulation, while unintentional killing, punishable by strangulation, usually involved only imprisonment and the payment of a fine.

A final reason for foreign objection to Chinese jurisdiction resulted from the application of the Chinese principle of community responsibility. In cases of homicide or of any other violations of Chinese law the authorities imposed upon the entire foreign community—or, in case the nationality of the offender was known, upon the national group concerned—the duty of discovering and handing over the guilty party. Failure or refusal to fulfill this duty was punished by seizing as hostages the chief men of the offending nationality or by suspending trade until the demand had been satisfied. Although this procedure appeared in Chinese eyes eminently "reasonable" and although some justification for the practice can be found in the fact that the foreign community often conspired to smuggle the accused person out of the reach of the Chinese authorities, thereby becoming "accessories after the fact," it was an arrangement which was thoroughly repugnant to Western ideas of justice. The entire foreign community was unanimous, therefore, in its opposition to a system whereby the lives and property of innocent men were held in jeopardy to answer for the actions of an individual over whom they had no control.

In spite of the imperial decrees against the importation and sale of opium the early nineteenth century saw a steady increase in the amount of the drug brought in from abroad. During the last six years of the East India Company's monopoly, 1828–1834, the amount of opium reaching Canton in the "country ships" trading under the company's licenses totaled 92,957 chests, an average of 15,493 chests—slightly more than 1000 tons—per year, and the value of this prohibited importation during the same six years made up 54 per cent of all the imports carried in the annual balance sheets of the company. Additional imports in American, Dutch, French, and Portuguese ships brought the average annual amount for these years up to about 18,000 chests. The five years which followed the abolition of the company's monopoly saw an even more rapid increase, the amount imported during the fiscal year 1838–1839 being estimated at more than 40,000 chests, while the average for the five-year period is fixed at not less than 30,000 chests per year.

The steady growth of the trade in the face of the prohibitory imperial decrees was made possible by the connivance of imperial officials who accepted munificent bribes from the smugglers. During the period prior to 1834 the foreigners had only a small direct part in this aspect of the trade; the opium hulks at the mouth of the river delivered the opium to the Chinese buyers, who made all the necessary "arrangements" for the safe landing of the forbidden drug. After 1834 the situation changed. The British "free traders" who supplanted the East India Company, as well as the American and other non-British merchants, began to push the opium trade with great energy, both at Canton and at a number of other ports to which foreigners had no right of access. From this time the foreigners not merely brought opium to the coast of the empire but also had a direct hand in the bribery of the officials and in the landing of the opium on Chinese soil.

From the accession of the emperor Tao Kuang, who came to the throne in 1820, the subject of the opium trade attracted increasingly the attention of the imperial authorities at Peking. In 1836 the question of "enforcement or modification" of the existing prohibition was debated at great length, and at the end of 1838 the emperor finally decided upon strict enforcement. The agent for the execution of the imperial will was Lin Tse-hsu, formerly viceroy of Hukuang (the two provinces of Hupeh and Hunan), who arrived at Canton on March 10, 1839, clothed with the dictatorial powers of imperial high commissioner and under instructions to "go, investigate, and act."

For eight days after his arrival Commissioner Lin investigated; on March 18 he acted. A cordon of troops was thrown around the factories, and foreign merchants were ordered to hand over for destruction all the opium in the opium hulks and to sign bonds pledging themselves never to import any more opium. Any violation of this pledge was to be punished by death and by the confiscation of the offending ship, together with its entire cargo. The senior British superintendent of trade, at this time Captain Charles Elliot, promptly hastened up from Macao to protest against this arbitrary and unwarranted procedure. With the British headman also within his grasp, Commissioner Lin reiterated his demand for the surrender of the opium and took new steps to enforce compliance. On the evening following Captain Elliot's arrival at Canton all the Chinese servants were ordered to leave the factories, and the imprisoned foreigners were cut off from all intercourse with the people of Canton.

Resistance being out of the question, the British superintendent was compelled to comply with the Chinese demands, at least so far as they concerned the surrender of British-owned opium. As soon as the delivery of the opium into the hands of the Chinese officials was commenced, the coercive measures against the foreign community were modified; first they were allowed a more abundant supply of food, and later their domestic servants were permitted to return to the factories. When the entire amount, 20,291 chests, had been surrendered, the armed cordon around the factories was withdrawn, and the British were informed that, when they had given the required bond against further participation in the forbidden trade, commerce would be continued as usual. Much to the surprise of the entire foreign community, the surrendered opium was carefully destroyed; Commissioner Lin may have been "brutally harsh" in his methods, but there was no question as to his scrupulous honesty.

Instead of giving the required bond and resuming the normal commercial relations the British community, on orders from Captain Elliot, promptly left Canton and retired to Macao, while a number of the British ships found safe anchorage in the excellent harbor of the small island of Hongkong. Early in July a conflict between some Chinese and a party of British and American sailors on the mainland opposite Hongkong resulted in the death of a Chinese, and Commissioner Lin demanded that the guilty persons be handed over for trial and punishment by the Chinese authorities. Captain Elliot refused this demand and also refused to allow any of his fellow nationals to give the required bond with reference to the nonimportation of opium. On August 15, therefore, the imperial commissioner threatened to blockade Macao unless the British withdrew from the town; the English community thereupon transferred itself to Hongkong Island, where two weeks later it was comforted and encouraged by the arrival of two British warships. On November 3 the two British ships and a fleet of Chinese war junks met in the river which leads up to Canton. The British opened fire, sinking four of the junks and creating at last a state of war between Great Britain and the Chinese Empire. To the Chinese the war which commenced in this impromptu fashion had but one cause: opium. To the British and to the majority of the Westerners who at that time had dealings with China opium was nothing more than the incidental occasion for a struggle the real purpose of which was to force upon the Chinese government a modification of its arrogant attitude toward the outside world.

For more than seven months after the initial armed clash between British warships and Chinese junks no fresh acts of war occurred; it was not until June, 1840, that a fleet of twenty British warships, accompanied by twenty-eight transports loaded with troops, arrived in Far Eastern waters for the purpose of settling Britain's dispute with the ancient empire. Even then the war was fought in an extremely desultory manner. Attacks by the British forces at Canton and at the mouth of the Yangtze produced no apparent effect upon the Chinese government, while a naval demonstration at Taku led only to the negotiation of a treaty which was repudiated by both governments. In the spring of 1842, however, the British commander in chief commenced energetic operations at the mouth of the Yangtze. On July 20 the British attacked and took Chinkiang, where the Grand Canal crosses the Yangtze, and on August 9 they arrived off the city of Nanking. This irresistible advance along the great interior waterway of the empire brought the Peking government to terms; on August 29, 1842, there was signed at Nanking a treaty of peace between Sir Henry Pottinger, the British plenipotentiary, and three representatives of the Chinese emperor.

The terms of the Treaty of Nanking attested the utter defeat of the Chinese. An indemnity of $21,000,000 (Mexican) was paid: $6,000,000 as compensation for the destroyed opium, $3,000,000 to settle the debts owed to British merchants by members of the Canton Co-hong, and $12,000,000 for Great Britain's war expenses.

"It being obviously necessary and desirable that British Subjects have some port whereat they may careen and refit their ships, when required, and keep stores for that purpose," the island of Hong-kong was ceded in perpetuity to the British crown.

In satisfaction of the British demand for increased commercial opportunities the treaty conferred the right of residence and trade "without molestation or restraint" at the five ports of Canton, Amoy, Foochow, Ningpo, and Shanghai. At these five "treaty ports" the British government was entitled to appoint superin-tendents or consular officers "to be the medium of communication between the Chinese authorities and the said (British) merchants, and to see that the just duties and other dues of the Chinese gov-ernment, as hereafter provided for, are duly discharged by Her Britannic Majesty's subjects."

A further concession to the demands of the victorious foreigners was the provision that the imperial government would draw up and promulgate for general information "a fair and regular tariff of import and export customs and other dues." After the payment of the established customs British merchandise should enjoy the privi-lege of being conveyed, by Chinese merchants, to any part of the interior of the empire without being liable to any additional tax other than a publicly promulgated transit tax.

By Article XI of the treaty the right of British officials to com-municate on terms of equality with the officials of China—a right vainly asserted eight years earlier by Lord Napier—was conceded, and in order to preclude the possibility of misunderstandings this article established the precise forms to be employed in correspond-ence between officials of various ranks.

The Treaty of Nanking brought an end to the Anglo-Chinese hostilities and laid the foundations for future relations between the two belligerents. During the course of the next two years three additional treaties were concluded by the Chinese Empire: the Treaty of the Bogue, with Great Britain, on October 8, 1843; the Treaty of Wanghia, with the United States, on July 3, 1844; and the Treaty of Whampoa, with France, on October 24, 1844. To-gether with the Nanking Treaty these three later treaties consti-tuted what is usually called the First Treaty Settlement between China and the maritime powers of the West, and until revised by the treaties of 1858–1860 they served to regulate China's relations with the outside world. For a thorough understanding of the changed conditions under which the foreigners henceforth were to reside and trade in China these three treaties should be studied in detail, but it will suffice here to point out briefly their most important provisions.

Shortly after the conclusion of the Nanking Treaty the Chinese, apparently in response to the representations of Commodore Kearny, assured the Americans that the privileges extended to the British should be enjoyed also by all the foreigners formerly trading at Canton. In the Treaty of the Bogue the British plenipotentiary therefore secured the inclusion of the following article:

> The Emperor of China having been graciously pleased to grant to all foreign countries whose subjects or citizens have hitherto traded at Canton the privilege of resorting for purposes of trade to the other four ports of Fuchow, Amoy, Ningpo, and Shanghai, on the same terms as the English, it is further agreed that, should the Emperor hereafter, from any cause whatever, be pleased to grant additional privileges or immunities to any of the subjects or citizens of such foreign countries, the same privileges and immunities will be extended to and enjoyed by British subjects.

As a result of this clause and similar clauses which are to be found in practically all the general treaties signed by China during the nineteenth century, China's treaty commitments to the outside world became "interlocking." Each of the countries having treaties with the Chinese Empire was entitled to claim for its citizens or subjects all the rights and privileges which China might be persuaded to grant to the nationals of the "most favored nation," and any concession henceforth extracted from China by the diplomacy of one power became automatically the vested right of all.

Article II of the Treaty of Nanking, by providing for the appointment of consuls as a medium of communication between British merchants and Chinese authorities at the treaty ports, had by implication removed the persons and property of these merchants from the jurisdiction of the Chinese. In the General Regulations issued by the Chinese government in July, 1843, this implied limitation upon Chinese jurisdiction was made more definite, and the clauses bearing on this point were incorporated into the Treaty of the Bogue, of October 1843.

It remained for the American treaty of the following year, however, to establish in explicit terms the exclusive jurisdiction of the treaty powers over their nationals resident in China. Article XXI of the Treaty of Wanghia made the following provision:

Subjects of China who may be guilty of any criminal act toward citizens of the United States shall be arrested and punished by the Chinese authorities according to the laws of China, and citizens of the United States who may commit any crime in China shall be subject to be tried and punished only by the Consul or other public functionary of the United States thereto authorized according to the laws of the United States; and in order to secure the prevention of all controversy and disaffection, justice shall be equitably and impartially administered on both sides.

Article XXIV of the same treaty provided that "if controversies arise between citizens of the United States and subjects of China which cannot be settled amicably otherwise, the same shall be examined and decided conformably to justice and equity by the public officers of the two nations acting in conjunction." All cases which might arise between citizens of the United States were made subject, by Article XXV, to the jurisdiction of the authorities of the United States, and the same article provided that "all controversies occurring in China between citizens of the United States and subjects of any other Government shall be regulated by the treaties existing between the United States and such Governments, respectively, without interference on the part of China."

This establishment of the jurisdiction of a foreign government, in lieu of that of the territorial authorities, over the persons and property of its nationals is known as extraterritoriality. A demand for such an arrangement had long existed among the various nationalities residing at Canton, and the clauses of the American treaty, whose provisions immediately became through the operation of the most-favored-nation clause the common property of the other treaty powers, constitute the foundation upon which extraterritorial jurisdiction in China was based.

The French Treaty of Whampoa, signed on October 24, 1844, contained nothing important which is not found in the British and American treaties. During the course of his negotiations, however, the French plenipotentiary, M. de Lagrené, succeeded in persuading the Canton viceroy to memorialize the emperor on behalf of the Chinese Christians, with the result that two imperial edicts were issued: on December 28, 1844, and on February 20, 1846, respectively. The first of these edicts canceled the ancient proscription against Christianity and declared that adherents of the foreign religion, so long as they refrained from crime, were not to be troubled by the authorities. The second provided that equal tolerance was to be shown to those who professed Protestant Christianity and Catholic Christianity, but the latter were to have restored to them, where possible, the buildings which they had erected for religious purposes during the reign of K'ang Hsi. The imperial decrees still maintained the prohibition against foreign missionaries' going about through the empire to propagate their religion; but the Canton viceroy is said to have informed M. de Lagrené that if the missionaries acted with discretion, no real objection would be raised to their presence in the interior.

Despite the outcome of her war with Great Britain, China remained in 1844 a great and impressive empire, still supremely satisfied with the excellence of her ancient civilization and still able to command the healthy respect of the Western countries whose merchants visited her coasts in search of profitable trade. The victories won by British arms and the ports recently opened to foreign residence directly affected only the southern coastal districts of the empire and the lower reaches of the Yangtze valley; the security of the imperial court and the serenity of the nation as a whole had been unshaken by the course of events. Yet the empire of Tao Kuang, powerful though it still was, had been forced to surrender a not insignificant portion of its once perfect sovereignty. Formerly China had laid down the conditions upon which the foreigner might dwell and trade at her ports; now, bound by the treaty stipulations imposed upon her by outside force, she had ceased to be completely the mistress of her own house.

SUGGESTED REFERENCES

BRAAM, A. E. VAN An Authentic Account of the Embassy of the Dutch East India Company . . . in 1794 and 1795.

DENNETT, T. Americans in Eastern Asia.

ELLIS, SIR H. Journal of the Proceedings of the Late Embassy to China [Amherst embassy].

KEETON, G. W. The Development of Extraterritoriality in China.

LATOURETTE, K. S. The Chinese: their History and Culture.

LATOURETTE, K. S. A History of Christian Missions in China.

LATOURETTE, K. S. History of the Early Relations between the United States and China, 1784–1844.

MACNAIR, H. F. Modern Chinese History: Selected Readings.

MORSE, H. B. The East India Company Trading to China.

MORSE, H. B. The International Relations of the Chinese Empire, Vol. I.

MORSE, H. B. and MACNAIR, H. F. Far Eastern International Relations.

OWEN, D. E. British Opium Policy in China and India.

QUINCY, J. The Journals of Major Samuel Shaw.

STAUNTON, SIR G. L. An Authentic Account of an Embassy . . . to the Emperor of China (Macartney embassy).

STAUNTON, SIR G. T. (translator). Ta Tsing Leu Lee.

WILLIAMS, E. T. A Short History of China.

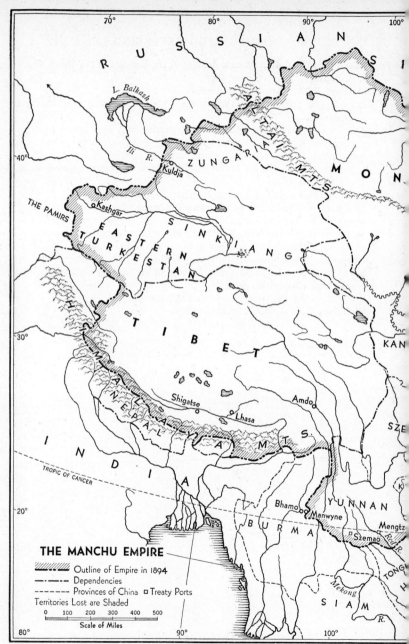

THE MANCHU EMPIRE

///// Outline of Empire in 1894
—··—··— Dependencies
———————— Provinces of China   ▫ Treaty Ports
Territories Lost are Shaded

0   100   200   300   400   500
Scale of Miles

Map Plate, Patented July 5, 1921 · Method of Making Maps, Patented July 5, 1921

XXIII

China's First Half-Century under the Treaties: 1844–1894

Continuation of Friction · Anglo-French Co-operation in the Far East · The *Arrow* War · The Tientsin Treaties of June, 1858 · The Renewal of Hostilities · The Supplementary Treaties of Peking (October, 1860) · Effect of the Second Treaty Settlement · Religious-Toleration Clauses · Legalization of the Opium Traffic · Cessions of Territory · The T'aiping Rebellion · Suppression of the T'aipings · Ward, Gordon, and the Ever Victorious Army · End of the Rebellion · China and the Treaty Powers · The Imperial Maritime Customs; Sir Robert Hart · The Empress Dowager Tzu Hsi · Internal Disorders · Anson Burlingame and his Mission to the Powers · The Sino-American Treaty of July, 1868 · Burlingame in Europe · The Sino-Russian Dispute over Kuldja · French Expansion in Annam; the Tongking War · The British in Burma · The Margary Case and the Chefoo Convention · Relations with Japan · The Continuance of China's Prestige · Tentative Adoption of Western Devices; Persistent Conservatism

THE First Treaty Settlement in 1842–1844 had made sweeping changes in the conditions of foreign residence and trade in China, but the conflict between China and the West was not yet over. The imperial government had been forced to guarantee to the foreigners certain rights and privileges, but it remained to be seen whether the local officials and the Chinese people would abide by the new arrangements. At the four newly opened ports, although the people still regarded the foreigners as essentially barbarians, there was comparatively little trouble. At Canton, however, friction began to develop almost immediately; the Cantonese, embittered by the war, were stubbornly opposed to the fulfillment of the treaty stipulations, while the foreigners, on the other hand, were soon claiming rights which they had neglected to incorporate in the treaties.

The American and French treaties both contained clauses providing for treaty revision at the end of twelve years, and the British, by virtue of the most-favored-nation clause, claimed the same right. Long before the expiration of the twelve-year period the three treaty powers were fully determined to insist upon changes which would assure to their nationals the full enjoyment of the privileges which the original treaties had been intended to secure. But the Chinese government had no desire for further negotiations of any sort. When the British government in 1854 announced its intention of demanding treaty revision, the Chinese viceroy at Canton refused to recognize the legality of the claim; and a similar answer was returned two years later to a like demand from the representative of the United States.

In October, 1856, the British and French governments, which had been allied against Russia in the Crimean War, determined to extend their co-operation to the Far East and to undertake a joint expedition against China. The French had found cause for action in the execution of a French Catholic missionary, Père Auguste Chapdelaine, by the authorities of Kwangsi Province. The British government at the moment of reaching its decision for joint action with the French lacked any clear-cut *casus belli* but was prepared to use force simply for the purpose of securing from the Chinese a general revision of those portions of the earlier treaties which now seemed inadequate to the growing needs of British commerce.

Even while the British government was reaching its decision to employ force, however, the Canton viceroy was providing them with the necessary justification. On October 8, 1856, Viceroy Yeh Ming-ch'en sent his officers to arrest as notorious pirates the Chinese crew of the "lorcha"[1] *Arrow*, which was lying at anchor in the harbor of Canton. The case of the *Arrow* involves a number of complicated points. The vessel was Chinese-owned but had been registered at Hongkong—under a Hongkong ordinance to which the British government had refused its approval—and had been authorized by the Hongkong authorities to fly the British flag, under which it was engaged in the still illegal opium trade. Unknown to the Chinese officials, the license to fly the British flag had at the moment of the arrest actually expired; but there was a provision in the Hongkong ordinance to the effect that a vessel

[1] A "lorcha" is a vessel combining a European-styled hull with sails of Chinese pattern.

whose license expired while it was away from the colony might continue under the British flag until its return to the port of Hongkong. These interesting complications, however, had little practical bearing upon the development of the case. The British consul at Canton, Mr. Parkes, demanded the immediate return of the arrested seamen and an apology for the insult to the British flag, while Viceroy Yeh, although eventually returning the men, denied that there had been any violation of British rights and refused to make an apology.

The *Arrow* episode was merely a convenient pretext for war and not its cause. The British government had already decided upon the use of force, and the ultimatum which Lord Elgin, as British plenipotentiary, sent in December, 1857, to Viceroy Yeh contains only a passing allusion to the case. Lord Elgin's own opinion of the case is enlightening: "I have hardly alluded in my ultimatum to that wretched question of the *Arrow* which is a scandal to us, and is so considered, I have reason to know, by all except the few who are personally compromised."[1]

British military activity was delayed by the outbreak of the Sepoy Mutiny in India, which necessitated the diversion to India of the expeditionary force intended for operations in China. In July, 1857, Lord Elgin arrived at Hongkong. In December he dispatched his ultimatum to the Canton viceroy, and later in the same month Lord Elgin and the French plenipotentiary, Baron Gros, authorized a joint attack by the available British and French naval forces upon the city of Canton. After this move the British and French endeavored to secure the active support of Russia and the United States. These two countries, however, refused to co-operate in any military undertaking, although their diplomatic representatives, Count Putiatin and Mr. W. B. Reed, accompanied the allied expedition to the north and took advantage of the Anglo-French success as a means of securing the revision of their own treaties.

In April, 1858, the Anglo-French warships, now supported by adequate military forces, arrived off Taku at the mouth of the Pai Ho. On May 20 they demanded the surrender of the Taku

[1] Walrond, T. (editor), *Letters and Journals of James, Eighth Earl of Elgin*, p. 209.

forts, and upon the refusal of this demand the forts were taken by force. Nine days later the plenipotentiaries arrived at Tientsin, where after a few days of delay they were met by representatives of the Chinese emperor duly accredited for the negotiation of new treaties. Three weeks of negotiation sufficed to bring about the conclusion of four new treaties: the Russian treaty, signed on June 13; the American, on June 18; the English, on June 26; and the French, on June 27.

The conclusion of the four Tientsin treaties served only to effect a truce between China and the Western allies. When the British, French, and American envoys in June, 1859, arrived at Taku on their way to Peking for the purpose of exchanging treaty ratifications, they were informed by the Chinese authorities that they should proceed to the capital by land from Peitang, a port some ten miles to the north of Taku. At Taku itself the fortifications had been greatly strengthened, while booms and heavy chains had been stretched across the river in order to bar the entrance of vessels. Although the British and French treaties both provided that the exchange of ratifications should take place at Peking, Tientsin had not been made a treaty port; nor had any of the treaties established the right of warships to go up the Pai Ho. However, the British and French envoys regarded the barring of the river as a violation of their treaty rights, and the naval escort by which the British envoy was accompanied attempted to force a passage. This attempt was repulsed with heavy losses. The American plenipotentiary, Mr. J. E. Ward, proceeded to Peking by the route which the Chinese had indicated; but the British and French envoys retired to Shanghai, where they awaited the arrival of fresh forces and new instructions.

The final scenes of the war were enacted during the late summer of 1860. On July 30 a new British and French expeditionary force arrived at Peitang. On August 21 the Taku forts were attacked and taken. By September 5 the allied forces were at Tientsin. On September 21 the Chinese were defeated in battle almost under the walls of the capital, and the imperial court fled to Jehol, north of the Great Wall, leaving to the emperor's brother, Prince Kung, the task of settling with the invaders.

It is extremely doubtful whether the artillery of the allied armies could have made any impression upon the massive walls of the Chinese capital; but the defenders were now thoroughly intimidated, and on October 13 they responded to an allied ultimatum by surrendering the Anting gate in the north wall. On the eighteenth, in reprisal for the earlier treacherous capture and cruel treatment of a British "parley" party, the Yüan Ming Yüan—Summer Palace—was utterly destroyed. On the twenty-fourth the ratifications of the British Treaty of Tientsin were exchanged inside the capital, and a "supplementary" treaty was signed, the French exchange of ratifications and the signing of the French supplementary treaty taking place on the following day.

The Second Treaty Settlement between China and the West consisted of eight treaties signed during the years 1858–1860 by the representatives of the empire. In addition to the four treaties signed at Tientsin and the British and French supplementary treaties concluded at Peking two further treaties had been signed with Russia: one at Aigun on May 28, 1858, and the other at Peking on November 14, 1860. These formal treaties were supplemented by tariff schedules, which were drawn up after consultation between the foreign plenipotentiaries and the Chinese commissioners and which had the binding force of treaties.

In general the effect of this new array of treaties was the sweeping extension of foreign control over the conditions of residence and trade in China. In addition to paying indemnities to Britain and France for the expenses of the war and to the United States for property losses suffered during the hostilities at Canton, China was forced to open for trade ten additional treaty ports, one of which was in Manchuria, one in Shantung, and four on the Yangtze River. The right of extraterritoriality was definitely incorporated in the treaties of each of the four treaty powers, and the right of maintaining resident diplomatic representatives at Peking—a right hitherto enjoyed only by the Russians—was now extended to the three maritime countries. As a medium through which these resident diplomats might hold regular communication with the imperial government China was forced to establish a Foreign Office—(the *Tsungli Yamen*), while the British treaty of 1858 provided that British ships of war, "coming for no hostile purpose or being engaged in the pursuit of pirates," were to be at liberty to visit "all the ports within the dominion of the Emperor of China." From 1860, therefore, the foreign powers were able, both at Peking and in the provinces, to give vigorous expression to their dissatisfaction at any nonperformance of treaty commitments.

Despite the imperial edicts of 1844 and 1846 granting toleration to Chinese Christians, the missionaries of the four treaty powers had insisted that the revision of the treaties should provide more adequate guaranties for themselves and their converts. The four Tientsin treaties of 1858 therefore included clauses whereby the toleration and protection of Christianity by the imperial government was made a matter of treaty obligation. Although there was wide difference between these four clauses in wording, Article XXIX of the American treaty may be regarded as typical:

> The principles of the Christian religion, as professed by the Protestant and Roman Catholic churches, are recognized as teaching men to do good, and to do to others as they would have others do to them. Hereafter, those who quietly profess and teach these doctrines shall not be harassed or persecuted on account of their faith. Any persons, whether citizens of the United States or Chinese converts, who according to their tenets peaceably teach and practice the principles of Christianity shall in no case be interfered with or molested.

The French and Russian treaties both secured the right for missionaries and other nationals of the two countries, when provided with regular passports, to travel through the empire.

The devoted labors of many Christian missionaries were to confer great and unquestioned benefits upon the Chinese people; Christian medical and educational institutions especially were to play a leading part in bringing to China the best of Western civilization. But the positive benefits from Christian missions were to be partly vitiated by the mistaken policy which had made religion the subject of special treaty stipulation. Christianity, thus involved in the fabric of China's new diplomatic obligations, has never ceased to be a "foreign doctrine,"[1] and the acceptance

[1] In earlier times Chinese converts were often called "foreign slaves"; more recently they have been designated by the epithet "running dogs of imperialism."

of its teachings has often been regarded by non-Christian Chinese as evidence of an unpatriotic willingness to acquiesce in the injuries inflicted upon China by the West.

The First Treaty Settlement between China and the Western powers had left opium in an anomalous position. The American treaty had provided that American citizens engaging in the importation of opium or of any other contraband should be entitled to no protection from the government; but the British treaty, save in the article relating to the indemnity which China was to pay, made no mention of the drug. In spite of the fact that nothing was done to legalize this trade, which the Chinese regarded as the sole cause of their disastrous war with Great Britain, the imperial authorities had made no further attempts to check the open activities of the smugglers; and by the year 1858 the importation of opium, engaged in by the nationals of all countries, had increased until it amounted annually to not less than five thousand tons.

The treaties concluded at Tientsin made no change in this situation, save for the fact that the American treaty omitted the stipulation depriving smugglers of government protection; but the Americans encouraged the British in their efforts to obtain recognition of the trade, and the supplementary tariff schedule drawn up by the British plenipotentiary and the Chinese commissioners legalized the importation of opium by providing for an import tax of 30 *taels* ($21.60 in United States money) per chest of $133\frac{1}{3}$ pounds. At last, after two decades of conflict and two foreign wars, the Chinese government had been forced to abandon its efforts to exclude the drug from its ports.

During the period between 1842 and 1856 the British had leased from China for the better protection of the port of Hongkong a small portion of Kowloon peninsula which projects from the mainland opposite Hongkong Island. By Article VI of the supplementary treaty at Peking in October, 1860, this strip of land was ceded outright to the British crown.

The few square miles of territory thus secured by the British fade into insignificance, however, when compared with the splendid prize obtained on the northern boundary of the empire by the Russians. For more than a century and a half the boundary between the Russian and Chinese empires had remained, as fixed by the Treaty of Nerchinsk, the watershed to the north of the Amur River. But the Russians had never definitely abandoned their hope of securing a "rectification" of the frontier, and China's war with the British and French furnished an opportunity for the fulfillment of this hope.

On May 28, 1858, Count Nicholas Muravieff concluded at Aigun a treaty whereby the Amur River, from the confluence of the Shilka to that of the Ussuri, became the boundary between the two empires, while the territory to the east of the Ussuri and of the lower Amur was to be held in common. The ratification of this treaty by the Chinese emperor took place on June 14, the day following the conclusion of the Russian treaty at Tientsin. During the allied occupation of Peking in October, 1860, the Russian minister at Peking, General Ignatief, took advantage of the Chinese panic to conclude a new treaty, signed on November 14, granting to Russia sole possession of the coastland to the east of the Ussuri and the Amur.

Weakened and humiliated by two wars against the West, the Manchu government was shaken to its foundations by the outbreak of the most serious rebellion that China had seen since the death of Wu San-kuei, nearly two centuries earlier. The T'aiping Rebellion, which for fifteen years spread ruin and desolation throughout southern China and the Yangtze valley, resulted in part from the hostility of the Chinese for their Manchu conquerors and from the general discontent aroused by the misgovernment of the early nineteenth century.

In part, however, this outbreak was a result of China's increasing contact with the outside world. During the war against Great Britain, 1840–1842, the imperial authorities at Canton, by encouraging local volunteer forces to resist the foreign invaders, had made it possible for large quantities of weapons to fall into the hands of the hitherto carefully repressed secret societies. The defeat of the imperial forces in this struggle had greatly lessened the government's prestige and had diminished its ability to suppress local disorders. Finally, the religious fanatic whose followers became the nucleus of the rebellion obtained some, at least, of his religious ideas from contact with Christian missionaries and their literature.

Hung Hsiu-ch'üan, the T'ien Wang ("Heavenly King") of the T'aipings, was a native of Kwangtung Province and was born in 1813. Although he was decidedly bright as a boy and passed with credit the district and prefectural literary examinations, Hung failed repeatedly in his attempts to pass the provincial tests for the Chü Jen degree. In 1847, after the last of these numerous failures, the disappointed aspirant came for a brief period under the instruction of Mr. I. J. Roberts, an American missionary. Several years earlier Hung had read with considerable interest a number of missionary tracts and leaflets, and in 1848 he organized a religious society, the "Society of God," to destroy idolatry and to spread the worship of the one true God. By 1850 the activities of the new society had attracted the attention of the imperial authorities, and in August of that year troops were sent against it for the purpose of breaking it up. These imperial troops were routed, and the movement, hitherto essentially religious, was promptly transformed into a rebellion against the Manchus.

In China nothing succeeds so spectacularly as successful resistance to a discredited and unpopular political regime. With their repulse of the government's armed forces, Hung Hsiu-ch'üan and his followers became the nucleus of a rapidly growing horde recruited from all the discontented and anti-Manchu elements of south China.

The rebels were poorly supplied with weapons and in spite of their increased numbers found themselves too weak to stand against the full force of the imperial troops in the Liang-Kwang viceroyalty. In the spring of 1852, therefore, they moved northward from Kwangsi into Hunan. Changsha, the capital of Hunan, beat off the rebel attacks; but Yochow, at the junction of the Siang and Yangtze rivers, was taken, and here the insurgents found an arsenal which furnished them with an abundance of weapons. From Yochow the now fully armed forces swept irresistibly down the Yangtze valley until in March, 1853, they established themselves at Nanking, the ancient capital of the Ming dynasty.

In the autumn of 1852, while besieging Changsha, Hung Hsui-ch'üan had assumed the imperial title and had proclaimed his new dynasty the T'ai Ping ("Great Peace"). At the same time, moreover, the rebel leader had asserted his pretensions to even more exalted powers. The edicts which he issued after this time were proclaimed in the name of a new "Christian" Trinity: God the "Heavenly Father," Jesus Christ the "Divine Elder Brother," and the T'aiping T'ien Wang the "Divine Younger Brother."

For a while many Protestant missionaries looked with favor upon this quasi-Christian movement, and the American Department of State, on the strength of early favorable reports, instructed its representative in China to recognize the new government if, in his opinion, this step should seem expedient. After the establishment of his capital at Nanking, however, the T'aiping emperor abandoned himself to luxury and dissipation. The early favor of the missionaries was alienated by the increasing arrogance of his divine pretensions, while the inefficient administration of the territories under their sway destroyed all hope that the T'aipings would be able to establish an organized government. After the conclusion of the Second Treaty Settlement (1858–1860), therefore, the Western governments determined upon a policy of supporting the Manchus against the rebels.

In the spring of 1852, when the T'aiping rebels moved northward into the Yangtze valley, the available government forces in that region consisted only of the various provincial armies and the Manchu garrisons at a few of the more important cities. These had been quickly overwhelmed; and before the slow-moving Peking authorities were able to take adequate measures against the uprising, the outbreak of hostilities with Britain and France made it necessary for them to concentrate their forces against the foreign invader. Under these conditions the local authorities of the Yangtze area between 1852 and 1860 received little assistance from Peking. Only after the conclusion of the foreign war in the north was it possible for the imperial government to do more than issue proclamations calling for energetic action by the provincial authorities. The latter were forced to raise by their own efforts the men, money, and munitions required for the suppression of the rebels.

In the long struggle against the T'aipings four men played especially prominent parts: Tseng Kuo-fan, Li Hung-chang, Frederick Townsend Ward, and Charles George Gordon.

Tseng, a native of Hunan and a scholar of brilliant attainments, happened to be, at the time the rebels moved northward from Kwangsi, out of the government service, living as a private subject in his native province. Without waiting for orders he promptly raised a volunteer force and embarked upon a military career. Li, a native of Anhui, was also a man of letters and a holder of the highest literary honors; like Tseng he recognized the need for men of action and, laying aside the pen of the scholar, took up the sword. The services of these two volunteer leaders, whose energy and ability were in striking contrast to the ineptitude displayed by the responsible officials, were promptly recognized by the imperial government. Both were appointed to office and entered upon public careers which in each case ended only with death. Tseng, after restoring order in Hunan Province, was transferred to the Liang-kiang viceroyalty (consisting of Kiangsu, Kiangsi, and Anhui) as viceroy, while Li Hung-chang, his junior, was associated with him as governor of Kiangsu. As viceroy and governor, Tseng and Li eventually accomplished the destruction of the T'aiping movement.

Frederick Townsend Ward, an American born in Salem, Massachusetts, arrived on the coast of China about 1851. In 1860, while he was serving as first officer on the Chinese gunboat *Confucius*, he entered into an agreement with a Chinese banker at Shanghai, an agent of Li Hung-chang, for the organization of a force to reconquer from the rebels the city of Sungkiang, the chief city of the prefecture in which Shanghai is located. In July, 1860, after an initial failure, he succeeded in this project, whereupon he undertook the organization of a permanent force of Chinese, drilled along Western lines by European officers, for regular service under the imperial authorities.

For just a year, from September, 1861, until his death in September, 1862, Ward led his little force through a series of brilliant successes which fully justified the honorific title "Ever Victorious Army" bestowed upon it by an imperial decree of March, 1862.

On September 20, 1862, Ward was mortally wounded in an assault upon the town of Tzeki, a few miles from the city of Ningpo. His services and his death were reported to the throne in a memorial by Li Hung-chang, and an imperial decree, conferring posthumous honors upon the valiant hero, ordered the local authorities of Sung-kiang and Ningpo to erect special temples to his memory.

During the six months after the death of Ward a number of officers, none of them satisfactory, succeeded to the command of his Ever Victorious Army. At the end of this period the British government permitted Major Charles George Gordon to assume command of the force. The new commander retained his post for fourteen months and co-operated with the regular imperial troops in taking from the rebels a number of walled cities, including the great city of Soochow, which surrendered on December 4, 1863.

The fall of Soochow was the occasion of a violent altercation between Gordon, who had guaranteed the safety of the capitulating T'aiping leaders, and Li, who had promptly had these leaders beheaded. The dispute was smoothed over, and Gordon continued in the Chinese service five months longer; but upon his resignation the Ever Victorious Army was disbanded.[1] Nanking, now on the verge of surrender, was the only important city remaining in rebel hands, and the Chinese authorities were anxious to avoid the complications which after the restoration of peace might result from the presence of such a formidable force under the control of foreign commanders.

On the last day of June, 1864, the T'ien Wang committed suicide, and on July 19 Nanking was taken by storm. After the fall of the T'aiping capital isolated bodies of rebels continued to hold a number of less-important walled towns; but in May, 1865, the last of these rebels had been routed and the rebellion was at an end. For fifteen years it had spread ruin and desolation through the most prosperous provinces of the empire; directly or indirectly it is estimated to have caused the death of twenty million people. Even today extensive ruins in many Yangtze-valley cities bear mute testimony to the completeness of the destruction wrought by the followers of Hung Hsiu-ch'üan.

[1] Gordon was killed in 1885 at Khartoum in the Sudan.

The treaty settlement of 1858–1860 had conceded to the foreign powers, on paper, practically every right or privilege which they had hoped to secure. During the years which followed the conclusion of these treaties, therefore, the four original treaty powers and such other Western countries as joined their ranks were chiefly concerned with realizing upon the full value of these paper concessions and with developing to the utmost the apparently unlimited possibilities of China as a market for their surplus commodities, the output of a steadily growing industrial system.

Three of these first treaty powers—Britain, France, and Russia —held territories on the frontiers of China, and the expansion of their territorial holdings was destined to create friction between themselves and the ancient empire. For the first decade or so, however, all three were interested in maintaining the status quo. Great Britain, whose commerce with China exceeded that of any other foreign country, was especially anxious to aid in every possible way the development of conditions increasingly favorable to trade; Russia, whose territories bordered on China from central Asia to the Pacific, sought to establish cordial relations with the Chinese court and to win its confidence; France, primarily interested in the protectorate over Catholic missions, sought to foster conditions under which the work of the missionaries could be freely carried on.

The fourth major treaty power, the United States, had no Asiatic possessions and consequently was in no danger of becoming involved in frontier disputes. After 1865, moreover, American commercial activity in the Far East greatly declined, partly because of the destruction of the American merchant marine during the Civil War and partly because Americans were turning their energies to the development of the internal resources of their own country.

One of the most important consequences of the T'aiping Rebellion was the establishment of the Imperial Maritime Customs. In 1853 the Triad Society, an organization in sympathy with the T'aipings, took Shanghai and overthrew the imperial administration at that port. In order to facilitate the regular collection of the treaty tariff the British, French, and American consuls at Shanghai entered into an arrangement whereby a committee of three, one appointed by each consul, was vested with authority to collect import and export duties on behalf of the Chinese government. This temporary arrangement proved so satisfactory, both to the Chinese government and to the foreign trader, that the tariff agreements drawn up in connection with the treaties of 1858 provided that the Chinese government would establish, in imitation of the Shanghai experiment, a foreign-administered custom service whose operations were to be extended to all the treaty ports. This service ensured to the Chinese government the efficient collection of the tariffs levied upon foreign trade and at the same time guaranteed to the foreign merchants freedom from continual friction with the old-style Chinese officials.

In November, 1863, Mr. (later Sir) Robert Hart succeeded to the office of inspector general of the newly organized service. Hart soon proved himself to be an unusually capable organizer and administrator. Under his direction, which continued until his death in 1911, the customs became an elite service, cosmopolitan in membership and attracting into its ranks men of the highest quality. In addition to performing the functions usually associated with a customs service the Imperial Maritime Customs carried on hydrographic work along the Chinese coast, established a public health service, and organized a modern postal system.[1]

Nor did even this extreme diversity of activities complete the services which Hart rendered to the Chinese government. The "I. G.," as he was usually called, became the confidential adviser of the imperial government upon all questions of international relations, and his advice frequently proved to be of inestimable value.

Two years before Robert Hart became inspector general of the Maritime Customs the control of the imperial government passed into the hands of one of the most remarkable women in the history of China. The Empress Dowager Tzu Hsi, the widow of Hsien Feng, was twenty-six years of age when her husband's death brought to the throne her five-year-old son, T'ung Chih. Throughout the next forty-seven years she dominated the government of China: first, as regent for her son; from 1875 until 1889 as regent for the

---

[1] The Imperial Maritime Customs also became the training school of a number of extremely able Sinologues.

infant Kuang Hsu, whom she placed on the throne after the death of T'ung Chih; between 1889 and 1898 as the power behind the throne; and from 1898 until her death as regent for the second time in the name of Kuang Hsu.

Brilliant, strong-willed, and unscrupulous, frequently and not inaptly compared with Elizabeth of England and with Catherine of Russia, Tzu Hsi did much to check the rapid disintegration of the Manchu empire. Conservative by nature and until nearly the end of her life bitterly anti-foreign, she never really appreciated, prior to the collapse of the Boxer movement, the necessity of re-adjusting China's institutions so as to meet the conditions of a new world environment; nor did she succeed in putting an end to the widespread graft and corruption in the imperial court. But she possessed the ability to choose capable subordinates and to inspire them with personal loyalty to their sovereign. Jung Lu, Prince Kung, and Prince Ching (among the Manchus), Tseng Kuo-fan, Tso Tsung-t'ang, Li Hung-chang, Chang Chih-tung, Liu Kun-yih, and Yüan Shih-k'ai (among the Chinese) are merely a few of the better-known of the officials who under the leadership of the empress dowager restored to the old governmental machinery such energy and efficiency that China was able to command once more the respect and consideration of the outside world.

The situation of the Manchu government during the early years of Tzu Hsi's regency was decidedly precarious. Besides losing prestige through the disastrous foreign wars, the Manchus, under the treaty settlements, had assumed obligations which conflicted with established Chinese tradition, and the fulfillment of these obligations necessitated an unaccustomed interference by the central authorities in local affairs. After the suppression of the T'aiping Rebellion, therefore, the empire was torn by disturbances in various parts of the country. Some of these disorders were anti-Manchu revolutionary movements instigated by secret societies. Others were caused by bands of armed robbers who seized upon the general confusion as an opportunity for unrestrained banditry. Still others took the form of anti-foreign or anti-Christian outbreaks and were the result of popular opposition to the new treaty rights which had been granted to the Western "barbarians."

In the matter of its newly assumed treaty obligations the imperial government thus found itself "between the devil and the deep sea." If it attempted in the face of popular disapproval to enforce full observance of the treaty stipulations, it risked the danger of involving itself in the anti-foreign hostility and of precipitating fresh disorders which, through destruction of foreign lives or property, would bring from the foreign diplomats demands for compensation and more adequate protection. If, on the other hand, the government attempted to conciliate Chinese public opinion by preventing the full exercise of treaty rights by the European merchant and missionary, diplomatic complaints and demands were equally certain to pour in upon the Tsungli Yamen.

In November, 1867, Anson Burlingame, American minister to China, resigned his post and accepted appointment as head of a diplomatic mission which the Chinese government dispatched to the governments of the Western powers. As the first resident minister of the United States at Peking, Burlingame between 1861 and 1867 had consistently advocated a conciliatory policy toward China and had been able to secure the cordial co-operation of his British, French, and Russian colleagues; at the same time he had gained the confidence of the leading Chinese statesmen. For some time prior to the date of Burlingame's resignation the Chinese government had been considering the advisability of dispatching a mission to the various Western countries; and when they learned of his intention to retire, they welcomed the opportunity of securing him as their representative.

Arriving in America at the end of March, 1868, China's "envoy to the world" made a number of public addresses in which he explained the difficulties confronting China and urged the Western nations not to be too insistent upon the immediate and literal fulfillment of all the treaty concessions which had been forced from her. "Let her alone; let her have her independence," he urged; "let her develop herself in her own time and in her own way. Let her do this and she will initiate a movement which will be felt in every workshop of the civilized world."

At Washington, in July, Burlingame and his two Chinese associates concluded a new treaty with the United States. In Article V of this treaty the Chinese government, as a concession to the American desire for a plentiful supply of cheap labor, recognized "the inherent and inalienable right of man to change his home and allegiance, and also the mutual advantage of the free migration and emigration of their citizens and subjects respectively from one country to the other for purposes of curiosity, of trade, or as permanent residents." Article VI guaranteed that Chinese visiting or residing in the United States should "enjoy all the privileges, immunities, and exemptions enjoyed by the citizens or subjects of the most favored nation, naturalization alone being excepted." Article VIII allayed China's fears by a disavowal on the part of the United States of "any intention or right to intervene in the domestic administration of China in regard to the construction of railways, telegraphs, or other material internal improvements."

The assurance contained in Article VIII of the Burlingame Treaty was faithfully adhered to by the United States, but the provisions in Articles V and VI subsequently led to serious friction between the two countries. As early as 1876, complaints against the competition of "cheap Oriental labor" began to reach Washington from organized labor on the Pacific coast, and two years later Congress passed an act prohibiting the immigration of Chinese laborers. This act was vetoed by President Hayes on the ground that it was in violation of the 1868 treaty with China, and in 1880 an American treaty commission was sent to Peking for the purpose of securing a revision of the immigration clauses.

By the new treaty the Chinese government agreed that the United States might "regulate, limit, or suspend such coming or residence [that is, of Chinese laborers] but may not absolutely prohibit it." In 1882 Congress took advantage of this right by "suspending" Chinese immigration for a period of ten years. Six years later, in violation of the revised treaty, a new act of Congress absolutely prohibited the immigration of Chinese laborers. China's assent to the policy of complete exclusion was incorporated into the Chinese-American treaty of 1894; but in 1904, when this treaty expired, the Chinese government refused to renew it, and the Chinese people by a boycott of American goods showed their resentment of the humiliating discrimination against Chinese in America.

After the conclusion of the Chinese-American treaty Burlingame crossed the Atlantic and carried to the courts of Europe his plea for a conciliatory nonaggressive policy toward China. At London, although less cordially received than in Washington, his arguments had a noticeable effect upon the Foreign Ministry, while Paris and Berlin both responded favorably to his plea not to endanger peace by attempts to "force China into paths of progress." At St. Petersburg also the mission was well received; but here, in February, 1870, Burlingame died of pneumonia, and the undertaking came to an end.

In Europe, as in America, Burlingame's enthusiastic speeches undoubtedly aroused expectations which were doomed to disappointment, but the general effect of his mission was beneficial. China's difficulties, arising out of the problems of readjustment, were adequately presented to the Western countries for the first time; and the Western governments, hitherto dependent upon such information as was supplied by people directly interested in the extension of treaty privileges, began to receive real enlightenment with regard to China's side of the question.

In spite of the beneficial effect of the Burlingame mission, the next two decades were marked by friction between China and all three of the Western powers—Russia, Britain, and France—whose Asiatic possessions bordered upon the empire.

In 1863 the Mohammedan tribes of Chinese Turkestan rose in revolt against the Chinese authorities, and an able leader, Yakub Beg, putting himself at the head of the movement, set up an independent state with its capital at Kashgar. On the ground that the disturbances in this region threatened the peace and safety of Russian territories the Russian government in 1871 sent forces to occupy the district of Kuldja (on the Ili) in the northern part of Chinese Turkestan, promising to evacuate the occupied region as soon as China should have succeeded in restoring order in the rebellious province.

When this promise was given, no one seriously expected that the Chinese would be able to re-establish their authority in Turkestan. Yakub Beg's power was so formidable that the British in 1870 and in 1873 sent two missions to his court, while the Russians in 1872 recognized his sovereignty by negotiating a commercial treaty with him. But China's military power was not yet a negligible quantity. In 1870 General Tso Tsung-t'ang, who had been engaged in suppressing another Mohammedan insurrection in Yunnan, was ordered to undertake the restoration of order in Turkestan. Tso Tsung-t'ang's advance was very slow (on two occasions he halted his army long enough to plant and reap a crop of grain to provide food for its own use), but in the fall of 1876 he finally led his forces into the western portion of Turkestan. Yakub Beg was defeated, and before the end of 1877 Chinese authority over the rebellious Mohammedans was completely restored.

As the time had now come for Russia to evacuate Kuldja in accordance with her promise, the Chinese government in December, 1878, sent a special representative to St. Petersburg for the purpose of arranging for the withdrawal of the Russian forces. Chung Hou, the official to whom this mission was entrusted, was interested only in settling the matter as quickly as possible; and in October of the following year he concluded an agreement (the Treaty of Livadia) whereby Russia was to retain about three fourths of the occupied territory, to receive a sum of five million rubles as compensation for the costs of occupation, and to secure the opening of a new caravan trade route.

The treaty was promptly repudiated by Peking, Chung Hou narrowly escaped the penalty of death as a reward for his diplomatic incompetence, and the Chinese repeated their demand for the restoration of the territory. The army of Tso Tsung-t'ang was still in Turkestan, and the Russian governor of western Siberia informed his government that he had at his disposal no forces capable of dealing with the army under General Tso. Under these circumstances the Czar's ministers reluctantly gave way, and by a new treaty, signed on February 12, 1881, at St. Petersburg, practically the whole of the disputed territory was restored to China, while China paid Russia nine million rubles for the cost of the occupation.

The French acquisition of Cochin China in 1862 and the establishment, in the next year, of a protectorate over Cambodia were followed by a steady expansion of French interests and influence into other parts of the kingdom of Annam. In 1866 an expedition under Francis Garnier explored the Mekong River, seeking a possible trade route into the Chinese province of Yunnan. The upper reaches of the Mekong proved to be unnavigable; but Garnier, when he reached Yunnan, discovered another stream—the Red River—which offered a practicable trade route into Yunnan from Annam. In 1873, therefore, he was sent with a force of two hundred and twelve men to Hanoi to secure from the Annamese government permission for the French merchants to send their goods up the Red River. When the Hanoi authorities refused to grant this permission, hostilities resulted. Garnier and his little army, after some initial success, were defeated, and the leader was slain. Following this check, the French had recourse to diplomacy, and in 1874 concluded a treaty of peace with Annam. By the treaty France recognized the independence of Annam but received the right to trade along the Red River and to "advise" the Annamese government upon all matters involving foreign relations.

The French-Annamese treaty of 1874 was officially communicated to the Chinese government in May, 1875. Although the treaty, by establishing a quasi protectorate over Annam, infringed upon China's ancient rights of suzerainty, the Tsungli Yamen offered no immediate objection to the new arrangement, while the Annamese king, by sending his regular "tribute missions" to Peking in 1876 and 1880, indicated that he recognized no modification of his traditional relationship with the Dragon Throne. In 1880, however, the Chinese minister at Paris formally inquired as to the intentions of the French in Annam, and in 1881 he protested against the French assertion that Annam was an "independent state."

By the beginning of 1882, French intentions in Annam were made perfectly clear both to the Annamese and to the Chinese, and the king of Annam, alarmed at French encroachments upon his powers, appealed to the Chinese for help. In April a French force took Hanoi by storm, and in August, 1883, France compelled the king to conclude a new treaty whereby his kingdom was openly transformed into a French protectorate. After the taking of Hanoi, Chinese troops were sent into Tongking, the northern province of Annam, to co-operate with the Annamese irregular forces in war against the conquering European, and a state of war, although not formally proclaimed by either belligerent, actually existed between France and China.

The Chinese and the French were both anxious to avoid war. In May, 1884, therefore, Li Hung-chang and a French officer, Commandant Fournier, entered into a convention at Tientsin for the cessation of hostilities; China recognized the French treaty with Annam and agreed to withdraw her troops from Tongking. Before this arrangement could be communicated to the Chinese military officials in Tongking, a clash occurred at Langson between the French and the Chinese forces. Both governments made charges of bad faith, the Li-Fournier convention was repudiated, and hostilities continued on land and sea for another year. On the sea the French were overwhelmingly superior, but on land the Chinese forces showed themselves quite capable of holding their own against the foreign enemy. After several unsuccessful efforts to open negotiations peace was finally restored by a new Treaty of Tientsin, signed on June 9, 1885. Neither government received any war indemnity, the provisions of the Li-Fournier convention were reaffirmed, and arrangements were made for trade between Annam and the adjoining provinces of the Chinese Empire.

While the French on the eastern side of the Indo-Chinese peninsula were building up a colonial empire by the conquest of Annam, the British, on the west, were completing the annexation of Burma —also an ancient vassal of China. Like the French, the British hoped to make their expansion in Indo-China a steppingstone to the development of trade with the southwestern provinces of China. Their attempt to realize this hope brought Britain and China to the verge of war.

In 1874 the British government of India secured China's permission to send an exploring party into Yunnan from Burma, and Mr. A. R. Margary, a British consular officer at Hankow, traveled overland through Yunnan to join the party at Bhamo on the Burmese side of the frontier. A month after his arrival the party, which numbered about two hundred persons and included a strong armed escort, left Bhamo for the Yunnanese frontier. Because of rumors that certain frontier tribes in Yunnan were arming to oppose the party Margary and a few attendants went ahead of the main party to "talk peace" and to allay the hostility of the tribesmen. On February 19, 1875, he entered Yunnan; three days later his small party was massacred at Manwyne by an armed mob, apparently alarmed by the approach of what appeared to be a foreign army of invasion.

When the news of Margary's murder reached Peking, the British minister, Sir Thomas Wade, demanded immediate satisfaction for the outrage. The imperial government executed a number of tribesmen said to have been implicated in the murder, and compensation was made to the families of the murdered men; but the British minister's demand that the viceroy of Yunnan be punished for negligence was rejected. After some futile insistence upon this point Wade entered upon a general discussion of outstanding questions between Britain and China. In September, 1876, after long negotiations, Wade and Li Hung-chang concluded at Chefoo a convention which settled most of these questions in an equitable manner. The new convention was promptly ratified by the Chinese government; but the British commercial community in China raised a storm of objections to certain provisions, and it was not ratified by Great Britain until 1885, after the inclusion of an "additional article" safeguarding the still important opium trade.

In 1871, four years after the inauguration of the Meiji era (see next chapter), the Japanese government established relations with China by a treaty signed at Tientsin. Unlike the treaties which each of these countries had been compelled to conclude with the Western powers, the treaty between China and Japan contained no provision for extraterritorial jurisdiction; each government agreed that its people while residing in the territory of the other should be subject to the jurisdiction of the regular local authorities.

The relations established between the two Far Eastern empires were almost immediately embittered by a dispute arising out of the murder of some Luchuan fishermen who, in the same year that saw the conclusion of the treaty, were shipwrecked on the island of Formosa and murdered by the Formosans. The Luchu Islands, a southern continuation of the Japanese Archipelago, are inhabited by people closely related to the Japanese; the Japanese government therefore regarded them as part of its empire and demanded that China pay compensation for the murder of the shipwrecked men. On the ground that the Luchus were vassals of China and that Japan therefore had no right to intervene in the matter the Chinese rejected the demand. In 1874 the Japanese government dispatched an expedition to Formosa to secure by force the satisfaction which China refused to grant. For a few weeks war between China and Japan appeared unavoidable, but the Peking government finally gave way and paid Japan the sum of five hundred thousand taels: a hundred thousand as compensation for the murders, the balance as payment for the expenses of the expedition. This settlement, which tacitly admitted Japan's sovereignty over the Luchus, was a complete victory for the Japanese and encouraged them a few years later to challenge China's authority over another of her ancient vassal states: Korea.

In spite of the various encroachments upon her outlying territories and dependencies, China continued to command the respect of the Western world for three decades after the Second Treaty Settlement. Japan had successfully disputed China's claim to suzerainty over the Luchu Islands, but the islands lay far from the Chinese coast and actually were, geographically, a part of the Japanese chain. The British had absorbed the once vassal state of Burma, but even while annexing this former dependency they had considered it wise to conciliate the Chinese court by guaranteeing that the decennial tributary mission should continue to go as usual from the Burmese capital to Peking. France had compelled the Manchus to abandon their claim to suzerainty over Annam, but the successful stand of the Chinese troops against the French in the Tongking war had added to China's prestige more than had been lost by the surrender. Even greater prestige had been gained by the military efficiency displayed in the overthrow of Yakub Beg and by the unexpected outcome of the Kuldja controversy. Russia had retained a part of the disputed region, but China, to the surprise of the Western world, had compelled the Russians to retreat and to surrender territory over which they had once raised their flag. Surely a nation which could accomplish this could not be dismissed as a negligible power.

Not only had China recovered from her extreme helplessness of 1860; she even appeared to have entered, somewhat cautiously, upon a policy of adopting some of the more obviously useful institutions of the West. A portion of the army had been armed and organized in accordance with European methods. A beginning was made in the development of a modern navy, Chinese students being sent to study in Western countries and a few Western naval officers being employed to take command of warships purchased abroad. A number of Chinese merchants were encouraged to organize a Chinese steamship company and to engage in foreign trade as well as in trade between the coast and river ports of their own country. Within a decade after the Burlingame mission the imperial government had finally made up its mind to maintain resident ministers at the courts of the principal treaty powers, and this step was followed by the establishment of consuls at a number of ports where Chinese commercial interests had assumed importance. In 1873, after the young emperor had attained his majority, the members of the diplomatic corps were finally admitted to an imperial audience.

An attempt in 1876 to establish a railway between Shanghai and Wusung was abandoned in the face of local opposition, but in 1887 a railway was put into operation in Chihli Province between the Kaiping coal mines and Tongshan, while 1890 saw the erection of a modern ironworks at Hanyang, across the river from Wuchang. In 1862 a "language school" was established at Peking under the auspices of the Tsungli Yamen, for the purpose of providing the government with competent interpreters. Three years later, courses in modern science were added to the curriculum, a number of foreign instructors were employed, and the school was transformed into the Tungwen College.

In spite of these hesitating steps toward the introduction of Western ideas China, after nearly four centuries of intercourse with Europe and after half a century of treaty regime, was still stubbornly opposed to any modification of her own ancient institutions. With the exception of the decision to receive the diplomatic corps, which was forced upon the reluctant Peking authorities by the foreign diplomats, practically every innovation was the work of a few outstanding individuals: Li Hung-chang, Chang

Chih-tung, and the inspector general of customs, Robert Hart. By the great majority of the officials and by the overwhelming mass of the Chinese people the West was hated, despised, and feared. Although they realized China's inability to resist foreign demands, the officials and literati felt that the introduction of foreign ideas and methods would result in the destruction of the very foundations of their own civilization, while the mass of the common people, often knowing the foreigner only as a purveyor of strange and disturbing religious doctrines, resented his upsetting influence in the affairs of the town or village community. From time to time this resentment, often incited by the literary class, flared out in violent attacks upon the missionary and his Chinese convert; more generally, however, all classes combined in what may best be described as a sullen determination that the aggressive Westerners, having secured an inch, should not be permitted to take an ell. In 1894, therefore, as fifty years earlier, the Manchu government was chiefly desirous of keeping the foreigner at arm's length, and in this policy it had the approval of the nation at large.

SUGGESTED REFERENCES

BLAND, J. O. P., and BACKHOUSE, E. China under the Empress Dowager.
BREDON, J. Sir Robert Hart.
COOLIDGE, M. R. Chinese Immigration.
DENNETT, T. Americans in Eastern Asia.
GUNDRY, R. S. China and her Neighbors.
HAIL, W. J. Tsêng Kuo-Fan and the Taiping Rebellion.
KEETON, G. W. The Development of Extraterritoriality in China.
LANE-POOLE, S., and DICKINS, F. V. Life of Sir Harry Parkes.
LATOURETTE, K. S. The Chinese: their History and Culture.
LATOURETTE, K. S. A History of Christian Missions in China.
LEAVENWORTH, C. The Arrow War.
MACNAIR, H. F. The Chinese Abroad.
MACNAIR, H. F. Modern Chinese History: Selected Readings.
MORSE, H. B. The International Relations of the Chinese Empire, Vols. I and II.
OLIPHANT, L. The Mission of Lord Elgin to China and Japan.
RANTOUL, R. S. Frederick Townsend Ward.
WILLIAMS, E. T. A Short History of China.
WILLIAMS, F. W. Anson Burlingame and the First Chinese Mission to Foreign Powers.
WILLIAMS, S. W. The Middle Kingdom.

XXIV

Japan under the Tokugawa Shogunate

WHEN the third Tokugawa Shogun in 1638 decreed the expulsion of all Portuguese merchants from Japan, he inaugurated for his country a period of almost unbroken seclusion which lasted for more than two centuries. With the final departure of the Portuguese during the following year the Dutch East India Company's agents at Hirado were the only Europeans legally remaining on Japanese soil. In 1641 the Dutch merchants were forced to abandon their Hirado factories and to take up their residence, under conditions which reduced them practically to the status of prisoners, on the artificial islet of Deshima in Nagasaki harbor. Henceforth this little handful of Europeans and a limited number of Chinese merchants permitted to trade at Nagasaki under equally strict surveillance were the only connecting links between the Japanese Empire and the outside world.

The adoption of strict isolation as a national policy coincided with the beginning of an equally extensive period of internal peace. The Shimabara Revolt of the winter of 1637–1638, an uprising of some thirty thousand persecuted Christian peasants and discontented samurai, was finally suppressed by the Shogunal forces in the early spring of 1638. This was the last occasion, for two and a quarter centuries, on which the Tokugawa rulers were compelled to draw the sword because of a serious revolt against their dictatorial power. Not until 1864, when the western clans seized upon the abandonment of the isolation policy as a pretext for defying the Shogunate, were armed forces again assembled on Japanese soil for domestic conflict.

Shut off from the outside world and enjoying to an unprecedented degree the blessings of domestic tranquillity, the Japanese people for the two centuries and more of the Tokugawa "Great Peace" devoted themselves to the task of elaborating and perfecting their national culture.

Most of the credit for this long period of peace, so sharply contrasting with the incessant warfare of the preceding era, must be accorded to Tokugawa Iyeyasu, whose shrewd measures for guaranteeing the future of the Tokugawa family, briefly described in a previous chapter,[1] are entitled here to a careful re-examination.

Profiting by the lessons that were to be learned from the success of Yoritomo's Kamakura Shogunate and from the failure of the various post-Kamakura dictatorships, Iyeyasu had selected as the permanent capital of his new regime the hitherto insignificant town of Yedo, in the Kwanto. Here, safely removed from the corrupting luxury of Kyoto and from the dangerous intrigues of the court nobility (the *kuge*), the founder of Tokugawa fortunes followed the example of Yoritomo by establishing a Bakufu (literally, "camp office"), an administrative organization to aid in the management of military matters and in the performance of the increasingly complicated political and financial functions which devolved upon him.

A sweeping rearrangement of fiefs effected during the months following the battle of Sekigahara (October 21, 1600) put the Tokugawa family and its hereditary retainers, the fudai daimyo, in possession of an expanse of contiguous territory extending from the northeastern limits of the Kwanto to the shores of the Inland Sea and comprising approximately the central half of the main island, Honshu. By this rearrangement the "outside lords," the tozama daimyo, those who had made their submission to the Tokugawa chief after Sekigahara, were relegated to the northern

[1] See Chapter XVII, pp. 407–408.

Tokugawa Japan

and western extremities of Honshu and to the islands of Yezo, Shikoku, and Kyushu, in which regions most of them were compelled to accept fiefs much less extensive than their former holdings. Of the tozama daimyo, only Shimadzu, the lord of Satsuma and Osumi, in southern Kyushu, suffered no diminution or change in his possessions; all the others were reduced in land, in income, and in military resources. The daimyo whose holdings were thus changed, moreover, found their new fiefs so located with respect to those of their traditional enemies that ancient hostilities and reciprocal suspicions served as a strong deterrent to the formation of anti-Tokugawa combinations.

The rearrangement of feudal holdings was followed in the spring of 1601[1] by a demand that all the daimyo, tozama as well as fudai, subscribe to a solemn pledge of loyalty to the Tokugawa lord. In this pledge each daimyo specifically bound himself (1) to obey all the commands of Iyeyasu, (2) to refuse asylum to anyone who had defied or opposed Iyeyasu, and (3) not to enroll as a retainer any samurai accused of being a traitor or an assassin.

In September, 1615, after his successful siege of Osaka castle and the destruction of the powerful military group supporting the rival claims of Hideyoshi's son, the now aged Iyeyasu[2] collaborated with his son and successor, Hidetada, in promulgating two sets of regulations: "The Laws of the Military Houses" and "The Rules of the Imperial Court and the Court Nobles." These codes were subsequently re-enacted by each successive Shogun on his accession to office, and the first of the two was of such fundamental importance that it is often called the Tokugawa constitution.

The "Laws of the Military Houses" began by proclaiming the duty of the buke, or military class (the daimyo and their samurai retainers), to divide their time between the study of literature and practice in warlike exercises: "Literature first and arms next was the rule of the ancients. They must be cultivated concurrently." Several articles of the code were given over to prohibitions relating to private morals and established what may be termed a professional standard of behavior for the individual member of the military caste: the daimyo and their men of arms were to refrain from drunkenness, frivolous or licentious behavior, and ostentation. The remaining sections dealt with important matters of an essentially public and political nature: the feudal lords were forbidden to harbor criminals, to enroll rebels or murderers among their retainers, or to allow social intercourse between the people of their domains and those of neighboring fiefs; marriages between daimyo families, the building of castles, and even the undertaking of repairs upon already existing strongholds were permissible only if approved in advance by the Shogun; strictly accountable for the proper administration of his own fief, each daimyo was also under

---

[1] Still two years before Iyeyasu received his Shogunal commission.
[2] He died in February, 1616, at the age of 74.

the obligation of keeping a close watch upon his neighbors and of reporting to the Shogunal government any inclination toward the introduction of unauthorized innovations or toward the formation of cliques.

The "Rules of the Imperial Court and the Court Nobles" were intended to give to the Shogun the same absolute control over the members of the court as over the military class; for Iyeyasu overlooked no potential source of danger, and he knew that the court nobles (kuge), incompetent though they might be in the actual administration of public affairs, were past masters in the art of intrigue. Just as the code for the warriors opened with the command to divide their time between literary and military pursuits, so the first rule for the court emphasized the all-importance of scholarship: "Learning is the most essential of all accomplishments. Not to study is to be ignorant of the doctrines of the ancient sages, and an ignorant ruler has never governed a nation peacefully." This exhortation to scholarly pursuits, apparently intended to encourage among the courtiers a form of activity that would keep them out of serious mischief, was followed by a number of regulations more directly contributory to Tokugawa domination. Appointments to high posts in the court were to be made only after the nomination had been submitted to and had been approved by the Shogun, whose assent was also necessary before any important court official could resign or be dismissed from his office. As a precaution against possibly dangerous combinations among the kuge families it was ordered that an adopted son should always be chosen from the family of the adopter, while the practice of adopting a daughter to become the heir of the family fortunes was absolutely prohibited. The most important of the regulations, however, was one which forbade any communication between the emperor and persons outside the court except through certain definitely prescribed channels; inasmuch as the designated channels of communication were either Tokugawa officers residing in Kyoto or court officials dependent upon the Shogun for their positions, the restriction enabled the Yedo authorities to isolate the emperor so completely as to eliminate all possibility of his becoming an active political factor.

Of the fourteen Tokugawa Shoguns who followed Iyeyasu two only were conspicuous for their ability: Iyemitsu, the third Shogun, who held office from 1622 until 1651; and Yoshimune, the eighth, who ruled between 1716 and 1745. With these two exceptions none of Iyeyasu's successors rose far above mediocrity, while several fell decidedly below that level. Yet so carefully had the first Tokugawa stabilized the social order that little ability or originality was needed to maintain the family's ascendancy and to impose discipline upon the daimyo.

The administration of the extremely capable Iyemitsu saw the only important additions to, or modifications in, the work of Iyeyasu. In 1626 the young Shogun decreed that henceforth every daimyo, tozama or fudai, should spend equal and alternate periods in residence at Yedo and upon his fief;[1] during the absence of the daimyo from the Shogunal capital, moreover, they were required to leave behind them as hostages their wives and eldest sons.

Having thus reinforced the already existing guaranties against disloyalty on the part of his vassals, Iyemitsu turned his attention to other possible points of weakness in the Tokugawa system and appears to have become convinced that the most serious threat to the permanence of the regime lay in Japan's commercial contacts with the outside world, contacts which by that time were confined almost exclusively to those parts of the empire under the jurisdiction of the tozama daimyo. As a result of this conviction he embarked upon an increasingly restrictive policy which culminated in 1638 in the almost total seclusion already described.[2]

Iyemitsu's third and perhaps most important contribution to the strength of the system established by his grandfather was his transformation of the Bakufu into a carefully organized piece of

[1] For the tozama daimyo the regulations provided alternate periods of a year, while for the fudai the periods were six months in length.

[2] I am unable to agree with those who look upon the seclusion policy as inspired primarily by fear of attack and conquest by the Christian powers of Europe; the fact that the Dutch were forced to transfer their headquarters from Hirado to Nagasaki, a city governed directly by Tokugawa officers, and the further fact that the Chinese were also compelled to limit their trading activities to Nagasaki both indicate that the Shogun was extremely anxious to prevent any direct contact between the daimyo and the foreign traders.

governmental machinery. In the days of Iyeyasu and Hidetada the Bakufu had been a somewhat informal group of administrative assistants selected from among the most capable and trustworthy of the fudai daimyo, since Iyeyasu had laid down the rule that no tozama lord should ever be permitted to take part in the direction of affairs at Yedo. With the third Shogun this loosely organized body became a thoroughly regimented bureaucracy, practically self-perpetuating and capable of functioning efficiently even in the absence of any real leadership on the part of its nominal head. After Iyemitsu, indeed, the Shogun gradually became more and more of a figurehead in whose name the governmental powers were exercised by the bureaucrats.

At the head of the administrative machine stood the *tairo*, an officer who acted as prime minister in normal times and as regent whenever the Shogunal office happened to be held by a minor. Under the tairo were two councils: the *roju* ("Council of State"), entrusted with such matters of "high policy" as the supervision of the daimyo and the maintenance of proper relations with the imperial court; and the *wakadoshiyori* ("Junior Council"), whose specific duty it was to exercise jurisdiction over vassals of less than daimyo rank.[1] Vacancies in the Council of State were usually filled by promotion from the Junior Council, whose members in turn were selected from among those who had displayed conspicuous ability in administrative posts. Only fudai daimyo, of course, were eligible to either council, and political power was so divided between them as to make each a check upon the other.

Appointed by the councils and responsible to them were various special boards or commissions charged with the administration of finance, of military affairs, of religious institutions, of education, and of police matters, as well as the officials entrusted with the government of the important cities of Kyoto, Osaka, Sakai, and Nagasaki. Here, as in the division of powers between the two councils, the principle of checks and balances was observed, while a large number of *metsuke* ("censors," or spies) appointed by the Council of State kept that august body at all times fully informed as to

---

[1] A daimyo was one who held in fief land with an estimated annual yield of not less than 10,000 koku — approximately 50,000 bushels — of rice.

the conduct of officials and the loyalty of the daimyo in all parts of the empire.

In its dealings with the daimyo, both fudai and tozama, the Bakufu was ever on the alert to punish shortcomings and to avert political dangers.

The military preponderance of the Tokugawa family and the efficiency of its hereditary retainers were, in the last analysis, the foundation of the Shogun's power. Hence every fudai daimyo, even though himself of Tokugawa ancestry, held his fief "on good behavior" as judged by the standards of strict military discipline. Incompetence, dissipation, or a failure to obey promptly the commands of the Bakufu authorities resulted almost invariably in the transfer of the offender to a less desirable fief or in the reduction or total confiscation[1] of the lands entrusted to his care.

Toward the tozama daimyo a different policy was adopted. In the case of these lords danger to the Shogunate lay not in their dissipation or incompetence but in their accumulation of too much wealth and power. Nor was it usually convenient or desirable to alter their holdings and thus to upset the balance of power among them so carefully established by Iyeyasu. The Bakufu therefore followed the policy of leaving these feudatories undisturbed in the possession of their fiefs and of taking every possible precaution against their becoming wealthy. Whenever any tozama lord by frugality and by careful administration of his fief seemed likely to become dangerously prosperous, the Yedo authorities promptly commanded him to undertake the restoration of a temple, the erection of a Shogunal castle, or some other costly public work, with the result that he soon found himself reduced to an innocuous condition of financial embarrassment.

It is necessary at this point to note one important and—for the Tokugawa—extremely dangerous outcome of the policy adopted in dealing with the tozama lords: the development in the regions under tozama rule of a strong clan spirit which served to unite ever more closely these daimyo and their people. Whereas the frequent transfer of fudai daimyo from fief to fief tended to prevent

---

[1] In such extreme cases the culprit was usually "graciously permitted" to commit suicide.

the growth of clannishness in the regions assigned to these trusted "hereditary retainers," the tozama families, holding the same fiefs for generation after generation, steadily increased their local prestige and in their own domains eventually attained a position not unlike that of the clan chieftain of pre-Taikwa Japan. Iyeyasu's "Laws of the Military Houses," which prohibited unauthorized marriages between daimyo families and forbade the retainers of one lord to transfer their allegiance to another or even to travel outside their lord's fief except by special permission, helped to foster this growth of particularism and clan spirit, while the policy of excluding the tozama daimyo from positions in the central government had a similar effect.

Of the numerous clans which thus grew up in the regions under tozama rule, four in the western part of the empire gradually attained outstanding importance: Satsuma, in southern Kyushu; Hizen, in the northwestern part of the same island; Tosa, on the southern side of Shikoku; and Choshu, holding the modern provinces of Nagato and Suwo, in the western extremity of Honshu. The heads of these clans, like all the other tozama lords, acknowledged no inferiority to the Tokugawa in birth or in noble tradition. The Mori family of Choshu, during the half-century preceding the battle of Sekigahara, had held sway over no less than thirteen provinces in the west. The Shimadzu of Satsuma were, like the Tokugawa, of Minamoto descent and could boast that the provinces of Satsuma and Osumi had been in possession of their family without interruption since the closing years of the twelfth century. Others, although hardly able to rival these two in the greatness of their past, could point to the time when their own families stood high in comparison with the Tokugawa "bumpkins" of the Kwanto. When once the power of the Bakufu began to decline, therefore, it was in these great tozama families (or, more accurately, in the powerful clan organizations of which they were the titular heads) that the anti-Tokugawa movement found inspiration and leadership.

At the close of the sixteenth century Yedo was, as has been pointed out, a comparatively insignificant country town. After the battle of Sekigahara, however, the victorious Iyeyasu turned his attention to the task of transforming this country town into a more appropriate setting for the dictator of all Japan. A new and imposing castle was constructed, wide areas of waste land were reclaimed, and the Tokugawa retainers were encouraged to erect new homes for themselves on sites allotted to them; special inducements to artisans and merchants resulted in a rapid development of the city's industry and trade, and efforts were made—unsuccessfully, as we have seen (see Chapter XVII)—to persuade first the Dutch and later the English to make Yedo their principal trading post in Japan. After the establishment of the Shogunate the city continued to grow by leaps and bounds. By the middle of the seventeenth century its population probably exceeded two hundred thousand; an official census in 1723 gave a figure of more than half a million; and it has been estimated that in 1800 upward of a million people resided in the Tokugawa capital.

Iyemitsu's policy of national isolation and his decree requiring the daimyo to spend half their time in residence at Yedo, although both were inspired by political considerations, contributed in no small degree to make his city economically and culturally as well as politically the center of the empire. The restriction of foreign commerce to the single port of Nagasaki and the imposition of drastic limitations even upon the trade at that point were serious blows to the hitherto prosperous commercial cities of Osaka, Sakai, Nagoya, Hirado, and eventually to Nagasaki itself. Thenceforth all these cities steadily declined in wealth and population as their merchants, moneylenders, artists, and artisans sought fortune in the shadow of the Shogun's castle. Under the decree of "alternate residence" it became necessary for every daimyo to provide for himself and his family a suitable permanent domicile at Yedo, and the mansions of some three hundred great nobles, with their numerous occupants, constituted an important addition to the growing city.

Wealthy merchants were no rarity in pre-Tokugawa Japan, but hitherto they had been found only in such purely commercial centers as Osaka, Sakai, and the like, safely removed from intimate contact with daimyo or samurai. At Yedo, however, a new and unprecedented situation developed: the Shogun and his Bakufu officials, daimyo from all parts of the empire with their families and retainers, and thousands of samurai found themselves permanently located in the heart of a great and growing commercial city. Living in aristocratic idleness, with regular incomes and with only the peacetime routine of garrison duty to occupy their time, the members of the military caste turned for diversion to the attractions offered by the city around them.

All too soon the simple-minded buke discovered that their incomes, although regular, did not enable them to enjoy to the full the manifold attractions which the city offered; but they also discovered obliging and usurious moneylenders who were always willing to advance ready cash for their spending. In vain did successive Shoguns issue solemn decrees ordering their retainers to observe the rules of frugality and sobriety laid down in the "Laws of the Military Houses." In vain did the Bakufu frame sumptuary laws designed to keep the bourgeoisie in their place. The military caste, lordly daimyo and humble samurai alike, gave themselves up more and more shamelessly to the luxuries, frivolities, and vices of their city environment, while the once despised merchant class, now hated and feared by those who no longer dared to despise them, held their nominal rulers in the bondage of an ever increasing debt.

Disastrous as was the influence of Yedo upon the character of the professional soldier, the spectacular growth of the city in population and wealth had an equally unfortunate effect upon the relations between the Tokugawa government and the outlying portions of the empire.

In the first place, the increase in population altered and weakened the Shogun's military position. So long as the population of his capital was such as could be maintained on the resources of the Kwanto, with little or no importation of food or other necessities, the Tokugawa ruler was able in case of need to withstand a siege by the combined forces of the rest of the country. Once this limit was exceeded, however, the military situation became fundamentally different: in case of a war against the rest of Japan, Yedo and the Kwanto could now be starved into submission unless the Shogunal armies were strong enough to take the offensive and win a speedy victory.

In the second place, the steady flow of wealth from the provinces to the new metropolis served to broaden and intensify provincial hostility to the Shogunal government. From the days of Iyeyasu, as we have seen, it was the policy of the Tokugawa rulers to weaken the tozama daimyo by calling upon them from time to time to spend great sums in public works, usually on some project outside the boundaries of their respective fiefs. While the cost of these undertakings drained the treasuries of the feudatories upon whom the work was imposed, the money thus put into circulation had a generally beneficial effect upon the economic life of the country. The extravagant expenditures of the daimyo at Yedo undoubtedly aided the Shogun's effort to keep the tozama lords in a reassuring state of financial embarrassment; but this money, on the other hand, seldom found its way back to the provinces, with the result that central and western Japan, drained of their monetary wealth, suffered from steadily advancing economic anemia. To the inveterate hostility of the tozama daimyo, who had never loyally acquiesced in the supremacy of the Tokugawa "upstarts," there was thus added a growing anti-Tokugawa popular sentiment, engendered by economic conditions and affecting not only the regions under tozama rule but also many of the areas held in fief by fudai vassals.

Attention has already been called to the emphasis which the first Tokugawa Shogun placed upon the cultivation of scholarship by the military men and the court nobles. The ulterior motives of the astute Iyeyasu are fairly obvious. Realizing the difficulty of maintaining a large body of professional soldiers in military inaction without serious loss of military discipline and esprit de corps, he hoped that the addition of scholarly pursuits to the dull routine of military exercises would sufficiently occupy the warrior's time and, by making him a member of the "aristocracy of letters," serve to keep alive his sense of caste superiority and solidarity. In much the same way he appears to have hoped that the court nobles at Kyoto, if encouraged to devote themselves to literature and philosophy, would be diverted from any temptation to active participation in political affairs. As the new political order became more and more strongly organized under an increasingly bureaucratic Bakufu, the Yedo authorities came to feel that an excess of martial zeal among the samurai constituted a serious threat to the stability of their civilian institutions. Accordingly the later Shoguns, in the hope of fostering an alternative and less dangerous enthusiasm, continued to encourage the development of scholarship, especially among the military classes.

The Tokugawa government, however, had no desire to avoid the Scylla of excessive martial zeal only to be engulfed in the Charybdis of dangerous thought. Under their patronage, therefore, Japanese scholarship was directed almost exclusively to the presumably safe study of the Confucian Classics. Schools of Confucian philosophy were founded, professorships and lectureships were established, the available copies of ancient writings were collected into libraries, and encouragement was given to the publication of new editions. Several of the Shoguns, including Iyeyasu himself, made a point of attending the lectures of prominent scholars, while one at least showed his enthusiasm for learning by delivering public lectures on the Classics.

The immediate effects of the revival of Confucian learning were decidedly beneficial to the new regime. Well-trained scholars, thoroughly grounded in the social philosophy of the Chinese Sage, rendered valuable assistance to the Bakufu in various administrative capacities. Others, educated in the same school of thought, performed equally important service in popularizing among the Japanese people the ethical principles upon which a civilian government must rest. During this period the development of a new ethical outlook was especially apparent among the military classes, whose code of behavior—*Bushido* (literally, "Way of the Soldier")— underwent marked change through the injection of philosophical ideas.[1] The changed outlook did not stop, however, with the warrior. Bushido, thus transformed by the addition of philosophical refinements, ceased to be the exclusive property of the soldier and, although retaining its ancient military title, became an accepted standard of behavior for buke and bourgeoisie alike.

[1] The fact is that Bushido in the 18th century was no longer what it was before, a customary code developed among soldiers under the stress of war, but a system of practical ethics evolved out of the disagreements of philosophers and in process of adaptation to the needs of peaceful society.—SANSOM, *Japan: a Short Cultural History*, pp. 491–492

Over against these beneficial effects of scholarly activity, however, must be placed other consequences of less happy augury for the Tokugawa rulers. It is true that the ethical teachings of Confucius constantly emphasized the duty of loyalty; but the state envisaged by the Chinese philosopher knew no such officer as the Shogun, and the loyalty upon which he laid most stress was that of minister to sovereign. Historical research, moreover, despite the efforts of pro-Tokugawa authors to rewrite the nation's history in such manner as to justify the existence of the Shogun, carried the student back to the pre-Shogunal days of Shotoku and the Taikwa reforms and centered his attention upon the emperor as the fount and origin of all lawful political power. History and philosophy alike, therefore, provided the critically inclined with grounds for questioning the Tokugawa pretensions to unlimited sovereign power; and even before the end of the seventeenth century a few daring scholars were beginning to assert that the Shogun was nothing more than a creation of the emperor, who could revoke at any time the powers which he had granted.

The seventeenth-century revival of Confucian scholarship was attended by an almost total eclipse of Buddhism as a positive force in the life of the Japanese people. Splendid new temples at Yedo, Nikko, Kyoto, and elsewhere gave, indeed, an outward appearance of continued prosperity, while Iyemitsu strengthened the illusion by decreeing that every daimyo should enroll himself and his people as adherents of some recognized Buddhist sect; but these outward appearances of activity served only as a cloak to conceal the complete absence of any real spiritual or intellectual influence on the part of the Buddhist clergy. In part, this decline in influence must be attributed to the deliberate policy of the Tokugawa rulers, who, although openly patronizing the Buddhist church, overlooked no opportunity of transforming it into a useful and obedient tool of government. To an even greater extent, however, the loss of importance by this once all-powerful religious force resulted from the inveterate hostility of the Confucianists, in whose eyes there was little to choose between the superstitions of Buddhism and those of the now proscribed Christianity.

The spiritual vacuum created by the decline of the Buddhist

faith was filled by a reviving interest in the ancient but long-neglected cult of Shinto. Throwing off the bodhisattva role to which they had been reduced by the triumph of Buddhism, the native Kami once more assumed the status of independent deities demanding the reverent worship of every Japanese patriot. Fostered though it undoubtedly was by the revival of classical studies and by the contemptuous attitude of the Confucianists toward the spiritual teachings of Buddha, the Shinto revival eventually developed into a reaction against Confucianism itself. To those advocating a return to the simple cult of the indigenous Shinto Kami the Chinese sage was as much a foreigner as was the Hindu saint, and the moralizings of the philosophers were as meaningless as the theological subtleties of the monks.

The effect of the Shinto renaissance upon political thought was obvious and inevitable. The worship of the old national deities focused attention upon the divine ancestry of the imperial family, and the believer in Shinto was led to the inexorable conviction that the emperor not only was the source of all political power but should, in his own sacred person, exercise that power to the full.

Thus wrote Motoori Norinaga at the end of the eighteenth century:

> The Mikado is the sovereign appointed by the deities who created this country. The Sun-Goddess never said "Disobey the Mikado if he be bad," and therefore, whether he be good or bad, no one attempts to deprive him of his authority. He is the Immovable Ruler who must endure to the end of time so long as the sun and moon continue. In ancient language the Mikado was called a god, and that is his real character. Duty, therefore, consists in obeying him implicitly without questioning his acts.

The ideas of Motoori and his followers appear to have influenced the immediate political situation as little as did the occasional academic questionings of the Confucian scholars. Two generations later, however, when changing conditions finally brought about the collapse of the Shogunate, these earlier assertions of the emperor's divine character proved extremely useful to the reformers who undertook the restoration of the imperial power.

The revival of classical scholarship and the return of Shinto, although of far-reaching importance, were but two aspects of

Japan's cultural development during her long period of isolation and peace. Of equal or greater importance were the rise and spread of new popular forms of artistic and literary expression. These forms, originating in the soil (or, more accurately, in the city streets) of the empire, differed from those of earlier times in that they were less strongly influenced by Chinese standards and were, therefore, a more natural expression of Japanese genius.

Even during pre-Tokugawa days the wealthy commercial cities of Osaka and Sakai had begun to develop a culture of their own which, although certainly influenced by the artistic and literary forms of Kyoto, was essentially "middle class" in taste and expression. With the rise of Yedo this culture was quickly transplanted to the growing Kwanto metropolis, where it took root and flourished, first among the bourgeoisie but eventually among the ruling classes as well. Vigorous, outspoken, and addicted to bold colors rather than to fine shading, the new art and literature of bourgeois origin overwhelmed the more delicate and refined forms of the earlier schools and became the dominant element in Tokugawa culture. In the temples and tombs erected by the Tokugawa rulers at Yedo and Nikko the architect, caring little for exact proportion or for gracefully sweeping curve, dazzles the beholder with intricate carving and a veritable blaze of color. On the stage, melodrama and farce take the place of the "No" dancers whose restrained posturings delighted their aristocratic audiences. Delicate brush drawings of flowers and landscapes give way to the caricatures of Matahei or the color prints of Hokusai and Hiroshige, while poetry and prose, instead of gracefully suggesting, blurt out with brutal frankness the tender sentiment or the scandalous tale.

In spite of the exclusion policy inaugurated by Iyemitsu and continued by his successors in the Shogunal office, Tokugawa Japan was never wholly cut off from the influence of foreign ideas. The principal point of contact, of course, was Nagasaki, where the Dutch commercial establishment throughout its two centuries and more of imprisonment at Deshima served the Japanese government as an official intelligence bureau for foreign news. Periodic missions (annually until 1790 and at four-year intervals after that date) were dispatched to Yedo by the Deshima factory, and the "chief factor," who headed these missions, was regularly required to furnish the Shogun with a written report on all the important world events of the preceding year or years. In addition to the information provided by the Dutch a certain amount of outside news was obtained through the medium of Chinese traders at Nagasaki, and the eighteenth-century contact with the Russians in Yezo and the Kurils furnished the Shogunate with a fresh source of information concerning events which occurred beyond the limits of the empire.

Under Iyemitsu and the next four Shoguns these efforts to keep the government fully informed on important developments in the outside world were accompanied by equally determined efforts to prevent the spread of foreign ideas among the people. The importation of foreign books was strictly prohibited, and no one except those officially authorized to act as interpreters was permitted to study the Dutch language. At Nagasaki elaborate precautions were taken to prevent any unauthorized contact between the foreign merchants and the people, while the periodic Dutch missions to Yedo were carefully isolated from everyone except the officials entrusted with the duty of escort and supervision.

The capable and open-minded eighth Shogun, Yoshimune (1716–1745), radically modified this aspect of Iyemitsu's policy. The prohibition upon the importation of foreign books (except those relating to the Christian religion) was repealed (1720). An eminent Yedo scholar, Aoki Konyo, was dispatched to Nagasaki to study the Dutch language and to compile a Dutch-Japanese dictionary. The Gregorian calendar was translated into Japanese, and Yoshimune appears to have been so impressed by its superiority that only the opposition of his more conservative ministers prevented the adoption of the Western calendar in place of the Chinese.

Even before Yoshimune's abolition of the ban on foreign learning a few daring individuals had engaged in the surreptitious study of Western sciences, especially anatomy and medicine. After the adoption of a more liberal policy there was a steady increase both in the number of students interested in foreign studies and in the range of the subjects studied. Anatomy and medicine continued to attract most attention, but works on geography, astronomy, botany, and other scientific subjects were studied and translated into the Japanese language. Before the end of the eighteenth century one enthusiastic student of Western learning had succeeded in constructing workable pieces of electrical apparatus, and the account of Perry's first visit, in 1853, reports that the Japanese were "not unacquainted with the general principles of science and of [*sic*] the facts of the geography of the world."[1]

Even after the lifting of the ban upon foreign learning the Tokugawa authorities permitted no relaxation in the restrictions on foreign trade; from this time, however, a number of patriotic and progressive Japanese became increasingly critical of the Bakufu for its stubborn adherence to the policy of national isolation. Among these critics of the established foreign policy were some who felt that continued seclusion was resulting in cultural stagnation and decay. Others believed that Japan's refusal to engage actively in world trade was the chief cause of all the economic ills by which she was afflicted. Still others, among whom must be counted some of her shrewdest thinkers, argued that Japan's feudal warriors with their obsolete equipment were no longer capable of defending her against a serious attack by a foreign foe and that only by resuming intercourse with the outside world could she so revise and modernize her military organization as to have any hope of maintaining her national independence.

Not all this domestic criticism was inspired by hostility to the Tokugawa regime. It is true that many, perhaps a majority, of those emphasizing the economic disadvantages of isolation were

[1] The report continues:

When a terrestrial globe was placed before them, and their attention was called to the delineation on it of the United States, they immediately placed their fingers on Washington and New York, as if perfectly familiar with the fact that one was the capital and the other the commercial metropolis of our country. They also, with equal promptitude, pointed out England, France, Denmark, and other kingdoms of Europe. Their inquiries in reference to the United States showed them not to be entirely ignorant of the facts connected with the material progress of our country; thus, when they asked if roads were not cut through our mountains, they were referring (as was supposed) to tunnels on our railroads. And this supposition was confirmed on the interpreter's asking, as they examined the ship's engine, whether it was not a similar machine, although smaller, which was used for travelling on the American roads . . . The engine was evidently an object of great interest to them, but the interpreters showed that they were not entirely unacquainted with its principles.—F. L. HAWKS, *Narrative of the Expedition of an American Squadron to the China Seas and Japan*, pp. 286–287

men dwelling in the provinces under tozama control, the southwestern part of the empire, where foreign trade had formerly flourished and where the anti-Tokugawa attitude of the tozama lords found popular support in the discontent aroused by the overconcentration of wealth at Yedo. On the other hand, however, not a few loyal supporters of the Bakufu, including even some thoughtful members of the Tokugawa family, were to be found among those who openly voiced the fear that isolation, if continued, would result in cultural decay and military disaster. In view of these facts it is obvious that the question of foreign policy had not yet assumed the aspect of a political issue between the Tokugawa government and its enemies, but by the end of the eighteenth century it had become the object of critical attack from various quarters and for a variety of reasons.

Coincident with this awakening internal criticism the closed-door policy of the Tokugawa government found itself subjected to increasing pressure from without. At first this pressure came chiefly from the Russians. During the eighteenth century, as we have seen (Chapter XX, pp. 499–500), the Czar's representatives made repeated efforts to establish diplomatic and commercial relations with Japan. Captain Spanberg's voyage in 1739 and the official embassies of 1792 and 1804 were equally fruitless; but the steady Russian advance into the Kurils, Sakhalin, and even Yezo spelled a danger that could not long be kept at arm's length merely by ignoring it.

The Far Eastern ramifications of the Napoleonic wars brought the ships of other Western countries into Japanese waters and aroused additional foreign interest in Japan as a possible field for commercial enterprise. The depredations of British cruisers between 1795 and 1810 drove the Dutch authorities at Batavia to make use, where possible, of American vessels for their Far Eastern trade, and during these years several American ships sailing under the Dutch flag made voyages between Batavia and Nagasaki. In 1807 an American ship was chartered by a Russian trading company and dispatched to Nagasaki on an unsuccessful trading venture. The following year saw Japan visited by the British warship *Phaeton*, which, ignoring Japan's neutral rights as well as the

Shogun's exclusion edict, entered Nagasaki harbor in search of Dutch merchantmen and withdrew only when threatened with attack by the massed forces of the hastily summoned Kyushu daimyo. In 1813—after the British conquest of the Dutch East Indies—British agents arriving from Java in a ship displaying the Dutch flag attempted to force the staff of the Deshima factory to transfer their allegiance to the new masters of the East Indies. To this demand the chief factor returned a flat refusal; and Deshima remained an outpost without a homeland until 1815, when the Vienna settlement restored to the Dutch their national independence and their East Indian possessions.

For about twenty years after the close of the Napoleonic struggle British and American interests in the Far East were so fully occupied with the development of Chinese trade that no attempt was made to extend operations to Japan. In 1837, however, some Americans at Canton decided to make an effort to open trading relations with the Japanese. A number of Japanese seamen, picked up off the coast of North America, had been sent to Macao for repatriation, and the owners of the American ship *Morrison*, like the Russians a century earlier, attempted to utilize the return of these unfortunate castaways as a means of securing Japanese good will. The plan did not work. Arriving off the southern coast of Kyushu, the *Morrison* was fired on by the coast-defense batteries and was compelled to abandon its attempt to enter a Japanese port.

With the close of the first Anglo-Chinese war the knocking at Japan's door became increasingly insistent; between 1844 and 1849 at least seven separate attempts were made—by Americans, Dutch, English, or French—to negotiate some sort of commercial agreement with the government of the Island Empire.

In the face of growing internal criticism and increasing external pressure the Yedo authorities clung stubbornly—almost desperately—to the time-honored policy of isolation. Realizing that it no longer wielded the absolute power of earlier times, the Bakufu feared to attempt any essential modification of the status quo, lest such a step involve it in new and fatal complications. Yet even the timid conservatism of the Shogun's advisers was moved to make some concession to changing conditions. In 1825 a new general order from Yedo had reiterated the death penalty for any Japanese subject who, having left the country, attempted to return, and had commanded that any foreign vessel approaching the coast be driven away by force; it was in compliance with this command that the daimyo of Satsuma had driven away the *Morrison*. But in 1842 this order was modified. It was now decreed that foreign ships in distress might enter Japanese ports and receive hospitable treatment, while Japanese castaways might be repatriated if brought to Nagasaki in Dutch or Chinese vessels. Thus far and no farther was the Tokugawa government prepared to go in its abandonment of isolation.

To the European peoples of that time, even the Russians, Japan was still a comparatively unimportant collection of islands lying on the far edge of the Far East. From early in the nineteenth century, however, the government of the United States had begun to feel that the opening of at least a few Japanese ports was a matter of vital importance to the American people. American whaling ships operating in the north Pacific and American trading vessels carrying furs from the Oregon coast to Canton felt increasingly the need of ports at which they might stop for supplies and repairs. In 1848, as a result of the war with Mexico, the United States obtained possession of California, with its splendid harbor of San Francisco, and by 1850 California was ready to be admitted into the Union as a state, while San Francisco had become a flourishing seaport anxious to develop a trans-Pacific trade with China.

As early as 1849 the authorities at Washington had informed the European governments of America's intention to dispatch an expedition to Japan for the purpose of securing the opening of Japanese ports to the trade of the outside world. The Dutch chief factor at Deshima, to whom his home government transmitted the American statement of plans, promptly informed the Shogunate of the impending arrival of an American naval force. In 1851 Commodore Aulick, then in command of the United States squadron in the Far East, received instructions ordering him to visit Japan with his forces, for the purpose of delivering to the Japanese emperor a letter from President Fillmore. Before this instruction could be carried out, however, Commodore Aulick was recalled from his command, and the mission was entrusted to his successor, Commodore Matthew Calbraith Perry.

On July 8, 1853, Commodore Perry with a squadron of four ships, including the first two steamships ever to enter Japanese waters, arrived at Uraga in the Bay of Yedo. Upon the arrival of this formidable force the local Japanese officials promptly notified the Americans that no intercourse with foreigners was permitted at that port; if, therefore, they had anything to communicate, they must proceed to Nagasaki, where they would find officers authorized to negotiate with them. In response to this communication Commodore Perry announced that he had a letter from the President of the United States addressed to the emperor of Japan and that he would not go to Nagasaki but would deliver the letter either at Uraga or, if necessary, at Yedo itself.

After six days of preliminary discussions, during which the American plenipotentiary, refusing to communicate directly with anyone below the rank of councilor of state, was represented by his subordinate officers, the Japanese authorities formally accepted the President's letter. On July 17 the squadron departed for Chinese waters, leaving the Shogun and his advisers to decide what answer should be made to the American President's request for "friendship, commerce, a supply of coal and provisions, and protection for our shipwrecked people."

Seven months later, on February 13, Perry was back at Uraga, this time with a squadron of seven ships, to receive the answer of the Japanese government. During his absence, however, the Bakufu had been unable to reach any decision. Six long weeks of patient negotiation followed, and finally, on March 31, the American commodore and the representatives of the Shogun concluded a treaty in which Japan agreed to grant all the fundamental requests of the United States. Shimoda, in Izu Province, and Hakodate, on the island of Yezo, were to be opened to American ships, and at these two ports Americans were to have the privilege of purchasing wood, water, provisions, coal, and other necessities. Shipwrecked American sailors, if cast away on any part of the Japanese coast, were to be treated kindly and conveyed to one of the above-mentioned ports. After the expiration of eighteen months the United States was to appoint a consul or agent to reside at Shimoda if "either of the two governments" decided that such an arrangement was necessary. It was also agreed, in cautious phrases insisted upon by the Japanese representatives, that "ships of the United States, resorting to the ports open to them, shall be permitted to exchange gold and silver coin, and articles of goods, for other articles of goods, under such regulations as shall be temporarily established by the Japanese government for that purpose."

The success of the American representative in concluding with the Japanese government an agreement of even such limited scope was the signal for the other foreign powers to come forward with demands for similar concessions. In October, 1854, Rear Admiral Stirling secured for Great Britain a treaty granting British ships the right to trade at the ports of Hakodate and Nagasaki. In February, 1855, Count Putiatin, the envoy of the Russian government, secured for Russian merchants the right to carry on trade, under Japanese regulations, at Hakodate and Shimoda. In November of the same year the Dutch negotiated a convention abolishing the humiliating restrictions under which for two hundred and fourteen years the merchants of Holland had transacted business at Nagasaki, and admitting them to the trade of the newly opened ports. All three of these new treaties, as well as that negotiated by Commodore Perry, contained most-favored-nation clauses; as a result of these clauses the international obligations assumed by Japan, like those of her continental neighbor, were quickly knit together into a compact body to which additions were easily made but from which any subtraction was extremely difficult.

In the negotiation and conclusion of the treaties whereby Japan abandoned her long-continued isolation the Tokugawa Shogun, through his representatives, had passed himself off upon the foreign diplomats as the reigning sovereign of the empire. But the ruler whom the foreign officials were led to regard as the *de facto* "temporal" emperor, in contrast with a "spiritual" emperor residing at Kyoto, exercised no longer the undisputed authority of earlier days, and the dilemma in which he was placed by the events of these twenty-eight months weakened still further the foundations of his already precarious position.

Two centuries earlier Iyemitsu upon his own authority had decreed the expulsion of foreigners and the closing of Japan to foreign trade; in 1853, however, the Yedo Bakufu had neither the power to enforce this decree nor the courage and prestige necessary to adopt and carry out a reversal of the earlier policy. Even before Commodore Perry's arrival at Uraga the Shogun and his advisers had become fully aware of the weakness of their hold upon the empire. In the summer of 1853, therefore, instead of deciding on their own responsibility the questions raised by the letter from the American President, they transmitted a copy of the letter to Kyoto for consideration and called a general council of the daimyo to discuss the policy that should be adopted. Although the great majority of the daimyo expressed themselves in favor of maintaining the isolation policy, the Bakufu succeeded in obtaining the approval of the emperor Komei (1846–1867) for the original treaty with the Americans and also for those concluded during 1854 and 1855 with the British, the Russians, and the Dutch. But the evil had been done. By referring the matter to Kyoto and by using the imperial approval as justification for a step to which the great majority of the fudai retainers were opposed, the Bakufu had restored to the emperor an active share in the administration of national affairs and had, in effect, acknowledged itself to be directly subject to imperial command. All that was now needed to complete the discomfiture of Yedo was that the emperor should change his attitude and order the re-expulsion of the foreign intruders. For in that case the Shogun must either attempt the impossible or, admitting his inability to execute his sovereign's orders, surrender into the imperial hands the military powers so long held by the Tokugawa family.

Nor were the anti-Tokugawa elements in the empire slow to take advantage of the Bakufu's mistake. The tozama daimyo of the western clans, many of whom had formerly criticized the Shogunate for its stubborn adherence to the exclusion policy, raised an outcry against the Bakufu for its abandonment of Japan's time-honored policy. The nobles of the imperial court, equally inspired by opposition to the Tokugawa rule, joined their voices to those of the tozama lords, and the conversion of the emperor from complaisance to disapproval was not difficult. Although he had given his assent to the first four treaties, the emperor opposed any further concessions to the foreign nations and demanded that the treaties already concluded be so limited in their application as to bar any real commerce with the outside world.

The Shogunate, unable to resist the pressure of foreign demands, had bound itself by a series of treaty engagements whose fulfillment was bitterly opposed by all the anti-Tokugawa elements in the empire, by a majority of the fudai daimyo, and even by a strong minority inside the Bakufu organization. Divided among themselves and confronted by an apparently impossible dilemma, the Tokugawa clansmen during the fourteen and a half years following Commodore Perry's first appearance in Japanese waters struggled vainly to retain the power which had been consolidated by Iyeyasu and his immediate successors, while the question of foreign relations was compelled to serve as a football in this game of domestic politics.

The eleventh article of the Perry treaty conferred upon the government of the United States the right to appoint—after the expiration of eighteen months—a consul or agent to reside at the port of Shimoda, but it was not until August, 1856, that Townsend Harris arrived to take up his residence at that port as consul general. The Yedo authorities, whose understanding of the treaty differed somewhat from that of the American government, reluctantly acquiesced in the establishment of a permanent American representative on Japanese soil; but Harris by his tact and persistence gradually succeeded in winning the confidence of those officials with whom he came into frequent contact. In March, 1857, therefore, he was able to conclude a supplementary convention whereby American citizens were accorded the rights of residing permanently at Shimoda and Hakodate and of carrying on trade at Nagasaki. In November of the same year he proceeded to Yedo, where he was admitted to an audience with the Shogun; and on July 29, 1858, after long and patient negotiation he finally succeeded in concluding with the Shogunal representatives a regular commercial treaty. Whereas the Perry treaty had merely opened to American ships two ports where they might secure wood, water, and coal and exchange "articles of goods" under such regulations as the Japanese government should temporarily establish, the Harris treaty of 1858 provided for the opening of five Japanese ports—Hakodate, Hyogo, Kanagawa, Nagasaki, and Niigata—to the Americans for residence and unrestricted trade. Customs duties were to be levied according to a schedule appended to the treaty, and the American government received full extraterritorial authority—in civil as well as in criminal cases—over its citizens resident in Japan.

By virtue of the most-favored-nation clauses in the already existing treaties the new concessions obtained for the United States by Harris were automatically extended to all the other powers having treaties with Japan. But the Harris treaty had been concluded by the Shogun on his own responsibility, despite the fact that the emperor had refused his assent, and the foreign powers were soon to discover that the opposition of the conservatives was sufficient to nullify most of the concessions secured by the negotiations at Yedo.

From this point the Bakufu began to pay the penalty for its initial failure to deal boldly with the thorny question of foreign policy. In persuading the emperor to give his approval to the first treaties the Shogunal officials had argued the need of temporizing with the formidable intruders, avoiding a conflict until such time as the reorganization of the army and navy should make possible the successful use of armed force against them. Subsequent communications to Kyoto, prior to 1858, also represented the Shogun as tolerating the presence of the foreigners only as a subterfuge, a time-gaining preliminary to their forceful expulsion at some later date. By disregarding the emperor's orders in the matter of the Harris treaty the Shogun, although persisting in his efforts to carry water on both shoulders, committed himself irrevocably to the policy of increasingly close commercial intercourse with the West. This decision, if it had been announced boldly in 1853, might have evoked only mild opposition; made five years later, however, it roused the imperial court to open hostility and eventually rallied all the anti-Tokugawa elements in the country to a violent attack upon the feeble and vacillating foreign policy of Yedo.

Taking as their slogan the cry *Son-O-Jo-I* ("Revere the sovereign and expel the barbarian"), the conservative and patriotic adherents of the imperial party lashed out furiously at every concession granted by the Shogun to the importunate Westerners, not only in the Harris treaty but also in the earlier treaties of 1854 and 1855. Nor was the indignation of the conservatives to exhaust itself in noisy denunciations. An imperial edict angrily reprimanding the Shogun for having dared to conclude the Harris treaty was followed by direct action on the part of anti-Bakufu fighting men determined either to bring the Bakufu to a proper performance of its duty or, failing in that, themselves to purge Japan's sacred soil from the desecrating presence of the foreigner.

On July 7, 1859, Harris, now promoted to the rank of minister, took up his residence in the newly established American legation at Yedo. The preceding day had seen the installation of Rutherford Alcock[1] as British minister, and these two were soon joined by the diplomatic representatives of France, Holland, and Russia. The establishment of diplomatic residence was a signal for the commencement of a campaign of terrorism on the part of the enraged conservatives. Early in August the British and American ministers found themselves compelled to protest to the Bakufu concerning the frequent insults, threats, and acts of violence against their nationals and even against the members of their legation staffs at Yedo and at the recently opened neighboring port of Yokohama. On August 25 two Russians, an officer and a seaman of the warship on which the Russian minister had just arrived, were cut down in the street at Yokohama by unidentified samurai swordsmen, and during the next four years the terroristic activities of the conservative samurai resulted in a steadily lengthening list of fatal attacks.

Although the patriotic swordsmen most frequently vented their wrath upon the foreigner, the "guilty" Bakufu officials who had failed in their sacred duty were neither forgotten nor allowed to go unpunished. The outstanding figure in the Tokugawa government at this time was the tairo Ii Naosuke, who had been responsible for disregarding the imperial commands in connection with the Harris treaty and who subsequently had used an iron hand in dealing with those daring to question the Shogunal authority.

[1] Later, Sir Rutherford Alcock.

On March 24, 1860, while the tairo was proceeding in a palanquin from his own residence to the Shogun's palace, he was suddenly attacked and slain in the very midst of his armed escort by a score of samurai in the service of Nariaki, the conservative daimyo of Mito. A little less than two years later—on February 14, 1862— Ando Tsushima-no-kami, a prominent member of the Shogunal ministry on foreign affairs, was similarly attacked, although only wounded, by another small band of desperate samurai.

Down to the close of the year 1861 much of the opposition to the Shogun's foreign policy had come from the discordant elements within the Tokugawa clan; for example, Nariaki of Mito, whose retainers had murdered Ii Naosuke, was the chief of a great Tokugawa family and the father of Keiki, the lord of Hitotsubashi, who subsequently became the last of the Shoguns. This internal dissension on the Tokugawa side, dangerous though it was, had its compensations in that it confused the issue and tended to prevent unity of action on the part of the powerful and bitterly anti-Tokugawa western clans. With the death of Nariaki, in September, 1861, opposition within the ranks of the Tokugawa practically came to an end; but from this point the western clans, hitherto divided by their own private jealousies and by the fact that there were important Tokugawa leaders on both sides of the question, lined up solidly with the extreme anti-foreign party at Kyoto.

In May, 1862, Shimadzu Idzumi, father of the Satsuma daimyo and actual head of that great clan, arrived in Kyoto, where, a few days later, he was joined by the daimyo of Choshu, Mori Motonori. Choshu had always been closely associated with the anti-foreign group, but Satsuma, although equally anti-Tokugawa, had been inclined to favor the opening of the empire to foreign trade. Laying aside all past differences, the two daimyo now joined forces in support of the court against Yedo and promptly became the recognized leaders of the imperial party. The "Sat-Cho" (Satsuma-Choshu) alliance has continued to the present and has ensured to the allies predominant power in the post-Tokugawa government of Japan,[1] but the immediate result of the new combination was

[1] As is pointed out later, the Satsuma clique now controls the navy, while Choshu enjoys a similar pre-eminence in army affairs.

to put the two western clans into the forefront of the anti-foreign movement and to bring them into direct conflict with foreign armed force.

Satsuma was the first to become thus involved. On September 14, 1862, a party of British subjects, three men and a woman, were riding on the highway near Yokohama when they crossed the path of Shimadzu Idzumi, who, accompanied by a large force of retainers, was on his way homeward from Yedo. Because of a breach of etiquette, real or fancied, on the part of the foreigners they were attacked by the daimyo's armed followers, one of the men, Mr. C. L. Richardson, being killed and the two others seriously wounded. On reporting this outrage to his government the British chargé d'affaires was instructed to demand the arrest, trial, and capital punishment of the guilty samurai, together with the payment of an indemnity to the amount of £125,000; of this sum, £100,000 was to be paid by the Bakufu and the remainder by the Satsuma daimyo. After long discussion the Yedo officials agreed to pay the entire indemnity, Satsuma's share as well as their own, but they were compelled to confess their inability to secure the imposition of any punishment upon the guilty samurai. Under these circumstances the British representative invoked the support of his naval authorities, and on August 11, 1863, a British squadron entered the Bay of Kagoshima for the purpose of securing from the Satsuma daimyo full satisfaction of the British demands. In reply to an ultimatum demanding the immediate trial and execution of the murderer the Satsuma authorities declared that the guilty person had escaped but would be arrested and punished as soon as his whereabouts could be ascertained. Refusing to enter into any discussion of the points covered by their ultimatum, the British on August 14 and 15 bombarded Kagoshima and destroyed the greater part of the town, after which exploit the squadron returned to Yokohama.

Armed conflict between Choshu and the Western powers actually began before the British bombardment of Kagoshima, but it was not until the autumn of 1864 that this second member of the Sat-Cho combination was treated to a convincing demonstration of the superiority of foreign war machinery.

During the early months of 1863, while the Richardson affair was still a subject of negotiation at Yedo, the extremists at Kyoto, under Choshu leadership, renewed their agitation for the cancellation of all existing treaties; and in April the Shogun and his prime minister, who had been summoned to Kyoto for the purpose of receiving the imperial commands, acquiesced in the demand for the early expulsion of the foreigner—by peaceful negotiation if possible but by force if negotiation proved unavailing. The imperial edict on this point fixed no definite date for the execution of the new policy, and the evasiveness of the Tokugawa authorities during the subsequent month and a half convinced the court party that Yedo had no honest intention of undertaking the task. On June 5, therefore, a second meeting was convened in the presence of the emperor to consider the situation. The expulsion of the foreigner by force was reaffirmed; June 25 was fixed upon as the date for executing the decision, and instructions to this effect were issued by the imperial officials *directly to all the daimyo*.

To most of the daimyo, other than the Tokugawa rulers of the Kwanto, the new imperial decree was a matter of merely academic interest; but to the lord of Choshu, who had strongly advocated the policy and whose territories lay along the northern shore of the Strait of Shimonoseki, it was a call to prompt effective action. On June 26, 1863, the American steamer *Pembroke*, anchored at the entrance of the strait, was fired upon by two armed vessels belonging to the Choshu daimyo; twelve days later a similar attack was made upon the small French gunboat *Kienchang*, and on July 11 the Choshu ships and shore batteries fired upon the Dutch steamer *Medusa*. In immediate reprisal for the first of these belligerent acts the American warship *Wyoming*, on July 16, arrived at Shimonoseki and destroyed the two Choshu ships; on the twentieth of the same month two French warships under Admiral Jaurès punished the attack on the *Kienchang* by burning a small village and destroying one of the shore batteries. Undismayed by these sharp reprisals, however, the remaining batteries continued throughout the next year to fire quite impartially upon every foreign ship that ventured within range of their guns.

While the Bakufu continued to temporize with the foreigner,

the war party, with Choshu at its head, became steadily more powerful at Kyoto and in the empire at large. Scores of daimyo from all parts of the country deserted Yedo for the imperial capital, and in August it was announced that the emperor would himself take the field at the head of his loyal vassals in the campaign against the foreigner. Overreaching themselves in their ambition, the Choshu daimyo and his advisers now sought to make themselves the absolute masters of the imperial court; the *coup* failed, and on September 30 they were compelled to withdraw in disgrace to their fief. The disgrace of Choshu, coming, as it did, shortly after the British bombardment of the Satsuma port, weakened the war party at Kyoto; but the exiled Choshu daimyo continued with unabated zeal his singlehanded campaign against foreign shipping in the Strait of Shimonoseki.

In March, 1864, Sir Rutherford Alcock returned to Yedo from a two-year leave of absence and promptly assumed leadership of the foreign diplomatic corps. His vigorous arguments convinced his colleagues that the forceful opening of the Strait of Shimonoseki was the only means of ensuring Japanese observance of the treaties, and on May 30 the representatives of France, Great Britain, the Netherlands, and the United States formally announced their intention of acting in concert for the protection of existing treaty rights. As a result of this agreement an allied fleet of seventeen ships[1] arrived on September 5, 1864, at Shimonoseki. During this day and the following three days the foreign fleet silenced and systematically disabled fifteen batteries along the Choshu coast of the strait. After the completion of these operations the allied commanders negotiated with representatives of Choshu an agreement assuring free passage and non-fortification of the strait, the payment of the expenses of the expedition, and the right of call at Shimonoseki for foreign merchant ships.

[1] It consisted of nine British, four Dutch, and three French warships and, in the absence of an available American warship, a specially chartered merchant steamer, equipped with a single cannon, to represent the United States.

THE END OF THE SHOGUNATE

The bombardment of Kagoshima in August, 1863, the expulsion of the Choshu clansmen from the imperial capital six weeks later, and the joint naval expedition against Shimonoseki in September of the following year were serious blows to the power and prestige of the two leading anti-Tokugawa clansmen; but these events, although they brought temporary relief to the embarrassed Bakufu, effected little real improvement in its difficult situation. Choshu, of course, was now under a cloud because of the attempted *coup d'état* at Kyoto; but Satsuma, still remaining secretly on friendly terms with its disgraced partner, now united with the two other outstanding western clans—Hizen and Tosa—to carry on with unabated zeal the campaign against the Tokugawa organization.

From this point, moreover, the anti-Tokugawa party adopted a new and even more embarrassing line of attack. Realizing that a continuance of anti-foreign activity on their part would only serve to strengthen the alliance between the Shogunate and the treaty powers, they abandoned their earlier policy and endeavored to convince the foreign diplomats of their own essential friendliness, of the nation-wide hostility to Yedo, and of the serious error which the foreign powers would commit if they continued to make common cause with the Tokugawa. This note was first sounded in the summer of 1864 by two young Choshu clansmen, Inouye Kaoru and Ito Hirobumi,[1] who volunteered their services as intermediaries in the hope of averting the conflict between the powers and their clan. Inouye and Ito explained that the belligerent acts of Choshu were inspired entirely by hostility to the Shogunate; and they specifically urged that the representatives of the powers, if they wished to establish permanent friendly relations with Japan, should ignore Yedo and, proceeding to Osaka, enter into direct communication with the officers of the imperial court.

As early as the summer of 1863 certain of the foreign diplomats had considered the advisability of a naval demonstration at Osaka for the purpose of securing imperial ratification of the existing

[1] Both were later to attain outstanding prominence among the statesmen of the Meiji era.

treaties, and the American minister, in a dispatch to the Secretary of State, recommended that such action be authorized. For more than two years after this date nothing was done. At the end of October, 1865, however, the representatives of the four treaty powers decided to take advantage of the fact that the Shogun and his principal ministers were at Osaka and to go there in a body, accompanied by all their available naval forces, for the purpose of discussing certain outstanding matters and, if possible, securing the emperor's ratification of the treaties.

On November 4, as a result of this decision, an international fleet of nine ships[1]—five British, three French, and one Dutch— arrived off the port of Hyogo, near Osaka. On November 14, after the foreign diplomats had openly hinted at the possibility of their treating directly with certain of the western daimyo, the Shogun's spokesman solemnly promised that the emperor's approval of the treaties would be given. The fulfillment of this promise was no easy matter, since the reactionary element, which included many of the leading members of the court nobility, was still supreme at Kyoto; but on the afternoon of the twenty-fourth the Bakufu was able to communicate to the foreign representatives the following text of an imperial rescript addressed to the Shogun: "The Imperial consent is given to the treaties, and you will therefore undertake the necessary arrangements in connection therewith."

In September, 1866, ten months after the emperor had given his reluctant assent to the foreign treaties, the fourteenth Shogun, Iyemochi, died and was succeeded in office by Keiki, the daimyo of Hitotsubashi, who since 1862 had played a leading role in the affairs of the Bakufu. Five months later the emperor Komei was succeeded on the throne by his fourteen-year-old son Mutsuhito. The almost simultaneous accession of a new emperor and a new Shogun suggested to more than one patriotic Japanese leader the possibility of a much-needed readjustment of internal political conditions. The old emperor had occupied the throne since 1846 and had long been under the influence of the extreme reactionary elements of the court; his son and successor, too young to have crys-

---

[1] The United States again had no warship available, and the American chargé d'affaires was compelled to accept transportation on one of the British ships.

tallized his opinions, could easily be led to accept the views of a different group of advisers. On the other hand, the new Shogun, having spent four years in unsuccessful efforts to solve the problems of the Yedo administration, was not unwilling to accept any honorable path of escape from his increasing difficulties.

The solution came from the western clans. In October, 1867, the Tosa daimyo, with the support and approval of Satsuma, Choshu, and Hizen, presented to the Shogun a memorial in which he pointed out that the division of political authority was endangering the very existence of the nation and urged him to sacrifice upon the altar of patriotism the decentralizing power so long held by the Tokugawa family. On November 3 the Shogun complied with this advice by tendering to the emperor a formal resignation of his Shogunal commission, and nine days later the offer was accepted in the following curt decree: "Tokugawa Keiki's proposal to restore administrative authority to the Imperial Court is accepted by the Emperor."

Even after the surrender of his Shogunal title the Tokugawa leader was the greatest landholder and the most powerful daimyo of the empire. He therefore expected that in the reorganized government he and his relatives would be assigned positions commensurate with the actual importance of the family. Reasonable though such an expectation may have seemed, the ex-Shogun was quickly disillusioned. On January 3, 1868, seven weeks after the imperial assumption of administrative authority, the ban against Choshu was lifted. A large number of Choshu clansmen promptly entered Kyoto, and the military control of the imperial city, hitherto in the hands of Tokugawa retainers, was taken over by the combined forces of the four western clans: Satsuma, Choshu, Hizen, and Tosa.[1] Four days later, after lodging a formal protest against the presence of the Choshu "rascals" in the capital, Keiki withdrew to Osaka.

The withdrawal of the ex-Shogun from Kyoto was soon followed by the promulgation of an imperial edict commanding him to resign his court titles and to surrender his fiefs. Realizing at last that his enemies would be satisfied with nothing short of his com-

[1] The so-called Sat-Cho-Hi-To combination.

plete destruction, the unfortunate lord, at the end of January, retired to Yedo and prepared for war. Against the forces now arrayed under the imperial banners, however, the Tokugawa party could offer but feeble resistance. In May, Keiki surrendered his city and his fiefs and was allowed to retire into private life. For something more than a year his adherents in the north kept up the struggle, but in July, 1869, the submission of the last of these rebellious forces marked the end of the Tokugawa chapter in Japanese history.

SUGGESTED REFERENCES

ALCOCK, SIR R. The Capital of the Tycoon.

BRINKLEY, F., and KIKUCHI, D. A History of the Japanese People.

COSENZA, M. E. (editor). The Complete Journal of Townsend Harris.

HAWKS, F. L. Narrative of the Expedition . . . to . . . Japan.

LATOURETTE, K. S. The Development of Japan.

MURDOCH, J. A History of Japan, Vol. III.

NITOBE, I. Bushido, the Soul of Japan.

SANSOM, G. B. Japan: a Short Cultural History.

TREAT, P. J. The Early Diplomatic Relations between the United States and Japan, 1853–1865.

XXV

The Development of Modern Japan

The Meiji Era and its Leaders · The Organization of the New Government · The New Capital and the Abolition of Feudalism · The Adoption of Western Innovations · The Aftermath of Feudalism: the Samurai Revolt · Economic Reorganization · The Modern Army and Navy · The Demand for a Parliament · The Granting of a Constitution · The Powers of the Emperor: a Constitutional Autocrat · The Imperial Diet and its Limitations · The Cabinet, the Privy Council, and the Elder Statesmen · Japan's Struggle for Treaty Revision · The Aoki-Kimberley Treaty with Great Britain · New Japan and her Oriental Neighbors · China, the Luchus, and Formosa · Renewal of Relations with Korea · Russia, Sakahalin, and the Kuril Islands · Korea as a Storm Center · The Li-Ito Convention · Port Lazareff and Port Hamilton · The Sino-Japanese War · Shimonoseki and the Three-Power Intervention · The Consequences of the War · Japan in 1899

ON NEW YEAR'S DAY, 1868, the government of the young emperor proclaimed the *nengo* (year-name) of the new reign. These year-names have often lacked real or lasting significance, but the "auspicious designation" *Meiji* ("Enlightened Government") selected for the reign of Mutsuhito reflected the purposes and foreshadowed the achievements of the ardent reformers by whom the emperor was surrounded. During the forty-five years of the period thus happily designated a group of unusually capable and far-sighted men—among whom the emperor himself eventually assumed a worthy place—gave to Japan a government enlightened in fact as well as in name; under this government the Japanese Empire was transformed from a weak and backward state into a world power.

During the long, unbroken peace of the Tokugawa era the actual administration of affairs in the domains of the feudal lords had fallen from the hands of the daimyo, their titular rulers, into those of capable samurai subordinates. Even as at Yedo the Shogun had gradually become a mere puppet under the control of his Bakufu, so also in the provinces the great feudatories with few exceptions had degenerated into useless idlers and men of fashion, in whose

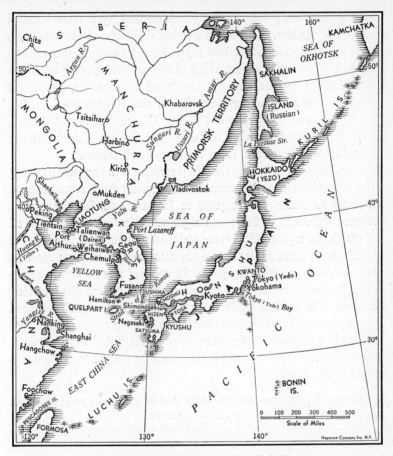

Nineteenth Century Japan and its Neighbors

name the "samurai of the gown"—so called to distinguish them from the more numerous "samurai of the sword"—managed the affairs of fief and clan.

It was from this class of capable and educated subordinates, experienced in the management of affairs and keenly alive to the weakness of Japan's existing institutions, that the leaders of the imperial restoration and of the subsequent Meiji reforms were chiefly recruited. From the kuge nobility came Sanjo, Iwakura, and some half a dozen others less well known to history, while the feudal aristocracy was similarly represented by a mere handful of reform leaders. The overwhelming majority of the men who laid the foundations of modern Japan were drawn from the samurai class. Nor was this pre-eminence of the samurai merely quantitative. Except for the already mentioned kuge nobles, Sanjo and Iwakura, the outstanding statesmen of the Meiji era—Kido, Ito, Yamagata, and Inouye, from Choshu; Okubo, Saigo, and Oyama, from Satsuma; Soyeshima, Okuma, and Enomoto, from Hizen; Itagaki, Goto, and Tani, from Tosa—were all samurai.

The first steps taken by the Meiji reformers in the establishment of a new administrative organization were far from revolutionary. A series of edicts, promulgated in January and February, 1868, created a Council of State and eight administrative boards, in all of which the higher offices were assigned to princes of the imperial family or to great nobles, while the reformers themselves received only subordinate advisory posts. In spite of this moderate beginning, however, evidence of a more radical program was not long delayed. On April 6, while the imperial forces were still engaged in suppressing the Tokugawa rebels, the young emperor at Kyoto set forth in a solemn declaration, usually referred to as the Charter Oath, the principles by which he would be guided in the government of the empire:

The practice of discussion and debate shall be universally adopted, and all measures shall be decided by public argument.

High and low shall be of one mind, and public order shall thereby be perfectly maintained.

It is necessary that the civil and military powers be concentrated in a single whole, the rights of all classes be assured, and the national mind be completely satisfied.

The uncivilized customs of former times shall be broken through and the impartiality and justice displayed in the workings of nature be adopted as a basis of action.

Intellect and learning shall be sought for throughout the world, in order to establish the foundations of the Empire.

Although the first three articles of this imperial declaration were later interpreted as explicitly promising the establishment of a parliamentary form of government, it is hardly probable that such was the intention of the emperor's advisers. With one or two exceptions[1] the leading Meiji reformers were by temperament and conviction bureaucrats rather than politicians; their theories of government were more in line with modern Fascism than with the ideas of democracy, and the establishment of a constitutional parliamentary government two decades later came as a grudging concession to popular agitation rather than as the premeditated elaboration of their original program. It seems more reasonable, therefore, to interpret this portion of the emperor's oath as a pledge that no new Shogunate—under Shimadzu, Mori, or some other great feudatory—should interpose itself between the sovereign and the empire. Convinced of the fundamental weakness of the old system and all too conscious of the political incompetence of their own respective daimyo, the samurai statesmen of the new era were determined that the emperor henceforth should be *his own Shogun,* holding all civil and military powers, and that no great territorial lord or group of court nobles should enjoy exclusive access to his sacred ear.

The surrender of Yedo to the imperial forces in May, 1868, set the stage for the next open break with the old regime. From the beginning of their work of reorganization the men around the throne had been fully aware of the fact that the old capital was poorly suited to serve as the seat of a modern government. Thirty miles distant from the nearest seacoast and located in the heart of the mountains, Kyoto was an admirable location for a puppet court; Yedo, on the other hand, was situated at the head of Yedo (now Tokyo) Bay and had been for more than two and a half centuries the administrative center of the empire. Kyoto, moreover, was steeped in conservative tradition and still resented the impious intrusion of the "outside barbarian," while Yedo, already accustomed to the foreign merchant and the diplomat, could more easily adjust itself to the changing order. On September 3, 1868, therefore, an imperial edict changed the name of the Kwanto metropolis from Yedo to Tokyo ("Eastern Capital"), and two months later the entire administrative organization of the government was transferred to the former Tokugawa headquarters. Kyoto—now

[1] Itagaki and possibly Okuma.

officially renamed Saikyo ("Western Capital")—continued to be regarded as the "spiritual" capital of the empire, the appointed place for coronations and for weddings and funerals in the imperial family, but henceforth all the civil functions of the government were administered from the new capital in the east.

As a consequence of the ex-Shogun's surrender and the confiscation of all the fiefs held by rebellious Tokugawa partisans the emperor became the greatest daimyo of the empire, with direct authority over the entire Kwanto and over extensive portions of the neighboring provinces. Even before the transfer of the capital, therefore, the imperial government faced the task of devising for these lands a centralized system of administration, and on June 13, 1868, a decree was issued establishing three classes of local administrative districts: the great cities (*fu*), the fiefs (*han*) of the loyal daimyo, and the imperial domains (*ken*) created from the confiscated estates of the Tokugawa. While the han were left to the undisturbed rule of their old feudal lords, the fu and the ken were placed under newly created administrative officers appointed by and responsible to the imperial government.

Although the loyal daimyo were thus left in full enjoyment of their ancient powers, the samurai leaders of the new regime probably never intended that this arrangement, whereby one part of the country continued to be ruled feudally while the rest was administered imperially through appointed officials, should be more than a temporary makeshift. On March 5, 1869, the four great western lords—Shimadzu of Satsuma, Mori of Choshu, Nabeshima of Hizen, and Yamanouchi of Tosa—presented to the throne a humble memorial, said to have been drafted by Kido, the leading statesman of the reform group, asking permission to surrender to the emperor all the administrative powers which they held in their respective fiefs. The memorialists entreated the emperor "to issue Imperial Decrees as may be deemed necessary to deal with the lands and the people of the four clans represented in this memorial, and to make such changes as Your Majesty may think proper." On the following day this petition was graciously approved, and the example thus set by the powerful Sat-Cho-Hi-To lords was quickly followed by all but seventeen of the remaining two hundred and seventy-two daimyo. Four and a half months later, on July 25, a decree was issued abolishing the old distinction between the court nobles and the feudal lords, kuge and buke, and ordering the immediate surrender of the few fiefs that had not been given up voluntarily. This decree, however, established the dispossessed feudatories as local administrative officials in their former fiefs, which continued to be designated as han.

As local officials upon whom the imperial government could depend for the execution of its new policies the former daimyo were not a success. The experience of two years, during which time the reformers had been consolidating their position at the capital, demonstrated the unsatisfactory nature of the compromise. On August 29, 1871, therefore, there appeared a decree which, since it marked the abolition of feudalism in fact as well as in name, deserves to be quoted in full:

> We are of the opinion that in a time of radical reform like the present, if We desire by its means to give protection and tranquillity to the people at home, and abroad to maintain equality with foreign nations, words must be made to mean in reality what they claim to signify, and the government of the country must center in a single authority.
>
> Some time ago We gave Our sanction to a scheme by which all the clans restored to Us their registers; We appointed Chiji for the first time, each to perform the duties of his office.
>
> But owing to the lengthened endurance of the old system during several hundred years, there have been cases when the word only was pronounced and the reality not performed. How is it possible for Us, under such circumstances, to give protection and tranquillity to the people, and to maintain equality with foreign nations?
>
> Profoundly regretting this condition of affairs, We now completely abolish the Clans (Han) and convert them into Domains (Ken), with the object of diligently retrenching expenditure and arriving at convenience of working, of getting rid of the unreality of names and of abolishing the disease of government proceeding from multiform centers.
>
> Do ye, Our assembled servants, take well to heart this Our will.[1]

The abolition of feudalism placed the Meiji reformers in full control of the governmental machinery, local as well as central,

[1] W. W. McLaren (editor), *Japanese Government Documents, 1867–1889*, pp. 32–33.

and removed the last element which might seriously have interfered with their plans for transforming Japan into a powerful modern state, able "to maintain equality with foreign nations." These plans had been stated, briefly but adequately, in the last two articles of the young emperor's Charter Oath: "The uncivilized customs of former times shall be broken through . . ." and "Intellect and learning shall be sought for throughout the world, in order to establish the foundations of the Empire." While the Chinese, with unshaken confidence in the superiority of their own ancient civilization, persisted for nearly half a century longer in their opposition to foreign innovations, their Japanese neighbors "went to school" to the West and open-mindedly welcomed every Western institution, idea, or mechanical invention which in the judgment of their new rulers might serve to put the empire on a footing of economic and military equality with the nations of Europe and America.

Even before the decision in favor of Westernization had been reached by the imperial authorities, a number of daring spirits had made their way surreptitiously, and at the risk of their lives, to Europe for the purpose of securing first-hand knowledge of the West and its civilization. After the official adoption of the new policies the government dispatched hundreds of selected students to the various Western countries in order that they might be educated in all branches of Occidental learning.

This method of introducing new ways and new ideas, however, was too slow to satisfy the statesmen who set their hand to the task of radical reform. Scientists and engineers from all parts of the world were taken into the government service in order that they might become the instructors of the Japanese in the mysteries of Western mechanical achievement. Military officers, first from France and later from Germany, were employed to organize and drill a new Western-style army. British naval experts were brought to Japan to aid in laying the foundation of a modern navy. American educationalists were invited to help in the establishment of a nation-wide system of public education.

Japan had been introduced to the electrical telegraph and to the steam railway by Commodore Perry, whose gifts to the Shogun in 1854 included a complete set of telegraphic apparatus and a workable model railway; but it was left for the Meiji government to make practical use of these two means of communication. The first telegraph lines were put into operation in 1868. Two years later, work was begun on Japan's first railway, a line running from Tokyo to Yokohama, and in December, 1870, a Department of Public Works was created "for the purpose of taking charge of mines, the iron industry, light-houses, railways, telegraphs, etc."

The final step in the abolition of feudalism was, of course, the outstanding event of 1871, but other innovations adopted during this year and the following year were hardly less revolutionary. On January 3, 1871, it was decreed that, commencing on January first of the following year, the armed forces of the empire would be recruited by conscription, "enforced in all parts of the country without regard to social position." The same month saw the promulgation of a revised penal code and the beginning of efforts in the field of prison reform. In August the old Board of Censors was abolished and its functions were merged into that of a modernized Department of Justice. In September came the creation of two new major departments, education and finance; during the following year the first of these justified its existence by formulating a nation-wide program for compulsory primary education, while the second took steps toward the organization of a modern banking system. And on January 1, 1873, the Gregorian calendar replaced the ancient lunar calendar of the Chinese as the official method of recording dates.

When the Meiji reformers in the autumn of 1871 took from the feudal lords the last vestige of their ancient powers, they were obliged to make some provision for the support of the former daimyo and their samurai retainers. These two classes, with their dependent families, comprised some two million of the country's population, and the first arrangement took the form of a pension bill whereby the ex-daimyo received one tenth and the samurai one half of the incomes which they had enjoyed under the feudal system. For the daimyo this arrangement was more than generous; as feudal lords comparatively few of them, after meeting the administrative expenses of their fiefs, had been able to count upon net incomes equal to the pensions thus bestowed upon them. The samurai, on the other hand, were compelled to accept a 50 per cent cut in their net incomes. Partly for the purpose of alleviating the hardship inflicted upon the samurai and partly for the purpose of bringing about the disintegration of the samurai caste, an imperial decree promulgated simultaneously with the pension bill permitted these hereditary warriors to lay aside their two swords and abolished the ancient regulations which forbade their engaging in industry and trade.

In December, 1873, an imperial notification offered to the recipients of small pensions the privilege of commuting their pensions for a lump payment of six years' income in the case of hereditary pensions or four years' income if the pension was only for the lifetime of the recipient, one half of the commutation to be paid in cash and the other half in government bonds bearing 8 per cent interest. The avowed purpose of this offer was to provide capital to those pensioners who desired to purchase agricultural land or to engage in some other profitable undertaking, but there is reason to believe that the imperial government was already finding the burden of the 1871 pension bill too heavy for its resources.

During the next two and a half years approximately one third of the samurai took advantage of this offer, and in August, 1876, a new imperial notification on the subject made compulsory the commutation of all pensions. Hereditary pensions were to be exchanged for payments—half in cash and half in bonds—on a sliding scale which ranged from five years' income in the case of pensions exceeding 70,000 yen to fourteen years' income if the annual pension was less than 25 yen.[1] Those holding life pensions

[1] The bonds which constituted half of these commutations bore varying rates of interest. In the case of pensions exceeding 1000 yen per year the bonds paid 5 per cent interest; if the pension was between 1000 yen and 100 yen, the interest on the bonds was 6 per cent; if the pension was less than 100 yen, the bonds bore 7 per cent interest. A pension of 100,000 yen was therefore commuted for a cash payment of 250,000 yen and bonds yielding an annual return of 12,500 yen. A pension of 50,000 yen was commuted for five and a half years' income: 137,500 yen in cash and bonds yielding 6875 yen per year. For a pension of 1000 yen the commutation was seven and a half years' income: 3750 yen in cash and bonds for the same amount yielding 187.50 yen per year. For a pension of 100 yen the holder received eleven years' commutation: 550 yen in cash and an equal amount in 6 per cent bonds yielding 33 yen per year.

were to receive commutation for half the number of years allowed for hereditary incomes of the same annual amount.

The drastic scaling down of the government's commitments may have been necessary in the interest of sound national finance, but in the case of the small pensioners it was productive of much economic hardship. Untrained for business and unskilled in any occupation save that of war, many of the samurai quickly frittered away their cash payments and found themselves compelled to eke out a beggarly existence on incomes amounting to 10 or 20 per cent of those which they had enjoyed prior to the abolition of the feudal system.

To the economic hardships inflicted on the proud and once powerful samurai was added an even more serious cause for bitterness against the new government. In August, 1871, as we have seen, an imperial order had been issued *permitting* them to lay aside the two swords which for generations had been the distinctive badge of their class, while the following January had been marked by the calling up of the first conscript recruits for a modern army organized along Western lines. In August, 1876, simultaneously with the notification which made compulsory the commutation of pensions, there now appeared a decree forbidding the wearing of swords by any except those who were members of the newly organized army.

Stirred to fury by this addition of insult to injury, bodies of samurai in various parts of the empire promptly rose in revolt. Most of these uprisings involved small isolated groups and were easily suppressed; but in southern Kyushu, where the samurai of Satsuma rose en masse under the leadership of Saigo,[1] the movement assumed a serious aspect. The Satsuma rebels, some forty thousand warriors equipped with modern weapons, offered a real test to the newly organized conscript army. Beginning on January 29, 1877, the struggle continued until September 24 of the same year, but in the end the imperial forces proved their superiority over the flower of the ancient military caste. The rebellion was crushed, and the surviving samurai, bowing to the inevitable, were gradually absorbed into the body of the nation's population.

[1] One of the original reformers.

During the years following the suppression of the samurai revolt the Meiji statesmen were able to devote a large part of their attention to the task of strengthening the country's economic foundations. Especially difficult in this period of economic reorganization were the financial problems consequent upon the centralization of governmental powers and the expansion of governmental functions. Even after the drastic scaling down of pension obligations in 1876 the treasury was compelled to pay out eight or ten million yen annually as interest on the commutation bonds, while far greater amounts were required to meet the ordinary expenses of civil administration. The extraordinary expenses involved in the construction of railway and telegraph lines, in the organization of a postal system, in the institution of agricultural and educational reforms, in the building of a modern navy, and in the maintenance of the new army were on a scale hitherto unprecedented in the history of the nation and threw a heavy strain upon its recently improvised financial system.

In order to make it possible for the nation to carry an increasing burden of taxation the government fostered and encouraged every means of increasing national production. The former samurai were offered the opportunity of securing at a low price the lands necessary to make them self-supporting. An imperial colonization commission was created for the purpose of locating settlers on hitherto unused lands in the Hokkaido (Yezo). Modern methods of machine production, especially in the textile industry, were introduced, and the factory system was rapidly developed. Currency reform and the newly established banking system provided the empire with credit facilities adequate to the needs of modern industrialism, while the development of trade associations and the growth of a merchant marine, under government subsidy, enabled the Japanese to secure for themselves a constantly increasing share of the profits from their trade with the outside world.

There is probably no country on earth where the professional fighting man, throughout the ages, has been held in higher esteem or has wielded greater political influence than in Japan. Such being the case, the early development of Japan's modern army and navy and the rise of the powerful military and naval cliques are entitled to something more than the casual mention accorded them in the preceding pages.

From the beginning of their contact with the West the rulers of nineteenth-century Japan were deeply impressed by the superiority of Western war machinery, and even before the overthrow of the Tokugawa power some progress had been made in the introduction of Western armament. In 1854 the Shogun received from the Dutch government the gift of a small steam warship, and other vessels of war were subsequently purchased by the Yedo government from Europe and America. Some of the western daimyo, notably those of Satsuma and Choshu, also purchased warships, while they as well as the Shogunal government equipped their forces with modern weapons. Although the Meiji restoration was conceived and executed by statesmen drawn largely from the ranks of the so-called samurai of the gown, these civilian reformers fully appreciated the need for adequate means of national defense and made the modernization of army and navy an important part of their program. For several years the two services were administered by the single Department of Military Affairs, but on April 7, 1872, an imperial decree abolished this office and divided its functions between the two newly created departments of War and Navy.

The foundation of a thoroughly modern army, as we have seen, was laid by the first conscription law, which went into operation on January 1, 1872. Called to the colors in their twentieth year, the conscripts were to serve three years in active service and four years in the reserve, after which their "military responsibility" for emergency service continued until the age of forty. This law was calculated to provide a standing army with a peacetime strength of 240,000 and, after 1878, a wartime strength of 420,000; this latter number, of course, was supplemented by the effectives available from the ranks of those who had completed their service in the reserve. In 1878 the General Staff, hitherto subordinate to the War Office, was made independent; the following year saw the creation of a Board of Supervision, having charge of military inspection and general military education; and in 1882 a military academy was established for the training of officers. In 1885 the French military advisers were replaced by German officers, and in 1889 the military-service law was revised by the addition of five years' service in a second reserve after the three years of training and the four years in the first reserve.

When the two services were separated in 1872, the navy con- /
sisted of fourteen ships with a total displacement of slightly more than 12,000 tons. Except for one small vessel of 138 tons' displacement all these ships were foreign-built; but shipyards had been established at Nagasaki and Yokohama even before the fall of the Shogunate, and in 1869 an academy had been founded at Tokyo for the education of naval officers. In 1873 work was begun at Yokohama on the construction of two warships, one of 900 and the other of 1450 tons, the first of which was completed in 1875 and the second a year later; but during the next thirty years most of the additions to the Japanese navy were built in foreign shipyards, chiefly in England. Although the Japanese thus continued to rely upon foreign countries for naval construction, they soon took into their hands all the details of management. During the early days Dutch, French, and English experts were employed as technical advisers, but in 1882 the last of these were dismissed, and thenceforth foreigners were employed by the Navy Department only as instructors in Western languages.

During the closing years of the Tokugawa regime Satsuma and Choshu, as has been noted, were especially active in providing themselves with modern armaments both on land and on sea. Partly because of this and partly because of the pre-eminence of these two clans in the restoration movement the administration of the imperial forces was from the first delegated to a small group of Satsuma and Choshu men. When the two services were separated, naval affairs were practically monopolized by the Satsuma members of the group, while their Choshu colleagues concentrated on the army. The dominance of Satsuma and Choshu in the respective services has continued down to the present.[1] Not all high naval officers have been Satsuma men, nor have all the generals of the army come from Choshu; but promising young clansmen of the two clans have seldom found it difficult to gain admission to the

[1] In very recent years, however, there has appeared among the younger officers a growing tendency to resent and challenge this tradition.

military or the naval academy, as the case might be, and those giving proof of real ability have always seemed to enjoy a measurable advantage over non-clansmen in the important matter of promotion.

The dominating position of Satsuma and Choshu in the administration of the armed services ensured, on the one hand, a further development of the already powerful spirit of clannishness among the members of the two clans. On the other hand, this strong clan feeling, reinforcing the esprit de corps of the services, has given the army and navy cliques an unusual degree of solidarity. Although the two cliques have sometimes been found pitted against each other in support of incompatible budgetary demands, they have usually worked together on other questions; and their combined strength has not infrequently enabled them, in important matters of national policy, to force their will upon the civil branches of the government.

Chief of all the problems confronting the men in control of the new regime was the creation of a truly national government which would command the loyal support of the entire Japanese people. Even before the samurai revolts of 1876 and 1877 the dominant power of the favored clans had aroused widespread opposition, and the malcontents, basing their demands upon the pledge contained in the coronation oath, had begun to cry out for the creation of a national elective assembly. In 1881 the agitation for a constitution and a parliament received fresh impetus from the revelation of a scandal in connection with the Hokkaido colonization bureau. Riots in Tokyo resulted in the burning of a number of police stations and necessitated the proclamation of martial law. The disturbance quickly abated, but the ruling oligarchy now realized the necessity of giving way to the popular demand. On October 12 an imperial decree declared that a parliament would be established in the twenty-third year of Meiji (1890) and that a commission would in the meantime make all necessary preparations to that end.

Shortly after the publication of this decree Ito Hirobumi was sent abroad for the purpose of studying the constitutional systems of the West. After a year spent in Europe and America, during which he became convinced that the governmental system of Prussia most nearly met the needs of Japan, Ito returned home. On March 21, 1883, he was appointed Minister of the Imperial Household and was placed at the head of a special bureau entrusted with the task of drafting a constitution for the empire.

Between 1883 and 1889, while the elaboration of the constitution was being carried on in profound secrecy by the special bureau, a number of minor changes were made to prepare for its ultimate establishment. In July, 1884, the old orders of nobility were replaced by a new nobility consisting of five hundred peers distributed among five ranks: prince, marquis, count, viscount, and baron. The new peerage, which included thirty-five former commoners, provided a membership for the House of Peers in the coming parliament. In 1885 the Council of State, which had been created in September, 1871, was replaced by a cabinet of ten ministers: the Minister President of State, and the ministers of Foreign Affairs, Home Affairs, Finance, War, Navy, Justice, Education, Agriculture and Commerce, and Communications. Three years later a privy council was established, with Ito, who now resigned his post as the Minister President of State in the cabinet, as its president. Finally, on February 11, 1889, the long-awaited constitution was promulgated.

The new instrument of government fully protected the ancient prerogatives of the throne and the powers of those who spoke in its name. Article I declares that "the Empire of Japan shall be reigned over and governed by a line of Emperors unbroken for ages eternal." Article III proclaims that "the Emperor is sacred and inviolable," while the succeeding article declares that "the Emperor is the head of the empire, combining in himself the rights of sovereignty, and exercises them according to the provisions of the present Constitution."

Subsequent articles state the powers of the sovereign in detail. He "exercises the legislative power with the consent of the Imperial diet"; "convokes the Imperial Diet, opens, closes, and prorogues it, and dissolves the House of Representatives"; "issues, when the Imperial Diet is not sitting, Imperial Ordinances in the place of law"; "determines the organization of the different branches of the administration, and salaries of all civil and military officers, and appoints and dismisses the same"; "has supreme command of the Army and Navy"; "determines the organization and peace standing of the Army and Navy"; and "declares war, makes peace, and concludes treaties." Inasmuch as it is provided, both in the preamble and in Article LXXIII of the constitution, that amendments to the constitution are to be made only on the initiative of the emperor himself, any diminution of these almost autocratic powers appears to be extremely improbable.

The Imperial Diet, which met for the first time in November, 1890, consisted of a House of Peers and a House of Representatives. The hereditary members of the House of Peers consisted of the princes of the imperial family and the two higher ranks— princes and marquises—of the reorganized nobility. From among the counts, viscounts, and barons a number not exceeding one fifth of the members of each order were elected by their fellows to sit in the house for terms of seven years. In addition the House of Peers contained an indefinite number of members "nominated by the Emperor on account of meritorious services to the State or erudition," together with one member from each prefecture and from each of the three great cities, elected from among themselves by the fifteen greatest taxpayers in each of those administrative units.

The members of the House of Representatives, three hundred in number in this first diet, were elected by the adult male subjects of the empire who paid direct taxes of fifteen yen annually. This high property qualification restricted the suffrage to about four hundred and sixty thousand out of a population of some thirty million. In 1900 the franchise was extended to those paying direct taxes to the amount of ten yen, thereby more than doubling the number of voters. In 1919 the qualification was further reduced to a payment of three yen in direct taxes, again doubling the number of electors, and in 1925 the suffrage was extended to all male subjects over twenty-five years of age. The members of the House of Representatives are elected for a term of four years. Only three times since the establishment of the diet has a house served its full term, while on twelve occasions general elections have resulted from a dissolution of the diet because of disagreement between the government and the majority in the elected branch.

Whether or not Count (later Prince) Ito and his collaborators were unreasonably conservative in their work is a question upon which there was, and is, some difference of opinion. Most of the criticism directed against the new constitution has focused upon the inadequacy of the powers which it granted to the legislative body. Here, more than in any other phase of his work, Ito gave evidence of his indebtedness to the Prussians. The ministers were responsible not to the diet but to the emperor, by whom, according to Article X, they were appointed and dismissed. Article LXVII provided that certain expenditures—those based upon powers appertaining to the emperor, those which may have arisen by the effect of law, and those appertaining to the legal obligations of the government—could be neither rejected nor reduced by the diet without the government's concurrence. Article LXXI incorporated into the constitution the following Bismarckian expedient: "When the Imperial Diet has not voted the Budget, or when the Budget has not been brought into actual existence, the Government shall carry out the Budget of the preceding year." In diet after diet attempts were made to establish the responsibility of the ministers or legislative control over the budget; but the government, practically independent of the diet for its immediate running expenses, was always able to punish an irreconcilable House of Representatives by dissolving the diet and forcing its members to incur the expense of a new election.

In one respect, at least, the results of this constitutional weakness appear to have had an unfortunate effect upon Japan's political development. Deprived of any real power in the affairs of the empire, the members of the diet, especially of the House of Representatives, have been slow to develop any sense of political responsibility. Only as a member of the opposition was the Japanese representative able to attract attention, and, unlike the opposition member in most other parliamentary bodies, he seldom had to consider the possibility of being at some future time called upon to provide a substitute for the measures which he attacked.

Although constitutional responsibility for the direction of affairs rested upon the cabinet and privy council as advisers of the sovereign, the last two decades of the Meiji era saw the influence of these two bodies frequently overshadowed by that of a body unknown to the constitution: the Genro, or Council of the Elder Statesmen. Composed of the surviving members of the small group who had laid the foundations of Japan's new government, this informal council exercised a powerful influence upon the emperor's decisions. When it contained among its members Ito, Inouye, Yamagata, Oyama, and Matsukata, all retired from active political leadership, its influence was particularly strong. With the death of its original members the Genro, although recruited by the co-option of certain of the more prominent juniors, gradually lost some of its importance as a factor in the nation's affairs.

Throughout the twenty-two years between 1872 and the summer of 1894 the Meiji government's efforts at political and economic reconstruction were complicated by repeated attempts to secure from the Western powers a satisfactory revision of the treaties by which Japan had been opened to intercourse with the outside world. The privilege of extraterritoriality, which had been secured for the foreign residents on Japanese soil, was bitterly resented by the Japanese and was often presumed upon by those who enjoyed it; the treaty-imposed tariff, alterable only with the consent of all the outside powers, made it impossible for Japan to make the tariff a source of additional revenue or to adopt a protective policy for the benefit of her newly established industries, while the participation of foreign ships in Japan's coastal carrying trade, an activity which no fully sovereign country permits to alien vessels, was regarded as a serious obstacle to the development of a national merchant marine.

The task of revising the treaties was made more difficult by the interlocking effect of the most-favored-nation clauses. In 1878 the United States agreed, on condition of similar action by the other powers, to tariff autonomy and to abolition of the American right to engage in the coastal trade. Between 1882 and 1886 Inouye, at that time Minister of Foreign Affairs, conferred frequently with the foreign representatives at Tokyo in the hope of arriving at some solution of the problem.

During the winter of 1886–1887 a series of conferences between Inouye and the foreign diplomats brought almost to completion a simultaneous treaty revision whereby Japan was to secure immediate control of the coasting trade, the right to increase her import duties to 10 per cent, and the gradual abolition of extraterritoriality. When, however, the details of this arrangement began to leak out in July, 1887, and it was discovered that it provided for a transition period during which foreign judges would sit in the Japanese courts in cases involving foreign interests, a storm of popular protest compelled the government to break off negotiations.

In the fall of 1887 Viscount Tani, Minister of Agriculture and Commerce, memorialized the prime minister in favor of the unilateral denunciation of the treaties by Japan. Tani wrote:

I think there will be few European nations which will refuse to adopt the proposals we make, and which will threaten to maintain their privileges by force . . . In the present condition of Europe and America, if any country showed hostility toward us another country would proceed to form an alliance with us.

In spite of the government's efforts to suppress it the contents of this memorial were made public and served to increase popular agitation on the subject.

In 1888 and 1889 Count Okuma as Foreign Minister made a fresh attempt to secure revision by negotiation. Like Inouye, Okuma found that mixed tribunals for cases involving foreign interests were a *sine qua non* to the principal treaty powers. Once more a storm of popular protest broke out; an unsuccessful attempt was made on Okuma's life, and Okuma resigned.

With the establishment of the Imperial Diet in the fall of 1890 the popular agitation for treaty revision was transferred in part to the floor of the House of Representatives, where it became a favorite topic for the opposition orators in their attacks upon the ministry. In December, 1893, the opposition leaders in the lower house proposed an address to the throne demanding that the government enforce strictly the existing treaty stipulations as a method of compelling the foreign powers to give way on the matter of revision. Before this address could be brought to a vote, the diet was dissolved. When the new diet assembled on May 15, 1894, the struggle on this point was promptly resumed, and on May 30 an address to the throne condemned the ministry for its failure to safeguard the national interests. Three days later, on June 2, the diet was again dissolved.

While the treaty question was causing this protracted storm in the House of Representatives, Japanese diplomacy, under the leadership of Foreign Minister Mutsu, achieved its first real progress toward freeing the country from its humiliating obligations. By means of negotiations conducted through Japan's representatives at London, and carefully kept from the knowledge of the press, the British government had been brought to the point of agreeing to a thorough revision of the existing treaties, and on July 16, 1894, six weeks after the dissolution of the diet, the Aoki-Kimberley Treaty with Great Britain was signed. Extraterritoriality was to be abolished after the expiration of five years, this delay being agreed upon in order to allow time for the completion of Japan's judicial reorganization. The treaty provided for duties ranging from 5 to 15 per cent on a limited number of imported articles; with this exception Japan was to enjoy complete tariff autonomy. In all other respects the subjects of the two contracting powers were to enjoy most-favored-nation treatment. Before the end of the year 1894 the United States, appreciative of the benefits which the British had secured, followed their example. The other treaty powers quickly fell into line, and by August, 1899, Japan—save for certain still-existing tariff limitations—was in full enjoyment of her sovereign rights.

During the first twenty-five years of the Meiji era the program for internal reorganization and the struggle for treaty revision were paralleled by a third series of important problems: those arising out of the relations between "new" Japan and her immediate neighbors of the Oriental world. Tokugawa Japan had closed her doors almost as effectively against intercourse with the Asiatic continent as against the dangerous European. Once reopened to intercourse with the West, however, it became necessary for Japan to establish satisfactory relations with the adjacent mainland.

In this, as in the other two great problems of the early Meiji period, the policies of the responsible statesmen were frequently disapproved by the belligerently patriotic and demagogic orators of the opposition. A decade before the fall of the Shogunate one of the leading exponents of the imperial cause, Yoshida Shoin, had advocated, as a consequence of the restoration of the emperor's rightful authority, the beginning of an expansionist policy whereby Korea, Manchuria, eastern Siberia, and all the islands along the coast should be brought under Japanese rule. Yoshida's doctrines survived him, and the patriots of the Meiji era were ever ready to voice their protest against a policy which fell short of the ideals expressed by this prophet of Japanese chauvinism.

In 1871, the fourth year of Meiji, a commercial treaty concluded at Tientsin established upon a modern basis the age-old relations between Japan and China. By their treaties with the Western countries both China and Japan had been forced to consent to the establishment of extraterritorial jurisdiction within their frontiers; in this first treaty between themselves no such provision entered. The subjects of each emperor, while residing in the territories of the other, were to submit to the jurisdiction of the territorial authorities.

The same year which saw the conclusion of this treaty also witnessed the beginning of the first modern controversy between the two neighboring empires: the dispute with regard to China's responsibility to Japan for the murder of certain Luchuan fishermen shipwrecked on the shores of Formosa. The peaceful settlement with China was bitterly criticized in Japan by the militantly patriotic samurai class. At the very beginning of the affair the two-sword warriors, inspired by the expansionist ideals of Yoshida, loudly insisted that prompt steps be taken to secure by force full satisfaction of Japan's just demands. To this attempt of the militarists to gain control of the government the civilian oligarchy offered a stubborn resistance, and not until the spring of 1874 did they make a partial concession by dispatching against the guilty Formosan tribesmen a punitive expedition of some three thousand men. Despite this concession the war party was not satisfied, and the dissatisfaction aroused among the members of the samurai clans by this question appears to have been a contributing cause of the Satsuma Rebellion in 1877.

Throughout the two centuries and a half which followed Hideyoshi's Korean adventure the intercourse between Japan and Korea had been extremely limited. The first of the Tokugawa Shoguns had succeeded in regaining for his countrymen the privilege of residing for commercial purposes at the port of Fusan, and forty Japanese vessels each year were permitted to enter the port. At the same time Iyeyasu had secured from the Korean court an agreement to dispatch to Yedo a congratulatory mission to each new Shogun. Inasmuch as the expenses of these missions on their journey from Tsushima to Yedo were borne by the Japanese, the Yedo authorities arranged in 1790 that the congratulations of the Korean court might be delivered at Tsushima. In 1811 one such mission is reported to have come to Tsushima, but after that date no further missions were sent.

Upon the establishment of the Meiji regime an attempt was made by the Japanese government to secure a resumption of the old congratulatory missions; but Korea refused to comply with this request, and her refusal was accompanied by a severe denunciation of the Japanese for having become a renegade among the peoples of the Orient. In 1869 and again in 1871 the government of the peninsula kingdom refused to receive missions from the Japanese court. At this point the Japanese became involved in the Luchu-Formosa dispute with China, but in 1875 a Japanese gunboat was sent to make a detailed survey of the Korean west coast. In the course of the survey, while taking soundings in the mouth of the Han River, a Japanese party was fired upon by the batteries guarding the river. The Japanese gunboat promptly avenged this insult by landing a party and destroying the fort, after which it returned home to report the occurrence.

In the face of renewed clamor by the war party the Tokyo government followed a policy of studied moderation. Advising China of her intentions and securing the reluctant approval of the Chinese government, Japan dispatched to Korea an expeditionary force accompanied by two warships. A demand for the establishment of friendly relations was presented to the Korean government, and on February 26, 1876, after peaceful negotiations a treaty was signed. By this treaty, in which Korea was formally declared to be a sovereign and independent state, Japan received the right of unrestricted trade at Fusan and at two additional ports, together with the right to maintain a permanent legation at Seoul. Japanese subjects residing in Korea were to enjoy the very extra-territorial privileges whose inclusion in their own treaties with the West the Japanese so bitterly resented.

Brilliant as was the diplomatic success of the Japanese government in securing the opening of Korea to Japanese trade and in undermining, by the phraseology of the treaty, China's ancient claim to suzerainty over the peninsula, the result of the expedition brought little applause from the Japanese people. Once more the samurai had been disappointed in their hope for a war of conquest.

Apart from the unwillingness of the Meiji statesmen to see the control of the government pass even temporarily into the hands of the war party, a peaceful solution of the Korean episode was dictated by the fear that a war might result in bringing into the peninsula a foreign power far more dangerous than China. Ever since the first half of the seventeenth century, when their exploring vanguard reached the shores of the Pacific, the Russians had been slowly but steadily strengthening their control over the Asiatic coast north of the Korean frontiers. In 1860, as a result of the treaty whereby Russia secured from China the Primorsk territory lying between the Korean boundary and the mouth of the Amur River, this control became complete, and a Japanese invasion of Korea might easily have resulted in the offer of Russian assistance to Korea against the invader.

That the fear of a conflict with Russia was not without foundation is demonstrated by the fact that Japanese and Russian aspirations had already begun to clash in the insular regions to the north of Japan: in the Kuril chain of islands, extending from Yezo to the southern tip of Kamchatka, and in the large island of Sakhalin, which lies opposite and south of the mouth of the Amur. Geographically and historically, there was little to choose between the claims of the two empires to sovereignty over these islands. The Kuril Islands may be regarded either as a northeasterly continuation of the Japanese Archipelago or as a southwesterly extension of Kamchatka, and La Perouse Strait, between Yezo and Sakhalin, is slightly wider than the strait which separates the latter island from the nearest point of the Asiatic mainland. In pre-treaty days the Japanese administration made little or no pretension to authority over Sakhalin, where the first Russian and Japanese explorations both date from the first half of the seventeenth century, while the eighteenth-century Russian explorers of the Kuril group, following the chain southward from Kamchatka, found the Japanese established only on the three southernmost islands of the group.

In the summer of 1859 the Russian government attempted to secure a clear title to Sakhalin by sending Count Muravieff-Amursky to Japan with the proposal that the Japanese recognize the Strait of La Perouse as the frontier between the two empires. This proposal was rejected by the Yedo Bakufu, and no agreement resulted from the negotiations. Subsequently the Japanese, on their side, proposed alternatively the division of the island between the two empires or the purchase of Russia's claim by Japan, but both these proposals were rejected by Russia. In the meantime the island was being steadily colonized by Russian immigrants; the Japanese, who had as yet made little progress in the occupation of the northern portions of Yezo, were able to offer no effective competition to their rivals. In 1875, less than a year after the Formosan expedition, the two empires reached a settlement whereby Russia abandoned all claims to the Kuril Islands in return for Japanese recognition of Russian sovereignty over all of Sakhalin.

The Japanese treaty of 1876, which forced the Koreans to abandon their policy of strict non-intercourse with the outside world, transformed the peninsula kingdom into the storm center of the Far East.

In the eyes of the Chinese, Korea was one of the ancient vassals of the imperial throne and, bound to her suzerain by a sense of cultural indebtedness, served as a buffer state against the invasions of outside barbarians. In case of dire necessity the vassal should be succored by the armed forces of the suzerain; in response to an appeal for aid the suzerain might even dispatch forces to enable the vassal government to re-establish internal order, but otherwise

the vassal was fully sovereign and was expected to solve its problems, external as well as internal, without the interference of the
Dragon Throne.

Even before the conclusion of the Japanese treaty several of
the Western powers had attempted, without success, to negotiate
with the Seoul government. In 1879 Li Hung-chang, in charge of
China's relations with her peninsula vassal, privately advised the
Koreans to conclude treaties with as many of these powers as
possible; and beginning in May, 1882, Korea signed treaties of
friendship and commerce with the United States, Great Britain,
Germany, Italy, Russia, and France. Despite the conclusion of
these treaties, which were expected to establish a body of foreign
interests sufficiently extensive to block the dangerous expansion
of Japanese influence, the situation in Korea steadily developed
into a conflict between the conservatives, who desired adherence
to old institutions, and a progressive party, composed of those
in favor of Japanese innovations.

In 1883 the Chinese government, alarmed by the growth of
Japanese influence, determined to appoint a resident at the Korean
capital, and Yüan Shih-k'ai, later to become president of the Chinese Republic, was sent to Seoul in this capacity. During the next
eleven years Yüan, as Chinese resident, was the mainspring of the
conservative organization. During the same period the Japanese
legation staff and perhaps a majority of the Japanese who came
to Korea in a private capacity were active agents in the upbuilding
of the pro-Japanese party.

Clashes between the two parties were frequent and violent. In
1882 a Seoul mob attacked the Japanese legation, and the minister,
with his suite and the Japanese civilians in the city, had difficulty
in escaping to the seacoast. For this attack the Korean government
was compelled to pay an indemnity of four hundred thousand yen
and to open fresh ports to the Japanese. In 1884 the progressives
and their Japanese friends, with or without the complicity of the
Japanese legation, attacked the palace and gained possession of the
king and queen. When Yüan Shih-k'ai and his Chinese troops
arrived to protect the royal family, they found the palace occupied
by the Japanese minister and his legation guards. The Chinese

forces opened fire on the Japanese, who cut their way out of the city and found safety on a Japanese merchant ship in the harbor of Chemulpo.

For the moment it seemed probable that the 1884 outbreak would eventuate in war between Korea's two neighbors, but neither China nor Japan was at this time anxious to engage in hostilities. Although the Peking government probably underrated the military strength of the Japanese, China at the time was engaged in the Tongking war with France, and even after this conflict was settled in the spring of 1885 it was in no condition to embark upon another armed struggle. In Japan, on the other hand, the peace party was still in power and was still unwilling to interrupt its domestic program by engaging in a foreign war. In the spring of 1885, therefore, Count Ito was dispatched to China, and on April 18, at Tientsin, he concluded with Li Hung-chang the Li-Ito convention[1] dealing with the status of Korea and the rights of the two empires in Korean affairs. The forces under the Chinese resident, as well as the Japanese legation guards, were to be completely withdrawn from the kingdom. The Korean king was to be invited to organize a Korean army, in the formation of which neither Chinese nor Japanese were to be employed. In case any serious disturbance in Korea made it necessary for either China or Japan to send troops into the peninsula the country sending the troops must notify the other, previously and in writing, of its intention to do so, and the troops should be withdrawn when the matter had been settled. For a period of nine years, during which it may be said to have kept the peace between two countries which did not desire war, the Li-Ito convention regulated the status of Korea.

In part the conclusion of the Li-Ito convention appears to have been facilitated by a common fear that Russia might utilize to her own advantage the unsettled condition in Korea. In 1884 the Korean government had anticipated one provision of the convention and had invited Russian military officers to assist in the organization of the Korean army. Early in 1885 it became known that Russia was to receive, as compensation for the services of her military experts, the right to use Port Lazareff, on the Korean coast,

[1] Commonly referred to as the Tientsin convention.

as a coaling station and naval base. Against this new danger Japan / and China promptly combined diplomatic forces. To the Japanese the establishment of a Russian ice-free naval base on the Korean coast would constitute an ever present threat to national security, while the Chinese, well acquainted with Russian methods, realized that this might prove to be the first step in the Russian absorption of Korea. Stern protests from Peking and Tokyo were sent to Seoul, and the proposed lease of Port Lazareff was not concluded.

Russia's unsuccessful attempt to establish herself on the Korean coast also brought prompt action from another quarter. On May 12, 1885, the British Asiatic squadron occupied Port Hamilton, an anchorage in the group of islands which lie between Quelpart Island and the southern tip of the Korean peninsula. This occupation called forth immediate protest from the Korean government, as well as from China and Japan, who were no more anxious to have the British power established in this region than to see the Russians in control. In the face of these protests the British retained Port Hamilton until February, 1887; then, partly because the Russian aspirations to Port Lazareff had been abandoned and partly because Port Hamilton had proved to be thoroughly unsuited as a naval base, the anchorage was evacuated.

The Li-Ito convention of 1885 had effected a temporary compromise between the two governments which at that time were equally anxious to avoid the dangerous adventure of a foreign war, but it had brought no essential harmony between their respective policies and aspirations in Korea. The open clash was merely postponed, and in 1894 developments in all three countries brought matters at last to the breaking point. In March of that year Kim Ok-kiun, a pro-Japanese Korean who had been residing in Japan since 1884, was lured to Shanghai and murdered by Koreans of the anti-Japanese faction. When the Chinese government, instead of punishing the murderers, allowed them to return in triumph to / Korea, Japanese public opinion expressed itself in no uncertain terms against China and against the feeble policy of the Tokyo administration, whose protest to the Chinese government was regarded as inadequate.

In Korea, almost simultaneously, a conservative religious party known as the *Tong Hak* ("Eastern Learning") had fomented a serious outbreak, and on June 2, 1894, the Korean court applied to Peking for military assistance to suppress the revolt. Formally notifying the Japanese of their intention, as required by the Li-Ito convention, the Chinese sent a force of fifteen hundred men into Korea and later reinforced them with about as many more. Japan, although not appealed to by the Korean court, replied to the Chinese move by sending in troops of her own, and by the end of June about eighteen thousand Japanese soldiers were in the peninsula.

For the Japanese statesmen the gathering of the Korean storm clouds coincided with a parliamentary crisis at home. On the second of June, the day upon which the Korean king appealed to China for military aid, the Japanese diet had been dissolved for the second time within six months, and the opposition leaders were preparing to base their coming campaign upon a sweeping denunciation of the government's foreign policy. The revision of the British treaty was going on, and on July 16 the government was to be able to announce a brilliant success in this direction; but for the moment the Korean question had overshadowed even the "unilateral treaties," and the newspapers were loudly demanding that the question of Korea be settled once and for all.

The Tong Hak disturbance had been successfully crushed by the Korean government before the arrival of the Chinese and Japanese forces, but on June 17 Japan proposed to China that the two empires combine to force upon Korea such reforms of her administration as might seem desirable. The logic of the Chinese reply was difficult to refute: "Even China, whose vassal Korea has always been, would not interfere in the internal administration of the kingdom; Japan, having from the beginning recognized Korea as an independent state, cannot claim any right to interfere."

On July 14 the Japanese government, undeterred by the Chinese reply, notified the Tsungli Yamen (Chinese Office of Foreign Affairs) that Japan would proceed without China's co-operation to institute in Korea such reforms as were necessary to prevent the recurrence of dangerous disturbances of the peace. The conclusion of the British treaty revision two days later apparently encouraged the Japanese to cut the Gordian knot. On the twenty-third the Japanese troops at Seoul attacked the palace, seized the royal family, and set up a new government by which on the following day a decree was issued denouncing all existing treaties with China and calling upon the Japanese to drive the Chinese from the kingdom. War had commenced.

The formal declaration of a state of war did not come until August 1, but on the twenty-fifth of July the Japanese naval forces succeeded in crippling a Chinese gunboat and in sinking a transport, the chartered British steamer *Kowshing*, carrying twelve hundred Chinese reinforcements to Korea. Contrary to the expectations of most foreign observers, who felt that Japan would be no match for her enemy, the war was an almost unbroken series of victories for the smaller nation. The Chinese were swept out of Korea; a single naval battle gave Japan complete mastery of the sea. Port Arthur and Weihaiwei were besieged and taken, and the armies of the Mikado were advancing upon Tientsin when Li Hung-chang, in March, 1895, appeared at Shimonoseki to sue for peace.

From the outset of the war the governments of the Western powers, although recognizing that a Japanese victory must result in the abandonment of China's suzerainty over Korea, had given evidence of their unwillingness to see any part of the Chinese mainland transferred to Japan. As early as October, 1894, Great Britain proposed that the powers intervene in the war, to secure the restoration of peace on the following terms: the cession of Formosa and the payment of a suitable war indemnity to Japan, independence for Korea, and territorial integrity for China. The British intervention proposal was not accepted by the other neutrals, but Japan was repeatedly warned that the Western powers would not approve the permanent annexation of any Chinese territory upon the continent of Asia.

In the peace negotiations at Shimonoseki, Li Hung-chang did his best to secure a modification of the Japanese demands, but the treaty which he was finally compelled to sign on April 17, 1895, spelled utter humiliation to his country. China was forced to recognize the independence of Korea; to cede to Japan Formosa, the Pescadores, and the Liaotung peninsula; to pay a war indemnity of 200,000,000 taels; to open four new treaty ports to Japanese trade and residence; to agree to negotiate with Japan a new commercial treaty, until the conclusion of which Japan was to enjoy most-favored-nation treatment.

When Li arrived at Shimonoseki, however, he was not completely at the end of his resources. Even before he had left Peking he had received definite assurance that Russia would interpose a veto to any cession of a part of the Manchurian mainland to Japan. When the terms of the treaty became known, Russia, supported by France and Germany, intervened to force the Japanese government to modify the treaty in so far as it related to the Liaotung area. On April 23, six days after the treaty was signed, the ministers of the three powers called at the Tokyo Foreign Office and presented identic notes to the Japanese government, advising Japan, "in the interest of the peace of the Far East," to renounce her claim to the cession of any territory on the mainland. Realizing the futility of attempting to resist this powerful combination, the Japanese government gave way and re-ceded to China the area in question, receiving in its stead an additional indemnity to the amount of 30,000,000 taels.

Despite her retreat from Manchuria at the behest of the three intervening powers Japan had gained a spectacular triumph over her neighbor. Her military efficiency, in striking contrast with the ineptitude of the Chinese armed forces, had excited the admiration of the West; Korea, definitely detached from all connection with China, was henceforth to become more and more dependent upon and subject to the Mikado's empire; the 230,000,000 taels of war indemnity received from China enabled the Meiji statesmen to reorganize the currency of the empire and place it upon a gold basis; and the new commercial treaty with China, subsequently negotiated in accordance with the provision in the treaty of peace, placed Japanese trade and traders in that country upon a footing of complete equality with those of Europe and America. The United States, as we have seen, had followed the British example and had revised her treaty with Japan before the end of 1894, but the outcome of the war unquestionably helped to persuade the other treaty powers to fall into line in the matter of treaty revision.

Over against these more or less tangible benefits, however, must be set certain less desirable consequences of the war. The appeal to arms in 1894 enabled the imperial cabinet to end for the time its embarrassing struggle with the parliamentary opposition, but it also resulted in putting into the hands of the army and navy a dominant power over the civil administration. At the outbreak of the war an imperial ordinance provided that the Ministry of War and the Ministry of Navy could be filled only by officers in active service holding at least the rank of lieutenant general or vice admiral. Inasmuch as officers in active service are subject to the orders of the General Staff of the army and the navy, respectively, it became possible from this time for either General Staff to wreck —or to prevent the formation of—any cabinet whose civilian members refused to follow in domestic or foreign affairs policies satisfactory to the armed services. At the close of the war the acquisition of the Pescadores and Formosa served as an excuse for increasing the peace strength of the army, and still further entrenched in power the military officials, to whom were entrusted the tasks of colonial administration.

The triumph of the military element in domestic politics had an especially unfortunate effect upon Japan's relations with Korea, for whose "independence" the war ostensibly had been waged. Count Inouye was recalled from Korea in September, 1895, and was replaced as Japanese minister by Viscount Miura. Inouye had attempted to cultivate among the Koreans a cordial friendship for Japan, but his successor treated independent Korea as a conquered province in which every obstacle to Japanese domination was to be ruthlessly swept aside. On October 8, 1895, a mob of Koreans and Japanese, instigated by Miura and assisted, at his command, by the Japanese troops in Seoul, invaded the palace, murdered the queen, and seized the person of the king.[1] For four months the Korean king was a puppet in the hands of his Japanese captors; but in February, 1896, he escaped to the Russian legation, and Japanese influence over the government was replaced by that of Russia. Within ten months after the conclusion of their vic-

---

[1] For the findings of the Japanese court of investigation see F. A. McKenzie, *The Tragedy of Korea*, pp. 263–268.

torious treaty the Japanese had thus thrown away their opportunity of cultivating cordial relations with Korea. Instead they had aroused against themselves a national hatred more intense than any since the days of Hideyoshi; they had thrown the Korean government into the arms of the Russians and had thereby helped to create the situation which was to lead, within a decade, to the Russo-Japanese War.

JAPAN IN 1899

On August 4, 1899, the old-style French treaty, the last of the series, expired; on that date, by international agreement, the revised treaties between Japan and the various Western powers came into full force. Extraterritoriality was abolished, foreign ships ceased to enjoy the right of engaging in coastal trade, and Japan, save for a "conventional" tariff upon a limited number of imports, was restored to full and unconditional sovereignty with respect to the outside world. Almost exactly forty-six years had elapsed since Commodore Perry, on July 8, 1853, dropped anchor in Uraga Bay; less than thirty-two years had passed since the last of the Tokugawa Shoguns had surrendered his administrative powers into the hands of the young emperor Mutsuhito.

In this brief period of time Japan had passed through a transformation whose speed and completeness were little short of marvelous. In 1899 Mutsuhito still occupied the throne, surrounded by many of the advisers who had participated in laying the foundations of the Meiji regime. Many were still alive who had gazed with awe and apprehension at Perry's "black ships," who had raised the clamor against commerce with the outside world, and who had joined in attempts to drive the hated foreigner from Japanese soil. But these survivors of the earlier age looked out upon the world in 1899 through different eyes. Japan's own black ships had recently been employed to force upon her neighbors the acceptance of the foreign culture whose introduction she had once so bitterly opposed. Her merchant marine was engaged in carrying to distant ports the output of a growing factory system as well as the products of her older industries. Railroads and telegraph had quickened internal communication. A reorganized school system had opened to the coming generation the storehouse of Western scientific knowledge. Hotels, tourist agencies, and steamship lines were beginning to seek the patronage of the once hated "barbarian." For better or for worse, Japan in 1899 had definitely committed herself to Westernization.

SUGGESTED REFERENCES

BRINKLEY, F., and KIKUCHI, D. A History of the Japanese People.

DENNETT, T. Americans in Eastern Asia.

GUBBINS, J. H. The Making of Modern Japan.

HEARN, L. Japan: an Attempt at Interpretation.

HOLTOM, D. C. The Political Philosophy of Modern Shinto.

ITO, H. (English translation by M. Ito). Commentaries on the Constitution of the Empire of Japan.

JONES, F. C. Extraterritoriality in Japan.

KITAZAWA, N. The Government of Japan.

LATOURETTE, K. S. The Development of Japan.

MCLAREN, W. W. (editor). Japanese Government Documents, 1867–1889.

MCLAREN, W. W. A Political History of Japan in the Meiji Era.

OKUMA, COUNT S. (editor). Fifty Years of New Japan.

QUIGLEY, H. S. Japanese Government and Politics.

REIN, J. J. The Industries of Japan.

UYEHARA, G. E. The Political Development of Japan, 1867–1909.

XXVI

Developments in Colonial Policies: 1850–1914

Russia in Northern Asia · Russian Pressure toward the South · The Trans-Siberian Railway · A Check to Russia in the Far East · The Consolidation of British Rule in India · Administration under the Crown · Safeguarding the Northern Frontier · Frontier Annexations · Relations with Afghanistan · The British and Yakub Beg · Relations with Tibet: the Younghusband Expedition · British Expansion in Burma and the Malay Peninsula · Economic and Social Development in India · The Beginnings of Indian Participation in Government · The Growth of Indian Disaffection · The Indian Councils Act of 1909 · The Dutch in the Malay Archipelago · The Inauguration of Reforms · Benefits to Dutch Trade · The Establishment of an Educational System · The Achin War · The French in Indo-China · Paul Doumer and Administrative Reforms · Effects of the Russo-Japanese War · The Independence of Siam · Internal Reforms · The Partial Abolition of Extraterritoriality

I N ASIA the last half of the nineteenth century and the opening years of the twentieth century were marked by the steadily increasing imperialistic activities of the various European countries. Occupying extensive zones in northern and southern Asia, respectively, Russia and Great Britain were incomparably the most important European powers in the Far East. Holland, Spain, and France possessed valuable, if localized, areas; Germany and the United States were later to join the ranks of the imperial powers; but the empires of Russia and Britain, dominating vast regions of Asia even before the middle of the nineteenth century, easily overshadowed all the others. The expansionist policies of these two powers and the jealous suspicion with which each regarded the growth of the other seemed at times to resolve the entire question of the Far East into a struggle between the Russian bear and the British lion.

RUSSIA IN NORTHERN ASIA

Unlike the other portions of Asia which have come under European control, the greater part of the area occupied by Russia has been the scene of a genuine process of colonization. The non-

European peoples whom the advancing Russians conquered and dispossessed, including the population of the areas ceded by China in 1858 and 1860, were probably no more numerous than the American Indians who once inhabited the present area of the United States. Russian migration into this vast, thinly occupied region, as we have already seen, was led by the Cossacks, who, as explorers, hunters, and fur-traders, quickly swept across the continent to the shores of the Pacific. In western Siberia, between the Ural Mountains and Lake Baikal, a steady peasant migration followed upon the heels of the Cossacks and brought under cultivation the more desirable land in the newly acquired territory.

In the regions east of Lake Baikal colonial occupation was, during the earlier period, less spontaneous. The Russian government, adopting a policy which had been followed by the English in some of their possessions, first utilized this area as a place for the disposal of undesirables. Criminals and political offenders, to the number of several hundred thousand, were sent as exiles into the Far East. In many cases the families of the banished men followed them, and even when the term of exile was not for life a large portion of these people remained in eastern Siberia as permanent inhabitants.

The founding of Vladivostok in July, 1860, greatly increased the economic possibilities of the region. The abolition of serfdom in Russia the following year made available a large number of potential colonists, since for many of the former serfs the land adjustment at home made no adequate provision. It has been estimated that during the decade which followed the emancipation two and a half million peasants moved from Russia into Siberia. The great majority of these settled between the Urals and Lake Baikal, but the more eastern section also received from this wave of migration an addition to its population sufficient to make the region definitely Russian in culture and blood.

As has been pointed out in an earlier chapter, the eastward progress of Russia's first Cossack explorers was constantly deflected toward the north by the mountain system which runs diagonally across the continent. The fur-trading interests of these early pioneers and their dependence upon the use of great rivers for con-

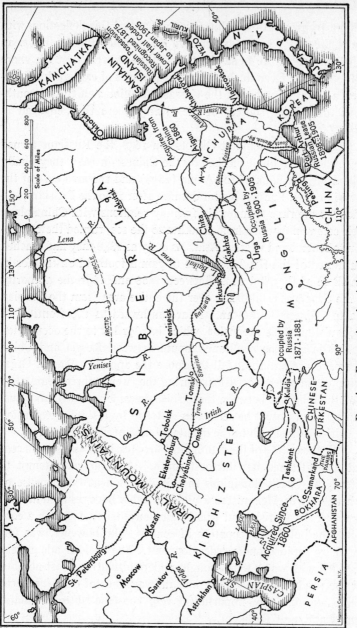

Russian Expansion in Asia since 1850

venient transportation inclined them to accept this deflection, with the result that Russian exploration had reached the Arctic Ocean at the mouth of the Lena six years before it arrived at the shore of the Pacific. Even during the earliest stages of exploration, however, a certain number of the Cossack frontiersmen turned southward toward the sources of the rivers, where they engaged in mining for gold.

Reaching the Pacific at Okhotsk in 1638, the Russians turned southward. Although checked by the Chinese in 1689, they finally gained the left bank of the Amur (1858) and the area east of the Ussuri (1860). For nearly four decades after 1860 the Russians, satisfied for the time to maintain friendly relations with China along their common frontier from Kiakhta to the sea, turned their attention to central and western Asia. As early as 1848 they had reached southward of the Kirghiz Steppe to gain a foothold on the northern shore of the Aral Sea. Between 1868 and 1891 the authority of the Czar was established over the entire area from the Caspian Sea to Chinese Turkestan, as far southward as the frontiers of Afghanistan. This expansion, which in 1871 led to the occupation of Kuldja and the resultant dispute between Russia and China (see page 556), did not fail to arouse the apprehensions of Great Britain. On several occasions during the twenty-three years after 1868 the relations between these rivals became strained, and Russian activity, as will be seen, was matched by a similar expansion of British influence into the debatable land of central Asia.

With the taking of the Pamirs in 1891 Russian expansion in central Asia attained its "farthest south." Any further attempt to extend the Czar's dominions in this direction at the expense of either Persia or Afghanistan would inevitably have resulted in open war with the British, and Russia was not anxious for such a conflict. The political occupation of central Asia, however, was followed by rapid economic development. The regions adequately provided with water were brought under cultivation, most notably for the production of cotton, and railway lines of combined economic and military importance were constructed to Bokhara, Samarkand, and Tashkent.

The construction of the Trans-Caspian Railway into the recently acquired Asian territories was followed in 1891 by a more ambitious railway project—a line across Siberia to link European Russia with the eastern stronghold, Vladivostok. The building of this line was commenced on May 31, 1891, when the Russian Czarevitch (later Nicholas II) officially inaugurated the work on the section between Vladivostok and Khabarovsk.

The original purpose of the Trans-Siberian Railway appears to have been primarily economic. It was the pet project of the non-militant Alexander III and was carried to completion by the essentially pacifist Minister of Finance, Count Witte. Alexander and his finance minister, who had no interest in any fresh territorial acquisitions in the East, hoped that the projected railway would aid tremendously in the exploitation of the territory already acquired; and such, indeed, was one consequence of its construction. The agricultural regions through which the line passed obtained, at last, satisfactory means of getting their products to market, the settlement of the country rapidly increased, a number of flourishing cities grew up along the railroad, and Vladivostok—its eastern terminus—became a seaport of first importance.

The building of the Trans-Siberian Railway, however, had consequences which were wholly foreign to the plans of Alexander and Count Witte. Even if the building of the line had not been undertaken, it is possible that the Russian government would have intervened in 1895, as it did, to prevent the cession of the Liaotung area to Japan. The difficulties involved in running the railway from Vladivostok to Khabarovsk and thence along the northern bank of the Amur to Chita, however, suggested to the Russian government the compensation which China should pay for Russia's intervention; namely, the privilege of carrying the railway across northern Manchuria on a direct line to Vladivostok. This concession, which will be considered in detail in a later chapter (see page 679), profoundly affected the subsequent course of events in the Far East. The right of way of the Chinese Eastern Railway (this short cut granted to the Trans-Siberian) became a Russian zone of influence stretching across northern Manchuria, and within two years after the acquisition of this zone the Russians reached southward to secure for themselves a lease on a part of that Liaotung area which they had so recently rescued from the hands of the Japanese.

The attempt of Nicholas II and his advisers to absorb Manchuria and to secure in Port Arthur the long-sought ice-free port on the Pacific, coinciding with Russia's assumption of the role of protector over the Korean royal family, brought the Czar's empire into direct conflict with the expansionist aspirations of Japan. The development of this conflict and its culmination in the Russo-Japanese War will be discussed in connection with Japanese history (see pages 720–722).

To the Russians the outcome of the Russo-Japanese War was a humiliating check, but except for the southern half of Sakhalin Island it involved no loss of Russian territory. After the war, indeed, Russia's position in the Far East appears to have been actually strengthened. Although Port Arthur and the South Manchuria Railway (the line running southward from Changchun to Port Arthur) were surrendered to Japan, the important Chinese Eastern line across northern Manchuria remained in Russian hands, while Vladivostok, in spite of its winter handicap, continued to grow in commercial importance. Owing to the predominantly Russian character of the population in Siberia the military reverses, far from leading to any separatist movement, strengthened the allegiance of the region to the Czar. Moreover, this Russian population was greatly increased through fresh colonization, since many of the soldiers who had served in the war remained as colonists after demobilization, in preference to returning to European Russia. Finally, the results of the war were beneficial to Russia's relations with the Chinese Empire, whose growing suspicion and fear of Russia were now considerably modified by the presence of the Japanese in southern Manchuria.

THE CONSOLIDATION OF BRITISH RULE IN INDIA

At the close of the period of company rule, India consisted of two parts: one part absolutely subject to British rule; the other composed of the Indian states, officially known as "protected states," which were bound to the British only by treaties of friendship and commerce. With respect to the area under direct rule the transition from company rule to crown government after the pacification of the mutiny was a comparatively simple process. Such of the former officials as desired to continue at their posts were retained as officers of the crown; the forces, European and Indian, were reorganized as a branch of the royal army; and necessary changes were made in the organization of the courts of justice.

With respect to the protected states, however, the transfer of India to crown rule led eventually to a decided modification of their earlier status. In the queen's proclamation of November 1, 1858, which announced the establishment of the royal government over India, all treaties and engagements entered into by the East India Company with the independent Indian princes were declared to be binding upon the British crown, which desired "no extension of our present territorial possessions" and declared that it would "respect the rights, dignity, and honor of the native princes as our own." For eighteen years, indeed, there appears to have been no change in the status of the princes; but the proclamation of Victoria as empress of India (Kaisar-i-Hind) on January 1, 1877, inevitably transformed the independent rulers from allies into vassals. The British government, since that time, has maintained the form of treating the princes as independent sovereigns, but it has never hesitated to interfere in their affairs when interference seemed desirable.

Although the independent ruling princes have lost much of their independence, the policy of the British government has added to their secure tenure of such sovereignty as remains to them. In 1848 the company's governor-general, Lord Dalhousie, had proclaimed the *doctrine of lapse*, that is, the rule that, whereas the adopted son of a sovereign prince might inherit the personal property of his adopting father, the rights of sovereignty in such a case lapsed to the East India Company as "the paramount power in India." During the last ten years of the old regime this rule was frequently applied by the company's representatives, but in 1858 the first royal governor-general, Lord Canning, announced that henceforth an adopted son would be recognized as a legal heir to sovereign powers as well as to property rights.

With the transfer of India from the rule of the company to that of the crown the supervisory powers formerly exercised by the company's directors and by the Board of Control passed into the hands of a Secretary of State for India and a newly created Council of India. As in the earlier days, however, most of the real administrative responsibility devolved upon the officials residing in India, and here the organization was little changed from the form which it had taken under the company.

The supreme authority in India was vested in the viceroy, or governor-general, whose court (until transferred to Delhi in 1911) was located at Calcutta. In the performance of his duties the viceroy was assisted by an Executive Council, composed of members appointed by the crown, and by a Legislative Council, which included the members of the Executive Council together with additional members named by the viceroy. Under the viceroy the directly governed portions of India were administered by governors, lieutenant governors, or commissioners, the particular title depending in each case upon the importance of the area involved. The two great presidencies, Bombay and Madras, were administered by governors, with the assistance of executive councils, and similar advisory bodies existed for the lieutenant governors or commissioners of the smaller provinces.

The efficient functioning of the whole system was fundamentally dependent upon the carefully recruited and well-trained members of the Indian civil service. Selected (since 1854) by rigorous competitive examination and usually making their service in India a life career, the members of this elite corps filled all the offices below the viceroyalty and the two great governorships; from them also were selected men to serve as residents at courts of the more important protected states.

The rulers of the protected states, save for the influence exerted by the residents just mentioned, enjoyed a free hand in their administration of local affairs. Here the governments, although sometimes borrowing ideas and institutions from the British, were administered by Indian officials, many of whom showed themselves to be fully as capable as the European administrators of the neighboring crown territories.

During the half-century which followed the Sepoy Mutiny and the substitution of the direct rule of the British crown for that of the East India Company the outstanding fact in Indian history was the gradual extension and consolidation of British authority over the entire peninsula and over certain strategically important regions on the northern frontier.

British interest in the states on the northern frontier of India and the gradual extension of British influence in this direction were the result of three major considerations: a desire to open fresh areas to commerce, the need of putting an end to raids by frontier tribes, and the fear aroused by Russian expansion in central Asia. Until about 1870 the first two considerations were preponderant; but after this date the advance of Russia toward the mountain passes on the northwest frontier was a cause of keen apprehension to the British government and to its representatives in India. When the Russians after 1891 turned their attention to eastern Siberia, Manchuria, and Korea, British anxiety as to the safety of India was somewhat allayed; yet it was not until Russia had been checked in the Far East by Britain's Japanese ally that the fear of the "bear that walks like a man" definitely subsided.

In 1865 the small Himalayan state of Bhutan, on the northern frontier of Bengal, was punished for its raiding activities by an invasion and was forced to cede to the British government some four thousand square miles of territory along the frontier. Eleven years later a more important annexation took place in the extreme west. The protected state of Baluchistan was induced to cede to the British crown the district of Quetta, extending the full length of its northern frontier. The occupation of Quetta was undertaken for the purpose of enabling the Anglo-Indian government to maintain a closer watch upon developments in Afghanistan. In 1891 and 1892, apparently in response to the Russian seizure of the Pamirs, the British occupied Hunza and Nagar in the Gilgit valley, thus strengthening their defenses against any attempted invasion through the passes of the Hindu Kush. In 1895 internal disturbances in the petty state of Chitral, to the west of Gilgit, led to the invasion of that region and to the establishment of a government satisfactory to the British.

In 1839–1840 the East India Company had involved itself in a disastrous attempt to drive the Afghan Amir, Dost Muhammad, from his throne and to replace him by a prince more subservient to British interests. After sustaining heavy military losses the company abandoned the attempt and recognized Dost Muhammad, who continued to rule until his death in 1863. Upon the death of the old Amir the British governor-general, Sir John Lawrence, proclaimed that the British government had no interest in Afghan affairs and would recognize as the lawful ruler any claimant who might triumph over his rivals.

After a five-year struggle Sher Ali, a son of Dost Muhammad, secured the throne and received British recognition. The new Amir, although offered an annual subsidy by the Indian government, soon inclined toward the Russians, whom he found willing to enter into formal treaty relations such as the British persistently refused. The British occupation of Quetta in 1876, undertaken as a check to the Afghan power, still further alienated Sher Ali, and in 1878 the Amir publicly received a Russian envoy at Kabul, refusing at the same time to allow a British envoy to enter his domain. As a result of this display of hostility a punitive expedition was dispatched into Afghanistan; Sher Ali was driven from the country and compelled to seek refuge among his Russian friends, and his successor on the throne was forced to cede Kalat, the Khyber Pass, and the valley of Kurram to the British.

In spite of their success the British losses in this undertaking were so severe that the Indian government was brought to realize the necessity of revising its policy toward the court of Kabul. Lord Dufferin, who became governor-general in 1884, therefore exerted himself to cultivate the good will of the new Amir, Abdurrahman. Early in 1885 a frontier clash between the Afghans and the Russians, which brought Russia and Great Britain to the verge of war, enabled the British to pose as the defenders of Afghan independence. From this date the British guaranteed Afghanistan against Russian attack, granted the Amir a generous annual subsidy, and made it a part of their fixed policy not to send their own troops into Afghan territory.

When Yakub Beg, taking advantage of the Mohammedan revolt

in Chinese Turkestan, established himself as an independent ruler (see page 555), the Indian government was much alarmed lest the new sovereign become an ally of Russia. In spite of the danger of antagonizing the Chinese government, therefore, several embassies from India were sent to Kashgar. Yakub was recognized as an independent sovereign, and in February, 1874, he concluded a commercial treaty with the British. In May, 1877, however, Chinese authority was re-established over the region.

As early as 1774, during the administration of Warren Hastings, the East India Company had attempted, with little success, to establish permanent relations with the mysterious theocratic state to the north of the Himalayas. The mission in 1774, under George Bogle, and another in 1783, under Samuel Turner, each succeeded in paying its respects to the Tashilunpo lama at Shigatse, but the Tibetans refused to be drawn from their seclusion. In the closing years of the nineteenth century the desire for commercial expansion combined with the still lively fear of Russian progress in central Asia to inspire a renewal of British attempts for closer relations with Tibet.

In March, 1890, a boundary dispute of long duration between the Tibetans and the people of Sikkim, annexed by the company in 1850, was brought to a close by a convention between the Indian and Chinese governments. In accordance with Article IV of this convention, which provided for the establishment of a Tibetan mart for British trade, the Chinese government, by a commercial agreement signed in December, 1893, opened to British trade the town of Yatung. The new mart proved to be utterly unsuited for commerce, and the British authorities attempted in vain to secure the opening of a more satisfactory trading post.

At the beginning of 1899 Lord Curzon of Kedleston was appointed viceroy of India. The new viceroy, who was a firm believer in energetic policies, promptly revived the effort to obtain an improvement in commercial arrangements and attempted to open direct communication with the Dalai lama. In June, 1901, an emissary from the Dalai lama, a Mongol named Dorjieff, arrived in Russia, where he was officially received by the Czar; later in the same year Lord Curzon's letter to the Dalai lama was returned with seals unbroken, the lama alleging that diplomatic communications could be received only through the hands of the Chinese imperial government.

In view of this apparently anti-British attitude of the Tibetans Lord Curzon urged the dispatch of an expedition, and in November, 1903, he finally received permission to send a limited force —the Younghusband expedition—as far as Gyantse. When the Tibetans offered armed resistance to this advance, the expedition was reinforced and was authorized to proceed to Lhasa, which it entered in August, 1904. The Tibetan government was forced to undertake the payment of a small indemnity, part of which was subsequently remitted; China's suzerainty over the country was reaffirmed; and the British government secured the right to maintain a representative at Lhasa. Although the convention of 1904 recognized China's suzerainty over Tibet, the British government after that date repeatedly intervened to prevent any move for the incorporation of Tibet as an integral part of China; and this almost inaccessible mountain region tended to become a focal point of British, Russian, and Chinese diplomatic intrigues.

As we have seen in an earlier chapter, the British conquest of Burma, which was partially accomplished by the East India Company's wars of 1825 and 1852, was completed by the Third Burmese War in 1885. On January 1, 1886, the annexation of the hitherto independent fragment of Burma was formally proclaimed. By 1891 the opposition of the last Burmese patriot fighting forces had been crushed, and in 1897 Upper Burma and Lower Burma were united into a single administrative district of the Indian Empire. Although Burma has thus been ruled by the British as a part of India, there is little real connection between the two regions; and for a long time there has been a growing feeling among qualified British authorities that this more eastern possession would be better administered as a completely separate unit.[1]

In the Malay peninsula, as in Burma, the royal government of India continued to build upon foundations which had been laid by the East India Company. Mention has already been made of the

[1] It should be noted that one of the recommendations of the Simon Commission (1930) was to that effect.

northward extension of British influence, between 1874 and 1888, from its base at Singapore. During this period Perak, Selangor, Negri Sembilan, and Pahang became British protectorates, and in 1896 these four petty states were united to form the Federated Malay States. In 1909 the area of British control in the peninsula was increased by the establishment of protectorates over four additional states (Trengganu, Kedah, Perlis, and Kelantan), and five years later the state of Johore agreed to accept a British adviser. Since 1909, especially because of the rapid development of plantation rubber, British Malaysia has become an extremely prosperous and profitable possession.

When we turn from questions of foreign policy and territorial expansion, the most impressive feature of Indian history during the half-century which followed the establishment of the direct rule of the crown was the progress achieved in the development of communications, public-welfare services, and modern education. Under the company's rule some efforts had been made to develop irrigation as an insurance against drought; a few miles of railway had been constructed; some three thousand miles of telegraph had been set up; and in the year of the mutiny provision had been made for the establishment of modern universities at Calcutta, Madras, and Bombay.

Under the new regime all these undertakings were carried on with increased energy. In 1880 the area under irrigation in the Punjab and in Sind amounted to some six million acres; by 1902 this acreage had been doubled. In 1880 the few miles of railway existing at the time of the mutiny had increased to nearly ten thousand miles, and this mileage had nearly doubled by the end of the century. These two developments have done much to safeguard against, or to enable the government to cope with, the recurrent famines which have throughout all ages been a scourge to India's people. In 1864 a beginning was made in public sanitation by the appointment of sanitary boards in each presidency. The first boards were concerned primarily with measures for safeguarding the health of the armed forces, but this step marked the inauguration of a service which has helped to improve living conditions and to check the spread of disease among the entire population.

Of particular importance during the period under review was the development in the field of modern education. Institutions of higher learning were established in all parts of India, not only in the areas under British administration but also in a number of the self-governing Indian states. Although the languages, literature, and philosophy of their native land were not wholly neglected, the students in the Indian universities displayed especial zeal for the acquisition of purely Western knowledge, devoting much of their time to the English language, natural science, history, political theory, economics, and law. The result of this education has been to provide India with a large number of capable officials, lawyers, teachers, and political leaders. But it has also inspired thousands of Indians with a belief in their ability to dispense with British rule and to manage for themselves the political and economic affairs of the nation.

By the act of 1853, which renewed for the last time the charter of the East India Company, Parliament had created a Legislative Council to assist the governor-general in the enactment of such laws as might be necessary for the government of the company's possessions. In 1861 a new act of Parliament revised the organization of this body, which was now to consist of the viceroy's Executive Council with not less than six nor more than twelve additional members. The additional members were to be appointed by the viceroy, and not more than half of them were to be government officials. The Legislative Council had little actual power, since its decisions were subject to veto by the viceroy and by the Secretary of State for India; but in 1862 Lord Canning, then viceroy, took advantage of the absence of any racial limitation upon his appointing power and named three Indians as non-official members of the body. The 1861 act established similar legislative councils, with even less real power, for the provinces of Bombay and Madras, and here also the provincial governors promptly adopted the policy of appointing Indian members. In 1892 Parliament again modified the composition of the viceroy's Legislative Council by providing that the additional members should number not less than ten nor more than sixteen. The same act also enlarged the provincial legislative councils. The most important provision of this act,

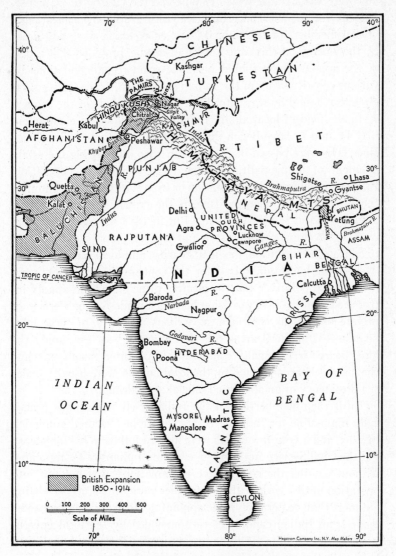

The Development of British India

however, was a clause which empowered the viceroy to make permanent regulations concerning the future appointment of non-official members of the council. The rules which were laid down by the viceroy, at this time Lord Lansdowne, provided that a part of the appointments should be made upon recommendations by various constituencies of the Indian population. The elective principle thus found its way into the selection of a part of the council.

In the field of local affairs Indian participation in government may be said to have begun during the days of the company rule, since laws were passed in 1842 and in 1850 authorizing the establishment of municipalities in the larger centers of population. Little resulted from this legislation or from the attempt of Canning, the first viceroy under the rule of the crown, to encourage the growth of local self-government. But in 1870 serious efforts were made to develop local interest in and supervision of "funds devoted to education, sanitation, medical, charity, and local public works." At first the bodies organized for the control of such affairs were primarily appointive; but the elective principle was gradually introduced, and by 1884 provision had been made for the election of private persons as chairmen, as well as members, of these local boards. In the rural areas this development was less rapid: the local boards were usually composed of appointed members, while the district boards, elected by the local boards, were usually under the presidency of an appointed official as chairman.

Until 1879 membership in the Indian civil service was practically impossible for Indians. S. N. Tagore had secured admission in 1863, and a very few others were able to follow in his footsteps; but the Civil Service Act of 1870, enabling Indians to be appointed without passing the competitive examinations, was not put into operation until 1879. At that date rules were drawn up permitting not more than 20 per cent of the appointments in any one year to be made from Indian candidates recommended by the local government boards. In spite of this new provision the Europeans continued to constitute an overwhelming majority in the civil service.[1]

[1] H. H. Dodwell, in *A Sketch of the History of India*, p. 217, states that between 1867 and 1903 the number of Europeans receiving salaries of over 1000 rupees ($400) a month rose from 638 to 1278.

These extremely cautious extensions of the right to participation in governmental affairs failed to satisfy the aspirations of the Indian people, who with the development of modern education were becoming increasingly political-minded and correspondingly unwilling to acquiesce in the assumption of European superiority. In 1878 the Indian government passed the Vernacular Press Act, which required the editor of any publication in an Oriental language to give bond not to publish articles objectionable to the government. Four years later Lord Ripon, the new viceroy, repealed the Press Act, and the vernacular papers in all parts of India became the medium of a widespread agitation for more extensive grants of self-government.

In December, 1885, Indian discontent was made manifest by the organization of the Indian National Congress, a self-constituted body of outstanding leaders who assembled to discuss the political condition of the country and to suggest necessary changes. At its first meeting the congress was decidedly moderate in tone; its members, fully appreciating the substantial benefits of British rule, were primarily interested in establishing, by the "constitutional" method of constructive criticism, a possible basis of co-operation with the British authorities for the increase of those benefits. Even at this first meeting, however, the congress put on record a far-reaching program of reform. It demanded the abolition of the Council of India and the establishment of simultaneous examinations in England and in India for the Indian civil service; it attacked the excessive military expenditure and the oppressive salt tax; it proposed that Indians be granted commissioned offices in the Indian army; it insisted that the legislative councils be enlarged; and it demanded the introduction of the elective principle for these councils.[1]

During the first twenty years of its existence, 1885–1904, the Indian National Congress, although handicapped by the fact that it contained few delegates from the Moslem part of the population, steadily increased its prestige. Originally composed of some seventy members, all of whom had attended merely as irresponsible volunteers, it developed into a truly representative body

[1] As we have seen (p. 644), these demands were partially met in 1892.

whose several hundred members, elected by various public or semipublic groups in all parts of the country, reflected with reasonable accuracy the wishes of the Hindus. Throughout this period of development the early leaders were able to maintain control, and the congress, in co-operation with liberal-minded Britons in India and Great Britain, continued to seek its ends by nonviolent means. Even during the late 1890's, however, the increasingly representative character of the organization had resulted in the appearance of a strong "left wing" minority, advocates of direct action and terrorism as the best methods of forcing compliance with India's demands. The opening years of the new century saw rapid growth in the strength of the left wing, and the meeting of 1904 was the last occasion on which the moderate leaders were able to exercise effective control over the action of the congress.

In 1906 a combination of circumstances convinced the British government that the time had come for conceding to the Indian people a more important share in the administration of their country's affairs. At this time the success of Japan in her war with Russia had given a fresh impetus to the nationalistic movement in India, as in other parts of the Far East, and Lord Curzon, the recent viceroy, had aroused violent protest by two unpopular measures: the Universities Act of 1904[1] and the partition of Bengal in 1905.

As a result of these conditions the new viceroy, Lord Minto, proposed certain reforms which met the approval of Lord Morley, the Secretary of State for India; a new Indian Councils Act was accordingly introduced into Parliament and passed in the spring of 1909. By the new act, commonly known as the Morley-Minto Reform, the viceroy's Legislative Council was enlarged to a membership of sixty, of whom thirty-three were to be appointed by the viceroy, while the remaining twenty-seven were to be elected. The provincial legislative councils of Bombay, Bengal, Madras, and the United Provinces were similarly enlarged to fifty members,

[1] The Universities Act modified the constitution of the executive bodies of the universities and provided for official inspection of the affiliated colléges; it was popularly regarded as an attempt to fetter the academic independence of these institutions.

and in each of these it was provided that the elected members should be in the majority.

In view of the fact that antagonism existed between Moslem and Hindu, provision was made, by the system of "communal representation," for securing to minority groups in the several provinces, Moslem or Hindu as the case might be, adequate (and numerically disproportionate) representation in the provincial and central legislative assemblies. Similar provision was also made for the representation of the European community, of the universities, and of special economic groups.

In 1907, while the reforms were still under discussion, Lord Morley appointed two Indians to membership in the council of the Secretary of State for India. As soon as the act had been passed, the viceroy appointed an Indian member to his own Executive Council, and Indian members were subsequently appointed to the executive councils of Bengal, Madras, Bombay, and Bihar and Orissa.

Although the new arrangement fell far short of putting political control into Indian hands, it gave to the representatives of the Indian people some measure of real influence in governmental affairs. The Indian minority members of the viceroy's Executive Council and of the Supreme Legislative Council could secure a hearing, if not acceptance, for a non-European point of view, while the majorities in the provincial legislative councils could, and frequently did, make public their dissent by passing resolutions of disapproval with regard to taxation and other questions of internal administration. After fifty-one years of crown rule the British government admitted that it could hold India only by conceding to the Indian people some share in the administration of their affairs.

In 1911, for the purpose of further strengthening the bond of loyalty between the Indian people and the British crown, George V and Mary—the king-emperor and his queen-empress—paid a royal visit to the country. Never before had a reigning British sovereign set foot on Indian soil, and on December 12, 1911, a great durbar (court) was held at Delhi, the ancient Mogul capital. Here, surrounded by his British and Indian officials and by a brilliant assemblage of ruling Indian princes, the King-Emperor proclaimed that Delhi would be henceforth the seat of his viceroy's government. The general feeling of satisfaction resulting from the 1909 reforms and from the royal visit notably improved the Indian situation, and three years later, on the outbreak of the World War, an overwhelming majority of the Indian population rallied with enthusiasm to the support of the empire against its foreign foes.

THE DUTCH IN THE MALAY ARCHIPELAGO

In the Far Eastern insular possessions of Holland—an empire which comprises the greater part of the Malay Archipelago[1]— such economic and social reforms as have occurred since the middle of the nineteenth century have come almost purely as the result of humanitarian agitation in the ruling country. The greater part of the population under Dutch rule has offered little opposition to foreign domination and has taken little part in the process by which the harshness of this domination has been modified. Only in the Mohammedan state of Achin, in northwestern Sumatra, have the Dutch during the last eighty years found themselves confronted by an organized opposition of sufficient strength to have any serious effect upon their policy.

As we have seen in an earlier chapter, it was only in 1848, as a result of the constitutional reforms of that year, that the Estates-General of the Netherlands obtained a legal right to interfere in the administration of the overseas possessions; prior to that date the king and his ministers were responsible to no one for their actions and decisions relating to this great empire in the East. Even after this constitutional change had taken place, it was several years before the Estates-General began to make itself felt in colonial questions. Few of its members were qualified to deal with matters of colonial policy; and although there was a general feeling that something should be done for the reform of glaring abuses, no one knew where to begin.

---

[1] The northern part of the island of Borneo became a British possession during the nineteenth century, and in 1884 the eastern portion of New Guinea was divided between the British and the Germans.

In 1854 a beginning was made by the adoption of a colonial constitution which laid down the general principles upon which the colonial government was to be based. Among other important provisions this document provided for the abolition of slavery, the establishment of institutions for the education of the subject peoples, the leasing of unused lands to European planters, the imposition of a land tax, and the regulation of the hitherto almost unlimited demands for forced labor.

Even after this reform program had been committed to paper, some time elapsed before any specific improvements were made in the administration of the island possessions; but in 1860 a liberal government came into power at the Hague and undertook to translate the program into a series of definite enactments. In the first year of its tenure of power the new government enacted a civil-service law whereby the colonial administration was completely reformed by the establishment of a body of competent civil servants. In 1867 it abolished the system of "land grants"—involving absolute lordship over the people on the land—which had been utilized by the earlier governments in lieu of the payment of salaries. Between 1860 and 1865 the "culture system" of securing staple export commodities—the system of compelling individuals and communities, under penalties for failure, to furnish prescribed quantities of a certain commodity at an arbitrarily fixed price—was abandoned with respect to tea, indigo, tobacco, and cinnamon. By 1870 the culture system had been abolished for everything except sugar and coffee. Between 1878 and 1890 the production of sugar by forced labor gradually gave way to production by free labor, and after 1900 the forced production of coffee gradually disappeared.

Every step taken by the liberal government in the abolition of this archaic method of production was bitterly opposed by the conservative business element, which feared that any change would spell ruin for Dutch commerce. These fears certainly were not justified. The decade between 1855 and 1865, which included the first five years of reform, saw the actual imports into and the exports from Java—the most important of the islands—increased by more than 30 per cent, while the twenty-five years from 1875, when the reform program was almost completed, until the end of the century witnessed a 47 per cent increase in the value of exports from the entire region of Dutch Malaysia and a 56 per cent increase in the value of goods imported into these possessions. In other words, under the reformed system the subject peoples not only produced an increasing volume of commodities for export but also provided an even more rapidly increasing market for foreign products.

The economic reforms in the Dutch East Indies were accompanied by the establishment of a system of public education. Prior to the drafting of the colonial constitution in 1854 the Dutch government appropriated for the education of the non-European population an annual amount of less than fifteen thousand dollars, and this sum was devoted entirely to the training of the necessary subordinate officials. In 1866 the liberal administration in power at the Hague launched a serious program for the education of the common people. Normal schools were founded in 1872, by which date the expenditure for the education of non-Europeans had risen to about two hundred thousand dollars per year; and by the end of the century the annual expenditure for this item was in the neighborhood of a million dollars. For a region containing a population of approximately fifty million people even this sum was ridiculously inadequate; but a real start had been made, and the early years of the twentieth century saw a steady extension of the government's efforts to provide the mass of the people with at least a primary education.

By the irony of fate the one serious struggle in which the Dutch became involved after 1848, the war against the Sumatran state of Achin, resulted in part from the attempt to carry out in that portion of their domains the enlightened reforms which have proved so beneficial elsewhere. The Achinese rose in arms in 1873 against the Dutch attempt to abolish debt slavery, an institution which had long existed among the Mohammedan states of the archipelago; and the war dragged on for more than thirty years. In 1905 the Sultan of Achin surrendered to the Dutch armies, but it was not until two years later that the termination of guerrilla warfare finally restored peace to the troubled region of the island.

Following the termination of the costly and long-continuing war with Achin, the Dutch East Indies enjoyed increasing prosperity and a comparative freedom from political controversy. The prosperity of the Dutch Islands, as of the neighboring regions of British Malaysia, was greatly increased by the rapid development of plantation rubber, which after the beginning of the present century largely replaced the wild rubber of Brazil and the Congo. Although the British port of Singapore was the principal center of the rubber trade, a very large part of the world's rubber supply was produced in Java, Sumatra, and Dutch Borneo. Among the people under Dutch rule this growing prosperity was reflected in an increase of population rather than in a rising standard of living, but the increased consumption of European commodities indicated that some progress had been made in spreading among the people an appreciation of various Western products.

The French in Indo-China

By the end of 1867 the French, as the result of ten years of activity (see page 484), had succeeded in obtaining a permanent foothold in the southeastern part of Indo-China. In 1862 the government of Annam had concluded a treaty ceding to France the region known as Cochin China, and the following year saw the establishment of a French protectorate over what remained of the once important state of Cambodia. In 1867 Siam recognized the protectorate over Cambodia, and in the same year the French forced the Annamese to cede the three districts of southern Annam bordering on Cochin China.

After 1867 the government of Emperor Napoleon III was so fully occupied with European affairs as to have little time or energy for Far Eastern adventures; two years after the termination of the Franco-Prussian War the newly established republic of France turned its attention to the expansion of the French interests in Indo-China. The French-Annamese treaty of 1874, like the Japanese-Korean treaty signed two years later, marked the beginning of the process by which the Chinese Empire was to be deprived of one of its ancient vassals (see pages 557–558), but after 1885 the expansion of French Indo-China was mainly at the expense of its neighbor on the west, Siam. In 1893 the murder of a French officer on Siamese soil gave the French government a pretext for making demands upon Siam. Hitherto the watershed east of the Mekong valley had been recognized as marking the western boundary of the French possessions, but in October, 1893, the Siamese government was forced to cede to France all the territory to the east of the river. In 1904 Siam was obliged to cede to Cambodia two provinces lying on the western frontier of Cambodia, and three years later France forced the cession of the land between the Mekong and the hills to the west of that river, thus completing its acquisition of the entire lower-Mekong valley.

For about a decade after the close of the Tongking war with China the government of French Indo-China reflected little credit upon the French Republic. Swarms of greedy officials, ignorant of local customs and languages, imposed excessive taxes which roused the people to frequent outbreaks against French rule. In 1896, however, an honest and energetic official, M. Paul Doumer,[1] was appointed to the post of governor-general. It was under this new administration that the policy of expansion into the Mekong valley was carried to a conclusion, but M. Doumer also distinguished himself by his efficient management of internal affairs. The colonial finances were reformed, the worst of the old group of officials were dismissed, and the people under French rule began at last to enjoy the benefits of an honest administration of justice. By 1907, when the French had completed the westward extension of their possessions, the program of internal reform had removed many of the old causes for popular discontent and had greatly strengthened the position of France in the peninsula.

In spite of this improvement in the situation the French statesmen were greatly disturbed by the outcome of the Russo-Japanese War. Annam, like other parts of the Far East, soon began to stir with a new spirit of nationalism and to echo the cry "Asia for the Asiatics." In response to the demonstrations of nationalism the French government made prompt concessions which, for the mo-

---

[1] On May 13, 1931, M. Doumer was elected to the presidency of France; less than a year later, May 6, 1932, he fell at the hands of an assassin.

ment, appeared to satisfy the people. But the internal unrest was not the only cause for French anxiety. During the war France, although remaining nominally neutral, had given a good deal of assistance to the Russians. Japan had protested at the time against this unfriendly action, and after the close of the war the French had some reason to fear a Japanese attack upon Indo-China. This fear was finally dispelled by the conclusion on June 10, 1907, of a Franco-Japanese agreement wherein the two contracting powers pledged themselves to respect reciprocally each other's rights and special interests in the Far East. Two years later a similar agreement, adjusting their rival claims in the Indo-Chinese peninsula, was entered into by France and Great Britain. With the conclusion of these two agreements France felt reasonably secure against outside attacks upon her Eastern possessions.

THE INDEPENDENCE OF SIAM

Siam, the one state in Indo-China and one of the few states in all Asia that has succeeded in preserving its autonomy, owes its independence, at least in part, to its geographical position. By 1886 Siam was almost completely surrounded by the possessions of France and Great Britain. The French on the east had completed in 1885 the establishment of their authority from the southern point of Cochin China to the Tongking-Yunnan frontier. On the west the British absorption of Burma, commenced in 1826 by the acquisition of the Tenasserim coast, had just been completed by the annexation of Upper Burma, while British Malaysia, at the extremity of the Malay peninsula, was beginning to encroach upon territories which formerly had acknowledged the overlordship of the Siamese king. The mountainous frontier between Siam and British Burma lessened the danger of any trouble with Great Britain in that direction, but the British in the south and the French on the east were both ready to seize any opportunity for expansion.

Fortunately for Siam, Britain and France until after the commencement of the twentieth century were bitterly jealous of each other, and each was anxious to preserve at least a portion of Siam as a buffer state. In 1893, when Siam was forced to surrender the left bank of the Mekong, the aggressive action of France nearly resulted in war between that country and Great Britain. Three years later the two Western powers concluded a treaty guaranteeing the integrity of the remaining territory of Siam and marking out the kingdom into three zones. The eastern zone was to be a French "sphere of influence," the western zone, including the Malay peninsula, was to be a British "sphere," while the central (Menam) valley was to be neutral.

As a guaranty of Siam's territorial integrity the Anglo-French treaty of 1896 appears to have been subject to "necessary rectifications of the frontier." In 1904 and in 1907, as we have seen above, the French secured additional Siamese territory to the west of the Mekong, while the British, in 1907 and again in 1909, compensated themselves by establishing their protectorate over fresh areas in the Malay peninsula. The process of paring down the kingdom appears, however, to have ended with the last cession to Great Britain; and although the division into three zones was reasserted by the Anglo-French agreement of 1904, the tendency of the two powers to interfere in Siamese affairs steadily decreased after 1909.

Although the continuance of Siamese independence is attributable in no small part to the fact of Anglo-French rivalry, even this fact by itself probably would not have sufficed to prevent the eventual partition of the country between its two powerful neighbors. From the accession of Phra Maha Mongkut (Rama IV) in 1851, however, Siam was ruled by a succession of unusually capable monarchs whose continued policy of internal reform served to eliminate all pretexts for foreign aggression. On the death of Rama IV, in 1868, there succeeded to the throne Phra Maha Chulalonkorn (Rama V), who reigned until 1910.

In matters of internal policy the long reign of Rama V may be compared not unfavorably with the almost exactly contemporaneous Meiji era in Japan. Although Siam remained essentially agricultural in its economic activities, the forty-two years of this reign saw the institution or continuance of a series of reforms which affected every aspect of the national life. Slavery was abolished; the law codes and courts were reformed; a system of public education was established; internal communications were improved by building roads, railroads, and telegraph lines; and the maintenance of order was assured by the organization of a small but efficient modern army.

Like Japan also, although less rapidly, Siam was able to free herself from practically all traces of foreign extraterritorial jurisdiction[1] within her frontiers. In 1903 an American, Mr. E. H. Strobel, was employed by the Siamese government as adviser-general, to succeed M. G. Rolin-Jaequemyns, a Belgian who had formerly held the post. Acting on Mr. Strobel's advice, the Siamese in 1904 concluded the treaty with France whereby the French secured territory to the west of the Mekong. In return for this concession the French government abandoned its extraterritorial jurisdiction over protégés and Asiatic subjects. On the death of Mr. Strobel, in 1906, the position of adviser-general was filled by the promotion of his assistant, Mr. J. I. Westengard, also an American. On July 15, 1909, after negotiations lasting two years, the new adviser secured from the British an even more important concession: Great Britain abolished her existing courts in Siam and placed all British subjects in Siam under the jurisdiction of Siamese courts, with a provision for diplomatic revision in case of injustice. Siam thus secured an opportunity to demonstrate to the Western world the honesty and efficiency of her modern judicial institutions. Complete abolition of foreign extraterritorial jurisdiction was still to be achieved, but a long step had been taken toward that goal.

SUGGESTED REFERENCES

BOOKWALTER, J. W. Siberia and Central Asia.

CABATON, A. Java, Sumatra, and the Dutch East Indies.

CUMMING, SIR J. (editor). Political India, 1832–1932.

DAY, C. The Dutch in Java.

DIGUET, E. J. J. Annam et Indo-Chine française.

DUTT, R. C. The Economic History of India in the Victorian Age.

FRANKE, O. Die Grossmächte in Ostasien von 1894 bis 1914.

HANNA, H. B. The Second Afghan War.

ILBERT, SIR C. P. The Government of India.

[1] Extraterritoriality in Siam was established by the treaties of 1855 and 1856.

KRAUSSE, A. Russia in Asia.

LAWTON, L. Empires of the Far East.

MAHAN, A. T. The Problem of Asia.

PASVOLSKY, L. Russia in the Far East.

REINSCH, P. S. Intellectual and Political Currents in the Far East.

ROBERTS, S. H. History of French Colonial Policy, 1870–1925.

SCOTT, J. G. France and Tongking.

SWETTENHAM, SIR F. British Malaya.

TORCHIANA, H. A. V. C. Tropical Holland.

VANDENBOSCH, A. The Dutch East Indies.

YAKHONTOFF, V. A. Russia and the Soviet Union in the Far East.

YOUNGHUSBAND, SIR F. India and Tibet.

XXVII

The United States as an Asiatic Power

America's New Interest in the Orient · The Philippines during the Nineteenth Century · Spanish Policy: Liberalism and Repression · The Philippine Revolution of 1896 · The Spanish-American War · Philippine Co-operation with the Americans · Cession of the Philippines to the United States · Organization of a Philippine Republic · Resistance to American Rule · The Establishment of a Civilian Government · The Friars' Lands · Education · Economic Development · Philippine Nationalism and the Extension of Political Rights · The Filipinization of the Administration · The Philippines in 1914 · America's New Orientation

FROM the establishment of its independence until the outbreak of the Civil War in 1861 the United States played an active and important part in the affairs of the Far East. During the four-year struggle between North and South, however, the Confederate commerce destroyers swept from the sea the greater part of the American merchant marine, while the quarter of a century which followed the close of the war found the American people so fully occupied with the task of developing the stupendous resources of their own West that they had little time or energy for exploring the economic possibilities of Asia.

It was during this quarter of a century and largely as a result of these circumstances that American policy in the Orient assumed its traditionally "negative" aspect. Anson Burlingame at Peking, Townsend Harris and Robert H. Pruyn at Tokyo, because of the comparative unimportance of American commercial interests, were able to assume an attitude of detachment and to urge upon their colleagues a policy of co-operative nonaggression, while Burlingame, as we have seen, later carried the same doctrine to the capitals of the various powers enjoying treaty relations with China.

Shortly before the close of the nineteenth century it became apparent that economic conditions in the United States had undergone a definite change. The Census of 1890 showed that the "frontier line"—the line separating the more populous area from the region containing a population of less than one person per square mile—had disappeared. The West still contained thousands of unoccupied square miles; but the free land no longer constituted a great contiguous area on the map, and it was on the verge of total disappearance. At the same time the United States, hitherto a borrowing nation, began to have a surplus of capital; there was so much money seeking investment that sound bonds reached prices at which they returned only 2½ or 3 per cent to the purchaser. Under these conditions the owners of surplus capital began to develop a new interest in foreign fields for investment, while the expanding industrial system of the United States began to consider the need of finding fresh markets for its output.

Up to this time the territory of the United States was wholly continental, but for many years the American government had looked upon the island kingdom of Hawaii as territory which should never be allowed to fall into the hands of any foreign power. In January, 1893, a revolution organized by the American business community of Honolulu overthrew Queen Liliuokalani and established a republic which promptly concluded with the American government a treaty of annexation. The treaty with Hawaii was submitted to the Senate by President Harrison on February 14, 1893; but before any action had been taken, Harrison was succeeded by Grover Cleveland, who disapproved of the treaty, and on March 9 it was withdrawn from the Senate's consideration.

On the far side of the Pacific, also, the United States during the early nineties was giving evidence of renewed interest in the course of events. Although the Cleveland administration in October, 1894, rejected a British proposal for a five-power intervention in the Sino-Japanese War, the American representatives at Tokyo and Peking a month later made an independent offer of American good offices for the restoration of peace. At the conclusion of the war the American minister at Peking drew up and presented to the Department of State an elaborate program for the reorganization of China under foreign supervision, while the American business men at the treaty ports displayed far more activity than they or their predecessors had shown during the past three decades.

In April, 1898, a long controversy between the United States
and Spain, arising out of conditions in Cuba, culminated in the
outbreak of the Spanish-American War. Although the controversy
out of which the war had developed related exclusively to the
Caribbean area, the hostilities promptly spread to the Far East.
Spain had at Manila a squadron of warships which might easily
inflict damage on American trade, and Commodore Dewey, commanding the Far Eastern naval forces of the United States, received orders to destroy this squadron. On the night of April 30
Dewey's ships entered Manila Bay, and on the following day the
Spanish naval force was destroyed.

Under three centuries of Spanish rule and under the unifying
influence of Catholic missions the Filipino people had made real
progress in the direction of national unity before the end of the
nineteenth century. Although using a variety of local dialects, the
overwhelming majority of the islanders spoke essentially one language; during the Spanish regime, as a result of improved interisland communication, the local differences in this language had
steadily diminished, while the increasing use of a corrupted Spanish
—"bamboo" Spanish—as a medium of intercourse had given an
added impulse to the development of cultural unity. Save for
the Mohammedan Moros and a small number of still-pagan hill
tribes the Filipinos had long since been converted to Christianity,
and the educational institutions maintained by the church had
become, contrary to the intentions of the ecclesiastical authorities,
a medium through which their students had gained some familiarity
with the nonreligious thought of the West. Through this medium
the ideas of post-Napoleonic Europe, including the epoch-making
idea of nationalism, had gradually gained a foothold in the islands.

After Spain's loss of her continental possessions in the Western
Hemisphere the government at Madrid departed from its earlier
economic policy with respect to its Far Eastern possessions and
endeavored to exploit more fully the rich commercial possibilities
of the Philippines. In 1830 the port of Manila was opened to foreign trade, and this concession proved so profitable to Spain that
the period from 1855 to 1862 saw the opening of five additional
Philippine ports.

Western Expansion in the East Indies

The rapid development of foreign commerce resulted in the rise of an influential Filipino middle class, increasingly interested in political questions. This growth of commercial and political interests was accompanied by a decline in the influence of the church, especially with respect to education. There was a demand for schools in which the children should be educated by the state, and in 1863 the Spanish government instituted a public-school system which was intended to make it possible for every Filipino boy and girl to secure a primary education. Religious as well as secular subjects were to be taught in the newly established schools, but the clergy, although still retaining a voice in the management of school affairs, were no longer in complete control of education.

Unfortunately for Spain and for the Philippines, the Spanish government appeared incapable of adopting a settled policy with regard to its possessions. The Philippine people were not anti-Spanish, and a consistently liberal policy would have resulted in the development of an enlightened and loyal Filipino nation; a policy of firm repression, on the other hand, might have maintained indefinitely the old absolute power of crown and church. Instead of following either policy the Spanish vacillated between liberalism and reaction. For a while the Filipinos would be given reason to expect far-reaching reforms and an extension of self-government; then these hopes would be rudely disappointed by the appointment of a dictatorial governor and by the unchecked ravages of corrupt subordinate officials. The irritation caused by the nonfulfillment of their hopes caused many of the Filipinos to lose sight of the numerous reforms which actually were instituted, while the harsh methods employed by some of their rulers created a belief that all Spaniards were cruel tyrants.

Few of the educated Filipinos during the early period of agitation regarded complete separation from Spain as either desirable or attainable, but they were insistent in their demands for general reforms, including the establishment of Philippine autonomy and the right of representation in the Spanish Cortes. As time went on, however, the Filipino leaders grew more and more revolutionary in their beliefs. Even the more conservative leaders became convinced that it was useless to look to the government for the desired reforms, while the more radical element began to organize revolutionary societies whose members were bound by oaths of obedience, brotherhood, and secrecy.

In August, 1896, the Spanish authorities secured definite information concerning the organization and the activities of the Katipunan, the most powerful of the revolutionary societies. The consequent arrest and execution of a large number of prominent reform leaders, some of whom were innocent of any connection with the Katipunan, resulted in the outbreak of open revolution. Issuing a declaration of independence in which they recited the manifold evils of Spanish rule, the Filipino revolutionaries took the field and for just a year maintained a fairly even struggle against the Spanish forces. In August, 1897, terms of peace were agreed upon; the government pledged itself to the immediate inauguration of certain fundamental reforms, while General Emilio Aguinaldo and a number of the other revolutionary leaders went into exile. The agreement of August, 1897, proved to be merely a truce. The Spanish authorities showed little intention of carrying out their promised reforms, and at the moment of Dewey's arrival in Manila Bay the Filipino leaders were busily organizing for a fresh insurrection.

For about ten weeks after the destruction of the Spanish fleet the Americans, although complete masters of Manila Bay and of Philippine territorial waters, had no troops available for land operations against the Spanish; not until the middle of July did the first detachments of the American army arrive in the islands to follow up Commodore Dewey's naval victory. During this interval, however, the absence of American land forces was made good by the active co-operation of the Filipino *insurrectos*. General Aguinaldo, who at the outbreak of the Spanish-American War was at Singapore, promptly returned to Manila, arriving there on May 19. An interview between Aguinaldo and the American consul at Singapore had convinced the former that the United States intended to aid the Filipinos in throwing off the Spanish yoke, and Commodore Dewey, although noncommittal as to the policy of his government, welcomed the co-operation of the Filipino insurgents and provided them with military supplies for use against the common enemy. By the end of May, Aguinaldo had organized a strong force, and the Filipinos embarked upon an energetic campaign against the Spanish detachments outside the capital. During the month of July the American forces at Manila were strengthened by the arrival of some ten thousand soldiers, and on August 13 the land and naval forces of the United States, with the assistance of the insurgents, compelled the Spanish to surrender Manila.

A few hours before the capitulation of the Philippine capital the governments of Spain and the United States had concluded an armistice, and in due course of time the plenipotentiaries of the two countries met at Paris for the conclusion of a permanent treaty. At the outbreak of the war and, apparently, even at the conclusion of the hostilities the government of the United States had little intention of securing possession of the Philippines. Indeed, some of the American peace delegates were strongly opposed to the acquisition of the islands and urged that they be either returned to Spain or given their independence. On the other hand, the four months which elapsed between the signing of the armistice and the conclusion of the peace treaty saw the development in certain American circles of a strong sentiment in favor of retaining the islands.

The strongest argument for the retention of the islands was based upon their possible importance in the development of American Far Eastern commerce. During the course of the war the United States had at last annexed the Hawaiian Islands; but even this new outpost in the Pacific was far distant from the potentially great Asiatic market, while France, Germany, Great Britain, and Russia, through the possession of ports on the Chinese coast, were so situated as to enjoy more convenient access to Chinese trade. The acquisition of the Philippines, it was believed, would put the merchants of the United States on a footing of equality with their European rivals as well as with the Japanese.

To those who urged that the Filipinos were as capable of self-government as the Cubans and that the United States should secure and guarantee Philippine independence the advocates of annexation replied that the two cases were not parallel. Whereas Cuba, it was argued, was protected by the Monroe Doctrine against any possible foreign interference, the Philippines, if accorded their independence, would inevitably fall into the hands of the Japanese or of some European power. In the end the advocates of annexation had their way, and the treaty of peace—signed on December 10, 1898, at Paris and ratified by the United States on February 6, 1899[1]—ceded to the United States the Spanish possessions in the Far East.

To the Filipino leaders the destruction of Spanish power in the islands could have but one result: the establishment of a sovereign and independent Philippine state. On May 24, 1898, five days after his return from exile, General Aguinaldo proclaimed himself dictator of a provisional government, and on June 12 the independence

[1] The exchange of ratifications took place on April 11, 1899.

of the Philippines was solemnly proclaimed. In September a congress assembled for the purpose of drafting a constitution. This task was completed on November 29, and on January 21, 1899, Aguinaldo as president of the Philippine republic promulgated the new instrument of government. In the meantime, however, the treaty transferring the archipelago to the United States had been concluded, and the American army, steadily reinforced by fresh contingents from home, had established its power in a number of the smaller islands as well as at the city of Manila. Although the treaty had not yet been ratified, President McKinley instructed the commander of the American forces that the sovereignty of the United States over the Philippines must be maintained.

The claims of the Filipinos and of the United States were so diametrically opposed as to admit no possible compromise. The Filipino leaders refused to recognize that Spain had any power to transfer the islands to the United States. They asserted that by the time the treaty was signed the Spanish authority had been completely overthrown, that a *de facto* government had been created, and that Spain therefore was no longer in possession of an actual sovereignty which could be transferred by treaty. The government of the United States, on the other hand, held that the Filipinos had not actually gained their independence from Spain, that the withdrawal of the American forces would have been followed by the suppression of the attempt to establish a republic, and that Spain at the time of the signing of the treaty was therefore the actual as well as the legal sovereign of the islands.

On February 4, 1899, two days before the United States Senate agreed to the ratification of the treaty with Spain, hostilities broke out between the Filipino forces and the American army of occupation. For a short time the Filipino leaders were able to maintain an organized government and to co-ordinate the operations of their armed forces; but in November, 1899, the last of their successive capitals was captured, and all semblance of a government disappeared. There followed a period of guerrilla warfare in northern Luzon and in some of the other islands. With the capture of President Aguinaldo in March, 1901, most of the resistance ended, but the last republican leaders did not surrender until June, 1902.

Even before the complete suppression of Filipino resistance the American authorities had inaugurated a program of far-reaching reforms such as the people of the islands had vainly attempted to secure from the Spanish. In March, 1899, a special commission appointed by President McKinley arrived at Manila for the purpose of securing reliable information upon which the government would be able to base its policy. The report of this commission was submitted early in 1900, and in June of the same year a permanent Philippine Commission, presided over by Judge William H. Taft, arrived in the Philippines. In several parts of the islands hostilities between the Americans and the Filipinos were still in progress; these districts were left under the direct rule of the military authorities, and martial law prevailed. In the regions where military operations had been brought to an end, however, the Taft commission promptly proceeded to organize and establish the machinery of civil government. On September 1, 1900, the commission was vested with legislative power, subject to the approval of the President of the United States; in this capacity its first act was to appropriate 2,000,000 pesos ($1,000,000) for the improvement of roads and bridges.

During the course of the next ten months the local administration in the pacified provinces was completely reorganized. Provincial and municipal governments (elected by the suffrage of the male inhabitants over twenty-one years of age who could read and write English or Spanish or who were the owners of taxable property) were established. The judiciary was reorganized, and in the newly established courts capable Filipino jurists were appointed to high positions. In January, 1901, the commission showed its appreciation of the importance of education as a factor in reorganizing the country, by creating a Department of Education.

By the spring of 1901, as we have seen, the armed resistance to American authority had practically come to an end; the government of the United States therefore decided that the time had come for transferring the supreme power in the islands to the hands of civil authorities. On July 4, 1901, in accordance with this decision, Mr. Taft assumed office as the first civil governor of the islands. In the work of administration Governor Taft was assisted by a council, composed of the four American members of the Philippine Commission and three Filipino members, which functioned as a cabinet and as a legislative body. In the districts where hostilities still continued the military governor retained his former powers until the abolition of that office a year later; but from July 4, 1901, the greater part of the Philippines passed completely under the control of the civil government.

During the two and a half years of Governor Taft's administration the newly organized government did much to lay the foundations for social and economic improvement. To combat the recurrent epidemics of smallpox and cholera a Bureau of Public Health was established, and a beginning was made toward the introduction of modern sanitation in the larger centers of population. The currency, which had steadily depreciated with the decline in the price of silver, was stabilized by the establishment of the gold standard. One of the members of the governor's cabinet was made Secretary of Public Instruction, and subsequently the direction of this department became the special function of the vice-governor.

One of the most difficult problems which Governor Taft was called upon to settle was that of adjusting the conflicting interests of church and state with respect to the extensive lands held, under Spanish rule, by the religious orders. These so-called friars' lands included about four hundred and thirty thousand acres, the income from which went to support the missionary work of the church. Even before the American occupation the relations between the ecclesiastical administrators and their tenants had given rise to much friction, and Governor Taft proposed that the government put an end to the trouble by purchasing the land from the church authorities and selling it to the occupants. After negotiations which involved a visit to Rome by Mr. Taft the matter was satisfactorily adjusted; the Philippine government bought the land for the sum of about seven and a quarter million dollars and then proceeded to dispose of it in small parcels to the Filipino peasants. The equitable adjustment of this affair resulted in transforming an important element of the agricultural population, much of it in the immediate vicinity of Manila, from serfdom to the status of free landholders.

From the very beginning of their regime the American authorities in the Philippines displayed the deepest interest in the development of education. Even before the conclusion of the treaty with Spain schools for instruction in the English language were established under the auspices of the American army of occupation; and the Taft commission, as we have seen, promptly created a Department of Public Instruction to have oversight over the entire educational system. By the summer of 1901 nearly a thousand American teachers were on their way to the islands, and an organized system of primary, intermediate, and secondary schools patterned after those of the United States had been put into operation. A normal school was established in Manila for the training of Filipino teachers, and in 1908 the system was completed by the establishment of the University of the Philippines. By 1915 there were over six hundred thousand students in the public schools of the islands, about 90 per cent of this number being in the primary grades. The main emphasis was placed upon the schools of primary education, which were giving instruction to about one third of the children of school age; but vocational, secondary, and technical education had not been neglected.

In the treaty of peace between Spain and the United States it was provided that for a period of ten years the American government should refrain from passing any legislation detrimental to the existing rights of non-Americans engaged in the Philippine trade. In spite of this provision, which kept the Philippines during this period outside the American tariff wall, the transfer of sovereignty was followed by rapid economic development of the islands. In part this development was the result of the reforms which have already been noted: the restoration of a sound currency, the improvement of roads and bridges, the curbing of epidemics, and the liberation of the agricultural population from a state of serfdom. The process was greatly facilitated, however, by the influx of large quantities of American capital in search of opportunities for profitable investment. The presence of an abundant supply of capital made it possible to carry out very promptly a number of necessary constructive enterprises. The harbor of Manila was improved by dredging and by building new piers and an extensive breakwater. The construction of a sewerage system for Manila was undertaken, and the city was provided with a more adequate water supply. Several hundred miles of railway were constructed and put into operation, while communications were still further improved by the establishment of additional interisland steamship lines and by the construction of a steadily expanding network of improved roads. New capital also found its way into Philippine industry, especially into the sugar and copra industries, where the introduction of modern machinery of European or American construction greatly increased the output over that of the earlier period.

When the ten-year period fixed by the Spanish treaty had elapsed, the Congress of the United States, by the Payne-Aldrich tariff bill of 1909, promptly brought the Philippines inside the tariff wall. The consequent increase of Philippine trade with the United States was tremendous. Hitherto Philippine tobacco and sugar had competed under a heavy handicap with the domestic and Cuban products; now they were on a basis of complete equality, while copra, hemp, grass linen, and other important items of export enjoyed in the American market advantages over similar products from other parts of the East Indies.

In spite of the extensive rights of local self-government which they enjoyed from the beginning of the American regime the Filipinos continued to look forward to national independence as the ultimate goal of their efforts. Indeed, their successful participation in the management of local and provincial affairs was taken by the Filipino leaders as conclusive proof that they were fully capable of complete self-government, while the material prosperity of the islands was regarded as evidence that the Philippines were entitled to independent national existence. Nowhere in the Orient, therefore, were the consequences of the Russo-Japanese War more promptly felt, and the year 1906 saw the recommencement of a strong nationalist movement for the establishment of Philippine independence.

The American government was not prepared to grant the Philippines independence or home rule, but it was ready to make substantial concessions to the aspirations of the Filipinos. An act of Congress in 1902 had authorized the President to take a census of the islands and two years after the completion of the census, if peace then prevailed, to establish an elective assembly as a branch of the Philippine legislature. The tabulation of the census returns was completed early in 1905, and orders were accordingly issued for the election of a representative body to take place in the summer of 1907. On July 30, 1907, the election took place, and on October 16 the first Philippine Assembly convened. The existing Philippine Commission, now consisting of five Americans and four Filipinos, all appointed by the President, became the upper house of a bicameral legislative body, and the elected Assembly, consisting of eighty-one members, constituted the lower house.

From the close of the Spanish-American War until March, 1913, the direction of American policy remained steadily in the hands of the Republican party; but in the election of 1912 the Democratic party succeeded in electing Woodrow Wilson to the Presidency and in gaining a majority of the seats in both branches of Congress. Inasmuch as the Democrats while out of power had consistently advocated an early grant of independence to the Philippine Islands, the result of this election was hailed with great enthusiasm by the Filipinos. President Wilson was inaugurated in March, 1913, and in October of that year Mr. Francis Burton Harrison, the first Democratic appointee to the post, arrived at Manila to take up his duties as governor-general of the Philippines.

In accordance with the policy advocated by the Democratic party the new administration at this time appointed two additional Filipino members to the Philippine Commission, thus giving the Filipinos control of both branches of the legislature. As the new governor-general immediately announced that he would submit to the decisions of the legislature in all matters, the Filipino statesmen now became, for the first time in their history, fully responsible for the management of the affairs of state. The immediate result of this transfer of authority was a rapid "Filipinization" of all branches of the insular administration. A great number of American officials were removed from office and replaced by Filipinos. This process was bitterly criticized by a majority of the American residents in the Philippines, and dire consequences were predicted. As a matter of fact the new administrative officers did commit a number of blunders, but the anticipated catastrophe never made its appearance.

Ten months after the arrival of Governor-General Harrison and the inauguration of his new policies for the administration of the Philippine government came the outbreak of the World War. Inasmuch as this conflict soon spread to eastern Asia and had far-reaching effects upon the affairs of even such countries as remained neutral, the summer of 1914, in the history of the Far East as in that of Europe, is an appropriate point at which to stop and take stock of the situation.

During the sixteen years following the surrender of the Spanish forces at Manila the cultural, economic, and political life of the Philippines had undergone a complete transformation. Modern means of communication had been developed; improvements in agriculture and industry had contributed to a rapid expansion of commerce; a large class of landless peons had been transformed into substantial agriculturalists tilling their own land; an extensive and steadily developing system of public education had been established; modern methods of sanitation and public health service had greatly reduced the death rate from contagious disease; the machinery of local self-government had been instituted in all parts of the islands; and by 1914 the representative Assembly enjoyed a large measure of control over the administration of general affairs.

Not all the policies adopted during this period by the American authorities had been wholly acceptable to the Filipinos; perhaps not all of them had been wholly beneficial either to the people of the islands or to the United States, but since the autumn of 1902 organized opposition to the new regime had been conspicuously absent. Although occasional difficulties arose with the Moros and with certain of the "uncivilized tribes" of the mountainous interior, the mass of the people of the Philippines, relying upon the frequently repeated assertion that the American tenure was not intended to be permanent, appeared to regard their relationship with the United States as a necessary and not distasteful prelude to ultimate independence.

AMERICA'S NEW ORIENTATION

To the men directing the policies of the United States the acquisition of the Philippine Islands was at the time not an end in itself but merely a means to an end. Important as were the changes in the islands resulting from the institution of the new regime, American statesmen were only incidentally interested in local cultural development or even in the exploitation of the archipelago's natural resources. Reversing the ancient policy of Spain, they intended to transform Manila into the chief commercial metropolis of the Orient, the center from which the "fabrications of American genius" should find their natural outlets in Eastern markets and in which should be assembled "products, brought from the isles of the Orient and the mainland in junks and proas, and thence distributed by American commerce to the markets of the world."

Despite a noticeable increase in commercial activity during the 1890's the influence of America in eastern Asia was, at the outbreak of the Spanish war, relatively insignificant. Partly because of this fact and partly because of preoccupation with the war, the international scramble for concessions and special rights in China during the spring and summer of 1898 attracted little attention in the United States.[1] Less than six months after the war with Spain was officially closed by the exchange (April 11, 1899) of the ratifications of the Paris Treaty, however, the government at Washington inaugurated the "open door" correspondence[2] with the other interested powers and thereby gave the world to understand that America was no longer indifferent to developments and policies which by circumscribing her existing treaty rights in China would lessen the value of her recently acquired commercial outpost in the Far East.

In January, 1900, Senator Beveridge declared:

China is our natural customer. She is nearer to us than to England, Germany, and Russia, the commercial powers of the present and the future. They have moved nearer China by securing permanent bases on her borders; the Philippines give us a base at the door of all the East. . . . Two years ago there was no land in all the world which we could occupy for any pur-

[1] See pages 681–683.   [2] See pages 685–686.

pose. Our commerce was daily turning toward the Orient, and geography and trade developments made necessary our commercial empire over the Pacific. And in that ocean we had no commercial, naval, or military base. Today we have one of the great ocean possessions of the globe, located at the most convenient commercial, naval, and military point of the eastern seas, within hail of India, shoulder to shoulder with China.[1]

Senator Lodge of Massachusetts, speaking to the Senate two months later in justification of the administration's policy, advanced similar arguments which may be briefly summarized as follows: After the Sino-Japanese War it became increasingly evident that Russia was closing in on China and planning to exclude other nations from Chinese markets. This danger became clearer as the months rolled by, but no one saw how America was to assert her rights and interests in the East. The acquisition of Hawaii was obviously the necessary first step in obtaining a just share in the trade of the Pacific. Then came the Spanish war, in which Admiral Dewey by his victory at Manila gave his countrymen the means of solving their problems in the Orient. He made the United States an Eastern power, "with the right to speak and with force behind that right." This new status was already demonstrated by the successful outcome of Secretary Hay's "open door" proposals, for the assent of the other powers "was given to the master of Manila."[2]

The transfer of the Philippines to American jurisdiction, important as were its consequences for the inhabitants of the islands, was therefore equally important for its influences upon the Far Eastern balance of power and upon the general world outlook of the American people. For better or for worse, the United States had once more assumed an active role in the Orient.

SUGGESTED REFERENCES

BARROWS, D. P. A History of the Philippines.
BLOUNT, J. H. The American Occupation of the Philippines.
CHAMBERLIN, F. The Philippine Problem.
COOLIDGE, A. C. The United States as a World Power.
DENNETT, T. Americans in Eastern Asia.

[1] Congressional Record, Vol. 33, pp. 704, 707.
[2] Summarized from the Congressional Record, Vol. 33, pp. 2628–2629.

ELLIOTT, C. B. The Philippines.

FORBES, W. C. The Philippine Islands.

KALAW, M. M. Self-government in the Philippines.

LE ROY, J. A. The Americans in the Philippines.

MILLER, H. H. Economic Conditions in the Philippines.

REYES, J. S. Legislative History of America's Economic Policy toward the Philippines.

RUSSELL, C. E. The Outlook for the Philippines.

WILLIAMS, D. R. The United States and the Philippines.

WORCESTER, D. C. The Philippines Past and Present.

XXVIII

China: 1895–1914

THE overwhelming defeat of China by Japan in the war of 1894–1895 marked the commencement of a fresh period of humiliation for the former empire. The irresistible advance of the Japanese armies and the total failure of China's newly acquired modern navy completely destroyed the military reputation which China had built up by her suppression of Yakub Beg's revolt and by her creditable operations against France in the Tongking war.

In the peace negotiations at Shimonoseki, Li Hung-chang found himself unable to wring from the Japanese spokesman, Count Ito, any abatement of Japan's demands. China was compelled to recognize the independence of Korea, to cede Formosa and the Pescadores to the conqueror, and to pay a heavy indemnity for the expenses of the war; only the intervention of Russia, France, and Germany, as we have seen, prevented the acquisition by Japan of a large portion of southern Manchuria. Defeated by her smaller but more progressive neighbor, China stood revealed to the outside world in all her weakness, a helpless giant totally incapable of defending herself against outside attack.

Outside the area of hostilities the war with Japan caused little excitement among the Chinese people, save at the treaty ports and among the members of the scholar class. A petition against the ratification of the treaty was drawn up by a young Cantonese scholar named K'ang Yu-wei and was signed by six hundred and four of the literati from all parts of the empire, but was never presented to the emperor. Among the mass of the people in the inland provinces the news of the war penetrated but slowly and aroused little comment.

In government circles, however, the outcome of the war was the cause of almost feverish activity. Li Hung-chang, who had long been in control of the country's foreign affairs and who was held responsible for the war, was forced into temporary retirement from official life. A number of military officials were dismissed for incapacity and cowardice, and this preliminary house-cleaning was followed by determined efforts to reorganize the national defenses on a basis of greater efficiency. General oversight over the army and navy was placed in the hands of a Grand Council of War Affairs, of which Yüan Shih-k'ai, recently Chinese resident in Korea, was appointed chief secretary. Large quantities of arms and munitions were purchased; foreign officers were employed to undertake the training and organization of a modern army; and a number of warships were ordered, some from England and some from Germany, to replace those which had been lost in the war.

The activities of the Chinese government were not limited to these purely military reforms. Impressed by the advantages which the Japanese had derived from their adoption of Western methods of production and transportation, the authorities at Peking now endeavored to strengthen their country by the introduction of similar Western innovations. Within four months after the conclusion of the Treaty of Shimonoseki decrees had been issued by the imperial government ordering the provincial authorities to foster the development of factories, arsenals, dockyards, and steamship lines, and to commence the construction of a number of strategic railways. All these undertakings were to be financed with Chinese capital, and the provincial authorities, with this end in view, were to enlist the co-operation of the wealthy people of their provinces in the formation of companies and syndicates.

If the Chinese government hoped, as seems probable, that the rapid introduction of mechanized industry and transportation could be accomplished without the aid of foreign capital, this hope was doomed to disappointment. The provincial officials, finding themselves unable to secure the necessary capital from exclusively Chinese sources, were compelled, more or less surreptitiously, to admit foreign capital into their newly formed syndicates. The railways and modern industries whose establishment had been ordered by the throne, moreover, constituted the merest beginning in a real industrialization of the empire, and foreign capital was prepared to support by strong arguments its right to undertake developments which China could not carry out alone and which the imperial government had publicly acknowledged to be beneficial and desirable.

When the three European powers intervened to force a modification of the Treaty of Shimonoseki, it was generally expected that China would be compelled to pay for the service which had been rendered. This expectation was not disappointed. France was the first of the three to present her bill. On June 20, 1895, a treaty was signed at Peking whereby the French secured a "rectification" of the Annamese frontier by the surrender of certain Chinese territories on the left bank of the Mekong. The same treaty also provided for the immediate ratification by the Chinese emperor of the earlier Franco-Chinese boundary convention. Eleven days after the conclusion of this treaty the French and Russian diplomats secured for their financiers the privilege of lending to China, at 4 per cent interest, the four hundred million francs needed to pay the first installment of the Japanese indemnity.

Both these agreements were extremely objectionable to the British government. British financial interests had hoped to arrange the indemnity loan for China, while the rectification of the Annamese frontier had involved the cession to France of territories which China held under a recently concluded agreement with Great Britain. As the German bankers also were anxious to lend money to China, the Germans resented being left out by their partners in the recent intervention; the British and German diplomats therefore joined forces to secure for an Anglo-German syndicate the privilege of arranging two loans, in March, 1896, and in March, 1898, for the payment of the remaining installments due to Japan. British objections to the Annamese boundary readjustment, however, were not satisfied until February, 1897, when China compensated Great Britain by surrendering certain territories on the Burmese frontier and by granting certain concessions to British trade.

Although Russia had combined with France in the matter of the first indemnity loan to the Chinese government, this was but empty satisfaction to the Czar's government; Russia had little money to lend, and the loan was actually taken up by French and Belgian financiers. In 1896, however, Li Hung-chang was sent to Russia, at the special request of the Russian government, to represent the Chinese emperor at the coronation of Nicholas II. During the course of the Chinese statesman's stay at Moscow he concluded with the Russian minister of foreign affairs, Prince Lobanov, a secret treaty in which the two empires bound themselves to common action against any renewed aggression by Japan.

At this time, as we have seen, the Russian government was engaged in building the Trans-Siberian Railway, and Count Witte, the Russian finance minister, succeeded in convincing Li Hung-chang that a Russian railway line across northern Manchuria would make it possible for Russia at any time to render more efficient military support against a Japanese attack. The treaty of alliance, therefore, was accompanied by an agreement permitting Russia to construct, as a link in her transcontinental system, the Chinese Eastern Railway. In order to prevent the outside world from suspecting that any serious business had been transacted at Moscow the formal agreement in regard to the Chinese Eastern Railway was signed on September 8 at Berlin. The line was to be built by the Chinese Eastern Railway Company, ostensibly a Russian-Chinese concern; at the end of thirty-six years the Chinese government might buy the railroad at cost, and eighty years after its opening to traffic it was to revert to the Chinese without payment.

In Article IV of the Li-Lobanov treaty it was stated that the building of this railway was not to "serve as a pretext for any encroachment on Chinese territory nor for any infringement of the rights of sovereignty of His Majesty the Emperor of China," while Article V of the railway agreement provided that the Chinese government should "take measures to assure the safety of the railway and of the persons in its service against any attack." According to Article VI of this latter document, however, the lands utilized by the railway company were to be exempt from all taxes, and the company—which actually meant the Russian government —was to have "the absolute and exclusive right of administration" of these lands. Inasmuch as Article VI of the railway agreement appears in the authoritative French version but not in the Chinese version of the contract, this ambiguity was certainly not accidental; and the Russian government, giving the broadest possible interpretation to its "absolute and exclusive right of administration," transformed the railway line into a Russian zone with an adequate police force of regular troops thinly disguised as "railway guards."

Within two years after the close of the Sino-Japanese War two of the intervening powers, France and Russia, had thus secured substantial rewards for their service to China, while Great Britain, although not a party to the intervention, had obtained, on the Burmese frontier, territorial compensation for the concession granted to her French neighbor. In addition the French, Russian, British, and German financiers had been given the privilege of lending to China a total of a hundred and sixty million dollars.

Although German financiers had shared with the British in the indemnity loan of March, 1896, the German government felt that its share in the rescue of China was still unrewarded. For two years and a half after the intervention Germany persistently but vainly attempted to convince the Chinese government that the cession of a Chinese port to be used as a German naval base would be a graceful recognition of Germany's recent services and an assurance of even more efficient support from the German fleet in any future danger. The Chinese statesmen, while admitting the strength of the German arguments, invariably pointed out that such a concession to Germany would be followed by a flood of similar demands from other foreign governments.

Finally, the government at Berlin was given a pretext for securing by force what it had been unable to obtain through diplomacy. On November 1, 1897, two German priests of the Catholic mission in Shantung Province were murdered by a band of armed Chinese robbers, or brigands. When the news of this murder reached Berlin five days later, the German government promptly wired instructions to the German naval forces in the Far East; and on November 14 a German squadron steamed into the Bay of Kiaochow, on the Shantung coast, to secure adequate compensation for the murders.

The demands of the German government were presented to the Tsungli Yamen (the Chinese Office for Foreign Affairs) on November 20, and on March 6, 1898, after negotiations lasting three and a half months, the Chinese government found itself compelled to give way. In addition to punishing the murderers, paying a heavy money indemnity, and dismissing the governor of Shantung, China leased to Germany for a term of ninety-nine years the port of Tsingtao, with two hundred square miles of surrounding territory on Kiaochow Bay, and granted to German financial interests a priority in all railroad or mining developments which might be undertaken in the province of Shantung.

The lease of Kiaochow to Germany, as had been foreseen by the Chinese statesmen, was a signal for all the other powers to insist upon compensatory grants. In the space of three months and three days after the conclusion of this first lease four other strategically important sections of Chinese coast had passed under European control on similar terms.

On March 27, 1898, the Russians secured a twenty-five-year lease of Port Arthur and thirteen hundred square miles of the Liaotung region, together with the privilege of building a railroad northward from Port Arthur to the Chinese Eastern link in the Trans-Siberian system.

On April 2 the British government, stirred to action by Russia's acquisition of Port Arthur, forced from the Chinese a pledge that

Weihaiwei, as soon as that port was evacuated by the Japanese,[1] would be leased to Great Britain for as long as the Russians remained at Port Arthur. Inasmuch as the British government recognized the province of Shantung as a German "sphere of interest," the Weihaiwei lease was not accompanied by any grant of economic privileges in the adjoining regions.

On the ninth and tenth of April the French minister at Peking, by an exchange of notes with the Tsungli Yamen, secured a ninety-nine-year lease of two hundred square miles of territory at Kwangchowwan, in the province of Kwangtung.

Finally, on June 9, 1898, the British secured a ninety-nine-year lease of three hundred and seventy-five square miles in extension of its existing holdings on the Kowloon peninsula opposite the island of Hongkong.

With the satisfaction of their demands for strategically located naval bases on the Chinese coast the diplomatic representatives of the four European powers turned their energies to the task of securing for their nationals adequate participation in the exploitation of the empire's economic possibilities. In order to minimize the chances of conflict between themselves the four governments mapped out definite spheres of interest, within which the concession-hunting of the "interested" power should not be impeded by the interference of another.

The claims to especial rights and interests within these spheres, in face of the most-favored-nation clauses in China's existing treaties, rested upon notes secretly exchanged with the Tsungli Yamen, upon verbal assurances received from officials at Peking or at the provincial capitals, or even upon nothing more substantial than the fact that the claiming nation was first in the field. This flimsy foundation, however, was buttressed by formal agreements and informal understandings whereby the several powers reciprocally undertook to respect the established spheres.

Russia was recognized as having predominant interests in Man-

[1] The Japanese evacuation took place on May 23 upon the payment of the last installment of the war indemnity, and the British flag was immediately hoisted at Weihaiwei; but the formal lease, which involved about three hundred square miles of territory, was not signed until July 1.

churia and Mongolia. The Yangtze valley was allotted to Great Britain. The German sphere was Shantung Province and an undefined extension toward the west along the Yellow River. France claimed and secured recognition for a preponderance of interest in the southern provinces bordering upon Indo-China. In addition to these four European powers Japan, by reason of her recent acquisition of Formosa, claimed a sphere of interest in the province of Fukien, occupying the coast across from that island.

The sphere-of-interest arrangement appears to have intensified the pressure of foreign demands. Each of the powers felt called upon to demonstrate its ability to undertake developments commensurate with the area over which it had established a claim for special consideration, and each demand for fresh concessions in one sphere became an occasion for additional similar demands in the others.

To the imperial government of China and to many outside observers the establishment of foreign leaseholds along the Chinese coast and the division of the country into spheres of interest had every appearance of being the preliminaries to an undisguised partition of the ancient empire. Inspired by the fear of this development, the government at Peking embarked upon a policy of vigorous Westernization which, it was hoped, would strengthen the country and at the same time gain the good will of the powers threatening China's national existence.

On June 11, 1898, two days after the conclusion of the Kowloon lease, the emperor Kuang Hsu, under the influence of a group of enthusiastic young reformers headed by K'ang Yu-wei, issued the first of a series of reform decrees. During the period between that date and September 22 of the same year (the so-called Hundred Days of Reform) there came from the imperial brush a veritable flood of decrees intended to bring about the complete reorganization of the Chinese government. The existing educational system was revised by the modification of the examinations and by the creation of an imperial university for modern studies, which was to serve as a model for similar provincial institutions. The number of provincial officials was reduced, and steps were taken to centralize political power in the hands of the imperial officials at Peking.

A decree issued on July 7 attempted, by the establishment of a copyright and patent law, to encourage "the writing of useful books and the invention of new machines." And one of the last of the series, promulgated on September 5, called for the formation of a national army, to be recruited by universal conscription and to be organized along Western lines.

If the young emperor and his reform advisers had been given time in which to carry out their experiment, they might have achieved some measure of success. Instead of showing new consideration for China, however, the Western powers continued throughout the summer of 1898 to press upon the Peking government fresh demands for mining and railway concessions in all parts of the empire. By the middle of September the condition of the country seemed so desperate that the more conservative of the officials, many of whom had accepted the reform program in the hope that it would bring relief from foreign aggression, began to urge the empress dowager to resume direct control over the government.

Tzu Hsi, who had been living in semiretirement since 1889, made no move to interfere in affairs until the emperor, who feared her and regarded her as the center of the opposition to his reform policies, attempted to strengthen his position by proceeding against her trusted supporters in official circles; then, however, she acted with characteristic decision and energy. By a *coup d'état* carried into execution on September 22 she removed the young emperor from power, put to death or drove into exile his recent advisers, and took the reins of government into her own hands.

With the *coup d'état* came the adoption of a new policy for the preservation of the empire. Kuang Hsu had hoped to make China strong by a rapid introduction of Western ideas and Western institutions. Tzu Hsi and her advisers were fully alive to the need for reform but were determined upon reform along more conservative lines; the old traditional institutions of government were to be strengthened, and the officials were to be aroused to a more vigorous performance of the duties delegated to them by the throne. The young emperor had proclaimed to the world China's readiness to open her resources for development and her ports for trade, to which the world had responded by a brusque presentation of fresh demands for economic concessions. The empress dowager, although anxious to avoid the danger of a conflict with any of the foreign powers, determined to command the respect of the West; she therefore gave notice to the several foreign legations that China, for the present, would not consider any further requests for concessions of any sort.

As at Peking, so also at Washington, the leasing of Chinese ports and the mapping out of Chinese territory into spheres of interest were causes for growing anxiety. The years immediately preceding the Sino-Japanese War had been marked by a reawakening of American interest in the Orient, and American capital, like that of the European countries, was now beginning to regard China as a possible field for profitable investment. The establishment of spheres of interest was a matter of especial concern to Americans. The history of European expansion had shown that the step from sphere of interest to protectorate was seldom long deferred, and the establishment of European political control over the greater part of China would result in the erection of barriers against the importation of American goods as well as against American investment.

At the commencement of the battle of concessions in March, 1898, the United States was on the verge of the war with Spain. During the period of land-leasing operations, therefore, the American government was too busily occupied elsewhere to take any important hand in Chinese affairs. By the summer of 1899, however, the authorities at Washington awoke to the fact that the value of the newly acquired Philippines, regarded as a base for an expanding commerce with China, might be nullified by the monopolization of trade within the several spheres of interest into which the empire was being divided.

In September, 1899, therefore, the American Secretary of State, John Hay, took steps to secure for American business and finance adequate guaranties for the continuance of "an open door and equal opportunities" in China.[1] Notes were addressed to the gov-

---

[1] The open door negotiations, if not inspired by British statesmen, had their hearty approval; but the British government was careful to exclude the Kowloon leased territory from the scope of the agreement.

ernments of Great Britain, France, Germany, Russia, Italy, and Japan, requesting assurance that the ships and merchants of all nations should be given equal treatment—with respect to import duties, harbor charges, and railroad rates—within any leased territory or sphere of interest that these six countries had secured or might at any future time secure in China. The notes also requested assurance that these six countries would not interfere with any treaty port or with any existing treaty rights inside their respective spheres of interest.

In their replies to these notes each of the six governments stated that, if all the other powers agreed to follow this policy, it would give the assurance requested by the United States. On March 20, 1900, Mr. Hay therefore informed each of the governments that satisfactory assurances had been received from all and that the United States henceforth would consider them all bound to maintain the policy of the "open door" in China.

The open-door negotiations of Secretary Hay had resulted in the desired assurance that there would be no unfair discrimination against American trade in China, but they brought no comfort to the imperial government at Peking. Even if the Chinese authorities had been kept informed of this diplomatic correspondence, as they were not, the notes contained little that might be expected to assuage the fear of continued foreign aggression. Mr. Hay recognized the spheres of interest as accomplished facts and raised no objection to leased ports, so long as such leases were not operated to the detriment of American treaty rights; indeed, while the exchange of notes was actually in progress, steps were taken by the American government to secure for the United States the lease of a naval base on the coast of Fukien, and this effort was abandoned in deference to the Japanese claim of a sphere of interest in that province.

For nearly a year before the inauguration of the open-door negotiations the Chinese government had been preparing to resist any fresh encroachments. Fully realizing that a refusal to grant new concessions might involve China in a conflict with some Western power, the empress dowager, immediately after her *coup d'état*, made vigorous efforts to reorganize the military defenses of the empire. The modern-armed troops of the north were strengthened by the creation of new brigades and were concentrated around Peking under a single supreme command. The viceroys of the provinces in which arsenals existed were instructed to increase to the utmost extent the production of rifles, cannon, machine guns, and ammunition. The provincial authorities of the Yangtze-valley provinces and those along the coast were ordered to modernize the forces under their command and to repel, without awaiting specific instructions from Peking, any foreign attack upon the territories under their jurisdiction.

The truculent attitude of the Chinese government became evident when the Italian government, in the early part of 1899, made a belated attempt to enroll Italy among the powers having footholds in China. On February 28 the Italian minister presented to the Tsungli Yamen a request for the lease of San-men Bay, in Chekiang Province, as a coaling station, and for the usual mining and railway concessions in the southern part of that province. Although the Italian request had the diplomatic support of the British minister, the Yamen refused to consider it and returned the note to its author. The Italian representative, on March 10, attempted to gain his point by presenting an ultimatum, but this action was repudiated by his government. The overzealous minister was recalled, and the demands were finally abandoned.

Insignificant as this episode may appear, it was the occasion for great activity and excitement in Chinese government circles and among the Chinese people. Troops from the distant province of Kansu were summoned to Peking, provincial officials of the coast provinces were exhorted to display redoubled vigilance against possible foreign attack, and rumors of an impending foreign invasion obtained wide currency among the people of all classes.

In the fall of 1898, when the available modern troops in north China were concentrated at Peking, the empress dowager had issued decrees calling upon the provincial and local authorities of the northern provinces to revive the ancient system of local militia, *tuan*, partly for the maintenance of local peace and partly as a reserve force in case of actual foreign invasion. The recruiting of these militia bands was facilitated by the presence of a large number of men who had been rendered destitute and desperate by a long period of drought affecting all the northern provinces. Many professional brigands also found their way into the tuan and utilized the new organization as a cloak for their customary acts of violence. By the summer of 1899 many of these bands in Shantung and Chihli (present Hopei) provinces had assumed the high-sounding title *I Ho Tuan* ("Bands of Righteous Harmony"). Sometimes, also, they were known as *I Ho Chuan* ("Fists of Righteous Harmony"), and it was by the second of these titles, promptly translated into the English equivalent "Boxers," that they first became known to the Western residents of the country.

From the very beginning of their formation the Boxer bands were intensely and patriotically anti-foreign. The organization developed in those provinces which were most intimately affected by the recent alienations of territory. The concentration of the regular forces for defensive purposes around the capital and the frequent naval demonstrations in the waters of northern China were matters of common knowledge, and teahouse gossip—China's equivalent of the Western newspaper—was permeated by exaggerated rumors as to the aggressive intentions of the dreaded foreigners. In anticipation of the coming conflict with the hitherto irresistible Westerner the Boxer bands developed and sedulously practiced an elaborate ritual of magic exercises and incantations which, they believed, would render them invulnerable to foreign bullets.

Second only to the dreaded foreigners who were believed to be plotting the destruction of the empire, the principal objects of Boxer hatred were the Chinese converts to Christianity, the so-called "secondary foreign devils." Although the later Boxer placards attributed the persistent drought and the consequent famine conditions to the diabolical influence of the foreign gods, hostility to the Christians was based only to a minor extent upon opposition to their religious beliefs. To a greater extent it appears to have resulted from the tendency of the missionaries—of all denominations—to intervene in the local courts in cases involving their converts. Most of all, however, the hatred for the Christians arose out of the fact that in many parts of the troubled area the Chinese

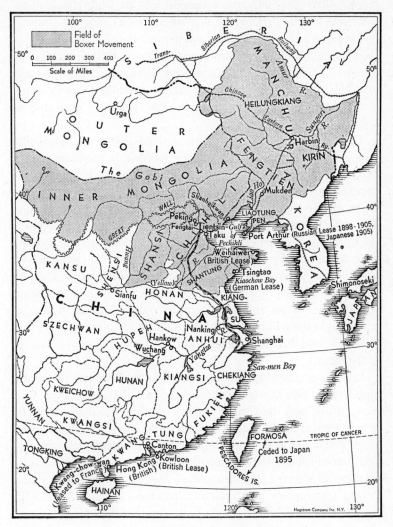

China, 1895–1914

converts and their missionary friends were the only visible manifestations of the dreaded foreign influence. During the summer
and autumn of 1899 the threats and depredations against the Christian communities in Shantung and southern Chihli steadily increased. None of the Christians were killed; but their property
was stolen or destroyed, and they were constantly given to understand that the near future held in store for them even greater
tribulation.

By November, 1899, those of the foreign diplomatic representatives at Peking whose nationals were engaged in missionary work
in Shantung Province began to bring pressure to bear upon the
imperial government and to demand that adequate measures be
taken for the suppression of the Boxer activities in that province.
The bitterly anti-foreign governor of the province, Yu Hsien, was
the object of especial criticism by the diplomats, and on December 6 he was replaced by General Yüan Shih-k'ai. On December 30,
before the new governor had fairly settled himself at his post, an
English missionary was murdered by some members of the Boxer
organization. Yüan Shih-k'ai promptly rounded up the murderers
and brought them to trial, with the result that two were condemned
to death, one to life imprisonment, and the remaining two to
banishment.

In spite of these apparently adequate punishments the representatives of five Western countries—Great Britain, France, Germany, Italy, and the United States—combined to demand of the
imperial government that it denounce the Boxers as an unlawful
organization and take immediate steps for their complete suppression. Inasmuch as the Boxer bands had been organized in response
to imperial decrees, the demand of the five powers placed the
Peking government in a difficult situation. If it complied with
the demand, the Chinese people, believing that the foreigners were
already in control of the government, might rise in rebellion
against the Manchu dynasty; if, on the other hand, the demand
was refused, the foreign powers might take the refusal as a pretext for a war against China and for the partition of the empire.
Faced by this dilemma the imperial authorities attempted to take
such measures as would satisfy the insistent demands of the diplo-

matic corps but at the same time would not draw upon themselves the hostility of the Boxers.

The first five months of the year 1900 were months of growing fear and suspicion. The diplomats at Peking suspected the imperial government of conspiring with the Boxers for the extermination of all foreigners residing in China. The imperial government and the patriotic bands suspected the foreign powers of planning the conquest of China. Some of the Western powers suspected each other of aiming to use the disorders as an excuse for seizing a portion of the empire or for acquiring special privileges detrimental to their rivals. The suspicions entertained by the foreign diplomats led to the presentation of more and more categorical demands to the Tsungli Yamen and to the concentration of strong naval forces in the Gulf of Pechihli (now known as Pohai). On the Chinese side the growing suspicion was reflected in a steady augmentation of the Boxer bands and in the spread of the movement from Shantung and southern Chihli into the region immediately around the capital. By the middle of May the districts between Peking and the seacoast were filled with Boxer organizations breathing hostility to the foreigners and threatening extermination to the Chinese Christians.

On May 28 the Fengtai station of the railway leading from Peking to Tientsin was attacked by a mob which destroyed several buildings and hurled threats at a French engineer in the employ of the Chinese government. Alarmed at the possibility of being cut off from the coast by the destruction of the railway, the diplomatic corps demanded permission to summon detachments of marines from their warships to guard the legations; and on June 1, despite the protests of the Tsungli Yamen, some four hundred and fifty guards were brought to Peking.

From this point the gathering storm developed with terrible rapidity. On the night of June 3-4 the Boxer bands, convinced that the invasion of the country had actually commenced, destroyed several sections of the railway between Peking and Tientsin. On the evening of June 9 the British and American ministers telegraphed to the naval commanders at Taku, asking that reinforcements be sent to Peking immediately and stating that if they did not come promptly, they would be too late. In response to this desperate request an international force of two thousand men under the command of the British admiral Seymour left Tientsin the following morning, repairing the damaged railway as it advanced toward the capital.

Like the summoning of the first legation guards, the start of the Seymour expedition produced immediate reaction on the Chinese side. At Peking an imperial decree appointed Prince Tuan, leader of the antiforeign party, to the presidency of the Tsungli Yamen; later in the same day telegraphic communication between the legations and Taku was cut; on the eleventh the chancellor of the Japanese legation, who had gone to the railway station to meet the expected reinforcements, was attacked and killed; on the thirteenth the Boxer bands made their first appearance inside the capital, where they immediately began to loot and to attack outlying foreign buildings, while the same date saw the column under Admiral Seymour hopelessly blockaded on the railroad, about halfway from Tientsin to Peking, by an overwhelmingly superior number of Boxers.

At Taku the severance of all communication with the Seymour column caused much anxiety among the commanding officers of the foreign naval forces. On the fourteenth a council decided that the railway station at Taku should be occupied in order to keep open the line of communications as far as Tientsin, and on the following day this step was taken. Two days later, after an ultimatum demanding the surrender of the Taku forts, these forts were bombarded and taken by storm by the combined operations of the warships and an international landing party.

As late as the morning of June 19, when the news of the seizure of the Taku forts became known to the Boxers at Peking, a strong peace party continued to exercise a steadying influence in governmental circles. On that date, however, the war party, headed by Prince Tuan, seized control of the government. On the afternoon of the nineteenth identic notes to each of the foreign legations informed the diplomats that, in consequence of the international attack upon the forts, a state of war existed between China and the outside world. The diplomats were further informed that they must prepare to leave the capital within twenty-four hours and that the government would provide transportation and an escort for the journey to Tientsin. Early on the morning of the twentieth the German minister, proceeding to the Tsungli Yamen for the purpose of protesting against this order, was shot and killed on the way. That afternoon, upon the expiration of the twenty-four hours of grace, the Boxers, with the co-operation of a part of the imperial troops, opened fire upon the legations.

In the violence and cruelty of its anti-foreign spirit, in the heroism and sufferings of the beleaguered foreign community at Peking and of their less fortunate missionary fellow nationals in the interior, and, unfortunately, in the ruthlessness with which the foreigners ultimately reasserted their superiority, the storm which raged over the northern provinces of China during the remaining summer months of 1900 can be compared only with the Sepoy Mutiny of half a century earlier in India.

At Peking the resident diplomats and missionaries, with the help of the legation guards, defended themselves against an almost continuous attack from June 20 until August 14, when an international relief force from Tientsin fought its way into the capital and raised the siege. The missionaries and their Christian adherents in the interior had little opportunity of defending themselves. In Chihli, Shansi, Manchuria, and Mongolia—the area in which the Boxer fury attained greatest intensity—scores of missionaries and thousands of Christian converts were ruthlessly hunted down and exterminated by infuriated mobs or by the forces under the command of the provincial officials. In the other provinces of northern China, although the officials gave some protection to the helpless foreigners, the missionaries were forced to seek safety in flight, while their abandoned converts suffered almost as severely as in the provinces already named. Nor were the atrocities of "Boxer Year" all committed by the Chinese. In their advance to Peking and after their occupation of the capital the troops of the international relief force treated the Chinese who fell into their hands with a brutality which, understandable though it may have been in the circumstances, aroused the horrified protests of many who accompanied the expedition.

When the Peking government decided upon war, orders were sent to the provincial officials throughout the empire, informing them that a state of war existed and instructing them to commence hostilities against the foreigners. These instructions were flatly disobeyed by the officials of central and southern China. Led by Chang Chih-tung, Liu Kun-yih, Li Hung-chang (viceroys, respectively, at Wuchang, Nanking, and Canton), and Yüan Shih-k'ai (governor of Shantung), the authorities of the Yangtze-valley and coast provinces declared that the movement was a rebellion and that the belligerent instructions issuing from Peking were not the commands of the lawful government. This neutral stand by the powerful provincial officials south of the Yellow River, since it greatly limited the area of the outbreak, undoubtedly aided the foreign governments in the task of rescuing their beleaguered nationals at Peking; but it also probably saved the Manchu dynasty. As the price of their neutrality the viceroys demanded that no foreign armies should be landed in their provinces and that no attack should be made upon the imperial family. Inasmuch as a refusal to comply with these demands might have resulted in the nation-wide expansion of a localized outbreak, the required assurances were given.

In their efforts to save China from destruction the neutral viceroys and governors were aided by the attitude of the United States. On July 3, 1900, Secretary Hay dispatched to all the other governments interested in China a circular note, stating that it was the policy of the United States to "preserve Chinese territorial and administrative entity . . . and safeguard for all the world the principle of equal and impartial trade with all parts of the Chinese Empire." This declaration of policy was promptly echoed by the other governments and was given much publicity in China as a means of allaying the suspicions of the Chinese people. An agreement signed on October 16, 1900, by Great Britain and Germany, wherein the two signatory countries pledged themselves not to utilize the present disturbances in China as an opportunity for gaining special territorial advantages, was also adhered to by the other leading treaty powers and served to block any move for the partition of the empire.

Although the efforts of the neutral provincial officials probably saved the imperial throne for the Manchus, they could not save their country from deep humiliation at the hands of the treaty powers. When the international forces entered Peking on August 14, 1900, the empress dowager and the court fled to Sianfu, the provincial capital of Shensi, leaving Li Hung-chang and Prince Ch'ing to face the problem of making peace with the foreigners. The negotiations lasted nearly thirteen months, but on September 7, 1901, the two Chinese plenipotentiaries and the representatives of eleven treaty powers signed the Peking protocol, setting forth the terms upon which the Manchu government was to be absolved from its complicity in China's anti-foreign outbreak.

As the price of peace the government was forced to put to death as "rebels" the outstanding leaders of the Boxer movement, to assume liability for an indemnity of four hundred and fifty million taels (about $330,000,000 in United States currency), and to agree to the permanent maintenance at Peking of such foreign military forces as the several governments considered necessary for the protection of their legations. The right was also accorded the foreign powers to maintain troops along the railway between Peking and Shanhaikuan; the forts at Taku and all other forts along the route from Peking to the sea were destroyed, never to be rebuilt; and an imperial decree was issued declaring membership in an anti-foreign society to be an offense punishable by death. In addition to imposing these punishments and giving these guaranties for the future safety of foreigners China was forced to replace the old Tsungli Yamen with a Ministry of Foreign Affairs (*Waiwupu*), which ranked above the six existing ministries or boards, and to agree to such modifications in the existing commercial treaties as the foreign powers might consider desirable.

In spite of oft-repeated assurances that no advantage was to be taken of the Boxer disorders as an opportunity for territorial acquisition the Russian government set out during the autumn of 1900 to gain for itself complete mastery over Manchuria. At Peking the Russian representative consistently advocated the modification of the demands made upon China, but in Manchuria the disturbances were made a pretext for sending strong forces to various points along the Chinese Eastern Railway and along the line of the newly granted concession leading to Port Arthur. In November, 1900, the overwhelming military power of the Russians in Manchuria enabled the Russian commander at Port Arthur to force upon the Chinese military governor of Manchuria an agreement providing for the complete military control of Manchuria. Pending the completion of the Manchurian railway lines China was not to maintain an army in the "three eastern provinces" and was to recognize Russia's right to keep there as many troops in addition to the railway guards as the Russian government might judge necessary. After the restoration of order and the completion of the railways the Chinese government was to consult with the Russian representatives as to the nature of the forces thereafter to be established by China. In addition to these military clauses the agreement contained the stipulation that China should not grant to the subjects of any other power, without Russian consent, railway or mining concessions in any part of Manchuria.

When the news of the agreement leaked out, as it did during the following January, the other treaty powers promptly protested at St. Petersburg and warned the Chinese plenipotentiaries against ratifying it. After a vain attempt to deny the existence of the alleged document the Russian government, on April 5, 1901, informed the British government that the arrangement, which dealt solely with the conditions upon which the Russian forces would evacuate Manchuria, had been dropped and that the Russian government would "await with calm the development of events."

After the conclusion of the Peking negotiations and the signing of the protocol the question of Russian evacuation of Manchuria was again taken up by the representatives of Russia and China. In October, 1901, the Russian government presented a new draft convention whose terms differed but little from those of the agreement which had been abandoned six months earlier. Again the other treaty powers, appealed to by the Chinese government, protested against the conclusion of an agreement which would make Manchuria practically a Russian protectorate, and on April 8, 1902, Russia finally agreed to evacuate Manchuria by zones, during the course of the next year and a half, as follows:

a. Within six months from the signature of the Agreement, [Russia agrees] to clear the southwestern portion of the Province of Mukden up to the river Liao of Russian troops, and to hand the railways over to China.

b. Within further six months to clear the remainder of the Province of Mukden and the Province of Kirin of Imperial troops.

c. Within the six months following to remove the remaining Imperial Russian troops from the Province of Hei-lung-kiang.

On October 8, 1902, in accordance with the terms of the agreement, the Russian troops were withdrawn from the first of these zones. The troops thus evacuated, however, were merely withdrawn to Port Arthur or to the two remaining zones of occupation, and on the expiration of the second six-month period the Russian government refused to proceed further with the agreed withdrawal unless China made additional economic and political concessions. These demands were rejected, and the Russian forces in the occupied zones, instead of being withdrawn, were actually increased in strength.

The disastrous consequences of the Boxer outbreak, following, as they did, upon China's humiliating defeat by the Japanese, convinced the Manchu government that the empire must adopt a new policy if it was to become strong enough to maintain its independent existence. When the aged Tzu Hsi, in January, 1902, finally returned from distant Sianfu and took up her residence in Peking, she immediately embarked upon a policy of sweeping reform in the direction of Westernization. Many of the reforms which had been hastily attempted four years earlier by the young emperor and his advisers were re-enacted by the empress dowager, especial emphasis being placed upon military reorganization and upon the establishment of modern educational institutions for instruction in Western science.

The spectacular success of the Japanese in their struggle with Russia, 1904–1905 (see Chapter XXIX), gave additional impetus to the enthusiasm for modernization. Thousands of Chinese students, with the approval and encouragement of their government, flocked to Japan to acquire from their once-hated neighbors the secrets of the process whereby Japan had raised herself to a footing of equality with the great powers of the West. An imperial decree issued in September, 1905, abolished the ancient system of literary examinations for the selection of government officials; henceforth the offices of government were to be filled not by the old-style Confucian scholars but by those who had mastered the political theories and scientific knowledge of the West. At the same time commissions were appointed to reform the law code and the legal system of China, in order to bring these into harmony with the codes and systems existing in Western countries.

On September 1, 1906, the reform program of the empress dowager culminated in the promise of a constitution. During the preceding year an imperial commission had been traveling abroad for the purpose of studying the methods and operation of constitutional government in the various foreign countries. Now, in response to the report of this commission, an imperial decree proclaimed the intention of the government to draft a constitution granting to the people a share in the management of the nation's affairs. After a preparatory period of ten years (subsequently shortened to seven years), during which the nation was to be educated for participation in its new responsibilities, an imperial parliament was to be established. Local and provincial elected bodies, however, were to be put into operation as soon as possible, in order to serve as a part of the educational process. In 1907 numerous self-government societies were formed under official auspices to train the people in the duties of citizenship, and the following year saw the beginning of arrangements for the election of the first provincial assemblies.

One other project in the reform program deserving special mention is the attack by the imperial government upon the sale and consumption of opium. By 1906 the amount of foreign opium annually imported into the country had risen to over three thousand five hundred tons, in addition to which more than ten thousand tons of the drug were produced in China. In September, 1906, the empress dowager and her advisers issued an edict for the progressive elimination of the domestic supply of opium. Each year for a period of ten years, one tenth of the acreage devoted to the cultivation of the poppy was to be turned to the production of cereals or other foodstuffs; during the same ten-year period the officials in all parts of the empire were to force the closure of opium dens within their several jurisdictions and were to furnish all possible assistance to opium addicts endeavoring to break themselves of the habit of smoking opium.

Like the other reforms decreed at this time, the campaign against opium was at first regarded with frank skepticism by foreign observers. In a short time, however, the imperial officials proved beyond question their determination to free the country from the evil effects of the opium habit, so far as that could be accomplished by action on China's part. In 1908 the British government was so favorably impressed by the efficiency and sincerity of China's effort that an agreement was concluded whereby the importation of Indian opium, which constituted more than 95 per cent of the foreign opium consumed in China, was also to be reduced by one tenth each year.

On November 14, 1908, the emperor Kuang Hsu died after an inglorious reign of thirty-three years, during most of which period he was a mere puppet in the hands of his strong-minded aunt. On the death of the emperor the empress dowager dictated the choice of his successor upon the dragon throne. This act, however, was the last act of a dying woman, and the following day saw the death of the remarkable figure who, for good or for evil, had played such a dominant role during nearly half a century of Chinese history.

Unlike her Meiji contemporary upon the throne of Japan, the empress dowager Tzu Hsi had come only late in life to an appreciation of her country's weakness and of the necessity for learning from the West. The emperor Mutsuhito lived to see Japan, through the reforms associated with his name, rise to a place in the ranks of the world powers; Tzu Hsi, dying in the midst of her belated activities for the modernization of China's institutions, left behind her an empire on the verge of ruin. Thirty-nine months after her death the Manchu dynasty was to fall, leaving to the Chinese people the task of creating, from foundations to pinnacle, a new and satisfactory political edifice to replace the ruined institutions of antiquity.

The almost simultaneous death of Kuang Hsu and of the empress dowager Tzu Hsi brought an infant emperor to the throne and placed the reins of government in the hands of a new regent. The dying empress had dictated the selection of Kuang Hsu's three-year-old nephew Pu Yi, who ascended the throne as the emperor Hsüan T'ung; during his minority the regency was to be assumed by the child's father, Prince Ch'un, a younger brother of the late emperor.

The new regent was a man of mediocre ability and of practically no experience in governmental affairs. Bitterly reactionary in his opinions, his first move was to dismiss from office Yüan Shih-k'ai, the organizer of China's modern army and the most influential Chinese supporter of the dynasty. At the same time Tuan Fang, the most liberal and one of the most capable of the Manchu officials, was also compelled to retire into private life, and it soon became apparent that the new regime was to be dominated by those who had "learned nothing and forgotten nothing" during the past twenty years.

Even during the last year of the empress dowager's regime there had been much protest against the ten-year period which must elapse before the first meeting of the national parliament would give the people's representatives an actual share in the government of the empire. With the accession of the infant emperor, and especially after the regent and his advisers had given evidence of their reactionary proclivities, the demands for an immediate summoning of parliament became increasingly insistent.

In the autumn of 1909 the elected assemblies of the several provinces had their first meetings, and in October, 1910, a national assembly (not a parliament) met for the first time at Peking. This body, which was purely advisory in character, consisted of a hundred members appointed by the throne and an equal number elected by the provincial assemblies. The hundred appointed members included twenty-two members of the imperial family, twenty-six members of the nobility (Manchu, Chinese, Mongol, and Tibetan), thirty-two government officials, ten distinguished scholars, and ten members chosen from among the greatest taxpayers. The elected members were apportioned among the provinces, each province having from two to nine representatives, according to population. In spite of the fact that half the Assembly was composed of nominees of the throne, the new body promptly turned

against the regent and repeated the demands which had been voiced
by the provincial assemblies: the immediate convocation of parliament with legislative power and the establishment of a "responsible" cabinet. In January, 1911, after having obtained from the
regent a reluctant promise that the parliament would be summoned
in 1913 instead of 1916, the Assembly was dissolved.

Even while the spokesmen of the Chinese people in all parts
of the empire were voicing the popular demand that the central
administration be placed under the control of the national representatives, the central government decided upon a fresh extension
of its functions at the expense of provincial autonomy, and in the
case of some provinces at the expense of private vested rights.

The wave of enthusiasm for Westernization which swept over
the country in 1905 had assumed particular strength in the matter
of railroad development, and the imperial government at that time,
inspired by the hope of keeping in Chinese hands as many as possible of China's interior lines of communication, encouraged the
wealthy elements of the various parts of the empire to undertake
the construction of the necessary railways within their respective
provinces. In 1909 the Peking authorities, reversing this earlier
policy, determined to bring all these projected railways under their
direct control as a national enterprise. Early in 1911, therefore, a
Board of Communications was established under the presidency
of Sheng Hsüan-huai, and on May 20 of the same year a foreign
loan was concluded with an Anglo-French-German-American financial group, or consortium, for the construction of these lines.

Although the new policy was unquestionably sound in theory,
it immediately called forth fresh and violent protests from the
most influential elements in several provinces where local railway
enterprises had been undertaken. The grounds for these protests
were varied. Much of the objection arose from the still-lively fear
of foreign domination. Much also can be attributed to the fact
that the change was regarded as an unwarranted encroachment
upon provincial rights by the central government. To a much
greater extent, however, the opposition was inspired by an absolute lack of confidence in the imperial government and in the newly
appointed head of the Board of Communications. Even those who

recognized the need for employing foreign capital and the desirability of consolidating China's railways into a unified system looked upon the move as a mere pretext for extending the power of a reactionary Manchu officialdom and of its corrupt Chinese henchmen.

In the province of Szechwan, where local investors had raised about three million dollars for the building of a provincial railway, the situation was complicated by the fact that a great part of this sum had been dissipated by the company's officers. The shareholders demanded that the government guarantee the return of their investment; and when this guaranty was not forthcoming, riots broke out in many parts of the province.

By the autumn of 1911 the entire empire was seething with discontent and honeycombed by revolutionary organizations plotting the overthrow of Manchu rule. It is probable that the rioting in Szechwan would have served to set in motion the full force of the antidynastic movement; but before developments in that province had reached the stage of open revolt, the revolution was precipitated by the outbreak of a mutiny among the provincial troops at Wuchang, capital of the Hukuang viceroyalty. On the night of October 8 an accidental bomb explosion at Hankow, across the river from Wuchang, led to the discovery of a revolutionary group in that city. Prompt action by the viceroy resulted in the arrest and summary execution of three of the conspirators; but the ramifications of this particular plot had spread even to the troops of the Wuchang garrison, and on October 10 these troops, fearing that their complicity had been revealed, rose in mutiny. The viceroy's *yamen* ("official residence") was destroyed, and the mutineers, finding themselves in command of the city, proclaimed rebellion against the dynasty.

Within a few days after the Wuchang outbreak the provinces of the Yangtze valley and southern China were in full revolt, while uprisings against the Manchus were beginning to occur even in the more northern portions of the empire. Hankow and Hanyang, which comprise with Wuchang the so-called Wu-Han metropolitan area at the junction of the Han River with the Yangtze, were captured; and the revolutionaries of the adjoining provinces established a republican government with Li Yüan-hung, the leader of the mutinying soldiers, as president.

From the very outbreak of the revolt the prince regent had shown his utter helplessness before the rising storm. On October 14, four days after the beginning of the mutiny, a hastily issued decree had appointed Yüan Shih-k'ai to the Hukuang viceroyalty with instructions to proceed at once to the restoration of order; but Yüan, after deliberation, declined the post on the ground of ill health. The regent's next move was to reassemble the Assembly which had been dissolved in January, and the Assembly, meeting on October 22, took advantage of the situation to demand the immediate establishment of a responsible government and the dismissal of Sheng Hsüan-huai, president of the Board of Communications. On November 1 the regent offered Yüan Shih-k'ai the post of prime minister, which he declined; on November 7 Yüan was elected to the premiership by vote of the Assembly, and on the fifteenth he finally agreed to accept the post.

Within two weeks after Yüan's acceptance of the premiership the northern armies, once more under the command of their old chief, had succeeded in recapturing from the rebels the cities of Hankow and Hanyang. Here, however, the advance of the imperialists stopped; Wuchang, on the south bank of the Yangtze, still remained in the hands of the revolutionists, together with most of the other important centers in the lower part of the Yangtze valley. Even if Yüan had felt strongly attached to the Manchu cause, the task of reconquering all the Yangtze valley and southern China would have dismayed him; and the now all-powerful premier felt little gratitude or obligation to the regent who, three years earlier, had driven him from public office. The cause of the Manchus was already ruined beyond possibility of restoration, and Yüan was concerned with reaching an adjustment which would be most beneficial to the country or most advantageous for himself.

On December 6 the prince regent was compelled to resign, and his functions were assumed by the empress dowager Lung Yu, widow of Kuang Hsu. A little more than two months later, on February 12, 1912, the new regent, in the name of the infant emperor, signed three decrees which announced to the world the end of Manchu rule in China. The first of these decrees abdicated the imperial power and ordered Yüan Shih-k'ai, as premier of the empire, to unite the country by the organization of a republican government. The second decree set forth the terms which had been agreed upon for the post-abdication treatment of the emperor, the imperial family, and the Manchu clansmen. In the third decree the abdicating emperor exhorted all the administrative officials of the old regime to continue under the new government their loyal services to the country.

The Republic and its Problems

Within two months after the outbreak of the revolution the republic which had been proclaimed at Wuchang, with Li Yüan-hung as president, had grown to include thirteen provinces of central and southern China. Early in December, Yüan Shih-k'ai, through reliable emissaries, had opened negotiations with the republicans for the purpose of arranging a satisfactory settlement of the nation's affairs, and these negotiations continued up to the date of the Manchu abdication. By December, also, the prominent revolutionary leaders from abroad, who had been quite as completely surprised by the developments as had the Manchus, began to return from exile to take part in the movement; and on December 27 Dr. Sun Yat-sen, generally recognized by the republicans as the most prominent organizer of prerevolutionary anti-Manchu societies, arrived at Shanghai.

Upon the arrival of Sun Yat-sen there was an immediate reorganization of the republican government. Although Li Yüan-hung had been elected president in October by the small group of revolutionary leaders at Wuchang, he was a man of no previous political prominence. He was now prevailed upon to resign from the presidency, and on December 29 Dr. Sun was elected to fill the vacant office. At the same time the republican capital was transferred from Wuchang to Nanking. After this reorganization Yüan Shih-k'ai's negotiations were conducted with the new Nanking administration.

The terms of the Manchu abdication were approved in advance by the Nanking government, and the Nanking leaders also agreed that Yüan should become president of the republic which they had already proclaimed. On February 14, two days after the valedictory decrees of the infant emperor, Dr. Sun and his cabinet offered to the "National Assembly" at Nanking their formal resignation. On the following day the resignations were accepted, and the Assembly elected Yüan Shih-k'ai as provisional president; north and south were reunited, and the republic, on paper at least, was established.

To the facile optimists the spectacular collapse of the Manchu regime and the prompt establishment of the republic appeared to mark the dawn of a new era of peace and progress for the Chinese nation. Forgotten or ignored were the half-century of turmoil between 1640 and 1689 in England, the eighty-two years of French history from the fall of the Bastille until the establishment of the Third Republic, and the problems of American internal organization which were not solved until 1865. Too much of China's past weakness was attributed to Manchu corruption and ineptitude, while the brilliant achievements of Meiji Japan and the general belief in the political ability of the Chinese people led many observers, foreign as well as Chinese, to underestimate the difficulties involved in erecting upon China's ancient foundations a new and modern political edifice.

Yet the difficulties involved in this task were, as a matter of fact, both numerous and complex. For something like two thousand years the Chinese people, while depending upon local democratic institutions for the direction of their local affairs, had been accustomed to an imperial overlordship operating, in normal times, through the agency of a scholarly official class. Even this imperial rule, moreover, had been extremely decentralized and had committed to the local and provincial officials a high degree of local autonomy; outside the scholar class the people, until very recently, had paid almost no attention to national or even provincial affairs and had been concerned only with their narrow local interests.

The first problem, therefore, if China was to become a republic in fact, was that of so organizing the local democratic institutions as to make them a foundation for a national government. This problem was rendered the more difficult by the absence of any nation-wide economic interest such as in most Western countries serves to create a general dependence upon a national government. Closely associated with the first problem were the equally fundamental tasks of organizing a centralized administration, of putting government finances on a systematic basis, and of elaborating a modernized legal code, all of which meant violent departure from the ancient traditions of the nation.

In addition to the purely internal problems involved in the task of national reorganization there were serious complications resulting from China's existing treaty relations with the various foreign powers. The extensive foreign interests in the country made it extremely possible that any long period of internal disorder, endangering foreign life or property, would call forth intervention by one or more foreign powers; indeed, it was not impossible that, even if no legitimate excuse was given, one or another treaty power might profit by China's disordered condition as an opportunity for expanding its sphere of interest. In the meantime foreign capital and foreign advisers were more than ready to put themselves at the service of the new republic, while the governments of the treaty powers quite naturally insisted upon adequate guaranties that their treaty rights would be fully respected.

The Manchu abdication on February 12, 1912, found the active or articulate political elements in China divided into two irreconcilable groups. On one side were the revolutionary republican agitators whose anti-Manchu conspiracies had done so much to prepare for the revolution and had made it possible for the Wuchang outbreak to sweep like wildfire through the central and southern provinces of the empire. Opposed to these were the Chinese members of the old officialdom, who recognized the need for sweeping changes in the country's political organization but whose ideas were less radical than those of their rivals. In each of these groups one individual stood out as a recognized leader and as the chief exponent of the policies of his party: Sun Yat-sen among the republicans, and Yüan Shih-k'ai among the conservative old-style bureaucrats.

Dr. Sun Yat-sen (also known as Sun Wen) was born in 1866 in Kwangtung Province. He had been educated in missionary institutions, first in an English church school at Honolulu and subsequently in an Anglo-American hospital at Canton and in a British medical school at Hongkong. In 1894 he became the leader of an antidynastic conspiracy at Canton, but the plot was discovered, and he was forced to seek refuge abroad. Taking advantage of the Boxer uprising in the summer of 1900, Sun returned to Canton and organized another unsuccessful revolt. From this time until the fall of 1911 he continued in exile his work for a revolution against the Manchus. Endowed with a magnetic personality and speaking English as fluently as he spoke Chinese, Dr. Sun was an accomplished orator in either language, and his constantly growing influence among the students studying abroad spread back into China to give him an unrivaled position among the revolutionary "Westerneducated" class in all parts of the country.

Yüan Shih-k'ai was perhaps the ablest and the most progressive survivor of the officials who had served under the empress dowager Tzu Hsi. Like a number of others who rose to prominence during the closing decades of the Manchu regime, Yüan had gained his entry into official life by favoritism rather than through the established examination routine. He was a native of Honan Province and was born in 1859. At the age of twenty he saw military service in Korea; and shortly thereafter he was taken into the service of Li Hung-chang, who sent him to Korea as Chinese resident to combat the growing influence of the Japanese.

After the Japanese war Yüan was given a prominent post in the newly organized Board of National Defense and was appointed to the command of one of the four modern army corps. In 1898 he took the side of the empress dowager, and he is generally credited with having betrayed Kuang Hsu's plans to that dominating old lady, thereby enabling her to accomplish her *coup d'état*. From the *coup d'état* until Tzu Hsi's death, ten years later, Yüan was a loyal and trusted supporter of the Manchu throne. Although he served as governor of Shantung, as viceroy of Chihli, and as Grand Secretary, his most important work was in the development of China's modern army. In his army reorganization and in his work

as a civil administrator Yüan had displayed a thorough appreciation of Western technical progress and had made free use of foreign
innovations. On the other hand, his attitude upon questions relating to the fundamental organization of the state was thoroughly
conservative, and he was therefore the accepted leader of all the
conservatives.

In accordance with the agreement between Yüan Shih-k'ai and
the Nanking revolutionary government Sun Yat-sen, at Nanking,
had resigned his presidential title on February 14, 1912, two days
after the Manchu abdication, and on the following day the Nanking
National Assembly had elected Yüan to the office of provisional
president. On February 20 the office of provisional vice-president
was conferred upon Li Yüan-hung in recognition of his prominent
part in the revolution. The Nanking Assembly attempted to have
the inauguration held at Nanking, but on March 10 the provisional
president and vice-president took their oaths of office at Peking,
and in April a new provisional parliament assembled at Peking for
the purpose of drafting a permanent constitution. In April, 1913,
the provisional parliament, a single-chamber body, was replaced by
a regular bicameral parliament, and in October of the same year
that part of the constitution which related to the national executive
had been completed. Accordingly, on October 6, 1913, Yüan was
elected constitutionally as president of the republic, Li Yüan-hung
was elected to the vice-presidency, and on October 10, the second
anniversary of the revolution, they were formally inaugurated.

The election and inauguration of Yüan in October, 1913, put
the control of the nation's affairs definitely in his hands and marked
the triumph of the conservatives in the bitter party struggle which
had begun a year and a half earlier. The principal point in dispute
during this long struggle had been the extent of the power to be
exercised by the president. Yüan had insisted that the power of
the executive should be free from any direct parliamentary control;
his republican opponents, the members of the *Kuomintang* ("National People's Party"), were determined that the presidential
office should be modeled after the French rather than the American
and that the real power should lie in the hands of the prime minister, who would be directly responsible to parliament.

The purely constitutional dispute was embittered by a growing distrust of Yüan Shih-k'ai in the ranks of the Kuomintang. In May, 1913, an insurrection against Yüan had broken out in the Yangtze valley and had spread into a number of the southern provinces. The uprising was ruthlessly suppressed, and a number of prominent Kuomintang leaders, including Sun Yat-sen, were compelled to seek safety in Japan or in other foreign countries.

Although the Kuomintang members constituted a majority of the parliament, Yüan's break with the party during the summer of 1913 did not prevent his election in October. The formal recognition of the republic by most of the treaty powers (the United States and Mexico had recognized the new government in April, upon the assembling of the national parliament) was withheld pending the election of a constitutional president, and even Yüan's political opponents, believing that the constitution would effectively check his vaulting ambition, were willing to vote for him as the price of foreign recognition.

Once firmly established as executive head of the government, Yüan proceeded to take drastic measures against his Kuomintang enemies. On November 5, less than a month after his election, he issued a presidential mandate dissolving the Kuomintang party and expelling from the houses of the parliament a total of four hundred and thirty-eight of the party's members. This "purge" effectively terminated the activities of parliament by permanently depriving it of a quorum, and Yüan proceeded to govern with dictatorial powers which were unchecked during the remaining two and a half years of his life.

Aside from his own unquestioned political and administrative ability, Yüan Shih-k'ai's dictatorship derived its strength from three sources. First of all, the great majority of the old-style officials, recognizing as valid the imperial decree which had authorized Yüan to "organize a republican government," gave him their support. In the second place, the old imperial army was an instrument largely of his own creation, and its generals, appointed by him as military governors of the various provinces, could be relied upon to support him in almost any emergency. Finally, but not least in importance, Yüan enjoyed the confidence of most of the foreign governments; Western statesmen had already adopted the theory that a "strong man" was needed to bring order out of chaos in China, and Yüan, so long as he remained in power, had comparatively little difficulty in securing by foreign loans the money necessary for carrying on the government of the country.

Even before the overthrow of the Manchu dynasty the steadily expanding economic domination of the Chinese in Tibet and Mongolia and the attempts of the imperial government to bring these two great dependencies more directly under its control had led in both regions to the growth of national sentiment and to open revolt against Chinese rule. While the "twenty-one provinces" (the eighteen south of the Great Wall and the "three eastern provinces" of Manchuria) are essentially homogeneous in population and culture, Tibet and Mongolia are inhabited by peoples only distantly related to the Chinese, speaking different languages and separated from them by differences in cultural heritage. After the Chinese revolution the Tibetan and Mongolian agitations for self-government, somewhat aided in each case by foreign intrigue, steadily gained ground, and the republican government, although insisting that the republic included all the territories of the recently abolished empire, found itself unable to maintain any effective authority in these two regions.

When the British expedition under Colonel Younghusband advanced into Tibet in the summer of 1904 (see page 642), the Dalai Lama, the temporal and spiritual head of the Tibetan state, fled northward into Mongolia, where he took refuge with the *hutukhtu* ("reincarnated Buddha") of Urga, leaving the affairs of Tibet to be adjusted by negotiations between the Anglo-Indian authorities and the Chinese government. In 1906 the British and Chinese governments concluded an agreement whereby Great Britain recognized Chinese suzerainty over Tibet and pledged herself not to annex any Tibetan territory or to interfere in the administration of the country. In August of the following year a treaty between Russia and Great Britain bound the two powers to recognize China's suzerainty over Tibet and to attempt no negotiations with the Tibetan government except through China as an intermediary.

In spite of these diplomatic guaranties of its suzerainty the imperial government had determined to safeguard its position in Tibet by administrative reforms which would more closely unite the dependency with the rest of the empire; and in December, 1909, when the Dalai Lama finally returned to Lhasa, this program was being energetically followed by the government of the prince regent. To the Tibetan people and to their theocratic ruler the domination of the Chinese was quite as objectionable as subjugation by the British. In January, 1910, rioting occurred at Lhasa; and when the Chinese government proposed to dispatch additional armed forces to the Tibetan capital, the British government, to which the Dalai Lama had appealed, questioned China's right to send troops into the country without previously informing Great Britain of her intentions. In February the Dalai Lama once more sought safety in flight; but this time he fled southward into India, where he was cordially received and entertained by the British authorities.

By the summer of 1912, when the Dalai Lama again returned to his capital, the revolution in China had taken place and the revolutionary government, which had proclaimed Tibet to be an integral part of the Chinese Republic, was preparing to send an army into the country for the purpose of rescuing the Chinese resident at Lhasa. Once more the British representative at Peking interposed a protest against Chinese military activity in Tibet.

Great Britain had not officially recognized the new Chinese government, and the Peking authorities were informed that British recognition would not be forthcoming until China had agreed to certain important modifications in the status of her mountainous dependency. The Chinese were not to interfere in Tibetan affairs without having first consulted Great Britain. Tibet was not to be represented in the parliament of China, and the Chinese government was to abandon its intention of sending an army to Lhasa. Under the circumstances the Peking government found it advisable to agree to these demands as a necessary price for British recognition, and in 1913 an Anglo-Tibetan-Chinese conference met at Simla, the "summer capital" of the Indian government, for the purpose of formulating the relations of Tibet with its two neighbors.

The Simla convention divided Tibet into two areas. In "Inner Tibet" China was to exercise direct administrative authority; but "Outer Tibet" was to be autonomous under Chinese suzerainty, and China was to maintain no officials there except the resident, who was allowed to have a military guard not exceeding three hundred men. The British government was to have the right to maintain a diplomatic representative at Lhasa, and any controversy which might arise between China and Tibet was to be submitted to the British for adjudication. Although the Chinese representative at the Simla conference "initialed" this convention, the Chinese government refused to ratify it. Great Britain and the Lhasa government both ratified the agreement and chose to regard it as a final solution of the situation, but from the Chinese point of view the entire Tibetan question was still open.

While the authorities of British India were taking advantage of the situation in Tibet as an opportunity to extend British influence in that region, the Russians were taking similar advantage of a like situation in Mongolia. By the secret Russo-Japanese agreements of 1907, 1910, and 1912 (see pages 732–734) "Outer" Mongolia and all of "Inner" Mongolia except the eastern portion (which was associated with southern Manchuria) were recognized by the Japanese government as constituting the special sphere of Russian interest in the Chinese Empire.

During the summer of 1911 a growing anti-Chinese sentiment among the Mongols—arising partly from the steady infiltration of Chinese traders and settlers, partly from the aggressive policy of the Chinese local officials, and partly from the active intrigues of Russian agents—resulted in an appeal to the Russian government by a number of Mongol princes for protection against Chinese tyranny. The Russian minister at Peking was promptly instructed to inform the Chinese government of this appeal and to give notice that Russia, on account of her natural concern in developments so near to her own frontier, would take steps to protect her interests unless the Chinese authorities immediately suspended the measures against which the Mongols had protested. In October, 1911, two months after the delivery of this warning, Russian troops were sent to Urga, the chief city of Outer Mongolia, for the alleged purpose of protecting the Russian consulate in case of serious disturbances. The outbreak of the revolution in China was promptly reflected in Mongolia; on October 30, 1911, the hutukhtu of Urga declared his independence of China, and his example was soon followed by a number of other Mongol princes.

Yüan Shih-k'ai's attempts, after his inauguration as provisional president, to negotiate directly with the Mongol secessionists were unsuccessful. The Mongols refused to enter into discussions with the Chinese government except through the Russians as intermediaries; and when the Chinese government indicated its intention of dispatching troops to Mongolia, the Russians gave notice that they could not "view with indifference" a move which would create a disturbance on the frontier of Siberia. After aiding the Mongols against the Chinese during the summer of 1912, the Russians in November of that year concluded an agreement with the Mongol princes. In return for a grant of all the rights which Russia had enjoyed under the treaties with China the Czar's government undertook to maintain the autonomy of Outer Mongolia and to forbid the entry of Chinese troops or colonists into Mongol territory.

The conclusion of the Russo-Mongolian agreement definitely transformed the Mongolian question into an issue between China and Russia. Inasmuch as the republic in 1912 was in no condition for a war with its northern neighbor, the Peking authorities were compelled to have recourse to diplomacy in the hope of saving as much as possible of China's ancient sovereign rights in the area under dispute.

The Russo-Chinese negotiations relating to Mongolia lasted a full year before resulting in any definite understanding, but on November 5, 1913, a protocol and an exchange of notes (requiring no ratification) recognized the autonomy of Outer Mongolia under the suzerainty of China. The Chinese government bound itself not to intervene in the internal administration of the region, not to send troops there, and not to permit colonization of the country by Chinese settlers; similar pledges were given by Russia. Russia recognized the right of the Chinese to maintain representatives at Urga and at a number of other important points, while China acquiesced in the maintenance of Russian consulates to safeguard Russian interests. Russia was to use her influence to secure Mongol agreement to this arrangement, and a conference was to be held between Russia, China, and the Mongols for the further discussion of all outstanding questions.

Manchuria is, and has been for many centuries, regarded by the Chinese as an integral part of their country. As early as the days of the Han dynasty the southern portion of this region was incorporated in the empire; since that time Chinese culture has been firmly established even among the non-Chinese elements of the population, and at the beginning of the twentieth century an overwhelming majority of the population was actually of Chinese descent. As in Tibet and Mongolia, however, the years immediately before and after the establishment of the republic saw Chinese sovereignty in Manchuria challenged by powerful neighbors. The details of this phase of China's difficulties are reserved for the next chapter, but it should be noted that here, as at other points on her frontier, plans for the partition of China were being actively pursued.

CHINA IN 1914

After the humiliating defeat by the Japanese and the dismal fiasco of the Boxer movement the Chinese had made desperate, if somewhat belated, efforts so to adjust their economic organization and political institutions as to make possible the continued existence of their national independence. As long as the old empress dowager remained in control of the government, it seemed possible that the necessary adjustment might be accomplished, as it had been in Japan, by building upon the ancient and traditional prestige of the throne; but with the death of Tzu Hsi the affairs of the imperial family fell into the hands of those who, by blundering incompetence, precipitated the revolution and brought about the overthrow of the dynasty.

In the two and a half years following the Manchu abdication it became increasingly evident that the adoption of a republican form of government had not brought China appreciably nearer to a solution of her difficulties. The situation of the Chinese state in the summer of 1914 was definitely worse than at any time since the end of the Boxer disturbance.

A constitution had been drawn up, and a president had been elected; but Yüan Shih-k'ai, although far more capable than the Manchu regent whom he replaced, was an official of the old school, opposed to and distrusted by the entire body of revolutionary reformers, and the armed dictatorship which he had established was arousing throughout the country the bitter opposition of elements that had had no part in the movement against the Manchus.

SUGGESTED REFERENCES

BERESFORD, LORD C. The Break-up of China.

BLAND, J. O. P., and BACKHOUSE, E. China under the Empress Dowager.

DENNETT, T. Americans in Eastern Asia.

HART, SIR R. These from the Land of Sinim.

KENT, P. H. B. Railway Enterprise in China.

LATOURETTE, K. S. The Chinese: their History and Culture.

LATOURETTE, K. S. A History of Christian Missions in China.

MACNAIR, H. F. Modern Chinese History: Selected Readings.

MORSE, H. B. The International Relations of the Chinese Empire, Vol. III.

MORSE, H. B., and MACNAIR, H. F. Far Eastern International Relations.

SMITH, A. H. China in Convulsion.

STEIGER, G. N. China and the Occident.

WEALE, P. The Fight for the Republic in China.

WILLIAMS, E. T. A Short History of China.

WILLOUGHBY, W. W. Constitutional Government in China.

YARMOLINSKY, A. (translator and editor). The Memoirs of Count Witte.

YEN, H. L. A Survey of Constitutional Development in China.

XXIX

Japan as a World Power

A Member of the Family of Nations · Japan and the Boxer Movement · Russia and Japan in Korea · The Anglo-Japanese Alliance · The Diplomatic Prelude to the Russo-Japanese War · The War · Japanese Successes by Land and Sea · The Peace of Portsmouth · The Sino-Japanese Agreements of December 22, 1905 · Renewal of the Anglo-Japanese Alliance · Asia for the Asiatics · The Passing of Korea · Japan's Post-War Relations with Russia · Relations with the United States · The South Manchuria Railway Company · The Root-Takahira Notes · The Chinchow-Aigun Railway and the Knox Neutralization Proposal · The Manchurian Industrial-Development Loan · Japanese Industrialization and Commercial Expansion · End of the Meiji Era and Beginning of the Taisho

IN AN earlier chapter we have followed the steps by which Japan, under the progressive government of the Meiji era, turned her energies to the task of reorganizing her economic and political institutions along Western lines. So successfully was the task accomplished that the closing decade of the nineteenth century saw the the Island Empire, although only recently forced from its earlier policy of jealous seclusion, accepted by Europe and America as a full-fledged member of the "family of nations." In part, at least, world opinion was undoubtedly influenced by the success of Japanese arms in the war with China; but the new respect for the Japanese Empire was due, perhaps even in greater part, to the real progress which the country had made in its assimilation of the science, the mechanical inventions, the economic organization, and the political and legal institutions of the West.

Remarkable as were the achievements of the Japanese during the closing years of the nineteenth century, the opening years of the twentieth century were to see these achievements, both in peace and in war, eclipsed by fresh victories and accomplishments. Before five years of the new century had passed, Japan, accepted as an ally by one of the great European powers, had waged single-handed a successful war against another power of first rank; nine

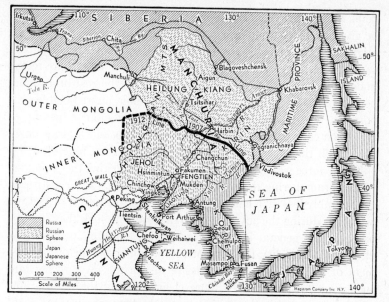

The Russo-Japanese Sphere of Interest

years later the Japanese, by virtue of their recognized strength on land and sea, were able to exercise a dominating influence in matters of international concern relating to eastern Asia. As in the earlier years of the Meiji era, moreover, this growth in military power is but one side of the picture. Equally important was the steady advance in the fields of industry, science, and education. For this advance by 1914 had transformed the Japanese empire into a highly industrialized state competing with Europe and America for world markets and struggling at home with the manifold problems of the modern economic system.

Hardly had the abandonment of extraterritorial rights by the treaty powers signalized Japan's formal admission into the family of nations when the outbreak of the Boxer movement in China threw upon the Japanese a heavy share in the international operations for the relief of the foreign community at Peking. Under decidedly embarrassing conditions the Japanese government acted with extreme circumspection. Although the British government proposed early in the development of the disorders that Japan, being most advantageously located of all the treaty powers, should be given an international mandate for such armed intervention as might be necessary for the relief of the legations, the Japanese carefully refrained from assuming a disproportionate share in the undertaking. Unwilling to burden itself with the cost of an independent military venture which might assume unpredictable proportions, the Japanese government was even more reluctant to serve as a cat's-paw for the other treaty powers and to draw down upon itself the concentrated antiforeignism of the Chinese.

In the force which ultimately advanced to Peking the Japanese, while outnumbering the troops from any other power, constituted considerably less than half of the total. After the taking of Peking, as well as during the advance, the Japanese, although they participated in the general looting, are credibly reported to have displayed less brutality than the other foreign troops in their treatment of the Chinese. Japan's desire to win the favor of her late enemy was displayed even more clearly during the negotiations which culminated in the Peking protocol. Throughout these negotiations the Japanese plenipotentiary, like the representatives of the United States and Russia, showed his friendship for China by voting consistently against the more violent of the punitive measures proposed by the other powers.

To the Japanese government more than to the government of any other power interested in the affairs of China, Russia's utilization of the Boxer movement as an opportunity for securing a permanent foothold in Manchuria was cause for growing anxiety. Even after the forced retrocession of the Liaotung region and after the lease of Port Arthur to Russia, Japanese statesmen had looked upon Manchuria as a region whose great natural resources and potential markets might be developed to the benefit of their country's growing industrial system. If Manchuria became a Russian province or even a Russian protectorate, the Japanese might easily find themselves excluded from any share in such development. Added to this danger was the possibility that Russia, once firmly established in Manchuria, would not stop at the Manchurian frontier but would continue to extend her influence across the Yalu River into Korea.

During 1896 and 1897, largely as a result of Japan's own blunders (see pages 628–629), Japanese influence in Korea had been completely overshadowed by that of Russia. In February, 1896, the Korean king, fleeing from the dictation of his pro-Japanese cabinet, left the palace to seek refuge in the Russian legation, where for slightly more than a year he remained as the guest of the Russian minister. From this safe haven the fugitive monarch dismissed the pro-Japanese members of his government, and during the succeeding months most of the Japanese officials in Korean service were replaced by Russians. In April and September, 1896, valuable mining and timber concessions along the Tumen and Yalu rivers were granted to Russian concession-hunters, while in May of the same year the Japanese-trained military forces, suspected of pro-Japanese tendencies, were disbanded to make way for a new army organized by Russian experts.

The Russian acquisition of Port Arthur in March, 1898, had served temporarily to improve the position of the Japanese in Korea. On April 25 of that year the Japanese Foreign Minister and the Russian representative at Tokyo concluded an agreement (the Nishi-Rosen protocol) whereby the two empires, recognizing the independence of Korea, reciprocally pledged themselves "not to take any measures regarding the nomination of military instructors and financial advisers without having previously arrived at a mutual accord on the subject." Although the Nishi-Rosen protocol, like earlier understandings between the two governments, contained an assertion of "the independence and perfect sovereignty of Korea," it also explicitly recognized Japan's vital interest in the "development of the commercial and industrial relationship" between herself and her less progressive peninsula neighbor. Interpreting the agreement to mean that Russia was willing to abandon her Korean aspirations in order to be able to concentrate her energies upon Manchuria, the Japanese therefore promptly applied themselves to the task of acquiring in Korea paramount interests and influence, political as well as economic. Concessions for railways and other public utilities were secured for Japanese capitalists; Japanese trade was rapidly expanded; with the encouragement of their own government large numbers of Japanese migrated to Korea; and Japanese experts of various sorts once more gained ascendancy in the government of the Korean monarch.[1]

It soon became evident, however, that Russia, in concluding the Nishi-Rosen agreement, had not intended to leave Japan an undisputed field in Korea. The appointment of a new Russian minister to Seoul early in 1899 was followed by an attempt to secure Masampo, near Fusan, as a Russian naval base. The vigilance of the Japanese representatives succeeded in frustrating this move; but early in 1901, when the attention of the world was still focused upon the international negotiations at Peking, there was a similar attempt to gain possession of Chinhai Bay, while Russian diplomacy at Seoul strove to bring Korean finances under Franco-Russian control and to enlarge Russia's concessionary rights along the Korean-Manchurian frontier.

By the summer of 1901 the question of Japan's future policy on the continent of Asia had divided the leading Japanese statesmen into two camps. One group, headed by Count Ito and Count Inouye, favored an alliance with Russia and the peaceful delimitation of the debated region into Russian and Japanese spheres of interest. A second and more numerous party, headed by Prime Minister Katsura, Marquis Yamagata, and the military authorities, believed that a peaceful settlement with Russia was impossible and that Japan, in anticipation of the unavoidable conflict with this powerful foe, should seek an alliance with Great Britain, Russia's inveterate enemy, as an assurance that she would not again find herself opposed by a European coalition. Although Ito was actually authorized to seek an understanding with the Russian government, conversations had already been commenced at London between Baron Hayashi and the British Foreign Minister. In November the diplomatic discussions at London bore fruit in the form of a tentative draft treaty. During the following month the comparative merits of the two policies were hotly debated at Tokyo, and on December 17 a meeting of the privy council, pre-

---

[1] In October, 1897, Yi Hyeung, hitherto satisfied with the title of King, had assumed the title of Emperor as indicative of the fact that Korea, now fully sovereign, was on an absolute equality with China and Japan.

sided over by the emperor, decided in favor of an alliance with the British. Baron Hayashi was accordingly authorized to take up the matter officially, and on January 30, 1902, the Anglo-Japanese Treaty of Alliance was formally concluded.

In their new treaty the two high contracting parties, while asserting the independence of China and Korea and declaring themselves to be "entirely uninfluenced by any aggressive tendencies in either country," recognized the fact that the interests "of Great Britain relate principally to China, while Japan, in addition to the interests which she possesses in China, is interested in a peculiar degree, politically as well as commercially and industrially, in Corea." In view of the above fact the two powers recognized that it would "be admissible for either of them to take such measures as may be indispensable in order to safeguard those interests if threatened either by the aggressive action of any other Power or by disturbances arising in China or Corea." In case either Great Britain or Japan in defense of the aforesaid interests became involved in war with another power, the other party to the alliance was to maintain strict neutrality and to use its efforts to prevent other powers from joining in hostilities against its ally. If, however, any other power or powers joined in the hostilities against the ally already involved in war, "the other High Contracting Party will come to its assistance, and will conduct the war in common, and will make peace in mutual agreement with it."

Having provided against the possibility of being involved single-handed in a war against a European coalition, the Japanese government was now in a position to secure from Russia, by force if necessary, adequate recognition of Japan's rights and interests in Korea. In June, 1903, after a year and a half of energetic military preparations, the Japanese decided to open negotiations with Russia concerning the respective rights of the two countries in Manchuria and Korea. On August 12 the Japanese formally proposed to Russia an agreement whereby the two countries, while pledging themselves to respect the independence and territorial integrity of China and Korea, should recognize reciprocally "Japan's preponderant interests in Korea and Russia's special interests in railway enterprises in Manchuria." Each country was to undertake not to interfere in the commercial and industrial enterprises of the other within its allotted sphere, and each country was to have the right to send into its own sphere of interest such troops as might be necessary to protect its undertakings. In addition, Russia was to recognize "the exclusive right of Japan to give advice and assistance in the interests of reform and good government in Korea, including necessary military assistance."

For nearly six months after the presentation of this proposal negotiations between the two governments were carried on in a desultory manner, the Tokyo government pressing for a satisfactory answer and the authorities at St. Petersburg consistently attempting to evade the issue. The Russians appear to have had no idea that the Japanese would ever resort to war, and the Japanese complained that the Czar's ministers, assuming an arrogant attitude, frequently allowed long periods to elapse before replying to the Japanese notes. In the meantime the Russian Yalu Lumber Company was busily exploiting the concession granted it by the Koreans, while the Trans-Siberian Railway, which would be of almost incalculable military importance, was rapidly nearing completion.

On February 6, 1904, the Japanese minister at St. Petersburg broke off negotiations and asked for his passports. Two days later the Japanese naval forces appeared off Chemulpo and Port Arthur, and hostilities commenced. By the majority of Western military experts Japan's appeal to arms was regarded as a suicidal blunder; Russia was a world power of the first rank, and few observers believed that Japan had any hope of success in a conflict against a first-rate European state. Only after the war was well under way did it become evident that the Japanese authorities had carefully considered all aspects of the situation and had opened hostilities under conditions which gave them at least an even chance of victory.

On paper the available naval forces of the two belligerents were approximately equal, but this paper equality was decidedly misleading in fact. The Russian fleet was not concentrated. Most of the ships were at Port Arthur, and two cruisers were in the port of Chemulpo, only twenty-four hours' sailing distance away; but the outbreak of the war found an important part of the Russian fleet icebound at Vladivostok, where they were absolutely useless.

The superiority of the Japanese land forces immediately available for operations in Korea and Manchuria, assuming that Japan was able to keep the sea open for her transports, was even more marked. At the outbreak of the war the Russian troops east of Lake Baikal numbered less than a hundred thousand; for supplies and reinforcements Russia was dependent upon the still-unfinished single-tracked Trans-Siberian line, and the total number of soldiers employed by her during the course of the war did not exceed a million. Japan, on the other hand, had about eight hundred thousand trained soldiers in readiness at the commencement of hostilities, and before the war was over she had landed a total of a million and a half men on the Asiatic mainland.

The prerequisite for Japanese success in the war was the establishment of superiority on the sea, and this superiority was secured during the first twenty-four hours after the commencement of hostilities. On February 9 the Japanese squadron which had been sent to Chemulpo destroyed the two Russian ships at that port. Some hours earlier, during the night of February 8–9, a Japanese torpedo attack upon the main Russian fleet at Port Arthur resulted in crippling two Russian battleships and a cruiser. From this moment the Russian naval forces were completely "bottled up" at Port Arthur and Vladivostok. Except for three torpedo boats which were sunk in the battle of Tsushima, practically the only Japanese naval losses during the war were caused by Russian mines, and the Japanese were able to pour their troops into Korea and Manchuria without any serious danger of interference by the enemy.

With their sea communications definitely assured, the Japanese military commanders were free to carry out their carefully planned campaign. As their best hope for victory lay in crushing the Russian armies before any great body of reinforcements from European Russia could be sent to the Far East, the Japanese generals constantly fought on the offensive. Korea was quickly overrun, and on May 1, 1904, the Japanese armies crossed the Yalu River into Manchuria. Five days after the crossing of the Yalu, Japan began to land troops on the coast of Liaotung for the purpose of cutting off the Russian leased territory and besieging the stronghold of Port Arthur.

By the end of August the Russian field forces outside Port Arthur had been driven northward almost to Mukden, and Port Arthur was completely invested. During the operations south of Mukden between the end of August and the middle of October, when both armies went into winter quarters, two hard-fought but indecisive battles forced the Russians a few miles farther northward. The failure of the Russians to push aside the Japanese field army and to reopen the communications of Port Arthur sealed the fate of that beleaguered fortress; on January 2, 1905, after a desperate siege, Port Arthur surrendered.

The fall of this stronghold practically determined the outcome of the war. In October, 1904, a Russian fleet composed of all the available ships in European waters had been dispatched to the Far East for the purpose of regaining the command of the sea, and the winter of 1904–1905 saw the arrival of strong reinforcements for the Russian army at Mukden. With the surrender of Port Arthur the Russian warships there were destroyed or captured, and the Japanese fleet was left free to concentrate against the approaching fleet from Europe. At the same time the Japanese land forces which hitherto had been engaged in the siege now became available as reinforcements for the army before Mukden. About the end of February the Japanese resumed the offensive and in a battle which lasted more than two weeks forced the Russians to withdraw to a new position some seventy miles north of Mukden. The losses on both sides were heavy; but the Russian army remained intact, and the success of the Japanese brought little apparent advantage.

Two months after the great battle around Mukden the Russian naval reinforcements arrived in Far Eastern waters. Port Arthur having fallen, the Russian commander had no choice but to attempt to reach Vladivostok. When the Russian fleet reached the strait between Korea and the island of Tsushima, it was met by the Japanese in full force; the battle at this point, fought on May 27–28, resulted in the almost total annihilation of the

Russian force, while the losses incurred by the Japanese were restricted to three torpedo boats.

Even before the battle of Tsushima it became evident that both belligerent powers were nearing the end of their resources. In Russia the war had never received popular support. The heavy burdens which it entailed and the long series of military reverses had aroused public discontent to the breaking point. Revolutionary movements were developing, and a longer continuance of the war might result in a complete overthrow of the government. Nor was Japan, despite the brilliant successes which had attended her efforts and the almost religious loyalty of the people to the emperor, in a much better condition. The costs of the war had been met by recourse to foreign loans; but the credit of the Japanese government was practically exhausted, and there was no money in sight for continuance of the conflict. For Japan the alternative was a quick peace or bankruptcy.

Three days after the battle of Tsushima the Japanese minister at Washington privately communicated to President Roosevelt an official request that he offer his services as a mediator so as to bring about the opening of peace negotiations. In response to this request the American President on June 8 formally proposed to Russia and Japan that they appoint plenipotentiaries to meet and arrange terms of peace. Japan announced on June 10 her acceptance of American "good offices," and the favorable reply of the Russian government was received two days later. On August 10 the representatives of the two belligerent powers met at Portsmouth, New Hampshire, and on September 5 a treaty of peace was signed.

Although the Japanese people were bitterly disappointed by the fact that the expected war indemnity was not obtained from Russia, the Treaty of Portsmouth gave Japan a great extension of rights and powers. Russia ceded to Japan that part of the island of Sakhalin lying south of the fiftieth parallel, recognized Japan's "paramount political, military, and economic interests" in Korea, and agreed to transfer to Japan, subject to the agreement of the Chinese government, the leased territory in Liaotung together with the railway between Changchun and Port Arthur and all the mining and other rights connected with the railway concession. The Russian government also agreed to pay the Japanese government the sum of twenty million dollars for the cost of maintaining the Russian prisoners of war during their captivity, and granted to the Japanese the right of fishing in the territorial waters of the Siberian coast.

Inasmuch as the transfer by Russia to Japan of the Liaotung leasehold and of the Port Arthur–Changchun railway (subsequently known as the South Manchuria Railway) required the consent of the Chinese government, Baron Komura was dispatched to Peking in November, 1905, for the purpose of obtaining this consent. At Peking, as at Portsmouth, the Japanese Minister of Foreign Affairs was highly successful. On December 22, after lengthy negotiations, he secured the signature of the Chinese plenipotentiaries to agreements which, during the ensuing quarter of a century, were to constitute the legal foundation for a steadily expanding body of "special rights" in Manchuria.

The basic document resulting from these negotiations was a brief treaty in which China acquiesced in "all the transfers and assignments made by Russia to Japan in Articles V and VI" of the Portsmouth Treaty, while the Japanese government agreed to conform, "so far as circumstances permit," to the original conditions under which the leased territory and the railway concession had been held by Russia. In thus securing what amounted to a right to nullify any and all of the conditions under which the lease and the railway contract had been granted, the Japanese obviously placed themselves in a far more privileged position than had been occupied by their predecessors.

An "Additional Agreement," signed at the same time, still further extended Japan's field of privileges. At Mukden, Yingkow, and Antung special areas—"concessions" or "settlements"—were to be set apart for Japanese residence under Japanese administration. Upon the withdrawal of the Russian and Japanese armed forces sixteen places in Manchuria were to be opened to international residence and trade. Japan received permission to rebuild on standard gauge and to operate until 1924 as a commercial line the narrow-gauge railway constructed during the war from Antung to Mukden. The timber concession on the west bank of the Yalu, formerly granted to the Russian Yalu company, was to be exploited by a joint company composed of Chinese and Japanese shareholders. As a *quid pro quo* for these various concessions Japan agreed that as soon as tranquillity had been restored in Manchuria, and China had "become capable of affording full protection to the lives and property of foreigners" in that area, she would withdraw her railway guards simultaneously with a like withdrawal by Russia.

The treaty and the additional agreement, both of which in due time were given publication, do not constitute a complete record of the concessions which the Japanese claim to have secured during the course of the negotiations. In February, 1906, the Tokyo Foreign Office communicated to the representatives of the powers chiefly interested in Far Eastern affairs a summary of certain "secret protocols" which, it was asserted, also had been concluded at Peking and were an integral part of the new arrangement entered into by China and Japan, but no *official text* of these alleged protocols, authorized by the two governments concerned, was ever made public. All the protocols related to the future of railway development in southern Manchuria, and one of them, according to the Japanese government, embodied the following pledge by China:

The Chinese Government engage, for the purpose of protecting the interests of the South Manchuria Railway, not to construct, prior to the recovery by them of the said railway, any main line in the neighborhood of and parallel to that railway, or any branch line which might be prejudicial to the interests of the above-mentioned railway.

During the subsequent quarter of a century this alleged protocol was repeatedly and, as we shall see, successfully invoked by the Japanese government as a binding treaty commitment on the part of China, entitling Japan to veto the construction of any railway that threatened to impair the value of the Japanese lines in Manchuria. On the other hand, T'ang Shao-yi, who was one of the Chinese plenipotentiaries at the Peking negotiations, stated in January, 1908, that the Japanese had sought such a pledge, that the question had been discussed and therefore appears in the minutes of the conference, but that no protocol or other legally binding agreement to this effect had been signed.[1]

Two days after the opening of the peace negotiations at Portsmouth the British Minister of Foreign Affairs and the Japanese minister at London signed a renewal—or a revision—of the treaty of alliance which had been concluded three and a half years earlier. This new and revised version of the Anglo-Japanese Alliance differed on a number of significant points from the original. In the preamble of the new document the maintenance of the "independence and integrity of the Chinese Empire" still appears as one of the objects of the agreement, but all reference to the preservation of Korean independence is omitted. India now appears for the first time as a part of the area within which the contracting parties agree to co-operate in defense of their special interests, while in Article III of the treaty Great Britain recognizes the right of Japan to take such measures as she may deem necessary to safeguard and advance her "paramount political, military, and economic interests in Corea."

The revised treaty of alliance, like the original, was *intended* to remain in force for a term of ten years but, also like the original, underwent revision before the expiration of that term. In 1911 the British government, anxious to allay any suspicion that the alliance

---

[1] For a fuller study of this important question the student is referred to K. Asakawa, "Japan in Manchuria," in the *Yale Review*, August, 1908; P. H. Clyde, *International Rivalries in Manchuria*, pp. 104 ff.; K. K. Kawakami, *American-Japanese Relations*, p. 34; J. V. A. MacMurray (editor), *Treaties and Agreements with and concerning China, 1894–1919*, Vol. I, pp. 549–554; W. W. Willoughby, *Foreign Rights and Interests in China* (revised edition), pp. 171–173; C. Walter Young, *Japan's Special Position in Manchuria*, pp. 87–105; and Report of the Lytton Commission (*League of Nations, Appeal by the Chinese Government, Report of the Commission of Enquiry*), p. 44. The following from the Lytton report may be regarded as conclusive:

In Tokyo, Nanking and Peiping, all the relevant documents were examined, and we are now able to state that the alleged engagement of the Chinese plenipotentiaries of the Peking Conference of November-December, 1905, regarding so-called "parallel railways" is not contained in any formal treaty; that the alleged engagement in question is found in the minutes of the eleventh day of the Peking Conference, December 4th, 1905. We have obtained agreement of the Japanese and Chinese Assessors that no other document containing such alleged engagement exists beyond this entry in the minutes of the Peking Conference.

was aimed at the United States, secured Japan's consent to the inclusion of the following stipulation:

> Should either of the High Contracting Parties conclude a treaty of general arbitration with a third power, it is agreed that nothing in this Agreement shall impose on such contracting party an obligation to go to war with the Power with whom such an arbitration treaty is in force.

This second revision, signed on July 13, 1911, was also for a term of ten years.[1]

To the nationalistic patriots in every country of the Far East the outcome of the Russo-Japanese War seemed to promise the dawn of a new era. For more than a century the Orient had been helpless in the face of the steady advance of Occidental domination, with the result that the peoples of the Orient had come to regard the West as irresistible and invincible. Japan's success in a single-handed combat against one of the greatest of European powers aroused a new spirit of hopefulness among the peoples of Asia who resented the economic and political domination of the West. Japan had proved that the European was not invincible, and what the Japanese had accomplished might also be accomplished by other Asiatics. Japan was taken as an ideal by the patriots of all parts of the Orient; "Asia for the Asiatics" became their common watchword; and even a "Pan-Asian Union" under the leadership of the Japanese Empire was advocated by orators and publicists in China and India, although this last enthusiasm was soon chilled by Japan's own actions on the Asiatic continent, particularly in Korea.

On January 21, 1904, the Korean government, anticipating the outbreak of war between Russia and Japan, had issued a declaration of neutrality. Any hope that this move would enable the feeble "empire" to avoid becoming involved in the approaching conflict was, however, doomed to speedy disappointment. Upon the out-

---

[1] At the expiration of the ten-year term the treaty was not renewed; it continued in force, however, by virtue of a provision for such continuation "until the expiration of one year from the day on which either of the High Contracting Parties shall have denounced it." During the Washington Conference (November, 1921, to February, 1922) the alliance was terminated by mutual consent as a condition to the conclusion of the Four-Power Pact between France, Great Britain, Japan, and the United States.

break of hostilities Japan, ignoring the Korean declaration, landed forty thousand soldiers at Chemulpo; and the major portion of this force proceeded directly to the capital, where the resident Japanese minister was pressing upon the court a treaty of alliance. After two weeks of futile resistance to Japanese pressure the Korean monarch, on February 23, gave way and signed the treaty; in return for a Japanese guaranty of Korean independence and territorial integrity he accepted Japan as an ally and pledged himself to follow Japanese advice in matters of internal reform. Six months later (August 22, 1904) a second agreement, also signed under pressure, bound the Korean emperor to accept a Japanese financial adviser and to consult the Japanese government on all matters affecting foreign affairs.

The termination of the Russo-Japanese conflict was to bring to Korea only an intensification of Japanese domination. The revised Anglo-Japanese Alliance, signed on August 12, 1905, contained no reference to Korean independence; on the contrary the British government therein explicitly recognized Japan's right "to take such measures of guidance, control, and protection in Corea as she may deem proper and necessary to safeguard" her "paramount political, military, and economic interests." By Article II of the Portsmouth Treaty, Russia accorded her late adversary, in almost identical terms, a free hand in the affairs of the peninsula, and even before the conclusion of these two treaties President Roosevelt, through his personal representative, had given the Tokyo Foreign Office an assurance that the reorganization of Korea by the Japanese would meet with no opposition from the United States.

Having thus made certain that a "forward" policy in Korea would evoke no protest from the powers chiefly interested in the Far East, the Japanese authorities lost little time in reducing the Korean Empire to the status of a thinly disguised protectorate. Early in November, 1905, Marquis Ito was dispatched to Seoul to secure a satisfactory revision of the treaty relations between the two empires, and on November 17 the Korean monarch—according to his own subsequent statement, "at the point of the sword and under duress"—authorized the conclusion of a new convention. Under the terms of the new treaty the Foreign Office at Tokyo was to have "control and direction of the external relations and affairs" of Korea; the Japanese government was to be represented at Seoul by a resident-general who should have the right of "private and personal audience" with the Korean emperor; Japan was also to appoint residents at the several ports and at such other places as she might deem necessary, to exercise the powers and functions formerly exercised by consuls and "to perform such other duties as may be necessary in order to carry into full effect the provisions of this agreement." These arrangements were to remain in force "until the moment when it is recognized that Corea has attained national strength."

The arrangement of November 17, 1905, remained in force less than two years. In the early summer of 1907 the Korean emperor, taking advantage of the fact that the Second Hague Conference was about to meet, secretly dispatched a mission to Europe for the purpose of laying before that august assembly Korea's case against her aggressive neighbor. Japan's representatives at the Hague prevented the Korean mission from obtaining a hearing, but at Seoul the unfortunate Yi Hyeung, for having thus dared to disregard the terms of his treaty with Japan, was forced to abdicate in favor of his son Yi Chuk. The abdication took place on July 9 (six days before the Hague Conference actually began its sessions); and fifteen days later the new emperor was compelled to give his assent to a fresh convention whereby the last vestiges of political power were taken from him, to be placed in the hands of the Japanese resident-general and other appointees of the Japanese government.

The new convention, like the one which it replaced, quickly proved unsatisfactory. Even the beneficial reforms initiated by the Japanese officials met with widespread opposition, while the popular hatred for Japan was constantly aggravated by the unscrupulous operations of numerous Japanese fortune-hunters. An outstanding object of Korean hatred was Ito Hirobumi (Prince Ito since 1905), who had negotiated the 1907 agreement as well as that of 1905; and in October, 1909, Ito was assassinated at Harbin, in Manchuria, by a fanatical Korean patriot. From this point events moved inexorably, but without unseemly haste, to their long-anticipated goal. On July 24, 1910, a newly appointed resident-general—General Terauchi, who simultaneously held the office of Minister of War in the Japanese cabinet—arrived at Seoul. On the following day Terauchi had an audience with the Korean emperor and empress. As a result of this interview Yi Chuk humbly petitioned for the annexation of Korea to the Japanese Empire, and on August 22, 1910, the treaty of annexation was signed.

The explanatory announcement published by the Tokyo Foreign Office said:

In its solicitude to put an end to disturbing conditions the Japanese Government made an arrangement in 1905, for establishing a protectorate over Korea, and they have ever since been assiduously engaged in works of reform, looking forward to the consummation of the desired end. But they have failed to find in the régime of a protectorate sufficient hope for a realization of the object which they had in view, and a condition of unrest and disquietude still prevails throughout the entire peninsula. In these circumstances, the necessity of introducing fundamental changes in the system of government in Korea has become entirely manifest, and an earnest and careful examination of the Korean problem has convinced the Japanese Government that the régime of a protectorate cannot be made to adapt itself to the actual condition of affairs in Korea, and that the responsibilities devolving upon Japan for the due administration of the country cannot be justly fulfilled without the complete annexation of Korea to the Empire.

The ratifications of the Treaty of Portsmouth were exchanged on November 25, 1905, and on August 1 of the following year the Changchun–Port Arthur section of the Chinese Eastern Railway was formally transferred to the possession of Japan. Upon the completion of the railway transfer, negotiations were promptly opened between the Russian Foreign Minister, Isvolsky, and Baron Motono, the Japanese representative at St. Petersburg, for the ostensible purpose of arranging the simultaneous evacuation of Manchuria by the opposing armies and of concluding the treaty of commerce and navigation and the fisheries convention stipulated in the Portsmouth Treaty. The actual scope of the negotiations, however, was much more extensive, and on July 30, 1907, the representatives of the recently warring empires affixed their signature to two political treaties, one intended for publication and the other to remain a carefully guarded secret. These two agreements laid the foundation for complete understanding and co-operation between the Russian and Japanese governments in the exploitation of their respective spheres of influence in eastern Asia.

In the brief published treaty the high contracting parties, after paying the now customary lip service to "the independence and territorial integrity of China and the principle of the Open Door," reciprocally agreed to maintain the existing status quo "by all the peaceful means within their reach." No definition of the status quo thus solemnly guaranteed was incorporated in the published document, but the terms of the companion secret treaty show that the two governments had reached a mutually satisfactory agreement on this point. From the northernmost point of the Korean-Siberian frontier a "demarcation line" was drawn in a northwesterly direction to the Sungari River, thence up the Sungari to the mouth of the Nonni (the "Nunkuang" in the treaty), up the Nonni to the mouth of the Tola, and up the course of this last river "to its intersection with the Meridian 122° East of Greenwich" in the eastern foothills of the Great Khingan range. To the north and south of the line thus drawn Russia and Japan, respectively, were to enjoy unmolested freedom in seeking concessions for railways and telegraph lines.[1] Russia, fully informed with respect to the conventions and arrangements governing the relations between Japan and Korea, undertook "not to interfere or to place any obstacle in the way of the further development of those relations," while the Japanese government, "recognizing the special interests of Russia in Outer Mongolia," agreed "to refrain from any interference which might prejudice those interests."

On July 4, 1910, a second pair of treaties, one to be published and the other to remain secret, were concluded at St. Petersburg by Isvolsky and Motono. In the published treaty of this date there appeared no reference to "the integrity of China" or to "the principle of the Open Door," and the two governments, instead of undertaking to maintain the existing status quo "by all the peaceful means within their reach," assumed a more bellicose stand. Article III reads:

[1] Although the demarcation line ran some seventy miles north of Changchun, it was explicitly understood that Russia's rights in the Chinese Eastern Railway down to Changchun were to remain undisturbed.

In case any event of such a nature as to menace the above-mentioned *status quo* should be brought about, the two High Contracting Parties will in each instance enter into communication with each other for the purpose of agreeing upon the measures that they may judge it necessary to take for the maintenance of the said *status quo*.

As in 1907, however, the more important points of agreement were set forth not in the published document but in the simultaneously concluded secret treaty. Here, after reaffirming the demarcation line fixed in 1907, the high contracting parties agreed to respect reciprocally "the special interests" of each in the spheres already indicated, and recognized "the right of each, within its own sphere, freely to take all measures for the safeguarding and defense of those interests." Each power undertook "not to hinder in any way the consolidation and further development" of the special interests of the other party within the limits of the above-mentioned spheres. In case these special interests were threatened, they pledged themselves to "agree upon the measures to be taken with a view to common action . . . for the safeguarding and defense of those interests."

On July 8, 1912, still another secret convention was concluded. "In order to avoid all cause of misunderstanding concerning their special interests in Manchuria and Mongolia," the Russian and Japanese governments decided "to prolong the line of demarcation and to define their spheres of special interests in Inner Mongolia." From its 1907 terminus on the eastern slopes of the Great Khingan Mountains the demarcation line was extended so as to bring within the Japanese sphere that portion of Inner Mongolia lying east of "the meridian of Peking (116° 27′ East of Greenwich)." Inner Mongolia to the west of that meridian, like all of Outer Mongolia, was henceforth recognized by Japan as belonging to the Russian sphere.

While the years following the close of the Russo-Japanese War were marked by the development of increasing cordiality between Japan and her recent enemy, the same period saw a corresponding decrease in the good will which had hitherto characterized the relations between Japan and the United States. Indeed, the various Russo-Japanese treaties mentioned above reflected and were, in large measure, inspired by the growing bitterness of Japanese-American relations.

This unfortunate development must be attributed to a number of factors. In Japan, although President Roosevelt had shown himself decidedly pro-Japanese during and at the close of the war, public opinion was encouraged to blame the American President for Japan's failure to secure from Russia the payment of a war indemnity; when the indemnity question had threatened to produce a deadlock at Portsmouth, Mr. Roosevelt had wired to the Japanese emperor, strongly urging that Japan should not break off negotiations on this point, and the Japanese press had found it convenient to hold him personally responsible for the disappointing character of the resultant treaty. In the United States, on the other hand, the people along the Pacific coast, and especially in California, were beginning to resent the competition of Japanese immigrant labor and to apply to the Japanese the "exclusionist" arguments which formerly had been used against the Chinese; this agitation, which first took definite form in the segregation of Japanese school children in the public schools of San Francisco, inevitably intensified the existing anti-American feeling on the Japanese side of the Pacific.

Underlying these superficial causes for friction, however, was the development of conflicting economic interests in the Far East. The decade between the Sino-Japanese and Russo-Japanese wars had been marked by a steady expansion of American commercial activity in the Orient and by the efforts of the American government to establish the open-door principle in China as a guaranty against the exclusion of its nationals from that important field. During this period the Russians had been looked upon as the most dangerous opponents of the open door, while the Japanese had been regarded as strong supporters of the principle. With the conclusion of the war Japan stepped into Russia's shoes in southern Manchuria and showed her intention of utilizing her new position in much the same way as it had been utilized by the Russians. Indeed, American commercial interests soon discovered that the substitution of Japan for Russia was, from their point of view, far from advantageous. Japan, unlike Russia, had a rapidly growing industrial system, and the Japanese industrialists demanded that their government secure southern Manchuria as an exclusive field for Japanese exploitation. Nor was the irritation which arose out of economic questions felt only on the American side. To the Japanese it appeared, not without reason, that the Americans, who had already brought Hawaii within their tariff wall and were soon to do the same with the Philippines, were attempting to force their way into the Manchurian field and to deprive Japan of the legitimate fruits of victory.

By Article VII of the Portsmouth Treaty, Russia and Japan formally proclaimed their intention "to exploit their railways in Manchuria exclusively for commercial and industrial purposes," while Article IV of the same document stated that the two governments would not "obstruct any general measure, common to all countries, which China may take for the development of the commerce and industry of Manchuria." At the conclusion of the war, as we have seen, the Japanese government was in serious financial straits, and the statesmen at Tokyo appear to have had little prospect of exploiting, without the aid of foreign capital, the concessions acquired by the treaty. In view of these circumstances American observers would seem to have been justified in regarding the expulsion of Russia from southern Manchuria as marking the dawn of a new era in which business opportunities, especially in the field of railway development, would be thrown open to American capital.

The first American attempt to take advantage of the situation momentarily confirmed this optimistic belief. In October, 1905, Mr. E. H. Harriman, who was then in the Far East for the purpose of securing a trans-Asiatic link for his projected round-the-world transportation system, was able to conclude with Prime Minister Katsura and Marquis Ito a preliminary agreement for the establishment of an American-Japanese syndicate which should finance and operate the Japanese railways and accompanying mining concessions in southern Manchuria, the profits from this operation to be divided equally between the syndicate and the Japanese government. Foreign Minister Komura, however, had different ideas, and on his return from America he strenuously opposed the arrangement, insisting that Japan should retain for herself both the control of and the profits to be derived from her newly acquired concession. The preliminary agreement with Mr. Harriman was therefore abrogated, and on June 7, 1906, an ordinance of the Meiji emperor authorized the formation of the "South Manchuria Railway Joint Stock Company," to which the government transferred its Manchurian railway rights.

The imperial ordinance creating the company provided that its shares should be "owned only by the Japanese and Chinese governments or by the subjects of Japan and China." The Chinese government, however, made no move to avail itself of the privilege offered it, while few, if any, of the shares were subscribed for by Chinese subjects. On the other hand, the Japanese government has always from the beginning held a majority of the stock. Inasmuch as the president and the vice-president of the company were appointed by the Prime Minister, with the emperor's approval, the South Manchuria Railway was in fact a government department and was entrusted with extensive political functions in Japan's Manchurian "sphere of influence."

In November, 1907, the Chinese government concluded a contract with an Anglo-Chinese syndicate for the construction of a fifty-mile extension of the Chinese Imperial Railway (subsequently known as the Peking-Mukden Railway) from Hsinmintun, at that time its northern terminus, to Fakumen, a city some fifty miles northwest of Mukden. On the ground that the proposed extension would violate the alleged "parallel lines" pledge given by China in 1905, Japan promptly announced her objection; she was upheld in this stand by the British government, and the contract was canceled.

Japan's veto of the Hsinmintun-Fakumen project, which seems to have been a deliberate challenge to her railway monopoly in southern Manchuria, amounted to a denial that the open-door principle applied to this portion of Chinese territory. No American financial interests were directly involved in this affair, and the government of the United States, officially at least, took no cognizance of the claims asserted by Tokyo; but a year later (November 30, 1908) Secretary of State Root, in an exchange of notes with Ambassador Takahira, associated the defense of the open door and of China's integrity and independence with the maintenance of the status quo in the Pacific area as points upon which the two governments were agreed.

In 1909, after a number of tentative proposals for new railroads in Manchuria, an Anglo-American syndicate entered into negotiations with the Chinese government for the construction of a railroad, some seven hundred miles in length, from Chinchow on the Gulf of Pechihli (Pohai) to Aigun on the Amur River. On January 20, 1910, the contract for the line received the approval of the Chinese government. Even before the contract received imperial confirmation the new American Secretary of State, Mr. Knox, took up the matter with the British government and suggested that, in conformity with the principles of the open door, the financiers of the other treaty powers be invited, with China's approval, to participate in the enterprise.

In connection with this railway project and in the hope of securing to China the undisturbed enjoyment of her political rights in the Manchurian provinces Mr. Knox also proposed, first to the British government and later to Japan and Russia, a scheme for "neutralizing" all the railways of Manchuria by bringing them under the control of an international consortium. According to this scheme the six great powers chiefly interested in China —America, Great Britain, France, Germany, Japan, and Russia— should float a loan of sufficient size to enable the Chinese government to repurchase the Chinese Eastern and South Manchuria lines and to build all the projected Manchurian lines, the Chinchow-Aigun as well as those arranged for by the Japanese or the Russians.

The success of the Knox proposal, which the British Foreign Minister approved "in principle," depended upon the willingness of Japan and Russia to allow the repurchase of the Chinese Eastern and South Manchuria lines before the date stipulated in the contracts under which those two lines were built. Upon this point, however, the proposal was hopelessly wrecked; both Russia and Japan promptly rejected the scheme. The Russian reply pointed out that the Chinese Eastern, constituting as it did a link in the Trans-Siberian system, could not properly become a part of an internationally controlled railway organization. To the Japanese the proposal was, if possible, even more objectionable than to the Russians. Before the Russo-Japanese War, Manchuria had been recognized as a Russian sphere of interest, and Japan had now secured, by force of arms, the southern portion of that sphere. The Japanese, moreover, could see no reason or justice in an attempt to internationalize and neutralize the Manchurian railways, in which they had vested interests, so long as the railways in the British, French, and German spheres were allowed to remain undisturbed in the possession of the financial interests of those countries.

Unanimous in their opposition to the neutralization scheme, the Russian and Japanese governments took somewhat different stands on the subject of the Chinchow-Aigun railway. Russia, in notes to Peking and Washington, promptly vetoed the project on the ground that such a railway, crossing the Chinese Eastern and tapping the resources of the region north of that line, would be injurious to her strategic and economic interests. Japan, although less openly defiant, was hardly less opposed to the new line and on January 31, 1910, informed the Chinese government that Japanese consent must be obtained before any new railway could be constructed. Two weeks later a note to the Waiwupu declared that Japan would participate in the undertaking on condition that the line be connected at some point with the South Manchuria Railway, but subsequent additional conditions on matters of detail were so unacceptable to China as to place the Japanese conditional approval almost on a par with the Russian veto. The contract for the line was therefore canceled.

Following the failure of the Chinchow-Aigun project, American capital, in combination with English, French, and German financial interests, made one more attempt to enter the Manchurian field. On October 27, 1910, the representatives of an American banking group signed a preliminary contract for a loan to China of £10,000,000, of which amount £1,000,000 was definitely earmarked as intended for "the promotion and extension of industrial enterprises in the three Manchurian provinces." The American banks involved in the negotiation were interested in the development of possibilities for investment throughout China and had previously entered into a working agreement to that end with certain banks of the three above-mentioned countries; the British, French and German banks were therefore admitted to participation in the new financial undertaking, and on April 15, 1911, the final contract for the loan was signed by the four-power banking group (generally known as the Four-Power Consortium) and the Chinese imperial government.

As early as November 19, 1910, Japan expressed to the Russian government her opposition to the Manchurian feature of the loan, and seven months later her ambassador at Paris informed the French Foreign Office that Japan could not view with indifference measures which tended to menace her "special rights and interests" in southern Manchuria. Japan's objections were ably seconded by Russia, and only £400,000 of the sum so designated was actually utilized in Manchuria.

The outbreak of the Chinese Revolution in the fall of 1911 put a temporary stop to these financial operations, but in the spring of 1912 Japanese and Russian banking interests were invited to join with the four-power group in financing a large "reorganization loan" to the Chinese Republic. In accepting this invitation both Japan and Russia laid down the condition that nothing in the proposed loan should operate to the prejudice of their special rights and interests in Manchuria and Mongolia; Japan even attempted to secure a guaranty that no part of the loan would be expended in those regions. The withdrawal of the American group in March, 1913, left the two new members in a position to dominate Consortium policies. In May of the same year a loan of £25,000,000 was actually floated, but the proceeds were employed by Yüan Shih-k'ai to meet his financial problems south of the Great Wall. Once more, Japan and Russia had succeeded in preventing the invasion of their special preserve by European and American rivals.

Turning from war, diplomacy, and territorial expansion to the less spectacular subject of domestic development, we find that during the years 1900–1914 Japan not only maintained but even quickened her pace in adopting the most modern Western methods of transportation, factory production, business organization, and finance. This steady progress is most strikingly illustrated by the statistics of foreign trade. In 1894 the total foreign trade of the empire, imports and exports, amounted to some two hundred and thirty million yen. Five years later the total value of imports and exports had increased to four hundred and thirty million yen. In 1904, the first year of the Russian war, the foreign trade for the year amounted to nearly seven hundred million yen. In 1913 this total was one billion three hundred and sixty million yen, while in 1914, the last year of the period under review, it exceeded a billion and a half.

From 1899 until 1914, when the whole trend of international trade was dislocated by the World War, Japan's balance sheet showed a substantial excess of imports over exports. In 1898 this excess amounted to about ten million yen, while the figures for 1913 showed imports valued at seven hundred and twenty-nine million yen as against exports to the amount of six hundred and thirty-two million. To some extent the unfavorable balance of trade was redressed by such "invisible exports" as tourists' expenditures in Japan and the earnings of a growing Japanese merchant marine, but Japan during these years was a borrowing country, utilizing foreign capital to purchase abroad the machinery needed for her rapidly developing industrial system. The foreign capital thus utilized for the upbuilding of Japanese industry amounted in 1914 to more than two billion yen, about two thirds of the amount which at that time had been invested by foreigners in China. Unlike their Chinese neighbors, however, the Japanese had been able to retain complete control over their railways, hydroelectric plants, mines, shipyards, and factories; for the foreign investor in Japan was only a bondholder and not, as in China, the owner of the enterprise for which his funds had been employed.

In the development of Japan's modern factory system the cotton-textile industry led the way. As early as 1898 the number of power-driven spindles in Japanese spinning mills had reached the million mark; after that date machine spinning and the output of yarn increased by leaps and bounds. The adoption of power-driven machinery for weaving was less rapid, the great advance in this direction coming after the Russian war. In 1905 the number of power looms in operation was only 19,000 as compared with more than 700,000 old-fashioned hand looms; by 1914, however, only

400,000 of the hand machines were still in use, while the number of power looms had increased more than sixfold to 123,000.

In 1890 there were 1700 miles of railway in Japan, 550 miles owned by the government and the rest by private companies. By the end of 1905 the total railway mileage had risen to about 4000, and in 1914 there were 8000 miles of railroads in operation. The greater part of new railway construction throughout the entire history of Japanese railways has been undertaken by private enterprise; but in March, 1906, a Railway Nationalization Law was enacted, under which the government, at the cost of four hundred and eighty-two million yen, took over some twenty-eight hundred miles of privately built lines. Under this act private companies were encouraged to build and operate local lines with the understanding that such lines, if they became of national importance, would be absorbed into the national system.

Prior to the Russo-Japanese War, Japan's shipbuilding industry was, as a recent Japanese writer has expressed it, "in an infantile stage." The shipyards at Yokohama, Kobe, and Nagasaki, founded in the early years of the Meiji era, were capable of producing small merchant vessels and auxiliary ships for the navy, but all the fighting members of the naval force with which Japan opened the war had been purchased abroad. During the struggle the government undertook to construct in its own yards two 13,000-ton armored cruisers. Immediately after the close of the war two battleships, ordered from Great Britain before the outbreak of hostilities, were delivered; but with these exceptions the only non-Japanese unit added to the navy since 1904 is the battle cruiser *Konjo*, completed in 1913.

On July 30, 1912, the emperor Mutsuhito died, and the epoch-making Meiji era, whose forty-five years had witnessed Japan's transformation from an isolated feudal state to a well-organized empire ranking high among the great powers of the world, came at last to an end. The death of the old emperor brought to the throne his son Yoshihito, whose accession inaugurated the year-period known as Taisho ("Great Righteousness"). In commerce and industry, as in the field of foreign relations, the first two years of the Taisho era saw steady progress along the lines which characterized the closing years of Meiji. While Japanese diplomacy maintained and even strengthened Japan's special position in Manchuria, the extension of railway and steamship lines, the erection of new and more modern factories, and the expansion of foreign trade continued to strengthen the empire's position in the economic world. It is only when we turn to the internal political situation that we find any break between the new reign and the one just ended.

During the closing decade of the Meiji era the relations between the Diet and the government had been far more harmonious than those during the earlier years of Japan's experiment with parliamentary government. From 1901 to 1912 the post of Premier was held alternately by two men, Katsura and Saionji,[1] and the three changes of government during this period were not caused by conflicts with a hostile majority in the Diet. This record of political tranquillity may be attributed in no small part to the general spirit of loyalty and intense nationalism aroused by the diplomatic struggle and the subsequent war against Russia and to the feeling, after 1905, that every patriotic subject of the emperor should devote his energies to the task of consolidating Japan's newly attained position as a world power. Even more important as insurance against the development of party strife was the positive influence of the emperor, to whom the ministers were responsible and in whose name they administered the nation's affairs. Surrounded and supported by an inner circle of trusted advisers known as the Genro[2] ("Elder Statesmen"), Mutsuhito was an active participant in governmental affairs, and his ministers, relying upon the prestige of the throne, had little cause to fear parliamentary opposition.

With the accession of the new emperor came party strife and political confusion. In November, 1912, Saionji, because of his

[1] Katsura, 1901–1905; Saionji, 1905–1908; Katsura, 1908–1911; Saionji, 1911–1912.

[2] The Genro first appeared as a recognized, albeit extralegal, body in 1900, but it was composed of men who from the beginning of the reign had played a prominent part in directing the policies of the government. Its original members were Yamagata Arimoto, Ito Hirobumi, Inouye Tsuyoshiaki, Oyama Iwao, and Matsukata Masayoshi. The first three were Choshu men; the last two were Satsuma. In 1911 and 1912 two new members were added: Katsura Taro, of Choshu, and Saionji Kimmochi, a descendant of the old kuge nobility. At present (September, 1935) Prince Saionji is the sole surviving member of the Genro.

refusal to acquiesce in the army's demand for two additional army divisions, was forced out of office by the military clique. On the recommendation of the Genro, Katsura was commanded to form a ministry; but in February, when the Diet met, the orators of the various political parties opened a violent attack upon the government and upon the anonymous counselors who had advised Katsura's appointment. Katsura promptly resigned and was followed as Prime Minister by Admiral Yamamoto. The Yamamoto ministry succeeded in gaining the support of the Seiyukai, at that time the majority party in the House of Representatives, and continued in office until March, 1914, when the disclosure of a serious naval scandal led to its resignation. The choice of the Genro now fell on the aged Count Okuma, an avowed "party politician" and the leader of the Kenseikai. Okuma had repeatedly stated his conviction that the ministry should be responsible to the elected branch of the Diet; but despite the fact that the Kenseikai held a minority of the seats in the House of Representatives, he undertook without hesitation the task of forming a government. In the face of a hostile Seiyukai majority the Okuma ministry, with the support of the civil and military bureaucrats, weathered the storm of public criticism until August, when Japan's entry into the World War aroused once more the militant patriotism of the nation and— temporarily at least—put an end to party politics.

SUGGESTED REFERENCES

CLYDE, P. H. International Rivalries in Manchuria.

DENNETT, T. Roosevelt and the Russo-Japanese War.

DENNIS, A. L. P. The Anglo-Japanese Alliance.

DILLON, E. J. The Eclipse of Russia.

FRANKE, O. Die Grossmächte in Ostasien von 1894 bis 1914.

KAWAKAMI, K. K. American-Japanese Relations.

KIKUCHI, BARON D. Japanese Education.

McGOVERN, W. M. Modern Japan, its Political, Military, and Industrial Organization.

McKENZIE, F. A. The Tragedy of Korea.

McLAREN, W. W. A Political History of Japan during the Meiji Era.

ORCHARD, J. E. Japan's Economic Position.

POOLEY, A. M. (editor). The Secret Memoirs of Count Tadasu Hayashi.

PORTER, R. P. Japan, the Rise of a Modern Power.

PRICE, E. B. The Russo-Japanese Treaties of 1907–1916.

ROSEN, BARON R. R. Forty Years of Diplomacy.

XXX

The World War in the Far East

Early Efforts to Neutralize the Far East · Japan's Ultimatum to Germany ·
Kiaochow and the Neutrality of China · The Fall of Kiaochow · The Twenty-one
Demands · Negotiations · The Sino-Japanese Treaties and Notes of May 25, 1915 ·
The Imperial Ambitions of Yüan Shih-k'ai · Yüan's Disappointment and Death ·
China's Entry into the War · Siam and the War · Russia and China in Mongolia,
1914–1916 · The Russo-Japanese Treaties of July 3, 1916 · The Allies and China's
Belligerency · The Lansing-Ishii Notes · Japanese Influence in China · The Far
East at the Paris Conference · The New International Consortium

WITH the outbreak of the World War in the summer of 1914
many parts of the Far East, being possessions of one
or another of the European belligerents, became automatically
involved in a struggle with which they had no natural concern. In
spite of the legal status of belligerency thus conferred upon the
British, French, Russian, and German territories in eastern Asia
and in the Pacific Ocean, early efforts were made by some of the
warring powers as well as by two interested neutrals, China and
the United States, to prevent as far as possible the spread of hostilities into the Far Eastern area.

On the third or fourth of August the diplomatic representatives
of the United States and of China, acting in concert, approached
the various belligerents and possible belligerents with the proposal
that they pledge themselves not to engage in hostilities in Chinese
territorial waters or on Chinese territory, including the leased
areas held by foreign powers.[1] Both at London and at Berlin the
proposal found a not unfavorable hearing, and the British Foreign
Minister, Sir Edward Grey, is reported to have said that the
maintenance of the status quo in the Far East would be advantageous to all concerned.

[1] Kwangchowwan, held by France; Kowloon and Weihaiwei, by Great Britain;
Kiaochow, by Germany; and Liaotung, by Japan.

Even before the receipt of the American-Chinese proposal, or at least independently, the British Foreign Office appears to have made an effort to prevent the spread of the war into this part of the world; for on August 4, when thanking the Japanese ambassador for his government's offer of assistance, Sir Edward Grey recalled the fact that Japan during the Russo-Japanese War "had demanded almost less than at one time it seemed she might have been entitled to have" under the terms of the Anglo-Japanese alliance, and added, "and now we in turn should avoid, if we could, drawing Japan into any trouble."[1] The Berlin authorities, perhaps because of the weakness of Germany's forces in the Far East, were even more favorable to the proposed neutralization of the area and went so far as to suggest a reciprocal agreement with Great Britain whereby each would refrain from attacking the colonies or commerce of the other in the regions east of the meridian 90° east of Greenwich.

In giving their approval and support to proposals calculated to preclude the extension of the war zone into eastern Asia the European powers were unquestionably actuated by a desire to preserve intact the prestige and the economic interests of the white race in that part of the world. Whether a self-denying ordinance to this end would have been respected by both sides throughout the conflict is an interesting academic question. The maintenance of the status quo in the Far East, however, did not rest with the Western belligerents; less than two weeks after the commencement of hostilities in Europe the imperial Japanese government, for reasons satisfactory to itself, entered the war on the side of the Allies.

Japan's decisive move took the form of an ultimatum to Germany on August 15, to which an unconditional acceptance within eight days was requested:

Considering it highly important and necessary, in the present situation, to take measures to remove all causes of disturbance to the peace of the Far East and to safeguard the general interests contemplated by the Agreement of Alliance between Japan and Great Britain, in order to secure a firm and enduring peace in eastern Asia, the establishment of which is the aim of the

[1] *British Official Documents on the Origin of the War*, Vol. XI, p. 329.

said agreement, the Imperial Japanese Government sincerely believe it their duty to give advice to the Imperial German Government to carry out the following two propositions:

(1) To withdraw their men-of-war and armed vessels of all kinds from Japanese and Chinese waters, and to disarm at once all that cannot be so withdrawn.

(2) To deliver up to the Japanese authorities, by September 15, without condition or compensation, the entire leased territory of Kiaochow with a view to the eventual restoration of the same to China.[1]

The German government made no reply to the ultimatum, and on August 23 Japan declared war.

In 1898, when Germany forced from China the lease of Tsingtao and of the adjoining territory on the shore of Kiaochow Bay, Emperor William and his advisers appear to have been primarily interested in the future of the leasehold as a naval base. During their sixteen years of occupancy, however, the Germans had devoted themselves to the task of developing the commercial possibilities of their foothold on Chinese soil and had made no serious effort to transform it into a second Port Arthur—a Far Eastern Gibraltar. Defensive fortifications had, indeed, been constructed on the hills behind the flourishing seaport; but these fortifications,

---

[1] Taken in conjunction with other pertinent facts, the above carefully worded reference to the Anglo-Japanese Alliance suggests that the Tokyo government found in that treaty a convenient pretext rather than a cause for participation in the war. Great Britain's earlier approval of efforts to prevent the spread of the war into the Far East has already been noted, and Dr. Reinsch, at that time the American minister at Peking, states that the British government was not informed of Japan's intended action until after the ultimatum had been delivered (*An American Diplomat in China*, p. 123). Until 1917, when Great Britain by special agreement with Japan secured the dispatch of Japanese destroyers to the Mediterranean for service against German submarines, Japan's activity against the Central Powers was limited to the seizure of German territories in the Far East and the protection of Japanese and Allied commerce against German warships in Eastern waters. In her wartime dealings with China, Japan's appreciation of the obligations entailed by the Anglo-Japanese Alliance did not prevent attempts on her part to secure extensive economic advantages in that portion of Chinese territory generally regarded as the British "sphere of interest." It is true that certain Japanese statesmen and writers have asserted that Japan's declaration of war upon Germany came in response to a British appeal based upon the terms of the Alliance; but others, equally entitled to speak with authority, have denied the existence of any treaty obligation to enter the war and have declared that Japan acted throughout as a free agent in the pursuit of vital national interests.

although decidedly modern, were not very extensive, and in the summer of 1914 the garrison of Kiaochow consisted of only sixteen hundred soldiers. Even when reinforced by reservists and volunteers hastily summoned from all parts of the Orient, the total force available for defense against impending attack amounted to not more than forty-five hundred men.

Despite the weakness of the force by which they were opposed the Japanese military authorities prepared and proceeded to carry out an elaborate plan of campaign against the German stronghold. On August 20, three days before the expiration of the ultimatum, the Japanese minister at Peking informed the Chinese Foreign Office that military considerations would make it necessary for Japanese troops in their operations against Kiaochow to occupy certain portions of Chinese territory outside the leased area. The Chinese government, which on August 6 had declared neutrality with respect to the European conflict, answered the Japanese notification with a statement that China's neutrality applied also to the impending German-Japanese hostilities and protested that any occupation of Chinese territory outside the leased area would constitute an infringement of China's neutral rights.

In utter disregard of the Chinese protest the Japanese dispatched to the northern coast of Shantung a fleet of transports carrying an expeditionary force of some twenty thousand men, and on September 2 these troops were disembarked at the port of Lungkow, about a hundred miles away from the nearest point of the leased area. From Lungkow a military railroad for the transportation of war material was constructed to Weihsien on the German-built Tsingtao-Tsinan Railway, and Kiaochow was methodically invested on the land side. Although justifying the occupation of Chinese territory on the ground of urgent military necessity, the Japanese subsequently discovered that it was possible to disembark their forces inside the German area; and after September 14 they began to land troops at Laoshan, some fifteen miles from Tsingtao and within the limits of the Kiaochow leasehold. On September 24, moreover, a British force of fourteen hundred men, sent to cooperate in the siege, also found it convenient to utilize Laoshan as a landing place.

On September 3, the day after the landing of the Japanese forces at Lungkow, the Chinese Foreign Minister, still protesting against Japan's violation of China's neutral rights, formally announced to the diplomatic representatives at Peking the creation of a war zone in conformity with the precedent established during the Russo-Japanese War. "As far as concerning Lungkow, Laichow, and places adjacent to Kiaochow Bay, within the narrowest possible limits absolutely necessary for military operations of the belligerent troops," stated the minister, "our government will not be wholly responsible as a neutral state; while in all other places within our territory the law of neutrality which has already been proclaimed shall remain in force." Even this concession, however, failed to accord with Japan's wishes, and Japanese forces during the course of the siege occupied the city of Weihsien as well as the German-built railway as far as Tsinan, 254 miles from the coast.

On October 31, after nearly two months of preliminary operations, the attacking forces were ready to commence the assault. The guns of the ships and the siege artillery of the land forces accordingly opened a heavy bombardment under cover of which the trenches of the besiegers were pushed steadily forward. On November 7 the garrison capitulated. Nine days later the Japanese and British troops, with flags flying and bands playing, entered the city in triumph.

With the fall of Tsingtao, involving as it did the surrender of practically every armed German on Chinese soil, it seemed to the government at Peking that there remained no reason for the continuance of the war zone. Early in December the Foreign Minister pointed out to Japan's representative at Peking that there was no longer any military necessity for the presence of Japanese troops in Chinese territory outside the leased area, and on January 7, 1915, he formally notified the Japanese and British legations that the war zone was abolished.

As was pointed out at the close of the preceding chapter, the post of Premier in the Japanese government at the outbreak of the World War was occupied by the aged Count Okuma, leader of the Kenseikai party. Called to the premiership by imperial command in spite of the fact that his party held but a minority of the seats in the elected branch of the Diet, Okuma during this first five months in office had carried on with difficulty in the face of a Seiyukai majority. Japan's entry into the war had caused a temporary abandonment of party politics; but as soon as the military operations in Shantung had been brought to a successful close, the Prime Minister once more found himself confronted by a hostile parliamentary majority whose spokesmen now demanded the adoption of a Chinese policy such as would secure for Japan the utmost possible advantage from the existing world situation.

Although customarily described by contemporary Western writers as a "liberal," Okuma's liberalism was purely a matter of internal politics; on questions of foreign policy his patriotic belief in Japan's "manifest destiny" was quite as ardent as was that of his most imperialistic Seiyukai opponent. The Kenseikai party, of which Okuma was the leader, derived its greatest strength from the support of the industrial elements; and the Premier had his own ideas as to how the situation might best be utilized for the benefit of Japanese industry and to the advantage of his political party.

On December 3, 1914, a list of demands to be made upon China was placed in the hands of Mr. Hioki, the Japanese minister at Peking; when, in the opinion of the minister, an auspicious occasion for their presentation arrived, he was to communicate with his government and ask for definite instructions. In December the Chinese government, as we have seen, raised the question of the continued presence of Japanese troops in Chinese territory outside the former German leasehold. On Christmas Day, Okuma dissolved the Imperial Diet and issued a call for a general election, to take place on March 25. Two weeks later, January 7, came the Chinese notification that the war zone was abolished, a notification to which Minister Hioki replied on the ninth that China's action was "improper and arbitrary, betraying want of confidence in international good faith, and regardless of friendly relations." The auspicious moment had arrived, and on January 18, 1915, Mr. Hioki, in a personal interview with President Yüan Shih-k'ai, presented the demands—twenty-one in number—which he had held in readiness for the past six weeks.

The demands thus presented by the Japanese government were divided into five groups.

The *first group* consisted of four demands relating exclusively to the province of Shantung. The Chinese government was to give its assent to any agreement which the Japanese, at the end of the war, might make with Germany respecting the disposal of German rights and interests in that province. A pledge was to be given that no territory in Shantung and no island along its coast would in the future be ceded or leased to any other power under any pretext. For the present, China was to consent to the construction of a railway by Japan from Lungkow or Chefoo to connect with the Kiaochow-Tsinan line and was to open to foreign trade, as soon as possible, a number of cities and towns in the province.

The *second group* of demands, which was prefaced by the statement that "the Chinese Government has always recognized the predominant position of Japan in South Manchuria and Eastern Inner Mongolia," contained seven articles relating to that area. China was to extend to ninety-nine years the terms of the leases of Port Arthur and of the Manchurian railways already under Japanese control. She was to grant to the Japanese additional railway, mining, and landholding rights in Manchuria and Inner Mongolia, and to recognize Japan's power to veto any railway proposal or any foreign loan secured upon the railways or the local taxes of the area. In addition to granting these concessions the Chinese government was in the future to employ only Japanese subjects as political, financial, or military advisers or instructors in this part of its territories.

The *third group* contained two demands relating to the Han-yeh-ping Company, which operates the Hanyang iron and steel mills, the Tayeh iron mines, and the Pingshan collieries—all in the Yangtze valley—and is the greatest iron-producing concern in the republic. China was to consent to the conversion of this company into a joint Sino-Japanese enterprise in which the Chinese interests were not to be sold without Japan's approval; in addition, the Chinese government was to pledge itself to obtain the permission of this company before it allowed the opening of any competing mines in the neighborhood of those controlled by the company or before taking any measure "which may likely affect the interest of the said company directly or indirectly."

The single demand in *group four* was for a pledge that the Chinese government would not "cede or lease to any Power any harbor or bay or any island along the coast of China."

The *fifth group* contained seven demands relating to a variety of matters. The Chinese central government was to engage "influential Japanese" as advisers in political, financial, and military affairs. Japanese hospitals, churches, and schools in the interior of China were to be granted the right to own land. The police service in certain parts of China was to be placed under joint Japanese and Chinese administration, or Japanese were to be employed in the police offices in such localities. China was either to purchase from Japan a stated proportion of her arms and munitions or to establish an arsenal as a joint Japanese-Chinese enterprise. Four railway concessions in the Yangtze valley were to be granted to Japanese syndicates. Japan's consent must be secured before China employed any foreign capital for industrial undertakings of any sort in Fukien Province. Finally, Japanese (Buddhist) missionaries were to enjoy the same rights in China as missionaries from other countries.

Although Minister Hioki in the course of his interview warned President Yüan that this affair must be kept absolutely secret, the subject matter of Japan's demands quickly became known, first to the diplomatic community at Peking and eventually to the outside world. Among the foreign residents of China, as well as among all classes of the Chinese population, the news of Japan's move aroused general indignation; even the British, shocked by the Group V demand for railway concessions in the Yangtze valley, were bitterly critical of the step taken by their Eastern ally. The Tokyo statesmen, however, had not erred in their calculations; Britain, France, and Russia were in no position to invite an open break with the Japanese, and the governments of these countries allowed the demands on China to pass without comment.

Of the interested Western powers only the United States was free to voice its objections. For more than a month after the presentation of the demands the American Department of State, in the face of reports from the American minister at Peking, accepted at face value Japan's assurances that she had no thought of impairing China's territorial integrity or the existing rights of foreign powers. By the end of February, however, Washington's belief in the reliability of these assurances began to evaporate, and on March 13 a memorandum from the Department of State pointedly called to the attention of the Japanese ambassador the obligations assumed by his government in the Root-Takahira notes of 1908. On May 13 the diplomatic representatives of the United States at Peking and Tokyo presented to the Chinese and Japanese governments identic notes stating that the government of the United States "cannot recognize any agreement or undertaking which has been entered into or which may be entered into between the governments of China and Japan impairing the treaty rights of the United States and its citizens in China, the political or territorial integrity of the Republic of China, or the international policy relative to China commonly known as the open door policy."

Supported only by the formal protests of the United States and so weak in military resources that war with Japan would have been suicidal, the Chinese government was compelled to rely upon its own diplomacy for any abatement of the Japanese demands. The less objectionable points were promptly conceded, but all of Group V and certain of the demands in the other groups were stubbornly resisted on the ground either that they were inconsistent with China's existing treaty obligations to other countries or that they would nullify the essential sovereignty of the republic. After March 25, the date of the general election in Japan, the Japanese minister appears to have adopted a somewhat less peremptory tone, and on April 26 he modified the original demands by withdrawing from present discussion all except one of the fifth group, the points thus withdrawn to be reserved for later consideration. This appearance of moderation on the part of Japan encouraged the Chinese government to present a list of counter proposals, but the Japanese government had reached the end both of its patience and of its willingness to make concessions. On the afternoon of May 7 Minister Hioki, in obedience to instructions from Tokyo, delivered his ultimatum: unless the Chinese government, on or before 6 P.M. of May 9, gave its assent to all the demands contained in the revised list presented on April 26, the imperial Japanese government would "take such steps as they may deem necessary."

Confronted at last with the clear alternative between surrender and war, China gave way, and on May 8 the Minister of Foreign Affairs announced his government's compliance with the terms of the ultimatum. Two weeks and a half later, May 25, Mr. Hioki and the Chinese Foreign Minister, Lou Tseng-tsiang, signed two treaties, one relating to Shantung Province and the other to southern Manchuria and eastern Inner Mongolia. In addition to these formal agreements, which settled in accordance with Japan's wishes most of the demands contained in the first two groups, a series of thirteen supplementary notes, exchanged by the two plenipotentiaries on the same date, elaborated certain of the treaty clauses or assured to the Japanese government a satisfactory adjustment of important questions not included in the treaties. Despite the postponement of the demands in Group V the treaties and notes of May 25, 1915, constituted a reasonable guaranty that Japan at least would not find the war unprofitable.

Even before the end of 1913, as we have seen in an earlier chapter, President Yüan Shih-k'ai had definitely parted company with the revolutionary leaders whose successful uprising against the Manchus resulted in the establishment of the Chinese Republic, and early in 1914 there was ample reason for believing that China's president was planning to make the republic a mere interlude between the Manchu empire and a new imperial regime in which he would be the founding sovereign.

In May, 1914, a new provisional constitution drafted by a specially appointed Political Council was promulgated by presidential mandate to replace the Nanking constitution. The new "fundamental law" of the republic, whose validity was never acknowledged by Yüan's political opponents, established an undisguised dictatorship. It contained a vague provision for the creation at some future date of an elected parliament; but for the present all power was concentrated in the hands of the president, who had authority to declare war, to make treaties, to direct the armed forces of the nation, to negotiate foreign loans, and to issue presidential mandates having the force of law.

China's obvious inability to resist the aggressions of her neighbors, as evidenced by her difficulties in Tibet and Mongolia and especially by the Japanese demands, appears to have encouraged the conservative supporters of Yüan in the belief that the nation would approve a return to the old monarchical system. During the spring and summer of 1915 a conservative organization known as the Chou An Hui busied itself in spreading propaganda in favor of the re-establishment of the empire with Yüan as emperor. As a result of Chou An Hui activities, telegrams from all parts of the country, represented as spontaneous expressions of public opinion, were sent to the president urging him to assume the imperial title.

Still posing as the disinterested patriot anxious only for the welfare of his country, Yüan requested his American political adviser, Dr. F. J. Goodnow, to draw up a memorandum discussing the relative merits of monarchy and republic as systems of government for China. Dr. Goodnow's memorandum, or such portions of the memorandum as were made public, favored a monarchy as more in harmony with China's history, her traditions, and her social and economic conditions.

Fortified by the expert advice of his foreign adviser, Yüan ordered a national convention to assemble and to vote upon the question. The outcome of this vote was a foregone conclusion; the members of the convention had been carefully selected, and each member, in voting upon the question, was required to sign his ballot. On December 9, 1915, the convention voted unanimously in favor of the proposed restoration of the imperial system, and Yüan, after some show of hesitation, accepted the honor.

Having determined to transform the government in accordance with the "unanimous request of the nation's representatives," Yüan Shih-k'ai announced that his assumption of the imperial title would take place on January 1, 1916. As early as October 29 the diplomatic representatives of France, Great Britain, and Russia, acting on the suggestion of the Japanese government, had joined with the Japanese representative at Peking in advising the Chinese Foreign Office not to continue with the monarchical movement; but this "friendly counsel" had been ignored. About the same time a prominent young military leader, Ts'ai Ao, fled from Peking to Japan, whence he proceeded to his native province of Yunnan in the extreme southwest of China. On Christmas Day, 1915, just a week before the date fixed for the coronation ceremonies, Peking received news that Yunnan had risen in revolt under Ts'ai Ao's leadership.

During the next few days the antimonarchical outbreak spread with such rapidity in Yunnan and in the neighboring provinces that Yüan, on the very eve of the coronation, issued an order postponing the ceremony. A second mandate, on February 23, indefinitely postponed the proposed change of government; on March 22 the president issued a decree declaring that he had been completely misinformed concerning the wishes of the nation; having now learned that the people were opposed to the restoration of a monarchy, he canceled his earlier acceptance of the imperial throne and rededicated himself to the service of the republic. On June 6, eleven weeks after this definite abandonment of his ambitious attempt to found a new dynasty, Yüan Shih-k'ai died, a broken and a disappointed man. He had never really believed in republican institutions, and he probably was sincere in his belief that China would be stronger as an empire than as a republic. If he had succeeded in his attempt, China might have been benefited; failing, he left behind him a disunited country destined to years of turmoil and civil wars.

Li Yüan-hung, who as vice-president succeeded to the presidency upon the death of Yüan Shih-k'ai, possessed little political ability, but he was loyal to the republican system of government and made an honest effort to re-establish the constitutional regime which Yüan had overthrown. Although the three-year term for which the members of the lower house and one third of the senators had been elected in 1913 had already expired, it was decided that this term should be extended for two years as compensation for the period during which Yüan had ruled without parliament, and the 1913 parliament was reassembled at Peking. The parliament immediately turned to the task of completing the drafting of a permanent constitution, and the next few months were unmarked by any serious trouble between the executive and legislative branches of the government.

In spite of these apparently satisfactory relations it was obvious that serious difficulty might easily develop between the parliament and the president's cabinet. Tuan Ch'i-jui, who had been appointed to the premiership by Yüan Shih-k'ai and who continued to hold that office under the new president, was senior general of the army and had the support of Yüan Shih-k'ai's former military subordinates. Because of his strong military connections Tuan was thoroughly distrusted by the Kuomintang majority in the two houses of parliament, while his own impatience with parliamentary procedure made him resentful of any criticism by the legislative body.

In February, 1917, when the United States broke off diplomatic relations with Germany, President Wilson instructed the American representatives in neutral countries to urge similar action by the governments to which they were accredited. On February 9 China responded to this suggestion by informing the German government that China would sever diplomatic relations unless Germany abandoned her submarine campaign, and on March 10, in the absence of a satisfactory reply from Germany, President Li Yüan-hung submitted to parliament a proposal to sever relations with the Berlin government. The proposal was approved by overwhelming majorities in both houses, and on March 14 relations with Germany were formally broken.

On May 7 President Li recommended to parliament that the severance of diplomatic relations be carried to its logical conclusion by a declaration of war, but this proposal immediately aroused strong opposition. Upon the fundamental question of entering the war against the Central Powers there was little difference of opinion. Although China's recent experiences with Great Britain, Russia, and Japan had left few illusions as to the high moral purposes of the Allies, it was generally believed that the right to representation at the eventual peace negotiations, on the Allied side, would be of inestimable value. The real objection to the proposed declaration arose out of the domestic political situation. Rightly or wrongly, the members of parliament suspected that a state of war would be utilized by the Premier and his military supporters as an opportunity for establishing once more a military dictatorship; and this suspicion was strengthened by the action of the Premier, who called a conference of the military governors (*tuchuns*) for the discussion of national policies while the question had yet to be submitted to parliament. Inasmuch as Tuan was also suspected of having concluded secret agreements with Japan to the detriment of China's national dignity, the parliament refused to take action on the declaration of war until the cabinet had been reorganized by the removal of the Premier and certain of his subordinates. In the face of this stand by the legislative body all the members of the cabinet, except Tuan and the Minister of Education, offered their resignations, and on May 23 President Li dismissed Tuan Ch'i-jui from his post as Premier.

The peremptory dismissal of Tuan, the recognized leader of the army clique, roused the tuchuns to the verge of revolt against the Peking government, and Chang Hsun, formerly a loyal supporter of the Manchu regime, proceeded northward from northern Kiangsu to mediate between the disputing parties. Arriving at Tientsin with a strong military force, Chang Hsun demanded that the president dissolve parliament. Despite the illegality of such a step Li Yüan-hung complied with the demand. On July 1 Chang Hsun entered Peking, where he took command of the city and proclaimed the restoration of the deposed Manchu emperor.

This startling attempt to restore the old dynasty was a complete failure. Tuan Ch'i-jui at the head of an overwhelming force advanced on Peking, Chang Hsun was forced to seek refuge in the legation quarter, and the republic was re-established. Li Yüan-hung, overcome by humiliation, resigned the presidency in favor of Vice-President Feng Kuo-chang, and Tuan Ch'i-jui resumed his former position as Premier. On August 14, two weeks after his assumption of the presidential office, Feng Kuo-chang issued a proclamation declaring war upon Germany and Austria-Hungary.

Following the dissolution of the national parliament by Li Yüan-hung in June, the Kuomintang majority of that body promptly reassembled at Canton and proceeded to set up a rival administration which declared itself the lawful government of

China. Although Sun Yat-sen, the outstanding leader of the southern group, had been very outspoken in his opposition to China's entry into the war on the side of the Allies, he and his colleagues realized that continued neutrality on their part would insure Allied support for the northern government in case of civil war. In due time, therefore, Canton followed the example of Peking and declared war upon Germany.

Despite its claim to be regarded as the true custodian of constitutional principles the government at Canton quickly developed much the same dependence upon militarist support as characterized its northern rival. In south China, as at Peking, all real power gravitated into the hands of the tuchuns, and the civilian officials enjoyed only such outward show of power as would enable them to pose as China's spokesmen in her dealings with the foreigners.

Siam also was included among the neutrals invited by President Wilson to follow the lead of the United States in breaking off relations with the Central Powers. This invitation was seconded by British diplomats, and on July 22, 1917, the Siamese government declared war on Germany and Austria-Hungary. The declaration was followed by the arrest and internment of all enemy aliens and by the confiscation of German and Austro-Hungarian vessels in Siamese ports, and in the summer of 1918 a small Siamese force was sent to Europe for the purpose of giving the kingdom at least a nominally active part in the prosecution of the war.

By virtue of her participation in the struggle Siam was entitled to representation in the Paris Peace Conference, thereby becoming a signatory of the peace treaties and a "charter member" of the League of Nations. In addition to her League membership Siam secured, through clauses inserted in the Versailles Treaty with Germany and in the Trianon Treaty with Austria-Hungary, the abolition of the extraterritorial rights formerly enjoyed at her expense by those two countries.

As we have seen in an earlier chapter (see page 713), the Chinese and Russian governments on November 5, 1913, arrived at a tentative solution of their conflicting interests in Mongolia; the autonomy of Outer Mongolia under Chinese suzerainty was recognized, and the two governments reciprocally agreed to specific limitations upon their respective activities in the region under discussion. As this arrangement was binding only upon the two signatories, it was decided to arrange a subsequent conference in which the Mongols also would be represented; in the meantime Russia undertook to use her influence to secure Mongol acquiescence in the situation thus established.

During the months following the conclusion of this agreement the Mongol princes, irritated by Russia's action in negotiating with China behind their backs, showed some inclination to retaliate by seeking an independent settlement with the Peking government. The Russian agents, however, succeeded in regaining the confidence of the suspicious Mongols, and on September 8, 1914, the tripartite Russo-Chinese-Mongol conference assembled at Kiakhta. By this time the European war was well under way, and the Russians, like their Japanese allies, were not averse to taking advantage of the general confusion as an opportunity for extending their Far Eastern influence. On September 30, three weeks after the opening of the tripartite conference, the Russian agent at Kiakhta privately concluded with the Mongol representatives two agreements, one of which provided for the establishment of a telegraph line while the other granted Russia a virtual monopoly over railway development in Outer Mongolia.

The triangular discussions at Kiakhta dragged on for almost exactly nine months, coinciding during the second half of this period with the Sino-Japanese negotiations over the Twenty-one Demands. On June 7, 1915, two weeks after the conclusion of Japan's negotiations at Peking, the Kiakhta conference finally reached an agreement on the various points at issue. In the new agreement the three governments accepted the formula "autonomy under Chinese suzerainty" as satisfactorily defining the status of Outer Mongolia. The Mongols were to enjoy the right of concluding treaties on questions relating to commerce and industry and were to be free from Russian and Chinese interference in internal affairs; as insurance against such interference the agreement definitely stipulated the number of resident representatives to be maintained in Outer Mongolia by China and by Russia, as well as the size of the military escort by which each of these representatives might be attended.

On the other hand, the suzerainty of China was maintained, nominally at least, by the stipulation that the government of Outer Mongolia was not empowered to make treaties dealing with political or territorial questions; but Chinese suzerainty was reduced to a mere shadow by the further provision that China herself must consult with the Russian government as well as with the Mongol authorities on all political and territorial matters affecting the region.

On the day the agreement was signed President Yüan proclaimed the nomination of the hutukhtu of Urga, the chief figure in Mongol Lamaism, as khan of Outer Mongolia, and Russo-Chinese-Mongol relations for the next year remained on a decidedly satisfactory basis. In January, 1916, the newly created Mongol khan sent a good-will embassy to Peking, and on July 8 his formal investiture took place at Urga. In no small measure the maintenance of friendly relations during this period seems attributable to the tactful policy of Yüan Shih-k'ai and of the Chinese resident at Urga, Chen Lu. After Yüan's death, in June, 1916, Chen Lu was replaced by a new resident, and friction between the Chinese and the Mongols immediately began to develop. Uprisings against the new resident occurred in various places, and by the end of 1916 the good effects of the tripartite agreement had been completely lost.

In the spring of 1916 the Russian government, desperately engaged in the European struggle and alarmed by the current rumor that Japan was contemplating a separate peace with the Central Powers, appears to have felt a need for an even closer understanding with its Far Eastern ally. At the same time the Japanese, in view of the concessions recently secured from China, were in a position which made it desirable to obtain from the Russian government formal and definitive recognition of their expanded interests. On July 3, 1916, after protracted negotiation, the two governments accordingly concluded still another set of agreements. As in 1907, 1910, and 1912, the results of the deliberations were embodied in two documents, one intended for publication and the other containing the provision that it should remain "strictly confidential."

The published treaty was brief and quite innocuous. In the first article the two powers reciprocally undertook that neither would become a party to "any arrangement or political combination" directed against the other. In Article II they agreed to confer with each other concerning the measures which should be taken in case "the territorial rights or the special interests" of either in the Far East should be menaced.

The secret treaty was far more precise, and the first two of its six articles deserve to be quoted in full:

Article I. The two High Contracting Parties, recognizing that their vital interests demand that China should not fall under the political domination of any third Power hostile to Russia or Japan, will enter frankly and loyally into communication whenever circumstances may demand, and will reach an understanding upon the measures to be taken to prevent the development of such a situation.

Article II. If, in consequence of measures taken by mutual agreement as provided in the preceding article, war should be declared between one of the Contracting Parties and one of the third Powers contemplated by the preceding article, the other Contracting Party, upon the demand of its Ally, will come to its aid, and in that case each of the High Contracting Parties pledges itself not to make peace without a previous agreement with the other Contracting Party.

The power or powers against which this treaty might eventually become effective remained unnamed, but the imperial governments of Russia and Japan were now bound in an alliance, offensive[1] as well as defensive, for the maintenance of their vital interests in Chinese territory. So long as the treaty remained in force, Russia and Japan were prepared for joint warfare against any power whose activities, in the opinion of the two governments, threatened to create in China a situation unfavorable to their special "rights."

At the outbreak of the war, as we have seen, two at least of the principal European belligerents, Britain and Germany, had made a serious effort to prevent the spread of hostilities into the Far East. Japan's entry into the war put an end to any hope of thus limiting the area of the conflict, and in August, 1915, President

---

[1] Article II, quoted above, did not limit its operation to a war in which the "contemplated" third power was the aggressor.

Yüan Shih-k'ai, at that time engaged in planning the restoration of the empire, was encouraged by the Russian and French ministers at Peking to propose that China enter the war on the side of the Allies. This suggestion was promptly opposed by Japan, and the British government, apparently fearing the possible consequences of such a move, supported the Japanese in their opposition. In the course of the next three months, however, Russian and French insistence upon the value of China's participation overcame Britain's doubts, and on November 23 the British ambassador at Tokyo joined his Russian and French colleagues in a formal request that the Japanese government co-operate in an effort to secure China's adherence to the Allied cause. To the joint representation of the three European Allies the Japanese Foreign Minister, Viscount Ishii, replied with a declaration of Japan's weighty reasons for objecting, and the suggestion was dropped.[1]

At the beginning of 1917 the European Allies, now almost at the end of their resources, turned once more to the Far East for aid. Great Britain and France wanted Japan to send her naval forces into the Mediterranean for service against the steadily increasing submarine menace, while both of these countries as well as Russia wanted China to break off relations with the Central Powers and to assume at least nominal belligerent status.

From the outbreak of hostilities in the summer of 1914 the Japanese government had made little effort to disguise the strictly local nature of its war interests. The dispatch of Japanese warships to the Mediterranean was as foreign to these interests as was China's participation in the war, and the Tokyo statesmen were not inclined to look favorably upon either proposal unless they were convinced that some definite advantage for Japan would

---

[1] Mr. T. F. Millard, in *Democracy and the Eastern Question*, p. 99, quotes Ishii as saying on this occasion that Japan, because of her need to keep a firm hand in China, "could not regard with equanimity the organization of an efficient Chinese army such as would be required for her active participation in the War." In a statement issued in April, 1919, at Washington, Viscount Ishii denied that he had expressed the sentiments attributed to him by Millard, and declared that Japan's opposition to China's entry into the war was based upon the conviction that such a move would throw the republic into a state of absolute chaos from which Japan, next to China, would be the chief sufferer.

thereby be secured. On February 3, however, America's breach with Germany and President Wilson's circular to the neutral powers, inviting them to adopt a policy harmonizing with that of the United States, altered the previously existing world situation and made necessary a material readjustment of Japan's policy. The probability that the war would end in a "peace by exhaustion" was greatly diminished; and it became practically certain that the United States, whose disapproval of Japan's recent actions in China was a matter of record, would play a prominent part in drafting the terms of the eventual post-war settlement of world affairs.

Faced by the necessity of securing dependable guaranties that the peace settlement—in so far as it related to the Far East—would be arranged with due consideration for Japan's important interests, Japanese diplomacy acted promptly. From Great Britain on February 16, from Russia on February 20, from France on March 1, and from Italy on March 28 the Japanese government obtained formal assurances that at the future peace conference these powers would give their support to Japan's desires "for the succession to all the rights and privileges hitherto possessed by Germany in Shantung Province and for the acquisition of the islands to the north of the equator which are now occupied by Japanese forces." In return for these pledges, which remained secret until after the armistice, Japan agreed to send three destroyer divisions into the Mediterranean, to withdraw her opposition to China's entry into the war, and to co-operate with her allies in their efforts to induce the Chinese government to take this step.

Hardly had the Japanese government adjusted itself to the impending entry of the United States into the war when the world situation was again fundamentally altered, this time by the outbreak of revolution in Russia. Unlike the Bolshevist seizure of power eight months later, the revolution of March, 1917, was hailed with enthusiasm by the United States and by the Allied nations of western Europe; but for Tokyo the fall of the Czarist regime was a real calamity. The Russo-Japanese secret treaties of 1907–1916 were, as we have seen, the cornerstone of Japan's position on the Asiatic continent, and it was hardly to be expected that the new democratic government at St. Petersburg would feel bound to maintain the partnership into which its autocratic predecessor had entered. The notes recently exchanged by Tokyo with the British, French, and Italian governments could be relied on to ensure adequate recognition of Japan's claims to the islands of Micronesia and to the former German rights in Shantung; but her even more vital interests in southern Manchuria and eastern Inner Mongolia, hitherto guaranteed by the agreements with Russia, were now seriously imperiled.

As matters thus stood, some understanding with the United States was obviously needed, and in the summer of 1917 Viscount Ishii, the former Minister of Foreign Affairs, was sent to America on a special mission. The ostensible purpose of the mission was the cultivation of good will by allaying American suspicions with regard to Japan's Asiatic policy, and Viscount Ishii, by a series of eloquent addresses in the principal cities of America, was highly successful in the performance of this task. The more important objective, American recognition of Japan's "special interests" in certain portions of Chinese territory, was pursued with equal success, and on November 2, after consultations which had been begun early in September, Viscount Ishii and the American Secretary of State exchanged the famous "Lansing-Ishii notes." The text of Secretary Lansing's communication, to which the Japanese representative replied in like terms, is as follows:

Department of State, Washington, November 2, 1917

Excellency:

I have the honor to communicate herein my understanding of the agreement reached by us in our recent conversations touching the questions of mutual interest to our Governments relating to the Republic of China.

In order to silence mischievous reports that have from time to time been circulated, it is believed by us that a public announcement once more of the desires and intentions shared by our two Governments with regard to China is advisable.

The Governments of the United States and Japan recognize that territorial propinquity creates special relations between countries, and, consequently, the Government of the United States recognizes that Japan has special interests in China, particularly in that part to which her possessions are contiguous.

The territorial sovereignty of China, nevertheless, remains unimpaired, and the Government of the United States has every confidence in the repeated assurances of the Imperial Japanese Government that while geographical position gives Japan such special interests they have no desire to discriminate against the trade of other nations or to disregard the commercial rights heretofore granted by China in treaties with other powers.

The Governments of the United States and Japan deny that they have any purpose to infringe in any way the independence or territorial integrity of China, and they declare, furthermore, that they always adhere to the principle of the so-called "Open Door" or equal opportunity for commerce and industry in China.

Moreover, they mutually declare that they are opposed to the acquisition by any Government of any special rights or privileges that would affect the independence or territorial integrity of China or that would deny to the subjects or citizens of any country the full enjoyment of equal opportunity in the commerce and industry of China.

I shall be glad to have Your Excellency confirm this understanding of the agreement reached by us.

Accept, Excellency, the renewed assurance of my highest consideration.

Robert Lansing.

Whatever may have been the purpose of the American government in entering upon a new understanding with Japan, the Lansing-Ishii agreement must be regarded as a piece of diplomatic ineptitude on the part of President Wilson and his Secretary of State.[1] The recognition of the fact that Japan possessed special interests in China was a high price to pay for a simple reaffirmation of the open-door doctrine, while the American expression of confidence in "the repeated assurances of the Imperial Japanese Government that . . . they have no desire to discriminate against the trade of other nations" justified the assumption that these "special interests," undefined in the notes, were such as to permit their utilization by Japan to the detriment of the other treaty powers if the Japanese government so desired.

As soon as the Japanese government gave its reluctant consent to China's participation in the war, the Terauchi ministry, which in October, 1916, had replaced that of Count Okuma, abandoned

[1] Dr. Reinsch asserts that the notes were agreed upon by the President and Mr. Lansing without the knowledge of the staff of the Department of State (*An American Diplomat in China*, p. 313).

the forceful tactics of its predecessor and undertook the task of
convincing the Chinese people and government that Japan was—
as she always had been—their only dependable friend. Upon the
widespread anti-Japanese sentiment of the Chinese people these
friendly gestures made little impression; if anything, the efforts
of the Japanese-inspired publications served only to arouse in the
general public increased suspicion and fear of their island neighbors. At Peking, however, Japan's official and unofficial representatives were more successful, and the years 1917 and 1918 were
marked by a steady growth of Japanese influence over the men who
controlled the affairs of the republic.

In large measure this growing Japanese influence was built upon
a financial foundation. The Chinese government, in view of the
impending declaration of war against the Central Powers, was in
great need of ready money, and Japan lost no time in demonstrating her willingness to supply this need. In the spring of 1917 a
certain Mr. Nishihara, the confidential agent of Premier Terauchi,
arrived at Peking with apparently unlimited funds at his disposal
for loans to China. Nishihara's negotiations with Premier Tuan
Ch'i-jui and his associates quickly aroused the suspicions of the
Chinese parliament, but after the dissolution of that body in June
(see page 758) his financial arrangements with the Peking military clique proceeded without effective opposition. The so-called
Nishihara loans, which during 1918 alone amounted to a total of
120,000,000 yen, secured for Japan binding options on a variety
of railway, mining, and industrial enterprises in the Manchurian
provinces; but the sums advanced on these contracts, instead of
being devoted to the projects named in the loans, were employed
entirely for political purposes by the authorities at Peking.

The money so lavishly advanced to Peking officialdom by Nishihara and other financial agents[1] was not, however, the only factor
in the development of Japanese influence. By the terms of an agreement concluded in January, 1918, the Japanese government undertook to provide Peking with expert military instructors and to
provide arms and munitions to the value of 40,000,000 yen. Two

[1] The Nishihara loans constituted about half of the total of Japanese advances
to China during 1918.

months later, on March 25, an exchange of notes at Tokyo proclaimed the intention of the two governments to take joint action against any Russian (that is, Bolshevist) threat to "the general peace and security of the Far East." On May 16 and May 19 the intention set forth in the above exchange of notes was embodied in two treaties, the first providing for the fullest measure of co-operation between the military forces of the two governments, and the second for similar co-operation between their navies. On September 6, 1918, a supplementary military agreement clarified the terms of the May 16 treaty by providing that in case of joint operations in Siberia the Chinese military forces were to act under Japanese direction. The final agreement of this series, signed on February 5, 1919, provided that the war and, consequently, the binding force of the military and naval pacts should be considered terminated "when both the Chinese and Japanese Governments shall have approved the Peace Treaty concluded with the enemy countries by the European Peace Conference and when both Chinese and Japanese troops stationed outside Chinese territory shall have been withdrawn simultaneously with the troops of the various Allied countries stationed in the same territories."

When the representatives of the "Allied and Associated Powers" assembled at Paris in January, 1919, for the purpose of drafting the terms of world peace, both the Japanese Empire and the Chinese Republic were vitally interested, and both were represented at the conference by strong delegations. The Japanese delegation was headed by Marquis Saionji, member of the Genro and former Premier, and included Japan's ambassadors to the three principal European Allies as well as a former Minister of Foreign Affairs, Baron Makino. The rival Chinese governments at Peking and Canton, abandoning for the moment their mutual recriminations, co-operated in sending a delegation headed by Lou Tseng-tsiang and C. T. Wang, two of China's ablest diplomats, with the Chinese ministers to the United States, Great Britain, and Belgium as their supporters.

In view of the fact that Japan was recognized as a world power, Marquis Saionji took his place with President Wilson, Mr. Lloyd George, M. Clemenceau, and Baron Orlando as a member of the

"Big Five" by whom all important points were ultimately decided. For the same reason Japan was given five seats in the general conference, and a Japanese member was customarily placed in each important committee of the main body. The Japanese government, however, was interested only in matters affecting the Far East. On purely European questions Japan's representatives refrained from expressing opinions and voted "with the majority," but in return for this scrupulous noninterference in European matters they demanded full consideration for Japan's wishes and claims in the Far East.

Compared with Japan in respect to military resources and industrial importance, China was only a minor state and could therefore hope to have little weight in the diplomacy of a war-torn world. Yet the Chinese people expected much from a conference which had assembled with the announced purpose of laying the foundations of an enduring world peace. Relying upon the idealistic program embodied in President Wilson's famous Fourteen Points, China's representatives arrived at the conference well equipped with arguments to support the justice of their claim for the complete restoration of political and economic rights in Shantung and for the nullification of the concessions extorted during the war by Japanese diplomacy.

Before an impartial tribunal of arbitration China's claims might have prevailed; at Paris they were doomed to failure. Of the four major powers sitting in judgment, three had already pledged themselves to support the cause of Japan, while President Wilson himself, confronted with the threat that Japan, if her claims were rejected, would withdraw from the conference and thereby wreck his cherished plan for a League of Nations, eventually agreed to her demands relating to Shantung. As for the notes and treaties of May 25, 1915, it was decided that the conference had no authority to question or to set aside agreements formally concluded between two of its members.

From the "Principal Allied and Associated Powers," in whose favor Germany renounced her title to all her overseas possessions, the Japanese Empire received a permanent mandate for the administration of the former German islands in the Pacific Ocean north of the equator. In Articles 156, 157, and 158 of the Versailles Treaty, Shantung was treated as a separate entity unaffected by the provisions (in Articles 128–134) relating to the rest of China. Japan thus received all the rights and privileges, "particularly those concerning the territory of Kiaochow, railways, mines, and submarine cables," and all the movable and immovable property formerly possessed by Germany in the Chinese province of Shantung, together with "the submarine cables from Tsingtao to Shanghai and from Tsingtao to Chefoo, with all the rights, privileges, and properties attaching thereto."

On one point alone, a point upon which she had the support of the Chinese delegation, did Japan fail to secure satisfaction for what she regarded as her reasonable aspirations; her proposal that the League Covenant should contain a clause recognizing "the principle of the equality of nations and the just treatment of their nationals" was rejected. Thus, although the Japanese Empire became one of the leading members of the League and received a permanent seat in the League Council, the other members of the League were left free to discriminate on racial grounds against Japanese immigration into their territories.

China's gains from her participation in the war were minor. Articles 128–134 of the Versailles Treaty provided for the renunciation by Germany of all the rights and privileges, outside the province of Shantung, resulting from pre-war treaties and agreements with China; German extraterritorial jurisdiction was abolished, the German concessions at Tientsin and Hankow were restored to Chinese control, and Germany's share in the Boxer indemnity was canceled. This portion of the treaty also provided that Germany should cede to China all public property outside Shantung, except her diplomatic and consular buildings.

In view of the storm of national resentment aroused in China by the claims relating to Shantung, the Chinese delegation refused to sign the treaty with Germany. By their subsequent signature on September 10, 1919, of the Trianon Treaty with Austria, China became a member of the League of Nations, in which, as a concession to her injured feelings, she received one of the temporary seats in the Council. Peace between China and Germany was formally established on September 15, 1919, by a mandate issued by President Hsu Shih-ch'ang, and on May 20, 1921, full diplomatic and commercial relations were restored by means of a treaty concluded at Peking.

Although the Japanese delegation at the Paris Conference was successful in its efforts to write into the Versailles Treaty clauses designed to secure for their coutry the enjoyment of all former German rights in Shantung, the other "Principal Allied and Associated Powers" were not yet willing to see Japan expand her influence over the Chinese Republic to the point of transforming China into a Japanese protectorate. During the years 1917 and 1918, as we have seen, the growth of Japanese influence was facilitated by a number of financial transactions resulting in the advance of some 250,000,000 yen to the Chinese government. This development eventually aroused the concern of the American government, and in the summer of 1918 the Department of State at Washington suggested to a number of American bankers already interested in Chinese finance that they associate themselves as a group with Japanese financial concerns in making such loans to China as might be needed for the stabilization of the country's financial situation.

The International Banking Consortium of 1911, from which the American banking group had withdrawn in March, 1913, had been still further depleted since that time by the exclusion of Germany and by the disappearance of Russia from the ranks of the capitalist countries; but the bankers of France, Great Britain, and Japan still remained bound, theoretically at least, by the terms of the Consortium agreement. With the approval of their government, therefore, the American group approached their former British, French, and Japanese colleagues with a proposal for the formation of a new Consortium which should underwrite all future loans to the Chinese government.

Before anything was accomplished in response to this proposal, the armistice was concluded; but during the peace negotiations at Paris, conferences were held by the representatives of the four banking groups, and steps were taken to arrive at an agreement whereby the lending of money to China would be conducted on a co-operative basis. In the early stages of these discussions the Japanese bankers, supported by their government, insisted that all the options which Japan had secured with respect to "future loans" in Manchuria and Mongolia should be excluded from the scope of the agreement. In view of the blanket option which Japan had secured from China in one of the notes exchanged on May 25, 1915, this proviso would have given the Japanese a complete monopoly of loans for Manchurian and Mongolian enterprises in addition to a pro rata share in all loans for developments in other parts of China; the Japanese proposal therefore was not acceptable to the other national groups or to their governments, and it seemed for a while that the negotiations would break down.

During the summer of 1920 an apparently satisfactory arrangement was reached. All extensions of the South Manchuria Railway, together with a number of specified lines for which definite loan contracts had already been concluded, were to be financed exclusively by the Japanese; all other railway projects, in Manchuria or Mongolia as well as in other parts of China, were to become part of the "common pool," and the financial operations connected with these undertakings were to be shared among the four national banking groups in accordance with an established ratio. On October 15, 1920, after negotiations which had occupied more than two years, a Consortium agreement on this basis was formally concluded.

SUGGESTED REFERENCES

HORNBECK, S. K. Contemporary Politics in the Far East.
LATOURETTE, K. S. The Chinese: their History and Culture.
MACNAIR, H. F. Modern Chinese History: Selected Readings.
MORSE, H. B., and MACNAIR, H. F. Far Eastern International Relations.
REINSCH, P. S. An American Diplomat in China, 1913–1919.
SCOTT, J. B. (editor). The Consortium.
TREAT, P. J. The Far East.
WHEELER, W. R. China and the World War.
WILLIAMS, E. T. A Short History of China.
WILLOUGHBY, W. W. Foreign Rights and Interests in China (revised edition, 2 vols.).

XXXI

The Russian Revolution and the Washington Conference

The Russian Revolution in the Far East · Allied Intervention in Siberia · The Consequences of the Intervention · The Kolchak Dictatorship and the Far Eastern Republic · Developments in China and Japan, 1917–1921 · War-Time Prosperity and Labor Problems in Japan · Korea's Bid for Self-Determination · Parliamentary Politics in Japan · China's Political Troubles · China and the Shantung Award · China and Soviet Russia, 1919–1921 · The Washington Conference · Far Eastern Danger Spots in 1921 · The Calling of the Conference · The Far East and the Limitation of Armaments · The Question of Siberia · China at the Conference · Attempts to Strengthen the Chinese Government · The Nine-Power Treaty · The Settlement of the Shantung Question

IN MARCH, 1917, the Russian people, weary of the corruption and stupidity of Romanov rule, forced the abdication of the Czar and set up a revolutionary government under the "liberal bourgeois" leadership of Alexander Kerensky. Eight months later, however, the Kerensky government was itself overthrown, and political control passed into the hands of the so-called majority communists (Bolsheviki), whose power lay in their domination of the recently formed councils (soviets) of soldiers and workingmen. The collapse of the Czarist regime in March and the subsequent triumph of Bolshevism in November were events of far-reaching importance. The first of these upheavals, as we have seen, seriously modified the existing balance of power in the Far East and led to certain diplomatic readjustments which have already been discussed. It now becomes necessary to consider, as fully as the limitations of space permit, the internal effects of the two revolutions upon Asiatic Russia and the consequent international reaction to the changing situation thus produced.

Siberia, it must be remembered, is an integral part of Russia, made so by an eastward frontier movement not unlike the westward expansion of the United States across the American continent. From the Ural Mountains to the shores of the Pacific the land-hungry Russian peasants, following on the heels of the trapper and fur-trader, crowded the Tartar tribesmen out of the more fertile areas and gradually came to constitute the majority of the population. Like the frontiersmen of other lands, the Russians of Siberia were hardy, self-reliant, and somewhat undisciplined; but the completion of the Trans-Siberian Railway brought coherence and prosperity to this far-flung frontier region, and the decade following the close of the Russo-Japanese War was marked by the development of numerous flourishing urban centers, the most important of which was the great eastern seaport and railway terminus, Vladivostok.

Even before the outbreak of the World War some progress had been made in Siberia, as in European Russia, toward the development of quasi-democratic institutions to deal with matters of local concern: assemblies (dumas) in the provinces and citizens' committees (zemstvos) in the towns. When, in March, 1917, news of the Czar's abdication was flashed eastward, these local bodies took over for a while the functions of government. But the local institutions of the old regime were poorly qualified to administer the affairs of a society suddenly freed from the bonds of an absolutism. The provincial dumas, constituted largely by imperial appointment, were thoroughly aristocratic, while the zemstvos, elected by a limited electorate, represented only the merchants and other wealthy classes among the townsmen. During the summer of 1917, therefore, the classes not represented in the zemstvos—the workingmen, the soldiers, and the peasants—organized soviets (councils) to "safeguard" the revolution and to protect their respective interests.

Between the newly constituted soviets and the old zemstvos, representative of the propertied class, there was inevitable conflict; but there were also decided differences of opinion within the soviets themselves, some of the leaders being thoroughgoing communists while others favored the retention of certain aspects of capitalism. On October 28, 1917, a convention of delegates from the soviets of eastern Siberia was held at Vladivostok, and an unsuccessful attempt was made to agree upon a generally acceptable

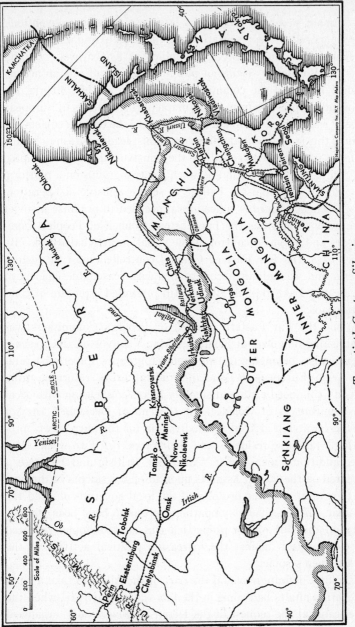

Twentieth-Century Siberia

government program. Six weeks later two separate conventions, one composed of representatives of the soviets and the other of delegates from the zemstvos, assembled at Khabarovsk. By this time the Bolshevist seizure of power at Petrograd was an accomplished fact, and the communist element in eastern Siberia, deriving added prestige from the triumph of their fellows in European Russia, had gained complete ascendancy in the eastern soviets. In spite of this fact the outstanding communist leader, Krasnoschekoff, believed it desirable to conciliate the zemstvo party and attempted to bring about co-operation between the two groups on a platform of modified communism. Failing to secure zemstvo co-operation, Krasnoschekoff and his colleagues proceeded to organize a soviet government known as the Far Eastern Council of People's Commissars and assumed control of the situation at Khabarovsk. By June, 1918, the Far Eastern Council controlled most of eastern Siberia and was administering affairs with reasonable efficiency; but west of Lake Baikal, Siberia still presented a picture of complete chaos.

While the Far Eastern Council of People's Commissars was establishing its power at Khabarovsk, in Vladivostok the presence of extremists belonging to two opposing groups—imperialist refugees from European Russia and radical exiles returning from abroad—produced a state of steadily increasing tension with occasional outbreaks of violence. At the end of December, 1917, a Japanese warship arrived at Vladivostok for the purpose of "protecting" Japanese residents and their property. Two weeks later three additional men-of-war—American, British, and Japanese—appeared on the scene. Assaults upon foreign residents of the port led to several consular protests to the local government; and the consular officials, whose sympathies appear to have been consistently on the side of the propertied classes, also found repeated cause to protest against the increasing political activity of the workingmen's soviet.

The first definite move on the part of the Allies to take a hand in Siberian affairs had come in the late summer of 1917, when the Americans, at the request of the Kerensky government, organized a corps of railway experts to take over the operation of the Trans-

Siberian Railway. The reasons for this step were purely military. The Western powers, now including the United States, hoped that the establishment of the new regime in Russia would lead to more efficient Russian participation in the war. The operations of the Russian armies, however, depended upon the supplies of imported war material, much of which entered the country by way of Vladivostok. Hence the maintenance of the Trans-Siberian was felt to be of vital importance to the Allied cause in Europe.

The overthrow of the Kerensky government by the Bolshevists and the growth of communist power in eastern Siberia as well as at Petrograd fundamentally altered the attitude of the outside powers. The conclusion of the Brest-Litovsk Treaty on March 3, 1918, between the Bolshevist government and Germany, brought denunciation of Russia as "a traitor to the Allied cause," promptly followed by suggestions of drastic Allied action in Siberia. Early in March a proposal that Japan assume the duty of intervening on behalf of her allies was strongly advocated by the Japanese press. On March 14 Mr. Balfour, in the British House of Commons, urged that Japan be invited to undertake this task in order to prevent the domination of Siberia by German and Austrian prisoners who, it was alleged, were being released and provided with arms by their Bolshevist dupes. In May the Japanese Foreign Office, with British and French support, formally proposed to the government of the United States that Japanese troops be sent to Vladivostok for the protection of Allied interests and for the preservation of peace in the Far East. Despite the alarming reports of German and Austrian activities President Wilson disapproved the Japanese proposal, and the idea of armed intervention was dropped for the moment.

Two months later, when intervention was actually decided on, the step was taken, ostensibly at least, for the purpose of aiding some fifty thousand Czechoslovakian soldiers to extricate themselves from the interior of Siberia. These Czechs, deserters from the Austrian armies, who had joined the Russian forces in order to fight against their Hapsburg oppressors, had arranged with the Bolshevik government, after the Brest-Litovsk Treaty, for transportation across Siberia to Vladivostok, from which point they hoped to go by sea to Europe for service with the Allied armies on the western front. By the beginning of May some eight thousand of the Czechs had arrived at their destination, while the remaining forty-odd thousand, in the trains placed at their disposal by the Bolshevist authorities, were strung out along the Trans-Siberian between the Urals and Irkutsk. In the last week of May conflict developed simultaneously all along the line between the Czech detachments and local revolutionary forces, with the result that the Czechs, gaining the upper hand, secured control of several important railway towns: Ekaterinburg, Cheliabinsk, Omsk, Novo-Nikolaevsk, Marinsk, Krasnoyarsk, and Irkutsk.[1] Following their initial success along the railway the Czechs extended their operations to other areas, disarming the adherents of the soviets and placing the reactionaries in control. On June 28 their forces at Vladivostok overthrew the Far Eastern Council of People's Commissars, who had recently gained control of the city, and restored the power of the zemstvo. Two weeks later they commenced to advance westward, and on July 27 the Czecho-Slovak National Council in Washington announced that "the Czecho-Slovaks, instead of withdrawing from Russia, are now in control of Siberia and of considerable territory west of the Urals."

The decision to intervene in Siberia was adopted, apparently, by the Supreme War Council in Paris on or about July 12, 1918; on July 17 a statement of American policy in this connection was drawn up by President Wilson; and on August 3, after the American government, by formally inviting Japan to co-operate, had made amends for the earlier rejection of the Japanese proposal,

---

[1] The origin of the Czech-Bolshevist conflict has been variously explained. A frequently repeated version is that the Russian authorities, under pressure from Germany, attempted to interfere with the Czech progress toward Vladivostok, and that the Czechs began to fight only after having been attacked by Russian forces. Against this must be placed the statement of Captain Kedlets, the Czech commander at Marinsk, who on May 29 informed Colonel Emerson of the American Railway Corps "that he and the other train commanders had instructions to stop where the instructions overtook them and capture the towns; that it was a concerted movement and that the director of the movement [General Gaida] was at this time in Novo-Nikolaevsk" (W. S. Graves, *America's Siberian Adventure*, p. 42). General Graves was the commander in chief of the American Expeditionary Force subsequently sent to Siberia.

the two governments issued simultaneous declarations of their intentions. The American government in its published declaration disclaimed any intention of interfering with the political integrity or the internal affairs of Russia. Military action in Russia was declared to be admissible "only to render such protection and help as is possible to the Czecho-Slovaks against the armed Austrian and German prisoners who are attacking them, and to steady any efforts at self-government or self-defence in which the Russians may be willing to accept assistance." The Japanese likewise asserted "the avowed policy of respecting the territorial integrity of Russia and of abstaining from all interference in her national politics." A British statement, issued on August 8, solemnly assured the Russians that "we shall not retain one foot of your territory. The destinies of Russia are in the hands of the Russian people. It is for them, and them alone, to decide their forms of Government and to find a solution of their social problems."

On August 3 a contingent of British troops landed at Vladivostok, and a week later they were joined by a battalion of Annamese under French command. Two days after the arrival of the Annamese the first Japanese force appeared. On August 15 and 16 two American infantry regiments from the Philippines arrived, to be joined on September 1 by an additional contingent from San Francisco. It was agreed among the intervening powers that each should be represented by a comparatively small force, not to exceed ten thousand men. The United States sent about that number; China did the same; the British, French, and Italian forces combined fell somewhat short of ten thousand; but Japan, by constant reinforcement, eventually increased the number of her soldiers on Russian soil to not less than seventy thousand.

It quickly became apparent that the various intervening powers variously interpreted the purpose of the intervention.

The French, who had issued no declaration of policy, were primarily interested in "reconstituting an eastern front" against Germany and Austria. This object they hoped to attain by aiding the Czechoslovaks to advance into Russia, where they were expected to rally all anti-Bolshevik elements, overthrow the Bolshevist regime, and tear up the Treaty of Brest-Litovsk.

The British, although not out of sympathy with the French plan, were more immediately interested in stamping out communism in the Russian Far East, in order to guard against its spread into China and India; therefore, in spite of the declaration that it was for the Russian people alone to decide their form of government and to find a solution of their social problems, the British representatives gave their whole-hearted support to the various reactionary leaders in the hope that eventually some combination would be found capable of consolidating all of Siberia into a definitely anticommunistic state.

Japan's attention was focused upon eastern Siberia, the region lying east of Lake Baikal and bordering on Manchuria, Korea, and the sea. Here Japanese support, like that of the British, was consistently given to the leaders of anticommunist and reactionary factions. Unlike the British, however, the Japanese representatives showed little interest in aiding the development of a stable government; and this fact, coupled with the presence and ceaseless activity of large numbers of Japanese troops, aroused in the Russians a suspicion (shared by some of Japan's associates) that the Japanese government sought to create a situation so chaotic as to furnish a pretext for taking over this area for "pacification" and eventual annexation.

The United States, as has been so often the case, appears to have had no definite policy. In his declaration of policy on July 17, 1918, President Wilson repudiated all intention of participating in Russia's internal affairs by giving partisan aid to any political group or groups, and General Graves, as commander of the American Expeditionary Force, adhered to the belief that his instructions imposed upon him the duty of remaining absolutely neutral in any conflicts between the communists and their reactionary opponents. In this attitude the American commander was upheld by his superiors in the War Department and by the President himself; the American diplomatic and consular representatives in Russia and in the Far East, however, as well as certain officials in the Department of State, agreed in the main with the British policy and attempted to secure for the Siberian conservative leaders the active support of the American armed forces.

The Allied intervention in Siberia was therefore an occasion for much discord and friction among the participants from the arrival of the first British contingent on August 3, 1918, until April 1, 1920, when the withdrawal of the last American troops brought to an end the international aspects of the undertaking and left the Japanese alone on the scene. Its net result, after rendering material assistance to a succession of anti-Bolshevik aspirants to dictatorial power, was the consolidation of the Russian people under communist rule.

Driven from Vladivostok in June, 1918, by the Czechoslovaks, the Far Eastern Council of People's Commissars continued for a short period to exercise political control in the Ussuri and Amur valleys. After the arrival of the Allied forces, however, the council was expelled from one point after another, and about the middle of September it ceased to exist. During the next year and a half a number of ambitious leaders attempted, with foreign support, to establish themselves as rulers over more or less extensive portions of Siberia. All were conservative to the point of being reactionary, all were guilty of atrocious cruelty in their treatment of the peasants and the laboring class, and all failed.

The one really impressive attempt at a dictatorship was that of Admiral Kolchak, who succeeded at least in dominating the Siberian picture from November, 1918, until December of the following year. Kolchak, a Czarist official, arrived in Vladivostok in June, 1918; and when the Czechoslovaks began their westward advance he was able to make his way to Omsk. Here he received appointment as Minister of War in the liberal but anti-Bolshevist government which had been organized by a combination between Kerensky liberals from Russia and the representatives of a Siberian peasant parliament. The diverse elements in the Omsk government failed to co-operate harmoniously, and on November 18 Kolchak took advantage of the discord to execute a *coup d'état*.

Admiral Kolchak was a Russian, not a Siberian, and his real interest lay in European Russia rather than in the people of Siberia. His seizure of power at Omsk, therefore, was followed by an ambitious attempt to push westward in co-operation with the Czechoslovaks in order to overthrow the Bolshevist government at Petrograd. Surrounding himself with other ex-Czarist officers and reactionaries, the new dictator conscripted a large peasant army, and in December, 1918, was able to advance as far as the Urals. This success, however, was only temporary. During the spring and summer of 1919, in spite of the abundant military supplies furnished him by the Allies, his army was steadily driven eastward by the opposing Red forces. In defeat his conscripted soldiers rapidly melted away, taking with them—often into the ranks of the Bolshevists—the arms, munitions, and uniforms provided by Kolchak's Allied supporters.

Realizing too late that his dictatorial policy and the brutality of his subordinates had hopelessly alienated the Siberian people, the admiral affected liberal principles and promised eleventh-hour reforms. By October, 1919, his power was definitely on the wane, and he soon had the added misfortune—or was guilty of the added stupidity—of getting into difficulties with the Czechs. In January, 1920, the Omsk government collapsed; and Kolchak, taken prisoner by the Czechs, was handed over by them to the Bolshevists, who executed him on February 6 as a counterrevolutionary.

Following the fall of Kolchak, western Siberia from the Urals to Lake Baikal was absorbed into the expanding Soviet Union. East of Lake Baikal, however, all was confusion. At Chita the murderous Cossack leader Semenov proclaimed himself Kolchak's successor as dictator of Siberia. At Khabarovsk and at Vladivostok, respectively, two other former allies of Kolchak—Kalmikov and Rozanov—continued their tyrannical domination. At the same time a long-repressed popular discontent flared up in all parts of the Trans-Baikal, Amur, and Maritime provinces. Peasant soviets were formed, and "partisan" bands, encouraged by the announcement on January 12 that the American troops were soon to be withdrawn, organized for guerrilla warfare upon the last remnants of the reactionary regime. Kalmikov at Khabarovsk, repudiated by his own Cossack followers because of his cruelty, was overthrown and put to death. On January 31 Rozanov was driven out of Vladivostok, where, in order to avoid fresh trouble with the foreign powers, the communists allowed the old zemstvo government to resume control. Semenov, at Chita, held out longer; but during the summer of 1920 his position became more and more untenable, and in October he finally took refuge abroad.

On April 1, 1920, the final American detachment, the last of the intervening forces except the Japanese, embarked at Vladivostok. The Japanese, who showed no intention of withdrawing, were in the meantime concentrating their forces in the coastal region, where they now proceeded to strengthen their position. On April 4 the zemstvo government at Vladivostok was overthrown by former adherents of Kolchak, with Japanese assistance, and a new government, completely subservient to the Japanese representatives, was established for the Maritime Province. On the following day the Japanese and reactionary forces carried out similar attacks at Nikolsk and at Khabarovsk. Three and a half weeks later—April 29—the puppet government of the Maritime Province was compelled to accept conditions which established a virtual Japanese protectorate over the region, and the massacre of a Japanese garrison at Nikolaevsk by a partisan band on May 27 was taken as justification for the occupation of Nikolaevsk and the Russian half of Sakhalin until such time as the Russians should offer adequate reparation for the crime.

While the Japanese were thus consolidating their position in the Maritime Province, the people of the Trans-Baikal and Amur provinces were proceeding to work out their own political problems. In March, 1920, delegates from the peasant councils assembled at Verkhne-Udinsk under the leadership of Krasnoschekoff, formerly head of the Far Eastern Council of People's Commissars, and on April 6 this assembly proclaimed the independent Far Eastern Republic of Siberia with Krasnoschekoff as president of a provisional government. Krasnoschekoff, although a believer in communism, also believed and was able to convince the other delegates that the Japanese would be aroused to hostile action by the establishment of a communistic state but would welcome a less radical organization as a convenient buffer between themselves and the Soviet Union. The constitution of the Far Eastern Republic, although decidedly liberal, therefore gave due recognition to the rights of private property and carefully avoided any strong tendency toward communism.

Events soon proved that Krasnoschekoff had not miscalculated the Japanese attitude. On May 11 the Japanese commander at Vladivostok telegraphed his approval of the new state and announced that his country would withdraw its remaining troops from the territory of the republic as soon as it gave evidence of ability to organize a stable government. Five days later formal recognition of the new state was similarly received from Moscow. During the summer of 1920 the partisan bands constituting the army of the Far Eastern Republic steadily closed in on Semenov at Chita. In August the Japanese withdrew the last of their troops from Trans-Baikal, and in October, as noted above, Semenov eliminated himself from the situation.

After the disappearance of Semenov the government of the republic transferred its capital from Verkhne-Udinsk to Chita and renewed its efforts to bring under its effective control the portions of eastern Siberia which were still occupied by Japanese forces. These efforts, although they accorded with the wishes of a large majority of the people in the territory in question, were bitterly resisted by Japan and the reactionary element of the population. In December, 1920, the Japanese authorities at Vladivostok issued a proclamation declaring that the Maritime Province would not be permitted to join the Far Eastern Republic, and attempted, without success, to keep the people from electing delegates to the constituent assembly at Chita. In April, 1921, in response to notes from the Chita government demanding that Japan withdraw her forces from Siberia and abandon her policy of interfering in the country's internal affairs, ten thousand additional Japanese troops were landed, and in May of the same year the former adherents of Kolchak and Semenov, with Japanese assistance, still further strengthened their hold on Vladivostok, Nikolsk, and Khabarovsk.

From the beginning of 1921 the authorities at Chita, finding that the role of buffer state exposed their country to constant and humiliating interference by Japan, turned more and more toward Moscow for aid and support. A note from the American government on May 31, 1921, expressing American disapproval of Japan's policy in Siberia and extending an invitation to participate in the Washington Conference, led the Japanese Foreign Office to seek some improvement in Japan's relations with the Far Eastern Republic. The Chita government was accordingly requested to send a delegation to Dairen for the purpose of discussing with the representatives of Japan the terms upon which Japanese forces would evacuate Siberian territory. At the Dairen Conference, which opened in August, 1921, the solidarity between Chita and Moscow became increasingly obvious. In reply to Japanese attempts to fix economic and military conditions upon which their forces would be withdrawn, the Chita delegation, supported by Moscow's unofficial observer, insisted upon unconditional evacuation; and the resultant deadlock persisted until April, 1922, when the conference broke up. At the Washington Conference, in the meantime, Japan's course of action in Siberia was pointedly criticized by Mr. Hughes, the American Secretary of State, and in the summer of 1922 the Japanese government, in the face of growing Japanese opposition to a continuance of the intervention, announced that its troops would be withdrawn from the Siberian mainland by the end of October.

On September 3, 1922, a second conference between the representatives of Japan and those of the Far Eastern Republic opened at Changchun,[1] at the junction of the Chinese Eastern Railway and the South Manchuria Railway. Like the earlier conference at Dairen, this meeting also developed into a deadlock, and after three weeks of fruitless negotiation it dissolved. Japan's decision, however, had been made: her forces in northern Sakhalin were to remain until Russia gave proper satisfaction for the Nikolaevsk massacre; her troops on the mainland would be withdrawn as announced. By November 1, 1922, the last Japanese troops had left the Maritime Province. Twelve days later, on November 13, the Far Eastern Republic, by the formal vote of the Chita government, abandoned its independent status and became a part of the Soviet Union.

DEVELOPMENTS IN CHINA AND JAPAN, 1917–1921

In Japan the period of the World War was marked by a great wave of commercial and industrial prosperity. With all the major European powers involved in war the demand for Japanese manu-

---

[1] Now Hsinking, the capital of Manchukuo.

factures, despite an energetic anti-Japanese boycott during 1915 in China, steadily increased in all parts of the Far East. At the same time the Russian Empire, almost completely cut off from its western allies, turned to Japan for enormous quantities of arms, munitions, and other wartime necessities. As Japan's own belligerent activities prior to the intervention in Siberia threw little strain upon her resources, she was able to take full advantage of these opportunities. From $287,715,000 in 1914 the total value of Japan's exports, chiefly manufactured goods, rose to $968,127,000 in 1918 and to an "all-time high" of $1,018,855,000 in 1919. In spite of greatly increased imports of such necessary raw materials as cotton, wool, and iron Japan during these years had a large favorable balance of trade. Her factory system and her merchant marine both rapidly expanded to meet the demands imposed on them. A new group of war millionaires arose to join the pre-war industrial princes, now grown to multimillionaires. At the same time prices, especially of foodstuffs, rose almost precipitously.

Prior to 1918 the position of the Japanese laborer was dominated by the Peace Regulations of 1900, which imposed upon "those who, with the object of causing a strike, seduce or incite others" the penalty of one to six months' imprisonment plus a fine of 3 yen to 30 yen. A Japanese Federation of Labor was organized as early as 1912, and in 1918 the right to form unions was tacitly recognized by the government; but such organizations, although tolerated, were not accorded actual legal status. While the Japanese government thus refused to approve organizations among the wage-earners, it was not until 1911 that any move was made to correct by legislation the glaring evils in the conditions of factory labor, and this initial effort, when made, was ridiculously inadequate. The Factory Act of March 29, 1911, which did not become effective until five years after the date of enactment, merely dealt with the employment of "young persons and women." Thereafter the lawful hours of labor for these two classes of employees were not to exceed twelve per day, while the employment of children under the age of twelve was forbidden except in certain specified industries, such as the manufacture of matches, in which children over ten years of age might be employed.

Forbidden to organize and unprotected by legislation on such matters as wages, hours of labor, or accident insurance, the working class in Japan was completely at the mercy of the employer. Hours of factory labor were reduced from fifteen hours to twelve only when the factory-owner discovered that two twelve-hour shifts made it possible to increase the efficiency of his machines. Fresh recruits from a teeming rural population replaced the injured, the ill, or the superannuated, who were allowed to become dependent upon their relatives. The same inexhaustible labor reserve made it possible for the employer, no matter how profitable his industry might be, to keep his wages at the bare subsistence level. The rapid rise of food prices resulting from war-time prosperity brought the underpaid factory laborers to the verge of starvation, and in the summer of 1918 the important industrial centers, particularly the great city of Osaka, were the scene of violent riots occasioned by the high price of rice. In September the Terauchi cabinet tendered its resignation, but the most important result of the rice riots was the subsequent tacit acquiescence in the existence of labor unions. Although not approving of these organizations, the Japanese authorities apparently came to realize that by forcing the employers to pay at least a living wage they might serve to prevent similar outbreaks in the future.

During the nine years following the annexation of their country to the Japanese Empire the Korean people were unwilling recipients of the blessings of progress as administered by alien rulers. To what extent they actually benefited from the changes effected by Japan it would be difficult to say. Apologists for Japan point to great improvements in transportation, production, and commerce; but the Koreans complain that the profits from these improvements, together with all the most fertile portions of their land, were monopolized by the Japanese themselves. At all events, the Koreans looked upon Japanese domination as oppression; accordingly they hailed with enthusiasm President Wilson's declaration in favor of self-determination for oppressed peoples and made unsuccessful efforts to lay their case before the Paris Conference.

Failing to secure a hearing at Paris, the people of the peninsula did not submit in silence to the rejection of their plea. On February 22, 1919, the old ex-emperor Yi Hyeung died, and on March 1, three days before the date set for his funeral, hundreds of thousands of Korean patriots assembled at Seoul and at other important cities to voice their demand for the restoration of their nation's sovereignty. At these points and at other centers to which the movement instantly spread, the procedure was everywhere the same, and on the Korean side everywhere remarkable for the absence of attempted violence.[1] The leaders read to the cheering multitudes a solemn declaration of Korea's independence; then, having made their gesture, they calmly awaited arrest and punishment. The revolt, if it may be so termed, was crushed with ruthless severity. More than two thousand of the demonstrators were killed or wounded by the soldiers employed to disperse the gatherings, and some thirty thousand were arrested. About one third of those arrested were released without trial, while a similar number were punished by summary flogging; of the nine thousand actually brought to trial, five thousand were found guilty of seditious behavior and received prison sentences.

Following this outbreak and its ruthless suppression the Japanese government, impressed by the evidence of widespread discontent, took steps to improve its administration of Korean affairs. The governor-general, an army officer, was replaced by Admiral Saito,[2] a capable and enlightened official. The Korean penal laws were reformed by the abolition of flogging, long since abandoned in Japan itself; police affairs were taken out of the hands of the army; and the Korean people, by the creation of local elective councils, were given at least a measure of self-government. The reforms thus put into force, although they greatly modified the former harshness of Japanese rule, did not wholly reconcile the Koreans to their condition, and subsequent years saw the migration of thousands of malcontents across the frontiers into Manchuria or into Russian territory. The settlement of Korean *émigrés* in Siberia, where they soon absorbed communistic ideas,

---

[1] It is reported that at only two of nearly six hundred centers of the movement did any of the Koreans use force.

[2] In May, 1932, Admiral Saito was called from retirement, by a state emergency, to become Prime Minister of Japan.

became a matter of great concern, and possibly of real danger, to Japan. The settlers in Manchuria, on the other hand, actually contributed to the expansion of Japanese influence in that region, since the Tokyo government, taking advantage of the presence of these Japanese subjects on Chinese soil, successfully asserted the right to send into the districts where they dwelt the officials necessary to maintain over them its extraterritorial jurisdiction.

When in October, 1916, the Okuma government was forced to resign, the new ministry which took its place was headed by Marshal Terauchi, a Choshu clansman and a protégé of the leading member of the Genro, Prince Yamagata. The Seiyukai, the opposition party during the Okuma administration, promptly entered into a working agreement with the new Premier, and in the general election of 1917 was able to secure a plurality (just short of an absolute majority) in the House of Representatives. Like Count Okuma's Kenseikai organization, the Seiyukai was closely allied with certain great business and financial interests,[1] and the Terauchi government, despite the fact that the Premier was a member of the military bureaucracy, had no objection to being drawn into this alliance. Because of the many favors exchanged between the government and the war profiteers the rice riots during the summer of 1918 were regarded as a popular protest against the Terauchi ministry, and in September of that year the Premier resigned.

Hara Takashi, selected by the Genro to fill the post left vacant by Marshal Terauchi's resignation, was the first commoner who had ever held the office of Premier in Japan. President of the Seiyukai since 1914 and even more of a party politician than was Okuma, Mr. Hara gave Japan its first real taste of party government, all the posts in the cabinet, except the ministries of war, navy, and foreign affairs, being given to members of the Seiyukai. In the Diet of 1918–1919, as a move to allay the popular discontent of the preceding summer, he introduced and carried to enactment a bill for the extension of the suffrage. By the new act the right of voting

---

[1] The allies, or patrons, of the Seiyukai are the powerful Mitsui interests; the Kenseikai, now known as the Minseito, has always been associated with the equally powerful Mitsubishi group.

was given to all adult males who paid direct taxes to the amount of three yen per year, instead of ten yen as formerly, and the number of qualified voters was thereby increased from 1,450,000 to 3,000,000. The political wisdom of the Seiyukai leader was soon demonstrated; in the election of 1920 the Seiyukai secured 282 (out of a total of 464) seats in the House of Representatives, a clear majority of exactly 100, and the control thus gained was lost in 1924 only because of a split within the party.

On November 4, 1921, a week before the opening of the Washington Conference, Premier Hara was cut down by the knife of an assassin. This shocking crime, the first of a series of political murders which during recent years have raised grave doubts as to the future of Japan's parliamentary form of government, appears to have been, in part at least, a consequence of the sudden collapse of the country's war-time prosperity.[1] Other factors, however, undoubtedly entered into the tragedy. Even at the height of the industrial boom the laboring class, as we have seen, had little share in the abounding prosperity, while the rising price of farm products failed to compensate the hard-working peasant for the accompanying rises in rent, taxes, and the prices of the goods which he must buy. The general spirit of discontent was aggravated during the Hara administration by the activities of the once all-powerful clan leaders, now overshadowed by the growing political influence of financial and industrial magnates. Resenting their political eclipse, these conservative patriots lost no opportunity to arouse popular indignation against the party politicians, who, while claiming to be the bulwarks of the imperial throne, "were content to be slaves of the millionaires."

In China the political schism of the summer of 1917, arising out of the controversy over participation in the war, left the republic with two rival governments. At Peking, Vice-President Feng Kuo-chang succeeded to the presidency upon the resignation of Li Yüan-hung and carried on the government with Marshal Tuan Ch'i-jui, the head of the military clique, as his Prime Minister,

---

[1] From $968,127,000 in 1918, $1,018,885,000 in 1919, and $926,983,000 in 1920 —a three-year average of $971,332,000—the total value of Japan's exports fell in 1921 to $578,545,000.

while at Canton the Kuomintang members of the dissolved parliament, under the leadership of Dr. Sun Yat-sen, declared themselves to be the legal representatives of the nation and the defenders of constitutional liberty. Both governments, as we have seen, issued declarations of war against the Central Powers, and after the armistice they collaborated in sending a strong delegation to represent China at the Paris Peace Conference. On all other points Peking and Canton were hopelessly divided, and the political situation was further complicated during the period 1917–1921 by much internal dissension at the two capitals.

In the north the presidential career of Feng Kuo-chang, who was merely finishing out the five-year term for which Yüan Shih-k'ai had originally been elected, came to an end in October, 1918. To fill the vacancy a pseudo parliament composed of representatives selected by the northern tuchuns assembled at Peking and elected Hsu Shih-ch'ang, a former viceroy of Manchuria. Under President Hsu, as under Li and Feng, the dominant figure at Peking was Premier Tuan Ch'i-jui, whose followers, drawn chiefly from the provinces of Anhui and Fukien, constituted the so-called Anfu Club. Opposed to Tuan and his Anfu organization, however, there were in the north two other influential politico-military cliques: a Fengtien group headed by Chang Tso-lin, who since the fall of the Manchu dynasty had enjoyed a practical dictatorship over the Three Eastern Provinces, and a Chihli group under General Ts'ao Kun, the tuchun of Chihli, and Wu P'ei-fu, his principal lieutenant. Throughout northern China and the Yangtze valley, adherents of one or another of these three groups held military domination over more or less extensive areas; all were nominally obedient to the Peking government, but the authority of the president and his Premier actually extended only to such regions as were under the control of Anfu supporters.

While the Peking government was thus able to maintain some semblance of unified power over the greater part of the republic, Canton was almost from the outset the scene of violent open conflict. Dr. Sun and his two principal associates, T'ang Shao-yi and the venerable Wu T'ing-fang, found it difficult to maintain their ascendancy over the Kuomintang members—or ex-members—of parliament, while the three leaders and the legislative body alike were soon at loggerheads with the southern military leaders upon whom they depended for support. In May, 1918, the triumvirate, as the result of a dispute with the militarists, withdrew from Canton to Shanghai; at the same time the parliamentarians, incensed at the presumption of the army officers, were on the point of transferring their headquarters to one of the western provinces, either Yunnan or Szechwan. Later in the year temporary harmony was restored, but in April, 1920, Dr. Sun and his two faithful colleagues were once more at Shanghai, having fled from Canton with the official seals of the government.

From his Shanghai haven of refuge Sun Yat-sen now entered into correspondence with Tuan Ch'i-jui, to whom he proposed an elaborate plan for the unification of the distracted country. The two rival governments should abdicate simultaneously in favor of a new national parliament elected in response to a joint summons. This new body, which should assemble at Peking on October 10, could then proceed, with the support of the whole nation, to the election of a president and to the organization of an effective national government.

By the spring of 1920, however, Marshal Tuan and the Anfu Club were nearing the end of their power at Peking. A year earlier the Chinese people, aroused by the Paris decision on the question of Shantung, had directed a large measure of their indignation against the authorities at Peking, whose avarice, stupidity, and subservience to Japan so fatally compromised China's claim for the complete restoration of her rights in Shantung. Three members of the Anfu Club, regarded as especially responsible for the betrayal of their country's interests, had been driven from public life; and Tuan Ch'i-jui, although he continued to hold the premiership, had lost much of his earlier prestige. Even as Tuan was voicing his approval of Dr. Sun's proposal, his rivals at Peking were preparing his overthrow. At the beginning of July, after a conference between Wu P'ei-fu, Ts'ao Kun, and Chang Tso-lin, Wu P'ei-fu's troops advanced upon Peking. The Anfu leader did not give up without a struggle, but on July 28 he resigned his post and withdrew to the seclusion of a Buddhist monastery.

Four months after the overthrow of the Anfu Club a change took place at Canton also, where the supporters of Sun Yat-sen once more gained the upper hand. Sun, T'ang, and Wu T'ing-fang again returned from Shanghai, and on May 5, 1921, after a formal election by the remnants of the old 1913 parliament Dr. Sun was inaugurated at Canton as the "constitutional" president of China.

CHINA AND THE SHANTUNG AWARD

The outburst of popular indignation in China following the receipt of news that the former German rights in Shantung had been awarded to Japan was directed in large measure, as noted above, against the Peking officials deemed guilty of betraying their country's interests. Back of these "traitors," however, was Japan, by whose agents the guilty Chinese officials had been bribed, out-witted, or coerced; and the infuriated Chinese patriots, while not neglecting to punish the faults of Peking, were determined to inflict punishment equally severe, if possible, upon their powerful and aggressive neighbor. Under the circumstances one weapon only seemed available, and this—a boycott of Japanese goods—was employed without delay.

The first news of the Paris decision was received in China on May 2; on the following day "The People's Determination Society" organized at Peking and declared itself in favor of a boycott, and on May 7, at a mass meeting of Shanghai students held to commemorate the fourth anniversary of Japan's 1915 ultimatum, the boycott was proclaimed for that city. The example of Peking and Shanghai was promptly followed at Canton, Tientsin, Hankow, and other ports.

The boycott was actively supported by the guilds and the chambers of commerce, but the principal driving force was provided by thousands of students banded together into hastily organized unions for the purpose of "saving the country." Throughout the summer of 1919 and during the years 1920 and 1921 normal activities in China's educational institutions were practically at a standstill while student orators, student organizers, and student pickets devoted themselves to the task of enforcing the ban against all things Japanese. Not satisfied with exercising pressure to prevent any backsliding on the part of the merchants, the student organizations conducted a systematic campaign among the buying public for the purpose of educating them to the part they must play in making the boycott effective. At Peking, where their demonstrations brought about the retirement of the "three traitors," the student agitators were also instrumental in preventing any negotiation with Japan for the restoration of the German holdings. "Young China" would permit no compromise. Kiaochow and the whole of Shantung must be evacuated without condition or reservations; until then the boycott would continue.

In spite of the energy and enthusiasm displayed by the student agitators the boycott of 1919–1921 appears to have had little actual effect upon the total volume of Japanese trade with China.[1] Yet the Japanese government, already the object of domestic criticism and of foreign suspicion, found itself seriously embarrassed by this persistent demonstration of Chinese hostility, and as early as January 24, 1920, it attempted to open negotiations with China for the restoration of Kiaochow. After a silence of nearly four months the Chinese government replied (on May 22) that China, not being a signatory to the Treaty of Versailles, "is not therefore in a position to negotiate directly with Japan on the question of Tsingtao on the basis of that treaty." For this reason and because of "the strongly antagonistic attitude" of the Chinese people in regard to the question it hoped that Japan would withdraw her troops from Shantung without delay. The approach of the Washington Conference gave Japan an additional reason for wishing to adjust her controversy with China, and two more attempts were made to inaugurate direct negotiations, but the opening of the conference found the two governments still deadlocked, unable to find any common ground upon which to open discussions.

[1] Professor C. F. Remer, in his *Study of Chinese Boycotts* (The Johns Hopkins Press, 1933), finds that although certain lines of Japanese trade were seriously affected there is no evidence that the trade as a whole suffered appreciably. Indeed, his examination of all the available trade reports convinced him that "the share of Japanese exports going to China was unusually great during the boycott years"; in other words, the sale of Japanese goods in China fell off less during these three years than did the sale in other countries.

While China's relations with Japan in the years following the close of the World War were thus embittered by the question of Shantung, her relations with Russia showed signs of definite improvement. As one of the Allied Powers, China had participated in the Siberian intervention, but, except for the presence of a small Chinese force at Vladivostok, her military activity in this connection was confined to Mongolia and the Chinese Eastern Railway zone in Manchuria.

In July, 1919, the Soviet authorities at Moscow, hoping to gain Chinese sympathy and support in the struggle against their "capitalistic" foes, issued a proclamation repudiating all the treaties and agreements whereby the Czarist government during the last twenty years of its rule had extended its power at China's expense. At the time this proclamation made little impression upon the Chinese authorities, who were pursuing their own plan for the recapture of certain rights recently alienated by Czarist aggression. A Chinese army, sent into Outer Mongolia for the purpose of setting aside the tripartite agreement of 1915 relating to that region, compelled the Mongols to submit to superior force, and in November, 1919, the hutukhtu of Urga renounced his rights as an autonomous ruler.

This resettlement of the Mongolian question in a manner so satisfactory to China was not destined to be permanent. In the summer of 1920 Baron Ungern von Sternberg, a former supporter of Admiral Kolchak, retreated from Siberia into Mongolia and prepared to establish there a base of operations against his Bolshevist enemies. Taking advantage of the anti-Chinese sentiment among the Mongols, Baron Ungern enlisted a large number of Mongols under his banner and advanced upon Urga. The first attack upon Urga, in October, 1920, was repulsed by the Chinese garrison; but in January, 1921, Baron Ungern, apparently with some assistance from the Japanese, succeeded in capturing the place. Ungern's triumph at Urga was followed almost immediately by a fresh invasion of Mongolia, this time by the forces of the Far Eastern Republic and their Bolshevist allies. In July, 1921, Ungern was defeated, and the Bolshevists promptly proceeded to organize a "Mongolian People's Revolutionary Government" at Urga.

On September 27, 1920, more than a year after their first friendly gesture to the Chinese, the Soviet authorities at Moscow repeated their desire to pave the way for better relations by surrendering to China without compensation "all that had been predatorily seized from her by the Czar's government and the Russian bourgeoisie." Four days before the date of this communication the Peking government canceled its recognition of the Russian diplomatic and consular agents in China, on the ground that these officers, having been appointed by the Kerensky government, no longer represented the *de facto* government of Russia, and on October 2 the authorities at Peking concluded with the Russo-Asiatic Bank an arrangement for the administrative control of the Chinese Eastern Railway by China pending the recognition by China of a Russian government with which a permanent agreement could be made. Both these steps by the Chinese government became the subject of correspondence between the diplomatic body at Peking and the Chinese Foreign Office. Although the Allied governments, in the treaties drawn up at Paris, had forced Germany and Austria to renounce their extraterritorial rights in China, the foreign diplomats at Peking were unwilling to admit China's right to cancel, by presidential mandate, Russian consular jurisdiction, while the modification of the status of the Chinese Eastern Railway, except by a formal treaty, was regarded as a dangerous precedent. In August, 1920, a mission from the Far Eastern Republic had arrived at Peking for the purpose of concluding a commercial treaty with the Chinese government, and in May of the following year the Peking authorities, despite the disapproval of the diplomatic body, announced their willingness to enter upon negotiations with a representative of the Moscow government.

The developments in Mongolia now became a cause for new friction between China and Russia. The hutukhtu of Urga appealed to Peking in the spring of 1921 for protection against the White Russians, but the establishment of the Mongolian People's Revolutionary Government in July, 1921, by the conquering Red forces, after their defeat of Ungern, was equally objectionable both to the former Mongol princes and to the Chinese government. When the Moscow embassy reached Peking in November, the Chinese were therefore determined to make the withdrawal of Russian influence from Outer Mongolia a *sine qua non* of any diplomatic arrangement. The Russian representative was unwilling to enter into any discussion on this point, and the negotiations consequently broke down. In spite of the Mongolian difficulty, however, Chinese opinion was not unfavorably impressed by the new Russian regime, and it was evident that a *rapprochement* between the two countries would be comparatively easy if the Russians agreed to abandon their Mongolian activities.

THE WASHINGTON CONFERENCE

In the spring of 1921 the Far East presented a number of conspicuously dangerous possibilities, conspicuous even in the generally chaotic condition of the post-war world.

First, there was the possibility that the leading Allied Powers, all interested in the Orient and all rapidly expanding their armaments, would be drawn by their conflicting Far Eastern interests into a new and perhaps more terrible world war. This danger was made more real by the development of Sino-Japanese friction over Shantung and, at least in American eyes, by the existence of the Anglo-Japanese Alliance.

Second, there was the possibility, amounting almost to a probability, of the disintegration of the Chinese Republic. A collapse of the Peking government, whose power and prestige had steadily declined since the death of Yüan Shih-k'ai, might easily lead to the revival of plans for the partition of China and thus to an intensification of already existing international jealousies.

Third, there was the fear of communism, the possibility that the doctrines of Bolshevist Russia would spread and take root among the discontented peoples of eastern Asia. It was especially in China that the expansion of Russian influence was to be feared; for the rising tide of Chinese nationalism, embittered by the Versailles Treaty and by the dispute with Japan over Shantung, had created a situation in which it was possible that the Chinese might turn to Moscow and seek Russian aid in freeing themselves from the treaty limitations upon their national sovereignty.

On May 26, 1921, the United States Senate unanimously adopted a resolution requesting the President to call a conference of the principal naval powers with a view to arriving at some mutual agreement on the subject of limiting or reducing the burden of naval expenditure. From the very outset, however, it was apparent that any agreement with respect to limitation of armaments must depend upon some solution of the trouble-breeding issues in the Pacific and the Far East. Only with the removal of these potential causes of international conflict would it be possible for the interested powers to approach with any hope of success the task of reducing the defensive forces which each was preparing against the danger of an attack by one or more of the others.

In view of the fact that the question of limiting the burden of naval preparedness was thus inseparably linked with the solution of questions relating to the Far East, the American government, with the consent of the governments whose co-operation it was seeking, determined to combine the two issues. On August 11, therefore, invitations were sent to Great Britain, France, Italy, and Japan—the four powers whose naval aspirations were of international consequence—inviting them to "participate in a conference on the subject of the Limitation of Armament, in connection with which Pacific and Far Eastern questions will also be discussed, to be held in Washington on the 11th day of November, 1921." At the same time the President formally invited China "to participate in the discussions of Pacific and Far Eastern questions, in connection with the Conference on the subject of the Limitation of Armament," and a similar invitation was subsequently extended to Belgium, the Netherlands, and Portugal, whose material interests in the Far East entitled them to seats at such a conference.

The part of the work of the conference which dealt with the limitation of naval armaments may be treated briefly. The Five-Power Naval Treaty concluded by the United States, Great Britain, Japan, France, and Italy established between the navies of these powers a tonnage ratio[1] in "capital" ships—battleships and armored cruisers. In the Far East the 5 : 3 ratio in capital ships between the American and Japanese navies and the similar ratio

[1] 5: 5: 3: 1.75: 1.75.

between the British and the Japanese established an adequate guaranty for Japan's national safety against either power, as it was universally agreed that no naval attack upon Japan from the nearest American or British base—Hawaii or Singapore—could hope for success unless undertaken by a force of at least double the strength of the Japanese navy.

The beneficial effect of this treaty in allaying national fears which had inspired the rival programs of naval preparedness was supplemented by a Four-Power Treaty between the United States, Great Britain, France, and Japan, and by an agreement maintaining the status quo in the matter of fortifications in the Pacific. The final article of the Four-Power Treaty provided that its ratification would bring to an end "the agreement between Great Britain and Japan which was concluded at London on July 13, 1911," that is, the Anglo-Japanese Alliance, thereby removing the American fear that a conflict with Japan would automatically involve Great Britain. At the same time Japanese fears were calmed by the agreement relating to the fortification of Pacific possessions, which provided that during the term of this treaty no new fortifications were to be erected in the islands of the Pacific to the east of the meridian of 110 degrees east longitude except upon islands "adjacent to the coast" of North America, of Australia, and of New Zealand. Thus Japan was insured against the danger of having the 5: 5: 3 capital-ship ratio nullified by the erection of British or American naval bases nearer than Singapore and Hawaii respectively.

Although Russia was not invited to send a delegation to Washington, the question of Siberia, in so far as it affected the conference powers, was somewhat clarified by the reading of formal statements by Baron Shidehara for Japan and by Secretary Hughes on behalf of the United States.

In the first of these statements the Japanese spokesman categorically denied that Japan sought the permanent acquisition of any portion of Siberian territory or was planning to make the withdrawal of her troops conditional upon the grant of special economic privileges to her nationals, and he reiterated the intention of his government to withdraw its troops as soon as conditions in Siberia were such as to afford a reasonable guaranty for the security of Japanese nationals there and for tranquillity on the frontier of Korea.

In reply Mr. Hughes, after repeating the views of the American government to the effect that "the continued occupation of strategic centers in Eastern Siberia . . . tends rather to increase than to allay the unrest and disorder in that region," expressed the gratification with which the American delegation had "listened to the assurances given by their Japanese Colleagues" and the friendly hope "that Japan will find it possible to carry out within the near future her expressed intention of terminating finally the Siberian expedition and of restoring Sakhalin to the Russian people."

Apart from the exchange of views on the subject of Siberia the Far Eastern deliberations of the Washington Conference were monopolized almost completely by the problems of China. The Chinese delegation lost no time in placing on record their country's objections to the policies of the powers and to the treaty stipulations imposed upon her in the past; and the other members of the conference, within the limits of action fixed by the requirement of unanimity,[1] endeavored to remove the more serious obstacles to China's national aspirations. The outcome of these endeavors must be considered under three headings: (1) the measures calculated to strengthen the existing Chinese government; (2) those intended to allay both China's fear of renewed foreign aggression and the growing reciprocal suspicion of "the powers other than China"; and (3) the arrangement between China and Japan—concluded outside the conference itself, but vital to the success of its labors—which laid the foundation for the ultimate solution of the Shantung question.

One important step toward strengthening the government of China was the conclusion of a customs treaty which, like most of the other agreements, was signed at the final session of the conference on February 6, 1922. In this treaty the eight other powers agreed to such immediate revision of the duties collected by the maritime customs as was necessary to raise the tariff rates to an

---

[1] The conference, it must be remembered, was a meeting of sovereign powers, and its decisions were therefore binding only upon such states as subsequently ratified them.

effective 5 per cent *ad valorem*. The same treaty further provided that "within three months after the date of the ratification of this convention" a special conference should assemble to prepare the way for the eventual concession of complete tariff autonomy to China.

China's financial difficulties, although serious, were not the only cause of her political weakness, and the members of the conference, in recognition of this fact, made a number of gestures intended to improve the Chinese government's prestige at home. On December 10, 1921, the eight other powers by unanimous resolution expressed their sympathy with China's desire for the abolition of extraterritoriality and agreed to the creation of a special commission to examine the laws and the administration of justice in China with a view to determining whether the surrender of extraterritorial rights was expedient. On February 1, 1922, China's protest against the continued maintenance of post offices on Chinese soil by four of the powers (France, Great Britain, Japan, and the United States) was met by a resolution declaring that all such foreign post offices should be abandoned on or before January 1, 1923. Other resolutions recognized "in principle" the justice of China's protests against the unauthorized maintenance of foreign armed forces on Chinese soil and the erection of foreign wireless stations, while on February 1, 1922, Mr. Balfour announced that the British government intended to restore to China the Weihaiwei leasehold and was prepared to open negotiations for the purpose of arranging the details of this restoration.

The removal of China's fears and of the mutual suspicions entertained by the other powers was accomplished by the Nine Power Treaty Relating to Principles and Policies concerning China, of which the first two articles deserve verbatim quotation:

ARTICLE I. The contracting powers, other than China, agree: (1) To respect the sovereignty, the independence, and the territorial and administrative integrity of China; (2) To provide the fullest and most unembarrassed opportunity to China to develop and maintain for herself an effective and stable government; (3) To use their influence for the purpose of effectually establishing and maintaining the principle of equal opportunity for the commerce and industry of all nations throughout the territory of China;

(4) To refrain from taking advantage of conditions in China in order to seek special rights or privileges which would abridge the rights of subjects or citizens of friendly states, and from countenancing action inimical to the security of such states.

ARTICLE II. The contracting powers agree not to enter into any treaty, agreement, arrangement, or understanding, either with one another, or, individually or collectively, with any power or powers, which would infringe or impair the principles stated in Article I.

In subsequent articles of the treaty (1) China and the eight other powers reiterated and elaborated the pledge to respect the principle of equal opportunity, (2) powers not represented at the conference but having treaty relations with China were invited to adhere to the treaty, (3) it was provided "that, whenever a situation arises which in the opinion of any one of them involves the application of the stipulations of the present treaty, . . . there shall be full and frank communication between the contracting powers concerned."[1]

THE SETTLEMENT OF THE SHANTUNG QUESTION

When the representatives of the nine powers assembled at Washington, the Sino-Japanese *impasse* over Shantung constituted the most serious immediate threat to peace in the Orient. China's refusal to admit the validity of the Shantung clauses in the Versailles Treaty rendered it impossible to bring the question before the conference, but it was obvious to all concerned that unless this controversy was adjusted the conference would fail to accomplish any of the purposes for which it had been called.[2]

[1] On April 14, 1923, "in the light of the understanding arrived at by the Washington Conference," the American and Japanese governments in a fresh exchange of notes agreed "to consider the Lansing-Ishii correspondence of November 2, 1917, as cancelled and of no further force or effect."

[2] It should be noted that Mr. Balfour's first suggestion of the restoration of Weihaiwei to China came on December 3, two days after the commencement of the "conversations" between the Chinese and Japanese representatives, and was conditional upon a satisfactory outcome of those conversations; his definite statement that Weihaiwei would be restored came on February 1, immediately following the announcement that an accord on the Shantung question had been reached. Equally significant is the fact that, with the exception of the Four-Power Treaty Relating to the Pacific, all the basic agreements concluded at the conference were signed on or after the date of this announcement.

Fortunately, both of the governments involved were anxious to arrive at a solution of the difficulty if a solution involving no loss of dignity could be found. This fact made it possible for Mr. Hughes and Mr. Balfour, chiefs of the American and British delegations, to tender their good offices and to arrange for conversations between the Chinese and Japanese representatives. The two parties agreed to set aside their conflicting juridical claims and to negotiate on a purely factual basis, the facts being that Japan was in possession of certain powers and rights in Shantung and was ready to surrender these, upon satisfactory conditions, to China. The conversations, at which representatives of the American and British governments were always present, therefore resolved themselves into an attempt to reach an equitable arrangement with regard to the conditions of the surrender.

On February 4, 1922, the Chinese and Japanese delegates signed a treaty which settled the fundamental issues of the controversy. Shantung, including Kiaochow, was to be evacuated by the Japanese forces within six months after the ratification of the treaty, and all public property at Tsingtao was to be transferred to the Chinese government without compensation except for the cost of improvements made by the Japanese during their occupancy. China undertook to respect all vested rights "lawfully and equitably acquired by foreign nationals" during the periods of German and Japanese administration. The mining concessions in Shantung, formerly held by Germans, were to be taken over by a specially chartered company in which Japanese capital might be invested to an amount not exceeding that invested by the Chinese. The Tsingtao-Tsinan Railway was to become the property of China; but in view of the fact that the Reparations Commission at Paris had deducted the value of this line from the amount which Japan had been entitled to receive from Germany, China was to pay Japan a sum equal to the valuation placed on the railway by the commission (53,406,141 gold marks), plus the value of improvements made by Japan and minus the amount of the profits which Japan had derived from her administration of the property.[1]

[1] The treaty was duly ratified on June 2, and on December 10 the evacuation of the Japanese troops was completed.

With the final session of the Washington Conference on February 6, 1922, the period of the World War in the Far East may be regarded as having come to a close. The work of the conference was, perhaps, hailed with unwarranted enthusiasm. It had actually succeeded in relieving for the time the dangerous tension in eastern Asia, but the future was to depend upon the spirit in which the various parties to the conference interpreted and gave effect to the principles that they had adopted.

SUGGESTED REFERENCES

BUELL, R. L. The Washington Conference.

GRAVES, W. S. America's Siberian Adventure.

MACNAIR, H. F. Modern Chinese History: Selected Readings.

MORSE, H. B., and MACNAIR, H. F. Far Eastern International Relations.

NORTON, H. K. The Far Eastern Republic of Siberia.

TREAT, P. J. The Far East.

WHEELER, W. R. China and the World War.

WILLIAMS, E. T. A Short History of China.

WILLOUGHBY, W. W. China at the Conference.

WILLOUGHBY, W. W. Foreign Rights and Interests in China (revised edition, 2 vols.).

Conference on the Limitation of Armament. Senate Document No. 126, 67th Cong., 2d Sess.

XXXII

Post-war Developments

The World War and Indian Nationalism · India's Participation in the War · The Montagu-Chelmsford Reforms · The Rowlatt Act · "Mahatma" Gandhi · Passive Resistance and Non-co-operation · The New Government in Operation · The Simon Commission · The Indian Nationalists and the Simon Report · Framing a Constitution for India · Self-government and Self-determination for the Philippines · The Jones Bill · Government under the Jones Bill · The Reassertion of American Control · Nationalism and Independence · The Dutch East Indies · French Imperialism in Indo-China · Progress and New Problems in Siam · The End of the "Unequal Treaties" · Revolution and a Constitutional Regime · China's Struggle for National Reorganization · The Rule of the Tuchuns · The Rise of the Kuomintang · The Northward Advance of the Kuomintang · The Nationalist Government of China · China's Intellectual Revolution · Nationalist China and the Powers · Diplomatic Successes · The Domestic Difficulties of the Nationalist Government · The Troubles of Post-war Japan · The Earthquake and the Depression · Japan's Struggle for World Markets · Political Problems · Beginning of the Showa Era · Dangerous Thought and the Threatened Breakdown of Parliamentary Government · Difficulties with the United States and with Soviet Russia · Relations with China, 1922–1931 · Manchuria, the Storm Center of the Far East · Aggressive Nationalism in New China · The Russo-Chinese Clash on the Chinese Eastern Railway · The Mukden Outbreak · The State of Manchukuo · The League of Nations and the Manchurian Question · Japan's Withdrawal from the League · Peace or War in the Far East?

AS A RESULT of the Indian Councils Act of 1909 and the royal visit two years later (see page 649) the Indian Nationalist movement, for the time, lost much of its bitterness, and in 1914 an overwhelming majority of the Indian people were definitely loyal to their British rulers in the struggle against the Central Powers. During the years 1914 and 1915, it is true, sporadic revolutionary outbreaks occurred in Bengal, the Punjab, and the Deccan; but the enactment in 1915 of the Defense of India Act, which conferred upon the government extraordinary wartime powers of arrest and imprisonment in cases of sedition, appears to have been generally approved by the people as a whole. Even the entry of Mohammedan Turkey into the war failed to cause any serious difficulty for British rule in India; the mass of the Indian people, Moslem as well as Hindu, believed that in showing themselves to be loyal supporters of the empire they were assuring the eventual attainment of India's aspirations. During the four years of the war India contributed to the Allied cause not less than eight hundred thousand fighting men and an additional half a million in the noncombatant services; Indian industry provided large quantities of munitions and other much needed war materials; and on March 1, 1915, the Indian government announced that India, as her contribution to imperial war financing, would undertake the flotation of a war loan amounting to £100,000,000.

Fully recognizing the importance of India's loyal co-operation, the British government early in the war began to make important concessions to the demands and wishes of the Indian people. Simultaneously with the announcement of the war loan the viceroy was able to inform the Indian people that with the approval of the British government the tariff on imported cotton goods was to be increased to 7½ per cent without any accompanying increase in the excise tax on cotton fabrics manufactured in India.[1] This change, which gave Indian manufactures a measure of protection against British competition, was hailed with general satisfaction, while the subsequent appointment of two eminent Indians, the Maharaja of Bikaner and Sir S. Sinha, to membership in the Imperial War Council was regarded as additional evidence of an intention to treat India as an equal and autonomous portion of the empire.

These measures did not long suffice to counteract the inevitable growth of war-weariness; and the Indian leaders, as the war dragged on, began to question the reality of its benefit to the Indian people. Nor was the questioning attitude of Indian Nationalists abated by the rumors that the close of the war would see a reorganization of the British Empire along lines which would give to the self-governing dominions a greater share in the direction of

---

[1] Since 1894 the tariff on cotton goods imported into India had been restricted, at the demand of Lancashire textile interests, to 3½ per cent, and the same group of British industrialists had successfully insisted upon the maintenance of a countervailing 3½ per cent excise tax on Indian-made cotton fabrics.

imperial affairs. In view of the fact that all the self-governing dominions had passed discriminatory legislation against their Indian fellow subjects, legislation which in the case of South Africa reduced Indian laborers to a condition of peonage, it was felt that the rumored reorganization of the empire would serve merely to impose upon India an additional number of masters. By the summer of 1916 the politically minded element of the Indian population had begun to turn toward the idea of "home rule." In September of that year a Home Rule League was formally established at Madras, and in December the Indian National Congress, composed of Hindus, and the Moslem League, both meeting at Lucknow, adopted joint resolutions in favor of co-operation for the attainment of home rule.

Even the absorbing task of carrying on the war did not prevent the British government from realizing the serious nature of the Indian Nationalist movement. As early as the spring of 1916 the India Office had sought to evolve some plan for the satisfaction of India's demands, and the resolutions passed by the Lucknow meetings in December inspired even greater activity at London. On August 20, 1917, the Secretary of State for India, Mr. Montagu, announced in the House of Commons:

The policy of his Majesty's Government, with which the Government of India are in complete accord, is that of the increasing association of Indians in every branch of the administration, and the gradual development of self-governing institutions, with a view to the progressive realization of responsible government in India as an integral part of the British Empire.

Following this epoch-making announcement of policy, the British authorities acted with unaccustomed speed. In the autumn of 1917 Mr. Montagu proceeded to India for the purpose of consulting with the viceroy, Lord Chelmsford, and on April 22, 1918, the result of these consultations was made public in the Montagu-Chelmsford report. Special committees were established to consider separately the recommendations of this report; on June 21, 1919, the new Government of India Act was introduced into the House of Commons, and on December 23 it became law.

By the new act all British India, as distinct from the Indian states ruled over by semisovereign princes, was divided into nine

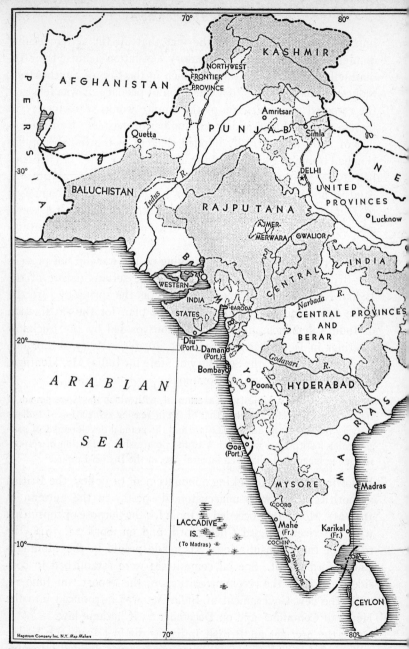

Map Plate, Patented July 5, 1921 · Method of Making Maps, Patented July 5, 1921

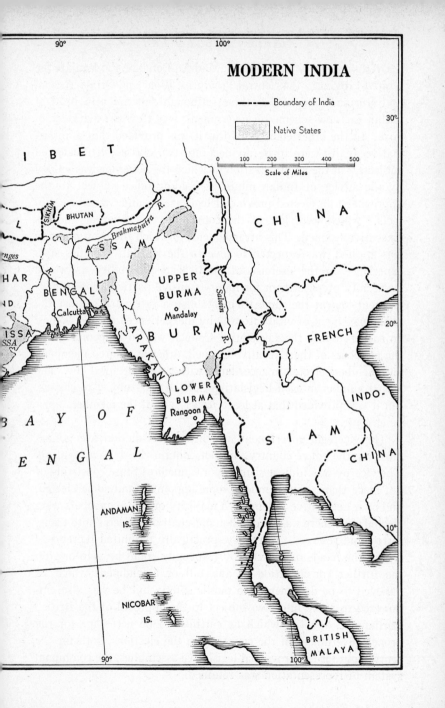

MODERN INDIA

------- Boundary of India

Native States

Scale of Miles

0   100   200   300   400   500

90°   100°   30°

T I B E T

CHINA

SIKKIM
BHUTAN

ASSAM

Brahmaputra R.

BENGAL
Calcutta
UPPER
BURMA
Mandalay

Salwin R.

BURMA

ARAKAN

HAR

ISSA
SSA

LOWER
BURMA
Rangoon

FRENCH   20°

INDO-

BAY OF
ENGAL

SIAM

CHINA

ANDAMAN
IS.

10°

NICOBAR
IS.

BRITISH
MALAYA

90°   100°

"governor's" provinces: Bengal, Madras, Bombay, the Punjab, the United Provinces, the Central Provinces, Bihar and Orissa, Assam, and Burma. The last of these, although subsequently brought within the new scheme of government, was treated separately in 1919. In the other eight provinces it was provided that administrative affairs were to be divided into two classes: "transferred subjects," in the administration of which the governor was guided by the advice of Indian ministers holding office subject to the approval of an elected provincial legislature; and "reserved subjects," which were left to the control of the governor and his Executive Council. This arrangement, to which the term *dyarchy* was applied, was expected to give to the legislative bodies such experience in the exercise of political responsibility as would eventually prepare them for more extensive participation in government and at the same time establish a safeguard against the mismanagement of vital interests by inexperienced elected bodies. In each province the Legislative Council was to be composed of the members of the Executive Council, other appointed members, and members elected in accordance with a new electoral law. The actual number in each Legislative Council was subject to change, but it was provided that at least 70 per cent of the members must be elective.

The viceregal government, which had jurisdiction over affairs affecting the entire country, did not contain the dyarchy feature. The viceroy was to be assisted by a Council of State consisting of not more than sixty members, some appointed and some elected, and by a Legislative Assembly, a majority of whose members were elected; but there was no division of "central subjects" into transferred and reserved. In reality, practically unlimited power was left in the hands of the viceroy. Not only could he veto or stop the further consideration of any bill or amendment which he believed to be detrimental to public safety, but he was also empowered to make into law, subject to the approval of the British Parliament, any bill which he certified to be necessary for the proper government of the country. In the elections, both for the central and for the provincial legislative assemblies, the communal system of representation was retained.

The new act also made some changes in the status of the Secretary of State for India. Hitherto the salary of this official and all the expenses of the India Office had been paid out of Indian revenues; henceforth they were to be paid out of money voted by the British Parliament. This change had long been demanded by Indian Nationalists and therefore met their approval; but the related demand, that the Secretary of State for India should have no more authority than was exercised by the Colonial Secretary with reference to the self-governing dominions, was not conceded; as agent of the British Parliament he was still clothed with authority to "superintend, direct, and control all acts, operations, and concerns which relate to the government or revenues of India," and the viceroy, in his administration of civil and military affairs, was required to "pay due obedience to all such orders as he may receive from the Secretary of State."

Unfortunately for the success of the new system of government its inauguration found India torn by a storm of anti-British feeling more intense than had appeared since the days of the Sepoy Mutiny. In January, 1919, when it was obvious that the conclusion of the peace treaty would soon bring the war to a close, the Indian government had introduced legislation to make permanent the extraordinary powers granted during the war by the Defence of India Act of 1915. Despite the violent protests of the Nationalist leaders in all parts of the country and despite the solid opposition of the elected minority in the Legislative Council the new legislation, the Rowlatt Act, was carried by the votes of the appointed members, and in March, 1919, it became law. The enactment of the Rowlatt Act was followed by serious riots and disturbances; and the rage of the Indian people reached its zenith in April, when the military commander at Amritsar dispersed a prohibited meeting by ordering his troops to open fire, with a resultant slaughter of 376 killed and some 1200 wounded.

In the storm which accompanied and followed the enactment of the Rowlatt Act there rose to nationwide prominence "Mahatma" (literally, "Great Soul") Gandhi. Mohandas Karamchand Gandhi was born in 1869 at Porbandar in Gujarat. At the age of nineteen, although the laws of his caste forbade ocean travel, he went to

England for the study of law, and in 1891 he was admitted to the English bar. Returning to India, Gandhi was asked in 1893 to conduct a case in Natal, South Africa, where during a stay of twenty years he devoted himself to the cause of his oppressed fellow Indians—indentured laborers and others. The success of his efforts was such that he returned to India in 1914 with an enviable reputation as a champion of the downtrodden. In his South African struggles for justice to Indian laborers and in his later Indian activities Gandhi consistently preached the doctrine of *Satyagraha* (literally, "insistence on truth" but usually translated as "passive resistance").

For four years after his return to India, Gandhi's belief in British justice remained unbroken. Although identifying himself with the Nationalist movement he was allied with the moderate wing, and as late as the end of June, 1918, he took the stand that home rule for India could best be attained through sincere cooperation between educated Indians and the British government. Less than a month after this expression of opinion came the publication of the report of the Rowlatt Committee and of the committee's recommendations which became the basis of the Rowlatt Act.

To Gandhi, as to all the other Nationalist leaders, the recommendations of the Rowlatt Committee and the legislation subsequently introduced into the Legislative Council appeared destructive of Indian liberties and nullified every promise that had been put forth by the Montagu-Chelmsford report. When the Rowlatt Act was passed, he proclaimed a *hartal* ("stoppage of business," or "boycott") on April 6 as a protest against the new law. Despite Gandhi's injunction that this demonstration must be nonviolent the *hartal* developed into serious riots. Horrified by the violence of the demonstration which he had inspired, the Mahatma imposed upon himself a three days' fast as atonement for the sins of his followers. Even greater, however, was the horror aroused in him by the Amritsar shooting, which in his eyes was the deliberate action of a "satanic government."

Up to this point Gandhi had been a loyal believer in the British rule; after this he was its uncompromising enemy. Early in 1920, when the plight of the Turkish Sultan, the caliph of all Islam, aroused the Moslems of India, Gandhi made common cause with the Mohammedans and secured their adherence to the program whereby he hoped to force British submission to Indian demands: the program of non-co-operation. At the elections held in the fall of 1920 for the establishment of the new legislative bodies created by the act of 1919 the "non-co-operators" refused to participate either as voters or as candidates. In spite of Gandhi's tremendous hold over the masses of the Indian people the non-co-operation movement soon began to disintegrate. In the spring of 1922 Gandhi prepared to proclaim a compaign of "civil disobedience": a general refusal to pay taxes, to obey the laws, or to perform any of the duties of citizenship. Knowledge of this intended move and a realization of the fact that the Mahatma's prestige had greatly declined during the preceding months convinced the authorities that it was both safe and necessary to place him under arrest. Brought to trial on a charge of sedition, he was sentenced to six years' imprisonment, but in January, 1924, the remaining portion of his sentence was remitted.

In the face of opposition on the part of Indian Nationalists the governmental machinery which had been created by the act of 1919 was put into operation. On February 9, 1921, the new Indian legislature, consisting of the Council of State and the Legislative Assembly, was formally opened by the viceroy and the Duke of Connaught, the personal representative of the king-emperor. Because of the fact that the non-co-operators had refused to participate in the elections of 1920 the elected members of the first legislature were drawn from the moderate elements among the Indian population. Even this first legislature, however, was far from being subservient to the executive, and the viceroy was compelled to have recourse to his power of certification to pass several measures which he considered essential to the government of the country. At the elections in November, 1923, the followers of Gandhi, breaking away from his leadership, entered the campaign and secured a majority of the elective seats. In this and in the subsequent legislatures the Nationalists overlooked no opportunity for advancing their demand that India be granted home rule, but they did not pursue a purely obstructionist policy. The probationary nature of the new government was fully appreciated, and the desire to prove that India was ready for a fuller measure of autonomy than had been granted by the act of 1919 compelled the elected members of both the central and provincial legislative bodies to take seriously their duties as representatives of the nation.

The success attained by the new government may be attributed, in part at least, to the disintegration of the non-co-operative movement and the repudiation of Gandhi's leadership by the politically minded Indians. This apparently beneficial result of the decline of the Mahatma's influence, however, was offset by growing difficulties between the two great religious groups, Moslem and Hindu. Even during the years 1920 and 1921, when Gandhi's influence was at its height, clashes between Moslems and Hindus had brought discredit upon his program of nonviolence. After his arrest these clashes had become more frequent, and by the beginning of 1927 the relations between rival religious groups in some parts of the country had become extremely bitter.

In the act of 1919 it was provided that after the lapse of ten years a parliamentary commission should be appointed to investigate the working of the new system and to make recommendations with respect to the increase or the modification of the powers therein granted to the Indian people. On November 8, 1927, two years earlier than the date established by this provision, the British government announced its decision to appoint a commission to report whether or not India was ready to receive more extensive rights of self-government. The commission consisted of seven members and was representative of the three parties in Parliament; Sir John Simon, its chairman, was a Liberal, and his associates included four Conservatives and two members of the Labor party.

Indian Nationalists immediately noted and resented one outstanding fact in the composition of the new commission: the absence of any representative of the nation whose political capacity was to be investigated. The appointment of an all-English commission was regarded as an unwarranted assumption of racial superiority, "an insult and an affront" to the Indian people. Nationalist resentment, which took definite form in resolutions of non-co-operation passed by the Indian Legislative Assembly, by the Provincial Assembly of the Central Provinces, and by the all-Indian Congress, was reflected in violent demonstrations and in a return of Indian nationalism to the intransigeant non-co-operative program of Gandhi. On this point India, however, was not wholly unanimous, and the Simon Commission on its arrival in February, 1928, at Bombay was welcomed by delegations representative of the Mohammedans, of various non-Brahman Hindu groups, and of the "untouchables" (outcastes), who comprise more than a fifth of the country's population.

The report of the Simon Commission was published in June, 1930, in two parts, the first consisting of an exhaustive survey of existing conditions and the second containing definite proposals for a larger measure of self-government for India. While recognizing the growing importance of Indian nationalism as "a phenomenon which can not be disregarded," the commission did not recommend the grant of home rule or of dominion status to India.

For the provinces it recommended "the maximum of provincial autonomy consistent with the common interest of India as a whole"; to this end it proposed that dyarchy be abolished and that "the boundary now set up between departments of which Indian Ministers may take charge and departments from which they are excluded should be removed." The provincial governors, however, were to retain their statutory power to override their legislatures in matters essential to the safety and tranquillity of the provinces.

In view of the hostility between the Moslem and Hindu elements of the population the commission recommended that the existing arrangement of "communal representation," whereby the two religions in the provinces in which they were respectively minority groups were guaranteed representation in excess of their numerical proportion, should not be discontinued. Similar provisions, indeed, were recommended for the Sikhs and for the "untouchables," in order that these elements should be safeguarded against oppression. Special representation was also recommended for the European residents, for those of mixed European and Indian parentage, for the Indian Christians, and for other distinct elements in the population.

Turning to the central government, the report recommended that the Council of State be retained, that the existing Legislative Assembly be transformed into a "Federal Assembly," and that the members of the latter body, instead of being elected by direct vote, be chosen by the provincial legislatures, due provision being made for the adequate representation of the minority elements in each province. In justification of this radical change the commission expressed the belief that a Federal Assembly thus constituted would be capable of becoming, without the necessity of statutory amendment, the central legislative body for a federation which would include not only the provinces of British India but also the now semisovereign Indian states. As in the case of the provincial executives the viceroy was to be left with unimpaired power in all matters vital to the defense of India and to the maintenance of internal peace.[1]

During the months preceding the publication of the Simon report the Indian government had made every effort to allay the suspicions of the extreme Nationalists and to secure their cooperation in the task of devising a satisfactory constitution. On October 31, 1929, the viceroy, Lord Irwin, declared that he had been "authorized on behalf of the Government to state clearly that in their judgment it is implicit in the declaration of 1917 that the natural issue of India's constitutional progress, as there contemplated, is the attainment of a dominion status." This declaration was accompanied by the statement that the publication of the commission's report was to be followed by the summoning of a "round table conference" at London, to be participated in by representatives of the British government, of British India, and of the semisovereign Indian states, for the purpose of deciding, in the light of the report, what changes in the existing political institutions of India should be recommended to Parliament.

These announcements strengthened and encouraged the moder-

---

[1] A special section of the report dealt with Burma, which since its acquisition had been governed as an integral part of India. The commission found that there existed no community of interest between Burma and India. It therefore recommended that the government promptly announce its intention of severing these two unrelated areas and that it undertake the task of providing a constitution for Burma as a separate unit in the British Empire.

ates of the Nationalist party, but as an olive branch to the extremists the vague promise of dominion status and the proposal for a round-table conference failed of their purpose. On December 28, 1928, the all-Indian Congress and the Moslem League, meeting at Calcutta, had passed a resolution calling upon the British government to accept in its entirety before the end of the year the dominion-status constitution for India which had been drafted by a committee of the Congress. On March 2, 1930, Gandhi, who had sponsored the Calcutta resolution, made public an ultimatum which he had delivered to the viceroy: unless the government acceded to his demand for national independence for India, the Mahatma within eight days would open his campaign of civil disobedience. On March 12 the campaign was launched, and on May 5, after the movement had resulted in serious riots in all parts of the country, Gandhi was again placed under arrest.

Such was the state of affairs in India when the Simon report was made public, and the publication of the commission's recommendations did little to improve the situation. The Indian press unanimously rejected the proposals contained in the report; the Liberals and the moderate Nationalists were bitterly disappointed at its failure to include a definite recommendation of dominion status; no Indian prince or Indian minister could be found to express approval of the report as a whole; and the viceroy, at the opening of the Legislative Assembly on July 8, found it necessary to announce that the Simon report should not be regarded as restricting in any way the deliberations of the round-table conference which was to be held at London. He declared that dominion status, although not mentioned in the report, was still to be regarded as the natural goal of Indian development.

Three round-table conferences[1] were held at London to formulate the principles upon which the future government of India should be based. The rough plan drawn up by the first round table, for a federal union which should include both British India and the territories of the princes, met with such general Indian approval that Gandhi, who had refused to participate in that conference,

[1] November 12, 1930, to January 19, 1931; September 14, 1931, to December 1, 1931; and November 17, 1932, to December 24, 1932.

attended the second as a delegate of the Congress party. As formulated by the second and third conferences, however, the proposed federal constitution conceded to India considerably less than the dominion status upon which even the moderates insisted. Upon his return from London at the end of 1931, therefore, Gandhi promptly launched a new civil-disobedience campaign and was as promptly put in jail, and in March, 1932, both the Indian Congress and the Moslem League voted to boycott the round table and to refuse any settlement which the London government might attempt to impose upon India without the assent of her people.

In the face of India's openly expressed dissatisfaction the British government proceeded with its plans, and in March, 1933, the proposed constitution was laid before the two houses of Parliament in the form of a "white paper." The document was bitterly criticized by all shades of Indian opinion, while the extreme conservatives in England denounced with equal vehemence what they regarded as an abject surrender of vital British interests. For a further period of nearly two and a half years the proposal was studied and debated, then on August 2, 1935—almost eight full years after the appointment of the Simon Commission—it received the royal signature and became law.

The new constitution (which, in the fall of 1935, has yet to be put into operation) creates a federal union for all India. In the administration of the central government the governor-general is to be assisted by a bicameral legislature and a responsible cabinet. The right of suffrage, previously enjoyed by some seven million Indians, is extended to about twenty-eight million new voters, provision still being made for communal voting in order to ensure adequate representation for minority elements of the population. So important, however, are the powers reserved for the governor-general and for His Majesty's government at Westminster that the full dominion status for which even the moderate Nationalists have contended seems still far in the distance. It is too soon to say whether the system of government which this document is intended to provide will command the support of the Indian people; too soon, therefore, to forecast India's future as a self-governing part of the British Empire.

SELF-GOVERNMENT AND SELF-DETERMINATION FOR THE PHILIPPINES

Three years after Governor-General Harrison inaugurated the policy of "Filipinizing" the government of the Philippines the Democratic administration at Washington took the next step in what was intended as "the progressive establishment of Philippine independence." On August 29, 1916, the so-called Jones bill, having been passed by both houses of Congress, was signed by President Wilson and thereby became the fundamental law for the government of the islands. After stating in its preamble that "it is, as it always has been, the purpose of the people of the United States to withdraw their sovereignty over the Philippine Islands and to recognize their independence as soon as a stable government can be established therein," the Jones bill created a new Philippine legislature in which, subject to certain restrictions, was vested complete legislative jurisdiction and authority.

The new legislature was to consist of a Senate of twenty-four members (two each from twelve senate districts defined by the bill) and a House of Representatives of ninety members (one from each of the existing eighty-one districts and nine additional members from the areas not already represented). The representatives from the eighty-one existing districts were to be elected triennially; the senators from eleven of the senate districts, except at the first election when one from each district was to be elected for a three-year term, were to be elected for terms of six years. The two senators from the twelfth senate district and the nine representatives from the new representative districts, all of which were in the twelfth senate district, were to be appointed by the governor-general and were to hold office until removed by him.[1] Senators must be over thirty years of age, and members of the House of Representatives must be over twenty-five; in both cases the ability to read and write either Spanish or English was required.

With the organization of the new legislature the Philippine Commission, which had existed since 1900, disappeared. The governor-

---

[1] The people of the twelfth senatorial district were considered to be not yet ready for the exercise of suffrage.

general, the vice-governor, and the judges of the Supreme Court were still appointed by the President of the United States; all the other officials of government were elected by the people of the islands or were appointed by the governor-general with the approval of the legislature.

The important limitations upon the power of the Philippine legislature were as follows:

a. The Legislature had no power to enact legislation "inconsistent with this Act," which included an elaborate Bill of Rights modeled after that contained in the American Constitution; to modify the trade relations between the Philippines and the United States, which "shall continue to be governed exclusively by the laws of the Congress of the United States"; or to levy port duties upon exports from the Philippines.

b. Any act of the Philippine Legislature with reference to the land of the public domain, timber, and mining; any act establishing or amending the tariff duties upon trade with foreign countries; or any act affecting immigration, or the currency or coinage laws of the Philippines, must be submitted to the President of the United States for his approval. If, however, the President within six months after such act had been submitted to him failed either to approve or disapprove the act, "it shall become a law the same as if it had been specifically approved."

c. The Governor-General, who possessed veto power similar to that given by the Constitution of the United States to the President, must submit to the President any bill or joint resolution which the Legislature passed over his (the governor-general's) veto. If the President disapproved, it should not become law; but if the President failed to approve or disapprove within six months, it became law.

On October 16, 1916, the newly constituted legislature convened for its first meeting and assumed the responsibilities entrusted to it by the Jones bill. During the remaining four and a half years of the Democratic regime in America the Philippine Islands enjoyed a degree of self-government which differed little, if at all, from that exercised by the "self-governing dominions" of the British Empire, and the representatives of the Filipino people applied themselves seriously to the task of perfecting their administrative organization.

In 1918 an executive order of the governor-general, approved by President Wilson, created a Council of State consisting of the governor-general, the president of the Senate, the speaker of the House, and the heads of the six executive departments. Except for the Department of Public Education, of which the vice-governor was ex-officio head, the heads of the executive departments were Filipinos appointed by the governor-general and confirmed by the Philippine Senate. The Council of State thus consisted of two American ex-officio members and seven Filipinos, and its creation was a move in the direction of a "parliamentary" government with a responsible cabinet. As President Wilson and Mr. Harrison both heartily approved of such a development, the powers of the governor-general during the remainder of Mr. Harrison's term became largely advisory, and the Council of State performed most of the functions which had been delegated by the Jones bill to the President's appointee.

In 1919 Governor-General Harrison reported to the President that a "stable government" existed in the islands, and President Wilson in conveying this information to Congress recommended legislation which would confer upon the Filipinos the complete independence that had been promised. At this time, however, the Democratic party no longer possessed a majority in Congress, and no action was taken.

In the Philippines, as in most other parts of the world, post-war economic readjustments were attended by financial difficulties, some of which may have been attributable to unwise policies adopted by the Filipinized administration. With the return to power of the Republican party in the United States, therefore, the stage was set for a modification of the Democratic program of increasing home rule. Early in 1921 a committee headed by General Leonard Wood and former Governor-General W. Cameron Forbes was appointed by President Harding to investigate and report on the condition of the insular government. Arriving at Manila in May, 1921, the Wood-Forbes mission after four months of investigation reported in favor of a greater amount of American control; and, in October, General Wood was appointed to the post of governor-general.

The policy of the new governor-general quickly brought him into conflict with the Filipino leaders, and in July, 1923, the members of the Council of State resigned in a body. During the course of the next three months the two houses of the Philippine legislature by joint resolution twice requested General Wood's recall. A more serious consequence of the friction, however, was the development of a new agitation in favor of immediate independence. In 1927 a joint resolution of the two houses of the legislature, providing for a plebiscite on the question of independence, was vetoed by the governor-general and was promptly passed over his veto, only to be vetoed again—this time decisively—by President Coolidge.

In August, 1927, the deadlock between the executive and the legislature was finally dissolved by the death of General Wood. Colonel Henry L. Stimson, who served a brief term as General Wood's successor, and Mr. Dwight F. Davis, who was appointed to the post in March, 1929, both reverted in no small degree to the Harrison policy of allowing the Filipino leaders to take over the administration of affairs. The person of the governor-general was withdrawn from the political arena, and the Council of State once more became, in effect, the responsible cabinet of a parliamentary government.

Neither the improved relations between executive and legislature nor the personal popularity of the successive governors-general served to allay the growing Filipino demand for national independence. Convinced that the government of the United States was irrevocably pledged to grant to the islands full independence as soon as a stable and effective government had been established, the people of the Philippines appeared to be equally convinced that this condition had been met. Their demand, therefore, was for the fulfillment of the American pledge, and the general election of June, 1931, resulted in an overwhelming victory for the Nacionalista party. On November 9 of the same year the recently elected legislature voted to approve a plan for a ten-year period of "autonomy with free trade," this transition period to be followed by a plebiscite on the question of independence, and in December a mission was dispatched to America for the purpose of laying the plan before the authorities at Washington. On November 6, 1932, two days before the American Presidential election, the legislature passed a new resolution, this time demanding immediate autonomy and the shortest possible period of transition to a status of complete independence.

While Philippine nationalism was thus urging an honorable fulfillment of the American pledge, opinion in the United States was reacting to other considerations. After the Washington Conference the Philippines, because of the agreement relating to the fortification of naval bases in the Pacific, were regarded by American naval strategists as a liability rather than an asset in the case of a war in the Far East. As a base for American commerce in the Orient, moreover, Manila had not come up to the expectations so confidently voiced in 1899 and 1900. Finally, the inclusion of the archipelago within the American tariff wall, although securing for American manufactures after 1909 an advantageous position in the Philippine market, had also enabled Philippine exports— sugar, tobacco, hemp, and other commodities which compete with American products—to enter the ports of the United States without payment of duty. With the deepening economic depression the last-mentioned consideration steadily acquired added weight, and the desire for protection against Filipino competition in American markets became a powerful motive for granting the islands at least enough independence to warrant placing them once more outside the tariff wall.

After two unsuccessful efforts to enact a measure which would satisfy both the American government and the Filipinos,[1] Congress passed and President Roosevelt signed, March 24, 1934, the Tydings-McDuffie bill. Several features of the previous bills objectionable to the Filipinos had been omitted from the new measure, and on May 1, 1934, the Tydings-McDuffie bill was accepted by the legislative body at Manila.

This bill provided that the Philippines, upon the establishment of a constitutional government, should be for ten years an autonomous commonwealth, still under American sovereignty and retain-

---

[1] The Hare bill was passed by the House of Representatives in April, 1932, but because of lack of time it was not taken up by the Senate. The Hawes-Cutting bill, passed by both houses on December 29, 1932, was vetoed by President Hoover and was passed over his veto on January 17, 1933, only to be rejected by the Philippine legislature.

ing limited rights of free trade with the United States. After the expiration of this period the commonwealth was to become an independent republic, all American military forces were to be withdrawn from the islands, and the question of the maintenance of naval bases in Philippine waters was to be settled by negotiation between the two governments. On February 8, 1935, a constitutional convention, assembled at Manila, completed the task of drafting a constitution, on March 23 the document was officially approved by President Roosevelt, and on May 14 it was ratified by the Philippine people. September 17 saw the election of the officers of the commonwealth, with Manuel Quezon as president; on November 15 the new government was inaugurated, and on July 4, 1936, begins the ten-year period which is to prepare the Philippines for complete independence.

THE DUTCH EAST INDIES

Of the various Western powers with extensive possessions in the Far East, Holland appears to have been the most successful during the last two decades in avoiding serious trouble with the people under her rule. Holding sway over an East Indian empire which measures three thousand miles from east to west and contains a population of more than fifty million, the Dutch have been able to maintain order with the support of an army of not more than forty thousand, and the greater portion of even this small armed force is non-European. At the close of the World War and during the subsequent years there were occasional outbreaks of local disorder, officially attributed to communistic intrigue,[1] but rampant nationalism and the demand for independence, so widely manifested in other Western-ruled parts of the Orient, appear to have made comparatively little headway among the people of the Dutch East Indies.

Like their seventeenth-century ancestors and like other Westerners of the present day, the Dutch are in the Far East primarily for profit; but three centuries of experience have taught them that

[1] The mutiny on the cruiser *Zeven Provincien*, in February, 1933, was a consequence of the "depression"; it was organized by the white minority of the ship's crew in protest against a recently announced pay cut.

the profitable exploitation of their empire depends upon the continued welfare and contentment of the East Indian people. Out of the fifty millions inhabiting the archipelago 80 per cent are to be found in the single island of Java,[1] and the increase of Java's population from an estimated fourteen million in 1890 to the present figure of forty million is perhaps the best evidence of the care that has been taken to improve the living conditions of the subject people. In 1890 the amount of land under cultivation in Java was 227,500 acres, less than 1 per cent of the area of the island; by 1931, as a result of extensive irrigation developments, the cultivated area had been increased to 2,700,000 acres. Although large areas are in the possession of the government, ownership of the land by "foreign" individuals, even though they be Hollanders, is forbidden by law. Long-term leases are permitted; but the use of land thus held is strictly regulated, and it is provided that land used by a foreign lessee for raising sugar cane must be restored to the Javanese owner on alternate years for the production of rice. With all the increase in export commodities—sugar, rubber, tobacco, tea, and coffee—the government has thus ensured an adequate supply of the great food staple.

In the government of the islands the Dutch have increasingly realized the necessity of enlisting the co-operation of the people. Some parts of Java and more extensive portions of the other islands are still ruled by vassal princes under the supervision of Dutch "residents." In the regions under direct Dutch rule the administration of local affairs has always been left to village headmen, who govern according to ancient tradition and are responsible for the maintenance of peace and order. In the larger administrative divisions, although Dutch officials hold the ranking positions, representatives of the people also have been given a voice in the direction of affairs.

The creation of the Volksraad (Legislative Council) in 1916 extended to the people the right of participation even in the central government. This body, consisting of twenty-four appointed and twenty-four elected members with a president appointed by the queen, includes Hollanders and East Indians in about equal

[1] The area of Java is 50,557 square miles.

proportions. The governor-general is appointed by the queen and is, in law, responsible only to the government at the Hague; but he is required to lay before the Volksraad for consideration the annual budget, all colonial loan agreements, and any proposed law relating to military service, and the presence of East Indian members in this advisory body ensures government action on these and other matters that will conform in some measure to the customs, traditions, and prejudices of the people.

Since 1932 the Dutch in the East Indies have had two outstanding causes for anxiety: Japan and the depression. Although represented at the Washington Conference, Holland was not included among the signatories of the Four-Power Treaty Relating to the Pacific, and her Eastern possessions were not expressly covered by the reciprocal guaranties set forth in that document. Japan's recent venture along the path of "manifest destiny" and her self-imposed championship of "Asia for the Asiatics" have therefore been cause for growing alarm. The fears of the Dutch were not allayed when Japanese diplomats, with assurances of peaceful intentions, announced a desire to co-operate in the development of the East Indies and urged the desirability of Japanese immigration into Dutch New Guinea. The impact of the depression upon the economic life of the Indies was terrific. From $575,000,000 in 1929 the total value of exports fell in 1932 to $217,000,000, a decline of more than 60 per cent. This decline in export trade was paralleled by an even greater falling off in imports from Europe, for European manufactures have met growing competition from the extremely low-priced products of Japanese industry, which have poured into the islands in rapidly growing volume. The principal sufferers from the commercial collapse were the Europeans, especially those engaged in trade or in the production of goods intended for export. Yet the mass of the people, in spite of the fact that the reduced demand for export goods led to a greater production of foodstuffs, suffered at least indirectly, since the insular government, with greatly reduced revenues, was compelled to make drastic reductions in the budget and to curtail many of its beneficial activities.

French Imperialism in Indo-China

The development of French Indo-China as a European outpost in the Far East can best be described as an adventure in deliberate imperialism, undertaken for the satisfaction of national dignity. Less highly industrialized than any other of the leading Western powers, France has had little need for, and has made little use of, her Asiatic possessions as markets for surplus factory production. Nor have the French people, with their low birth rate and an almost stationary population, displayed any inclination toward colonizing the regions brought under their political control. In the absence of strong commercial and colonizing motives, however, Napoleon III commenced and the republic continued the creation of an Indo-Chinese empire which has made possible the establishment and maintenance of a French policy in the Far East.

At the Washington Conference the French delegation, as a kindly gesture, offered the return of Kwangchowwan to China as their part in a general restoration of leased territories. French imperialism, however, has not yet begun a retreat. Although spheres of influence in China are, officially at least, things of the past, China's three southern provinces—Kwangtung, Kwangsi, and Yunnan—are regarded as a special field for French enterprise; and French activities in this field during recent years have frequently aroused the fears and suspicions of the Chinese government.

The inauguration and expansion of this empire have been discussed in earlier chapters. As now constituted it consists of four parts. Cochin China, the earliest acquisition, is ruled directly as a colony by a governor at Saigon; the other three divisions, Cambodia, Laos, and Annam-Tongking, are protectorates under the nominal rule of their own sovereigns but with all real power in the hands of French residents.[1] The administration is centralized in the hands of a governor-general located at Hanoi, who is invested with combined civil and military power and is responsible to the French Minister of Colonies. The governor-general's jurisdiction extends to the Kwangchowwan leasehold, and in 1923 he was also

---

[1] Annam and Tongking, although nominally a single state under the emperor of Annam, are administered as separate units by two residents.

given supervisory authority over the French insular possessions in the south Pacific: Tahiti, New Caledonia, the New Hebrides, and the Loyalty Islands.

After the close of the World War there were persistent demands in French Indo-China for some manner of self-government; these demands were met by the organization of communal councils, with a voice in local affairs, in the protectorates, and in 1922 by the addition of elected members to the Colonial Council at Saigon. In 1927, after further political agitation, the French government authorized the creation of a Government Council of sixty members to assist the governor-general in an advisory capacity. Of the sixty members in this new body thirty-five were to be French; six of the Indo-Chinese members were to be appointed by the governor-general, and three were to be elected by the larger property-owners, leaving only sixteen who could be regarded as representatives of the majority of the population.

While France has been slow to grant representative political institutions to her Indo-Chinese subjects, she has during recent years been equally careful to respect and maintain useful features of the old social order. Except in Cochin China, where annexation was promptly followed by the introduction of French language, law, and administrative procedure, it has been the policy of the French governors-general to strengthen by cautious modification rather than to replace the traditional institutions. The more farsighted of French colonial officials have expressed the conviction that Indo-China must, in the not distant future, be allowed to assume a status not unlike that of the self-governing dominions of the British Empire. Yet this development could only mean the end of French imperialism in the Orient; Indo-China, allowed to live its own life, would cease to serve as the cornerstone of French policy in the Pacific.

PROGRESS AND NEW PROBLEMS IN SIAM

By the treaties of Versailles, St. Germain, and the Trianon, at the close of the World War, Siam secured the abolition of German, Austrian, and Hungarian rights to the enjoyment of

extraterritoriality and a treaty-regulated tariff, but these unilateral rights were still enjoyed in full by the United States,
Japan, and ten European states. During the course of the Paris
Conference, however, President Wilson assured the Siamese representatives of America's readiness to relinquish her claim to such
privileges, and the promise was fulfilled in December, 1920, by
the conclusion of a new American-Siamese treaty. The tariff
clauses of the new treaty provided that, as soon as similar agreements had been made with the other treaty powers, the Siamese
government would be free to substitute for the existing 3 per cent
ad valorem tariff such a schedule of import duties as it might
consider desirable and appropriate. The abandonment of extraterritoriality was immediate and was conditioned only by a temporary arrangement whereby the American government, until five
years after the completion and promulgation of the new Siamese
law codes, should have the right to "evoke" any case in which an
American citizen was the defendant and to bring the case before
an American consular court.

More than three years elapsed before any of the other treaty
powers saw fit to follow the American example, but in March,
1924, a similar treaty revision was effected between Siam and
Japan. France, Holland, and Great Britain followed suit in
February, June, and July, 1925; later in the same year Spain,
Portugal, Denmark, and Sweden also agreed to revise their treaties
in the same direction; and Italy, Belgium, and Norway fell into
line during the spring and summer of 1926. With the exchange of
the last ratifications of these new treaties, in February, 1927,
Siam took her place alongside Japan as one of the two Far Eastern states which had succeeded in gaining freedom from the humiliating limitations of "unequal treaties."[1]

Apart from the task of securing tariff autonomy and the abolition of extraterritoriality, Siam's chief diplomatic concern during
the last twenty years has been the maintenance of satisfactory
relations with her powerful neighbors. Much has been accom-

[1] A large measure of the credit for Siam's successful campaign to regain her
lost sovereignty must go to an American, Francis B. Sayre, who during the years
1923–1925 served the Siamese government as adviser in foreign affairs.

plished in this direction. In addition to settling the tariff and extraterritoriality questions the Franco-Siamese treaty of February 14, 1925, provided for the submission either to arbitration or to the Permanent Court of International Justice of all disputes that might arise between the two countries, and the danger of disputes arising was greatly reduced by a special boundary convention, concluded on August 25, 1926, which established a demilitarized zone on either side of the Siamese-Indo-Chinese frontier. A treaty of general arbitration also was concluded, on November 25, 1925, between Siam and Great Britain. For the present, at least, these treaties and Siam's membership in the League of Nations seem to furnish adequate assurance against any renewed territorial encroachments by France or Great Britain.

On November 26, 1925, King Rama VI died after a reign of fifteen years, and his brother Prajadhipok succeeded to the throne. Siam's borrowings from the West had not at that time included any of the institutions of democracy, and the new monarch, unhampered by diet or parliament or by the existence of constitutional limitations, organized a purely personal government in which the administrative departments were committed to the charge of nobles enjoying the royal confidence. During the last years of the reign of Rama VI serious abuses had crept into the administration, and Prajadhipok, in addition to dismissing his late brother's favorites and taking steps to reduce governmental extravagance, created a Supreme Council of State, consisting of five princes of the royal family, to aid in supervising the work of those to whom he had entrusted the direct management of public affairs.

For six and a half years Siam under its new monarch was a conspicuously peaceful spot in a chaotic world, but the summer of 1932 was marked by a sudden, although bloodless, political upheaval. On June 24 the army and navy, acting under the leadership of a self-styled People's party, revolted and took complete control of the situation at Bangkok. All the outstanding members of the bureaucratic organization, the princes of the Supreme Council as well as the noble ministers, were forced to retire into private life, and on June 27 King Prajadhipok gave his royal assent to a constitution whereby his hitherto autocratic power was to be shared with a Senate, nominated for the present by the People's party but eventually to be elected by universal adult suffrage.

Although the leaders in the revolt called themselves the People's party, the general indifference of the population as a whole and the complete absence of bloodshed strongly suggest that the movement was in fact a *coup d'état* planned and executed by a small, well-organized group. In April, 1933, the king, convinced that the reformers were dangerous radicals tainted with communism, suspended the constitution and reassumed his traditional role of autocrat. Two months later, June 20, a second *coup d'état*, led by the commander in chief of the army, placed the alleged radicals once more in control of the capital. The revolutionary leaders hastened to assure the monarch of their devoted loyalty to his person, and he once more gave his approval to the recently suspended constitution.

The agreement between the Siamese monarch and his revolutionary subjects proved to be only temporary. Friction again developed in the late summer of 1934, and on March 2, 1935, the king, at that time visiting in England, announced his abdication of the throne. Four days later the ex-sovereign's eleven-year-old nephew, Prince Ananda Mahidol, was proclaimed as his successor.

China's Struggle for National Reorganization

In the summer of 1920, when the three northern tuchuns—Chang Tso-lin, Ts'ao Kun, and Wu P'ei-fu—overthrew the Anfu clique and established their authority at Peking, the Chinese Republic entered upon a period of turmoil which can best be characterized as "anarchy punctuated by civil war." Control over Peking, with the diplomatic and financial advantages resulting therefrom, was the glittering prize for which practically every ambitious tuchun of northern and central China fought, plotted, and changed sides. At times the tuchun or the group of tuchuns who controlled the capital was able to exercise authority over a respectable number of the provinces; at such times there appeared to be hope that the long-expected "strong man" would appear and unify

China under an efficient military rule. These moments of hopefulness, however, were always brief. As soon as an outstanding
military figure, a potential dictator, appeared at Peking, he inevitably became the object of a hostile combination of ambitious
rivals, and the prospects of national unification disappeared in the
clouds of a new war.

After the overthrow of the Anfu clique the triumvirate which
had accomplished this quickly dissolved, and during the year 1921
Marshal Chang Tso-lin was the power behind the Peking government. The invitation to participate in the Washington Conference
brought a temporary truce in China's internal conflict; but in May,
1922, Wu P'ei-fu, allied with Feng Yu-hsiang (formerly one of
Wu's subordinates) and Ts'ao Kun, drove Chang beyond the
Great Wall into Manchuria and set up a new regime at Peking.
In June, President Hsu Shih-ch'ang was forced to resign, and former President Li Yüan-hung, who since 1917 had been living in retirement at Tientsin, was induced to resume the presidential office.
With Li as a figurehead Wu P'ei-fu now attempted to bring about
a reconciliation between north and south, and the surviving members of the original parliament elected in 1912 were summoned
to Peking. In June, 1923, however, President Li once more fled to
Tientsin, and in October Ts'ao Kun, having secured election to
the presidency, assumed office and proclaimed a new constitution.

Following his retreat into Manchuria, Chang Tso-lin declared
himself independent of the Peking government and proceeded to
rule his Three Eastern Provinces as an absolute dictator.[1] In the
summer of 1924, having allied himself with the leaders of the old

[1] The report of the Lytton Commission of the League of Nations, in October,
1932, has the following comment on Chang's declaration of independence:

The independence declared by Marshal Chang Tso-lin at different times never
meant that he or the people of Manchuria wished to be separated from China. His
armies did not invade China as if it were a foreign country, but merely as participants in the civil war. Like the war lords of any other province, the Marshal
alternately supported, attacked, or declared his territory independent of the Central Government, but never in such a way as to involve the partition of China
into separate States. On the contrary, most Chinese civil wars were directly or
indirectly connected with some ambitious scheme to unify the country under a
really strong Government. Through all its wars and periods of "independence,"
therefore, Manchuria remained an integral part of China.—Appeal by the Chinese Government. Report of the Commission of Enquiry. League of Nations.
Pages 28–29.

Anfu clique, he once more led his forces against Peking. At a crucial moment in the campaign Feng Yu-hsiang deserted the cause of Wu P'ei-fu and occupied the capital. With his base of operations in hostile hands Wu P'ei-fu was defeated, but succeeded in escaping with a few of his troops to Honan.

On November 2, ten days after Feng Yu-hsiang's forces had occupied Peking, Ts'ao Kun resigned his presidential post. Three days later Feng demanded of the young Hsüan T'ung[1] that he abandon all pretension to the imperial title and accept a reduction in his pension. Refusing to agree to these demands, the ex-emperor fled from the palace, first to the home of his father and thence to the Japanese legation. From the legation quarter he subsequently withdrew to Tientsin, where, as "Mr. Henry Pu-yi," he remained in peaceful retirement until the events of 1931–1932 called him to a new career in Manchuria.

After the forced resignation of Ts'ao Kun on November 2, Chang, Feng, and the veteran Tuan Ch'i-jui organized a new coalition government; but during the following summer Feng turned against his allies, and in the autumn of 1925 a triangular conflict broke out between Feng, Chang, and Wu P'ei-fu. In this struggle, which lasted until the summer of 1926, Wu succeeded in driving Feng northward to Kalgan, while Chang, who now assumed the title of Acting Executive, was able to retain control of Peking and of his three Manchurian provinces. Such was the situation when the Cantonese Kuomintang ("Nationalist") government began their advance from the south to contest with the "northern militarists" the control over the nation's destinies.

In January, 1923, during his third period of "exile" at Shanghai, Dr. Sun Yat-sen came into contact with the Soviet envoy Adolf Joffe, who at that time was on his way to Japan for the purpose of opening negotiations with the Japanese. The Kuomintang leader previously had appealed in vain to the Western powers, particularly to the United States, for recognition and material assistance in the struggle against the military rulers of the north. He now

---

[1] Since his abdication in February, 1912, Hsüan T'ung and his "imperial" entourage had continued to occupy a portion of the Forbidden City, supported by an annual pension of $4,000,000 (Mex.) from the republican government.

found the Soviet envoy, who had been unsuccessful in his efforts to reach a satisfactory understanding with the authorities at Peking, full of sympathy for the Nationalist cause and ready to promise the assistance which Sun had vainly sought to obtain elsewhere. Shortly thereafter Dr. Sun once more returned to his position at the head of the Cantonese government, and in September, 1923, the first group of Russian advisers and experts, headed by Michael Borodin, arrived at Canton.

Under Borodin's guidance began the development which was to transform the Kuomintang from a "party of protest" into a militant factor in the political struggle. Drawing upon the example of the Russian Bolshevists, he was able to convince Dr. Sun of the necessity for strict party discipline and also for a program or statement of principles capable of arousing the enthusiasm of the party members. A new system of organization was worked out, and Sun Yat-sen himself provided the needed program in a series of lectures which were later published in book form as the *San Min Chu I* ("The Three Principles of the People"). At the same time there was established at Canton, with the aid of Russian and German experts, the Whampoa Military Academy, where party members received a training which would fit them for the task of leading the Kuomintang forces against the north.

In the midst of these labors, whose real benefit to the Kuomintang cause can hardly be questioned, Borodin and his fellow Russians found ample opportunity to spread the doctrine of communism among certain elements of the population. Sun Yat-sen is said to have been warned against the dangers which might result from utilizing Russian advisers and to have decided that the certain advantages outweighed the possible disadvantages. At first the effects of communist propaganda appeared so negligible as to justify Sun's decision, but eventually this phase of Russian activity became the source of complications which threatened ruin to the Kuomintang.

In December, 1924, following the defeat of Wu P'ei-fu, the new Peking triumvirate of Tuan Ch'i-jui, Chang Tso-lin, and Feng Yu-hsiang issued a call for a "Reorganization Conference" to meet on February 1, and on the last day of 1924 Sun Yat-sen, at the invitation of the triumvirs, arrived at Peking for the purpose of reaching some preliminary agreement as to the composition and scope of the proposed conference. Whether the Kuomintang leader, if he had lived, could have found any satisfactory basis for co-operation with the northern militarists is extremely doubtful. But Sun, when he reached Peking, was a dying man, and on March 12, 1925, his turbulent career came to an end.

With the death of its founder the direction of the Kuomintang organization passed into the hands of new leaders. Like Lenin in Russia, Dr. Sun was promptly canonized by his late followers, and these followers now turned more and more toward plans for making their government national in fact as well as in name. The year which followed Sun's death, therefore, saw active preparations at Canton for the adoption of a new forward policy. The triangular struggle between Chang, Feng, and Wu during the last part of 1925 and the first half of 1926 appeared to provide the southerners with a favorable opportunity for entering the field, and early in July, 1926, the northern advance was begun. Before the end of August the Kuomintang forces were in full control of Hunan Province, and by October they had established themselves in the three Wuhan cities—Wuchang, Hankow, and Hanyang—as well as at Nanchang, the capital of Kiangsi. The spring of 1927 saw them in possession of all the provinces south of the Yangtze, while to the north of that great river they had taken advantage of Feng Yu-hsiang's reappearance on the western flank of Chang Tso-lin's position and had driven Chang's forces out of Honan.

While the program of social reform set forth in the *San Min Chu I* created growing popular enthusiasm for the Kuomintang cause, the substantial successes of the Cantonese forces made additional converts from among those who for various personal reasons hoped to see the overthrow of the existing Peking regime. Besides numerous politicians and civilian officials these converts included at least two northern militarists of weight and standing: Feng Yu-hsiang, whose resumption of hostilities against Chang Tso-lin had materially aided the Kuomintang in its Honan campaign, and Yen Hsi-shan, who since the fall of the Manchus had been the military governor of Shansi. An attack of the Nationalists, thus reinforced, upon Chang Tso-lin in the summer of 1927 was checked partly by difficulties with the Japanese in Shantung but partly also by dissension within the ranks of the party.

In November, 1926, the headquarters of the Kuomintang organization were moved from Canton to Hankow. This move was followed by a rapid growth in the influence of the radical and communist elements, and in April, 1927, General Chiang Kai-shek (the commander in chief of the Kuomintang forces) and a number of moderate leaders established a rival organization at Nanking. From April until August the bitter recriminations exchanged between the two rival organizations threatened to destroy the Nationalist movement. To the Nanking allegations of communism and subservience to Russia the Hankow leaders replied with charges that Nanking was wholly militaristic and that Chiang Kai-shek was planning to make himself the dictator of all China.

On August 8, after much negotiation, a solution of the controversy was found. Chiang Kai-shek resigned his command and retired from public life, the Wuhan organization dismissed its Russian advisers and expelled its communist members, and the remaining members of the two groups combined to establish a reorganized party government at Nanking. But Nanking, with Peking still in the hands of the northern militarists, could ill afford to dispense with the services of its most successful general. Early in 1928, therefore, after the reorganization had been completed, Chiang was recalled and was placed again in supreme command of the Kuomintang armies.

In March, 1928, the Nationalist forces once more took the field against Peking. By the end of May the northern armies, defeated in the field and demoralized by the rapid spread of Kuomintang propaganda, were in full retreat; and early in June the Shansi troops of Yen Hsi-shan occupied the northern capital. Chang Tso-lin, withdrawing into Manchuria, lost his life in a mysterious bomb attack upon his private train as it was entering the city of Mukden, and all of China south of the Great Wall came, nominally at least, under the control of the National government.

The program of Sun Yat-sen, laid down in the *San Min Chu I*, divided the process of national reconstruction into three phases:

first, there was the obviously necessary period of *military unification*; this was to be followed by a period of *political tutelage*, during which a dictatorial revolutionary government would train the people in the duties of citizenship; when this training had been completed, the nation would be ready to enter upon the final stage, government under a *constitutional democracy*. With the defeat of Chang Tso-lin in June, 1928, the first phase, in theory, came to an end; the capital of the republic was promptly transferred from Peking—henceforth to be known as Peiping—to Nanking, and the country entered upon the second stage of its journey to national salvation.

On October 10, 1928, the seventeenth anniversary of the outbreak that overthrew the Manchus, the Government Council of the Kuomintang formally promulgated the governmental plan whereby the party, during the period of tutelage, was to administer the affairs of the nation. Under a State Council whose chairman was the titular head of the republic and the commander in chief of its armed forces the functions of government were apportioned among five *Yüan*, or departments. Three of these departments— the Executive Yüan, the Legislative Yüan, and the Judicial Yüan—were charged with the performance of the tasks usually regarded in Western political thought as comprising the whole duty of a government. The two remaining departments—the Examination Yüan and the Control Yüan—were to perform the functions which under the imperial regime had been cared for by the system of literary examinations and by the Board of Censors, the first certifying the competence of appointees to government office and the second exercising constant scrutiny over the official actions of every servant of the state. During the period of tutelage the members of the State Council and of the five Yüan were to be chosen by the Central Executive Committee and the party congress of the Kuomintang, which thus retained complete control over the machinery of the state.

Following the death of Chang Tso-lin military power in the Three Eastern Provinces (Manchuria) passed into the hands of his son Chang Hsueh-liang, popularly known as the Young Marshal, who was thoroughly in sympathy with the Nationalist cause.

In October, 1928, Chang Hsueh-liang was accepted as a member of the Kuomintang and was given a seat in the State Council of the Nanking government, and on the last day of the year, in official acknowledgment of Nanking's authority, the Nationalist colors were raised over the government buildings at Mukden.

No picture of China's political condition at the end of 1928 and no account of the political turmoil since that date would be complete without some indication of the intellectual revolution which has characterized the last two decades of the nation's history. During the first years after the overthrow of the Manchu dynasty republican China, while turning eagerly to Western science for "useful" knowledge, still looked to the ancient Classics for social guidance, and various Chinese scholars undertook the task of harmonizing republican practices with the fundamental principles of Confucian philosophy. About 1915 or 1916, however, this conservative attitude began to lose ground, and the subsequent years saw all the nation's traditional institutions subjected to increasingly destructive criticism by the patriots of "Young China."

As in other lands, the rising tide of radical thought may be attributed in no small part to the World War and to the post-war disruption of normal economic conditions. But in China these disturbing influences were supplemented by important developments of a more local character. The disintegration of the republic after the death of Yüan Shih-k'ai, the rise of the all-powerful tuchuns, and the consequent disappearance of the scholar as a positive factor in the administration of government, all combined to destroy the belief that the wisdom of antiquity had any present value or could contribute any useful material to the political and social fabric of a modern Chinese state. From this purely negative attitude to the denunciation of the old as positively harmful was a short step. The more extreme of the revolutionary thinkers, including the bulk of the students in the modern schools and colleges, quickly reached the point of repudiating all the rules, customs, beliefs, and traditions by which throughout the long centuries of the nation's existence the social order had been held together. Young China's radicals, like those of revolutionary France, thus embarked upon their work of national reconstruction obsessed with the idea of freeing their country, once and for all time, from the trammels of useless tradition and outworn superstition.

In the field of literature, where the radical writers turned their backs upon archaic classical forms in order to write in language more closely akin to the speech of the people, the spirit of rampant iconoclasm accomplished positive good. In the social and political fields, however, the destruction of the old was too often unattended by the ability to create anything new to fill the resultant vacancy. The rejection of ancient moral standards and social customs led to license rather than to liberty, and the abolition of time-honored institutions of government was followed by much aimless groping for some sort of political machinery with which to accomplish the purposes of organized society.

Even more important than the iconoclastic attitude of the young "intelligentsia" was the almost nation-wide determination of postwar China to free herself from the humiliating limitations imposed upon her sovereignty by existing treaties. At the Washington Conference, as we have seen, efforts were made to modify to some extent the causes for irritation, but the concessions granted by the conference fell far short of meeting the full demands of the Chinese people. The years that followed were therefore marked by frequent clashes at the various treaty ports and at Peking between the militant nationalism of an awakened China and the vested rights of the foreign powers.

The development of a Nationalist government in the south owed much to the popular demand for national equality, and, in the years immediately after the Washington Conference, Canton was one of the principal centers of agitation against the continuation of foreign privileges. During 1922 the Cantonese Nationalist organization gave its aid and support to a seamen's strike at Hongkong which, after almost completely paralyzing the British coastal steamship lines, eventually forced from the companies extensive concessions to their Chinese employees. The arrival of Borodin and his fellow Russians at Canton in the autumn of 1923 was followed by a marked intensification of anti-foreign spirit at that port, and the conclusion of an agreement between Peking and Moscow in May, 1924, in which the Soviet government abandoned all claim to extraterritorial jurisdiction, was a signal for renewed agitation in all parts of China for the total abolition of extraterritoriality and of all other special privileges enjoyed by the treaty powers.

In the early summer of 1925 two unfortunate "incidents" aroused the anger of the Chinese people against the "imperialistic" powers in general and against Great Britain in particular. The first of these incidents occurred on May 30, at Shanghai, when the police of the international settlement fired upon an unarmed crowd, or mob, of demonstrating students, killing twelve of their number and wounding some twenty more. The original cause of the trouble was a demonstration against the Japanese by student sympathizers with the striking employees of a Japanese factory, but the full force of popular indignation was turned against Great Britain by the fact that the police inspector who gave the fatal command and his superior officers in the international settlement police force all were British subjects.

The second incident, a direct result of the first, occurred three and a half weeks later at Canton. Here on June 23 the students and workmen showed their indignation over the Shanghai shooting by a great anti-British demonstration along the water front opposite the foreign settlement on the island of Shameen. During the course of the demonstration, in which a body of fully armed cadets from the Whampoa Military Academy took part, a shot was fired.[1] This shot was immediately followed by a heavy fusillade from rifles and machine guns by the armed defenders of the Shameen settlement and by such of the demonstrators as were armed. When the smoke had cleared away, it was found that the European casualties amounted to one man dead and four wounded; on the other side of the narrow stream the dead numbered fifty-two and the wounded more than a hundred.

The immediate outburst of popular feeling was directed primarily against the British, but the Nationalist leaders, now preparing to launch their expedition against the north, cited the Shanghai

[1] On the all-important question "Who fired this first shot?" the available testimony of eyewitnesses is hopelessly contradictory.

and Shameen affairs as arguments for the abolition of the "unequal treaties" and pledged themselves, when they succeeded in establishing their authority over all China, to put an end to the country's humiliation. This stand by the Kuomintang made it necessary for the authorities at Peking (Chang Tso-lin and his associates) to display an equal concern for the national dignity, and the abolition of the treaties now became the avowed program of all who held or hoped to hold any prominent position in Chinese politics.

Coincidentally with the northward advance of the Kuomintang forces in the summer of 1926 the British government reached the conclusion that the time had come for a thoroughgoing readjustment of its relations with China. On December 18, 1926, Great Britain therefore submitted to the other participants in the Washington Conference a circular note wherein, after reviewing the situation in China, she proposed to the other powers

that these governments shall issue a statement setting forth the essential facts of the situation; declaring their readiness to negotiate on treaty revision and all other outstanding questions as soon as the Chinese themselves have constituted a government . . . and . . . to pursue a constructive policy in harmony with the spirit of the Washington Conference but developed and adapted to meet the altered circumstances of the present time.

The tone of the British circular note found a ready response at Washington, and on January 27, 1927, the American Secretary of State declared that the United States was prepared to consider the revision of all its treaties with China. "The only question is, with whom shall it negotiate . . . if China can agree upon the appointment of delegates representing the authorities or the people of the country, we are prepared to negotiate such a treaty." From Tokyo on January 16, 1927, came a more guarded statement by the Japanese Foreign Minister, who declared that Japan was in full sympathy with "the legitimate aspirations of the Chinese people" and added: "If China should meet us half-way in the same spirit of moderation and good will, I have no doubt that negotiations will make satisfactory progress."

During the early months of 1927, events in the Yangtze valley put a heavy strain upon these benevolent intentions. The first week of January was marked by anti-foreign mob violence at

Hankow and at Kiukiang. On March 24, during the evacuation of Nanking by the northern forces and the simultaneous occupation by the Nationalists, serious outrages against foreign residents were perpetrated by soldiers in Nationalist uniforms. Six foreigners were killed, and many others were mistreated; foreign property was looted and burned; and a large number of foreign residents, including the American consul and his family, were perhaps saved from death or serious injury by an artillery barrage laid down by American warships. This violent attack upon foreign life and property brought to the responsible Nationalist leaders identic notes from the representatives of the five powers whose nationals had been involved,—France, Great Britain, Italy, Japan, and the United States,—demanding adequate punishment, a suitable apology, and complete reparation for injuries and property damage.[1]

Largely because of the fact that the American government refused to co-operate with the other powers in the presentation of an ultimatum, the danger of international armed intervention in China's internal struggle was averted. The successive manifestations of anti-foreign temper, however, led to the dispatch of troops and warships by the various interested powers to those Chinese ports at which the lives and property of their nationals seemed most in need of protection. Shanghai, because of the number of foreign residents and the extent of foreign property interests, was the object of especial concern, and even before the end of January, 1927, British fears for the safety of the international settlement were shown by the dispatch of a force of Rajput soldiers to assist in its defense. In the face of vehement protests both from the Nationalist leaders and from the government at Peking this force was landed. Britain's example was promptly followed by the other powers, and by the end of April foreign soldiers and marines to the number of forty thousand were either at Shanghai or on their way

[1] Subsequent investigation of the Nanking outrage established the fact that the attacks upon foreigners had been fomented by a small group of extremists for the purpose of involving General Chiang Kai-shek and the moderate wing of the Kuomintang in difficulties with the foreign powers. The affair was finally settled in the spring of 1928 by satisfactory agreements between the Nationalist government and the several aggrieved powers.

to the port. The greater part of the troops were soon withdrawn, but the British government, even after the panic had subsided, continued to maintain at Shanghai a defense force of regular soldiers as protection for its vital interests in China.[1]

With the transfer of all political power from Peking to Nanking the foreign diplomatic representatives were placed in an anomalous position. The treaty powers quickly recognized the Nanking government as the *de facto* and *de jure* government of the republic, but they also instructed their ministers to remain at Peiping (Peking), where, under the terms of the Boxer protocol of 1901, the legation quarter had been set apart as a special area under the exclusive jurisdiction of the diplomatic corps. In spite of this unusual arrangement, which made it necessary for the Nationalist Ministry of Foreign Affairs and the foreign diplomats to transact business at long range, the three years following the recognition of the Nationalist regime saw steady progress in the direction of an improvement in the relations between China and the governments of the outside powers.

The first notable diplomatic success of the Nationalist government was the achievement of tariff autonomy. The Washington Conference, as we have seen, had made some concessions to China's obvious need for an increase in tariff rates, but the special tariff conference which met at Peking during the winter of 1925–1926 had failed to reach any definite understanding on the subject of eventual tariff autonomy for the republic. Immediately after the triumph of the Nationalist armies, however, the American government decided to enter into separate negotiations with China on the subject. On July 25, 1928, the American minister and the Chinese Minister of Finance concluded a treaty at Peiping wherein the

[1] It should be noted that three developments in connection with the Yangtze-valley disturbances of the spring of 1927 were later cited by the Japanese government as precedents justifying Japanese action during 1931 and 1932 in Manchuria and at Shanghai. These were (1) the action of the British minister in concluding (February 19) with the Minister of Foreign Affairs of the as yet unrecognized Nationalist government an agreement relating to Hankow; (2) the action of the American naval commanders (March 24) in opening fire upon a part of Nanking for the protection of American residents; and (3) Great Britain's dispatch of troops to the international settlement at Shanghai without the prior assent of the Chinese government or of the other treaty powers.

United States recognized China's right to complete tariff autonomy as from January 1, 1929, subject only to the condition that American goods imported into China should enjoy treatment "in no way discriminatory" as compared with the treatment accorded to the goods of any other country. The example of the United States in this matter was quickly followed by most of the other countries whose existing treaties contained clauses restricting China's right to determine her own tariff schedules, and by the end of 1928 only Japan among the important powers had failed to conform to the new policy. Early in 1929 the Japanese government assented "in principle" to the exercise of tariff autonomy by China, and on May 6, 1930, after negotiations which had lasted nearly a year, a definitive Sino-Japanese treaty was finally signed. On May 16, ten days after the signature, this treaty went into effect, and China regained after nearly eighty-eight years the right to decide what duties should be levied on foreign goods entering her ports.

Nationalist China's efforts to secure the abrogation of extraterritoriality were less successful. On September 16, 1926, the Commission on Extraterritoriality, for which provision had been made at the Washington Conference, published a report expressing the opinion that the administration of justice in China had not been modernized to an extent which would warrant the surrender of extraterritorial rights. The establishment of the Nanking government and the apparent growth of civilian control in the new administration did much to weaken the specific objections upon which the commission had based its adverse opinion. During 1929 and 1930, therefore, the Nanking government succeeded in concluding with a number of the foreign countries new treaties in which the other "High Contracting Parties" agreed to surrender their extraterritorial jurisdiction if and when a similar surrender was agreed to by all the powers having treaties with China. In the summer of 1935 four great powers—France, Great Britain, Japan, and the United States—still adhered to their extraterritorial rights. Each of the four has expressed a willingness to negotiate on the question, but until negotiations with all four are brought to a satisfactory conclusion the extraterritorial rights of the other countries remain in force.

The Nationalist campaign for the recovery of China's lost sovereignty resulted also (at least until September, 1931) in some reduction in the amount of Chinese territory under foreign control. In February, 1927, while the Peking government was still the recognized government of the country, Great Britain entered into an agreement with the Nationalists for the restoration of the British concessions at Hankow and at Kiukiang to Chinese jurisdiction. After the recognition of the Nationalist regime two other British concessions, those at Chinkiang and at Amoy, as well as the Belgian concession at Tientsin, were similarly restored. On October 1, 1930, Great Britain returned to China the leased territory of Weihaiwei, thus fulfilling after a lapse of nearly nine years the promise made by Mr. Balfour at the Washington Conference. At Shanghai—by far the most important of the foreign concessions—the magnitude of foreign commercial interests prevented any real consideration of Chinese demands for restoration; but Chinese demands for a share in the government were met by granting to the Chinese taxpayers the right of electing—at first three and since 1930 five—members of the Municipal Council.

The defeat and death of Chang Tso-lin and the subsequent recognition of Nanking's authority by Chang Hsueh-liang did not mark an end of China's internal disorder. Instead of being able to lay aside the sword and to devote their energies to the pressing problems of economic and administrative reconstruction the Kuomintang leaders at Nanking found themselves compelled to deal with an almost endless series of revolts in all corners of China. These outbreaks, which led to a steady growth of military influence within the Nanking organization, may be classified under three headings: communist, militarist, and schismatic.

Communism, as we have seen, came into China with the Russian advisers who were invited to assist Sun Yat-sen in transforming the Kuomintang into an efficient political machine. Contrary to Dr. Sun's reported belief that communism had little chance of taking root in China, it developed within the party itself so rapidly as to bring about a serious party conflict in August, 1927. Expelled from the Kuomintang on this occasion, the followers of Marx and Lenin found among the masses of people eternally on the verge of starvation a ready hearing for their new doctrines, and communist or quasi-communist organizations grew up, especially in the interior, with startling rapidity. Many of the Chinese communists are said to have only a hazy understanding of the doctrines which they profess, and even more are said to be mere bandits using communist slogans as a cloak for their depredations. Whether communism or banditry, however, the desperate economic conditions of China's millions provided fruitful soil for growing disorder, and the Nanking government in its attempts to suppress the movement has been successful at one point, only to find itself confronted with a fresh outbreak in another province or district.

The militarist and schismatic revolts against the authority of the Nanking government cannot in most cases be clearly separated. The old-time tuchuns, who had joined the Nationalist camp during the triumphant days of 1927 and 1928, were soon alienated by a program intended to bring all the nation's armed forces under the effective control of a central administration, and the outbreaks headed by the less prominent of these former war lords were undisguisedly for the purpose of securing once more the full enjoyment of local dictatorial power. Men of such prominence as Feng Yu-hsiang and Yen Hsi-shan, however, found it necessary to consider their established reputations as patriotic public servants. Hence they were careful to build up a case for rebellion by denouncing the shortcomings of Nanking and by allying themselves with malcontents among the civilian members of the Kuomintang. On the other hand, the breaks in Kuomintang ranks, which at times led to alliances between schismatic party members and discontented tuchuns, were frequently the result of civilian opposition to the growth of military preponderance at Nanking, where Generalissimo Chiang Kai-shek appeared gradually to be attaining the status of an absolute dictator.

Even more than the government's failure to suppress communism, the recurrent difficulties with rebellious generals and the violent disputes inside the Kuomintang steadily weakened China's prestige in the eyes of the outside world, and many observers, ignoring the contemporary collapse of democratic institutions in other lands, reached the conviction that the Chinese were peculiarly incapable of administering the affairs of a modern state.

Yet these political disorders, even when complicated by the Yangtze floods of the summer of 1931 and by Japan's military activities after September 18 of the same year, have not proved to be an insuperable barrier to social and economic development. The Yangtze disaster, one of the most serious floods in the history of the country, was followed by the construction of a new and more adequate system of protective dikes. This undertaking, with the assistance of foreign technical advisers, was completed in time to hold in check the flood waters of 1932; and in 1935, although the Yangtze rose to a level even higher than that reached in 1931, the new dikes appear to have saved this densely populated area from a full repetition of the earlier disaster. A committee from the International Institute of Intellectual Coöperation, which in 1932 carried out a survey of China's national educational system, paid high tribute to the progress being made in that important field. During the years 1932–1935 thirty thousand miles of modern highways suitable for automobile traffic were completed. The National Economic Council, set up in 1931 by the Nanking government, has sought and obtained valuable assistance from League of Nations experts in a reconstruction program which includes not only the building of roads but also the development of the public health service, the improvement of rivers and harbors, and the introduction of new and more efficient methods of agriculture.

The last few years, moreover, have seen real progress in the direction of greater political stability for the Republic. In the spring of 1932 the Nationalist authorities announced that, except for operations against the communists, there would be no more civil wars in China. In other words, the central government, acquiescing in a larger measure of autonomy for various provinces, abandoned its efforts to impose its will by force upon the distant parts of the country and chose rather to consolidate its power in the provinces nearer at hand. The concession of greater provincial autonomy is a retreat, even if only temporary, from the original Nationalist program, but it is also a move toward traditional Chinese polity. An even more significant trend toward the traditional has been the noticeable swing from the extreme individualism of the 1920's back to the social philosophy of Confucius; for the teachings of the great Sage, once contemptuously rejected as outmoded and useless, are beginning to receive the serious attention of Young China. It now remains to be seen whether the nation's leaders will find in a revival of Confucianism that moral foundation without which, in ages past, no Chinese government has been able to endure.

THE PROBLEMS OF POST-WAR JAPAN

The closing months of 1922 found the affairs of the Japanese Empire in a most favorable state. Dominating eastern Asia and occupying a leading position in the newly organized League of Nations, prosperous and united at home, her relations with her two continental neighbors seemingly on the way to definite improvement, respected but not feared by the great powers of the West, Japan appeared to be the one country for which it would be reasonable to predict a peaceful and orderly adjustment to post-war conditions. The apparently favorable auguries of 1922, however, have not been fulfilled, and the subsequent thirteen years have been for Japan, perhaps even more than for the other countries of the Far East, a period of growing difficulties at home and abroad.

On September 1, 1923, one of the most destructive earthquakes in the history of the country laid in ruin the greater part of the Kwanto. In Tokyo and Yokohama the estimated loss of life was more than eighty thousand, and the property damage in these two cities and in the surrounding territory amounted to hundreds of millions of dollars. From all parts of the world came expressions of sympathy and generous contributions for relief; but the task of rebuilding the devastated area necessarily fell upon the Japanese people, who rose to the occasion with remarkable energy and ability. Within an amazingly short time the ruined urban districts were completely rebuilt, and the railways, waterworks, and hydroelectric systems were restored to a state of efficiency even surpassing that of the pre-earthquake period.

Irrevocably committed to the path of modern industrialism and driven forward along that path by a rapidly growing population,[1] the Japanese are convinced that their very existence depends upon a steadily expanding foreign trade. Even while they grappled with the task of reconstruction, therefore, they continued their efforts to increase the sale abroad of their industrial output; and the statistics of Japanese commerce, after a momentary decline in the later months of 1923, show a steady advance during the years 1924–1926. In 1927 the process of recovery was retarded and the economic structure of the empire was again shaken to its foundations by a serious bank crisis occasioned, in part at least, by the flotation of huge loans for relief and reconstruction. This financial debacle, which brought to light a number of scandals involving bank officials and prominent politicians, was but a prelude to still darker days, for the closing months of 1928 found Japan, along with the rest of the world, caught in the quicksands of the great depression.

With the development of the depression Japanese statesmen and business men turned with increasing energy to the task of winning new markets in every possible corner of the world in order to offset the inevitable shrinkage of certain pre-depression markets for their country's exports. Efforts to this end, although crowned with conspicuous success, necessarily conflicted with similar efforts on the part of other countries, whose industrialists viewed with growing alarm the invasion of their colonial and domestic markets by the cheaper competing products of Japanese factories. After the beginning of 1932, therefore, when the abandonment of the gold standard and the consequent depreciation of the yen in terms of foreign currencies made it possible to sell their goods abroad at astonishingly low prices, the Japanese exporters found themselves confronted by hastily erected barricades of quotas and increased tariffs, some designed for general protection against all foreign competitors but others undoubtedly discriminating in their operation against Japanese goods.

[1] With a present population of about 70,000,000 Japan has a birth rate of 34 and a death rate of 19 per thousand; the net increase of 15 per thousand has meant during the last few years the addition of approximately one million to the population each year. These figures are for Japan proper, exclusive of outlying parts of the empire.

On December 25, 1926, Emperor Yoshihito (the Taisho emperor) was succeeded on the throne by his son Hirohito, whose reign-period received the auspicious designation of *Showa* ("peace through justice"). During the five preceding years the imperial heir, acting as regent, had taken over the functions of his invalid father. Inasmuch as the death of Yoshihito involved no change in the actual tenure of power, the five years during which the crown prince acted as regent may be regarded as essentially a part of the present era, and the political developments of the last fourteen years may properly be considered without reference to the nominal change of sovereigns.

In Japan, as in the industrialized countries of the West, the economic difficulties arising out of the world depression have been equaled or even overshadowed by growing difficulties in the field of domestic politics. It will be recalled that in the opening years of the Taisho era (that is, in the years 1912 to 1914) dissatisfaction with certain of the Meiji political institutions had already begun to develop. The war years saw political questions forced into the background, but with the end of the war the earlier difficulties quickly reappeared. During the ten years and a half that followed the murder of Prime Minister Hara (from November 4, 1921, to May 15, 1932), Japan had ten premiers, of whom two[1] fell at the hands of assassins.

If it were not for the frequent recourse to physical violence and assassination,[2] this rapid succession of premiers might be interpreted as indicating a healthy political rivalry for the control of a constitutional parliamentary government. Careful investigation, however, reveals all too clearly the illusory nature of this party struggle. Even during the period from June, 1924, to May, 1932, when the Kenseikai (later transformed into the Minseito) and the Seiyukai alternated in nominal control of the administration, cabinets and prime ministers were made and unmade not by parliamentary majorities but by the operation of powerful forces behind

[1] Hamaguchi and Inukai, who, with Hara, are the only non-titled civilians ever to have held the post.

[2] The three prime ministers were but the most distinguished in a long list of prominent victims of murderous assaults.

the scenes. In countries with real parliamentary government the party successful at the polls forms the cabinet; in Japan the cabinet installed by extraparliamentary influence either holds office in the face of a numerically superior opposition or, dissolving the diet, so manipulates the election as to ensure the return of an acquiescent majority.[1]

During the last decade the peace of mind of the governing classes has been increasingly disturbed by the steady development of what is officially termed "dangerous thought." As early as 1925 the coalition ministry of Viscount Kato secured the enactment of a peace-preservation law which prescribed long terms of imprisonment for those advocating any alteration of the national constitution or working for the "fundamental negation" of the system of private ownership. In the spring of 1928 Baron Tanaka's Seiyukai ministry by imperial ordinance increased the penalties set forth in the earlier enactment, and this ordinance was approved by the diet at its next session. In spite of the fact that the death penalty or life imprisonment may now be imposed upon the organizers and the active members of any society adjudged to be revolutionary, and in the face of police activities resulting in the arrest of thousands of suspects, political and economic heresy has continued to spread at an alarming rate.

While the repressive efforts of the authorities have been directed almost exclusively against the radical organizations of the left, the most serious attacks upon Japan's constitutional system in recent years have come from the superpatriots of the conservative right. Loud in their protestation of devoted loyalty to the emperor, the "rightist" organizations, whose members are drawn largely from farmers and ex-service men, have been equally vociferous in denouncing not merely the culpable incompetence of party politicians but also the fundamental principles of parliamentary government. Nor do these conservatives content themselves with the mere expression of antiparliamentary opinion. On May 15, 1932,

---

[1] The election law of 1925, which extended the right of suffrage to all males over twenty-five years of age and increased by fourfold the number of qualified voters, seems to have made the manipulation of elections even less difficult than before.

when a group of civilian patriots joined with a number of army and navy cadets in the murder of Premier Inukai, their avowed purpose was to destroy the corrupt existing regime and to set up a military dictatorship in its place. The plot failed, and at least the outward semblance of parliamentary government was retained; but the outbreak did put an end—temporarily or permanently—to the system of party government.[1] It is possible that these recent developments mean no more than a temporary check in the evolution of Japan's constitutional system, but they justify the belief that the institutions borrowed from abroad by the Meiji statesmen are much less firmly rooted than was once supposed to be the case.

For nearly ten years after the adjournment of the Washington Conference (that is, until the Manchurian outbreak in September, 1931) cordial relations between Japan and the United States were disturbed only by a single serious issue: Japanese immigration into America. In 1907 this question had been settled, apparently to the satisfaction of both governments, by a "gentlemen's agreement" under the terms of which Japan issued passports for visiting the United States only to officials, merchants, students, and tourists, while the American government permitted Japanese laborers already in the country to re-enter after visits to their native land and to be joined in America by their wives and children from Japan. Although there is every reason for believing that the terms of this agreement were meticulously observed by Japan, the rapid growth of the Japanese population in certain Western states eventually led to renewed agitation for their exclusion; and the immigration bill of 1924, ignoring the existing arrangement, provided that no "alien ineligible to citizenship" should be admitted to the United States as an immigrant.[2] This provision was bitterly resented in Japan, where it was interpreted as a gratuitous insult;

---

[1] After the death of Inukai the aged Admiral Saito was called from retirement to head an emergency cabinet in which members of the two leading parties shared the portfolios with a number of non-party men. In July, 1934, Saito was succeeded as Premier by Admiral Okada, in whose cabinet the party politicians were forced to accept an even less prominent part.

[1] Officials, merchants, students, and tourists were still to be admitted, as before, on non-immigrant passports.

and outstanding Japanese leaders have insisted that unless the insult was withdrawn by placing immigrants from Japan on a legal equality with those from European countries, the relations between the two nations would be permanently embittered.

Japan's withdrawal of her forces from the Siberian mainland in October, 1922, opened the door for diplomatic relations with Russia, and early in 1923 the Soviet representative, Adolf Joffe, visited Tokyo for the purpose of arranging, if possible, a *modus vivendi* between the two countries. For nearly two years after the Joffe visit the conclusion of a satisfactory arrangement was obstructed by Japanese fears lest the resumption of normal relations be followed by the introduction and spread of communistic ideas from their dangerous neighbor. The conclusion of a Russo-Chinese agreement in May, 1924, however, seemed to leave Japan no alternative but to reach the best possible understanding with the Soviet regime. In August of that year, therefore, Russo-Japanese negotiations were begun at Peking, and on January 20, 1925, a convention was signed by M. Karakhan and Mr. Yoshizawa, the diplomatic representatives to China of their respective governments.

As a *quid pro quo* for Japanese recognition the Soviet government declared its willingness to grant concessions to Japanese subjects for the exploitation of minerals, forests, and other natural resources in certain regions, and, pending the conclusion of a new commercial treaty, agreed that Japanese fishermen should continue to enjoy fishing rights in the territorial waters of Siberia. Each high contracting power undertook to forbid any propaganda against the established institutions of the other and to expel from its domains "organizations or groups pretending to be the government for any part of the territories of the other party." The Soviet government recognized the validity of the Treaty of Portsmouth and expressed its regret for the massacre of Japanese subjects in 1920 at Nikolaevsk. Japan agreed to withdraw her armed forces from Russian Sakhalin and secured, in return, the right to exploit half the oil resources in that part of the island.

In 1928, coincidentally with the launching of their first Five-Year Plan, the Soviet government concluded a new fisheries convention under which Japanese interests received the right to exploit more than half the fishing grounds along the Siberian coast. Difficulties have inevitably arisen in the interpretation and execution of this agreement and others, but the Russian authorities, absorbed in the solution of their domestic problems, appear to have been genuinely anxious to avoid becoming involved in serious trouble in the Far East.

Since 1925, Russo-Japanese relations have failed to develop any great degree of cordiality, but this failure has little connection with the fears which so long deferred Japanese recognition of the Soviet regime. Although some of the already mentioned dangerous thinking in Japan undoubtedly found its inspiration in the Bolshevist experiment, there have been very few accusations against the Russians of having violated the no-propaganda pledge given at Peking. On the other hand, the growing power of the Soviet Union and the spread of Russian influence on the Asiatic continent have convinced many Japanese leaders that the new Russia is a dangerous rival against whom a war must some day be waged.

As we have already seen, the immediate effect of the Washington Conference upon Sino-Japanese relations was decidedly beneficial. The Nine-Power Treaty with its multilateral pledge to respect the sovereignty and integrity of China, and the amicable adjustment of the Shantung question, served to dissipate Chinese fears of their more powerful neighbor, while the Japanese, relieved of some of their own anxieties by the naval agreement, saw the wisdom of adopting toward China a policy less likely to drive the distracted republic into the arms of Russia. During the years following the conference the outstanding advocate of a more enlightened China policy was Baron Shidehara, who became Minister of Foreign Affairs in June, 1924, and continued at that post for nearly three years. Appreciating the fact that only in a friendly China could Japan hope to find a growing market for her exports, Shidehara strove to establish the relations between the two countries upon a basis of mutual respect, and he consistently opposed attempts to further Japanese political influence by means of intervening in China's internal affairs.

With the fall of the Wakatsuki cabinet in April, 1927, however, Shidehara's policies were set aside. General Baron Tanaka, who headed the new government and took into his own hands the management of the Foreign Office, was a frank expansionist and an advocate of a "strong" policy toward China.[1] The advent of Tanaka to the premiership and to the ministry of foreign affairs, moreover, closely coincided with the occupation of the Yangtze valley by the armies of the northward-moving Kuomintang, and the unusually troubled waters of China during his tenure of office would have been tempting even to a diplomat less naturally predisposed to the adventurous use of force for the extension of his country's prestige.

In May, 1927, barely a month after the new ministry had assumed office, the Japanese government decided to send troops into Shantung to protect Japanese interests in that province, a move which effectively blocked the Kuomintang advance upon Peking. In April of the following year, when the Nanking government launched a second campaign against the northern capital, Japanese forces were again sent to the interior of Shantung. On May 3 the Chinese and Japanese troops at Tsinan came into open conflict; and in the subsequent fighting some two thousand Chinese soldiers were killed or wounded, while the Japanese casualties amounted to about two hundred. War between the two countries was narrowly averted, and the Kuomintang armies, advancing against Peking along lines which did not cross the Japanese zone of occupation, brought their campaign to a successful conclusion. On May 18, when the capture of Peking by the southern forces was seen to be inevitable, Tanaka formally notified the two rival Chinese governments that Japan would not tolerate the spread of their civil war beyond the Great Wall into Manchuria. On June 4 Marshal Chang Tso-lin, withdrawing along the railway from Peking to Mukden, lost his life in a bomb explosion, and Chang Hsueh-liang, who succeeded his father as war lord of Manchuria, was promptly warned by Japan against entering into any arrangement with the Kuomintang.

[1] Although the authenticity of the famous "Tanaka Memorial," alleged to have been presented to the throne by Baron Tanaka in July, 1927, is open to serious question, the program contained in that document is in essential harmony with the steps subsequently taken by Japan under the leadership of men with whom Tanaka was closely associated.

In July, 1929, when General Tanaka was replaced as Premier by Mr. Hamaguchi, the leader of the Minseito party, Baron Shidehara resumed his place at the Foreign Office. For nearly two years and a half, as a member of the Hamaguchi and Wakatsuki cabinets, Shidehara continued his efforts to counteract the unfortunate effects of the Tanaka regime and regain by friendly gestures the good will of China. This return to more conciliatory tactics was followed by the termination of the anti-Japanese boycott which the Chinese Nationalists had maintained since the summer of 1928, and the Shidehara policy therefore found strong support among the Japanese merchants and industrialists. The eclipse of those advocating forceful measures was, however, only temporary. During the spring and early summer of 1931 the government's China policy was the target for increasing denunciation from army men and from the spokesmen of ultrapatriotic conservative groups. In August of the same year the Minister of War (General Minami), repudiating the policy of the cabinet in which he held a post, declared to an assembly of army officers that the outstanding issues between Japan and China could be settled only by the use of armed force.

Manchuria—the Storm Center of the Far East

Following the recognition of the Nanking government by the foreign powers in the summer of 1928, the Kuomintang leaders, urged on by an aroused and militant public opinion, turned to the task of strengthening the government's control over those territories which, although long regarded as parts of China, lay outside the eighteen provinces of China Proper. Most important of these territories, and the region in which China's sovereign rights were most dangerously threatened, was Manchuria, and it was here that prompt remedial action was most urgently needed. Even during his father's lifetime Chang Hsueh-liang had shown his sympathy with the program of the Chinese Nationalists. His accession to power in June, 1928, therefore opened the way to a *rapprochement* between Mukden and Nanking. The arrangement under which Chang, at the end of December, formally aligned himself with the

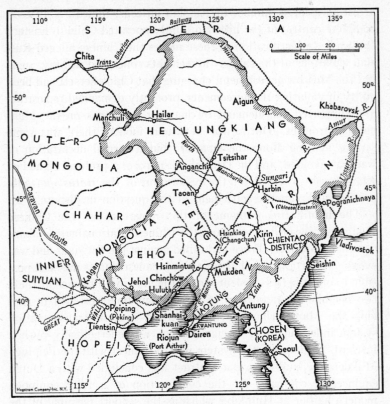

" Manchukuo "

Kuomintang left him in complete control of the internal administration of Manchuria, to which the province of Jehol was now
added; but it soon became evident that the young marshal was prepared to accept the guidance of the Nanking government in matters
of foreign policy and to co-operate loyally with its efforts to bring
Manchuria into more perfect union with the rest of China.

Of the two powers whose policies and vested interests in Manchuria seriously impeded the accomplishment of such a union,
Russia was apparently the more open to attack. In May and June,
1929, the Mukden authorities, taking their cue from Nanking,
therefore commenced action against Russian interests in northern
Manchuria. On July 10, after closing all Soviet trade agencies and

arresting a large number of Russian citizens, they forcibly took complete control of the hitherto jointly operated Chinese Eastern Railway. In justification of these moves the Chinese alleged Russian violations of the railway agreements concluded in May, 1924, but the Moscow government, charging that China herself had been guilty of violating the agreements, promptly demanded reparation and supported this demand by massing its troops on the Manchurian frontier. During the next four months there was some serious fighting along the frontier; but a formal declaration of war was avoided, and on December 22, 1929, a protocol signed at Khabarovsk provided for the restoration of the *status quo ante* pending a diplomatic settlement of the question in dispute.

The humiliating outcome of this move against the Chinese Eastern Railway did not cause the Chinese Nationalists to abandon their objective. Force had failed against the Russians and was even more certain to fail against the Japanese, but it was still possible to offset by less violent means the growing influence of these two neighbors. A program of railway-building, designed to provide the Manchurian provinces with a modern transportation system independent of foreign control, was energetically pushed forward.[1] This projected system was to connect with the Peiping–Mukden line, and in 1930 a contract was concluded with a Dutch engineering company for the construction of a fully equipped modern harbor at Hulutao,[2] which as the seaport terminal of the railway system was designed to keep in Chinese hands much of the traffic hitherto flowing through the ports of Dairen and Vladivostok. In the meantime, although Mukden jealously guarded its autonomy in the matter of local administration, the dissemination of Nationalist ideology was officially encouraged, and in September, 1930, Chang Hsueh-liang gave a practical demonstration of the reality of his alliance with Nanking by moving his troops south of the Great Wall to co-operate with the Kuomintang against the allied forces of Feng Yu-hsiang and Yen Hsi-shan.

---

[1] As early as 1926 Chang Tso-lin, primarily for military reasons, had undertaken the building of a number of independent railway lines; the new program looked to the consolidation of these lines into an effective system.

[2] On the Gulf of Liaotung near Chinchow.

The significance of these developments was not lost on the officials of the Japanese government. If the northeastern provinces were to the Chinese Nationalists an integral part of a China whose unity must be preserved, Japan's treaty rights in this area were to the Japanese the empire's economic "life line," to be guarded, by force if necessary, against Chinese attack. At Dairen and at Tokyo every phase of Chinese Nationalist activity in Manchuria was regarded as a deliberately hostile move against Japan's vested rights; yet the protests of the Tokyo authorities against the open encouragement of anti-Japanese propaganda, against the construction of competing "parallel" railway lines, and against other alleged violations of Japan's treaty rights served only to arouse in China fresh enthusiasm for the program of national unification.

During the summer of 1931 two incidents brought Sino-Japanese relations almost to the breaking point. A clash between Chinese landholders and Korean immigrants in June at Wanpaoshan, in the Manchurian province of Kirin, was followed early in July by serious anti-Chinese riots at Seoul and a number of other Korean cities. Charging that the Japanese authorities in Korea had fostered the outbreak by permitting the publication of exaggerated reports of the Wanpaoshan affair and that they had failed to take adequate measures after the riots started, patriotic Chinese organizations at Shanghai and other ports promptly declared a new boycott against Japanese trade. The second and practically simultaneous complicating incident was the arrest and execution on June 27, by Chinese troops, of Major Nakamura, a Japanese officer traveling in the interior of Manchuria. The Japanese charged that the Chinese authorities, after attempting to deny that the murder had taken place, failed to carry out in good faith their promise to arrest the guilty persons and bring them to trial. Baron Shidehara, still endeavoring to improve the diplomatic relations between Japan and China, appears to have made a genuine—and for a time successful—effort to keep the Nakamura affair from becoming public. In August, however, the news of the murder began to circulate in Japan, and the army leaders, impatient with Shidehara's weakness, began to voice their demand for the adoption of a more vigorous policy toward China.

On the night of September 18–19, 1931, the officers of the Japanese troops stationed at Mukden for the protection of the South Manchuria Railway took matters into their own hands. Alleging that Chinese regular soldiers had made an attempt to destroy the railway tracks at a point just north of Mukden, they launched an attack upon the local Chinese garrison forces and made themselves masters of the city. Following this outbreak the military authorities of the Liaotung Leased Territory assumed control of the situation. Under their energetic leadership the Liaotung garrison, heavily reinforced from Korea and Japan, occupied all the Chinese railways and proceeded to establish its control over all of southern Manchuria. Recognizing China's inability to offer effective military resistance, Marshal Chang Hsueh-liang appears to have instructed his troops to avoid conflict by withdrawing before the advancing Japanese. The extension of Japanese control was accordingly attended with little serious fighting; and by the end of December, when the Chinese forces were withdrawn from Chinchow, the subjugation of southern Manchuria was practically completed.

Although the Chinese government had officially adopted a policy of nonresistance, the Chinese public at Shanghai and other leading commercial centers was prompt to show by a new and more energetic boycott its resentment of Japan's Manchurian operations. In November and December, 1931, the total value of Japanese exports to China—exclusive of Manchuria—amounted to slightly less than four million yen instead of the average of twenty-three million in the corresponding two-month periods of each of the two preceding years.

In response to this paralyzing attack upon their trade the Japanese—on January 28, 1932—landed a force of fifteen hundred marines at Shanghai for the purpose of compelling the local authorities to put an end to the boycott. Here, for the first time, Japan's forceful methods met stubborn resistance in the form of the Chinese Nineteenth Route Army under the command of General Tsai Ting-kai. On March 2, after five weeks of furious fighting, the Chinese were finally driven from their defensive line of trenches by the Japanese forces, which by this time consisted of some seventy thousand regular troops. Following lengthy negotiations, in which the representatives of interested neutral powers participated as mediators, an agreement, signed on May 5, brought an end to the Shanghai struggle, and the Japanese forces began their evacuation of the war-torn metropolis.

When the Japanese army, on and after September 18, proceeded to expel all Chinese military forces from Mukden and southern Manchuria, one inevitable consequence of their action was the rapid disintegration of the hitherto existing administrative machinery of the entire area. Although the Tokyo Foreign Office assured the other interested governments that Japan's actions were not inspired by any thought of conquest, it soon became evident that Japanese military circles—if not the government itself—were irrevocably opposed to the resumption of authority at any future date by Marshal Chang Hsueh-liang and his supporters. The political vacuum left by the expulsion of the Chang regime did not long remain unfilled. Even before the end of September there began to appear in various districts self-government committees or associations in which Japanese business men, consular authorities, and resident officials of the South Manchuria Railway Company played dominant roles. These local committees gradually coalesced, and on February 18, 1932, they proclaimed the independence of the new state of "Manchukuo," consisting of the four provinces of Fengtien, Kirin, Heilungkiang, and Jehol. Deferring to Japanese wishes for complete control over the city of Mukden, the organizers of the new state established their capital at Changchun (renamed Hsinking), and on March 9 Pu Yi, the young ex-emperor of China, was formally installed as regent. In the government thus organized the various departments were placed in charge of Chinese ministers, some of whom had held responsible posts under the previous regime; but the administrative organization also contained numerous Japanese advisers and under-secretaries, of whom not a few were commissioned officers in the Japanese armed services or members of Japan's civilian bureaucracy.

On September 15, 1932, the governments of Japan and Manchukuo concluded a protocol in which the two countries, "recognizing that any threat to the safety of either of the High Contracting Parties constitutes at the same time a threat to the existence of the other," agreed to co-operate in the maintenance of their national safety. The conclusion of this alliance, which amounted to the proclamation of a Japanese protectorate, was followed by a vigorous campaign to make effective the jurisdiction of the Hsinking government over the full extent of the territory claimed by it. During the opening months of 1933, Japanese armies, conducting a remarkable campaign in subzero temperatures, invaded and subdued the hitherto recalcitrant province of Jehol.

Following the occupation of Jehol the Japanese military commanders in Manchuria, to safeguard the southern boundary of the newly acquired area, moved forces into the northeastern portion of Hopei (the former Chihli) province, clearing the region of Chinese troops and continuing their advance almost to the walls of Peiping. As a result of this military pressure the Chinese authorities, on May 31, 1933, concluded with the Japanese the agreement known as the Tangku Armistice, which established a demilitarized zone in northeastern Hopei. The agreement did not affect the Japanese forces which, in accordance with the Boxer Protocol of 1901, were stationed along the railway between Tientsin and Shanhaikuan, but all Chinese troops were to be withdrawn, and the zone was to be policed by a specially organized *gendarmerie* under the command of officers friendly to Japan.

While the foregoing adjustments were being made in Jehol and along the Great Wall the Japanese and Manchukuo forces, despite mild Russian protests, had carried their anti-rebel and anti-bandit operations beyond the line of the Chinese Eastern Railway to the banks of the Amur. In May, 1933, anxious to avoid complications which might easily lead to a second Russo-Japanese war, the Soviet government announced its willingness to dispose of its rights in the Chinese Eastern Railway. Tripartite negotiations (between Russia, Japan, and Manchukuo) for arranging the terms of the sale commenced in the summer of 1933. On January 22, 1935, an agreement on all points was at last reached, and on March 23 Russia's interests in the line were formally transferred to the state of Manchukuo. This transfer completed the liquidation of Russian property rights in Manchuria, and the line, renamed the North Manchuria, became an integral part of the system operated by the South Manchuria Railway Company.

At the end of 1933 the Manchukuo authorities determined to abandon the republican form of government and to transform their state into an empire. On March 1, 1934, after having held for two years the post of regent, Pu Yi was accordingly enthroned at Hsinking as emperor, taking as his regnal title *Kang Teh*. The resumption of imperial dignity by the last of China's Manchu rulers, although enthusiastically acclaimed at Tokyo, has not seriously affected the political actualities in the new state. Under the empire, as under the regency, the nominal heads of the administrative departments are Chinese, but the Japanese advisers and officials have continued to exercise what appears to be a dominating influence upon the decision of all important questions of policy.

The military operations at Mukden on September 18, 1931, were brought almost immediately to the attention of the Council of the League of Nations by simultaneous charges and countercharges from the representatives of the two governments involved. Nanking accused Japan of having made a premeditated attack upon China's sovereignty and territorial integrity, while the Tokyo government, asserting that the alleged attempt against the South Manchuria Railway line was but the culminating incident in China's deliberate campaign against Japan's existing treaty rights in Manchuria, insisted that the Japanese military forces, on and after the night of September 18, had taken no action other than could be clearly justified on the ground of necessary self-defense. Unable to reach any decision on the basis of these *ex parte* statements, the Council, on December 10, on the motion of the Japanese representative, unanimously resolved "to appoint a commission of five members to study on the spot and to report to the Council on any circumstance which, affecting international relations, threatens to disturb peace between China and Japan." The Commission of Enquiry established under this resolution, commonly known as the Lytton Commission, consisted of the Earl of Lytton (British) as chairman, Count Aldrovandi (Italian), General Henri Claudel (French), General Frank R. McCoy (American), and Dr. Heinrich Schnee (German).

Arriving at Yokohama on February 29, 1932, the commission spent slightly more than six months in Japan, China, and Manchuria, interviewing officials and private citizens of all three countries and examining the mass of evidence and opinion submitted to it by the representatives of the opposing parties. On September 4, 1932, the report of the investigation was completed, and on October 2 it was published simultaneously at Geneva and in the capitals of all the interested powers.[1] In its report the commission analyzed the situation out of which the conflict had developed, expressed its judgment upon the events in Manchuria on and after September 18, 1931, and laid down certain general principles upon which, in the opinion of its members, a satisfactory solution of the Manchurian question should be based. On two vital points the report of the commission supported China's contentions against those of the Japanese. On page 71, after describing the course of events on the night of September 18, it says: "The military operations of the Japanese troops during this night, which have been described above, cannot be regarded as measures of legitimate self-defense." Later, on page 97, the report states that, in the opinion of the commissioners, two factors without which the new state of "Manchukuo" could not have been formed "were the presence of Japanese troops and the activities of Japanese officials, both civil and military. For this reason the present regime cannot be considered to have been called into existence by a genuine and spontaneous independence movement."[2]

Taken up for consideration by the League Council on November 21, 1932, the Lytton report and its specific recommendations were debated at length, first by the Council, then by the Assembly, and finally by a special Committee of Nineteen to which the matter was referred by the Assembly. For three months the statesmen

[1] League of Nations. Appeal by the Chinese Government. Report of the Commission of Enquiry.

[2] The fighting at Shanghai, which commenced after the commission had received its instructions from the League Council and terminated before its arrival in China, was regarded as not falling within the scope of its investigations and was therefore not discussed in the report.

at Geneva attempted to find some arrangement whereby the League might mediate between its two disputing members, but their attempts broke down in the face of Japan's unalterable refusal to permit any outside element to participate in the necessary negotiations between herself and China. On February 24, 1933, by a vote of forty-two to one (Japan), with Siam not voting, the Assembly therefore approved the report of its special committee and recorded its decision that (1) the Manchurian dispute should be settled in accordance with the principles of the League Covenant, the Pact of Paris, and the Nine-Power Washington Treaty; (2) the members of the League should not recognize any situation, treaty, or agreement which might be brought about by means contrary to the obligations imposed by these solemn undertakings;[1] (3) Japanese military pressure upon China should cease; (4) the settlement should follow the lines of the ten recommendations of the Lytton report; (5) Sino-Japanese negotiations for the settlement of the dispute should be carried on under the supervision of the Assembly. Upon the passage of the foregoing resolution the Japanese representative left the meeting, and on March 27 the Tokyo government formally notified the League of Japan's intention to withdraw from membership in the organization, this withdrawal becoming effective, under the terms of the Covenant, two years after the date of the notice.

The Japanese note of withdrawal declared that Japan, devoted to the cause of peace, found herself divided from the League of Nations by an "irreconcilable divergence of views" concerning "the fundamental principles to be followed in the establishment of a durable peace in the Far East." Similar divergences appear also to separate Japan from the United States, which approved and supported the League in its stand on the Manchurian question, and from Soviet Russia.

[1] This second point of the League's decision incorporated the essential principle of the so-called Stimson Doctrine. On January 7, 1932, Mr. H. L. Stimson, the American Secretary of State, notified the Chinese and Japanese governments that the American government ". . . . does not intend to recognize any situation, treaty or agreement which may be brought about by means contrary to the covenants and obligations of the Pact of Paris of August 27, 1928, to which treaty both China and Japan, as well as the United States, are parties."

In the opinion of the Tokyo government peace can be assured only by a Japanese hegemony in eastern Asia, recognized and accepted as such by the powers. This policy—frequently referred to by Japanese spokesmen as Japan's Asiatic Monroe Doctrine—Japan is now prepared to maintain with or without Western approval. The most definite assertion of such intention came on April 18, 1934, when Eiji Amau, of the Japanese Foreign Office, declared that Japan assumed exclusive responsibility for peace in eastern Asia and would oppose, by force if necessary, any foreign activities in China that might lead to the disturbance of peace and order or might tend to alienate the friendly relations between China and Japan. Specifically indicated by Mr. Amau as objectionable were the granting of political loans or the supplying of war material or military advisers to China by any state, and joint operations of any sort undertaken by two or more powers. In response to this statement came immediate warnings that other signatories of the Nine Power Treaty could not recognize Japan's right to dictate in situations involving their rights and legitimate interests or to decide alone whether any particular action constituted a danger to the peace and integrity of China.

Although the Foreign Office, in reply, explained that Japan had no intention of infringing upon the existing treaty rights of other nations, the fact remains that Japan, since the summer of 1934, has been pursuing a "forward" policy in China. New demands in 1935, which the Chinese authorities did not dare to reject, have resulted in the establishment of virtual Japanese control over a steadily expanding area south of the Great Wall. At the same time there has been pressure upon Nanking to secure Chinese recognition of Manchukuo and the acceptance by China of Japanese leadership and advice.

A Japanese hegemony over China can hardly be harmonized with the provisions of the Nine Power Treaty or with the rights enjoyed by other nations under their existing separate treaties with the Chinese Republic. Japan's persistence in her present policy may therefore result in grave international complications. Once more, as in the summer of 1921, there exists in the Far East a situation fraught with danger for the peace of the world. For the moment the armed strength of Japan may suffice to establish a *pax Japonica* based upon force;[1] will the statesmanship of Japan, of China, and of the world at large show itself capable of organizing peace upon some more lasting basis?

SUGGESTED REFERENCES

ADACHI, K. Manchuria: a Survey.

ANDREWS, C. F. Mahatma Gandhi: his Own Story.

CONDLIFFE, J. B. China Today: Economic.

CUMMING, SIR J. (editor). Political India, 1832–1932.

DENNIS, A. L. P. The Foreign Policies of Soviet Russia.

DUTCHER, G. M. The Political Awakening of the East.

HARRISON, F. B. The Corner-stone of Philippine Independence.

HOLCOMBE, A. N. The Chinese Revolution.

HORNBECK, S. K. China Today: Political.

ILBERT, SIR C. P. The Government of India.

IWASAKI, U. Working Forces in Japanese Politics.

LATTIMORE, O. Manchuria: Cradle of Conflict.

LOVETT, SIR V. A History of the Indian Nationalist Movement.

MOOKERJI, R. The Fundamental Unity of India.

MOULTON, H. G., and KO, J. Japan: an Economic and Financial Appraisal.

PEAKE, C. K. Nationalism and Education in Modern China.

POOLEY, A. M. Japan's Foreign Policies.

QUIGLEY, H. S. Chinese Politics and Foreign Powers.

QUIGLEY, H. S. Japanese Government and Politics.

RAI, L. The Political Future of India.

REMER, C. F. Foreign Investments in China.

ROBERTS, S. H. History of French Colonial Policy, 1870–1925.

SAYRE, F. B. "Siam's Fight for Sovereignty," *Atlantic Monthly*, Vol. 140, pp. 674–689 (November, 1927).

SUN YAT-SEN. The Three Principles of the People.

VANDENBOSCH, A. The Dutch East Indies.

VAN TYNE, C. H. India in Ferment.

YAKHONTOFF, V. A. Russia and the Soviet Union in the Far East.

YOUNG, A. M. Japan in Recent Times.

YOUNG, C. W. Japan's Special Position in Manchuria.

YOUNG, C. W. The International Legal Status of the Kwantung Leased Territory.

YOUNG, C. W. Japanese Jurisdiction in the South Manchuria Railway Areas.

Appeal by the Chinese Government. Report of the Commission of Enquiry (Lytton Commission). League of Nations.

Report of the Indian Statutory Commission (Simon Commission).

[1] The Washington naval agreement and the London naval agreement of 1930 are to expire on December 31, 1936. After that date, in the absence of a new agreement, the several powers will be free to build such warships as they may consider necessary and can afford.

BIBLIOGRAPHY

I. *The Far East*[1]

1. GENERAL WORKS

BADDELY, J. F. Russia, Mongolia, China, being some record of the relations between them from the beginning of the XVIIth century to the death of the Tsar Alexei Mikhailovitch, 1602–1676 (2 vols.). Macmillan, London, 1919.

BARNES, J. (editor). Empire in the East. Doubleday, Doran, New York, 1934.

BASTIAN, A. Die Volker des östlichen Asien. Wigand, Leipzig, 1866.

BEAZLEY, C. R. The Dawn of Modern Geography. Clarendon Press, Oxford, 1897–1906.

BLAND, J. O. P. China, Japan, and Korea. Scribner, New York, 1921.

BOOKWALTER, J. W. Siberia and Central Asia. Stokes, New York, 1899.

BRANDT, M. VON. Drei Jahre ostasiatische Politik, 1894 bis 1897. Strecker & Moser, Stuttgart, 1897.

BRETSCHNEIDER, E. Mediaeval Researches from Eastern Asiatic Sources. K. Paul, Trench, Trübner & Co., London, 1910.

BUELL, R. L. The Washington Conference. Appleton, New York, 1922.

CAHEN, G. Histoire des relations de la Russie avec la Chine sous Pierre le Grand (1689–1730). Alcan, Paris, 1912.

CAMPBELL, W. Formosa under the Dutch. K. Paul, Trench, Trübner & Co., London, 1903.

CHABOT, J. B. Histoire de Mar Jabalaha III, patriarche nestorien. Paris, 1895.

CHAVANNES, E. Voyages des pèlerins bouddhiques. Leroux, Paris, 1895.

CHUNG, H. The Oriental Policy of the United States. Revell, New York, 1910.

COOLIDGE, A. C. The United States as a World Power. Macmillan, New York, 1908.

CORDIER, H. Le Christianisme en Chine et en Asie sous les Mongols. Paris, 1917.

[1] For the convenience of the student the works in this bibliography are arranged topically according to the following pattern:

COURANT, M. La Sibérie, colonie russe, jusqu'à la construction du Transsibérien. Alcan, Paris, 1920.

DENNETT, T. Americans in Eastern Asia. Macmillan, New York, 1922.

DENNETT, T. John Hay, from Poetry to Politics. Dodd, New York, 1934.

DENNETT, T. Roosevelt and the Russo-Japanese War. Doubleday, Page, New York, 1925.

DENNIS, A. L. P. Adventures in American Diplomacy, 1896–1906. Dutton, New York, 1928.

DENNIS, A. L. P. The Anglo-Japanese Alliance. Univ. of California Press, Berkeley, 1923.

DENNIS, A. L. P. The Foreign Policies of Soviet Russia. Dutton, New York, 1924.

DICKENSON, G. L. An Essay on the Civilizations of India, China, and Japan. J. M. Dent & Sons, London, 1914.

DOUGLAS, R. K. Europe and the Far East, 1506–1912 (revised edition). Cambridge Univ. Press, London, 1913.

DRIAULT, E. La Question d'Extrême-Orient. Alcan, Paris, 1908.

DUTCHER, G. M. The Political Awakening of the East. Abingdon Press, New York, 1925.

ELIOT, SIR C. N. E. Hinduism and Buddhism, an Historical Sketch (3 vols.). Arnold, London, 1921.

FERRAND, G. Relations de voyages et de textes géographiques arabes, persans et turcs relatifs à l'Extrême-Orient du VIIIᵉ au XVIIIᵉ siècles. Leroux, Paris, 1913.

FOSTER, J. W. American Diplomacy in the Orient. Houghton, Boston, 1903.

FOSTER, J. W. Diplomatic Memoirs (2 vols.). Houghton, Boston, 1909.

FRANKE, O. Die Grossmächte in Ostasien von 1894 bis 1914. Westermann, Braunschweig, 1923.

GALLAGHER, P. America's Aims and Asia's Aspirations. Century, New York, 1920.

GOLDER, F. A. Russian Expansion on the Pacific, 1641–1850. A. H. Clark & Co., Cleveland, 1914.

GRAVES, W. S. America's Siberian Adventure, 1918–1920. Jonathan Cape, New York, 1931.

GROOT, J. J. M. DE. Chinesische Urkunden zur Geschichte Asiens (2 vols.). De Gruyter, Berlin, 1921–1926.

GROUSSET, R. Histoire de l'Extrême-Orient (2 vols.). Geuthner, Paris, 1929.

HACKIN, J., and others. Asiatic Mythology (translated by F. M. Atkinson). George G. Harrap & Co., London, 1932.

HAMILTON, C. H. Buddhism in India, Ceylon, China and Japan: a Reading Guide. Univ. of Chicago Press, Chicago, 1931.

HARRIS, N. D. Europe and the East. Houghton, Boston, 1926.

HARRISON, E. J. Peace or War East of Baikal? Kelly & Walsh, Shanghai, 1910.

HINCKLEY, F. E. American Consular Jurisdiction in the Orient. Loudermilk, Washington, 1906.

HORNBECK, S. K. Contemporary Politics in the Far East. Appleton, New York, 1916.

HUC, É. R. Travels in Tartary, Thibet, and China, 1844–1846 (2 vols.; translated by William Hazlitt; introduction by Paul Pelliot). George Routledge & Sons, London, 1928.

HUNTINGTON, E. The Pulse of Asia: a Journey in Central Asia Illustrating the Geographic Basis of History. Houghton, Boston, 1907.

JONES, J. W., and BADGER, G. P. The Travels of Ludovico di Varthema, 1503–1508. Hakluyt Society, London, 1863.

KING-HALL, S. Western Civilization in the Far East. Scribner, New York, 1924.

KRAUSE, F. E. A. Geschichte Ostasiens. Vandenhoeck & Ruprecht, Göttingen, 1925.

KRAUSSE, A. Russia in Asia. Holt, New York, 1899.

KÜMMEL, O. Die Kunst Ostasiens. Cassirer, Berlin, 1921.

LAWTON, L. Empires of the Far East (2 vols.). G. Richards, London, 1912.

McCORDOCK, S. British Far Eastern Policy, 1894–1900. Columbia Univ. Press, New York, 1931.

MAHAN, A. T. The Problem of Asia and its Effect upon International Policies. Little, Boston, 1900.

MILBURN, W. Oriental Commerce. Black, Parry & Co., London, 1813.

MILLARD, T. F. America and the Far Eastern Question. Moffat, New York, 1909.

MILLARD, T. F. Conflict of Policies in Asia. Century, New York, 1924.

MILLARD, T. F. Democracy and the Eastern Question. Century, New York, 1919.

MILLARD, T. F. The New Far East. Scribner, New York, 1906.

MONTGOMERY, J. A. The History of Yaballaha III, Nestorian Patriarch, and of his Vicar, Bar Sauma. Columbia Univ. Press, New York, 1927.

MORSE, H. B., and MacNAIR, H. F. Far Eastern International Relations. Houghton, Boston, 1931.

NORMAN, H. The Peoples and Politics of the Far East. Scribner, New York, 1895.

NORTON, H. K. The Far Eastern Republic of Siberia. Holt, New York, 1923.

PARKER, E. H. A Thousand Years of the Tartars. Sampson Low, Marston & Co., London, 1895.

PASVOLSKY, L. Russia in the Far East. Macmillan, New York, 1922.

PEFFER, N. The White Man's Dilemma. Day, New York, 1927.

REINSCH, P. S. Intellectual and Political Currents in the Far East. Houghton, Boston, 1911.

REINSCH, P. S. World Politics at the End of the Nineteenth Century as Influenced by the Oriental Situation. Macmillan, New York, 1900.

RÉMUSAT, A. Mélanges asiatiques, ou choix de morceaux critiques et des mémoires relatifs aux religions, aux sciences, aux coutumes, à l'histoire et à la géographie des nations orientales (2 vols.). Doudey-Dupré, Paris, 1825–1826.

RÉMUSAT, A. Nouveaux mélanges asiatiques. Schubart et Heideloff, Paris, 1829.

ROBERTS, S. H. History of French Colonial Policy, 1870–1925. P. S. King & Son, London, 1929.

ROCKHILL, W. W. Notes on the Relations and Trade of China with the Eastern Archipelago and the Coast of the Indian Ocean during the Fourteenth Century. Brill, Leiden, 1915.

SIMPSON, B.L. An Indiscreet Chronicle from the Pacific. Dodd, New York, 1922.

SKRINE, F. H. The Expansion of Russia. Cambridge Univ. Press, London, 1903.

SOYESHIMA, M., and KUO, P. W. Oriental Interpretations of the Far Eastern Question. Univ. of Chicago Press, Chicago, 1925.

STAMP, L. D. Asia: an Economic and Regional Geography. Dutton, New York, 1929.

TREAT, P. J. The Far East, a Political and Diplomatic History. Harper, New York, 1928.

VINACKE, H. M. A History of the Far East in Modern Times. Knopf, New York, 1928.

VLADIMIR (pseudonym for Volpicelli, Z.). Russia on the Pacific and the Siberian Railway. Sampson Low, Marston & Co., London, 1899.

WARE, E. E. Business and Politics in the Far East. Yale Univ. Press, New Haven, 1932.

WESSELS, C. Early Jesuit Travellers in Central Asia, 1603–1721. Nijhoff, the Hague, 1924.

WOODHEAD, H. G. W., ARNOLD, J., and NORTON, H. K. Occidental Interpretations of the Far Eastern Problem. Univ. of Chicago Press, Chicago, 1926.

YAKHONTOFF, V. A. Russia and the Soviet Union in the Far East. Coward-McCann, New York, 1931.

YARMOLINSKY, A. (translator and editor). Memoirs of Count Witte. Doubleday, Page, Garden City, 1921.

YULE, SIR H. The Book of Ser Marco Polo (2 vols., revised by Henri Cordier). J. Murray, London, 1903.

YULE, SIR H. Cathay and the Way Thither (4 vols., revised by Henri Cordier). Hakluyt Society, London, 1913–1916.

Mémoires concernant l'Asie orientale: Inde, Asie centrale, Extrême-Orient (3 vols.). L'Académie des Inscriptions et Belles-Lettres, Paris, 1913–1916–1919.

The Washington Conference. Conference on the Limitation of Armament. Senate Document No. 126, 67th Cong., 2d Sess. Government Printing Office, Washington, 1922.

2. PERIODICALS

Asia Major. Leipzig, 1924– .

Bulletin de l'École française d'Extrême-Orient. Hanoi, 1901– .

Bulletin of the School of Oriental Studies. London, 1917– .

The Burlington Magazine. London, 1903– .

Current History. N. Y. Times Co., New York, 1914– .

Journal of the American Oriental Society. New Haven, 1880– .

Journal asiatique. Paris, 1822– .

Journal of the Royal Asiatic Society. London, 1834– .

Ostasiatische Zeitschrift. Berlin, 1912– .

Revue des arts asiatiques. Paris, 1924– .

T'oung Pao. Brill, Leiden, 1890– .

II. *China*

1. GENERAL WORKS

ALLEN, C. W. The Makers of Cathay. Presbyterian Mission Press, Shanghai, 1925.

AMIOT, J. M., and others. Mémoires concernant l'histoire, les sciences, les arts, les mœurs, les usages, etc., des Chinois: par les missionnaires de Pékin (Amiot, Bourgeois, Cibot, Ko, Poiret, etc.) (15 vols.). Nyon, Paris, 1776–1791.

BACKHOUSE, E., and BLAND, J. O. P. Annals and Memoirs of the Court of Peking. Houghton, Boston, 1914.

BASHFORD, J. W. China, an Interpretation. Abingdon Press, New York, 1916.

BAU, M. J. Modern Democracy in China. Commercial Press, Shanghai, 1923.

BENEDETTO, L. F. Marco Polo, Il Milione. Olschki, Florence, 1928.

BLAKESLEE, G. H. (editor). Recent Developments in China. Stechert, New York, 1913.

BLAND, J. O. P. Recent Events and Present Policies in China. Lippincott, Philadelphia, 1912.

BLAND, J. O. P., and BACKHOUSE, E. China under the Empress Dowager. Lippincott, Philadelphia, 1910.

BOULGER, D. C. China. Collier, New York, 1900.

BREDON, J. Sir Robert Hart. Dutton, New York, 1909.

BRINKLEY, F. China: its History, Arts, and Literature (4 vols.). Millet, Boston, 1902.

CANTLIE, J., and JONES, C. S. Sun Yat-sen and the Awakening of China. Jarrold & Sons, London, 1912.

CARTER, T. F. The Invention of Printing in China and its Spread Westward. Columbia Univ. Press, New York, 1924.

CHAVANNES, E. (translator). Les Mémoires historiques de Se-ma Ts'ien. Paris, 1895–1905.

CHEN TA. Chinese Migrations. U. S. Government Printing Office, Washington, 1923.

CHENG, S. G. Modern China: a Political Study. Clarendon Press, Oxford, 1919.

CLARK, G. The Great Wall Crumbles. Macmillan, New York, 1935.

CORDIER, H. Bibliotheca Sinica: Dictionnaire bibliographique des ouvrages relatifs à l'empire chinois (second edition; 4 vols.). Guilmoto, Paris, 1904–1908.

CORDIER, H. Bibliotheca Sinica: Supplement. Geuthner, Paris, 1924.

CORDIER, H. Histoire générale de la Chine (3 vols.). Geuthner, Paris, 1920.

COULING, S. Encyclopaedia Sinica. Clarendon Press, Oxford, 1917.

CROLY, H. Willard Straight. Macmillan, New York, 1924.

DUTCHER, G. M. The Political Awakening of the Far East. Abingdon Press, New York, 1925.

EDMUNDS, C. K. Modern Education in China. U. S. Government Printing Office, Washington, 1919.

FIELD, F. V. American Participation in the China Consortiums. Univ. of Chicago Press, Chicago, 1931.

FRANKE, O. Geschichte des chinesischen Reiches, Band I. De Gruyter, Berlin, 1930.

GAMBLE, S. D. Peking, a Social Survey. Doran, New York, 1921.

GILBERT, R. What's Wrong with China. J. Murray, London, 1926.

GILES, H. A. China and the Chinese. Columbia Univ. Press, New York, 1902.

GILES, H. A. China and the Manchus. Cambridge Univ. Press, London, 1912.

GILES, H. A. A Chinese Biographical Dictionary. Kelley & Walsh, Shanghai, 1898.

GILES, H. A. The Civilization of China. Holt, New York, 1911.

GILES, L. (editor and translator). Sun Tzu on the Art of War: the Oldest Military Treatise in the World. Luzac, London, 1910.

GOODNOW, F. K. China: an Analysis. Johns Hopkins Press, Baltimore, 1926.

GOWAN, H. H., and HALL, J. W. Outline History of China. Appleton, New York, 1926.

GRANET, M. Chinese Civilization (English translation by K. E. Innes and M. R. Brailsford). Knopf, New York, 1930.

GRANET, M. Danses et légendes de la Chine ancienne (2 vols.). Alcan, Paris, 1926.

GRANET, M. Fêtes et chansons anciennes de la Chine (second edition). Leroux, Paris, 1929.

GRAY, J. H. China, a History of the Laws, Manners, and Customs of the People (2 vols.). Macmillan, London, 1878.

GROUSSET, R. The Civilization of the East. China (translated by Catherine Alison Phillips). A. A. Knopf, New York, 1934.

GUTZLAFF, C. A Sketch of Chinese History, Ancient and Modern: comprising a Retrospect of the Foreign Intercourse and Trade with China (2 vols.). Smith, Elder & Co., London, 1834.

HAIL, W. J. Tsêng Kuo-Fan and the Taiping Rebellion. Yale Univ. Press, New Haven, 1927.

HIRTH, F. The Ancient History of China, to the End of the Chou Dynasty, 249 B.C. Columbia Univ. Press, New York, 1908.

HODGKIN, H. T. China in the Family of Nations. George Allen & Unwin, London, 1923.

HODOUS, L. Folkways in China. Probsthain, London, 1929.

HORNBECK, S. K. China Today: Political. World Peace Foundation, Boston, 1927.

HUC, E. R. Travels in Tartary, Thibet, and China, 1844–1846 (2 vols.; translated by W. Hazlitt; introduction by P. Pelliot). George Routledge & Sons, London, 1928.

HUMMEL, A. The Library of Congress, Division of Chinese Literature, Annual Reports. U. S. Government Printing Office, Washington, 1929–   .

KARLGREN, B. Sound and Symbol in China. Clarendon Press, Oxford, 1923.

KING, L. M. China in Turmoil, Studies in Personality. Heath, Cranton, London, 1927.

KULP, D. H. Country Life in South China: the Sociology of Familism. Columbia Univ. Press, New York, 1925.

KUO, P. W. The Chinese System of Education. Columbia Univ. Press, New York, 1915.

LATOURETTE, K. S. The Chinese: their History and Culture. Macmillan, New York, 1934.

LATOURETTE, K. S. The Development of China. Houghton, Boston, 1924.

LATTIMORE, O. The Mongols of Manchuria. Day, New York, 1934.

LEGENDRE, A. F. La Civilisation chinoise moderne. Payot, Paris, 1926.

LI UNG-BING. Outlines of Chinese History. Commercial Press, Shanghai, 1914.

MACGOWAN, J. Imperial History of China. Presbyterian Mission Press, Shanghai, 1906.

MACNAIR, H. F. China in Revolution. Chicago Univ. Press, Chicago, 1931.

MACNAIR, H. F. China's International Relations and Other Essays. Commercial Press, Shanghai, 1925.

MACNAIR, H. F. China's New Nationalism. Stechert, New York, 1925.

MACNAIR, H. F. Modern Chinese History: Selected Readings. Commercial Press, Shanghai, 1923.

MAILLA, J. A. M. DE M. DE. Histoire générale de la Chine (13 vols.). Pierres, Paris, 1777–1785.

MASPERO, H. La Chine antique. Broccard, Paris, 1927.

MAYERS, W. F. The Chinese Reader's Manual: a Handbook of Biological, Historical, Mythological, and General Literary Reference (second edition). Probsthain, London, 1910.

MEADOWS, T. T. The Chinese and their Rebellions. Smith, Elder & Co., London, 1856.

MILLARD, T. F. The Great War in the Far East. Mercantile Printing Co., Shanghai, 1915.

MONROE, P. China, a Nation in Evolution. Macmillan, New York, 1927.

PARKER, E. H. China: her History, Diplomacy, and Commerce. Murray, London, 1919.

PEFFER, N. China: the Collapse of a Civilization. Day, New York, 1930.

PLAYFAIR, G. M. H. The Cities and Towns of China. Kelly & Walsh, Shanghai, 1910.

POTT, F. L. H. A Sketch of Chinese History. Kelly & Walsh, Shanghai, 1923.

RANTOUL, R. S. Frederick Townsend Ward. Essex Institute, Salem, 1908.

ROSS, E. A. The Changing Chinese. Century, New York, 1911.

RUSSELL, B. The Problem of China. Century, New York, 1922.

SAINSON, C. Nan-tchao Ye-che, traduction d'une histoire de l'ancien Yunnan. Leroux, Paris, 1904.

SERGEANT, P. W. The Great Empress Dowager of China. Dodd, New York, 1911.

SIMPSON, B. L. ("Putnam Weale"). The Fight for the Republic in China. Hunt, London, 1918.

SIMPSON, B. L. ("Putnam Weale"). The Vanished Empire. Macmillan, London, 1926.

SIMPSON, B. L. ("Putnam Weale"). Why China Sees Red. Dodd, New York, 1925.

STAUNTON, SIR G. T. Miscellaneous Notices Respecting China (revised edition). Murray, London, 1850.

SUN YAT-SEN. The International Development of China. Putnam, New York, 1929.

T'ANG LEANG-LI. China in Revolt: How a Civilization Became a Nation. N. Douglas, London, 1927.

T'ANG LEANG-LI. The Inner History of the Chinese Revolution. Dutton, New York, 1930.

TERRIEN DE LACOUPERIE, A. Western Origin of the Early Chinese Civilization. Asher & Co., London, 1894.

TYAU, M. T. Z. China Awakened. Macmillan, New York, 1922.

TYAU, M. T. Z. China's New Constitution and International Problems. Commercial Press, Shanghai, 1918.

VAN DORN, H. A. Twenty Years of the Chinese Republic. Knopf, New York, 1932.

WERNER, E. T. C. China of the Chinese. Scribner, New York, 1919.

WIEGER, L. La Chine à travers les âges, hommes et choses. Impr. de la Mis. Cath., Hsienhsien, 1920.

WIEGER, L. Textes historiques. Impr. de la Mis. Cath., Hochienfu, 1903–1906.

WILHELM, R. A Short History of Chinese Civilization (translated by Joan Joshua). Viking Press, New York, 1929.

WILHELM, R. The Soul of China (English translation). Harcourt, New York, 1928.

WILLIAMS, E. T. China: Yesterday and Today (revised edition). Crowell, New York, 1927.

WILLIAMS, E. T. A Short History of China. Harper, New York, 1928.

WILLIAMS, S. W. The Middle Kingdom. Scribner, New York, 1883.

WILSON, A. The "Ever-Victorious" Army, a History of the Chinese Campaign under Lt.-Col. C. G. Gordon. Wm. Blackwood & Sons, Edinburgh, 1868.

WOODHEAD, H. G. W. The Truth about the Chinese Republic. Hurst & Blackett, London, 1926.

WU CHAO-CHU. A Nationalist Program for China. Yale Univ. Press, New Haven, 1929.

YEN, J. Y. C. The Mass Education Movement in China. Stechert, New York, 1925.

ZEN, S. H. C. (editor). Symposium on Chinese Culture. China Institute of Pacific Relations, Shanghai, 1931.

2. PERIODICALS

The China Review, Hongkong, 1872–1901.

China Weekly Review (formerly *Millard's Review*). Shanghai.

The China Year Book. Tientsin and Shanghai.

The Chinese Political and Social Science Review. Peking.

The Chinese Recorder. Shanghai.

The Chinese Repository. Canton, May 1832 to December 1851.

The Far Eastern Review. Shanghai.

Journal of the Royal Asiatic Society (North China Branch). Shanghai.

North China Herald (weekly edition of the *North China Daily News*). Shanghai.

Palaeontologica Sinica. Peking.

3. ARCHAEOLOGY, ANTHROPOLOGY, AND GEOGRAPHY

ANDERSSON, J. G. Children of the Yellow Earth: Studies in Prehistoric China. K. Paul, Trench, Trübner & Co., London, 1934.

ANDERSSON, J. G. "An Early Chinese Culture," *Bulletin of the Geological Survey of China,* Peking, 1923.

ANDERSSON, J. G. "Preliminary Report on the Archaeological Researches in Kansu," *Memoir of the Geological Survey of China,* Peking, 1925.

ARNE, T. J. "Painted Stone-Age Pottery from the Province of Honan," *Palaeontologica Sinica,* Peking, 1925.

BLACK, D. "The Human Skeletal Remains from the Sha Kuo T'un Cave Deposit in Comparison with those from Yang Shao Tsun and with Recent North China Skeletal Material," *Palaeontologica Sinica,* Peking, 1925.

BLACK, D. "The Lower Molar Hominid Tooth from the Chou Kou Tien Deposit," *Palaeontologica Sinica,* Peking, 1927.

BUXTON, L. H. D. China, the Land and the People. Clarendon Press, Oxford, 1929.

CHALFANT, F. H. "Early Chinese Writing (Yin Tortoise Shells)," *Memoirs of the Carnegie Museum*, Vol. IV, No. 1, 1906.

CHARDIN, T. DE, and LICENT, E. Paleolithic Industry in Northern China. Geological Survey of China, Peking, 1924.

CHAVANNES, E. "La Divination par l'écaille de tortue dans la haute antiquité chinoise d'après un livre de M. Lo Tchen-yu," *Journal Asiatique*, Vol. X, XVII, pp. 127–137, Paris, 1911.

CRESSEY, G. B. China's Geographical Foundations, a Survey of the Land and its People. McGraw, New York, 1934.

FORKE, A. Der Ursprung der Chinesen auf Grund ihrer alten Bilderschrift. L. Friederichson & Co., Hamburg, 1925.

FORKE, A. Die Völker Chinas. K. Curtius, Berlin, 1907.

HOPKINS, L. C. "Chinese Writing in the Chou Dynasty in the Light of Recent Discoveries," *Journal of the Royal Asiatic Society*, pp. 1011–1038, London, 1911.

LI CHI. The Formation of the Chinese People, an Anthropological Enquiry. Harvard Univ. Press, Cambridge, 1928.

LICENT, E. Comptes rendus de dix années (1914–1923) de séjour et d'exploration dans le bassin du Fleuve Jaune. La Librairie française, Tientsin, 1924.

RICHARD, L. Comprehensive Geography of China. T'ousèwè Press, Shanghai, 1908.

ROSS, J. The Origin of the Chinese People. Oliphants, London, 1916.

SHIROKOGOROFF, S. Anthropology of Eastern China and Kwangtung Province. North China Branch, Royal Asiatic Society, Shanghai, 1925.

SHIROKOGOROFF, S. Anthropology of Northern China. North China Branch, Royal Asiatic Society, Shanghai, 1923.

4. ART, PHILOSOPHY, AND LITERATURE

ARLINGTON, L. C. The Chinese Drama from the Earliest Times until Today. Kelly & Walsh, Shanghai, 1930.

ASHTON, L. Introduction to the Study of Chinese Sculpture. Benn, London, 1924.

AYSCOUGH, F. Tu Fu, the Autobiography of a Chinese Poet, A.D. 712–770. Arranged from his Poems. Houghton, Boston, 1929–1934.

BINYON, L. The G. Eumorfopoulos Collection, Early Chinese Frescos. Benn, London, 1927.

BINYON, L. Painting in the Far East (third edition). Arnold, London, 1923.

BIOT, E. Essai sur l'histoire de l'instruction publique en Chine et de la corporation de lettrés, depuis les anciens temps jusqu'à nos jours. Benjamin Duprat, Paris, 1847.

BOERSCHMANN, E. Chinesische Architektur (2 vols.). Wasmuth, Berlin, 1925.

BOERSCHMANN, E. Chinesische Baukeramik. Ludtke, Berlin, 1927.

BREWITT-TAYLOR, C. H. (translator). San Kuo, or Romance of the Three Kingdoms (2 vols.). Kelly & Walsh, Shanghai, 1925–1926.

BRUCE, J. P. Chu Hsi and his Masters, Introduction to Chu Hsi and the Sung School of Philosophy. Probsthain, London, 1923.

BRUCE, J. P. (translator). Chu Hsi: Philosophy of Human Nature. Probsthain, London, 1922.

BUSHELL, S. W. Chinese Art (revised edition; 2 vols.). H. M. Stationery Office, London, 1909.

BYNNER, W., and KIANG KANG-HU (translators). The Jade Mountain: a Chinese Anthology, being Three Hundred Poems of the T'ang Dynasty, 618–906. Knopf, New York, 1929.

CARUS, P. (translator). The Canon of Reason and Virtue: being Lao-tze's Tao-teh-king, Chinese-English, with Introduction, Transliteration, and Notes. Open Court Publishing Co., Chicago, 1927.

CHAVANNES, E. Mission archéologique dans la Chine septentrionale (2 vols.). Leroux, Paris, 1913–1915.

CHAVANNES, E. La Sculpture sur pierre en Chine au temps des deux dynasties Han. Leroux, Paris, 1893.

CREEL, H. G. Sinism. Open Court Publishing Co., Chicago, 1929.

D'ARDENNE DE TIZAC, H. Animals in Chinese Art. Benn Brothers, London, 1923.

D'ARDENNE DE TIZAC, H. L'Art chinois classique. Laurens, Paris, 1926.

DUBBS, H. H. Hsüntze, the Moulder of Confucianism. Probsthain, London, 1927.

DUBBS, H. H. (translator). The Works of Hsüntze. Probsthain, London, 1928.

DUYVENDAK, J. J. L. (translator). The Book of Lord Shang, a Classic of the Chinese School of Law. Probsthain, London, 1928.

FENOLLOSA, E. F. Epochs of Chinese and Japanese Art. Stokes, New York, 1913.

FISCHER, O. Chinesische Landschaftsmalerei. K. Wolff, Munich, 1921.

FISCHER, O. Die chinesische Malerei der Han-Dynastie. P. Neff, Berlin, 1930.

FORKE, ALFRED. Geschichte der alten chinesischen Philosophie. L. Friederichson & Co., Hamburg, 1927.

FORKE, ALFRED. Miscellaneous Essays of Wang Ch'ung. Berlin, 1911.

FORKE, ALFRED. Philosophical Essays of Wang Ch'ung. London, 1907.

FORKE, ALFRED. The World Conception of the Chinese. Probsthain, London, 1925.

FORKE, ANTON (translator). Yang Chu's Garden of Pleasure. J. Murray, London, 1912.

FUNG YU-LAN. A Comparative Study of Life Ideals. Commercial Press, Shanghai, 1927.

GILES, H. A. Chuang Tzü: Mystic, Moralist, and Social Reformer. Quaritch, London, 1926.

GILES, H. A. History of Chinese Literature. Appleton, New York, 1915.

GILES, H. A. Musings of a Chinese Mystic. J. Murray, London, 1920.

GILES, L. Taoist Teachings from the Book of Lieh Tzu. J. Murray, London, 1925.

HENKE, F. G. The Philosophy of Wang Yang-ming. Univ. of Chicago Press, Chicago, 1916.

HENTZE, C. Chinese Tomb Figures: a Study in the Beliefs and Folklore of Ancient China. Goldston, London, 1928.

HETHERINGTON, A. L. The Early Ceramic Wares of China. Scribner, New York, 1922.

HOBSON, R. L. Chinese Pottery and Porcelain (2 vols.). Cassell & Co., London, 1915.

HOBSON, R. L. George Eumorfopoulos Collection: Catalogue of the Chinese, Corean, and Persian Pottery and Porcelain (6 vols.). Ernest Benn, London, 1925–1928.

HOBSON, R. L. The Later Ceramic Wares of China. Ernest Benn, London, 1925.

HOBSON, R. L. The Wares of the Ming Dynasty. Benn Brothers, London, 1923.

HOBSON, R. L., and HETHERINGTON, A. L. The Art of Chinese Pottery from the Han to the Ming. Ernest Benn, London, 1923.

HU SHIH. Development of the Logical Method in Ancient China. Commercial Press, Shanghai, 1922.

JULIEN, S. (translator). Le Livre de la Voie et de la Virtu. L'Imprimerie Royale, Paris, 1842.

KOOP, A. J. Early Chinese Bronzes. Ernest Benn, London, 1924.

KÜMMEL, O. Chinesische Kunst. Cassirer, Berlin, 1930.

LAUFER, B. Beginnings of Porcelain in China. Field Museum of Nat. Hist., Chicago, 1917.

LAUFER, B. Chinese Clay Figures. Field Museum of Nat. Hist., Chicago, 1914.

LAUFER, B. Chinese Gravestone Sculptures of the Han Period. Stechert, New York, 1911.

LAUFER, B. Chinese Pottery of the Han Dynasty. Brill, Leiden, 1909.

LEGGE, J. The Chinese Classics (text, translation, and notes). The author, Hongkong, 1861–1872. Second edition, Clarendon Press, Oxford, 1893–1895.

MARGOULIÈS, G. Évolution de la prose artistique chinoise. Encyclopädie Verlag, Munich, 1929.

MEI, Y. P. (translator). The Ethical and Political Works of Motse. Probsthain, London, 1930.

OBATA, S. (translator). The Works of Li Po. Dutton, New York, 1922.

PELLIOT, P. Les Grottes de Touen-houang: peintures et sculptures bouddhiques des époques des Wei, des T'ang, et des Song (6 portfolios). Geuthner, Paris, 1914–1924.

PELLIOT, P. Jades archaïques de Chine, Collection Loo. Van Oest, Paris, 1925.

PETRUCCI, R. Chinese Painters. Brentano's, New York, 1920.

ROSTOVTZEFF, M. I. The Animal Style in South Russia and China. Princeton Univ. Press, Princeton, 1929.

SALMONY, A. Chinesische Landschaftsmalerei. Wasmuth, Berlin, 1920.

SIREN, O. Chinese Sculpture from the Vth to the XIVth century. Ernest Benn, London, 1925.

SIREN, O. Histoire des arts anciens de la Chine (4 vols.). Van Oest, Paris, 1929–1930.

SIREN, O. The Imperial Palaces of Peking (3 vols.). Van Oest, Paris, 1926.

SOOTHILL, W. E. The Analects of Confucius (text, translation, and notes). Fukuin Publishing Co., Yokohama, 1910.

STEIN, SIR M. A. The Thousand Buddhas: Ancient Buddhist Paintings from the Cave Temples of Tunhuang on the Western Frontier of China. Quaritch, London, 1922.

SUZUKI, D. T. A Brief History of Chinese Philosophy. Probsthain, London, 1914.

TCHEOU TO-YI. Bronzes antiques de Chine, Collection Loo. Van Oest, Paris, 1924.

VORETZSCH, E. A. Altchinesische Bronzen. Springer, Berlin, 1924.

WALEY, A. (translator). A Hundred and Seventy Chinese Poems. Constable & Co., London, 1918.

WALEY, A. Introduction to the Study of Chinese Painting. Scribner, New York, 1923.

WALEY, A. (translator). More Translations from the Chinese. Knopf, New York, 1919.

WALEY, A. (translator). "The Temple" and Other Poems (with an Introductory Essay on Early Chinese Poetry and an Appendix on the Development of Different Metrical Forms). Knopf, New York, 1923.

WALEY, A. The Way and its Power. A Study of the Tao Te Ching and its Place in Chinese Thought. Houghton, Boston, 1935.

WIEGER, L. Textes philosophiques. Impr. de la Mis. Cath., Hochienfu, 1906.

YETTS, W. P. Chinese Bronzes. Ernest Benn, London, 1925.

YETTS, W. P. George Eumorfopoulos Collection: Catalogue of the Chinese and Corean Bronzes, Sculpture, Jade, Jewelry, and Other Objects. Ernest Benn, London, 1929–1930.

ZÜCKER, A. E. The Chinese Theater. Little, Boston, 1925.

5. RELIGION

BEAL, S. (translator). Buddhist Records of the Western World; translated from the Chinese of Hiuen Tsiang (A.D. 629). K. Paul, Trench, Trübner & Co., London, 1906 (?).

BEAL, S. (translator). The Life of Hiuen Tsiang, by the Shaman Hwui Li. K. Paul, Trench, Trübner & Co., London, 1914.

BROOMHALL, M. Islam in China. Morgan & Scott, London, 1910.

CHAVANNES, E. (translator). Mémoire composé à l'époque de la grande dynastie T'ang sur les religieux éminents qui allèrent chercher la loi dans les pays d'Occident, par I-tsing. Leroux, Paris, 1894.

CHAVANNES, E., and PELLIOT, P. Un Traité manichéen retrouvé en Chine. (Reprint from *Journal asiatique*, 1911.) Paris, 1912.

CLENNELL, W. J. The Historical Development of Religion in China. Theosophical Publishing House, London, 1926.

D'OLLONE, C. A. M. C., and others. Recherches sur les musulmans chinois, par d'Ollone, de Fleurelle, Lepage, de Boyve, A. Vissière, et E. Blochet. Leroux, Paris, 1911.

DORÉ, H. Recherches sur les superstitions en Chine (14 vols.). Impr. de la Mis. Cath., Shanghai, 1911–1919. English edition (8 vols.; translated by Kennelly). Shanghai, 1914–1926.

EDKINS, J. Chinese Buddhism. K. Paul, Trench, Trübner & Co., London, 1890.

GETTY, A. The Gods of Northern Buddhism: their History, Iconography, and Evolution through the Northern Buddhist Countries (second edition). Clarendon Press, Oxford, 1928.

GILES, H. A. The Travels of Fa-hsien (399–414 A.D.). The Cambridge Univ. Press, London, 1923.

GRANET, M. La Religion des chinois. Gauthier-Villars, Paris, 1922.

GROOT, J. J. M. DE. Religion in China: Universism. Putnam, New York, 1912.

GROOT, J. J. M. DE. The Religion of the Chinese. Macmillan, New York, 1910.

GROOT, J. J. M. DE. The Religious System of China (6 vols.). Brill, Leiden, 1892–1910.

GROOT, J. J. M. DE. Sectarianism and Religious Persecution in China. Amsterdam, 1903–1904.

HAVRE, H. La Stèle chrétienne de Si-ngan-fu. Impr. de la Mis. Cath., Shanghai, 1895.

HODOUS, L. Buddhism and Buddhists in China. Macmillan, New York, 1924.

JOHNSTON, R. F. Buddhist China. Dutton, New York, 1913.

LATOURETTE, K. S. A History of Christian Missions in China. Macmillan, New York, 1929.

LEGGE, J. (translator). A Record of Buddhist Kingdoms: Being an Account by the Chinese Monk Fa-Hien of his Travels in India and Ceylon (A.D. 399–414). Clarendon Press, Oxford, 1886.

MOULE, A. C. Christians in China, before the Year 1550. Macmillan, New York, 1930.

NAU, F. L'Expansion nestorienne en Asie. Paris, 1913.

PORTER, L. C. China's Challenge to Christianity. Missionary Education Movement, New York, 1924.

SHRYOCK, J. K. The Temples of Anking and their Cults: a Study of Modern Chinese Religion. Geuthner, Paris, 1931.

SOOTHILL, W. E. (translator). The Lotus of the Wonderful Law. Clarendon Press, Oxford, 1930.

SOOTHILL, W. E. The Three Religions of China. Oxford, London, 1913.

WATTERS, T. (translator). On Yuan Chwang's Travels in India, 629–645 A.D. (2 vols.). Royal Asiatic Society, London, 1904–1905.

WIEGER, L. Bouddhisme chinois. Impr. de la Mis. Cath., Hochienfu, 1910.

6. POLITICAL INSTITUTIONS AND THEORIES

ALABASTER, E. Notes and Commentaries on Chinese Criminal Law and Cognate Topics, with Special Relation to Ruling Cases. Luzac, London, 1899.

BIOT, E. Le Tcheou-li, ou rites des Tcheou. A l'Imprimerie Nationale, Paris, 1851.

CHAPMAN, H. O. The Chinese Revolution, 1926–1927. Constable & Co., London, 1928.

CHEN WAN-LI. Le Développement des institutions politiques de la Chine. Jouve, Paris, 1926.

GALE, E. M. (translator). Huan K'uan, Discourses on Salt and Iron: Debate on State Control of Commerce and Industry in Ancient China. Brill, Leiden, 1931.

HOLCOMBE, A. N. The Chinese Revolution. Harvard Univ. Press, Cambridge, 1930.

HSIEH, P. C. The Government of China (1644–1911). Johns Hopkins Press, Baltimore, 1925.

JAMIESON, G. Chinese Family and Commercial Law. Kelly & Walsh, Shanghai, 1921.

LIANG CHI-CHAO. History of Chinese Political Thought (translated by L. T. Chen). Harcourt, New York, 1930.

LIANG J'EN-KIE. Étude sur la jurisdiction administrative en Chine. Jouve, Paris, 1920.

MAYERS, W. F. The Chinese Government (second edition). Kelly & Walsh, Shanghai, 1886.

QUIGLEY, H. S. Chinese Politics Today. Univ. of Minnesota Press, Minneapolis, 1924.

STAUNTON, SIR G. T. (translator). Ta Tsing Leu Lee: Fundamental Laws and Supplementary Statutes of the Tsing Dynasty. T. Cadell & W. Davis, London, 1810.

THOMAS, E. D. Chinese Political Thought. Prentice-Hall, New York, 1927.

VINACKE, H. M. Modern Constitutional Development in China. Princeton Univ. Press, Princeton, 1920.

WILLIAMSON, H. R. Wang An Shih. Probsthain, London, 1935.

WILLOUGHBY, W. W. Constitutional Government in China. Carnegie Endowment for International Peace, Washington, 1922.

WOO, J. Le Mouvement constitutionnel chinois. Giard, Paris, 1925.

WOO, T. C. The Kuomintang and the Future of the Chinese Revolution. George Allen & Unwin, London, 1928.

YAKHONTOFF, V. A. The Chinese Soviets. Coward-McCann, New York, 1934.

YEN, H. L. A Survey of Constitutional Development in China. Longmans, New York, 1911.

7. ECONOMIC HISTORY

ARNOLD, J. Commercial Hand-book of China (3 vols.). U. S. Department of Commerce, Washington, 1919–1920–1926.

ARNOLD, J. Some Bigger Issues in China's Problems. Commercial Press, Shanghai, 1928.

BUCK, J. L. Chinese Farm Economy: a Study of 2866 Farms in Seventeen Localities and Seven Provinces in China. Univ. of Chicago Press, Chicago, 1930.

CHU, C. The Tariff Problem in China. Longmans, New York, 1916.

CLARK, G. Economic Rivalries in China. Yale Univ. Press, New Haven, 1932.

COLLINS, W. F. Mineral Enterprise in China. William Heinemann, London, 1918.

CONDLIFFE, J. B. China Today: Economic. World Peace Foundation, Boston, 1932.

COONS, A. G. The Foreign Public Debt of China. Univ. of Pennsylvania Press, Philadelphia, 1930.

CORDIER, H. Les Marchands hanistes de Canton. Brill, Leiden, 1902.

CURTIS, L. The Capital Question of China. Macmillan, New York, 1932.

FRANKE, O. Kêng Tschi T'u, Ackerbau und Seidengewinnung in China. L. Friederichson & Co., Hamburg, 1913.

HIGH, S. H. China's Place in the Sun. Macmillan, New York, 1922.

HOSIE, SIR A. Szechwan: its Products, Industries and Resources. Kelly & Walsh, Shanghai, 1922.

HSU, M. C. Railway Problems in China. Columbia Univ. Press, New York, 1915.

HUNTER, W. C. The "Fan Kwei" at Canton (second edition). Kelly & Walsh, Shanghai, 1911.

JERNIGAN, T. R. China in Law and Commerce. Macmillan, New York, 1905.

KANN, E. The Currencies of China: an Investigation of the Silver and Gold Transactions Affecting China, with a Section on Copper. Kelly & Walsh, Shanghai, 1927.

KENT, P. H. B. Railway Enterprise in China: an Account of its Origin and Development. Arnold, London, 1907.

KING, F. H. Farmers of Forty Centuries: or Permanent Agriculture in China, Korea, and Japan. Mrs. F. H. King, Madison, 1911.

LEE, F. E. Currency, Banking, and Finance in China. U. S. Government Printing Office, Washington, 1926.

MALLORY, W. H. China: Land of Famine. American Geographical Society, New York, 1926.

MORSE, H. B. The East India Company Trading to China. Harvard Univ. Press, Cambridge, 1926.

MORSE, H. B. The Gilds of China. Longmans, New York, 1909.

MORSE, H. B. The Trade and Administration of the Chinese Empire. Longmans, London, 1908.

OVERLACH, T. W. Foreign Financial Control in China. Macmillan, New York, 1919.

REMER, C. F. Foreign Investments in China. Macmillan, New York, 1933.

REMER, C. F. Foreign Trade of China. Commercial Press, Shanghai, 1926.

REMER, C. F., and PALMER, W. B. A Study of Chinese Boycotts. Johns Hopkins Press, Baltimore, 1933.

SHAW, K. W. Democracy and Finance in China. Columbia Univ. Press, New York, 1926.

TAWNEY, R. H. Land and Labor in China. Harcourt, New York, 1932.

VINACKE, H. M. Problems of Industrial Development in China. Princeton Univ. Press, Princeton, 1926.

VISSERING, W. On Chinese Currency, Coin, and Paper Money. Brill, Leiden, 1877.

WAGEL, S. R. Chinese Currency and Banking. North-China Daily News & Herald, Shanghai, 1915.

WAGEL, S. R. Finance in China. North-China Daily News & Herald, Shanghai, 1914.

WARNER, W. Die Chinesische Landwirtschaft. P. Parey, Berlin, 1926.

8. FOREIGN RELATIONS

ANDERSON, A. A Narrative of the British Embassy to China in the Years 1792, 1793, & 1794. Rogers & Berry, New York, 1795.

ARIGA, N. La Chine et la grande guerre européenne. A. Pedone, Paris, 1920.

BAU, M. J. China and World Peace. Revell, New York, 1928.

BAU, M. J. The Foreign Relations of China. Revell, New York, 1922.

BAU, M. J. The Open Door Doctrine in Relation to China. Macmillan, New York, 1923.

BAUDEZ, M. Essai sur la condition juridique des étrangers en Chine. A. Pedone, Paris, 1913.

BAZANCOURT, C. L., BARON DE. Les Expéditions de Chine et de Cochin-Chine; d'après les documents officiels (2 vols.). Amyot, Paris, 1861–1862.

BERESFORD, LORD C. The Break-up of China. Harper, New York, 1899.

BLAKESLEE, G. H. China and the Far East. Crowell, New York, 1910.

BLAKESLEE, G. H. Conflicts of Policy in the Far East. World Peace Foundation, Boston; Foreign Policy Association, New York, 1934.

BOELL, P. Le Protectorat des missions catholiques en Chine. Institut scientifique de la libre-pensée, Paris, 1899.

BRAAM, A. E. VAN. An Authentic Account of the Embassy of the Dutch East India Company to the Court of the Emperor of China in 1794 and 1795 (English translation). R. Phillips, London, 1798.

CLYDE, P. H. International Rivalries in Manchuria. Ohio State Univ. Press, Columbus, 1926.

COOLIDGE, M. R. Chinese Immigration. Holt, New York, 1909.

CORDIER, H. Le Consulat de France à Canton au XVIIIᵉ siècle. Brill, Leiden, 1908.

CORDIER, H. L'Expédition de Chine du 1857–1858. Alcan, Paris, 1905.

CORDIER, H. L'Expédition de Chine de 1860. Alcan, Paris, 1906.

CORDIER, H. Histoire des relations de la Chine avec les puissances occidentales, 1860–1900 (3 vols.). Alcan, Paris, 1901–1902.

DEVÉRIA, G. Histoire des relations de la Chine avec l'Annam-Vietnam. Leroux, Paris, 1880.

DUYVENDAK, J. J. L. The Diary of His Excellency Ching Shan, being a Chinese Account of the Boxer Troubles. Brill, Leiden, 1924.

ELLIS, SIR H. Journal of the Proceedings of the Late Embassy to China. J. Murray, London, 1817.

ETHERTON, P. T., and TILTMAN, H. H. Manchuria: the Cockpit of Asia. Stokes, New York, 1932.

FIELD, F. V. American Participation in the China Consortiums. Univ. of Chicago Press, Chicago, 1931.

GÉRARD, A. Ma mission en Chine (1893–1897). Plon-Nourrit, Paris, 1918.

GUNDRY, R. S. China and her Neighbors; France in Indo-China, Russia and China, India and Thibet. Chapman & Hall, London, 1893.

HART, SIR R. These from the Land of Sinim. Chapman & Hall, London, 1901.

HERTSLET, E. Treaties etc. between Great Britain and China, and between China and Foreign Powers; and Orders in Council, Rules, Regulations, Acts of Parliament, Decrees, etc., affecting British Interests in China. In force on January 1, 1908. H. M. Stationery Office, London, 1908.

HIRTH, F. China and the Roman Orient. Kelly & Walsh, Shanghai, 1885.

HIRTH, F., and ROCKWELL, W. W. The Chu-fan-chi of Chau Ju-kua. Imperial Academy of Sciences, St. Petersburg, 1911.

HOLCOMBE, C. The Real Chinese Question. Dodd, New York, 1900.

HSÜ SHU-HSI. China and her Political Entity. Oxford, New York, 1926.

KEETON, G. W. The Development of Extraterritoriality in China. Longmans, New York, 1928.

KOO, V. K. W. China and the League of Nations. George Allen & Unwin, London, 1919.

KOO, V. K. W. The Status of Aliens in China. Columbia Univ. Press, New York, 1912.

KOTENEV, A. M. Shanghai: its Mixed Court and Council. North-China Daily News & Herald, Shanghai, 1925.

KOTENEV, A. M. Shanghai: its Municipality and the Chinese. North-China Daily News & Herald, Shanghai, 1927.

KUO, P. C. A Critical Study of the First Anglo-Chinese War. The Commercial Press, Shanghai, 1935.

LANE-POOLE, S., and DICKENS, F. V. Life of Sir Harry Parkes. Macmillan, London, 1894.

LATOURETTE, K. S. History of the Early Relations between the United States and China, 1784–1844. Yale Univ. Press, New Haven, 1917.

LATTIMORE, O. Manchuria: Cradle of Conflict (second edition). Macmillan, New York, 1935.

LEAVENWORTH, C. The Arrow War. Sampson Low, Marston & Co., London, 1901.

MACMURRAY, J. V. A. (editor). Treaties and Agreements with and concerning China, 1894–1919 (2 vols.). Carnegie Endowment for International Peace, Washington, 1919.

MACNAIR, H. F. The Chinese Abroad. Commercial Press, Shanghai, 1925.

MENG, C. China Speaks on the Conflict between China and Japan. Macmillan, New York, 1932.

MORANT, G. S. DE. Exterritorialité et interêts étrangers en Chine. Geuthner, Paris, 1925.

MORSE, H. B. The International Relations of the Chinese Empire (3 vols.). Longmans, London and New York, 1910–1918.

NORTON, H. K. China and the Powers. Day, New York, 1927.

OLIPHANT, L. The Mission of Lord Elgin to China and Japan (2 vols.). Harper, New York, 1860.

OWEN, D. E. British Opium Policy in China and India. Yale University Press, New Haven, 1934.

PAUTHIER, J. P. G. Histoire des relations politiques de la Chine avec les puissances occidentales, depuis les temps les plus anciens jusqu'à nos jours. Didot, Paris, 1859.

PAUTHIER, J. P. G. (translator). Mémoire secret addressé à l'Empereur Hien-Foung par un lettré chinois sur la conduite à suivre avec les puissances européennes. La Société Orientale, Paris, 1860.

PEAKE, C. K. Nationalism and Education in Modern China. Columbia Univ. Press, New York, 1932.

PINON, R. La Chine qui s'ouvre. Perrin, Paris, 1900.

POLLARD, R. T. China's Foreign Relations, 1917–1931. Macmillan, New York, 1933.

PRICE, E. B. The Russo-Japanese Treaties of 1907–1916 concerning Manchuria and Mongolia. Johns Hopkins Press, Baltimore, 1933.

QUIGLEY, H. S. Chinese Politics and Foreign Powers. Carnegie Endowment for International Peace, New York, 1927.

REID, G. China, Captive or Free? Dodd, New York, 1921.

REINSCH, P. S. An American Diplomat in China, 1913–1919. Doubleday, Page, Garden City, 1922.

REMER, C. F. Foreign Investments in China. Macmillan, New York, 1933.

REMER, C. F., and PALMER, W. B. A Study of Chinese Boycotts. Johns Hopkins Press, Baltimore, 1933.

ROCKHILL, W. W. China's Intercourse with Korea from the XVth Century to 1895. Luzac, London, 1905.

ROCKHILL, W. W. Diplomatic Audiences at the Court of China. Luzac, London, 1905.

ROCKHILL, W. W. Notes on the Relations and Trade of China with the Eastern Archipelago and the Coast of the Indian Ocean during the Fourteenth Century. Brill, Leiden, 1915.

ROCKHILL, W. W. Treaties and Conventions with or concerning China and Korea, 1894–1904. U. S. Government Printing Office, Washington, 1904.

SARGENT, A. J. Anglo-Chinese Commerce and Diplomacy. Clarendon Press, Oxford, 1907.

SCHEIBERT, J. Der Krieg in China, 1900–1901. A. Schröder, Berlin, 1901.

SCOTT, J. B. (editor). The Consortium. Carnegie Endowment for International Peace, Washington, 1921.

SMITH, A. H. China in Convulsion (2 vols.). Revell, New York, 1901.

SOOTHILL, W. E. China and the Occident. Oxford, New York, 1925.

STAUNTON, SIR G. L. An Authentic Account of an Embassy from the King of Great Britain to the Emperor of China. G. Nicol, London, 1797.

STAUNTON, SIR G. T. (translator). Tu-li-shin's Narrative of the Chinese Embassy to the Khan of the Tourgouth Tartars. J. Murray, London, 1821.

STEIGER, G. N. China and the Occident: the Origin and Development of the Boxer Movement. Yale Univ. Press, New Haven, 1927.

SZE, T. Y. China and the Most-Favored-Nation Clause. Revell, New York, 1926.

TAI, E. S. Treaty Ports in China. Columbia Univ. Press, New York, 1918.

THOMSON, H. C. China and the Powers, a Narrative of the Outbreak of 1900. Longmans, London, 1902.

TSCHEPE, A. Japans Beziehungen zu China (to 1600). Katholische Mis., Jentschoufou, 1907.

WHEELER, W. R. China and the World War. Macmillan, New York, 1919.

WILLIAMS, F. W. Anson Burlingame and the First Chinese Mission to Foreign Powers. Scribner, New York, 1912.

WILLOUGHBY, W. W. China at the Conference. Johns Hopkins Press, Baltimore, 1922.

WILLOUGHBY, W. W. Foreign Rights and Interests in China (revised edition, 2 vols.). Johns Hopkins Press, Baltimore, 1927.

WOOD, G. Z. China, the United States, and the Anglo-Japanese Alliance. Revell, New York, 1921.

WOOD, G. Z. The Chino-Japanese Treaties of May 25th, 1915. Revell, New York, 1921.

WOOD, G. Z. The Shantung Question, a Study in Diplomacy and World Politics. Revell, New York, 1922.

WOOD, G. Z. The Twenty-one Demands. Revell, New York, 1921.

YEN, E. T. The Open Door Policy. Stratford, Boston, 1923.

YOUNG, C. W. The International Legal Status of the Kwantung Leased Territory. Johns Hopkins Press, Baltimore, 1931.

YOUNG, C. W. Japanese Jurisdiction in the South Manchuria Railway Areas. Johns Hopkins Press, Baltimore, 1931.

YOUNG, C. W. Japan's Special Position in Manchuria. Johns Hopkins Press, Baltimore, 1931.

American Relations with China. Report of a Conference Held at Johns Hopkins University in September, 1925. Johns Hopkins Press, Baltimore, 1925.

Appeal by the Chinese Government. Report of the Commission of Enquiry. League of Nations, Geneva, 1932.

Report of Commission on Extraterritoriality in China. U. S. Government Printing Office, Washington, 1926.

Shanghai Municipal Council. Report of the Hon. Mr. Justice Feetham, C. M. G. (3 vols.). North-China Daily News & Herald, Shanghai, 1931.

Treaties and Agreements with and concerning China, 1919–1929. Carnegie Endowment for International Peace, Washington, 1929.

III. *India*

1. GENERAL WORKS

AIYANGAR, S. K. Ancient India. Luzac, London, 1911.

AIYANGAR, S. K. South India and her Muhammadan Invaders. Oxford Univ. Press, London, 1921.

CHIROL, SIR VALENTINE. India, Old and New. Macmillan, New York, 1921.

CODRINGTON, H. W. A Short History of Ceylon. Macmillan, London, 1926.

CUMMING, SIR JOHN (editor). Bibliography Relating to India (1900–1926). National Books Council, London, 1927.

DANVERS, F. C. The Portuguese in India. W. H. Allen, London, 1894.

DAS GUPTA, J. N. India in the Seventeenth Century. Calcutta Univ. Press, Calcutta, 1916.

DODWELL, H. H. A Sketch of the History of India. Longmans, London, 1925.

DUTT, R. C. The Civilization of India. J. M. Dent & Sons, London, 1900.

DUTT, R. C. The Economic History of India in the Victorian Age. K. Paul, Trench, Trübner & Co., London, 1906.

FORREST, SIR G. W. History of the Indian Mutiny (3 vols.). W. Blackwood & Sons, London, 1904–1912.

FORREST, SIR G. W. Life of Clive. Cassell & Co., London, 1918.

FOSTER, W. Early Travels in India. Oxford, London, 1921.

GLADWIN, F. The History of Jehangir. B. G. Paul & Co., Madras, 1788.

HAIG, T. W. Historic Landmarks of the Deccan. Pioneer Press, Allahabad, 1907.

HAVELL, E. B. A Short History of India. Macmillan, London, 1924.

HOLDERNESS, SIR T. W. People and Problems of India. Holt, New York, 1912.

HOLMES, T. R. E. History of the Indian Mutiny (fourth edition). W. H. Allen, London, 1891.

HUNTER, W. W. A History of British India. Longmans, London, 1900.

JOUVEAU-DUBREUIL, G. The Pallavas. Privately printed, Pondicherry, 1917.

KING, J. S. The History of the Bahmani Dynasty. Luzac, London, 1900.

LANE-POOLE, S. Aurangzib. (Rulers of India Series.) Clarendon Press, Oxford, 1893.

LANE-POOLE, S. Bábar. (Rulers of India Series.) Clarendon Press, Oxford, 1899.

LANE-POOLE, S. Medieval India. Putnam, New York, 1903.

LEVI, S. L'Inde et le monde. H. Champion, Paris, 1926.

LEVI, S. Le Népal. Étude historique d'un royaume hindou (3 vols.). Leroux, Paris, 1905–1908.

LYALL, A. Rise and Expansion of British Dominion in India. J. Murray, London, 1920.

MCCRINDLE, J. W. Ancient India as Described in Classical Literature. Constable & Co., Edinburgh, 1901.

MACPHAIL, J. M. Asoka. (Heritage of India Series.) Oxford, London, 1918.

MAJOR, R. H. (editor). India in the Fifteenth Century. Hakluyt Society, London, 1857.

MALLESON, G. B. Akbar. (Rulers of India Series.) Clarendon Press, Oxford, 1890.

MALLESON, G. B. Dupleix. Clarendon Press, Oxford, 1890.

MALLESON, G. B. History of the French in India (second edition). Grant, Edinburgh, 1893.

MARTINEAU, A. Dupleix et l'Inde française. H. Champion, Paris, 1920.

MASSON-OURSEL, P., WILLMAN-GRABOWSKA, H., and STERN, P. Ancient India and Indian Civilization. K. Paul, Trench, Trübner & Co., London, 1934.

MONCKTON-JONES, M. E. Warren Hastings in Bengal, 1772–1774. Clarendon Press, Oxford, 1917.

MOOKERJI, R. The Fundamental Unity of India. Longmans, London, 1914.

MOOKERJI, R. Harsha. Clarendon Press, Oxford, 1926.

PARKER, H. Village Folk-Tales of Ceylon (3 vols.). Luzac, London, 1910–1914.

PIERES, P. E. Ceylon and the Hollanders, 1658–1796. American Ceylon Mission Press, Ceylon, 1918.

RAGOZIN, Z. A. Vedic India. Putnam, New York, 1902.

RAPSON, E. J. Ancient India, from the Earliest Times to the First Century A.D. Cambridge Univ. Press, London, 1914.

RAPSON, E. J. (editor). The Cambridge History of India. Cambridge Univ. Press, London, 1922.

RAPSON, E. J. (editor). The Cambridge Shorter History of India. Macmillan, New York, 1934.

RAVENSTEIN, E. G. A Journal of the First Voyage of Vasco da Gama, 1497–1499. Hakluyt Society, London, 1898.

ROBERTS, P. E. History of India to the End of the E. I. Co. Clarendon Press, Oxford, 1916.

ROGERS, A., and BEVERIDGE, H. (translators). Memoirs of Jahangir (2 vols.). Royal Asiatic Society, London, 1909–1914.

RONALDSHAY, EARL OF (L. L. J. Dundas). India: a Bird's Eye View. Houghton, Boston, 1924.

SEWELL, R. A Forgotten Empire. S. Sonnenschein & Co., London, 1900.

SLATER, G. Dravidian Element in Indian Culture. Ernest Benn, London, 1924.

SMITH, V. A. Akbar, the Great Mogul. Clarendon Press, Oxford, 1917.

SMITH, V. A. Asoka: the Buddhist Emperor of India (second edition). Clarendon Press, Oxford, 1919.

SMITH, V. A. Early History of India. Clarendon Press, Oxford, 1904.

SMITH, V. A. The Oxford History of India (second edition). Clarendon Press, Oxford, 1923.

STEPHENS, H. M. Albuquerque. (Rulers of India Series.) Clarendon Press, Oxford, 1892.

STRACHEY, SIR J. Hastings and the Rohilla War. Clarendon Press, Oxford, 1892.

TAYLOR, M. Manual of Indian History. Longmans, London, 1895.

TILAK, B. G. Orion, or Researches into the Antiquity of the Vedas. Ashtekar, Poona, 1916.

VALLÉE-POUSSIN, L. DE LA. L'Inde aux temps des Mauryas et des barbares, Grecs, Scythes, Parthes, et Yue-Tchi. E. de Boccard, Paris, 1930.

VALLÉE-POUSSIN, L. DE LA. Indo-Européens et Indo-Iraniens: l'Inde jusque vers 300 av. J.-C. E. de Boccard, Paris, 1924.

WHITEWAY, R. S. The Rise of the Portuguese Power in India. Constable & Co., London, 1899.

2. PERIODICALS

Annual Report of the Archaeological Survey of India. Calcutta.
Bengal Past and Present. Calcutta Historical Society, Calcutta.
The Indian Antiquary. Bombay and London.
Journal of the Bengal Asiatic Society. Calcutta.

3. ARCHAEOLOGY, ANTHROPOLOGY, AND GEOGRAPHY

BARNETT, L. D. The Antiquities of India. P. L. Warner, London, 1913.

CHANDA, R. P. Note on Prehistoric Antiquities from Mohen-jo Daro. Calcutta, 1924.

CHILDE, V. G. The Aryans, a Study of Indo-European Origins. K. Paul, Trench, Trübner & Co., London, 1926.

COUSENS, H. An Account of the Caves at Nadsur and Karsambla. Government Central Press, Bombay, 1891.

COUSENS, H. The Antiquities of Sind. Government of India, Central Publication Branch, Calcutta, 1929.

FOOTE, R. B. Indian Prehistoric and Protohistoric Antiquities, Foote Collection (2 vols.). Government Press, Madras, 1914.

JOUVEAU-DUBREUIL, G. Archéologie du sud de l'Inde (2 vols.). Geuthner, Paris, 1914.

JOUVEAU-DUBREUIL, G. Pallava Antiquities. Probsthain, London, 1916.

LEVI, S., PRZYLUSKI, J., and BLOCH, J. Pre-Aryan and Pre-Dravidian in India (English translation by P. C. Bagchi). Calcutta Univ. Press, Calcutta, 1929.

LOGAN, A. C. Old Chipped Stones of India. Thacker, Spink, Calcutta, 1906.

MARSHALL, SIR J. H. (editor). Annual Report of the Archaeological Survey of India. Calcutta.

MARSHALL, SIR J. H. (editor). Mohenjo-Daro and the Indus Civilization (3 vols.). Probsthain, London, 1931.

REINACH, S. L'Origine des Aryans. Leroux, Paris, 1892.

4. ART, PHILOSOPHY, AND LITERATURE

BACHHOFER, L. Early Indian Sculpture (2 vols.). Harcourt, New York, 1929.

BHOTTACHARYYA, B. The Indian Buddhist Iconography. Clarendon Press, Oxford, 1924.

BLOCHET, E. Musulman Painting. XIIth-XVIIth Century (translated by C. M. Binyon). Methuen & Co., London, 1929.

CLARK, W. E. (translator). The Aryabhatiya of Aryabhata, an Ancient Indian Work on Mathematics and Astronomy. Univ. of Chicago Press, Chicago, 1930.

COOMARASWAMY, A. K. The Arts and Crafts in India and Ceylon. Foulis, London, 1913.

COOMARASWAMY, A. K. History of Indian and Indonesian Art. Weyhe, London, 1927.

COOMARASWAMY, A. K. Mughal Painting. Harvard Univ. Press, Cambridge, 1930.

COOMARASWAMY, A. K. Rajput Painting. Oxford, New York, 1916.

COOMARASWAMY, A. K. Visvarkama: examples of Indian Architecture, Sculpture, Painting, Handicraft. Luzac, London, 1914.

COUSENS, H. Bijapur and its Architectural Remains. Government Central Press, Bombay, 1916.

DAS GUPTA, S. A History of Indian Philosophy. Cambridge Univ. Press, London, 1922.

FERGUSSON, J. History of Indian and Eastern Architecture. J. Murray, London, 1910.

FOUCHER, ALFRED. L'Art Gréco-Bouddhique du Gandhara. Étude sur les origines de l'influence classique dans l'art bouddhique de l'Inde et de l'Extrême-Orient (2 vols.). Leroux, Paris, 1905–1918.

FOUCHER, ALFRED. The Beginnings of Buddhist Art and Other Essays in Indian and Central Asian Archaeology (translated by L. A. Thomas and F. W. Thomas). Geuthner, Paris, 1917.

FOUCHER, ALFRED, Étude sur l'iconographie bouddhique de l'Inde, d'après des documents nouveaux (2 vols.). Leroux, Paris, 1900–1906.

FRAZER, R. W. A Literary History of India. T. F. Unwin, London, 1898.

GOUGH, A. E. Philosophy of the Upanishads and Ancient Indian Metaphysics. K. Paul, Trench, Trübner & Co., London, 1882–1884.

GRIFFITHS, J. The Paintings in the Buddhist Cave Temples of Ajanta (plates by W. Griggs). By order of the Secretary of State for India in Council, London, 1896–1897.

HAVELL, E. B. The Ancient and Medieval Architecture of India. J. Murray, London, 1915.

HAVELL, E. B. A Handbook of Indian Art. J. Murray, London, 1920.

HAVELL, E. B. Indian Architecture (second edition). J. Murray, London, 1927.

HERRINGHAM, LADY. Ajanta's Frescos. Clarendon Press, Oxford, 1915.

HOPKINS, E. W. Ethics of India. Yale Univ. Press, New Haven, 1924.

HOPKINS, E. W. Legends of India. Yale Univ. Press, New Haven, 1928.

JOUVEAU-DUBREUIL, G. Dravidian Architecture. S. P. C. K. Press, Madras, 1917.

KEITH, A. B. Buddhist Philosophy in India and Ceylon. Clarendon Press, Oxford, 1923.

MACDONELL, A. A. A History of Sanscrit Literature. William Heinemann, London, 1900.

MASSON-OURSEL, P. Esquisse d'une histoire de la philosophie indienne. Geuthner, Paris, 1923.

MÜLLER, MAX. The Six Systems of Indian Philosophy. Longmans, New York, 1899.

MÜLLER, MAX (translator). The Upanishads. Clarendon Press, Oxford, 1879–1884.

Rosenberg, O. Die Problem der buddhistischen Philosophie. Harrassowitz, Leipzig, 1924.

Smith, V. A. A History of Fine Art in India and Ceylon from the Earliest Times to the Present Day. Clarendon Press, Oxford, 1911.

Strauss, O. Indische Philosophie. E. Reinhardt, Munich, 1925.

Tagore, Rabindranath (translator). One Hundred Poems of Kabir. Chiswick Press, London, 1914.

5. RELIGION

Cowell, E. B. (editor). The Jataka, or Stories of the Buddha's Former Births, translated from the Pali. Cambridge Univ. Press, London, 1895–1913.

Eliot, Sir Charles. Hinduism and Buddhism (3 vols.). Arnold, London, 1921.

Griswold, H. D. The Religion of the Rigveda. Clarendon Press, Oxford, 1923.

Hopkins, E. W. The Religions of India. Ginn, Boston, 1898.

Jaini, Jagmanderlal. Outlines of Jainism. University Press, Cambridge, 1916.

Kaegi, A. The Rigveda (English translation by Arrowsmith). Ginn, Boston, 1886.

Keith, A. B. The Religion and Philosophy of the Veda and Upanishads. Harvard Univ. Press, Cambridge, 1925.

Ketkar, S. V. The History of Caste in India. Luzac, London, 1911.

Macauliffe, M. A. The Sikh Religion. Clarendon Press, Oxford, 1909.

Pratt, J. B. The Pilgrimage of Buddhism, and a Buddhist Pilgrimage. Macmillan, New York, 1928.

Przyluski, J. Le Concile de Rajagrha: introduction à l'histoire du canon et des sectes bouddhiques. Geuthner, Paris, 1926.

Regnaud, P. Le Rig-Veda et les origines de la mythologie indo-européenne. Leroux, Paris, 1892.

Rhys-Davids, T. W. Buddhist India. (Story of the Nations Series.) Putnam, New York, 1903.

Senart, E. Les Castes dans l'Inde (second edition). Geuthner, Paris, 1927.

Stevenson, Mrs. S. The Heart of Jainism. Clarendon Press, Oxford, 1915.

Vasu, N. N. The Modern Buddhism and its Followers in Orissa. Hare Press, Calcutta, 1911.

Whitehead, H. The Village Gods of South India. Oxford, London, 1916.

Whitney, W. D., and Lanman, C. R. (translators). Atharva-Veda. Harvard Univ. Press, Cambridge, 1905.

6. POLITICAL INSTITUTIONS AND THEORIES

Andrews, C. F. Mahatma Gandhi: his Own Story. Macmillan, New York, 1930.

Banerjea, P. Public Administration in Ancient India. Macmillan, London, 1916.

Cumming, Sir J. (editor). Political India, 1832–1932, a Co-operative Survey of a Century. Oxford, London, 1932.

Gandhi, M. K. Hind Swaraj, or Indian Home Rule (second edition). Nateson, Madras, 1926.

Gandhi, M. K. Young India, 1919–1922. Huebsch, New York, 1923.

Ilbert, Sir C. P. The Government of India: Historical Survey. Clarendon Press, Oxford, 1922.

ILBERT, SIR C. P. The New Constitution of India. Univ. of London Press, London, 1920.

LAW, N. N. Studies in Ancient Hindu Polity. Longmans, London, 1914.

LOVETT, SIR V. A History of the Indian Nationalist Movement. J. Murray, London, 1920.

MARRIOTT, SIR J. A. R. The English in India. Oxford, New York, 1932.

MOOKERJI, R. Local Government in Ancient India. Clarendon Press, Oxford, 1920.

RAI, LAJPAT. The Political Future of India. Huebsch, New York, 1919.

RAI, LAJPAT. Young India. Huebsch, New York, 1917.

SHAMASASTRY, R. (translator). Arthasastra. Government Press, Bangalore, 1915.

TOPA, I. N. The Growth and Development of National Thought in India. J. J. Augustin, Hamburg, 1928.

VAN TYNE, C. H. India in Ferment. Appleton, New York, 1923.

Report of Indian Statutory Commission (Simon Commission). H. M. Stationery Office, London, 1930.

Montagu-Chelmsford Report. H. M. Stationery Office, London, 1918.

Report of Rowlatt Sedition Committee. Superintendent of Government Printing, London, 1918.

7. ECONOMIC HISTORY

BATCHELDER, C. C. Trade of British India with the United States, Japan, and Germany. U. S. Government Printing Office, Washington, 1923.

BRUCE, J. Annals of the Honorable East India Company. Black, Parry, and Kingsbury, London, 1810.

BUCHANAN, D. H. The Development of Capitalist Enterprise in India. Macmillan, New York, 1934.

COMPTON, H. Indian Life in Town and Country. Putnam, New York, 1904.

FOSTER, W. English Factories in India, 1618–1660. Clarendon Press, Oxford, 1906–1921.

FOSTER, W. The Founding of Fort St. George. Eyre & Spottiswoode, London, 1902.

KAEPPELIN, P. La Compagnie des Indes Orientales. A. Challamel, Paris, 1908.

MOOKERJI, R. A History of Indian Shipping and Maritime Activity from the Earliest Times. Longmans, Bombay, 1912.

MORELAND, W. H. India at the Death of Akbar. Macmillan, London, 1920.

OWEN, D. E. British Opium Policy in China and India. Yale Univ. Press, New Haven, 1934.

WARMINGTON, E. H. The Commerce between the Roman Empire and India. Cambridge Univ. Press, London, 1928.

8. FOREIGN RELATIONS

BANERJEE, G. India as Known to the Ancient World, or India's Intercourse in Ancient Times with Egypt, Western Asia, Greece, Rome, Central Asia, China, Indonesia. Clarendon Press, Oxford, 1921.

DAS, T. India in World Politics. Huebsch, New York, 1923.

HANNA, COL. H. B. The Second Afghan War, 1878–1879–1880 (3 vols.). Constable & Co., Edinburgh, 1899–1910.

NAG, K. Les Théories diplomatiques de l'Inde ancienne et l'Arthaçastra. Jouve et Cie, Paris, 1923.

RAWLINSON, H. G. Intercourse between India and the Western World (second edition). Cambridge Univ. Press, London, 1926.

IV. *Japan*

1. GENERAL WORKS

ALLEN, G. C. Modern Japan and its Problems. Dutton, New York, 1928.

ASTON, W. G. (translator). Nihongi. K. Paul, Trench, Trübner & Co., London, 1896.

BIGELOW, P. Japan and her Colonies. Arnold, London, 1923.

BRINKLEY, F. Japan: its History, Arts and Literature (8 vols.). Millet, Boston, 1901–1902.

BRINKLEY, F., and KIKUCHI, D. A History of the Japanese People from the Earliest Times to the End of the Meiji Era. Encyclopædia Britannica, Inc., New York, 1915.

BRYAN, J. I. Civilization of Japan. Holt, New York, 1928.

BRYAN, J. I. History of Japan. Ernest Benn, London, 1927.

BRYAN, J. I. Japan from Within. Stokes, New York, 1924.

CHAMBERLAIN, B. H. (translator). Kojiki. Asiatic Society of Japan, Tokyo, 1883.

CHAMBERLAIN, B. H. Things Japanese (fifth edition). J. Murray, London, 1905.

CLEMENT, E. W. A Short History of Japan. Univ. of Chicago Press, Chicago, 1915.

CORDIER, H. Bibliotheca Japonica. Leroux, Paris, 1912.

COURANT, M. Okoubo. Alcan, Paris, 1904.

D'AUTREMER, J. The Japanese Empire. Scribner, New York, 1910.

DAVIS, F. H. Japan. Stokes, New York, 1916.

DENING, W. The Life of Toyotomi Hideyoshi (third edition). J. L. Thompson & Co., Kobe, 1930.

EHLERS, J. H. Reconstruction and Development of the Tokyo-Yokohama District. U. S. Government Printing Office, Washington, 1928.

FUJISAWA, R. The Recent Aims and Political Development of Japan. Yale Univ. Press, New Haven, 1923.

GLEASON, G. What Shall I Think of Japan? Macmillan, New York, 1911.

GOWEN, H. H. Outline History of Japan. Appleton, New York, 1927.

GRIFFIS, W. E. Corea, the Hermit Nation (ninth edition). Scribner, New York, 1911.

GRIFFIS, W. E. The Mikado's Empire (2 vols.; twelfth edition). Harper, New York, 1913.

GUBBINS, J. H. The Making of Modern Japan. Lippincott, Philadelphia, 1922.

GUBBINS, J. H. The Progress of Japan, 1853–1871. Clarendon Press, Oxford, 1911.

GULICK, S. L. The Evolution of the Japanese. Revell, New York, 1903.

HARA, K. An Introduction to the History of Japan. Putnam, New York, 1920.

HEARN, L. Japan: an Attempt at Interpretation. Macmillan, New York, 1904.

HERSHEY, A. S. and S. W. Modern Japan, Social—Industrial—Political. Bobbs, Indianapolis, 1919.

HILDRETH, R. Japan as it Was and Is (edited by E. W. Clement). K. Paul, Trench, Trübner & Co., London, 1907.

HISHIDA, S. G. The International Position of Japan as a Great Power. Columbia Univ. Press, New York, 1905.

HULBERT, H. B. The History of Korea. Methodist Publishing House, Seoul, 1905.

HULBERT, H. B. The Passing of Korea. Doubleday, Page, New York, 1906.

INAGAKI, M. Japan and the Pacific. Scribner & Welford, New York, 1890.

IRELAND, A. The New Korea. Dutton, New York, 1926.

KAEMPFER, E. The History of Japan, together with a Description of the Kingdom of Siam, 1690–1692 (modern edition). J. MacLehose & Sons, Glasgow, 1906.

KENNEDY, M. D. The Changing Fabric of Japan. Constable & Co., London, 1930.

KIKUCHI, BARON D. Japanese Education. J. Murray, London, 1909.

LADD, G. T. In Korea with Marquis Ito. Longmans, New York, 1908.

LA MAZELIÈRE, A. R., MARQUIS DE. Le Japon, histoire et civilisation (8 vols.). Plon-Nourrit, Paris, 1907–1923.

LATOURETTE, K. S. The Development of Japan. Macmillan, New York, 1918.

LONGFORD, J. H. The Evolution of New Japan. Putnam, New York, 1913.

LONGFORD, J. H. Japan. Houghton, Boston, 1923.

LONGFORD, J. H. The Story of Korea. Scribner, New York, 1911.

LONGFORD, J. H. The Story of Old Japan. Chapman & Hall, London, 1910.

McGOVERN, W. M. Modern Japan, its Political, Military, and Industrial Organisation. T. F. Unwin, London, 1920.

McKENZIE, F. A. Korea's Fight for Freedom. Revell, New York, 1920.

McKENZIE, F. A. The Tragedy of Korea. Hodder & Stoughton, Ltd., London, 1908.

McLAREN, W. W. A Political History of Japan during the Meiji Era, 1867–1912. Scribner, New York, 1916.

MOUNSAY, A. H. The Satsuma Rebellion: an Episode of Modern Japanese History. J. Murray, London, 1879.

MURDOCH, J. A History of Japan (3 vols.). Greenberg, New York, 1926.

NACHOD, O. Geschichte von Japan (3 vols.). Asia Major, Leipzig, 1929–1930.

NITOBE, I. Japan. Scribner, New York, 1931.

NITOBE, I., and others. Western Influences in Modern Japan. Univ. of Chicago Press, Chicago, 1931.

OKAKURA, K. The Awakening of Japan. Century, New York, 1904.

OKUMA, COUNT S. (compiler). Fifty Years of New Japan. Smith, Elder & Co., London, 1909.

POOLEY, A. M. Japan at the Crossroads. George Allen & Unwin, London, 1917.

PORTER, R. P. Japan, the Rise of a Modern Power. Clarendon Press, Oxford, 1918.

ROBERTSON-SCOTT, W. J. The Foundations of Japan. J. Murray, London, 1922.

ROSS, J. History of Corea. J. & R. Parlane, Paisley, 1880.

SAITO, H. A History of Japan. K. Paul, Trench, Trübner & Co., London, 1912.

SANSOM, C. B. Japan: a Short Cultural History. Century, New York, 1931.

STEAD, A. (editor). Japan by the Japanese. William Heinemann, London, 1904.

TSURUMI, Y. Present Day Japan. Columbia Univ. Press, New York, 1926.

WILDES, H. E. Japan in Crisis. Macmillan, New York, 1934.

WILDES, H. E. Social Currents in Japan, with Special Reference to the Press. Univ. of Chicago Press, Chicago, 1927.

YOUNG, A. M. Japan in Recent Times. Morrow, New York, 1929.

2. PERIODICALS

Contemporary Japan. Tokyo.

Cultural Nippon. Tokyo.

Japan Chronicle. Kobe.

Japan Financial and Economic Monthly. Tokyo.

Japan Times. Tokyo.

Japan Times Year Book (1932–1933). Tokyo.

Japan Year Book (1905–1931). Tokyo.

Japanese Journal of Geology and Geography. Tokyo, 1922.

Japan-Manchoukuo Year Book (1934–   ). Tokyo.

The Near East. Tokyo.

Seismological Notes. Imperial Earthquake Investigation Committee, Tokyo, 1921–1924.

Transactions of the Asiatic Society of Japan (cited as T. A. S. J.). Yokohama.

3. ARCHAEOLOGY, ANTHROPOLOGY, AND GEOGRAPHY

HAUSHOFER, K. Das Japanische Reich in seiner geographischen Entwicklung. L. W. Siedel & Sohn, Wien, 1921.

HITCHCOCK, R. The Ancient Pit-dwellers of Yezo. U. S. Government Printing Office, Washington, 1891.

MUNRO, N. G. Prehistoric Japan. Yokohama, 1908.

REIN, J. J. Japan, nach Reisen und Studien im Auftrage der königlich preussischen Regierung. W. Engelmann, Leipzig, 1905.

SALWAY, C. M. The Island Dependencies of Japan. Morice, London, 1913.

Report upon Archeological Research in the Department of Literature. Kyoto University Archeological Institute, Tokyo, 1925–1927.

4. ART, PHILOSOPHY, AND LITERATURE

ANESAKI, M. Art, Life, and Nature in Japan. Marshall Jones, Boston, 1933.

ANESAKI, M. Buddhist Art in its Relation to Buddhist Ideals. Houghton, Boston, 1915.

ASTON, W. G. A History of Japanese Literature. Appleton, New York, 1899.

BÉNAZET, A. Le Théâtre au Japon. Leroux, Paris, 1901.

CRAM, R. A. Impressions of Japanese Architecture and the Allied Arts (second edition). Marshall Jones, Boston, 1930.

FENOLLOSA, E. F. Epochs of Chinese and Japanese Art. Stokes, New York, 1913.

GROSSE, E. Le Lavis en Extrême-Orient. G. Cres, Paris, 1929.

HEARN, L. (translator). Japanese Lyrics. Houghton, Boston, 1915.

INOUYÉ, T. Sur le développement des idées philosophiques au Japon. J. Maisonneuve, Paris, 1897.

KUKI, R. A History of Japanese Arts (3 vols.). Ryubun-kwan Publishing Co., Tokyo, 1908.

MIYAMORI, A. Masterpieces of Chikamatsu. K. Paul, Trench, Trübner & Co., London, 1926.

MORRISON, A. The Painters of Japan (2 vols.). T. C. and E. C. Jack, London, 1911.

MORSE, E. S. Japanese Homes and their Surroundings. Ticknor & Co., Boston, 1886.

NITOBE, I. Bushido, the Soul of Japan. Putnam, New York, 1905.

OKAKURA, K. Ideals of the East. J. Murray, London, 1920.

OMORI, A. S., and DOI, K. (translators). Diaries of Court Ladies of Old Japan. Houghton, Boston, 1920.

OTTO, A. F., and HOLBROOK, T. S. Mythological Japan: or the Symbolisms of Mythology in Relation to Japanese Art. D. Biddle, Philadelphia, 1902.

PAGE, C. H. Japanese Poetry. Houghton, Boston, 1923.

WALEY, A. The No Plays of Japan. Knopf, New York, 1922.

WALEY, A. (translator). The Pillow-Book of Sei Shonagon. Houghton, Boston, 1929.

WALEY, A. (translator). The Tale of Genji, by Lady Murasaki. Houghton, Boston, 1925–1934.

5. RELIGION

ANESAKI, M. History of Japanese Religion. K. Paul, Trench, Trübner & Co., London, 1930.

ANESAKI, M. Nichiren, the Buddhist Prophet. Harvard Univ. Press, Cambridge, 1916.

ANESAKI, M. Quelques pages de l'histoire religieux du Japon. Geuthner, Paris, 1921.

ASTON, W. G. Shinto: the Way of the Gods. Longmans, London, 1905.

CARY, O. A History of Christianity in Japan. Revell, New York, 1909.

CHARLEVOIX, P. F. X. DE. Histoire de l'établissement, des progrès, et de la décadence du christianisme dans l'empire du Japon. Perine Frères, Lyon, 1829.

ELIOT, SIR C. N. E. Japanese Buddhism. B. H. Blackwell, Ltd., Oxford, 1935.

HAAS, H. Geschichte des Christentums in Japan. Tokyo, 1902–1904.

HARADA, A. The Faith of Japan. Macmillan, New York, 1914.

HOLTOM, D. C. The Political Philosophy of Modern Shinto. Privately printed, Chicago, 1922.

KNOX, G. W. The Development of Religion in Japan. Putnam, New York, 1907.

LLOYD, A. The Creed of Half Japan: Historical Sketches of Japanese Buddhism. Dutton, New York, 1912.

NANJIO, B. A Short History of the Twelve Buddhist Sects. Bukkyo-sho-ei-yaku-shuppan-sha, Tokyo, 1886.

NUKARIYA, K. The Religion of the Samurai, a Study of Zen Philosophy. Luzac, London, 1912.

Pagés, L. Histoire de la religion chrétienne au Japon depuis 1598 jusqu'à 1651 (2 vols.). C. Douniol, Paris, 1869–1870.

Reischauer, A. K. Studies in Japanese Buddhism. Macmillan, New York, 1917.

Satow, Sir E. M. "Revival of Pure Shinto," T. A. S. J., Vol. III, Yokohama, 1875.

Suzuki, D. T. Essays on Zen Buddhism. Luzac, London, 1927–1934.

6. POLITICAL INSTITUTIONS AND THEORIES

Asakawa, K. Documents of Iriki. Yale Univ. Press, New Haven, 1929.

Asakawa, K. The Early Institutional Life of Japan. Tokyo Shueisha, Tokyo, 1903.

Asami, N. Japanese Colonial Government. New York, 1924.

Clement, E. W. Constitutional Imperialism in Japan. Columbia Univ. Press, New York, 1916.

De Becker, J. E. Commentary on the Commercial Code of Japan. Butterworth & Co., London, 1913.

De Becker, J. E. International Private Law of Japan. Butterworth & Co., London, 1919.

De Becker, J. E. Principles and Practice of the Civil Code of Japan. Kelly & Walsh, Yokohama, 1921.

Hall, J. C. (translator). "Joei Shikimoku (Law Code of the Kamakura Shogunate)," T. A. S. J. (Vol. XXXIV, Part I), Yokohama, 1906.

Hall, J. C. (translator). "Laws of the Military Houses (Tokugawa Shogunate)," T. A. S. J. (Vol. XXXVIII, Part IV), Yokohama, 1911.

Ito, H. (English translation by M. Ito). Commentaries on the Constitution of the Empire of Japan. Government Printing Office, Tokyo, 1889.

Iwasaki, U. Working Forces in Japanese Politics. Columbia Univ. Press, New York, 1921.

Iyenaga, T. The Constitutional Development of Japan, 1853–1881. Johns Hopkins Press, Baltimore, 1891.

Kitazawa, N. The Government of Japan. Princeton Univ. Press, Princeton, 1929.

McLaren, W. W. (editor). "Japanese Government Documents, 1867–1889," T. A. S. J. (Vol. XLII, Part I), Yokohama, 1914.

Matsunami, N. The Constitution of Japan. Maruzen & Co., Tokyo, 1930.

Nakano, Y. The Ordinance Power of the Japanese Emperor. Johns Hopkins Press, Baltimore, 1923.

Ogawa, G. The Conscription System in Japan. Oxford, New York, 1921.

Quigley, H. S. Japanese Government and Politics. Century, New York, 1933.

Uyehara, G. E. The Political Development of Japan, 1867–1909. Constable & Co., London, 1910.

7. ECONOMIC HISTORY

Butts, H. A. Trends in Japan's Trade and Industries. U. S. Government Printing Office, Washington, 1929.

Crocker, W. R. The Japanese Population Problem: the Coming Crisis. Macmillan, New York, 1931.

ELDRIDGE, F. R. Japan after the Earthquake. U. S. Government Printing Office, Washington, 1923.

KING, F. H. Farmers of Forty Centuries: or Permanent Agriculture in China, Korea and Japan. Mrs. F. H. King, Madison, 1911.

KUSHIDA, T. War and Armament Taxes of Japan. Oxford, New York, 1923.

MATSUKATA, M. Report on the Adoption of the Gold Standard. Government Press, Tokyo, 1899.

MOULTON, H. G., and KO, J. Japan: an Economic and Financial Appraisal. Brookings Institution, Washington, 1931.

OGAWA, G. Expenditures of the Russo-Japanese War. Oxford, New York, 1923.

ONO, G. War and Armament Expenditures of Japan. Oxford, New York, 1922.

ORCHARD, J. E. Japan's Economic Position. McGraw, New York, 1930.

REIN, J. J. The Industries of Japan. A. C. Armstrong & Son, New York, 1889.

SAINT-MAURICE, COMTE DE. La Civilisation du Japan (1908), son expansion en Extrême-Orient. G. Roustan, Paris, 1908.

TAKEKOSHI, Y. The Economic Aspects of the History of the Civilization of Japan (3 vols.). George Allen & Unwin, London, 1930.

TAKIZAWA, M. The Penetration of Money Economy in Japan. Columbia Univ. Press, New York, 1927.

UYEHARA, S. The Industry and Trade of Japan. P. S. King & Son, London, 1926.

WRIGHT, P. G. The American Tariff and Oriental Trade. Univ. of Chicago Press, Chicago, 1931.

Railway Nationalization in Japan: Ten Years' Progress under State Management, 1907–8 to 1916–17. Tokyo, 1919.

Report on Progress in Manchuria, 1907–1928. South Manchuria Railway, Dairen, 1929.

Second Report on Progress in Manchuria, to 1930. South Manchuria Railway, Dairen, 1931.

8. FOREIGN RELATIONS

ADACHI, K. Manchuria: a Survey. McBride, New York, 1925.

AKIMOTO, S. Lord Ii Naosuki and New Japan. Japan Times, Tokyo, 1909.

ALCOCK, SIR R. The Capital of the Tycoon: a Narrative of a Three Years' Residence in Japan. Longmans, London, 1863.

ARIGA, N. La Guerre russo-japonaise. Pedone, Paris, 1908.

ARIGA, N. La Guerre sino-japonaise. Pedone, Paris, 1896.

ASAKAWA, K. The Russo-Japanese Conflict. Houghton, Boston, 1904.

ASTON, W. G. Hideyoshi's Invasion of Korea. T. A. S. J., Vol. VI, Yokohama, 1878.

BLAKESLEE, G. H. Conflicts of Policy in the Far East. World Peace Foundation, Boston; Foreign Policy Association, New York, 1934.

BLAKESLEE, G. H. (editor). Japan and Japanese-American Relations. Stechert, New York, 1912.

BOXER, C. R. A Portuguese Embassy to Japan (1644–1647). K. Paul, Trench, Trübner & Co., London, 1928.

BUELL, R. L. Japanese Immigration. World Peace Foundation, Boston, 1924.

CHANG CHUNG-FU. The Anglo-Japanese Alliance. Johns Hopkins Press, Baltimore, 1931.

CHERADAME, A. Le Monde et la guerre russo-japonaise. Plon-Nourrit, Paris, 1906.

CHUNG, H. Korean Treaties. H. S. Nichols, New York, 1919.

CLYDE, P. H. International Rivalries in Manchuria. Ohio State Univ. Press, Columbus, 1926.

COSENZA, M. E. (editor). The Complete Journal of Townsend Harris. Doubleday, Doran, New York, 1930.

COWAN, T. The Russo-Japanese War. Arnold, London, 1904.

DENNETT, T. Roosevelt and the Russo-Japanese War. Doubleday, Page, Garden City, 1925.

DENNIS, A. L. P. Anglo-Japanese Alliance. Univ. of California Press, Berkeley, 1923.

GÉRARD, A. Ma mission en Japon (1907–1914), avec un épilogue de 1914 à 1919. Plon-Nourrit, Paris, 1919.

GREW, E. S. War in the Far East: a History of the Russo-Japanese War (6 vols.). Virtue & Co., London, 1905.

GRIFFIS, W. E. Matthew Calbraith Perry, a Typical American Naval Officer. Cupples & Hurd, Boston, 1887.

GRIFFIS, W. E. Townsend Harris, First American Envoy to Japan. Houghton, Boston, 1895.

GULICK, S. L. The American Japanese Problem. Scribner, New York, 1914.

HAWKS, F. L. Narrative of the Expedition of an American Squadron to the China Seas and Japan, Performed in the Years 1852, 1853, and 1854, under the Command of Commodore M. C. Perry (3 vols.). Appleton, New York, 1856.

HERSEY, A. S. The International Law and Diplomacy of the Russo-Japanese War. Macmillan, New York, 1906.

IYENAGA, T., and SATO, K. Japan and the California Problem. Putnam, New York, 1921.

KAWAKAMI, K. K. American-Japanese Relations. Revell, New York, 1912.

KAWAKAMI, K. K. Asia at the Door. Revell, New York, 1914.

KAWAKAMI, K. K. Japan and World Peace. Macmillan, New York, 1919.

KAWAKAMI, K. K. Japan's Pacific Policy. Dutton, New York, 1922.

KAWAKAMI, K. K. The Real Japanese Question. Macmillan, New York, 1921.

NITOBE, I. The Intercourse between the United States and Japan: an Historical Sketch. Johns Hopkins Press, Baltimore, 1891.

OLIPHANT, L. The Mission of Lord Elgin to China and Japan (2 vols.). Harper, New York, 1860.

POOLEY, A. M. Japan's Foreign Policies. Dodd, New York, 1920.

POOLEY, A. M. (editor). The Secret Memoirs of Count Tadasu Hayashi. Putnam, New York, 1915.

PORTER, R. P. The Full Recognition of Japan. H. Frowde, London, 1911.

PRICE, E. B. The Russo-Japanese Treaties of 1907–1916 concerning Manchuria and Mongolia. Johns Hopkins Press, Baltimore, 1933.

REMER, C. F. Foreign Investments in China. Macmillan, New York, 1933.

REMER, C. F., and PALMER, W. B. A Study of Chinese Boycotts. Johns Hopkins Press, Baltimore, 1933.

SATOH, H. Agitated Japan: the Life of Baron Ii Kamon-no-kami Naosuki. Dai Nippon Tosho Kabushiki Kaisha, Tokyo, 1896.

SATOH, H. Lord Hotta, the Pioneer Diplomat of Japan (second edition). Haku-bunkan, Tokyo, 1908.

SATOW, SIR E. M. A Diplomat in Japan. Seeley, Service & Co., London, 1921.

SATOW, SIR E. M. (translator). Japan, 1853–1864: or Genji Yume Monogatari. Tokyo, 1905.

SATOW, SIR E. M. (translator). Kinsé Shiriaku: a History of Japan, from the First Visit of Commodore Perry in 1853 to the Capture of Hakodate by the Mikado's Forces in 1869 (second edition). Naigwai Shuppan Kyokwai, Tokyo, 1906.

TREAT, P. J. Diplomatic Relations between the United States and Japan, 1853–1895. Stanford Univ. Press, Palo Alto, 1932.

TREAT, P. J. The Early Diplomatic Relations between the United States and Japan, 1853–1865. Johns Hopkins Press, Baltimore, 1917.

TREAT, P. J. Japan and the United States, 1853–1921. Houghton, Boston, 1921.

TREVOR, J. B. Japanese Exclusion. U. S. Government Printing Office, Washington, 1925.

WALROND, T. (editor). Letters and Journals of James, Eighth Earl of Elgin. J. Murray, London, 1872.

WILLIAMS, S. W. A Journal of the Perry Expedition to Japan (1853–1854). T. A. S. J. (Vol. 37), Yokohama, 1910.

WOOD, G. Z. The Chino-Japanese Treaties of May 25th, 1915. Revell, New York, 1921.

WOOD, G. Z. The Shantung Question: a Study in Diplomacy and World Politics. Revell, New York, 1922.

WOOD, G. Z. The Twenty-one Demands. Revell, New York, 1921.

YOUNG, C. W. The International Legal Status of the Kwan-tung Leased Territory. Johns Hopkins Press, Baltimore, 1931.

YOUNG, C. W. Japanese Jurisdiction in the South Manchuria Railway Areas. Johns Hopkins Press, Baltimore, 1931.

YOUNG, C. W. Japan's Special Position in Manchuria. Johns Hopkins Press, Baltimore, 1931.

Appeal by the Chinese Government. Report of the Commission of Enquiry. League of Nations, Geneva, 1932.

The Manchurian Question: Japan's Case in the Sino-Japanese Dispute as Presented before the League of Nations. Japanese Delegation to the L. of N., Geneva, 1933.

Traités et conventions entre l'empire du Japon et les puissances étrangères (2 vols.). Ministère des Affaires étrangères, Tokyo, 1908.

V. *Indo-China and Malaysia*

1. GENERAL WORKS

BELL, SIR H. H. J. Foreign Colonial Administration in the Far East. Arnold, London, 1928.

CRAWFURD, J. History of the Indian Archipelago. Constable & Co., Edinburgh, 1820.

FOWLER, J. A. Netherlands East Indies and British Malaya: a Commercial and Industrial Handbook. U. S. Government Printing Office, Washington, 1923.

GROENEVELDT, W. P. Notes on the Malay Archipelago from Chinese Sources. Bruining, Batavia, 1876.

IRELAND, A. The Far Eastern Tropics. Houghton, Boston, 1905.

2. FRENCH INDO-CHINA

AYMONIER, E. Un Aperçu de l'histoire du Cambodge. A. Challamel, Paris, 1918.

AYMONIER, E. Le Cambodge (3 vols.). Leroux, Paris, 1900–1904.

BARROW, SIR J. A Voyage to Cochinchina in the Years 1792 and 1793. T. Cadell & W. Davis, London, 1806.

BOSE, P. The Hindu Colony of Cambodia. Theosophical Publishing House, Madras, 1927.

BOSE, P. The Indian Colony of Champa. Theosophical Publishing House, Adyar, 1926.

CANDEE, H. C. Angkor the Magnificent, the Wonder City of Ancient Cambodia. Stokes, New York, 1924.

CHATTERJI, B. R. Indian Cultural Influences in Cambodia. Univ. of Calcutta Press, Calcutta, 1928.

COEDÈS, G. Le Temple d'Angkor-Vat (3 vols.). Van Oest, Paris, 1929–1932.

CORDIER, H. La France et la Cochinchine, 1852–1858. Brill, Leiden, 1906.

CORDIER, H. La Reprise des relations de la France avec l'Annam sous la restauration. Brill, Leiden, 1903.

DEVÉRIA, G. Histoire des relations de la Chine avec l'Annam-Vietnam du XVIe au XIXe siècle. Leroux, Paris, 1880.

DIGUET, E. J. J. Annam et Indo-Chine française. A. Challamel, Paris, 1908.

DIGUET, E. J. J. Les Montagnards du Tonkin. A. Challamel, Paris, 1908.

GROSLIER, G. Angkor. Laurens, Paris, 1924.

GROSLIER, G. Arts et archéologie khmèrs. Paris, 1921–1926.

GROSLIER, G. Recherches sur les Cambodgiens d'après les textes et les monuments depuis les premiers siècles de notre ère. A. Challamel, Paris, 1921.

GROSLIER, G. La Sculpture khmèr ancienne. G. Cres, Paris, 1925.

JEANNERAT DE BEERSKI, P. Angkor Ruins in Cambodia. G. Richards, London, 1923.

LAUNAY, A. Histoire ancienne et moderne de l'Annam. A. Challamel, Paris, 1880.

LECLÈRE, A. Le Bouddhisme au Cambodge. Leroux, Paris, 1899.

LECLÈRE, A. Histoire du Cambodge depuis le I^e siècle de notre ère. Geuthner, Paris, 1914.

LEUBA, J. Un Royaume disparu: les Chams et leur art. Van Oest, Paris, 1924.

MAJUMDAR, R. C. Ancient Indian Colonies in the Far East. Punjab Sanscrit Book Department, Lahore, 1927.

MASPERO, G. Le Royaume de Champa. Van Oest, Paris, 1927.

MAYBON, C. Histoire moderne du pays d'Annam. Plon-Nourrit, Paris, 1920.

NORMAN, C. B. Tonkin, or France in the Far East. Chapman & Hall, London, 1884.

PARMENTIER, H. The History of Khmer Architecture. *Eastern Art*, Vol. III, 1931, pp. 141–179. Philadelphia.

PAVIE, A. Recherches sur l'histoire du Cambodge, du Laos, et du Siam. Leroux, Paris, 1898.

PELLIOT, P. "Le Fou-nan." *Bulletin de l'École française d'Extrême-Orient*, 1903, pp. 248–303.

RÉMUSAT, A. (translator). Description du royaume de Cambodge, par un voyageur chinois qui a visité cette contrée à la fin du XIIIᵉ siècle. J. Smith, Paris, 1819.

SCOTT, J. G. France and Tongking. T. F. Unwin, London, 1885.

STERN, P. Le Bayon d'Angkor et l'évolution de l'art khmèr. Geuthner, Paris, 1927.

TCHEOU TA KOUAN. "Mémoires sur les coutumes du Cambodge" (translated by Paul Pelliot), *Bulletin de l'École française d'Extrême-Orient*, 1902, pp. 123 ff.

3. BURMA AND BRITISH MALAYA

BOULGER, D. C. The Life of Sir Stamford Raffles. H. Marshall & Son, London, 1897.

CLIFFORD, SIR H. Further India. Lawrence & Bullen, London, 1904.

COX, H. Journal of a Residence in the Burman Empire. Warren & Whitaker, London, 1821.

EGERTON, H. E. Sir Stamford Raffles: England in the Far East. T. F. Unwin, London, 1900.

FORCHAMMER, E. Notes on the Early History and Geography of British Burma. Superintendent of Government Printing, Rangoon, 1884.

FYTCHE, A. Burma, Past and Present. K. Paul, Trench, Trübner & Co., London, 1878.

GRAHAM, W. A. Kelantan: a State of the Malay Peninsula. J. MacLehose & Sons, Glasgow, 1908.

HARVEY, G. E. History of Burma. Longmans, London, 1925.

MARRYAT, F. S. Borneo and the Indian Archipelago. Longmans, Brown, Green, & Longmans, London, 1848.

MILLS, L. A. British Malaya, 1824–1867. Methodist Press, Singapore, 1925.

NEWBOLD, T. J. The British Settlements in the Straits of Malacca (2 vols.). J. Murray, London, 1839.

O'CONNOR, V. C. S. Mandalay and Other Cities of the Past in Burma. Hutchinson & Co., London, 1907.

PARKER, E. H. Burma, with Special Reference to her Relations with China. Rangoon Gazette Press, Rangoon, 1893.

PHAYRE, SIR A. History of Burma. K. Paul, Trench, Trübner & Co., London, 1883.

SKEAT, W. W., and BLAGDEN, C. O. Pagan Races of the Malay Peninsula. Macmillan, London, 1906.

STUART, J. Burma through the Centuries. K. Paul, Trench, Trübner & Co., London, 1909.

SWETTENHAM, SIR F. British Malaya. Dodd, New York, 1907.

SYMES, M. An Account of an Embassy to the Kingdom of Ava. Nicol & Wright, London, 1800.

WILKINSON, R. J. History of the Peninsula Malays (third edition). Kelly & Walsh, Singapore, 1923.

WILSON, H. H. Documents Illustrative of the Burmese War, with an Introductory Sketch of the Events of the War and an Appendix. Government Press, Calcutta, 1827.

WINSTEDT, R. O. Malaya—the Straits Settlements and the Federated and Unfederated Malay States. Constable & Co., London, 1923.

WRIGHT, A., and REID, T. H. The Malay Peninsula. T. F. Unwin, London, 1912.

YULE, SIR H. A Narrative of the Mission Sent by the Governor-General of India to the Court of Ava in 1855. Smith, Elder & Co., London, 1858.

Journal of the Burma Research Society. Rangoon.

4. THE DUTCH EAST INDIES

CABATON, A. Java, Sumatra, and the Dutch East Indies (translated by B. Miall). Scribner, New York, 1914.

CAMPBELL, D. M. Java: Past and Present (2 vols.). William Heinemann, London, 1915.

COLLET, O. J. A. Terres et peuples de Sumatra. Société d'édition Elsevier, Amsterdam, 1925.

DAY, C. The Dutch in Java. Macmillan, New York, 1904.

GONNAUD, P. La Colonisation hollandaise à Java. A. Challamel, Paris, 1905.

KATS, J. The Râmâyana in Reliefs of Javanese Temples. Luzac, London, 1925.

KROM, N. J. L'Art javanais dans les musées de Holland et de Java. Ars Asiatica, Paris, 1926.

KROM, N. J. Barabudur, Archaeological Description. Nijhoff, the Hague, 1927.

KROM, N. J. Die sumatraansche Period der javaansche Geschiedenis. Brill, Leiden, 1919.

MARSDEN, W. History of Sumatra. Longman, Hurst, Rees, Orme, & Brown, London, 1811.

RAFFLES, SIR T. S. The History of Java (second edition). J. Murray, London, 1830.

RENNEVILLE, R. A. C. DE. A Collection of Voyages Undertaken by the Dutch East-India Company (English translation). W. Freeman, London, 1703.

SCHELTEMA, J. F. Monumental Java. Macmillan, London, 1912.

SCIDMORE, E. R. Java: the Garden of the Far East. Century, New York, 1912.

SNOUCK-HURGRONJE, C. The Achehnese (2 vols.; English translation by R. J. Wilkinson). Luzac, London, 1906.

TORCHIANA, H. A. V. C. Tropical Holland. Univ. of Chicago Press, Chicago, 1921.

VANDENBOSCH, A. The Dutch East Indies. Erdmans, Grand Rapids, 1933.

VERNEUIL, M. P. L'Art à Java. Les Temples de la période classique indojavanaise: Tjandi Kalasan, Tjandi Mendont, Boroboudour, Tjandi Prambanan. Van Oest, Paris, 1927.

WITH, K. Bramanische, buddhistische und eigenlebige Architektur und Plastik auf Java. Folkwangverlag, the Hague, 1920.

5. SIAM

ANDERSON, J. English Intercourse with Siam in the Seventeenth Century. K. Paul, Trench, Trübner & Co., London, 1890.

CAMPBELL, J. G. D. Siam in the XXth Century. Arnold, London, 1902.

COCHRANE, W. W. The Shans. Government Printing Office, Rangoon, 1915.

DAMRONG, PRINCE. Historical Sketch of Lopburi. Journal of the Siam Society, Bangkok, 1908.

DAMRONG, PRINCE. Siamese History Prior to the Founding of Ayudhya. Journal of the Siam Society, Bangkok, 1919.

DÖHRING, K. Kunst und Kunst-Gewerbe in Siam. Asia Publishing House, Bangkok, 1926.

DÖHRING, K. Siam. Folkwangverlag, Darmstadt, 1923.

FRANKFURTER, O. Siam in 1688: a Narrative of the Revolutions in Siam in the Year 1688. Journal of the Siam Society, Bangkok, 1908–1909.

GRAHAM, W. A. Siam. De la More Press, London, 1924.

KAEMPFER, E. The History of Japan, Together with a Description of the Kingdom of Siam, 1690–1692 (3 vols.; modern edition). J. MacLehose & Sons, Glasgow, 1906.

LANIER, L. Étude historique sur les relations de la France et du royaume de Siam, de 1662 à 1703. E. Aubert, Paris, 1883.

LAUNAY, A. Histoire de la mission de Siam. Paris, 1921.

PALLEGOIX, J. B. Description du royaume thai ou Siam (2 vols.). Mission de Siam, Paris, 1854.

ROBERTS, E. Embassy to the Eastern Courts of Cochin-China, Siam and Muscat. Harper, New York, 1837.

SALMONY, A. Sculpture in Siam. Ernest Benn, London, 1925.

SALMONY, A. La Sculpture siamoise. Van Oest, Paris, 1925.

SEAUVE, CAPTAIN. Relations de la France et du Siam, 1680–1907. H. Charles Lavauzelle, Paris, 1908.

WALES, H. G. Q. Ancient Siamese Government and Administration. Quaritch, London, 1934.

WOOD, W. A. R. A History of Siam, from the Earliest Times to the Year 1781. T. F. Unwin, London, 1926.

Journal of the Siam Society. Bangkok.

6. THE PHILIPPINES

BARROWS, D. P. A History of the Philippines (second edition). Bobbs, Indianapolis, 1924.

BLAIR, E. H., and ROBERTSON, J. A. The Philippine Islands, 1493–1898 (55 vols.). A. H. Clark & Co., Cleveland, 1903–1909.

BLOUNT, J. H. The American Occupation of the Philippines. Putnam, New York, 1912.

BUTTERWORTH, H. The Story of Magellan. Appleton, New York, 1924.

CHAMBERLIN, F. The Philippine Problem. Little, Boston, 1913.

CHAPMAN, C. E. A History of California—the Spanish Period. Macmillan, New York, 1921.

COLE, F.-C., and LAUFER, B. Chinese Pottery in the Philippines. Field Museum of Nat. Hist., Chicago, 1912.

DE MORGA, A. The Philippine Islands, Moluccas, Siam, Cambodia, Japan, and China, at the Close of the Sixteenth Century (translated by H. F. J. Stanley). Hakluyt Society, London, 1868.

ELLIOTT, C. B. The Philippines (2 vols.). Bobbs, Indianapolis, 1916–1917.

FORBES, W. C. The Philippine Islands. Houghton, Boston, 1928.

HARRISON, F. B. The Corner-stone of Philippine Independence. Century, New York, 1922.

KALAW, M. M. Self-government in the Philippines. Century, New York, 1919.

KALAW, T. M. The Philippine Revolution. Manila Book Co., Manila, 1925.

KROEBER, A. L. The History of Philippine Civilization. The Trustees, New York, 1918.

LAUFER, B. The Relations of the Chinese to the Philippine Islands. Smithsonian Institution, Washington, 1907.

LE ROY, J. A. The Americans in the Philippines (2 vols.). Houghton, Boston, 1914.

MALCOLM, G. A., and KALAW, M. M. Philippine Government (revised edition). Heath, New York, 1932.

MILLER, H. H. Economic Conditions in the Philippines. Ginn, Boston, 1919.

MONCADA, H. C. America, the Philippines, and the Orient. Revell, New York, 1932.

REYES, J. S. Legislative History of America's Economic Policy toward the Philippines. Longmans, New York, 1923.

ROOSEVELT, N. The Philippines: a Treasure and a Problem. Sears, New York, 1926.

RUSSELL, C. E. The Outlook for the Philippines. Century, New York, 1922.

SALEEBY, N. M. Studies in Moro History, Law, and Religion. Bureau of Public Printing, Manila, 1905.

STOREY, M., and LICHAUCO, M. The Conquest of the Philippines by the United States. Doubleday, Page, Garden City, 1926.

WILLIAMS, D. R. The United States and the Philippines. Doubleday, Page, Garden City, 1925.

WORCESTER, D. C. The Philippines, Past and Present. Macmillan, New York, 1921.

Senate Document No. 180, 69th Cong., 2d Session (December 22, 1926; Mr. C. A. Thompson's report on political conditions in the Philippines).

VI. *Central Asia*

BACOT, J., and HACKIN, J. L'Art tibétain. Geuthner, Paris, 1911.

BARTHOLD, W. Turkestan down to the Mongol Invasion. Luzac, London, 1928.

BELL, SIR C. Tibet: Past and Present. Clarendon Press, Oxford, 1924.

BLOCHET, E. History of the Mongols of Central Asia (English translation by Denison Ross). Luzac, London, 1898.

BLOCHET, E. Introduction à l'histoire des mongols de Fadl Allah Rashid ed-Din. Luzac, London, 1910.

BOYER, A. M., RAPSON, E. J., and SENART, E. Kharoshti Inscriptions Discovered by Sir Aurel Stein in Chinese Turkestan. Clarendon Press, Oxford, 1920–1929.

BRETSCHNEIDER, E. Mediaeval Researches from Eastern Asiatic Sources. K. Paul, Trench, Trübner & Co., London, 1910.

BRETSCHNEIDER, E. Notices of Mediaeval Geography and History of Central and Western Asia. K. Paul, Trench, Trübner & Co., London, 1876.

CAHUN, L. Introduction à l'histoire de l'Asie. Turcs et mongols des origines à 1405. A. Colin et Cie, Paris, 1896.

CHAVANNES, E. Documents sur les Tou-kiue (Turcs) occidentaux. L'Académie impériale des sciences, St. Petersburg, 1903.

CHAVANNES, E. Les Documents chinois découverts par Aurel Stein dans les sables du Turkestan oriental. Clarendon Press, Oxford, 1913.

CLAVIJO, R. GONZÁLEZ DE. Embassy to Tamerlane, 1403–1406 (English translation). George Routledge & Sons, London, 1928.

CONRADY, A. Die chinesischen Handschriften und sonstigen Kleinfunde Sven Hedins in Lou Lan. Generalstabens Litografiska Anstalt, Stockholm, 1920.

COURANT, M. L'Asie centrale aux XVIIe et XVIIIe siècles. Empire kalmouk ou empire mantchou? A. Rey, Lyon, 1912.

CURTIS, W. E. Turkestan, the Heart of Asia. Doran, New York, 1911.

CZAPLICKA, M. A. The Turks of Central Asia in History and at the Present Day. Clarendon Press, Oxford, 1918.

DAS, S. C. (translator). History of Buddhism in India and Tibet. Presidency Jail Press, Calcutta, 1908.

DAS, S. C. Journey to Lhasa and Central Tibet. J. Murray, London, 1902.

DEASY, H. H. P. In Tibet and Chinese Turkestan: Being the Record of Three Years' Exploration. Longmans, New York, 1901.

D'OHSSON, C. Histoire des mongols, depuis Tchinguiz-Khan jusqu'à Timour Bey ou Tamerlane (4 vols.). F. Muller, Amsterdam, 1852.

DOUGLAS, R. K. The Life of Jenghiz Khan. K. Paul, Trench, Trübner & Co., London, 1877.

DUTREUIL DE RHINS, J. L. L'Asie centrale (Thibet et régions limitrophes). Leroux, Paris, 1889.

DUTREUIL DE RHINS, J. L., and GRENARD, F. Mission scientifique dans la Haute-Asie, Turkestan et Tibet (3 vols.). Leroux, Paris, 1897–1898.

FRANCKE, A. H. Antiquities of Indian Tibet. Superintendent of Government Printing, Calcutta, 1914–1926.

FRANCKE, A. H. A History of Western Tibet. S. W. Partridge & Co., London, 1907.

GIBB, H. A. R. The Arab Conquests in Central Asia. Royal Asiatic Society, London, 1923.

GRÜNWEDEL, A. Altbuddhistische Kultstätten in Chinesisch-Turkistan. Bericht über archäologische Arbeiten von 1906 bis 1907 bei Kuča, Qarašahr, und in der Oase Turfan. G. Reimer, Berlin, 1912.

GRÜNWEDEL, A. Alt-Kutscha. O. Elsner, Berlin, 1920.

GRÜNWEDEL, A. Bericht über archäologische Arbeiten in Idikutschari und Umgebung im Winter 1902–1903. K. B. Akademie der Wissenschaften, Munich, 1906.

GRÜNWEDEL, A. Mythologie des Buddhismus in Tibet und der Mongolei. F. A. Brockhaus, Berlin, 1900.

HEDIN, S. Central Asia and Tibet (2 vols.). Scribner, New York, 1903.

HEDIN, S. Southern Tibet: Discoveries in Former Times Compared with My Own Researches in 1906–1908. Lithographic Institute of the General Staff of the Swedish Army, Stockholm, 1917–1922.

HEDIN, S. Through Asia (2 vols.). Harper, New York, 1899.

HEDIN, S. Trans-Himalaya (3 vols.). Macmillan, New York, 1909–1913.

HOWORTH, SIR H. H. History of the Mongols from the 9th to the 19th Century. Longmans, London, 1876–1927.

IMBAULT-HUART, C. Recueil de documents sur l'Asie centrale. Leroux, Paris, 1881.

KOROSTOVETZ, I. J. Von Cinggis Khan zur Sowjet-republik. De Gruyter, Berlin, 1926.

KOZLOW, P. K. Mongolei, Amdo, und die tote Stadt Chara-Choto. Die Expedition der Russischen Geographischen Gesellschaft, 1907–1909. Neufeld & Henius, Berlin, 1925.

LAMB, H. Genghis Khan. McBride, New York, 1928.

LAMB, H. Tamerlane. McBride, New York, 1928.

LANDON, P. The Opening of Tibet. Doubleday, Page, New York, 1905.

LAUFER, B. Sino-Iranica: Chinese Contributions to the History of Civilization in Ancient Iran, with Special Reference to the History of Cultivated Plants and Products. Field Museum of Nat. Hist., Chicago, 1919.

LE COQ, A. VON. Bilderatlas zur Kunst und Kulturgeschichte Mittel-Asiens. D. Reimer, Berlin, 1925.

LE COQ, A. VON. Die Buddhistische Spatantike in Mittel-Asien (5 vols.). D. Reimer, Berlin, 1922–1933.

LE COQ, A. VON. Chotscho, Facsimile-Wiedergaben der wichtigeren Funde der ersten Königlich Preussischen Expedition nach Turfan in Ost-Turkistan. D. Reimer, Berlin, 1913.

MILLOUÉ, L. DE. Bod-Youl ou Tibet: Le Paradis des Moines. Leroux, Paris, 1906.

PELLIOT, P. Haute Asie. J. Goudard, Paris, 1931.

PELLIOT, P. Mission Pelliot en Asie centrale (8 vols.). Geuthner, Paris, 1914–1918.

PELLIOT, P. Les Mongols et la papauté (reprint from *Revue de l'Orient chrétien*). A. Picard, Paris, 1922–1923, 1924, 1931–1932.

PUMPELLY, R. Explorations in Turkestan. Carnegie Institution, Washington, 1903–1904.

PUMPELLY, R. Prehistoric Anau. Carnegie Institution, Washington, 1905–1908.

ROCKHILL, W. W. (translator and editor) The Journey of William of Rubruck to the Eastern Parts of the World, 1253–55, as Narrated by Himself, with two Accounts of the Earlier Journey of John Pian de Carpine. Hakluyt Society, London, 1900.

ROCKHILL, W. W. The Land of the Lamas. Century, New York, 1891.

ROERICH, G. Tibetan Paintings. Geuthner, Paris, 1925.

SCHMIDT, I. J. (translator). Geschichte der Ost-Mongolen und ihres Fürstenhauses, verfasst von Ssanang Ssetsen Chungtaiddschi der Ordus. St. Petersburg, 1829.

SKRINE, C. P. Chinese Central Asia. Methuen & Co., London, 1926.

SKRINE, F. H., and ROSS, E. D. The Heart of Asia: History of Russian Turkestan and Central Asian Khanates. Methuen & Co., London, 1899.

STEIN, SIR M. A. Ancient Khotan (2 vols.). Clarendon Press, Oxford, 1907.

STEIN, SIR M. A. Innermost Asia (3 vols.). Clarendon Press, Oxford, 1928.

STEIN, SIR M. A. Ruins of Desert Cathay. Macmillan, London, 1912.

STEIN, SIR M. A. Sand-buried Ruins of Khotan. T. F. Unwin, London, 1903.

STEIN, SIR M. A. Serindia (4 vols.). Clarendon Press, Oxford, 1921.

VLADIMIRTSOV, B. Y. The Life of Chingis-Khan (translated by Prince D. S. Mirsky). George Routledge & Sons, London, 1930.

WADDELL, L. A. The Buddhism of Tibet, or Lamaism (second edition). Heffer, Cambridge (Eng.), 1934.

WADDELL, L. A. Lhassa and its Mysteries. Methuen & Co., London, 1906.

YOUNGHUSBAND, SIR F. India and Tibet. J. Murray, London, 1910.

INDEX

(Following geographical names, the numbers in heavy face refer to maps.)

Abdu-r Razzak, description of India, 345, 347
Achin (Aceh), 302, 650, 652–653, **662**
Adams, Will, 415, 453 n.
Afghanistan, 152, **633**, 634, 639, 640, **645**. *See also* Bactria
Afghans, 155, 338, 475
Agra, **339**, 354, **645**
Aguinaldo, Emilio, 664, 665, 666
Ahmadnagar, **339**, 343, 344
Aigun, **537**, **633**, **717**, 738, **857**
Ainus (Yemishi), 213, 215, 226, 231
Ajanta, **132**; the fresco paintings of, 142
Ajodya, **132**, 140
Akbar, the Great Mogul, 354–358
Aksu, **65**, 70, **161**, 163
Alaska, Russian discovery of, 498
Alaungpaya, 479, 480, 512
Albazin, **487**; fortified Russian post on the Amur, 490, 492–493
Albuquerque, Alfonso de, Portuguese viceroy in India, 350–351, 362
Alcock, Sir Rutherford, first British minister to Japan, 589, 593
Aleutian Islands, **487**, 490
Alexander the Great, invasion of India by, 52–53
Allahabad, **132**, 145
Almeida, Francisco de, Portuguese viceroy in India, 350, 351
Altai mountains, **1**, **65**, **251**
Alternate residence at Yedo, 568, 572
Amau, Eiji, statement of Japanese policy by, 866
Amboyna, **361**, 363, 365, 454, 458–459
Amdo, 504, **536**
Amherst embassy, 520–521
Amoy, 421, 422, 430, 531, **537**, 845
Amritsar, **808**; massacre at, 811
Amu Daria (Oxus River), **1**, **65**, **161**, **251**
Amur river, **1**, **251**, **421**, **487**, 599, **857**; Russian activities on, 490–493, 509
Anawrata, 191–193
Andhra (Vengi), **57**, 60, **132**, 134–135, 139, 146, 149
Andrade, Fernão Perez de, 420
Andrade, Simon de, 421
Angkor, **179**, 187, 188, 189, **316**, 321

Anglo-Chinese War (Opium War), 530–531
Anglo-French-Chinese War (*Arrow* War), 539–542
Anglo-Japanese Alliance, 720–721, 728–729, 797, 799
Anhui, **292**, **537**, **689**
Annam, **75**, **179**, **316**, **361**, **451**, **662**; and China, 36, 180, 181–183; and the Mongols, 274, 280; independence of, 315–318; French expansion in, 482–484, 556–558; French administration in, 654, 827–828
Anti-foreignism, in China, 543–544, 552–553, 562, 688–693, 839–842; in Japan, 588–589, 590–593
Antung, **717**, **726**, **857**
Aoki-Kimberley treaty, 617
Arabs, in Central Asia, 86, 109, 170–171, 174, 175; in China, 91, 94, 114–115, 185, 420; in India, 135, 148, 345, 350; in Indo-China and Malaysia, 334–335, 361, 362, 372, 373
Arakan, **179**, 190, **316**, 326, **361**, 364, **809**
Archaeological discoveries, in China, 10–11; in India, 41–42; in Central Asia, 67, 163–165; in Japan, 213
Argun river, **487**
Arima, **387**; Christianity in, 410
Armagaon, **451**; English factory at, 467
Arrow, case of the, 539–540
Art: *in China*, pre-Han, 86; Han, 87; influence of Buddhism upon, 87, 90, 115–116; Northern Wei, 90; T'ang, 115–116; Sung, 127; Ming, 307; *in India*, 60; Greek influence on, 133; Gupta, 141–142; Mohammedan destruction of, 153, 155–156; *in Indo-China*, 181; Champa, 186; Cambodia, 188; Burma, 193; Annam, 317; *in Japan*, 228–229; Ashikaga, 392; Tokugawa, 578; *in Korea*, 205; *in Malaysia*, 197
Arthasastra, 60, 62
Aryans, arrival in India and early culture, 43–47
Ashikaga Takauji, founder of Ashikaga Shogunate, 388–389